PROVISIONS

EVERYWOMAN

Studies in History, Literature, and Culture

General Editors

SUSAN GUBAR AND JOAN HOFF-WILSON

PROVISIONS

A Reader from 19th-Century American Women

Edited with an Introduction
and Critical Commentary

BY

Judith Fetterley

*Indiana
University
Press*

BLOOMINGTON

Library of Congress Cataloging in Publication Data
Main entry under title:

Provisions: a reader from 19th-century American women.

Bibliography: p.
1. American prose literature—Women authors.
2. American prose literature—19th century.   3. Women—
United States—Literary collections.   I. Fetterley,
Judith, 1938–
PS647.W6P7   1985   818'.308'0809287   84-42840
ISBN 0-253-17040-0
ISBN 0-253-20349-X (pbk.)

4 5 6 7 95 94

TO

Ember Carianna

Ellen Mindel

Joan Schulz

WSS 210, "Introduction to Feminism"
1976–1978

Thesþian Feminists
1978–1983

CONTENTS

Contents

PROVISIONS

INTRODUCTION

When I first began to read extensively in the prose literature of nine-teenth-century American women, I was primarily curious. In four years of undergraduate and five years of graduate training, I had not been asked to read, much less study, a single piece of this literature. Once, in graduate school, a professor had suggested that, if I had the time, I might want to take a look at *Uncle Tom's Cabin*. I read it and then I wrote an essay on it for the local NAACP chapter newsletter. Obviously, the book interested me, but, also obviously, I could not find a place for that interest in my life as a graduate student with a specialization in nineteenth-century American literature; I could only find a place for it in my life as a civil rights activist. I was, of course, aware when I began this project of the critical attitude toward this material, of the scorn and contempt conveyed in the adjectives usually applied to it: sentimental, silly, soft, senseless, feminine, florid, frivolous. But, as a feminist with what I believed was a fairly clear understanding of the sexual politics of aesthetic judgments as they operate to shape literary history, I was not impressed by these adjectives nor convinced of their accuracy. So I began my reading, curious as to what I might find. And curious also to understand in the specific rather than the general why this material had been so thoroughly eliminated from the map of nineteenth-century American literature.

By the end of my first eight months of extensive reading, I had discovered that there was in fact an extraordinarily rich, diverse, and interesting body of prose literature written in the nineteenth century by American women. But I had also discovered that the desire to write a critical book on this material was for me at least premature. Without access to the primary texts, there could be no community of readers, and without such a community there could be, as I saw it, no finally intelligent criticism. Clearly, then, the first task of the reader-critic committed to this material was to get it into print. Furthermore, getting this material into print appeared a necessary first stage in the struggle to put this literature on the map of American literary history. For it had become increasingly clear to me during my first eight months of reading that the attempt to integrate the work of nineteenth-century American women into the definition of American literature would provide a good testing ground for the relationship between sexual politics and literary judgment. Having made these discoveries, I then proceeded to redesign my project. The result is the book you have before you: a critical anthology of the prose literature written by American women between 1830 and 1865.

In 1971, Ann Douglas [Wood] published an essay in the *American Quarterly* entitled "The 'Scribbling Women' and Fanny Fern: Why Women Wrote." In this essay, Douglas describes the context within which mid-nineteenth-century American women writers worked. This context was created by male critics and by women following their lead. These men and women undertook to define the nature of female writing and then, in somewhat contradictory fashion, they exhorted women to write only in the mode that was "natural" to them. According to Douglas, this context had major consequences for the work produced by women during this period. One of these consequences was reflected in the posture of authorial innocence adopted by many writers. Paradoxically, Douglas argues, these women presented themselves as writing unconsciously and she offers the example of Caroline Lee Hentz in *Ernest Linwood*, a novel published in 1856:

> Book! Am I writing a book? No, indeed! This is only a record of my heart's life, written at random and carelessly thrown aside, sheet after sheet, sibylline leaves from the great book of fate. The wind may blow them away, a spark consume them. I may myself commit them to the flames. I am tempted to do so at this moment.

When I began to read this literature for myself, I was struck by the difference between what I saw and what Douglas had described. This is not to argue that Douglas is wrong but rather to argue that the material at issue is more various than her thesis would suggest. For, as I read, what I discovered was not "innocence" but awareness. Indeed, many of the women whose work I read exhibited a considerable degree of self-consciousness about writing and a serious, sometimes direct, sometimes indirect, engagement with the issues raised by the conjunction of woman and writer. For example, Elizabeth Stuart Phelps's *The Angel Over The Right Shoulder* (1852) is essentially self-reflexive; a story written by a woman, its subject is women and writing. More striking, perhaps, because earlier, is Catharine Sedgwick's "Cacoethes Scribendi," first published in 1830. Twenty-five years before Hawthorne's infamous and endlessly quoted jibe against the "d----d mob of scribbling women" who dominated the American literary scene at mid-century and prevented, according to Hawthorne, his own chances for commercial success, Sedgwick analyzes the origins, implications, and consequences of the female "itch to scribble." In this story about a woman who determines on a career of letters after reading one of the latest instances of the periodic inundation of annuals and discovering in it the work of her female friends, Sedgwick evinces a clear understanding of the connections between women and writing and developments in the economics of publishing. Annuals became an item on the American scene in the late 1820s. Issued, as their name implies, once a year, many of them early adopted a policy of accepting American materials only. Thus they provided a major new market for the work of American writers, a category that of course included women. Sedgwick's Mrs. Courland is literally smitten by opportunity. Indeed, the motives Sedgwick assigns her would-be woman writer differ significantly from those presented by Douglas as the only ones women could legitimately claim. Mrs. Courland does not write because she is poor, nor because she is the sole support of husband and children; nor does she write in response to the pressure of male relatives, nor because she is possessed of a force that she can neither understand nor control. Nor does she write from the feminine urge to bring the values of the home into the world of the market place. Mrs. Courland writes because the opportunity is there and she enjoys doing it. A story about writing for annuals, itself written for and published in one of the first examples of the genre, "Cacoethes Scribendi" reflects the self-consciousness of its author. Inevitably, it raises the question, what is the difference between the writing of Sedgwick and the writing of Mrs. Courland? Obviously, Sedgwick's self-presentation is a far cry from Hentz's "Book! Am I writing a Book? No, indeed!"

Another early writer who self-consciously draws attention to herself as a woman writing is Caroline Kirkland. In *A New Home—Who'll Follow?* (1839), Kirkland insists on the twin facts of her authorship and her femaleness. Her preface, though filled with conventional apologies for the book's limitations, nevertheless defines her aesthetic principles; yet Kirkland concludes this preface with a "curtsey." Throughout the book Kirkland evinces authorial self-consciousness: "I trust the importance of [my subject] will be enhanced in the reader's estimation by the variety of figures I have been compelled to use in describing it." Equally, she indicates awareness of the current assumptions about "feminine" writing, and engages them with an ironic playfulness that exposes their absurdity. Declaring at one point to have discovered that "the bent of my genius is altogether towards digression," she continues with a parody of the twin assumptions that women have no will power and therefore can not write "serious," that is, logical and linear, literature: "Association leads me like a Will-o'-the-Wisp. I can no more resist following a new train of thought, than a coquette the encouraging of a new lover. . . ." In an essay entitled "Literary Women," published in *A Book for the Home Circle* (1853), Kirkland engages even more directly and sharply the conventional assumptions about women's writing. Playing with the posture of a literary woman about to defend literary women in a context that makes such defense impossible since such defense requires a self-consciousness and logic of which women are by definition incapable, Kirkland ironically delivers the required disclaimer: "we shall take care to deal with the subject after the desultory, unsystematic, and feminine manner. We repudiate learning; we disclaim accuracy; we abjure logic. We shall aim only at the pretty prattle which is conceded to our sex as a right, and admired as a charm."

Like Sedgwick in "Cacoethes Scribendi," Kirkland in *A New Home* seeks to seize the initiative in defining who is to represent the woman writer. To this end, she creates the character of Eloise Fidler, exemplar of the "female poetess," the figure conventionally asserted as the type of true female "genius." In parodying, exposing, and rewriting this figure, Kirkland distinguishes between herself and her character and thus implicitly argues for a different idea of the woman writer from that embodied in Eloise. In *A New Home*, Kirkland also argues implicitly for a broader definition of women's writing. In between realistic sketches designed to describe the facts of life on the Michigan frontier, Kirkland inserts stories more closely associated with the contemporary assumptions about the nature of women's writing. These stories contain conventional women's subjects—romantic love, courtship, marriage—treated in a relatively conventional fashion. Although there is a definite sense of play in the handling of these insert stories, Kirkland's intent is not to disavow this mode of writing, but rather, by containing it within the framework of a different kind of writing, to suggest that women can write successfully in more than this one mode.

In *The Pearl of Orr's Island* (1862), Harriet Beecher Stowe uses a similar technique to define the premises of her fiction and to distinguish implicitly between her text and the conventional assumptions about women's stories. Stowe, however, takes the issue further than Kirkland. Implicitly, she argues that the so-called woman's story is in fact a story written by men about men and for men. In *The Pearl of Orr's Island*, Stowe enfolds a lengthy narrative written by one male character and directed to another. This narrative tells of the fate of Dolores, mother of Moses, the book's male hero, who died while Moses was still a boy. In contrast to the text that surrounds it, the insert story presents as its heroine a male-identified woman—a woman whose only idea of life is romantic love; a woman thoroughly subject to male domination and completely dependent on men for identity, direction, and rescue; and a woman helpless and vulnerable. In his narrative, the male writer recounts his love for Dolores, his ineffectual efforts to save her, and her ultimate fate. Never marrying, he has remained true to this love, a love that seems inextricably connected to Dolores's vulnerability and doom. Through this artistically self-conscious technique of a tale within a tale, Stowe identifies the "love story" as men's work and defines the woman's story as something else.

In sum, then, I suggest that the work of many nineteenth-century American women writers before 1865 (and I could, of course, have discussed other writers in this context, most notably Alice Cary, Rose Terry Cooke, Rebecca Harding Davis, Gail Hamilton, Charlotte Forten Grimké) reflects a considerable degree of self-consciousness toward the act of writing. Furthermore, this self-consciousness is not of the kind implicit in the posture Douglas describes, which denies any intention of writing while in fact engaged in the act of writing, but is rather direct, straightforward, and often in conscious tension with the posture of "innocence." To take the issue a step further, I did not find in the work of the women included in this anthology (there are, of course, exceptions to this generalization) that same "anxiety of authorship" that Sandra Gilbert and Susan Gubar in *The Madwoman in the Attic* (1979) so eloquently describe as infecting the work of nineteenth-century English women writers, and that Mary Kelley in *Private Woman, Public Stage* (1984) perceives as informing the work of the nineteenth-century American "literary domestics," a group composed primarily of novelists. On the contrary, many of the writers I read seemed to manifest a considerable degree of comfort with the act of writing and with the presentation of themselves as writers and relatively little sense of disjunctiveness between "woman" and "pen." Indeed, I would suggest that mid-nineteenth-century American women writers were more comfortable with the idea of writing than were their male counterparts and that Gilbert and Gubar's analysis in "Toward A Feminist Poetics" more accurately interprets the work of Cooper, Poe, Hawthorne, and Melville than it does the work of nineteenth-century American women.

Women were early and significantly on the scene of American letters. According to Helen Papashvily, of the two-hundred-odd works of fiction produced by Americans between 1779 and 1829, "better than a third were written for or by women." Among the most popular of these fictions were two books written by women, Susanna Rowson's *Charlotte Temple* (1794) and Hannah Foster's *The Coquette* (1797), and one written by a man but attributed in the nineteenth century to a woman, William Brown's *The Power of Sympathy* (1789). In the 1820s and early 1830s, Sedgwick wrote a series of novels that received significant critical and popular acclaim and established for her contemporaries the right of women to the territory of American fiction. The 1830s and 1840s saw the

rise of annuals, gift books, and women's magazines with the consequences for women and writing that Sedgwick recognized in "Cacoethes
Scribendi." And in 1850, Susan Warner's *The Wide, Wide World* created
the category of "best seller" and gave it a uniquely feminine signature.
Thus, in mid-nineteenth-century America, although "women" and
"writing" were not synonymous, neither were they dichotomous, and
the woman who picked up her pen on this side of the Atlantic may have
felt that she was occupying essentially feminine territory. Conversely, the
American male who picked up the pen may well have felt contaminated
by an instrument peculiarly female and consequently engaged in an act
both eccentric and illegitimate. To view the fiction of American men as
written in a context of and in reaction to, on the one hand, the association
in nineteenth-century America of culture with the feminine, and, on the
other hand, the visibility of women as American writers may well provide
us with a new understanding of the origins of those particular features of
form and content that we currently associate with our "classic" literature.

But, one might argue that the comfort these women felt in the act of
writing derives from the fact that they did not, unlike perhaps their
English counterparts, think of themselves primarily as artists. Nina
Baym, discussing nineteenth-century American women novelists in
*Woman's Fiction: A Guide to Novels by and about Women in America,
1820–1870* (1978), argues that these women, in contrast to the later generation of regionalists, "saw themselves not as 'artists' but as professional
writers with work to do and a living to be made from satisfactory
fulfillment of an obligation to their audience." And in "The Literature of
Impoverishment: The Women Local Colorists in America 1865–1914"
(1972), Douglas makes essentially the same point about the "first" generation of American women novelists, claiming that "women in America
started to write in large numbers precisely at that time (the turn of the
nineteenth century) when a wide and competitive literary market was
becoming a reality. . . . In short, American women were drawn to writing
just when it became a possible business, and they were among the first to
sense and develop its business potential." Although these comments are
based on the careers of nineteenth-century American women novelists,
they may have an equal and even more pointed reference to the self-
concept of women who chose to write primarily in other modes. As the
more traditional, conventional and "big" form for nineteenth-century
fiction, the novel was also the most literary and artistic. Thus, to write an
essay, a sketch, or a letter may have compounded the differentiation
between woman and artist that Baym and Douglas describe. Aiming at
less than art and lower than immortality, the women represented by this
anthology may have avoided some of the psychic trauma that afflicted
those who aimed higher. In an essay entitled "On American Literature"
(1846), Margaret Fuller, anticipating the rise of a truly American artistic
genius, presents for a model "the great Latins of simple masculine minds

seizing upon life with unbroken power." It is rather doubtful, given this description, that any of the women I discuss would have presented themselves as candidates for the position of American artist.

Finally, I might note that my comments are based primarily on the texts I have chosen for inclusion in this anthology. Kelley in *Private Woman, Public Stage* has clearly identified the considerable degree of conflict that the "literary domestics" experienced between the privacy of woman and the publicity of writer. And although it may indeed be the case that further research into the letters, journals, and other published writings of the women represented in this anthology will reveal a similar pattern of conflict, this would not, I think, change my essential perception. For I would argue for a distinction between the cumulative voice derived from multiple sources and the particular voice developed for a specific text. For example, Kelley includes both Sedgwick and Sara Parton (Fanny Fern) in the category of "literary domestics" and analyzes them in terms of the conflict between private woman and public stage. Yet the voice that speaks to us in "Cacoethes Scribendi" and in the pieces by Fanny Fern is strong, clear, confident, unconflicted; it is a voice comfortable with the authority of the public forum, the written word. For such women, the text may have provided a temporary "world elsewhere" away from and outside of the general conflict.

If I was struck by the degree of self-consciousness and self-confidence that many mid-nineteenth-century American women writers exhibited in their writing, I was equally struck by the apparent ease with which they chose to write about women and their lives—or, in other words, with which they chose to write about themselves. Coming to the work of nineteenth-century American women from familiarity only with the work of nineteenth-century American men, I was understandably unprepared to find women inhabiting American texts. Yet the writers I read apparently did not feel that in writing about women they were being un-American. Perhaps because they did not see themselves as "artists" and did not aspire to fill the role of the American genius who would produce a uniquely American literature, these women were free to explore that other, "lesser" world of women. Or perhaps that fusion between "Americanness" and masculinity that has informed the twentieth-century interpretation of American literature was not in mid-nineteenth-century America so firmly fixed; thus nineteenth-century American women writers could consider themselves American artists and still write about women. A useful context for this question may be provided by the texts themselves. To what degree do the texts that these women produced suggest that they freely chose to write about women because the lives of women interested them and the woman's point of view struck them as significantly human? And, conversely, to what degree do these texts suggest that their authors felt they could only write about women? Among the writers included in this anthology, Davis is notable for her decision to focus on the lives of men. One could, I think, argue that some of her stylistic difficulties in "Life in the Iron Mills" (1861), the occasionally heavy, even clumsy quality of her prose, the sense it conveys of repression more than expression, derive from a discomfort with her subject matter, a conviction that the lives of men, even working-class men, do not constitute an appropriate subject for a woman writer. Yet there are other writers whose texts describe the focus on women as a choice freely made, not culturally enforced. In *The Angel Over The Right Shoulder*, for example, Phelps, though describing the woman's life as a restricted life, does not present herself as restricted by her choice of subject. She indicates no desire to follow Mr. James downtown and no interest in treating the "business" so important to him as to justify in his eyes the sacrifice of his wife's efforts to get time for herself. Rather Phelps's interest lies in the life thus sacrificed and for her subject she is willing to stay home. In *The Pearl of Orr's Island*, Stowe presents her preference in even more dramatic fashion. Although to Moses, his life is both story and history, Stowe drops him from her text when he sets out to sea; his masculine adventures take place off a stage occupied instead by the women who remain at home.

Much of the pleasure that the contemporary reader takes in this literature stems from its ratification of women as significant subjects. The focus of these writers provides an experience missing from most of our "classic" American fiction. But the fiction of nineteenth-century American women differs in other ways as well from that of nineteenth-century American men. One such additional difference may indeed be connected to the decision to focus on the lives of women. For most of the writers represented in this anthology, accurate and detailed recording of the realities of women's lives leads inevitably to an interest in social texture and settings. This interest in turn leads to a fiction of manners shaped by the perspective of realism. In "A Few Observations on American Fiction, 1851–1875" (1955), Lyle Wright laments the subjects that our early writers of fiction "missed": "They lived in the days of the masted schooners and flying clippers, stagecoaches and the early development of the railroads. . . . The frontier pushing westward was a throbbing movement of humanity bent on finding new homes and a new way of life. Trails were being blazed to the Pacific by the fur trappers and exploring parties, and marauding bands of Indians provided additional news." But if little of this "dash and daring on land and sea" can be found in their work, nevertheless, claims Wright, "a great deal can be learned about the way of life of the people, the clothes they wore, the food they ate, and their daily gossip." The gender bias implicit in Wright's definition of the truly interesting subject is obvious, but his comments are still useful in directing our attention to what women were actually doing. In *Woman's Fiction*, Baym contends that "if critics ever permit the woman's novel to join the main body of 'American literature,' then all our theories about American fiction, from Richard Chase's 'romance' to Richard Poirier's 'world elsewhere' to Carolyn Heilbrun's 'masculine wilderness' will have to be radically revised." One such theory, put to the test by the material in this anthology, is that which claims there was no fiction of manners in the United States before the Civil War. This position, based on the argument that pre–Civil War America did not present a social picture sufficiently dense and complex to support such a fiction, was initially articulated by Cooper, subsequently reiterated by Hawthorne, and dramatized after the Civil War by Henry James, who left America for England precisely in order to write such a fiction. But a look at the work of American women before the Civil War suggests that sufficient material for such fiction was indeed there and that other factors were at work in determining the choice of American men to write differently. These factors are perhaps implicit in the language of William Gilmore Simms's invidious distinction between the lesser world of manners and the higher realm of romance:

> The ordinary events of the household, or of the snug family circle, suggest the only materials [for the novel of manners]; and a large gathering of the set, at ball or dinner, affords incidents of which the novelist is required to make the highest use. Writers of much earnestness of mood, originality of thought, or intensity of imagination seldom engage in this class of writing. . . . [Scott] consoled himself with the reflection that male writers were not good at these things (quoted in James W. Tuttleton, *The Novel of Manners in America*, 1972).

Women, however, who were responsible for the ordinary events of the household and whose lives were centered in the family circle, whether "snug" or otherwise, were quite good at using such material in their fiction. And they did so, almost immediately. Unable, as Baym argues, to "imagine the concept of self apart from society," American women writers early concentrated on describing the social context that shapes the individual self, and thus they created a literature concerned with the connection between manners, morals, social class, and social value. In writing of Sedgwick's *Clarence*, published in 1830, Edward Foster claims for it the status of precursor to "the kind of social satire with which Edith Wharton was to prove especially capable." In 1832, Eliza Leslie won a prize for "Mrs. Washington Potts," a story that describes the fatal susceptibility of Americans to the lure of upward mobility and satirizes the bad manners and cruel behaviors that accompany this social disease.

Bad manners serve Kirkland equally well as an index of the negative consequences that attend the deracination produced by the "man's notion" of upward through westward mobility. Combing one's hair over the table and dropping the loose hairs on the floor, a nice habit of certain frontier women, symbolizes for Kirkland the loss of the values of hospitality and domesticity. In her view, bad manners reflect the worst faults of the frontier character: aggressiveness, irresponsibility, pretentiousness. Similarly, Harriet Jacobs in *Incidents in the Life of a Slave Girl* (1861) uses a description of manners to expose the fraudulence of the southern white claim to moral superiority. To ensure that her slaves will not eat the leftovers, the sadistic mother of Jacobs's child mistress spits in the pots after the food has been served. And when Cooke accords her "heroine" the name of Miss Lucinda Jane Manners, she focuses our attention on the role that manners play in the interactions and distinctions among classes within the supposedly classless American scene.

That all these writers were essentially middle-class in their assumptions, their values, and their point of view perhaps goes without saying. But it may be worth noting that the virtues they extol—kindness, courtesy, generosity, honesty, sympathy, integrity—however middle-class they may be in their origins, are presented as the standard for human behavior and are observed to occur in persons of all classes. Aware of the class divisions in American society, these writers were not, with certain notable exceptions such as Davis, essentially opposed to the idea of class. And in equating virtue with the best characteristics of the middle class, they produced in effect a fiction of middle-class manners.

Another theory of American fiction that would require revision if the work of nineteenth-century women were admitted to the category of American literature is that which claims the "rise of realism" as the significant event of post–Civil War American literary history. American women writers were realists well before the Civil War. In the preface to *A New Home*, Kirkland explicitly presents realism as her perspective; she describes her book as "very nearly—a veritable history; an unimpeachable transcript of reality; a rough picture, in detached parts, but pentagraphed from the life," and goes on to claim her work is "valuable only for its truth." In the second chapter of *Forest Life* (1842), Kirkland articulates her commitment in dramatic fashion. Donning the "magic glasses" of romanticism at the start of her tour of the Michigan frontier, she enjoys the view of "cottages . . . roofed with golden thatch, and enriched with mosses, like silk-plush; every casement was curtained with veined ivy, satin-leaved, and every door surrounded with its group of lovely mothers, and children . . ."—until one such "lovely mother" implores the "lovely lady" to let her "infant cherub" have the glasses for a moment. In an instant they are broken, the cherub converts to a "dirty little urchin," and for the rest of the trip Kirkland is committed to seeing through her own eyes what is really there.

Similarly, Lydia Maria Child in *Letters from New York* (1843), though wishing to resist the tendency of the "Practical" to suffocate the "Ideal" within her, nevertheless feels compelled to recount what the practical side of her actually sees. Her letters record with minute fidelity to both fact and feeling the life she observes on the streets of New York. Cary, in the opening paragraph of "Uncle William's" (1853), identifies herself as on the side not of "ingeniously [woven] probabilities," but of "a simple statement of facts," a position that commits her to language "after the manner of our landlord at the Clovernook Hotel" and to the histories of the young women with whom she went to school rather than to "a flight in the realms of fancy." In her history, *The Pearl of Orr's Island*, Stowe makes her young woman a painter whose art is characterized by "a fidelity to Nature that showed the most delicate gifts of observation." Mara's achievement in realism is accomplished "by herself" and against the grain of her "training," for at schools like Miss Plucher's, where Mara has been "finished," girls are encouraged to paint pictures that, according to her friend Sally, "needed [one] to write under them what they were made for." For a writer like Gail Hamilton, realism provides a necessary caution against the dangers of romantic self-delusion. Her comic perspective works the contrast between the vision conjured up by the phrase, "my garden," and the dismal reality that usually results from following that particular flight of fancy. In the work of writers like Jacobs and Davis, describing things as they are, not as popular myth, self-serving delusion, or cultural romance would have them, serves as the primary, if not the only, way to change the reality they describe. For such writers, the commitment to realism is closely connected to the commitment to social change.

Many of the writers included in this anthology were significantly involved with one or more of the movements for social change that played such a large part in the mid-nineteenth-century American milieu. Furthermore, they believed in the power of words to effect change. Thus, as a group, they produced a literature characterized by a sensitivity to and a protest against what they saw as injustice. Grimké, for example, writing about the experiments that took place during the Civil War on the sea islands off the coast of South Carolina, experiments in land redistribution, cooperative labor, and education that might have served as a model for southern Reconstruction, articulates a vision of the injustice of slavery and protests the racism that produced such a system, a system which she fears will survive its legal demise. Child, a dedicated abolitionist—indeed, when she wrote *Letters from New York* she was serving without pay as editor of the *National Anti-Slavery Standard*—in her letters focuses equally on the issue of class, reflected in the growing gap between the rich and the poor in America. In *Letters from New York*, the political dominance of those with money and the almost conscious creation of an impoverished and hence "criminal" class becomes for Child the primary horror at the heart of so-called democratic America. Davis reiterates this perception. In "Life in the Iron Mills" she asks "why"—why are some people born rich, free, and self-determinant, while others are born poor, slave, and self-destructive? Her passionately posed question symbolizes the collective voice of this group of American writers.

Different selections for this anthology would have underscored the predominance of the concern with social issues in the work of these writers. For example, excerpts from Sedgwick's *Hope Leslie* (1827) would have illustrated the early concern of American women writers with the treatment of Native Americans. Frequently appalled by the virtual genocide of these peoples, American women writers took a very different position on the subject than did their white male counterparts. In writing *Ramona* (1884), Helen Hunt Jackson could draw on a tradition of protest that included, among others, Child's *Hobomok* (1824), Sedgwick's *Hope Leslie*, and Ann Stephens's *Malaeska* (1860). Similarly, excerpts from Gail Hamilton's "Men and Women" (1863) would have placed her firmly in the tradition of protest. In this essay, Gail Hamilton addresses at considerable length and with marvelous wit "women's wrongs" from the oppressive nature of women's clothing to the restrictions placed on their mobility to the failures of female education and finally to the pressures placed on women to shut up and stop writing.

Yet, the example of Gail Hamilton notwithstanding, there was one aspect of the nineteenth-century concern for social justice that these writers found difficult to address directly. On the subject of women's oppression, the collective voice of mid-nineteenth-century American women writers is essentially muted and indirect. Although this period saw the rise of self-conscious and organized feminism in the United States and although many of the writers represented in this anthology were personally sympathetic to various aspects of the nineteenth-century women's movement, they produced no literary expression of feminism comparable to *Uncle Tom's Cabin*, the literary analogue of the abolitionist movement. In the period after the Civil War, Elizabeth Stuart Phelps's *The Story of Avis* (1877) constitutes such an expression, as does to some degree Kate Chopin's *The Awakening* (1899), but from the earlier period no text exists that I know of that addresses the oppression of women as *Uncle Tom's Cabin* addresses the oppression of black people—clearly, directly, with passionate conviction, intellectual coherence, and aesthetic power.

The text that comes the closest is *The Pearl of Orr's Island*, a book that Stowe interestingly enough began shortly after she finished *Uncle Tom's Cabin*. Yet the difference between the two books is marked. In both, the protagonist dies. In *Uncle Tom's Cabin*, however, Tom's death measures the full horror of the system of slavery, a system that gave white people power over black people and rationalized that injustice by a spurious distinction between the humanity of whites and that of blacks. Although he chooses to die rather than to violate his Christian principles, Tom does not die because he is a Christian; slavery kills him. Nor is Tom a Christian because he is a slave; his moral superiority and his status as a slave are not causally connected. For the better world that *Uncle Tom's Cabin* envisions is a Christian world in which whites and blacks, perceived as similarly human and treated as equals, equally embody Christian principles. Tom dies to bring into being a world where he could live.

In *The Pearl of Orr's Island*, Mara's death has no similar transformative power because Stowe can not imagine a world without distinctions between men and women. And this imaginative failure in turn stems from the fact that in Stowe's view Mara's moral superiority is causally connected to her status as a woman. Mara dies because as a woman she is too good for the world she inhabits. Stowe can not envision a world in which Mara could live because she can not imagine men becoming women or women becoming men. In committing herself in this later text to an ideology that claims a distinction between the humanity of women and the humanity of men, Stowe cuts herself off from the imagination of a possibly different future. In *Uncle Tom's Cabin*, Stowe can imagine black becoming "white" because it means slave becoming free. In *The Pearl of Orr's Island*, she can not imagine men becoming women because she realizes, despite the ideology of female superiority that the book proposes, that it would mean free becoming slave. Yet even less can she or does she wish to imagine women becoming men, for this would entail morally superior becoming morally inferior. Thus if movement in time and space defines the world of *Uncle Tom's Cabin*, stasis defines the world of *The Pearl of Orr's Island*. And Mara's death, a self-contained event, testifies finally to the dead end of the ideology that produced it.

Although mid-nineteenth-century American women writers could choose to write about women and their lives, they could not apparently choose to write directly about the injustices of those lives. The reasons for this are obviously multiple and well beyond the scope of this introduction to explore. Yet certainly the pressures on women to be selfless, pressures that led in the work of the literary domestics to the promulgation of, as Kelley puts it, "the supreme ethic of selfless service," impaired their ability to speak out in their own behalf. Furthermore, the ideological confusion apparent in a text like *The Pearl of Orr's Island* may have made it difficult for women to see their own oppression as clearly as they could see that of others. Again, as Kelley comments in relation to the literary domestics, "woman's immersion in her own peculiar history made ultimate self- and social knowledge elusive and the foreboding nature of the life to be understood forestalled personal resolution. To criticize or perhaps condemn the life was to criticize or condemn the self." And, finally, the personal risks of direct confrontation with the oppression of women must have seemed considerable. Yet that many of these women were aware of such oppression is apparent from their texts. Instead of direct confrontation, they chose to treat this subject indirectly—as a secondary theme or a side issue, as a subtext beneath and interfering with the surface text, or even as a text within the text.

In the first half of *The Pearl of Orr's Island*, Stowe records with considerable detail and some bitterness the differing attention accorded male and female development. In addition, she traces the divergent sense of self that results from this difference and implicitly connects Mara's early death to her culturally induced lack of self-esteem, an injury personalized by the pervasive contempt for girls exhibited by her "brother," Moses. Thus Stowe's text within the text tells a rather different story from that contained in the book's explicit ideology. Similarly, the subtext of Phelps's *The Angel Over The Right Shoulder* undercuts the easy resolution offered by the surface text. The narrator's illusion of compatibility between the needs of self and the pressure to serve others is exposed by the severe drama of choice presented in her dream of opposing angels. In effect, Phelps's story articulates the trauma of a life defined as valueless in itself.

Other examples of this consciousness of women's oppression, expressed as an aspect of a different subject, can be cited. In her lectures, Maria Stewart alludes to the criticism leveled at her as a woman daring to speak in public. Kirkland clearly recognizes the cost to women of the decision to uproot and move west. Fanny Fern satirizes the lies served up to women as guides for living. And in a single sentence, Jacobs says it all: "Slavery is terrible for men; but it is far more terrible for women."

I have not chosen to include in this anthology any examples from that body of nineteenth-century American women's writing that Baym designates as "woman's fiction" (Baym explicitly excludes *The Pearl of Orr's Island* from this category) and that Kelley identifies with the "literary domestics"—that is, novels. In part my reasons were strategic. I do not think that excerpts from these novels can adequately convey to the contemporary reader their thematic concerns, emotional force, or artistic form; their power to move rests on the cumulative effect of their completed design. Yet my decision also involved an act of judgment that is still problematic for me. I do not think that the novel represents the best work of nineteenth-century American women prose writers. Rather, I think that these writers did their best work in other forms—the letter, the sketch, the personal essay, the newspaper column, short fiction. There are several reasons why this might be so. First, as I have suggested earlier, the novel was the "big" form for nineteenth-century women's fiction. It was the most serious and most literary form; it was also the most popular and the most profitable, and the one most calculated to produce notoriety, if not fame. And for these very reasons, I would argue, it also received the most interference from the male literary establishment; it was the form most highly programmed and most heavily burdened by thematic and formal conventions. Significantly, Douglas's description in "The 'Scribbling Women' and Fanny Fern" of internalized interference refers primarily to the experience of the novels. More recently, the work of Kelley ("The Sentimentalists: Promise and Betrayal in the Home," 1979) and Myra Jehlen ("Archimedes and The Paradox of Feminist Criticism," 1981) argues in this direction, Jehlen going so far as to claim that the mid-nineteenth-century American women novelists "were conceptually totally dependent." Writers who wished to avoid such conceptual dependency or who wished to experiment with artistic form might well have chosen to work in genres less formalized, less pretentious, and less predetermined, and therefore more open, fluid, and malleable to their uses. As Gilbert and Gubar have stated, "most Western literary genres are, after all, essentially male-devised by male authors to tell male stories about the world"; in territory less clearly marked, the women's story that these writers wished to tell could perhaps be better told.

Similarly, one could argue, for the reasons suggested in the discussion of self-consciousness and self-confidence, that nineteenth-century American women found it easier to write well in forms that appeared less literary, artistic, and serious because such efforts more accurately coincided with their sense of who they were and what they could do; aiming lower enabled them to produce better work. For what would it have taken for a nineteenth-century American woman to have had the sense of self necessary for the creation of a work like *Moby Dick?* Stowe did not, after all, set out to write the epic she ultimately produced with *Uncle Tom's Cabin.* She initially conceived the work as a relatively brief series of sketches to be published in a friendly paper. In a very real sense, *Uncle Tom's Cabin* just "grow'd," and I would argue that Stowe's achievement is intimately connected to this fact. For it is not, I think, accidental that the genres at issue are all short forms. For reasons that again are beyond the scope of this introduction to explore, the short form best served the interests of these writers. Suffice it to say that the greatest of all nineteenth-century American women artists, Emily Dickinson, in choosing to write some 1,770 very short poems, defined the "tiny tale" as the ultimate mode of self-expression for her community.

Finally, one might note that novels require plots and plots present problems for women writers. As Joanna Russ has argued in "What Can a Heroine Do? Or Why Women Can't Write" (1972), there is very little that heroines can do and thus it is difficult for women to write books about them. The group of women represented by this anthology, wishing to write about women, avoided the problem of plot by writing short stories, sketches, essays, letters in which the focus could be on character, manners, setting, atmosphere. While Baym has argued for a qualified but positive reassessment of the woman's story embodied in "woman's fiction," and Jane Tompkins has argued for a radical re-vision of the so-called sentimental novels, claiming that they are powerful and important in their own right and equal in value to the fictions produced by nineteenth-century American men, the work of Douglas, Jehlen, and Kelley suggests why this literature is still hard for us to take. To this discussion, I would simply add the point made above, that the issue of plot is part of the problem. Cary can serve as an example. To go from the

"Clovernook" sketches to one of Cary's novels is to discover precisely
the degree to which the requirements of plot can sabotage a substantial
talent. In *Hagar* (1852), all of Cary's gifts for creating character, setting,
atmosphere, and tone are evident in the sections of the novel that treat the
rural scene; yet saddled, by virtue of her form, with the necessity for
creating both heroine and action, Cary fails to produce more than a blank
face passively suffering in an empty space.

Nevertheless, much of the significant work being done on nineteenth-
century American women writers focuses on the novelists. This fact suggests their centrality to the tradition explored in this anthology and
interested readers should consider, as they investigate this material
further, the degree to which the comments I have made above apply as
well to the novelists as to those working in other genres. Possibly my
own view of this tradition has been skewed by my decision to exclude the
novels from my deliberations. Such an extension of inquiry is, of course,
the work to be done by that growing community of readers to whose
increment this anthology is dedicated.

II

It would, I think, be no exaggeration to state that the work of
nineteenth-century American women before 1865, the work of the
women represented in and by this anthology, simply does not exist in the
field of nineteenth-century American literature as it is currently defined.
This literature forms no part of the context from which generalizations
about the period are made, it is not included in contemporary anthologies
of American literature, and it makes virtually no appearance in the standard histories of American literature. Of the writers represented in this
anthology, for example, nine do not appear in the *Literary History of the
United States* (revised fourth edition, 1974), five are merely mentioned in
passing, Sedgwick gets a paragraph, and only Stowe receives any
significant attention. In *The Literature of the American People* (1951),
Arthur Hobson Quinn treats in detail only Sedgwick and Stowe; of the
fourteen other writers included in this anthology, nine are not named and
the other five are mentioned only in passing.

Equally telling is the situation with anthologies. For a session at the
1981 Modern Language Association Convention, a colleague and I
undertook a survey of recent and current anthologies of American literature to determine the quality of their representation of women writers.
Of the writers included in this anthology, only Stowe appeared in any of
the texts examined. Like Stowe, Margaret Fuller made an occasional,
minimal appearance. Otherwise, as far as the editors of these anthologies
were concerned, there were no women writing during the period from
1830 to 1865 whose work is worth reprinting for the contemporary
reader—which is to say, there is nothing written by women during this
period that is aesthetically interesting, culturally representative, or his-
torically important. For the editors of many of these anthologies are

committed to broad principles of inclusion; their introductions proudly proclaim the goal of a more comprehensive and more accurate view of American literature based on the inclusion of more diverse, more representative, and noncanonical works. Yet in no instance did this agenda lead these editors to the work of the writers represented in this anthology, though it did lead them to the work of, for example, Theodore Parker, John Brown, Horatio Greenough, Abraham Lincoln, John James Audubon, and James Kirke Paulding.

The same pattern emerges from the scrutiny of yet another set of documents—the annual bibliographies of the *PMLA*. For example, the bibliography for 1941 carries an entry on "Matthew Franklin Whittier," "brother of the poet" who wrote dialect letters under the name "Ethan Spike." In 1944, we could read about William Cox, author of *Crayon Sketches* (1833), who is presented to us as a "minor essayist with 'authentic claims to remembrance'"; and we could discover that Ebenezer Starves, not William Tappan Thompson, was the author of *The Slaveholder Abroad* (1860). Nineteen hundred and forty-eight was a big year for Parton's brother, with articles appearing on "N. P. Willis and the American Language" and "Social Criticism in the Fiction of N. P. Willis." In 1949 and 1950, concern for rediscovering lost American fiction surfaced in a series of articles—"An Unfinished Novel by Nicholas Biddle"; "R. M. Bird's Plans for Novels of the Frontier"; "A 'Lost' American Novel" (on J. G. Ingraham's *Pierce Fleming, or The Lugger's Chase*); and "Timothy Flint's 'Lost Novel.'" In the same period of time, not a single article appeared on Sedgwick, Stewart, Sigourney, Kirkland, Phelps, Cary, Fanny Fern, Cooke, Davis, Spofford, Jacobs, Gail Hamilton, or Grimké. This pattern is duplicated for every decade up to and including the present.

Working with the bibliographies from *American Literature*, a journal that began publication in the 1920s, Paul Lauter finds a similar situation. With the exception of Dickinson, Lauter notes,

> the *only* article on a woman writer until volume ten was one on American comments, mostly by men, on George Sand. In volume ten one finds a piece, by a male scholar, on Cather, as well as another trying to show that Ann Cotton derived her material from husband John. It is not, I should add, that the journal confined itself to 'major' writers or to authors from the early or mid-nineteenth century. Quite the contrary, it ran pieces on stalwarts like John Pendleton Kennedy, not to speak of *Godey's Ladies' Book*, as well as articles dealing with a number of twentieth-century male authors ("Race and Gender in the Shaping of the American Literary Canon: A Case Study From the Twenties," 1983).

And in "The Politics of Bibliography" (1982), Deborah Rosenfelt points out that the "staggering disproportion between male and female writers" represented in Jacob Blanck's *Bibliography of American Literature*, published from 1955 through 1969, can not be explained by the single criterion stated in the preface—recognition during the author's lifetime. Instead, she argues, women writers were eliminated by hidden criteria never explicitly articulated. One such criterion, according to Rosenfelt, is the assumption that "minor women writers are more minor than minor male writers." Commenting on the invisibility of the suffragists in the category of nonfiction prose, a category that for Blanck includes, among others, the work of Silas Weir Mitchell, Rosenfelt notes that "nonfiction prose is more likely to qualify as 'literature' when written by men than when written by women—particularly, perhaps, when the content is explicitly feminist."

Rosenfelt's language here is unnecessarily tentative and generous. In "Sentimental Power: *Uncle Tom's Cabin* and the Politics of Literary History" (1981), Tompkins states the situation more forcefully and more accurately. In writing of Sacvan Bercovitch's *American Jeremiad,* Tompkins notes that "invaluable as Bercovitch's book is, it provides a striking instance of how totally academic criticism has foreclosed on sentimental fiction; since, even when a sentimental novel fulfills a man's theory to perfection, he cannot see it. For him, the work doesn't even exist." Tompkins makes the essential point. For what these examples in their cumulative effect demonstrate is that within the conceptual framework that informs the study of nineteenth-century American literature there exists a fusion between "American" and "writer" and "male" so complete that it simply never occurs to an editor seeking to define American literature through an anthology, or to a literary historian or bibliographer committed to recording and describing the development of American literature, or to a critic interested in exploring the American literary imagination, to consider the work of nineteenth-century American women. For them, it is as if it does not exist.

It may indeed be the case, as Lauter has argued in "Race and Gender in the Shaping of the American Literary Canon," that this identification of the American writer with white middle-class Anglo-Saxon men is of relatively recent origin. Certainly the following example from a contemporary critic suggests in rather dramatic fashion the accuracy of Lauter's thesis. Describing a portrait painted by the American artist, Thomas Hicks, which presents "a stylized representation of a group of American writers whose careers spanned the first half of the nineteenth century," Louis Simpson comments:

> To us today, although probably not to people of the time, it seems grossly indiscriminate. Present are not only Cooper, Bryant, Irving, Emerson, Lowell, Holmes, Poe, Hawthorne, and Whittier (Thoreau, Melville, and Whitman are to our present-day eyes conspicuously absent), but also Mrs. (sic) Sedgwick, Mrs. Selby, Mrs. Sigourney, Mrs. Southworth, and others of that subliterary "d---d mob of scribbling women" Hawthorne complained about.

Yet this comment appears in a book entitled *The Man of Letters in New England and the South* (1973). Simpson's title suggests a fusion of much earlier than twentieth-century origin. Indeed, I find it difficult to imagine a time in the history of American literature when the phrase, "the man of letters," did not mean just that. In *Perish the Thought: Intellectual Women in Romantic America, 1830–1865* (1976), Susan P. Conrad argues that the concept of a "woman of letters" was no more possible in 1850 than in 1970. Claiming Fuller as the definitive example of her thesis, Conrad argues that if a "woman of letters" could have existed in mid-nineteenth-century America, Fuller would have been it. Instead, according to Conrad, Fuller conceived of the artist as a "divinely masculine hero."

Obviously, the question posed by Lauter's thesis can not be answered until the literary climate of mid-nineteenth-century America has been examined with an eye to exploring its gender biases and in particular to determining the implicit and explicit bias behind the various "calls" for a distinctively national literature that dominated the period. Nevertheless, even F. L. Pattee, whose negative opinion of mid-nineteenth-century American women writers as presented in *The Feminine Fifties* (1940) is notorious, notes the critical bias against them:

> The aristocracy of letters as recognized by such editorial boards as those of the *North American Review,* or *Knickerbocker's* or *Graham's* or the *Atlantic Monthly,* the baby of the magazines in the late fifties, were, in heart at least, with Dr. Samuel Johnson, whose opinion of "blue-stockings" is well known. In 1854, *The Knickerbocker Gallery,* a volume issued as a testimonial and benefit to its editor, Lewis Gaylord Clark, with contributions from the leading writers whose work had appeared in the magazine since its start in 1833—fifty-four writers in all, contained the work of no woman.

No doubt the issue here is one of degree for invisibility would appear to be a twentieth-century phenomenon. In *The Prose Writers of America* (1846), for example, Rufus W. Griswold includes selections from Sedgwick, Leslie, Child, and Kirkland; and the later *Cyclopedia of American Literature,* edited by Evert and George Duyckinck and published in 1855, more comprehensive, as its name suggests, than Griswold's anthology, contains the work of Leslie, Sigourney, Sedgwick, Child, Kirkland, Stowe, Fanny Fern, and Cary, as well as selections from several other contemporary women writers. In 1873, John S. Hart published his *Manual of American Literature,* a book often cited as marking the beginning of the systematic study of American literary history. In this manual, Hart makes at least passing reference to Sedgwick, Leslie, Sigourney, Kirkland, Child, Phelps, Cary, Fanny Fern, Gail Hamilton, Stowe, and Spofford. (Conspicuously missing from his manual are, of course, the black writers.) By 1891, however, it was possible for Houghton Mifflin to publish an anthology entitled "Masterpieces of American Literature," which predictably included no work by women writers, and in 1920 Pattee produced a more "representative" anthology that reiterated the judgments he saw operative in the nineteenth century and excluded the work of all these writers except Stowe. Since then, the pattern described by Joan Schulz and myself in our dialogue was set; anthologies from the thirties, forties, fifties, and sixties, though replete with selections from minor male writers, contain not a single reference, with the very occasional exception of Stowe and Fuller, to the work of mid-nineteenth-century American women prose writers.

It is perhaps worth noting here that the women whom Lauter refers to in his analysis are primarily the post–Civil War regionalists. Despite his evidence, however, I would argue that writers such as Sarah Orne Jewett, Mary E. Wilkins Freeman, and Kate Chopin have never been as thoroughly obliterated from the map of American literary history as have the writers from the earlier period. Indeed, I would argue that Jewett's achievement lies to a considerable degree in the fact that, for a moment at least, she broke the bond between "American" and "writer" and "male" and made tangible the possibility that a woman could be an American writer. Yet one might also ask what price Jewett paid for her achievement or, alternatively, what strategy she adopted to accomplish this feat. It is, I think, no accident that Jewett chose to work in the genre of regionalism. In the history of American literature, regionalism consistently appears as a minor or secondary strain, an interesting side path off the main road of development. Since the vast majority of regionalists were women, the definition of this genre as inherently minor functions to contain the work of American women in a separate category and to accord it secondary status; it is, if you will, the literary equivalent of apartheid or purdah. Thus Jewett can appear on the map of American literature precisely because her significance can be contained through the politics of genre.

For the women writing before 1865, no such obvious container exists. To some degree, the category of "domestic" or "sentimental" novel, or even of "novel" itself, functions in this way, since it was primarily women who wrote novels during this period in which men were writing romances. And certainly the overwhelming emphasis in our literary history and criticism on the romance as the essential American form automatically excludes from the category of American literature the work of many nineteenth-century women writers. Yet, as I have argued above, the best work done by women during this period was not in the genre of the novel. To obliterate their achievement, something more is required. Although the conceptual fusion between "American writer" and "male" is sufficient to produce invisibility, it is not the only operative factor. By examining some of the other factors that operate to exclude the work of the women represented in this anthology from the map of nineteenth-century American literature, it is possible to understand more fully not only the sexual politics of literary judgments but also the nature of the challenge that this material presents to the current definitions of what constitutes American literature. It is, in other words, possible to understand more fully the origins and utility of the conceptual fusion.

We might begin our analysis by considering the contempt that characterizes most references to the work of mid-nineteenth-century American women. It is apparently impossible to discuss this material, even casually, without quoting Hawthorne's comment about "the d---d mob of scribbling women" whom he saw as his competitors (see, for example, the remarks of Louis Simpson above). One waits for its appearance like one waits for a nervous tic. By his comment, Hawthorne has evidently relieved scholars of the necessity for further definition. This contempt shows up as well in the cavalier approach to facts when the subject is mid-nineteenth-century women writers. So pervasive is this sloppiness that one must perforce conclude that those who write on this material feel not simply that they will not endanger their reputation as scholars by such carelessness, but rather that were they to take this material seriously enough to perform even the most minimal tasks of scholarship, this accuracy would endanger their reputations. In brief, the material is too trivial for scholarship. Thus it does not matter that Elizabeth Stuart Phelps, who was married to Austin Phelps, becomes Miss Phelps in the commentary of one critic, or that her daughter, who wrote under the same name and who did not marry until late in life, becomes in the commentary of another Mrs. Phelps. Nor does it matter that *The Sunny Side; or, The Country Minister's Wife*, the work of Elizabeth Stuart Phelps the elder, is ascribed by one critic to Almira Lincoln Phelps and that this Phelps is described as having "cashed in on the success of her first book with a second one called *The Last Leaf from Sunnyside*," a work in fact published by Austin Phelps as a posthumous tribute to his wife. Nor does it matter that Sedgwick is consistently confused with her sister-in-law and frequently referred to as the "principal of a famous school for girls." Nor does it matter that Child's biography of Isaac Hopper is referred to by one critic as a novel or that the *Literary History of the United States* has her editing the *National Anti-Slavery Standard* from 1841 to 1849.

Particularly appalling is the combination of factual sloppiness with a tone of absolute authority. This combination becomes even more deadly when one realizes that many of these authorities have obviously not bothered to read the material they discuss. Evidently, Hawthorne's jibe has removed not only the necessity of further definition but even the need for any further reading. Thus, one critic can label the work of the "galaxy of female writers" who for thirty years wrote for *Godey's* as "sentimental drivel, untutored trash," and dismiss all of it as "insipid, affected, stilted, verbose." And another critic can summarize the period as one in which "sentimental fiction was much in vogue . . . giving way reluctantly to realism which crystalized in the works of Eggleston and Howells in the seventies." And yet another can contend that "the style of these women was as 'fine' in its superlative decoration as the bindings in which their gift-book contributions appeared or as the pen names they chose." Baym, in *Woman's Fiction,* remarks on such misinterpretation. Critics after Hawthorne, she kindly notes, in commenting on Fanny Fern, "have been led astray by her flowery pen name and classed her with a mythical sisterhood of rhapsodic rhetoricians. In fact, Fanny Fern's newspaper pieces are jaunty, irreverent, and colloquial, written in a style highly responsive to the rhythms and vocabulary of ordinary speech." One such "misled" critic is Pattee who, in *The Feminine Fifties,* describes *Fern Leaves* as "a tear-drenched section of goody-goody inanity, carved alive from the feminine fifties." He follows this "analysis" with a comment from a contemporary review that welcomed the book as a "classic" and described the sketches as "acute, crisp, sprightly, knowing," evincing "a keen power of observation, lively fancy, and humorous as well as pathetic sensibilities." For Pattee this description is "Amazing!" But truly amazing, of course, is Pattee's apparent failure to read the material he is writing about.

The corollary of invisibility is silence. Contempt, delivered with such authority, legitimates the refusal to read this literature and in effect silences these writers. In *The Feminine Fifties,* Pattee interrupts his text to reproduce, "since no one to-day reads" it, the "bombshell surprise ending" of Sylvanus Cobb's *The Gunmaker of Moscow.* He makes no similar interruption to let the women speak for themselves. In chapter 9, predictably entitled "A D----D Mob of Scribbling Women," Pattee quotes, in addition to Hawthorne's comment, a male parody of Maria Cummins's *The Lamplighter,* apparently written by Willis; a male critic on *The Lamplighter;* Thomas Beers, biographer of Willis, on Fanny Fern's *Ruth Hall;* a male reviewer's estimate of Hentz's *The Planter's Northern Bride;* a publisher's blurb for a novel by Southworth; and "Orpheus C. Kerr" on the "disease" of "feminine fiction." For Pattee, and he is representative, voice is male. Thus "to be perfectly fair to *Ruth Hall,* I shall reproduce the review in *Harper's Magazine* one month after the volume was published." This seems a strange idea of fairness. Indeed, it seems hard to avoid the conclusion that Pattee actually does not want to let his readers hear what these women in fact have said. Let us not forget the example of Philomel whose tongue was cut out by her violator because she threatened to tell the truth.

What truth might mid-nineteenth-century American women writers be trying to tell that requires such silencing? In "Melodramas of Beset Manhood" (1981), Baym has demonstrated how "theories of American fiction exclude women authors" because these theories are based on the premise that content determines the "Americanness" of American fiction and the content so identified is invariably male. Arguing from the critical dismissal of "the ubiquitous melodramas of beset womanhood" as not the stuff of which serious American literature can be made, Baym points out that "the certainty here that stories about women could not contain the essence of American culture means that the matter of American experience is inherently male." Thus in the study of American literature there exists an equation between "masculinity" and "Americanness" parallel to the fusion discussed above between "male" and "American writer."

But, as I have suggested in the first section of this introduction, the literature of mid-nineteenth-century American women is essentially about women. Thus the first truth that the women have to tell is that not all Americans are male and the assumption that an American text must be a man's story told by men is partisan to say the least. Were this truth to be told, of course, it would require a redefinition of what constitutes an American theme; it would require the possibility that a story by a woman about women could be an American text. Yet the situation is more complicated still, for at issue here is not simply the insertion of women as subject; at issue equally is the matter of perspective. For a man's story told by a man is not necessarily the same as a man's story told by a woman.

In the literature of nineteenth-century American women the experience of American men looks different. For example, in *Love and Death in the American Novel* (1960), Leslie Fiedler argues that "the typical male protagonist of our fiction has been a man on the run, harried into the forest and out to sea, down the river or into combat—anywhere to avoid 'civilization,' which is to say, the confrontation of a man and a woman which leads to the fall to sex, marriage, and responsibility." Yet what happens to this theme if we take as the norm for "our fiction" a text like Sigourney's "The Father" or Stowe's *The Pearl of Orr's Island*, texts that present men as struggling to return home and tragedy as the failure to get there? Or consider in this context Louisa May Alcott's *Little Women* (1868). Here the boy, Laurie, looks out the window of his grandfather's house and longs, not for the sea or the forest or the river or the war, but rather for a home; he yearns to be asked to play with the girls and to be included in the world of women. If our definitions were to be taken from *Little Women* rather than, say, *The Adventures of Tom Sawyer* (1876), the essential American theme would look rather different. Lee Edwards and Arlyn Diamond make this same point, although from a different direction, in their introduction to *American Voices, American Women* (1973): "the women American men were rushing to the sea and to the woods to escape were not wistfully expecting the return of their husbands and sons so they could tidy them up and send them out to work. They too had fantasies of escaping, if necessary over the dead bodies of the men who thought their women really preferred tatting and waiting."

Other examples of specific thematic differences can be cited to demonstrate the redefinition of American subject and perspective required if the work of nineteenth-century American women were to be seen and heard. Male bonding, for instance, a theme central to the literature of nineteenth-century American men and central to the current definition of the "Americanness" of American texts, figures only rarely in the work of nineteenth-century American women; it is replaced by alliances between women. When male-bonding does appear, as for example in Stowe's *Uncle Tom's Cabin* in the alliance of Quimbo, Sambo, and Simon Legree, it symbolizes a demonic union that makes earth approximate hell. But regardless of the number of examples, the point is the same—namely, the truths that nineteenth-century American women have to tell are quite different from those of nineteenth-century American men. Thus to accept as American the literature written by women would involve a loss of that simple sense of assurance which comes from believing that the man's story is the whole, the only, or the only important story. For, as Annette Kolodny has put it in "Dancing Through the Minefield: Some Observations on the Theory, Practice and Politics of A Feminist Literary Criticism" (1980), "what is really being bewailed in the claims that we feminist critics distort texts or threaten the disappearance of the great Western literary tradition itself is not so much the disappearance of either text or tradition but, instead, the eclipse of that particular *form* of the text, and that particular *shape* of the canon, which previously reified male readers' sense of power and significance in the world."

This loss in itself would be sufficient to produce invisibility and silence. But there is, I think, something more at issue here. As the examples cited above suggest, men's truths when viewed from a woman's perspective are not true. "Man struggling to reach home" and "woman struggling to escape" invert the perception behind "man on the run"; Stowe's parody of male-bonding inverts the value usually accorded such alliances and suggests a completely different judgment on the behavior of men in groups. For it is not simply the case that our women writers offer an alternative view of reality; the reality they offer is often incompatible with that proposed by our male writers. Since in a sexist society the interests of men and women are unfortunately, despite the mythology to the contrary, mutually antagonistic—note Fiedler's "confrontation" and Edwards and Diamond's "dead bodies"—it is not surprising that the realities they describe are incompatible. Furthermore, while the literature of American women before the Civil War is certainly not man-hating and contains no equivalent for the misogyny that afflicts many of our "classic" texts, it is frequently, implicitly and on occasion explicitly, critical of men. Thus to read the literature of mid-nineteenth-century American women requires that one identify as a woman and examine the world through a woman's eye. This requirement no doubt has much to do with the phenomena of silence and invisibility.

Resistance to reading the literature of mid-nineteenth-century American women, however, is never presented in these terms. Rather it is presented, as we have seen in some of the comments quoted above, as an aesthetic judgment. In particular, this literature has been dismissed as "sentimental." Yet since many of the critics who use this term do little more toward defining it than to count the number of tears shed by Ellen Montgomery in *The Wide, Wide World,* one might well ask whether "sentimental" is not in fact a code word for female subject and woman's point of view and particularly for the expression of women's feelings. To dramatize this issue, let me propose a scene that could serve as an opening for a fiction written by a mid-nineteenth-century American woman: a little girl sits in front of a house; she is alone; her clothes are torn, her apron is dirty; any one of a number of casually brutal events may have happened to her; she is crying. How many readers, trained in the current environment of American literary criticism, could take this work seriously? How many readers would not automatically characterize it as sentimental and dismiss it? Yet how different is this scene from the opening of Mark Twain's *Adventures of Huckleberry Finn*? Isn't Huck a little boy, alone, brutalized, and on the edge of tears, if not actually crying, though Huck does in fact "blubber" rather frequently in his narrative? The issue, then, is not tears but whose tears. When we open the pages of an American book, we expect to encounter the figure of a boy or man, and we assume that this figure has the potential for generating a serious fiction, so if he is crying we begin to ask why. We do not expect to encounter the figure of a little girl, and if we do, we are primed to assume that the fiction can not be serious; for many readers the very idea of a little girl itself is inherently sentimental. And if, in addition, this little girl is crying, then we can be sure that the work is merely another of those "ubiquitous melodramas of beset womanhood."

But the entanglement of gender and judgment in relation to the literature of mid-nineteenth-century American women goes well beyond the bias implicit in the term "sentimental." Indeed "sentimental" is only one of many buzz words used to silence these voices and it is not the one most likely to be applied to the writers represented in this anthology. In the first part of this introduction, I discussed the degree to which the literature of mid-nineteenth-century American women is concerned with issues of social justice, has, as Tompkins puts it, "designs upon the world" and seeks "to influence the course of history." In addition, I argued that this literature is predominantly realistic, treating the contemporary scene with considerable fidelity to current social settings and textures. In the work of these writers, in contrast to that of nineteenth-century American men, there is little use of the past as either history or myth. Indeed, when Davis sets "Life in the Iron Mills" thirty years in the past, the gesture seems pointless and unintelligible. Similarly, the work of these writers rarely contains that note of nostalgia so frequent in the work of American men. For women, hope lay more in a future that their texts were intended to effect than in a past, either historic or mythic.

In contrast to the literature of nineteenth-century American women, the literature of nineteenth-century American men seems apolitical and asocial, more concerned with the personal, the private, the psychological; their texts frequently serve as the means for projecting, encountering, and exploring their own psychic territory. Once again, American literature inverts the usual assumptions about the effect of gender on text, assumptions that inform a work like *The Madwoman in the Attic,* since in our literature the women are more concerned with the world and the men are more concerned with the self. But men, of course, set the terms for definition and evaluation; and in this context, the literature of American women appears obvious, simplistic, propagandistic, and given to special pleading. Indeed, it appears narrow precisely because attention is given to a specific social issue rather than to such "universals" as men identify when they probe their particular psychic space. As long as the definition of what constitutes a great American book is taken from the work of American men, texts that are "political," have "designs upon the world," and seek "to influence the course of history" will be perceived as neither American nor good.

Yet the situation is more complicated still. For the texts of nineteenth-century American men are not really apolitical, they only appear so in contrast to works that are more overtly political. Thus the distinction between a great American text and one that is neither American nor good is often in effect a preference for one set of politics rather than another. For example, it would, I think, be a mistake to sever *The Scarlet Letter* (1850) from the context provided by the 1848 Seneca Falls women's rights convention and the subsequent emergence of organized political feminism in the United States. In *The Scarlet Letter,* Hawthorne defines as the first important American event the opening of a prison door and the emergence into the marketplace of Hester Prynne—woman, mother, artist, powerful, sexual. In this opening scene, Hawthorne articulates his perception of the possible meaning of America for women, a perception sharpened by the event of Seneca Falls. *The Scarlet Letter* is designed to foreclose on that possibility, for the containment of Hester constitutes a primary action of the text. Although flashes of Hester's power occur and reoccur, they serve essentially to rationalize the systematic reduction of her power: her sexuality is imprisoned beneath her drab clothing and severe cap; her artistry is diverted from rebellious self-expression into works of charity; her maternal force is converted into the ineffectual fumblings of a mother with a "bad" child whom she cannot control. The treatment of Pearl doubles the reduction of Hester. Throughout most of the book, Pearl is everything a little girl should not be—bold, aggressive, vengeful, resistant to authority, disloyal to her mother, independent, a law unto herself, tempestuous, demonic, and shameless. In the penultimate chapter, however, she is "humanized." She kisses her dying father and "as her tears fell upon her father's cheek, they were the pledge that she would grow up amid human joy and sorrow, nor forever do battle with the world, but be a woman in it." A woman now, silent and silenced, she disappears from history and from story. Such a text is certainly political but its politics are not those of the women represented in this anthology.

Or consider the example of *Huckleberry Finn,* a book many readers would cite as proof that their rejection of the fiction of nineteenth-century American women is not based on politics. For both *Uncle Tom's Cabin* and *Huckleberry Finn* are about and against slavery, so if one is good and the other is bad, the distinction must be aesthetic. But what finally are the politics of *Huckleberry Finn*? Surely there is a difference between a book attacking slavery written before the Civil War and a book attacking slavery written after the Civil War. This difference shows in the distinction between slavery as fact and slavery as metaphor. In Mark Twain's book, the historical experience of black people under slavery is converted and co-opted into a metaphor for the condition of the poor little white boy, enslaved to his conscience, enslaved to civilization, enslaved to growing up, and enslaved finally to his alter ego, Tom Sawyer, who represents his inevitable adult identity.

Another ideological feature that distinguishes the literature of mid-nineteenth-century American women from that of their male contemporaries and that frequently appears disguised as a purely aesthetic criterion is the explicitly Christian perspective that informs so many of the texts by women. In my experience, this feature presents the largest stumbling block to those contemporary readers genuinely seeking to review the work of nineteenth-century American women. Yet although the difficulty is usually couched as a difference between the religious views of reader and writer, under pressure the truth comes out as a set of assumptions about the nature of American texts that readers bring with them to a work like *Uncle Tom's Cabin.* Our "classic" American fictions present a certain view of human nature and human behavior. In this context, Uncle Tom is simply too good to be true, and so *Uncle Tom's Cabin* can not be truly good. Poe's stories are not similarly rejected as bad because his characters are impossibly evil—who would shut his sister living in the tomb? who would axe his wife while "aiming" at the cat? Obviously, definitions of human nature and its possibilities are both relative and political. Yet in the study of nineteenth-century American literature, "the power of blackness" has been enshrined as the requisite position. To be a great American book, a text must explore the dark, perverse, demonic side of human nature; "lurid," "hell-fired," and "wicked," it must carry as its secret motto *ego non baptizo te in nomine patris, sed in nomine diaboli.*

Such a criterion automatically excludes the work of most mid-nineteenth-century American women from the category of great American fiction. Under considerable pressure to write of and from the "sunny side," they did not produce demonic texts. (The work of Elizabeth Stoddard provides an exception to this generalization.) Yet their resistance to the demonic has its origins as well in their Christian perspective and commitment. Phelps, author of *The Sunny Side,* had an imagination of blackness "ten times black" but she fought its visions because she believed them to be unchristian. In writing as Christians, nineteenth-century American women writers aligned themselves with a different kind of power, one that they saw as essentially female. They wrote, not on the side of the devil, who was most definitely male, but on the side of Christ who stood for women. Thus, behind the paradigm, so frequently disguised as an issue of aesthetics, that no Christian book can be an American "classic," as can no book that is "sentimental" or "political" or "radical," lurks the familiar gender bias.

Before I was a feminist, I accepted the statement, once uttered in my hearing, that there was nothing written by nineteenth-century American women worth reading because there was nothing of theirs comparable to *Moby Dick.* In the early stages of my feminist awakening, I accepted an amendment to this statement, also articulated in my presence, that, although it is true that no nineteenth-century American woman wrote a work comparable to *Moby Dick,* the reason for this is not biological but cultural: no woman wrote *Moby Dick* because, since women in the nineteenth century did not go whaling, no woman had the experience necessary to write such a book. Now the issue seems infinitely more complex than either of these formulations would suggest. The stories of Jewett alone tells us that women frequently did accompany their whaler husbands on voyages; thus women did have access to the experience behind *Moby Dick* and could, presumably, have chosen to write about it. Given what I have said throughout this introduction, however, about nineteenth-century women writers, subject matter, perspective, and choice, it seems likely that, had a woman gone whaling and decided to write about it, she would not in fact have written *Moby Dick;* she would have written a book about the experience of women on whalers and about what whaling meant from a woman's point of view. Yet in theory her text could have been comparable to *Moby Dick* in scope, intensity, and power. But in fact there is no work by a nineteenth-century American woman thus comparable to *Moby Dick* and so we must look further into the implications of this use of whale as touchstone.

I have argued above that the long fictional form did not elicit the best work of nineteenth-century American women writers and thus, when the touchstone involves quality plus length, their work will not be comparable. And of course I could point out that the very fact that nineteenth-century American women, when they did write long fictions, chose to write novels, not romances, ensures that their work will not be comparable, as indeed it ensures that their work will be automatically excluded from the category of great American books, since for the mid-nineteenth century that category is inextricably associated with the formal features of the romance. Writing novels, women writers produced texts with a very different conception of plot, character, point of view, and art from those produced by men writing romances. But I would rather focus on another issue that seems to me to be at work here. Although it was clearly possible for nineteenth-century American women to write realistically and well about the details of their daily lives and about the social texture in which these lives took place, it was not possible for these writers, or perhaps it was not of interest to them, to extrapolate from their lives, their experience, and their perspective, and to see themselves as representative, universal, symbolic. To put it another way, although nineteenth-century American women might have gone whaling, they would not have seen themselves in the whale nor would they have imagined themselves as whale. Such attitude toward and subsequent use of the self was not, I would argue, available to women writing in America in the nineteenth century as it was to men, and as a result a certain imaginative quality that we currently identify with great American texts does not appear in their work. Dickinson, of course, transcended this limitation, but she was a poet who did not publish during her lifetime. And still this aspect of Dickinson's work causes difficulty for certain critics, so powerful is the identification of the representative, the universal, the symbolic with the male. In my reading, Stowe comes the closest to achieving this quality in fiction—as when, for example, in *Uncle Tom's Cabin* she symbolizes the moral disorder of slavery through the chaotic kitchen of Dinah, head cook in the "shiftless" household of Augustine St. Clare. Yet modern readers find it difficult to see in the world of "kitchen things" symbols of "universal" significance. Their difficulty is instructive of the problem facing nineteenth-century American women writers.

In part, the problem has to do with the body. *Moby Dick*, after all, makes an explicitly sexual reference, and the ease with which Melville moves from self to whale depends literally on his ability to contemplate his body as a subject and project it into his text. It would have been difficult indeed for nineteenth-century American women writers to have achieved a similar comfort with the idea of their flesh. An imagination so physical would certainly have been deemed inappropriate and might well have been labeled narcissistic, exhibitionistic, and even immoral. Thus one is particularly struck by those moments in the fiction of nineteenth-century American women when such projections of the self occur. Harriet Prescott Spofford's "Circumstance" (1860) is a case in point. In this story of a woman, alone in a forest, held prisoner by a wild cat from sunset to sunrise, Spofford conveys graphically the female experience of physical vulnerability and rape. Unimaginable as a man's story, it depends for its power on the fact of female flesh.

Yet such imaginative acts are rare in the literature of nineteenth-century American women. And when one reads their work in conjunction with the texts of nineteenth-century American men, one is struck by the relative ease with which the men convert themselves, their experience, and their bodies into symbols built to the dimensions of the whale. Emerson turns himself into a transparent eyeball through which streams universal truth; Whitman leans on the grass, makes love to the earth, and across the sky diffuses his flesh in eddies and jags. Poe converts his mind into the house of Usher; Thoreau looks into Walden pond and sees his soul. Hawthorne's "man of god" possesses passions of the flesh that encode their secret message on his breast. And in "Cock-A-Doodle-Do," Melville dramatizes the assumption that in democratic America a crowing cock licenses men to self-possession and self-expression.

Although it is beyond the scope of this introduction to examine in detail the reasons why the literary imagination of nineteenth-century American women did not work in the same way as the literary imagination of nineteenth-century American men, and thus why they produced no text comparable in this way to *Moby Dick,* and thus why this judgment is indeed gender-linked and gender-biased, there is one text that can provide us with a set of suggestive hypotheses. The text is Stowe's *The Pearl of Orr's Island,* which takes for part of its subject women and imagination. On the island lives old Captain Kittredge, a wonderful teller of tales, for whom "there was no species of experience, finny, fishy, or acquatic,—no legend of strange and unaccountable incident of fire and flood,—no romance of foreign scenery and productions, to which his tongue was not competent." His wife, "a sharp-eyed, literal body," regularly challenges the truth of her husband's narratives but is always forced to give it up because, as she says, "there's never any catchin' you, 'cause you've been where we haven't." In making Captain Kittredge the primary purveyor of the world of the imagination, Stowe suggests that it is easier for men to dream, fantasize, and fabricate than it is for women. Early in the book we are given a typical scene of female initiation—Sally Kittredge forced to sew the seams on a sheet. The endless, dreary, deadly monotony of such female tasks readily turns girls like Sally into women like her mother, literal to the point that they can find no value in the stories of men like Captain Kittredge. Freed from such drudgery, men are freed from the literal. Moreover, they have access to worlds that stimulate rather than inhibit the imagination. And finally, they can not be caught in the stories they tell for who knows where they have really been.

Mara, however, the book's heroine, unlike the Captain's wife and daughter, loves the Captain's stories. She listens to them with passionate intensity, absorbs their every detail, and uses them as the stuff of which her own dreams are made. Stimulated by the work of yet another male fabricator, Shakespeare's *The Tempest,* Mara elaborates the world of her own imagination. But "one attribute of the child was a peculiar shamefacedness and shyness about her inner thoughts, and therefore the wonder that this new treasure excited, the host of surmises and dreams to which it gave rise, were never mentioned to anybody." When Mara finally tries to share her world with Moses, she is met with indifference, incomprehension, and finally hostility.

What Stowe's text suggests, then, is not only that the conditioning of women in mid-nineteenth-century America was not likely to develop their imagination. It equally suggests that for those exceptional women who avoided this conditioning there was good reason for them to keep their thoughts to themselves. Dickinson knew well enough that her "madness" was "divinest sense," but she was also sensible enough not to make the claim public, lest she be labeled "dangerous and handled with a chain." Thus, regardless of what might have been going on inside their heads, nineteenth-century American women writers may well have chosen, for their own safety and survival, to speak publicly in a voice that was grounded in the real, the observable, the daily, the "sane." Although not the madness of Ahab, this sanity has much to tell us. And although we will need new eyes and new ears to see this literature and hear its voice, it is more than time to look and listen.

A NOTE ON SELECTION AND FORMAT

In preparing this anthology, I have had to make difficult choices. This volume could easily be twice its present size, and it could easily be different. Each text included here stands for many not included. To illustrate this point and to demonstrate the wealth of this body of literature, I have included at the end of this introduction an alternate table of contents, which can also, of course, serve as suggestions for further reading.

Originally, naively, I projected a volume that would cover the entire nineteenth century. When I lost my innocence of numbers and began to count words per page, I decided to limit this anthology to the literature in prose written by women between 1830 and 1865. Although this decision cost me some of my favorite writers and texts—Marietta Holley's *My Opinions and Betsey Bobbet's* (1872), Celia Thaxter's *The Isles of Shoals* (1873), Elizabeth Stuart Phelps's *The Story of Avis* (1877)—it seemed the most reasonable. When the literary history of nineteenth-century American women is written, it will most likely diverge significantly from the patterns set by American men. A single glance at my table of contents suggests one such divergence. During the period 1860 to 1865, the years of the Civil War, American men published few works of significance. In contrast, 50 percent of the material in this anthology comes from this period. Clearly, the Civil War played a different role for women than for men in the history and development of their literature. Indeed, major changes in the direction of women's writing would seem to have come later, in the 1870s and 1880s. Nevertheless, until this history has been written, I have chosen to work within the parameters of most contemporary American literature courses.

I should perhaps note that, when I realized I could do only a portion of what I wished, I chose to present the writers from the earlier rather than the later half of the century. Although later writers like Jewett, Freeman, and Chopin are safely contained by the politics of genre, they are at least on the map. The writers included in this anthology are currently nonexistent in the field of nineteenth-century American literature; even the investigations of contemporary feminist scholars focus primarily on the work of the novelists. And, of course, it is true that to understand fully the work of the later writers, we must know their origins.

Fairly early in the process of preparing this anthology, I made the decision to provide relatively substantial biographical and critical introductions to each writer. Since most of these writers will be unfamiliar to most readers, it seemed essential to provide a context for reading their work. In addition, I felt that such introductions offered me an opportunity to develop my ideas about this material. Although I began this introduction with a series of generalizations, I have also used the individual introductions to suggest larger patterns of theme and form and to trace developments and continuities, interconnections and influence, as well as discontinuities and differences.

My decision was also inspired by the desire to break the silence surrounding these writers. I wished to contradict the prevailing assumption that their voices are not heard because their texts have nothing to say and thus nothing can be said about them. I wished instead to demonstrate the counter position, that these texts are capable of sustaining significant critical inquiry and discourse. And in so doing, I sought to begin the process of developing that discourse and the concomitant community of readers so central to the work of recovering and re-viewing the literature of nineteenth-century American women.

Writing these introductions, however, was by no means an easy task. To a considerable extent this difficulty was caused by the sheer absence of information. For many of these writers, there are no existing biographies and virtually no criticism; indeed, it seems likely that the contemporary scholar who seeks to fill these gaps in American literary history will find that much information is simply lost forever. For other writers, only the critical assessments of their contemporaries exist; no subsequent analyses have been made. For a very few of these writers, more recent assessments do exist, but in no instance is there anything that could be called a standard critical biography, and, with the possible exception of Stowe, for none of these writers is there any substantial body of criticism. Furthermore, much of the material that does exist is riddled by inaccuracy, confusion, and contradiction, products of that pervasive contempt for the subject discussed above. Thus, not only must the feminist critic who works with this material fight off the malign effect of this attitude and continually process a rage for which there is no adequate outlet; she must also reckon with the fact that what she says about these writers and their work may simply not be true. I have tried to take account of this fact in writing the individual introductions by being tentative, and even on occasion intentionally vague, at those points where I have encountered disagreement or contradiction among sources; and I have tried to indicate as carefully as possible exactly what is and is not "known" about a writer and her work and precisely what the nature of our current "knowing" is. To this end, I have, wherever possible and appropriate, quoted from my sources, particularly those of the nineteenth century. Not only does this allow the reader to hear a few more nineteenth-century voices; it also allows the reader to challenge the assumptions I have made and the inferences I have drawn from this material. Since nothing I have said in these introductions is intended to be definitive and since such challenge is in fact the intent of my work, I can only hope that further research will correct my inevitable inaccuracies.

At the end of each of the individual introductions, I have provided two brief bibliographies. One is a selected list of primary materials intended as a guide to further reading for those interested in pursuing the work of a particular writer. The other is a list of secondary materials, selected on the basis of my assessment of their value for the study of the writer in question. Two standard and invaluable sources that I have used extensively in preparing these introductions need to be mentioned here: *Notable American Women,* edited by Edward T. James, Janet Wilson James, and Paul S. Boyer and published in 1971 by Harvard University Press; and *American Women Writers,* edited by Lina Maneiro and published in four volumes between 1979 and 1982 by Frederick Ungar.

Neither of these bibliographies is intended to be complete. Nor is the bibliography included at the end of this general introduction so intended. Comprised of secondary materials more general in nature than those found in the bibliographies following the individual selections, it is designed to provide the reader with a list short enough to be manageable and rich enough to be useful.

A PERSONAL NOTE ON PROCESS

When I was eleven years old, my mother began reading to me the novels of James Fenimore Cooper. For my tenth birthday, I received an illustrated copy of Mark Twain's *The Adventures of Tom Sawyer.* Previously, I had seen a movie version of *Tom Sawyer,* which gave me the first nightmare I can remember, and I had watched Mickey Rooney in an equally chilling *Adventures of Huckleberry Finn.* In junior high school, despite the librarian's warning that the book was a "little advanced" for readers of my age, I took *The Scarlet Letter* out of the school library and read it, convinced to the end that Hester had been literally branded. At the same time, at night in bed, I read Poe, the complete tales, in two small volumes, another gift, bound in a beautiful, soft, dark blue leather. In high school, college, and graduate school, I reread the work of Cooper, Mark Twain, Hawthorne, Poe, and added to my list Melville, Thoreau, James, Emerson. I have taught *The Last of the Mohicans, The Scarlet Letter, Moby Dick, Adventures of Huckleberry Finn, The Portrait of A Lady,* "The Black Cat" many times. And I have read many articles and books on these texts and on the tradition in nineteenth-century American prose literature that they represent and define. In all this time and in all these encounters, whether *Huckleberry Finn* was a book worth reading was never an issue. I "knew" *Huckleberry Finn* was a great book before I ever read a page of it.

Working with the literature of nineteenth-century American women has taught me the difference a context can make. During my first few months of reading this literature, an image began to take shape in my mind. I saw the male American "classics" surrounded by placentas; I saw them each firmly centered in a rich nutrient mass composed of critical books and articles, scholarly biographies, exhaustive bibliographies, special and regular MLA sessions, hundreds of discussions in hundreds of classrooms, cheap and accessible paperback editions, richly elegant coffee-table editions, government-funded standard text editions. I saw each of these texts connected to a life-support system that constantly fed them and endlessly testified to their worthiness to be fed. On the other hand, I saw the books of nineteenth-century American women—library copies not taken off the shelves in fifty years; old copies found in second-hand bookstores, musty, water-soaked, costing twenty-five or fifty cents, or first editions in excellent condition costing sometimes a dollar fifty; copies available only on microfilm or in outrageously expensive reprints or once available as part of a reprint project now defunct. When I first started work on this project, no one I knew had ever heard of, much less read, these texts; no body of scholarly material or critical commentary existed to assist me; I had neither been taught nor had I taught any of these texts. In *Women and Madness* (1972), Phyllis Chessler describes women in modern Judeo-Christian societies as "motherless children." The fictional children of nineteenth-century American women were equally motherless. Unlike their fat and well-fed brothers, they were thin, starving, and on their own.

The first task of the would-be mother-daughter is to begin the task of feeding—to get this literature back into print; to talk about it, write about it, and teach it; and to share it with others who in turn will begin to talk about, write about, and teach it. This task seems simple enough until one starts to do it, at which point the interference begins. Harold Bloom devotes an entire book to exploring "the anxiety of influence"; his explicit subject is the creative artist but implicitly he is talking about the literary critic as well. But when one works with the prose literature of nineteenth-century American women writers, there is no "anxiety of influence";

there is rather the "anxiety of absence." Indeed, there were many times during my work on this project when I would have given a great deal for a little "influence." I can remember quite clearly the emotions that attended my gradual discovery of others who were working on this material. Crumbs do convert to loaves when one is famished. Yet while a passion of relief from the anxiety of absence ensued each time I found my perceptions and convictions shared by even one other person, such relief was only temporary. In choosing the material for this anthology, I was, like the texts of my study, essentially on my own.

The difficulties associated with the selection process pale, however, in comparison with those associated with the process of beginning to write the introductions for the authors and texts I had selected. Although I can recollect it now with relative tranquility, I came closer than I like to recall to taking the two hundred pages I had so painfully composed during my first few months of writing, tying them up with my copy of *A Room of One's Own* and a large stone, and sinking the whole bundle to the bottom of the lake on whose shores I had written most of it.

Only over time did it become clear to me that struggling with my own prose reflected serious doubts about the value of my project. But how could this be otherwise, given the "anxiety of absence" I have described above and the long history of denigration and contempt that it reflects? Moreover, my doubt and disbelief were not alleviated by those few existing materials that deal with the literature of mid-nineteenth-century American women; rather they were intensified, for in the shoddiness and inaccuracy of much of this work I saw explicitly expressed both denigration and contempt. Thus each day, when I sat down to write, I had to summon up the energy and the strength to believe in the literature of these women. And each day the process had to be repeated; the work of the previous day gave me no assurance that I could write again the following day. The cumulative effect of this daily struggle registered finally as the complete erosion of my confidence in my material. Eventually, I came face to face with the cruel question of whether these writers deserved or could support the kind of attention I claimed for and was trying to give them. Temporarily, I stopped writing.

What happened over the next few months, however, led me to a major shock of recognition. Rather than backing off from this material, rather than genuinely putting it on the shelf, I found myself instead creating different ways to engage it. I began to xerox copies of the texts and to distribute them to colleagues in my own department and elsewhere; I reorganized courses so that I could teach this material; I designed a program of public readings drawn from the works of these writers. Obviously, I did believe in the value of this material, in the importance of working on it, and of sharing my work with others. And as I saw, through the various engagements I had set in motion, that my belief in these writers was shared, I began to realize that I had indeed committed myself to this project. But if the material was not the problem, what was? Prompted by this question, I began to examine the other half of the critical context—namely, myself—and I began to see that what I had gone through during those first few months of writing constituted nothing less than a major crisis in my own self-concept as a critic, in my definition of my critical persona, and in my vision of my critical function.

I can remember quite clearly the response of one editor to an early chapter of *The Resisting Reader.* "You write," she told me, "with such authority. Your voice is strong and authentic. I find this rare in women critics and refreshing." This was 1972 and I was still sufficiently sexist to enjoy being told I did not write like a woman; I was still sufficiently sexist to associate authority in voice with maleness in body. By the time I wrote the final version of *The Resisting Reader,* I had moved beyond such self-destructive pleasures and I had come to associate authority with the persona of the feminist critic. Yet, as I began to reflect on my experience during the first few months of writing on this project, I began to realize that there was a certain sexism inherent in the "authority" of *The Resisting Reader.* For as I struggled to express the meaning and value I perceived in nineteenth-century American women writers, I wondered what it would mean to speak authoritatively about texts I had read only a handful of times, had never taught or had taught to me, had discussed with others only rarely, if at all, and for which there existed no body of critical commentary? Clearly, *The Resisting Reader* was itself both product and part of the placental phenomenon described above, was itself a luxury of sexism. It is possible to be authoritative about texts that one has read numerous times, read numerous articles and books about, studied for years, taught again and again, and endlessly discussed. In a very real sense, a sexist culture had admirably prepared me to be a feminist critic of male texts. For writing about the literature of nineteenth-century American women it had prepared me not at all. And if I had cracked under the pressure, if I had quit doing what I felt I did not know how to do and gone back to doing what I felt I did know how to do, the sexist cycle of feeding the already fat would have been once again complete.

But if I could not use my old voice, could I find a new one? And what did I want this new voice to do? In the process of working on this material had my perception of my critical function changed as well? In *The Resisting Reader* I had wanted a voice that would interpose between the reader and the text so as to transform the relationship between the reader and the text; I wished to arm the reader against the text and thus to disarm the text for the reader. To do this, I wrote to make my own words a primary text. Now, I wanted a voice that would facilitate receptivity rather than resistance. I wanted my prose to impede as little as possible the reader's own relation to what I saw as the primary text. I wanted my words to serve as medium and instrument, not interference and armament. Obviously, the critical postures implicit in these two ideas of function differ radically from each other. I was no longer an antagonist, I was a lover—though, of course, as an antagonist I had loved and as a lover I quarreled.

The posture of lover, especially when one is a woman loving women, is not the most conventional one for a critic to assume, nor is it particularly comfortable or safe. Clearly my struggle to write reflected a sense of vulnerability. I had left a safe place and moved into one that was unknown and frightening. It may seem strange to identify the position of antagonist as safe. Certainly I expected *The Resisting Reader* to generate criticism, even hostility. But I believed the book would work for its intended audience and that was what mattered to me. Moreover, in the style of the book I felt safe. It was familiar, authoritative, self-assured. Now I was on entirely new ground, having to create a new style, one which by definition I had not tested, one which by definition could not provide the satisfactions of the past. Thus, not surprisingly the event that precipitated the near decision to destroy my work was the receipt of a "reader's report," based on one of the first individual introductions I had written. The reviewer, disappointed in the piece, called it unfocused and uninformed by any clear critical perspective, and labeled my style loose and impressionistic. In my state of extreme vulnerability, this report had an effect far in excess of either its actual content or its intent. I read it as a confirmation of my worst fear—the fear that in choosing to work on the literature of nineteenth-century American women I had lost my voice and that, in failing to find a new one, I had failed as an advocate for the writers and the texts I had come to love.

As I look back on it now, it seems to me that my vulnerability and anxiety make sense in the most obvious way. In the process of working on women writers, I had changed my critical persona, style, function, and stance from "masculine" to "feminine." I had exchanged the authoritative for the tentative, the impositional for the instrumental, and the antagonist for the lover. And I had given up imprinting for process. For the final factor that traumatized my first few months of writing was my recognition of what would constitute success. If I did what I set out to do right, my words would rapidly become obsolete, overwritten by the dialogue they had started.

As an experiment in style, the process of preparing this anthology has had a profound effect on my life. I can best summarize this effect by saying that in coming to know my past, I have begun to dream my future.

In the process of my work on this project, I have been immeasurably helped by the members of that small but growing community of readers who take seriously the work of nineteenth-century American women writers. In particular, I wish to thank Elizabeth Ammons, Nina Baym, G. J. Barker-Benfield, Mary Kelley, Carol Farley Kessler, Marjorie Pryse, Jane Tompkins, and Jean Yellin. Without their encouragement and example, my task would have been far harder. I wish also to pay tribute and give thanks to that group of readers who in the spring of 1983 shared with me my first experiment in teaching this material: Elissa Goldstein, Michael Kiskis, Mary Kuykendall, Bernadette Lamanna, Hazel Moore, Marilyn Sandberg, Susan Shafarzek, Megan Taylor. Their enthusiastic, wholehearted engagement in this experiment gave me a practical laboratory of inestimable value and provided me with much needed personal encouragement; their intelligent and frank appraisals of the material helped me to sharpen and focus my own readings and added significantly to their content; and above all their willingness to share the personal meaning of this material for themselves reaffirmed my conviction of its value. My last and greatest thanks I reserve for Joanne Dobson. Her own work in this field has served me as a steady source of inspiration; her conversation never failed to remind me that the literature of nineteenth-century American women stirs the imagination, moves the heart, and works the mind. She continually nourished my faith in my material, and she read my text in all its different stages, consistently encouraging me in my work while she provided crucial criticism. In a word, and in the fullest sense of that word, she enabled me to complete this project.

The literature of nineteenth-century American women speaks to the contemporary reader. In my various experiences of sharing it with others, I have found this to be so. It nourishes and feeds. In the spirit of feeding, I offer it to you.

Alternate Table of Contents

E. D. E. N. Southworth (1819–1899)
  The Hidden Hand, 1859
Elizabeth Stoddard (1823–1902)
  The Morgesons, 1862
Susan Warner (1819–1885)
  The Wide, Wide World, 1850
Frances Whitcher (1811–1852)
  The Widow Bedott Papers, 1856
Harriet E. Wilson (ca. 1801–1870)
  Our Nig: or, Sketches from the Life of A Free Black, 1859
Anne Seemuller (1838–1872)
  Emily Chester, 1864

Selected Secondary Works

Ammons, Elizabeth. "Heroines in *Uncle Tom's Cabin*." *American Literature,* 49 (1977), 161–79.
Baym, Nina. *Woman's Fiction: A Guide to Novels by and about Women in America, 1820–1870.* Ithaca: Cornell University Press, 1978.
———. "Melodramas of Beset Manhood: How Theories of American Fiction Exclude Women Authors." *American Quarterly,* 33 (1981), 123–39.
Brown, Herbert Ross. *The Sentimental Novel in America, 1789–1860.* Durham, N.C.: Duke University Press, 1940.
Conrad, Susan. *Perish The Thought: Intellectual Women in Romantic America, 1830–1860.* New York: Oxford University Press, 1976.
Dobson, Joanne. "Emily Dickinson and Mid-Nineteenth-Century American Women Writers: A Community of Expression." Ph.D. dissertation, University of Massachusetts, 1985.
Douglas, Ann. "The 'Scribbling Women' and Fanny Fern: Why Women Wrote." *American Quarterly,* 23 (1971), 3–24.
———. "The Literature of Impoverishment: The Women Local Colorists in America 1865–1914." *Women's Studies,* 1 (1972), 3–45.
———. *The Feminization of American Culture.* New York: Knopf, 1977.
Fetterley, Judith and Joan Schulz. "The Status of Women Authors in American Literature Anthologies." *MELUS,* 9 (1982), 3–17.
Gilbert, Sandra and Susan Gubar. *The Madwoman in the Attic: The Woman Writer and the Nineteenth-Century Literary Imagination.* New Haven: Yale University Press, 1979.
Jehlen, Myra. "Archimedes and the Paradox of Feminist Criticism." *Signs,* 6 (1981), 575–601.
Kelley, Mary. "The Sentimentalists: Promise and Betrayal in the Home." *Signs,* 4 (1979), 434–46.
———. *Private Woman, Public Stage: Literary Domesticity in Nineteenth-Century America.* New York: Oxford University Press, 1984.
Kolodny, Annette. *The Land Before Her: Fantasy and Experience of the American Frontiers, 1630–1860.* Chapel Hill: University of North Carolina Press, 1984.
Lauter, Paul. "Race and Gender in the Shaping of the American Literary Canon: A Case Study from the Twenties." *Feminist Studies,* 9 (1983), 435–63.
Loewenberg, Bert James and Ruth Bogin, eds. *Black Women in Nineteenth-Century American Life: Their Words, Their Thoughts, Their Feelings.* University Park: Pennsylvania State University Press, 1976.

Majors, Monroe A. *Noted Negro Women: Their Triumphs and Activities.* Chicago: Donohue and Henneberry, 1893.

Moers, Ellen. *Literary Women.* Garden City, N.J.: Doubleday, 1976.

Mossell, N. F. *The Work of the Afro-American Woman.* Philadelphia: George S. Ferguson, 1894.

Mott, Frank Luther. *A History of American Magazines.* Cambridge: Harvard University Press, 1938.

Papashvily, Helen. *All The Happy Endings.* New York: Harper, 1956.

Pattee, Fred L. *The Feminine Fifties.* New York: D. Appleton-Century, 1940.

————. *The First Century of American Literature, 1770–1870.* New York: Cooper Square, 1966.

Rosenfelt, Deborah S. "The Politics of Bibliography: Women's Studies and the Literary Canon." In *Women in Print I: Opportunities for Women's Studies Research in Language and Literature,* edited by Joan Hartman and Ellen Messer-Davidow, pp. 11–35. New York: Modern Language Association of America, 1982.

Rush, Theressa Gunnels, Carol Fairbanks Myer, and Esther Spring Arata, eds. *Black American Writers Past and Present: A Biographical and Bibliographical Dictionary.* Metuchen, N.J.: Scarecrow Press, 1975.

Russ, Joanna. "What Can a Heroine Do? Or Why Women Can't Write." In *Images of Women in Fiction,* edited by Susan Koppelman Cornillon, pp. 3–20. Bowling Green: Bowling Green University Popular Press, 1972.

Saum, Lewis O. *The Popular Mood of Pre–Civil War America.* Westport, Conn.: Greenwood Press, 1980.

Showalter, Elaine. *A Literature of Their Own: British Women Novelists from Bronte to Lessing.* Princeton: Princeton University Press, 1977.

Smith, Henry Nash. "The Scribbling Women and the Cosmic Success Story." *Critical Inquiry,* 1 (1974), 47–70.

Sterling, Dorothy. *We Are Your Sisters: Black Women in the Nineteenth Century.* New York: Norton, 1984.

Stetson, Erlene. "Black Women in and out of Print." In *Women in Print I,* edited by Hartman and Messer-Davidow, pp. 87–107. New York: MLA, 1982.

Tompkins, Jane. "Sentimental Power: *Uncle Tom's Cabin* and the Politics of Literary History." In *Glyph 8.* Baltimore: Johns Hopkins University Press, 1981.

————. "The Other American Renaissance." Paper delivered at English Institute, 1982.

Voloshin, Beverly. "A Historical Note on Women's Fiction: A Reply to Annette Kolodny." *Critical Inquiry,* 2 (1976), 817–20.

Walker, Nancy. "Wit, Sentimentality and the Image of Women in the Nineteenth Century." *American Studies,* 22 (1981), 5–21.

Watts, Emily Stipes. *The Poetry of American Women from 1632 to 1945.* Austin: University of Texas Press, 1977.

Welter, Barbara. *Dimity Convictions: The American Woman in the Nineteenth Century.* Athens: Ohio University Press, 1976.

Williams, Kenny. *They Also Spoke: An Essay on Negro Literature in America, 1787–1930.* Nashville: Townsend Press, 1970.

Yellin, Jean Fagan. "Afro-American Women, 1800–1910: Excerpts from a Working Bibliography." In *But Some of Us Are Brave: Black Women's Studies,* edited by Gloria T. Hull, Patricia Bell Scott, and Barbara Smith, pp. 221–44. Old Westbury: Feminist Press, 1982.

CATHARINE SEDGWICK

(1789–1867)

Cacoethes Scribendi

Atlantic Souvenir (Philadelphia: Carey, Lea and Carey),
1830.

Born on December 28, 1789, in Stockbridge, Massachusetts, Catharine
Maria Sedgwick was the third daughter and sixth surviving child of
Pamela Dwight and Theodore Sedgwick. Only Charles, born two years
later, challenged her position as youngest member of this family of
seven. In her own words, her schooling was "fragmentary" and "miscellaneous"; it included attendance at local district schools and later at private academies in New York, Albany, and Boston, institutions that
emphasized nonacademic subjects such as dancing and etiquette. Her
intellectual curiosity and aspirations, stimulated by her family environment, received little encouragement from her formal education. In a
memoir written for her grandniece, Sedgwick asserted that "my school
life was a waste. My home life my only education" (Kelley, p. 67).
Throughout her life Sedgwick felt "the want of more systematic training," but she found compensation in the love of reading inspired by her
father who, whenever he was home, kept her up while he read aloud to
the family from "Hume or Shakespeare, or Don Quixote, or Hudibras"
(Dewey, pp. 46, 45).
    Theodore Sedgwick was a self-made man who raised himself from
relative poverty to a position of considerable wealth and political influence. Repeatedly a member of Congress during the early years of
national government, he was intensely Federalist in his sympathies and
devoted to a life of public service and public responsibility. Thus, Sedgwick grew up in an atmosphere pervaded by politics and informed by a
commitment to translating political beliefs into public acts. Sedgwick
may well have been following her father's example when she later decided to translate her own more democratic sympathies into one of the

41

few forms of public action available to her as a woman, namely the writing of "conduct" books.

Pamela Dwight Sedgwick, who came from the colonial aristocracy of the Connecticut River Valley, played an equally important role in determining the pattern of Sedgwick's life. During Sedgwick's childhood, her mother suffered from poor physical health and from mental depression so severe as to verge on insanity. Sedgwick herself attributed her mother's condition to medical ignorance and cruelty, but even more to "the terrible weight of domestic cares" that she was left to bear alone while her husband pursued his devotion to public life (Dewey, p. 29). This early lesson in the consequences of the "self-negation" of wifehood was apparently not lost on Catharine (Kelley, p. 50). As early as 1813, only six years after her mother's death and when she was still in her early twenties, Sedgwick indicated, in a letter to her brother Robert, her predilection for remaining single. Clearly, this choice brought with it certain pains: "It is difficult for one who began life as I did, the primary object of affection to many, to come by degrees to be first to none, and still have my love remain in its entire strength, and craving such returns as have no substitute"; "If I had a home (alas! how many sweet visions are comprised within that impossible *if*)" (Dewey, pp. 198, 216). Yet she never seriously considered marriage. Instead, she seems to have accommodated her conflicting needs for autonomy and love by becoming the surrogate wife of her brothers, Robert and Charles, and the surrogate mother of her niece and namesake, Kate.

As part of this accommodation and perhaps also out of economic necessity, Sedgwick early began a pattern that was to last for over fifty years: in the winters she lived at the homes of her married brothers, Harry and Robert, both lawyers in New York City; in the summers she alternated between the family home in Stockbridge where her oldest brother, Theodore, lived, and the home of her younger brother, Charles, in Lenox where a special wing was built for her residence. These Berkshire summers from 1835 to 1860, to which Sedgwick was socially and intellectually central, are famous in American literary history for providing the meeting ground of virtually every American author of note during the period. Yet the heart of Sedgwick's life was essentially domestic and revolved around the families of her married brothers and sisters. Although devoted to her brothers, Sedgwick also formed strong bonds with her various sisters-in-law and established a number of primary friendships with women. In an observation that echoes the opening of "Cacoethes Scribendi," Frederika Bremer, who visited Sedgwick in the summer of 1851, commented on the absence of "gentlemen" in her circle:

> I spent four-and-twenty hours with the excellent and amiable
> Catharine Sedgwick and her family, enjoying her company and that of
> several agreeable ladies. There were no gentlemen—gentlemen, in-
> deed, seemed to be rare in social circles of this neighborhood. But
> they were less missed here than is generally the case in society, be-
> cause the women of this little circle are possessed of unusual intellec-

tual cultivation—several of them endowed with genius and talents of a high order. . . . The scenery is beautiful; these ladies enjoy it and each other's society, and life lacks nothing to the greater number (Foster, p. 36).

Between 1822 and 1835, Sedgwick wrote five major novels. *A New England Tale* (1822) began as a Unitarian tract designed to expose the narrowness and bigotry of orthodox Calvinism. (Sedgwick's father had converted to Unitarianism shortly before his death in 1813; in 1821, she joined the Unitarian church in New York, along with her brothers, Harry and Robert.) Developed into a novel and published with her brothers' encouragement, it became an immediate success. Sedgwick quickly followed this initial work with the much more ambitious and self-consciously artistic *Redwood* (1824). Written in the tradition of the novel rather than the romance, *Redwood* provides an early instance of the different direction that the development of American women's fiction took from that of American men. Since it was published anonymously, however, and since it was both American and good, many took *Redwood* to be the work of James Fenimore Cooper. Sedgwick's distance from Cooper, if not fully apparent in *Redwood,* was clearly demonstrated by her third, and what many consider to be her best, novel, *Hope Leslie* (1827). Based on her interest in the history of colonial New England, *Hope Leslie* is sharply informed by Sedgwick's desire to counteract racist attitudes toward Native Americans and to present a balanced view of the conflict between the early English settlers and the Indian tribes who inhabited the region. Thus the behavior of the Indians takes place in a context set by the treachery and aggression of the white man. In addition, *Hope Leslie,* in contrast to Lydia Maria Child's *Hobomok* (1824), contains an interracial marriage in which the white woman is not "redeemed" back to "civilization," but chooses instead to remain with her Indian husband and people. *Clarence* (1830) is Sedgwick's only novel of this period whose subject matter, the fashionable New York of her own day, is both urban and contemporary. *The Linwoods* (1835) returns to the pattern of the historical novel and depicts colonial New York at the time of the American Revolution.

Sedgwick was remarkable in her day for the degree of positive, and even enthusiastic, critical acclaim accorded her works. During her lifetime, critics consistently linked her name with those of Cooper, Washington Irving, and William Cullen Bryant and identified her as one of the founders of American literature. The sources of her popularity and reputation are perhaps fairly easy to define. To Sydney Smith's notorious question of 1820, "in the four quarters of the globe, who reads an American book," Sedgwick provided an answer. Her novels were noteworthy for their use of American materials—settings, characters, manners, history—and frequently for their realism in the handling of these materials. In addition, they reflected a commitment to the current mythology of American democracy—that is, to the belief that the only operative basis for class distinction in America was that of manners. Moreover, in marked contrast to Cooper's male-centered world, infiltrated by the occasional "female," Sedgwick's fictional world centered on women and contained a variety of female characters, often both interesting and realistic but always larger and more complex than the current literary stereotypes. Indeed, Edward H. Foster suggests that *Hope Leslie* may have been written in part as an answer to Cooper's systematic division of women into the categories of light and dark, passive and active, good and evil. Hope Leslie, the heroine, is colorful, self-reliant, energetic, successful, and good. Finally, Sedgwick's fictional prose is notable for its ease, grace, clarity, and directness. In sum, Sedgwick gave her country a writer to be proud of, a writer who could answer Smith's question, and to whom Americans could point as an example of what American genius could do with American materials.

After the publication of *The Linwoods,* Sedgwick stopped writing fiction for twenty years, not to return to the genre until *Married or Single?* (1857), and turned her energies instead to the writing of a series of didactic tales intended to address and solve a variety of social problems. Although Sedgwick's solutions seem woefully uninformed and inadequate, based as they are on the assumption that differences in manners form the primary source of class distinctions in America and that teaching the poor to be well behaved will equalize American society, these works nevertheless reflect her profound belief in the American democratic experiment and her deep commitment to devoting her talents, as her father did before her, to the service of her country. It may also be the case, as Elizabeth Williams has suggested, that such works fit more comfortably into Sedgwick's definition of appropriately feminine behavior than did success as a major novelist. Writing to Lydia Maria Child in 1830, Sedgwick noted that she was "not just now at all in love with novel-writing" (Kelley, p. 286). Perhaps her disenchantment stemmed in part from a belief that it was difficult to "do good" through novels. Certainly, by her own account, Sedgwick's literary life took second place to her domestic life: "My *author* existence has always seemed something accidental, extraneous, and independent of my inner self. My books have been a pleasant occupation and excitement in my life. The notice, and friends, or acquaintance they have procured me, have relieved me from the danger of ennui and blue devils, that are most apt to infest a single person. But they constitute no portion of my happiness . . ." (Dewey, p. 249).

Sedgwick died on July 31, 1867, at the age of 77, and was buried in Stockbridge. Her contribution to the development of nineteenth-century American women's literature was substantial. No small part of that contribution lay in the fact that she provided a role model, an image, and a name for her successors to invoke. In effect, she marked the territory of American literature for women; with her example before them, American women could legitimately feel American literature was a field open to them.

In "The 'Scribbling Women' and Fanny Fern: Why Women Wrote" (1971), Ann Douglas identifies the prescriptive matrix laid out for women writers in mid-nineteenth-century America. According to Douglas, in order to accommodate these prescriptions, women adopted a posture of artistic unself-consciousness and readily disavowed any conscious involvement in the act of writing. Remarkable in many ways, "Cacoethes Scribendi" (the phrase comes from the seventh *Satire* of Juvenal and can be roughly translated as the "writer's itch") is perhaps particularly noteworthy for its early sounding of an alternate note. In this story, Sedgwick reveals not only her own artistic self-consciousness but also her understanding of the context that produced much of the "unconscious" literature written by nineteenth-century American women. "Cacoethes Scribendi" thus provides an early instance of the effort on the part of American women writers to possess, define, and even police their own literary territory. Implicit in the story is not only a definition of who should write and why, but also a set of aesthetic criteria against which the productions of female pens are to be measured.

Sedgwick sets her investigation of the subject of women and writing in the context of a community of women, perhaps suggesting thereby that this is a women's issue; what women write will be read by and will primarily affect other women. It is also the case, however, that Sedgwick's description of the village of "H" as a community of women derives from a perception that anticipates the work of later writers such as Mary Wilkins Freeman and Sarah Orne Jewett: American men have left rural New England to women, and thus to write about the New England village is inevitably to write about women. Sedgwick's female community is remarkably unperturbed by the predominance of women. Indeed, the absence of "beaux" has distinct advantages for the young women of "H," for it frees them from mincing, affectation, envy, and insolence, and allows instead the reign of good will and good humor. Although expectations of future mating support this youthful content, the young women appear to be without anxiety about this future. Indeed, marriage seems potentially irrelevant in the face of the present pleasure that the women take in each other. Three spinster aunts attend the heroine of the story; their single state receives no comment nor does it serve in any way to distinguish them from the heroine's mother, the sister who has married. The atmosphere here is far different from the miasma of anxiety surrounding spinsterhood that pervades and infects a text like Louisa May Alcott's *Little Women* (1868). But Alice Courland, unlike Alcott's Jo March, does not wish to write; on the surface level, at least, Sedgwick's text appears less threatening to masculine dominance.

Ralph Hepburn and Alice Courland constitute Sedgwick's model Americans. Significantly enough, their virtues are similar; no separate definition of masculine and feminine virtue emerges from this text. Ralph is first notable for his ability to be the only "beau" in a world of women without losing his head. Ralph's good sense, for such it is, equally enables him to make a fair and realistic estimate of his own abilities. A great writer he is not, but he is "useful, good, and happy— the most difficult and rare results achieved in life." Ralph serves as an emblem of balance and proportion; and he makes the point that, in America, good manners, good morals, and good taste are the only real bases for personal distinction.

Also characterized by good sense and the absence of pretensions, Alice Courland presents a contrast to her aunts and mother and serves to engage directly the issue of women and writing. When Ralph presents her with samples from the "periodical inundation of annuals," she sits down to read them, "as if an annual were meant to be read" rather than merely bought and displayed on parlor tables. Sedgwick's tender sarcasm makes a self-referential point: "Cacoethes Scribendi" itself appeared in one of the earliest instances of this "inundation" that over the next twenty years was to reach the proportion of a major literary phenomenon. Sedgwick here identifies, records, and comments on a significant moment in the history of women and writing in America. The development of the publishing industry, with its attendant explosion of gift books and annuals and later of magazines and periodicals, provided scores of women with the opportunity to write—for money, for fame, for self-expression and emotional release, for something to do. In a very real sense, as Sedgwick implies, much of this literature was not meant to be read but only to be written.

In Mrs. Courland, Sedgwick has both named and identified the phenomenon Hawthorne would later describe so venomously and derivatively as that "d---d mob of scribbling women." Although Sedgwick is critical of Mrs. Courland, her portrait contains no trace of venom. Indeed, an undercurrent of sympathy and affection for this character threatens to subvert the very premises of the text. Both literate and literary, Mrs. Courland has for the first time reached a point where she is free to do something for herself. That something is her "call" to authorship, and, as she discovers her calling, she is both attractive and compelling. Her intense concentration, her sense of revelation, and her expanding vision of her own possibilities combine to produce this effect. Central to her epiphany is the discovery of role models. Mrs. Courland determines on her "career of letters" when she realizes that the exalted realm of authorship is inhabited by "some of the familiar friends of her childhood and youth." From them she learns how to write; she studies their productions and reads them from "beginning to end—faithfully. Not a sentence—a sentence! not a word was skipped." Having thus learned the "art and magic of authorship," Mrs. Courland is more than willing to become herself a role model; she immediately encourages her sisters to write. While Sedgwick presents this encouragement as a kind of communicable disease, nevertheless her description testifies to the importance women writers had for each other and provides a significant variation on the theme of the happy community of women with which the story begins.

Yet Alice is the heroine and Alice resists the itch to write. Or, perhaps, to put it more accurately, Alice is the heroine because she resists and thereby illuminates what is wrong with the itch. In a remark that anticipates the career of Emily Dickinson, who was born the year "Cacoethes Scribendi" was published, Sedgwick defines the problem:

"Mrs. Courland did not know that in literature, as in some species of manufacture, the most exquisite productions are wrought from the smallest quantity of raw material." Mrs. Courland mistakenly believes that subject matter alone constitutes the essence of literature and, further, that subject matter is an already defined and measurable commodity existing out there in the world to be encountered. In her view of authorship, subject matter has nothing to do with personal vision, nor has it anything to do with how something is said. In effect, then, Mrs. Courland has nothing to say and, with nothing to say, the literary act becomes detached, unreal, distorted, even cannibalistic. So desperate is Mrs. Courland for what she conceives as subject matter that "a sudden calamity, a death, a funeral" become "fortunate events to her" and the result is schizophrenia, not integration: "she wept as a woman, and exulted as an author." Thus the career of letters, when carried on in this context, simply reinforces the basic cultural assumption of the incompatibility of woman and author.

This hunger for subject matter also leads Mrs. Courland to violate the principle of realism. Though to the realist the village of "H" might seem a "barren field," Mrs. Courland's "zeal" works "wonders," converting everything into what it is not. When Alice protests that the literary "capital" that Mrs. Courland ascribes to Ralph, the product of his greater opportunity to encounter subject matter, consists in fact of a drunken officer, a runaway milliner, and a mercenary widower, Mrs. Courland reveals her "aesthetic" principle: " 'Pshaw! Alice: do you suppose it is necessary to tell things precisely as they are?' " In this context, which implicitly defines Sedgwick's own commitment to realism, Ralph emerges as the genuine writer. His is a "true story," based on real feelings, and he writes only what he has to say.

The craving for subject matter that afflicts the writer with nothing to say disrupts as well the social unit in which it occurs. For Alice, who must serve as the raw material for four scratching pens, the consequences are disastrous. Forced against her will to be a character in her mother's text, she is transformed into a caricature. Afraid to speak or act at home for fear of stimulating the itch, she is equally afraid to speak or act in public for fear of provoking references to her inadvertent career as a character. Indeed, her mother's assumption of published speech deprives Alice of her tongue. For the "pretty circle of girls" there is poison in the pen as well; instead of "good will and good humor," now "winks and smiles, and broader allusions" predominate. And "oh! what a changed place was that parlour!" The "talking women" are all silently gathering material or "driving their quills in their several apartments" and the social life of the village is in abeyance.

When Alice discovers that she has been made an *author* against her will, she finally acts. How are we to interpret this symbolically potent behavior? How are we to avoid the conclusion that Sedgwick is rejecting the possibility of woman as writer and advocating instead the role of woman as talker, whose words should be heard in the parlor not the annual? And how do we avoid the conclusion that Sedgwick is engaging in an act of self-denial, if not self-hatred? No doubt Sedgwick's ambivalence toward her own career as a writer is part of the subject matter of her text. Yet clearly a distinction can and should be made between the author of "Cacoethes Scribendi" and the authors presented in it. Unlike Mrs. Courland, Sedgwick has something to say. But is it that women should not write?

Perhaps a final comparison with *Little Women* is useful here. Unlike Jo March, Alice does not burn her book because she fears that writing violates some primary gender taboo and therefore makes her un-feminine. Alice burns her book because she realizes she is not a writer and does not want to be forced to become one. Her resistance is an act of self-definition, expression, and assertion, not, like Jo March's, an act of self-denial, renunciation, and mutilation. Consequently, her behavior is both positive and individual. Alice is finally just Alice, not "woman" or "women." Remarkably enough, Sedgwick may be free to write about a woman's not wanting to write simply because it never occurs to her that women should not write if they can.

The question the story engages, then, is not whether women should or should not write, but rather whether Mrs. Courland or her sisters or Alice should write. Neither the question nor the answer is inevitably gender related for nowhere does the story assert that a woman with something to say can not exist. Indeed, it asserts the contrary for its author is such a woman. And, finally, we should note that, though, by the end of the story, Alice's mother and aunts have relinquished their hope of ever seeing her an AUTHOR, they have not themselves stopped writing. Despite Sedgwick's criticisms, these women remain with us, one image of the woman writer—happy, self-confident, and irrepressible.

Source:

The Atlantic Souvenir (Philadelphia: Carey, Lea and Carey) 1830.

Selected Primary Works:

A New England Tale; or Sketches of New England Character and Manners, 1822; *Redwood*, 1824; *Hope Leslie*, 1827; *Clarence*, 1830; *The Linwoods*, 1835; *Tales and Sketches*, 1835; *Tales and Sketches*, second series, 1844; *Married or Single?* 1857; *Life and Letters*, ed. Mary E. Dewey, 1871.

Selected Secondary Works:

Nina Baym, *Woman's Fiction* (Ithaca: Cornell University Press), 1978; Michael D. Bell, "History and Romance Convention in Catharine Sedgwick's *Hope Leslie*," *American Quarterly*, 22 (1970), 213–21; Gladys Brooks, *Three Wise Virgins* (New York: Dutton), 1957; William Cullen Bryant, review of *Redwood*, *North American Review*, 20 (1825), 245–72; Edward H. Foster, *Catharine Maria Sedgwick* (New York: Twayne), 1974; Richard B. Gidez, "A Study of the Works of Catharine Maria Sedgwick," (Ph.D. dissertation, Ohio State University), 1958; Mary Kelley, "A Woman Alone: Catharine Maria Sedgwick's Spinsterhood in Nineteenth-Century America," *New England Quarterly*, 51 (1978), 209–25; ———, *Private Woman: Public Stage* (New York: Oxford University Press), 1984; Elizabeth Williams, "Catharine Sedgwick: A Study in Nineteenth Century Womanhood" (M.A. thesis, Cornell University), 1980.

Contexts:

1826—Cooper, *The Last of the Mohicans; The Atlantic Souvenir* (first American annual); *Juvenile Miscellany* (first American magazine for children)
1827—Cooper, *The Prairie;* Hale, *Northwood;* Poe, *Tamerlane and Other Poems;* Sigourney, *Poems*
1828—Hawthorne, *Fanshawe;* Webster, *An American Dictionary of the English Language*
1829—Irving, *The Conquest of Granada*
1830—Child, *The Frugal Housewife; Godey's Lady's Book;* Webster, *Speeches*

BY THE AUTHOR OF HOPE LESLIE.

> Glory and gain the industrious tribe provoke.
> Pope.

THE LITTLE SECLUDED and quiet village of H. lies at no great distance from our 'literary emporium.' It was never remarked or remarkable for any thing, save one mournful preeminence, to those who sojourned within its borders—it was duller even than common villages. The young men of the better class all emigrated. The most daring spirits adventured on the sea. Some went to Boston; some to the south; and some to the west; and left a community of women who lived like nuns, with the advantage of more liberty and fresh air, but without the consolation and excitement of a religious vow. Literally, there was not a single young gentleman in the village—nothing in manly shape to which these desperate circumstances could give the form and quality and use of a beau. Some dashing city blades, who once strayed from the turnpike to this sequestered spot, averred that the girls stared at them as if, like Miranda, they would have exclaimed—

> 'What is't? a spirit?
> Lord, how it looks about! Believe me, sir,
> It carries a brave form:—But 'tis a spirit.'

A peculiar fatality hung over this devoted place. If death seized on either head of a family, he was sure to take the husband; every woman in H was a widow or maiden; and it is a sad fact, that when the holiest office of the church was celebrated, they were compelled to borrow deacons from an adjacent village. But, incredible as it may be, there was no great diminution of happiness in consequence of the absence of the nobler sex. Mothers were occupied with their children and housewifery, and the young ladies read their books with as much interest as if they had lovers to discuss them with, and worked their frills and capes as diligently, and wore them as complacently, as if they were to be seen by manly eyes. Never were there pleasanter gatherings or parties (for that was the word even in their nomenclature) than those of the young girls of H. There was no mincing—no affectation—no hope of passing for what they were not—no envy of the pretty and fortunate—no insolent triumph over the plain and demure and neglected,—but all was good will and good humour. They were a pretty circle of girls—a garland of bright fresh flowers. Never were there more sparkling glances,—never sweeter smiles—nor more of them. Their present was all health and cheerfulness; and their future, not the gloomy perspective of dreary singleness, for somewhere in the passage of life they were sure to be mated. Most of the young men who had abandoned their native soil, as soon as they found themselves *getting along,* loyally returned to lay their fortunes at the feet of the companions of their childhood.

The girls made occasional visits to Boston, and occasional journeys to various parts of the country, for they were all enterprising and independent, and had the characteristic New England avidity for seizing a 'privilege;' and in these various ways, to borrow a phrase of their good grandames, 'a door was opened for them,' and in due time they fulfilled the destiny of women.

We spoke strictly, and à la lettre, when we said that in the village of H. there was not a single *beau.* But on the outskirts of the town, at a pleasant farm, embracing hill and valley, upland and meadow land; in a neat house, looking to the south, with true economy of sunshine and comfort, and overlooking the prettiest winding stream that ever sent up its sparkling beauty to the eye, and flanked on the north by a rich maple grove, beautiful in spring and summer, and glorious in autumn, and the kindest defense in winter;—on this farm and in this house dwelt a youth, to fame unknown, but known and loved by every inhabitant of H., old and young, grave and gay, lively and severe. Ralph Hepburn was one of nature's favourites. He had a figure that would have adorned courts and cities; and a face that adorned human nature, for it was full of good humour, kindheartedness, spirit, and intelligence; and driving the plough or wielding the scythe, his cheek flushed with manly and profitable exercise, he looked as if he had been moulded in a poet's fancy—as farmers look in Georgics and Pastorals. His gifts were by no means all external. He wrote verses in every album in the village, and very pretty album verses they were, and numerous too—for the number of albums was equivalent to the whole female population. He was admirable at pencil sketches; and once with a little paint, the refuse of a house painting, he achieved an admirable portrait of his grandmother and her cat. There was, to be sure, a striking likeness between the two figures, but he was limited to the same colours for both; and besides, it was not out of nature, for the old lady and her cat had purred together in the chimney corner, till their physiognomies bore an obvious resemblance to each other. Ralph had a talent for music too. His voice was the sweetest of all the Sunday choir, and one would have fancied, from the bright eyes that were turned on him from the long line and double lines of treble and counter singers, that Ralph Hepburn was a note book, or that the girls listened with their eyes as well as their ears. Ralph did not restrict himself to psalmody. He had an ear so exquisitely susceptible to the 'touches of sweet harmony,' that he discovered, by the stroke of his axe, the musical capacities of certain species of wood, and he made himself a violin of chestnut, and drew strains from it, that if they could not create a soul under the ribs of death, could make the prettiest feet and the lightest hearts dance, an achievement far more to Ralph's taste than the aforesaid miracle. In short, it seemed as if nature, in her love of compensation, had showered on Ralph all the gifts that are usually diffused through a community of beaux. Yet Ralph was no prodigy; none of his talents were in excess, but all in moderate degree. No genius was ever so good humoured, so useful, so practical; and though, in his small and modest way, a Crichton, he was not, like most universal geniuses, good for nothing for any particular office in life. His farm was not a pattern farm— a prize farm for an agricultural society, but in wonderful order con- sidering—his miscellaneous pursuits. He was the delight of his grandfather for his sagacity in hunting bees—the old man's favourite, in truth his only pursuit. He was so skilled in woodcraft that the report of his gun was as certain a signal of death as the tolling of a church bell. The fish always caught at his bait. He manufactured half his farming utensils, improved upon old inventions, and struck out some new ones; tamed partridges—the most untameable of all the feathered tribe; domesticated squirrels; rivalled Scheherazade herself in telling stories, strange and long—the latter quality being essential at a country fireside; and, in short, Ralph made a perpetual holiday of a life of labour.

Every girl in the village street knew when Ralph's wagon or sleigh traversed it; indeed, there was scarcely a house to which the horses did not, as if by instinct, turn up while their master greeted its fair tenants. This state of affairs had continued for two winters and two summers since Ralph came to his majority and, by the death of his father, to the sole proprietorship of the 'Hepburn farm,'—the name his patrimonial acres had obtained from the singular circumstance (in our *moving* country) of their having remained in the same family for four generations. Never was the matrimonial destiny of a young lord, or heir just come to his estate, more thoroughly canvassed than young Hepburn's by mothers, aunts, daughters, and nieces. But Ralph, perhaps from sheer good heartedness, seemed reluctant to give to one the heart that diffused rays of sunshine through the whole village.

With all decent people he eschewed the doctrines of a certain erratic female lecturer on the odious monopoly of marriage, yet Ralph, like a tender hearted judge, hesitated to place on a single brow the crown matrimonial which so many deserved, and which, though Ralph was far enough from a coxcomb, he could not but see so many coveted.

Whether our hero perceived that his mind was becoming elated or distracted with this general favour, or that he observed a dawning of rivalry among the fair competitors, or whatever was the cause, the fact was, that he by degrees circumscribed his visits, and finally concentrated them in the family of his aunt Courland.

Mrs. Courland was a widow, and Ralph was the kindest of nephews to her, and the kindest of cousins to her children. To their mother he seemed their guardian angel. That the five lawless, daring little urchins did not drown themselves when they were swimming, nor shoot themselves when they were shooting, was, in her eyes, Ralph's merit; and then 'he was so attentive to Alice, her only daughter—a brother could not be kinder.' But who would not be kind to Alice? she was a sweet girl of seventeen, not beautiful, not handsome perhaps,—but pretty enough— with soft hazel eyes, a profusion of light brown hair, always in the neatest trim, and a mouth that could not but be lovely and loveable, for all kind and tender affections were playing about it. Though Alice was the only daughter of a doting mother, the only sister of five loving boys, the only niece of three single, fond aunts, and, last and greatest, the only cousin of our only beau, Ralph Hepburn, no girl of seventeen was ever more disinterested, unassuming, unostentatious, and unspoiled. Ralph and Alice had always lived on terms of cousinly affection—an affection of a neutral tint that they never thought of being shaded into the deep dye of a more tender passion. Ralph rendered her all cousinly offices. If he had twenty damsels to escort, not an uncommon case, he never forgot Alice. When he returned from any little excursion, he always brought some graceful offering to Alice.

He had lately paid a visit to Boston. It was at the season of the periodical inundation of annuals. He brought two of the prettiest to Alice. Ah! little did she think they were to prove Pandora's box to her. Poor simple girl! she sat down to read them, as if an annual were meant to be read, and she was honestly interested and charmed. Her mother observed her delight. "What have you there, Alice?" she asked. "Oh the prettiest story, mamma!—two such tried faithful lovers, and married at last! It ends beautifully: I hate love stories that don't end in marriage."

"And so do I, Alice," exclaimed Ralph, who entered at the moment, and for the first time Alice felt her cheeks tingle at his approach. He had brought a basket, containing a choice plant he had obtained for her, and she laid down the annual and went with him to the garden to see it set by his own hand.

Mrs. Courland seized upon the annual with avidity. She had imbibed a literary taste in Boston, where the best and happiest years of her life were passed. She had some literary ambition too. She read the North American Review from beginning to end, and she fancied no conversation could be sensible or improving that was not about books. But she had been effectually prevented, by the necessities of a narrow income, and by the unceasing wants of five teasing boys, from indulging her literary inclinations; for Mrs. Courland, like all New England women, had been taught to consider domestic duties as the first temporal duties of her sex. She had recently seen some of the native productions with which the press is daily teeming, and which certainly have a tendency to dispel our early illusions about the craft of authorship. She had even felt some obscure intimations, within her secret soul, that she might herself become an author. The annual was destined to fix her fate. She opened it—the publisher had written the names of the authors of the anonymous pieces against their productions. Among them she found some of the familiar friends of her childhood and youth.

If, by a sudden gift of second sight, she had seen them enthroned as kings and queens, she would not have been more astonished. She turned to their pieces, and read them, as perchance no one else ever did, from beginning to end—faithfully. Not a sentence—a sentence! not a word was skipped. She paused to consider commas, colons, and dashes. All the art and magic of authorship were made level to her comprehension, and when she closed the book, she *felt a call* to become an author, and before she retired to bed she obeyed the call, as if it had been, in truth, a divinity stirring within her. In the morning she presented an article to *her* public, consisting of her own family and a few select friends. All applauded, and every voice, save one, was unanimous for publication—that one was Alice. She was a modest, prudent girl; she feared failure, and feared notoriety still more. Her mother laughed at her childish scruples. The piece was sent off, and in due time graced the pages of an annual. Mrs. Courland's fate was now decided. She had, to use her own phrase, started in the career of letters, and she was no Atalanta to be seduced from her straight onward way. She was a social, sympathetic, good hearted creature too, and she could not bear to go forth in the golden field to reap alone.

She was, besides, a prudent woman, as most of her countrywomen are, and the little pecuniary equivalent for this delightful exercise of talents was not overlooked. Mrs. Courland, as we have somewhere said, had three single sisters—worthy women they were—but nobody ever dreamed of their taking to authorship. She, however, held them all in sisterly estimation. Their talents were magnified as the talents of persons who live in a circumscribed sphere are apt to be, particularly if seen through the dilating medium of affection.

Miss Anne, the oldest, was fond of flowers, a successful cultivator, and a diligent student of the science of botany,. All this taste and knowledge, Mrs. Courland thought, might be turned to excellent account; and she persuaded Miss Anne to write a little book entitled 'Familiar Dialogues on Botany." The second sister, Miss Ruth, had a turn for education ('bachelor's wives and maid's children are always well taught'), and Miss Ruth undertook a popular treatise on that subject. Miss Sally, the youngest, was the saint of the family, and she doubted about the propriety of a literary occupation, till her scruples were overcome by the fortunate suggestion that her coup d'essai should be a Saturday night book entitled 'Solemn Hours,'—and solemn hours they were to their unhappy readers. Mrs. Courland next besieged her old mother. "You know, mamma," she said, "you have such a precious fund of anecdotes of the revolution and the French war, and you talk just like the 'Annals of the Parish,' and I am certain you can write a book fully as good."

"My child, you are distracted! I write a dreadful poor hand, and I never learned to spell—no girls did in my time."

"Spell! that is not of the least consequence—the printers correct the spelling."

But the honest old lady would not be tempted on the crusade, and her daughter consoled herself with the reflection that if she would not write, she was an admirable subject to be written about, and her diligent fingers worked off three distinct stories in which the old lady figured.

Mrs. Courland's ambition, of course, embraced within its widening circle her favourite nephew Ralph. She had always thought him a genius, and genius in her estimation was the philosopher's stone. In his youth she had laboured to persuade his father to send him to Cambridge, but the old man uniformly replied that Ralph 'was a smart lad on the farm, and steady, and by that he knew he was no genius.' As Ralph's character was developed, and talent after talent broke forth, his aunt renewed her lamentations over his ignoble destiny. That Ralph was useful, good, and happy—the most difficult and rare results achieved in life—was nothing, so long as he was but a farmer in H. Once she did half persuade him to turn painter, but his good sense and filial duty triumphed over her eloquence, and suppressed the hankerings after distinction that are innate in every human breast, from the little ragged chimneysweep that hopes to be a *boss*, to the political aspirant whose bright goal is the presidential chair.

Now Mrs. Courland fancied Ralph might climb the steep of fame without quitting his farm; occasional authorship was compatible with his vocation. But alas! she could not persuade Ralph to pluck the laurels that she saw ready grown to his hand. She was not offended, for she was the best natured woman in the world, but she heartily pitied him, and seldom mentioned his name without repeating that stanza of Gray's, inspired for the consolation of hopeless obscurity:

'Full many a gem of purest ray serene,' &c.

Poor Alice's sorrows we have reserved to the last, for they were heaviest. 'Alice,' her mother said, 'was gifted; she was well educated, well informed; she was every thing necessary to be an author.' But Alice resisted; and, though the gentlest, most complying of all good daughters, she would have resisted to the death—she would as soon have stood in a pillory as appeared in print. Her mother, Mrs. Courland, was not an obstinate woman, and gave up in despair. But still our poor heroine was destined to be the victim of this *cacoethes scribendi;* for Mrs. Courland divided the world into two classes, or rather parts—authors and subjects for authors; the one active, the other passive. At first blush one would have thought the village of H. rather a barren field for such a reaper as Mrs. Courland, but her zeal and indefatigableness worked wonders. She converted the stern scholastic divine of H. into as much of a La Roche as she could describe; a tall wrinkled bony old woman, who reminded her of Meg Merrilies, sat for a witch; the school master for an Ichabod Crane; a poor half witted boy was made to utter as much pathos and sentiment and wit as she could put into his lips; and a crazy vagrant was a God-send to her. Then every 'wide spreading elm,' 'blasted pine,' or 'gnarled oak,' flourished on her pages. The village church and school house stood there according to their actual dimensions. One old *pilgrim* house was as prolific as haunted tower or ruined abbey. It was surveyed outside, ransacked inside, and again made habitable for the reimbodied spirits of its founders.

The most kind hearted of women, Mrs. Courland's interests came to be so at variance with the prosperity of the little community of H., that a sudden calamity, a death, a funeral, were fortunate events to her. To do her justice she felt them in a twofold capacity. She wept as a woman, and exulted as an author. The days of the calamities of authors have passed by. We have all wept over Otway and shivered at the thought of Tasso. But times are changed. The lean sheaf is devouring the full one. A new class of sufferers has arisen, and there is nothing more touching in all the memoirs Mr. D'Israeli has collected, than the trials of poor Alice, tragi-comic though they were. Mrs. Courland's new passion ran most naturally in the worn channel of maternal affection. Her boys were too purely boys for her art—but Alice, her sweet Alice, was preeminently lovely in the new light in which she now placed every object. Not an incident of her life but was inscribed on her mother's memory, and thence transferred to her pages, by way of precept, or example, or pathetic or ludicrous circumstance. She regretted now, for the first time, that Alice had no lover whom she might introduce among her dramatis personæ. Once her thoughts did glance on Ralph, but she had not quite merged the woman in the author; she knew instinctively that Alice would be particularly offended at being thus paired with Ralph. But Alice's *public life* was not limited to her mother's productions. She was the darling niece of her three aunts. She had studied botany with the eldest, and Miss Anne had recorded in her private diary all her favourite's clever remarks during their progress in the science. This diary was now a mine of gold to her, and faithfully worked up for a circulating medium. But, most trying of all to poor Alice, was the attitude in which she appeared in her aunt Sally's 'solemn hours.' Every aspiration of piety to which her young lips had given utterance was there *printed.* She felt as if she were condemned to say her prayers in the market place. Every act of kindness, every deed of charity, she had ever performed, were produced to the public. Alice would have been consoled if she had known how small that public was; but, as it was, she felt like a modest country girl when she first enters an apartment, hung on every side with mirrors, when, shrinking from ob- servation, she sees in every direction her image multiplied and often distorted; for, notwithstanding Alice's dutiful respect for her good aunts, and her consciousness of their affectionate intentions, she could not but perceive that they were unskilled painters. She grew afraid to speak or to act, and from being the most artless, frank, and, at home, social little creature in the world, she became as silent and as stiff as a statue. And, in the circle of her young associates, her natural gaiety was constantly checked by their winks and smiles, and broader allusions to her multi- plied portraits; for they had instantly recognized them through the thin veil of feigned names of persons and places. They called her a blue stock- ing too; for they had the vulgar notion that every body must be tinged that lived under the same roof with an author. Our poor victim was afraid to speak of a book—worse than that, she was afraid to touch one, and the last Waverley novel actually lay in the house a month before she opened it. She avoided wearing even a blue ribbon, as fearfully as a forsaken damsel shuns the colour of green.

It was during the height of this literary fever in the Courland family, that Ralph Hepburn, as has been mentioned, concentrated all his visiting there. He was of a compassionate disposition, and he knew Alice was, unless relieved by him, in solitary possession of their once social parlour, while her mother and aunts were driving their quills in their several apartments.

Oh! what a changed place was that parlour! Not the tower of Babel, after the builders had forsaken it, exhibited a sadder reverse; not a Lan- caster school, when the boys have left it, a more striking contrast. Mrs. Courland and her sisters were all 'talking women,' and too generous to encroach on one another's rights and happiness. They had acquired the power to hear and speak simultaneously. Their parlour was the general gathering place, a sort of village exchange, where all the innocent gossips, old and young, met together. 'There are tongues in trees,' and surely there seemed to be tongues in the very walls of that vocal parlour. Every thing there had a social aspect. There was something agreeable and con- versable in the litter of netting and knitting work, of sewing implements, and all the signs and shows of happy female occupation.

Now, all was as orderly as a town drawing room in company hours. Not a sound was heard there save Ralph's and Alice's voices, mingling in soft and suppressed murmurs, as if afraid of breaking the chain of their aunt's ideas, or, perchance, of too rudely jarring a tenderer chain. One evening, after tea, Mrs. Courland remained with her daughter, instead of retiring, as usual, to her writing desk.—"Alice, my dear," said the good mother, "I have noticed for a few days past that you look out of spirits. You will listen to nothing I say on that subject; but if you would try it, my dear, if you would only try it, you would find there is nothing so tranquillizing as the occupation of writing."

"I shall never try it, mamma."

"You are afraid of being called a blue stocking. Ah! Ralph, how are you?"—Ralph entered at this moment—"Ralph, tell me honestly, do you not think it a weakness in Alice to be so afraid of blue stockings?"

"It would be a pity, aunt, to put blue stockings on such pretty feet as Alice's."

Alice blushed and smiled, and her mother said—"Nonsense, Ralph; you should bear in mind the celebrated saying of the Edinburgh wit—'no matter how blue the stockings are, if the petticoats are long enough to hide them.'"

"Hide Alice's feet! Oh aunt, worse and worse!"

"Better hide her feet, Ralph, than her talents—that is a sin for which both she and you will have to answer. Oh! you and Alice need not exchange such significant glances! You are doing yourselves and the public injustice, and you have no idea how easy writing is."

"Easy writing, but hard reading, aunt."

"That's false modesty, Ralph. If I had but your opportunities to collect materials"—Mrs. Courland did not know that in literature, as in some species of manufacture, the most exquisite productions are wrought from the smallest quantity of raw material—"There's your journey to New York, Ralph," she continued, "you might have made three capital articles out of that. The revolutionary officer would have worked up for the 'Legendary;' the mysterious lady for the 'Token;' and the man in black for the 'Remember Me;'—all founded on fact, all romantic and pathetic."

"But mamma," said Alice, expressing in words what Ralph's arch smile expressed almost as plainly, "you know the officer drank too much; and the mysterious lady turned out to be a runaway milliner; and the man in black—oh! what a theme for a pathetic story!—the man in black was a widower, on his way to Newhaven, where he was to select his third wife from three *recommended* candidates."

"Pshaw! Alice: do you suppose it is necessary to tell things precisely as they are?"

"Alice is wrong, aunt, and you are right; and if she will open her writing desk for me, I will sit down this moment, and write a story—a true story—true from beginning to end; and if it moves you, my dear aunt, if it meets your approbation, my destiny is decided."

Mrs. Courland was delighted; she had slain the giant, and she saw fame and fortune smiling on her favourite. She arranged the desk for him herself; she prepared a folio sheet of paper, folded the ominous margins; and was so absorbed in her bright visions, that she did not hear a little by-talk between Ralph and Alice, nor see the tell-tale flush on their cheeks, nor notice the perturbation with which Alice walked first to one window and then to another, and finally settled herself to that best of all sedatives—hemming a ruffle. Ralph chewed off the end of his quill, mended his pen twice, though his aunt assured him 'printers did not mind the penmanship,' and had achieved a single line when Mrs. Courland's vigilant eye was averted by the entrance of her servant girl, who put a packet into her hands. She looked at the direction, cut the string, broke the seals, and took out a periodical fresh from the publisher. She opened at the first article—a strangely mingled current of maternal pride and literary triumph rushed through her heart and brightened her face. She whispered to the servant a summons to all her sisters to the parlour, and an intimation, sufficiently intelligible to them, of her joyful reason for interrupting them.

Our readers will sympathize with her, and with Alice too, when we disclose to them the secret of her joy. The article in question was a clever composition written by our devoted Alice when she was at school. One of her fond aunts had preserved it; and aunts and mother had combined in the pious fraud of giving it to the public, unknown to Alice. They were perfectly aware of her determination never to be an author. But they fancied it was the mere timidity of an unfledged bird; and that when, by their innocent artifice, she found that her pinions could soar in a literary atmosphere, she would realize the sweet fluttering sensations they had experienced at their first flight. The good souls all hurried to the parlour, eager to witness the coup de théatre. Miss Sally's pen stood emblematically erect in her turban; Miss Ruth, in her haste, had overset her inkstand, and the drops were trickling down her white dressing, or, as she now called it, writing gown; and Miss Anne had a wild flower in her hand, as she hoped, of an undescribed species, which, in her joyful agitation, she most unluckily picked to pieces. All bit their lips to keep impatient congratulation from bursting forth. Ralph was so intent on his writing, and Alice on her hemming, that neither noticed the irruption; and Mrs. Courland was obliged twice to speak to her daughter before she could draw her attention.

"Alice, look here—Alice, my dear."

"What is it, mamma? something new of yours?"

"No; guess again, Alice."

"Of one of my aunts, of course?"

"Neither, dear, neither. Come and look for yourself, and see if you can then tell whose it is."

Alice dutifully laid aside her work, approached and took the book. The moment her eye glanced on the fatal page, all her apathy vanished—

deep crimson overspread her cheeks, brow, and neck. She burst into tears of irrepressible vexation, and threw the book into the blazing fire.

The gentle Alice! Never had she been guilty of such an ebullition of temper. Her poor dismayed aunts retreated; her mother looked at her in mute astonishment; and Ralph, struck with her emotion, started from the desk, and would have asked an explanation, but Alice exclaimed—"Don't say any thing about it, mamma—I cannot bear it now."

Mrs. Courland knew instinctively that Ralph would sympathize entirely with Alice, and quite willing to avoid an éclaircissement, she said— "Some other time, Ralph, I'll tell you the whole. Show me now what you have written. How have you begun?"

Ralph handed her the paper with a novice's trembling hand.

"Oh! how very little! and so scratched and interlined! but never mind—'c'est le premier pas qui coute.' "

While making these general observations, the good mother was getting out and fixing her spectacles, and Alice and Ralph had retreated behind her. Alice rested her head on his shoulder, and Ralph's lips were not far from her ear. Whether he was soothing her ruffled spirit, or what he was doing, is not recorded. Mrs. Courland read and re-read the sentence. She dropped a tear on it. She forgot her literary aspirations for Ralph and Alice—forgot she was herself an author—forgot every thing but the mother; and rising, embraced them both as her dear children, and expressed, in her raised and moistened eye, consent to their union, which Ralph had dutifully and prettily asked in that short and true story of his love for his sweet cousin Alice.

In due time the village of H. was animated with the celebration of Alice's nuptials: and when her mother and aunts saw her the happy mistress of the Hepburn farm, and the happiest of wives, they relinquished, without a sigh, the hope of ever seeing her an AUTHOR.

MARIA W. STEWART
(1803–1879)

Why Sit Ye Here and Die
lecture delivered at Franklin Hall, Boston, September 21, 1832.

> I was born in Hartford, Connecticut, in 1803; was left an orphan at five years of age; was bound out in a clergyman's family; had the seeds of piety and virtue early sown in my mind; but was deprived of the advantages of education, though my soul thirsted for knowledge. Left them at 15 years of age; attended Sabbath Schools until I was 20; in 1826, was married to James W. Stewart; was left a widow in 1829; was, as I humbly hope and trust, brought to the knowledge of the truth, as it is in Jesus, in 1830; in 1831 made a public profession of my faith in Christ (*Meditations from the Pen of Mrs. Maria W. Stewart*, 1879, iii–iv).

Biographical information about Maria Stewart is extremely sketchy. If nineteenth-century white American women writers have been neglected, nineteenth-century black American women writers have been even more so, and their work has fallen even further outside the definition of American literature than has the work of white women. Nevertheless, the survival of even a sketchy record of Stewart's career suggests the richness and complexity of that excluded material and its capacity for disrupting both racist and sexist assumptions. For consider this one fact alone: five years before the Grimké sisters began addressing mixed audiences of white men and women, thus eliciting the wrath of the Massachusetts Congregational clergy for such an unprecedented departure from the feminine sphere, Stewart, young, black, and "deprived of the advantages of an education," was lecturing in public in Boston to mixed groups of black men and women.

Sometime after the religious conversion described above, Stewart found her way to the Boston office of William Lloyd Garrison and Isaac Knapp, who had recently begun publishing the *Liberator*, and, "hearing that those gentlemen had observed that female influence was powerful," placed in Garrison's hands, "for criticism and friendly advice," a manuscript of devotional thoughts and of essays on the condition of black people in America (*Meditations*, pp. 75, 76). Garrison printed the manuscript as a pamphlet, "Religion and the Pure Principles of Morality, the Sure Foundation on Which we Must Build" (1831), and published excerpts from it in the *Liberator*. This pamphlet was followed by a second one, also printed by Garrison, "Meditations from the Pen of Mrs. Maria W. Stewart" (1832). A collection of fourteen poems and seven prayers, it is perhaps Stewart's most self-consciously literary effort. During 1832 and 1833, Stewart gave three public lectures in Boston, each of which was subsequently reprinted in the *Liberator*: before the Afric-American Female Intelligence Society of Boston, reprinted in the *Liberator*, April 28, 1832; at Franklin Hall, on September 21, 1832 (reprinted below); and at the African Masonic Hall on February 27, 1833. In 1835, Garrison published the collected *Productions of Mrs. Maria W. Stewart*.

Stewart was evidently discouraged by her audiences' lack of response to her exhortations and, apparently, particularly hurt by criticisms directed against her as a woman for daring to assume the role of public leader. Much of her "farewell" address of September 21, 1833, is devoted to establishing the particular capacity and right of women for spiritual leadership.

Stewart left Boston in 1833 and moved to New York. Here, "full of the greed for literature and letters," she made contact with a group of black intellectuals, at least one of whom, Alexander Crummell, was much impressed by her arrival on the scene: "I remember very distinctly the great surprise of both my friends and myself at finding in New York a young woman of my own people full of literary aspiration and ambitious of authorship. In those days, that is at the commencement of the anti-slavery enterprise, the desire for learning was almost exclusively confined to colored young *men*" (*Meditations*, p. 10). According to Crummell, however, there were in New York City a number of black women willing to meet Stewart's need: "Her eagerness for instruction was gladly met by the school teachers of New York, and in the circle of my own acquaintance young women willingly aided her in the study of arithmetic, geography, grammar, and other branches. Ere long she became a member of a 'Female Literary Society,' and I remember listening, on more than a few occasions, to some of her compositions and declamations" (*Meditations*, p. 10). Stewart eventually became a teacher in the public schools of New York and Brooklyn.

In 1852, after losing her job in Brooklyn, she moved to Baltimore, "hearing the colored people were more religious and God-fearing in the South" (*Meditations*, p. 13). Any illusions she might have had about the South were presumably dispelled by her experiences there. To support herself, she opened a school in Baltimore, stating that she "would teach reading, writing, spelling, mental and practical arithmetic, and whatever other studies called for. Not knowing the prices, I found myself teaching every branch for 50 cents per month, until informed by another teacher that no writing was taught for less than $1 per month. Bought wit is the dearest wit" (*Meditations*, pp. 13–14). The school was never very profitable and, toward the beginning of the Civil War, when her economic difficulties increased, Stewart approached some friends, asking them to organize an entertainment for her benefit. Unfortunately, Stewart had not learned to be sufficiently circumspect where money was concerned. Her "friends" "got up the festival with the help of others; made $300, gave me $30 to pay my rent; paid expenses, then divided the remainder among themselves and then laughed ready to kill themselves to think what a fool they had made of me" (*Meditations*, p. 14).

During the Civil War, Stewart moved to Washington, D.C., where, after much difficulty, she once again succeeded in establishing a school. Her commitment to the education of black children is movingly described in one of the letters prefatory to the 1879 edition of her work: "I have seen her going through the streets in the dead of winter looking up the little children who should be attending school; and whether their parents could pay or not, she was perfectly willing to give her time and strength in teaching them" (*Meditations*, p. 12). Stewart was equally committed to religious instruction; on Sundays, she converted her rooms into a Sabbath school and added another day of work to her week. At one time, she taught day school, night school, and Sunday school, and, in addition, held prayer meetings during the week. After the establishment of the Freedmen's Hospital in Washington, Stewart lived there and worked in it as a matron. In 1871, she raised two hundred dollars, bought a building in the neighborhood of the hospital, and opened a Sunday school under the direction of the Episcopal church.

In 1878, Congress passed a pension law under which, as the widow of a veteran of the War of 1812 (her husband had served as a seaman on American warships), Stewart was entitled to a claim. In order to establish her claim, she needed proof of her marriage. She commissioned a friend who was traveling to Boston to collect such proof. In the process, the friend uncovered a copy of the book Stewart had published forty-three years ago and apparently forgotten. Stewart herself returned to Boston to collect further information and here she met Garrison again after forty-six years. This reunion no doubt helped influence her decision to republish the volume. With the money she got from the government, she brought out a new edition in 1879, calling it *Meditations from the Pen of Mrs. Maria W. Stewart* and adding a prefatory section of testimonial letters and biographical data on the intervening years.

Research into Stewart's years in Boston produced another significant document: her husband's will. For the first time, Stewart saw the will and realized that his executors had cheated her out of the inheritance he had left her. In her first pamphlet, Stewart had exhorted black people to be more intelligent about money matters. Nevertheless, she herself was evidently trapped in a permanent poverty, not simply by being black, but also by being female. In the autobiographical section prefatory to the 1879 edition of her works, she indicates the connection between being a "lady" and being poor: "I would make enough just to supply

my wants for the time being, but not a dollar over. I did not make any
charge for wood and coal. And always had that refined sentiment of
delicacy about me that I could not bear to charge for the worth of my
labor" (*Meditations*, p. 14).

Stewart died in Washington, D.C. on December 17, 1879.

Virtue, piety, unity, self-improvement—these are some of the reme-
dies Stewart proposes for the ills she sees afflicting the black community. Her style is exhortation and her business agitation. Since both
exhortation and agitation convey an implicit charge to, and even against,
her audience, it is not perhaps too difficult to see why she may have
elicited hostility—particularly since the charge, coming from a woman,
was often directed against men: "Had those men among us, who have
had an opportunity, turned their attention as assiduously to mental and
moral improvement as they have to gambling and dancing, I might have
remained quietly at home, and they stood contending in my place"
(*Meditations*, p. 69). In the lecture reprinted below, Stewart indicates an
awareness of criticism: "I have come forward and made myself a hissing
and a reproach amongst the people." In her farewell address, she confronts the issue directly: "What if I am a woman; is not the God of
ancient times the God of these modern days? Did he not raise up Deborah, to be a mother, and a judge in Israel? Did not queen Esther save the
lives of the Jews? And Mary Magdalene first declare the resurrection of
Christ from the dead?" (*Meditations*, p. 76).

Stewart's exhortation to black people to improve themselves occurs,
however, in a context that takes into account the full force of white
racism. Scoffing at the notion that southern "slavery" differs
significantly from northern "freedom," Stewart identifies the situation
of black people in America as one of permanent servitude. White civilization is built on the back of black labor: "the Americans have practised
nothing but head-work these 200 years, and we have done their
drudgery"; "we have pursued the shadow, they have obtained the substance; we have performed the labor, they have received the profits; we
have planted the vines, they have eaten the fruits of them" (*Meditations*,
pp. 32, 69). And white "civilization" intends to perpetuate this situation; thus white women will not grant black women equal economic
opportunity because, "for their own part, they had no objection; but as
it was not the custom, were they to take them into their employ, they
would be in danger of losing the public patronage." As a result, they
consign black women to a life of servitude. Stewart's recoil from this
fate, so powerfully expressed in the address reprinted here, informs the
words of her autobiographical statement ("bound out in a clergyman's
family"), and creates a context for understanding Crummell's description of her as "full of the greed for literature and letters." Although
poverty and hard work characterized her career as a teacher, it seems
likely that this profession represented a significant escape from the
physical drudgery and mental stupefaction she saw designed for her as a
black woman in white America.

In the lecture reprinted below Stewart explicitly addresses both
white women and black men. From her "fairer sisters" Stewart claims

empathy based on similarity: "And why are not our forms as delicate, and our constitutions as slender, as yours? Is not the workmanship as curious and complete?" Stewart perceives white women as both directly and indirectly responsible for the slavery of black women, and she urges them to "go learn by experience" what might happen to their "acquirements" were they to live the life of a black woman. Certainly her vision of white women, "nursed in the lap of affluence and ease," and claiming exemption from labor on the basis of their "delicate" female "constitutions" while allowing black women to drag out "a miserable existence of servitude," strikes at the heart of the intersection of gender and race in mid-nineteenth-century America. In addition, Stewart indirectly raises the issue of class, for in her eyes all white women are middle or upper class. Fighting mythologies of race and class as they affect black women, Stewart nevertheless participates in such mythologies in relation to white women.

In her first pamphlet, Stewart directly addresses black women: "O, ye daughters of Africa, awake! awake! arise! no longer sleep nor slumber, but distinguish yourselves. Show forth to the world that ye are endowed with noble and exalted faculties" (*Meditations*, p. 25). In particular, she exhorts black women to raise money to build a school so that it may no "longer be said of the daughters of Africa, they have no ambition, they have no force" (*Meditations*, p. 31). In the lecture reprinted here, however, Stewart implies that black men have the primary responsibility for changing the conditions of servitude under which black women labor, since the black woman "depends" on them and has little power beyond that of "influence." And when she invokes the example of the Pilgrims, we can assume she is thinking of "fathers" as she addresses the "brethren."

Stewart's remedy for the condition of blacks in America rarely includes an explicitly political dimension. In her third lecture, she suggests that "every man of color throughout the United States, who possesses the spirit and principles of a man, sign a petition to Congress, to abolish slavery in the District of Columbia"; this suggestion, however, is as close as she comes to advocating direct political action (*Meditations*, p. 71). Primarily concerned with the internal affairs of the black community—education, morality, enterprise—she emphasizes black self-reliance: "Do you ask, what can we do? Unite and build a store of your own, if you cannot procure a license. Fill one side with dry goods, and the other with groceries. Do you ask, where is the money? We have spent more than enough for nonsense, to do what building we should want" (*Meditations*, p. 32).

Stewart has, on occasion, a political focus to what she opposes. In particular, she opposes colonization, an early attempt to "solve" the "problem" of black people in America. To those who favor it, she replies that one can die as easily in Africa as in America, on the way back as on the way over. She clearly recognizes the essential racism of the colonization movement:

> Or, if the colonizationists are real friends to Africa, let them expend
> the money which they collect, in erecting a college to educate her

injured sons in this land of gospel light and liberty. . . . But ah! methinks their hearts are so frozen towards us, they had rather their money should be sunk in the ocean than to administer it to our relief; and I fear, if they dared, like Pharaoh, king of Egypt, they would order every male child among us to be drowned (*Meditations*, pp. 70–71).

Although Stewart generally uses the term "American" to refer to white people, she correctly perceives colonization as in effect forced emigration: "They would drive us to a strange land. But before I go, the bayonet shall pierce me through" (*Meditations*, p. 73).

Stewart's rhetorical power derives from her belief in the principles of self-reliance and from her passionate invocation of these principles to fight racism. Concerned that her community not commit moral and intellectual suicide by internalizing white attitudes and thus becoming the creatures whites would have them be, she urges her people to fight back. Stewart's own courage and willingness to fight back are remarkable. Although she finally could not avoid internalizing sexism and allowed her perception of hostility and criticism to drive her from the field of public speech, she provides nevertheless a primary model of one who refuses to "sit . . . here and die."

Source:

Productions of Mrs. Maria W. Stewart (Boston: Friends of Freedom and Virtue), 1835.

Primary Works:

"Religion and the Pure Principles of Morality, the Sure Foundation on Which We Must Build," 1831; "Meditations from the Pen of Mrs. Maria W. Stewart," 1832; Productions of Mrs. Maria W. Stewart, 1835; Meditations from the Pen of Mrs. Maria W. Stewart, 1879.

Selected Secondary Works:

Gerda Lerner, *Black Women in White America* (New York: Vintage), 1973; *Black Women in 19th Century American Life: Their Words, Their Thoughts, Their Feelings*, ed. Burt James Loewenberg and Ruth Bogin (University Park: Pennsylvania State University Press), 1976; Dorothy Porter, *Early Negro Writing, 1760–1837* (Boston: Beacon), 1971.

Contexts:

1831—Poe, *Poems;* Whittier, *Legends of New England; Liberator*
1832—Bryant, *Poems;* Irving, *The Alhambra;* Poe, tales published in the Philadelphia *Saturday Courier*

WHY SIT YE HERE and die? If we say we will go to a foreign land, the famine and the pestilence are there, and there we shall die. If we sit here, we shall die. Come, let us plead our cause before the whites: if they save us alive, we shall live—and if they kill us, we shall but die.

Methinks I heard a spiritual interrogation—"Who shall go forward, and take off the reproach that is cast upon the people of color? Shall it be a woman?" And my heart made this reply—"If it is thy will, be it even so, Lord Jesus?"

I have heard much respecting the horrors of slavery; but may heaven forbid that the generality of my color throughout these United States should experience any more of its horrors than to be a servant of servants, or hewers of wood and drawers of water! Tell us no more of southern slavery; for with few exceptions, although I may be very erroneous in my opinion, yet I consider our condition but little better than that. Yet, after all, methinks there are no chains so galling as the chains of ignorance—no fetters so binding as those that bind the soul, and exclude it from the vast field of usefulness and scientific knowledge. O, had I received the advantages of early education, my ideas would, ere now, have expanded far and wide; but, alas! I possess nothing but moral capability—no teachings but the teaching of the Holy Spirit.

I have asked several individuals of my sex, who transact business for themselves, if providing our girls were to give them the most satisfactory references, they would not be willing to grant them an equal opportunity with others? Their reply has been—for their own part, they had no objection, but as it was not the custom, were they to take them into their employ, they would be in danger of losing the public patronage.

And such is the powerful force of prejudice. Let our girls possess what amiable qualities of soul they may, let their characters be fair and spotless as innocence itself; let their natural taste and ingenuity be what they may; it is impossible for scarce an individual of them to rise above the condition of servants. Ah! why is this cruel and unfeeling distinction? Is it merely because God has made our complexion to vary? If it be, O shame to soft, relenting humanity! "Tell it not in Gath! publish it not in the streets of Askelon!" Yet, after all, methinks were the American free people of color to turn their attention more assiduously to moral worth and intellectual improvement, this would be the result: prejudice would gradually diminish, and the whites would be compelled to say, unloose those fetters!

> Though black their skins as shades of night,
> Their hearts are pure, their souls are white.

Few white persons of either sex, who are calculated for any thing else, are willing to spend their lives and bury their talents in performing mean, servile labor. And such is the horrible idea that I entertain respecting a life of servitude, that if I conceived of there being no possibility of my rising above the condition of a servant, I would gladly hail death as a welcome messenger. O, horrible idea, indeed! to possess noble souls aspiring after high and honorable acquirements, yet confined by the chains of ignorance and poverty to lives of continual drudgery and toil. Neither do I know of any who have enriched themselves by spending their lives as house-domestics, washing windows, shaking carpets, brushing boots, or tending upon gentlemen's tables. I can but die for expressing my sentiments; and I am as willing to die by the sword as the pestilence; for I am a true born American; your blood flows in my veins, and your spirit fires my breast.

I observed a piece in the *Liberator* a few months since, stating that the colonizationists had published a work respecting us, asserting that we were lazy and idle. I confute them on that point. Take us generally as a people, we are neither lazy nor idle; and considering how little we have to excite or stimulate us, I am almost astonished that there are so many industrious and ambitious ones to be found: although I acknowledge, with extreme sorrow, that there are some who never were and never will be serviceable to society. And have you not a similar class among yourselves?

Again. It was asserted that we were "a ragged set, crying for liberty." I reply to it, the whites have so long and so loudly proclaimed the theme of equal rights and privileges, that our souls have caught the flame also, ragged as we are. As far as our merit deserves, we feel a common desire to rise above the condition of servants and drudges. I have learnt, by bitter experience, that continual hard labor deadens the energies of the soul, and benumbs the faculties of the mind; the ideas become confined, the mind barren, and, like the scorching sands of Arabia, produces nothing; or, like the uncultivated soil, brings forth thorns and thistles.

Again. Continual hard labor irritates our tempers and sours our dispositions; the whole system becomes worn out with toil and fatigue; nature herself becomes almost exhausted, and we care but little whether we live or die. It is true, that the free people of color throughout these United States are neither bought nor sold, nor under the lash of the cruel driver; many obtain a comfortable support; but few, if any, have an opportunity of becoming rich and independent; and the employments we most pursue are as unprofitable to us as the spider's web or the floating bubbles that vanish into air. As servants, we are respected; but let us presume to aspire any higher, our employer regards us no longer. And were it not that the King Eternal has declared that Ethiopia shall stretch forth her hands unto God, I should indeed despair.

I do not consider it derogatory, my friends, for persons to live out to service. There are many whose inclination leads them to aspire no higher; and I would highly commend the performance of almost anything for an honest livelihood; but where constitutional strength is wanting, labor of this kind, in its mildest form, is painful. And doubtless many are the prayers that have ascended to heaven from Afric's daughters for strength to perform their work. Oh, many are the tears that have been shed for the want of that strength! Most of our color have dragged out a miserable existence of servitude from the cradle to the grave. And what literary acquirements can be made, or useful knowledge derived, from either maps, books or charts, by those who continually drudge from Monday morning until Sunday noon? O, ye fairer sisters, whose hands are never soiled, whose nerves and muscles are never strained, go learn by experience! Had we the opportunity that you have had, to improve our moral and mental faculties, what would have hindered our intellects from being as bright, and our manners from being as dignified as yours? Had it been our lot to have been nursed in the lap of affluence and ease, and to have basked beneath the smiles and sunshine of fortune, should we not have naturally supposed that we were never made to toil? And why are not our forms as delicate, and our constitutions as slender as yours? Is not the workmanship as curious and complete? Have pity upon us, have pity upon us, O ye who have hearts to feel for others' woes; for the hand of God has touched us. Owing to the disadvantages under which we labor, there are many flowers among us that are

> born to bloom unseen,
> And waste their fragrance on the desert air.

My beloved brethren, as Christ has died in vain for those who will not accept of offered mercy, so will it be vain for the advocates of freedom to spend their breath in our behalf, unless with united hearts and souls you make some mighty efforts to raise your sons and daughters from the horrible state of servitude and degradation in which they are placed. It is upon you that woman depends; she can do but little besides using her influence; and it is for her sake and yours that I have come forward and made myself a hissing and a reproach among the people; for I am also one of the wretched and miserable daughters of the descendants of fallen Africa. Do you ask, why are you wretched and miserable? I reply, look at many of the most worthy and interesting of us doomed to spend our lives in gentlemen's kitchens. Look at our young men, smart, active and energetic, with souls filled with ambitious fire; if they look forward, alas! what are their prospects? They can be nothing but the humblest laborer, on account of their dark complexion; hence many of them lose their ambition, and become worthless. Look at our middle-aged men, clad in their rusty plaids and coats; in winter, every cent they earn goes to buy their wood and pay their rent; their poor wives also toil beyond their strength, to help support their families. Look at our aged sires, whose heads are whitened with the frosts of seventy winters, with their old wood-saws on their backs. Alas, what keeps us so? Prejudice, ignorance and poverty. But ah! methinks our oppression is soon to come to an end; yea, before the Majesty of heaven our groans and cries have reached the ears of the Lord of Sabaoth. As the prayers and tears of Christians will avail the finally impenitent nothing; neither will the prayers and tears of the friends of humanity avail us any thing, unless we possess a spirit of virtuous emulation within our breasts. Did the pilgrims, when they first landed on these shores, quietly compose themselves, and say, "the Britons have all the money and all the power, and we must continue their servants forever?" Did they sluggishly sigh, and say, "our lot is hard, the Indians own the soil, and we cannot cultivate it?" No; they first made powerful efforts to raise themselves, and then God raised up those illustrious patriots, Washington and Lafayette, to assist and defend them. And, my brethren, have you made a powerful effort? Have you prayed the Legislature for mercy's sake to grant you all the rights and privileges of free citizens, that your daughters may rise to that degree of respectability which true merit deserves, and your sons above the servile situations which most of them fill?

ELIZA LESLIE

(1787–1858)

Mrs. Washington Potts

Godey's Lady's Book, 5 (October), 1832.

Eliza Leslie was born in Philadelphia on November 15, 1787, the eldest
of five children of Lydia Baker and Robert Leslie. Her father was a
watchmaker and, in her own words, "a man of considerable natural
genius, and much self-taught knowledge, particularly in natural philosophy and mechanics." He was a close friend of both Benjamin Franklin
and Thomas Jefferson and a member of the American Philosophical Society. Her mother she described as a "handsome woman, of excellent
sense, very amusing, and a first-rate housewife." When Leslie was five,
the family moved to London, England, where her father set up business
exporting clocks and watches to Philadelphia. During the six years of
English residence, Leslie's father superintended her education that took
place in large part at home and that consisted primarily of her favorite
activities of reading and drawing. Mismanagement of the business and
the death of the Philadelphia partner required a return to America and,
shortly thereafter, in 1803, Leslie's father died, leaving her and her
mother to support themselves and the remaining children. Together they
opened a boarding house and Leslie herself taught drawing.

Perhaps in an effort to improve boarding-house fare, perhaps as
training for a life she never lived, perhaps as a way of continuing her
education, Leslie attended and graduated from Mrs. Goodfellow's
Philadelphia cooking school. In his introduction to the selection from
Leslie, one of five women included in *The Prose Writers of America*
(1846), Rufus W. Griswold comments that "the education of women
was managed much better than now in that period which our fathers are
wont to describe as the golden age of America. Among the institutions
that flourished here then were cooking-schools, in which the most im-

70

portant of sciences was taught in a manner that contributed largely to the comfort of the people." Apparently Griswold believed that learning to cook was essential to the success of a woman writer. Ironically, there was a connection for Leslie between her cooking and her writing. Her original literary impulse was poetic, but "at thirteen and fourteen, I began to despise my own poetry, and destroyed all I had," and for many years she abandoned "the dream of my childhood, the hope of one day seeing my name in print." Dream became reality as a result of her experience at Mrs. Goodfellow's. Having gathered while there "a tolerable collection of receipts" and having received "many applications from my friends for copies of these directions," Leslie decided to simplify matters by publishing them. The result was *Seventy-Five Receipts for Pastry, Cakes, and Sweetmeats,* which first appeared in 1827.

Her talent for writing must have been apparent even in this genre because the publisher of her cookbook urged her to try her hand at more imaginative forms. Not surprisingly, she began to write stories for children, a field just recently opened up for women by the work of Lydia Maria Child, and in 1828 she published *The Mirror,* a collection of juvenile fiction. Several other works for children followed in rapid succession; *Atlantic Tales* (1833) collected the best of her stories in this genre.

The decision to write adult fiction required more courage. In her memorial sketch of Leslie, Alice B. Haven records the self-doubt that attended the writing of "Mrs. Washington Potts": "So distrustful was she of her own power that, after the manuscript of this prize tale was finished (late at night, after returning from a party), she threw it into the grate, intending to burn it in the morning. But, reading it over once more before lighting her bonfire, she thought the experiment, at least, would be no loss, and sent it to the committee of award." The story won the prize offered by *Godey's* and was published in its October, 1832 issue.

Her concern with American manners, particularly those of women, evident in the stories collected in *Pencil Sketches,* led her to contribute to the numerous works on etiquette typical of the period. *The Behavior Book* (1835), later *Miss Leslie's Behavior Book* (1859), contained chapters on "Conduct to Literary Women" and "Suggestions to Inexperienced Authors." The first of these essays reveals much about Leslie's aesthetic principles, as well as presenting her sense of the particular pressures to which literary women are subjected. The second shows her generosity in assisting others seeking to enter her profession by sharing with them the fruits of her own experience. Not surprisingly, perhaps, her books on domestic economy provided her largest and most steady source of income. Among these, *Directions for Cookery: Being a System of the Art, in Its Various Branches* (1837) and *The House Book; or, A Manual of Domestic Economy* (1840) were best sellers and frequently reprinted.

Setting up residence in the United States Hotel, Leslie became for years a Philadelphia institution, meeting visiting celebrities and being herself sought out as one. She was often feared for her sarcastic tongue and strong opinions, but was, in fact, according to Haven, a delightful companion whose "table talk" would have made "a most entertaining article" and whose personal warmth reached almost "Quixotic" proportions in her benevolence to the needy, to all those who "had struggled courageously as she had done in early life, for themselves or others, with adverse fortune." She died on January 1, 1858 at Gloucester, New Jersey, at the age of seventy and was buried in St. Peter's churchyard in Philadelphia.

Eliza Leslie's subject in *Pencil Sketches* is American social life, its pretensions, absurdities, and even insanities. "Mrs. Washington Potts" is a good example both of Leslie's literary skills and of her thematic concerns.

When Bromley Cheston arrives home after a "three years' cruise in the Mediterranean," he finds his aunt, Mrs. Marsden, and cousin, Albina, "bewitched." Are they surprised to see him after three year's absence? Are they interested in his adventures? No, indeed; their only concern is Mrs. Washington Potts of whom they are "sure." In pursuit of their obsession, they have turned the house upside down and are performing herculean labors in parlor and kitchen at enormous personal and financial expense.

And what is the source of this obsession? At issue, however indirectly, is the particular situation of women. The world that Albina and her mother seek to negotiate is a women's world, a world that Bromley turns his back on for three years at a time and that most contemporary male writers equally ignored. Her dying husband enjoined Mrs. Marsden to remove to a country town so that she may live within her income. But life in a village on the Delaware, with a modest income and a nephew in the navy, is likely to be quite dull. Having been exiled from "society" without choice, Mrs. Marsden and Albina are perhaps understandably attracted to what they perceive as an opportunity to rejoin it. Equally understandable is their susceptibility to Mrs. Washington Potts's presentation of herself as the embodiment of "society." Isolated and "innocent," desirous of entering the women's world of social life and with no context for comparison, they present an altogether easy mark.

Mrs. Washington Potts, in turn, represents the susceptibility of Americans, and in particular of American women, to mistaken values. Herself a victim, and to some extent an innocent one, of machinations whose origin she does not understand, she is treated with some sympathy. She is not really at home in the world she pretends to inhabit. Nevertheless, she has succumbed to false values and is passing them on to others. In imitation of her, Mrs. Marsden and Albina try to exclude old Aunt Quimby from the party and they invite young Miss Boreham only because her "dress was expected to add prodigiously to the effect of the rooms." But Miss Boreham appears "in an old faded frock of last year's fashion," and Aunt Quimby refuses to stay put, for Leslie's point consists in demonstrating that such behavior can have no positive issue. Indeed, it results in cruelty. Later in the story, when Bromley Cheston arrives at Mrs. Washington Potts's party, he finds Albina "standing alone in the centre of the room, and the company whispering and gazing at her." Leslie's tone is in general comic, but this scene touches on the painful. Albina's isolation, bewilderment, and powerlessness compel the reader's identification with this quintessentially female experience of social humiliation.

Although Albina is "saved" by the arrival of Cheston, he is less of a hero and she less of a victim than this structure might indicate. Obviously intended as both measure and model, Bromley nevertheless has his foibles. Leslie's comic touch strikes early, identifying him as a man with a myth: " 'What a lovely spot,' exclaimed Cheston—and innocence—modesty—candour—contentment—peace—simple pleasures—intellectual enjoyments—and various other delightful ideas chased each other rapidly through his mind." Once reality has disrupted fantasy, other ideas chase each other through his mind and he swings back and forth on the impulse of the moment, unable to decide whether or not Albina really deserves his affection. He is both a bit of a fool and a bit of a prig. As for Albina, perhaps if Bromley had not arrived, she might have fought rather than fainted for by this time she is no longer bewitched; she has recovered her senses and in so doing has recovered the self that Bromley ought to have had sense enough to believe in. Bromley may doubt Albina but Leslie does not. Indeed, the optimistic tone that informs this story derives primarily from the confidence that Leslie places in the essential soundness of the American girl. We can understand the reasons for Mrs. Marsden's decision not to show Albina the disinviting note—she is trying to promote what she thinks are her daughter's interests. But we also recognize the mistake in her decision. Albina's judgment is clearer than her mother's; she would not have gone had she known and she should have been allowed to make the decision. Thus early in American literature, the American girl figures as the representative American character and the repository of truly American values.

The American reference, implicit in the character of Albina, is sounded early in the story with the arrival of the English Montagues at the Marsden party. Sneeringly, they attribute their premature appearance to their desire to comply with "the simplicity of republican manners" and, while they help themselves to cake "with impudent familiarity," they watch to see just how much insult republican Americans will take in order to have the distinction of contact with foreign aristocracy. Leslie's position is clear. The disease to which Mrs. Washington Potts has succumbed, and which she is busy spreading, consists of imitating foreign values. Although the susceptibility is American, the etiology is not. In the last paragraph we discover that the ultimate puppeteer is an English publisher with the political agenda of adding yet "another octavo to the numerous volumes of gross misrepresentation and real ignorance that profess to contain an impartial account of the United States of America." To accomplish his purpose, he has converted a third-rate reporter into an English lord by the simple device of substituting Montague for Wilkins because the former is a name "well calculated to strike the republicans with proper awe."

Leslie's comic perspective and her ability to capture social texture are

perhaps her greatest strengths. We see in all its particularity that freshly
papered parlor, the center table carefully arranged with souvenir books
opened "at their finest plates" and a volume of Mrs. Hemans's poems
marked with rose-leaves. We understand the contribution that Bromley's sketches of Mediterranean scenery will make to the "effect." We
know what the people at the party had to eat and we taste the salted ice
cream, runny macaroons and the sponge cake that "contradicted its
name." We tug along with Albina as she struggles to stretch her badly-
made dress into some appearance of symmetry. And, above all, we hear
the characters—the nasty whining of LaFayette Potts and the vapid af-
fectations of his mother; the loud whispering of the impudent Montagues and the pointless argument of the mother and daughter. And
certainly we hear the voice of Aunt Quimby who, being of "a sociable
disposition" and a truly American spirit, insists on talking to "anyone
that was near her, however high or however low," and in compelling
tones shares with the Montague women her example of their common
experience of the unsatisfactoriness of men: "and to this day I don't
know the price of that shad."

Leslie's gifts, however, do not inform her portrayal of Drusa, the
black servant in the Marsden home. Though clearly intended as comic,
this character never rises above the level of stock figure and stereotype.
Furthermore, though Cheston may contend that "in our country the
only acknowledged distinction should be that which is denoted by
superiority of mind and manners," servants come in for regular abuse
by many of the middle-class characters in the story. Mrs. Marsden talks
"much of the carelessness of servants" and blames Dixon for the salt in
the ice-cream; old Aunt Quimby speaks casually of "Peter, the stupid
black boy." Such biases obviously reveal the limitations of Leslie's portrayal of the American social scene.

Aunt Quimby presents the best example of Leslie's comic gift exer-
cized in the creation of character. Less central to the plot, she is more
free to be unpredictable, disruptive, and funny. But, of course, the situation itself provides the primary comedy of the piece. Although Bromley Cheston is "by no means *au fait* to the mysteries of confectionary,"
not having had the advantages of Mrs. Goodfellow's training, even he
realizes that too much "making out" is going into this party and that the
means are not fitted to the ends.

Leslie's comic perspective certainly contributes to the self-confidence
and optimism that characterize her voice. Like Sedgwick, she believes
that writing as a woman primarily for women can accomplish a good
deal in the way of education. Unlike Sedgwick, however, Leslie's position does not seem to be complicated by any ambivalent attitude toward
women and writing. For Leslie, there is no inherent contradiction between good sense and good writing where women are concerned. Indeed, the essay referred to earlier, "Conduct to Literary Women,"
provides primary evidence of her conviction that the best writers "have
generally a large portion of common sense to balance their genius, and
are therefore seldom guilty of the queerness unjustly imputed to the
whole fraternity." For Leslie, writing is not the communicable disease

but rather the remedy for it; if Mrs. Washington Potts could read "Mrs. Washington Potts," she might indeed be saved.

Source:

Pencil Sketches; or Outlines of Character and Manners (Philadelphia: Carey, Lea and Blanchard), 1833.

Selected Primary Works:

Atlantic Tales; or, Pictures of Youth, 1833; *Pencil Sketches,* 1833, 1835, 1837; *Amelia; or, A Young Lady's Vicissitudes,* 1848.

Selected Secondary Works:

Alice B. Haven, "Personal Reminiscences of Miss Eliza Leslie," *Godey's Lady's Book,* 56 (1858), 344–50 (includes Leslie's autobiographical sketch of 1851); Ophia D. Smith, "Charles and Eliza Leslie," *Pennsylvania Magazine of History and Biography,* 74 (1950), 512–27.

"The course of *parties* never does run smooth."
—Shakespeare.

BROMLEY CHESTON, an officer in the United States navy, had just returned from a three years' cruise in the Mediterranean. His ship came into New York; and after he had spent a week with a sister that was married in Boston, he could not resist his inclination to pay a visit to his maternal aunt, who had resided since her widowhood at one of the small towns on the banks of the Delaware.

The husband of Mrs. Marsden had not lived long enough to make his fortune, and it was his last injunction that she should retire with her daughter to the country, or at least to a country town. He feared that if she remained in Philadelphia she would have too many temptations to exercise her taste for unnecessary expense; and that, in consequence, the very moderate income, which was all he was able to leave her, would soon be found insufficient to supply her with comforts.

We will not venture to say that duty to his aunt Marsden was the young lieutenant's only incentive to this visit: as she had a beautiful daughter about eighteen, for whom, since her earliest childhood, Bromley Cheston had felt something a little more vivid than the usual degree of regard that boys think sufficient for their cousins. His family had formerly lived in Philadelphia, and till he went into the navy Bromley and Albina were in habits of daily intercourse. Afterwards, on returning from sea, he always, as soon as he set his foot on American ground, began to devise means of seeing his pretty cousin, however short the time and however great the distance. And it was in meditation on Albina's beauty and sprightliness that he had often "while sailing on the midnight deep," beguiled the long hours of the watch, and thus rendered more tolerable that dreariest part of a seaman's duty.

On arriving at the village, Lieutenant Cheston immediately established his quarters at the hotel, fearing that to become an inmate of his aunt's house might cause her some inconvenience. Though he had performed the whole journey in a steamboat, he could not refrain from changing his waistcoat, brushing his coat sleeves, brushing his hat, brushing his hair, and altering the tie of his cravat. Though he had "never told his love," it cannot be said that concealment had "preyed on his damask cheek;" the only change in that damask having been effected by the sun and wind of the ocean.

Mrs. Marsden lived in a small modest-looking white house, with a green door and green venetian shutters. In early summer the porch was canopied and perfumed with honey-suckle, and the windows with roses. In front was a flower-garden, redolent of sweetness and beauty; behind was a well-stored potager, and a flourishing little orchard. The windows were amply shaded by the light and graceful foliage of some beautiful locust trees.

"What a lovely spot," exclaimed Cheston—and innocence—modesty—candour—contentment—peace—simple pleasures—intellectual enjoyments—and various other delightful ideas chased each other rapidly through his mind.

When he knocked at the door, it was opened by a black girl named Drusa, who had been brought up in the family, and whose delight on seeing him was so great that she could scarcely find it in her heart to tell him that "the ladies were both out, or at least partly out." Cheston, however, more than suspected that they were wholly at home, for he saw his aunt peeping over the bannisters, and had a glimpse of his cousin flitting into the back parlour; and besides, the whole domicile was evidently in some great commotion, strongly resembling that horror of all men, a house-cleaning. The carpets had been removed, and the hall was filled with the parlour-chairs: half of them being turned bottom upwards on the others, with looking-glasses and pictures leaning against them; and he knew that, on such occasions, the ladies of a family in middle life are never among the missing.

"Go and give Lieutenant Cheston's compliments to your ladies," said he, "and let them know that he is waiting to see them."

Mrs. Marsden now ran down stairs in a wrapper and morning cap, and gave her nephew a very cordial reception. "Our house is just now in such confusion," said she, "that I have no place to invite you to sit down in except the back porch."—And there they accordingly took their seats.

"Do not suppose," continued Mrs. Marsden, "that we are cleaning house: but we are going to have a party to-night, and therefore you are most fortunate in your arrival, for I think I can promise you a very pleasant evening. We have sent invitations to all the most genteel families within seven miles, and I can assure you there was a great deal of trouble in getting the notes conveyed. We have also asked a number of strangers from the city, who happen to be boarding in the village; we called on them for that purpose. If all that are invited were to come, we should have a complete squeeze; but unluckily we have received an unusual number of regrets, and some have as yet returned no answers at all. However, we are sure of Mrs. Washington Potts."

"I see," said Cheston, "you are having your parlours papered."— "Yes," replied Mrs. Marsden, "we could not possibly have a party with that old-fashioned paper on the walls, and we sent to the city a week ago for a man to come and bring with him some of the newest patterns, but he never made his appearance till last night after we had entirely given him up, and after we had had the rooms put in complete order in other respects. But he says, as the parlours are very small, he can easily put on the new paper before evening, so we thought it better to take up the carpets, and take down the curtains, and undo all that we did yesterday, rather than the walls should look old-fashioned. I *did* intend having them painted, which would of course be much better, only that there was no time to get *that* done before the party, so we must defer the painting now for three or four years till this new paper has grown old."

"But where is Albina?" asked Cheston.

"The truth is," answered Mrs. Marsden, "she is very busy making cakes; as in this place we can buy none that are fit for a party. Luckily Albina is very clever at all such things, having been a pupil of Mrs. Goodfellow. But there is certainly a great deal of trouble in getting up a party in the country."

Just then the black girl, Drusa, made her appearance, and said to Mrs. Marsden, "I've been for that there bean you call wanilla, and Mr. Brown says he never heard of such a thing."

"A man that keeps so large a store has no right to be so ignorant," remarked Mrs. Marsden. "Then, Drusa, we must flavour the ice-cream with lemon."

"There a'n't no more lemons to be had," said the girl, "and we've just barely enough for the lemonade."

"Then some of the lemons must be taken for the ice-cream," replied Mrs. Marsden, "and we must make out the lemonade with cream of tartar."

"I forgot to tell you," said Drusa, "that Mrs. Jones says she can't spare no more cream, upon no account."

"How vexatious!" exclaimed Mrs. Marsden. "I wish we had two cows of our own—one is not sufficient when we are about giving a party. Drusa we must make out the ice-cream by thicking some milk with eggs."

"Eggs are scace," replied the girl, "Miss Albinar uses up so many for the cakes."

"She must spare some eggs from the cakes," said Mrs. Mardsen, "and make out the cakes by adding a little pearl-ash. Go directly and tell her so."

Cheston, though by no means *au fait* to the mysteries of confection-ary, could not help smiling at all this making out—"Really," said his aunt, "these things are very annoying. And as this party is given to Mrs. Washington Potts, it is extremely desirable that nothing should fail. There is no such thing now as having company, unless we can receive and entertain them in a certain style."

"I perfectly remember," said Cheston, "the last party at which I was present in your house. I was then a midshipman, and it was just before I sailed on my first cruise in the Pacific. I spent a delightful evening."

"Yes, I recollect that night," replied Mrs. Marsden. "In those days it was not necessary for us to support a certain style, and parties were then very simple things, except among people of the first rank. It was thought sufficient to have two or three baskets of substantial cakes at tea, some almonds, raisons, apples, and oranges, handed round afterwards, with wine and cordial, and then a large-sized pound-cake at the last. The company assembled at seven o'clock, and generally walked; for the ladies' dresses were only plain white muslin. We invited but as many as could be accommodated with seats. The young people played at forfeits, and sung English and Scotch songs, and at the close of the evening danced to the piano. How Mrs. Washington Potts would be shocked if she was to find herself at one of those obsolete parties!"

"The calf-jelly won't be clear," said the black girl, again making her appearance. "Aunt Katy has strained it five times over through the flan-nen-bag."

"Go then and tell her to strain it five-and-twenty times," said Mrs. Marsden, angrily—"It must and shall be clear. Nothing is more vulgar than clouded jelly; Mrs. Washington Potts will not touch it unless it is transparent as amber."

"What Nong tong paw again," said Cheston. "Now do tell me who is Mrs. Washington Potts?"

"Is it possible you have not heard of her?" exclaimed Mrs. Marsden.

"Indeed I have not," replied Cheston. "You forget that for several years I have been cruising on classic ground, and I can assure you that the name of Mrs. Washington Potts has not yet reached the shores of the Mediterranean."

"She is wife to a gentleman that has made a fortune in New Orleans," pursued Mrs. Marsden. "They came last winter to live in Philadelphia, having first visited London and Paris. During the warm weather they took lodgings in this village, and we have become quite intimate. So we have concluded to give them a party, previous to their return to Philadel-phia, which is to take place immediately. She is a charming woman, though she certainly makes strange mistakes in talking. You have no idea how sociable she is, at least since she returned our call; which, to be sure, was not till the end of a week; and Albina and I had sat up in full dress to receive her for no less than five days: that is, from twelve o'clock till three. At last she came, and it would have surprised you to see how affably she behaved to us."

"Not at all," said Cheston, "I should not have expected that she would have treated you rudely."

"She really," continued Mrs. Marsden, "grew quite intimate before her visit was over, and took our hands at parting. And as she went out through the garden, she stopped to admire Albina's moss-roses: so we could do no less than give her all that were blown. From that day she has always sent to us when she wants flowers."

"No doubt of it," said Cheston.

"You cannot imagine," pursued Mrs. Marsden, "on what a familiar footing we are. She has a high opinion of Albina's taste, and often gets her to make up caps and do other little things for her. When any of her children are sick, she never sends anywhere else for currant jelly or preserves. Albina makes gingerbread for them every Saturday. During the holidays she frequently sent her three boys to spend the day with us. There is the very place in the railing where Randolph broke out a stick to whip Jefferson with, because Jefferson had thrown in his face a hot baked apple which the mischievous little rogue had stolen out of Katy's oven."

In the mean time, Albina had taken off the brown holland bib apron which she had worn all day in the kitchen, and telling the cook to watch carefully the plum-cake that was baking, she hastened to her room by a back staircase, and proceeded to take the pins out of her hair; for where is the young lady that on any emergency whatever, would appear before a young gentleman with her hair pinned up. Though, just now, the opening out of her curls was a considerable inconvenience to Albina, as she had bestowed much time and pains on putting them up for the evening.

Finally she came down "in prime array," and Cheston who had left her a school-girl, found her now grown to womanhood and more beautiful than ever. Still he could not forbear reproving her for treating him so much as a stranger, and not coming to him at once in her morning-dress.

"Mrs. Washington Potts," said Albina, "is of opinion that a young lady should never be seen in dishabille by a gentleman."

Cheston now found it very difficult to hear the name of Mrs. Potts with patience.—"Albina," thought he, "is bewitched as well as her mother."

He spoke of his cruise in the Mediterranean, and Albina told him that she had seen a beautiful view of the bay of Naples in a souvenir belonging to Mrs. Washington Potts.

"I have brought with me some sketches of Mediterranean scenery," pursued Cheston. "You know I draw a little. I promise myself great pleasure in showing and explaining them to you."

"Oh! do send them this afternoon," exclaimed Albina. "They will be the very things for the centre-table. I dare say the Montagues will recognize some of the places they have seen in Italy, for they have travelled all over the south of Europe."

"And who are the Montagues?" inquired Cheston.

"They are a very elegant English family," answered Mrs. Marsden, "cousins in some way to several noblemen."

"Perhaps so," said Cheston.

"Albina met with them at the lodgings of Mrs. Washington Potts," pursued Mrs. Marsden, "where they have been staying a week for the benefit of country air; and so she enclosed her card, and sent them invitations to her party. They have as yet returned no answer; but that is no proof they will not come, for perhaps it may be the newest fashion in England not to answer notes."

"You know the English are a very peculiar people," remarked Albina.

"And what other lions have you provided?" said Cheston.

"Oh! no others except a poet," replied Albina. "Have you never heard of Bewley Garvin Gandy?"

"Never!" answered Cheston. "Is that all one man?"

"Nonsense," replied Albina; "you know that poets generally have three names. B. G. G. was formerly Mr. Gandy's signature when he wrote only for the newspapers, but now since he has come out in the magazines, and annuals, and published his great poem of the World of Sorrow, he gives his name at full length. He has tried law, physic, and divinity, and has resigned all for the Muses. He is a great favourite of Mrs. Washington Potts."

"And now, Albina," said Cheston, "as I know you can have but little leisure to-day, I will only detain you while you indulge me with 'Auld lang syne'—I see the piano has been moved out into the porch."

"Yes," said Mrs. Marsden, "on account of the parlour papering."

"Oh! Bromley Cheston," exclaimed Albina, "do not ask me to play any of those antediluvian Scotch songs. Mrs. Washington Potts cannot tolerate anything but Italian."

Cheston, who had no taste for Italian, immediately took his hat, and apologizing for the length of his stay, was going away with the thought that Albina had much deteriorated in growing up.

"We shall see you this evening without the ceremony of a further invitation," said Albina.

"Of course," replied Cheston.

"I quite long to introduce you to Mrs. Washington Potts," said Mrs. Marsden.

"What simpletons these women are," thought Cheston, as he hastily turned to depart.

"The big plum-cake's burnt to a coal," said Drusa, putting her head out of the kitchen door.

Both the ladies were off in an instant to the scene of disaster. And

Cheston returned to his hotel, thinking of Mrs. Potts, (whom he had made up his mind to dislike) of the old adage that "evil communications corrupt good manners," and of the almost irresistible contagion of folly and vanity. "I am disappointed in Albina," said he; "in future I will regard her only as my mother's niece, and more than a cousin she shall never be to me."

Albina having assisted Mrs. Marsden in lamenting over the burnt cake, took off her silk frock, again pinned up her hair, and joined assiduously in preparing another plum-cake to replace the first one. A fatality seemed to attend nearly all the confections, as is often the case when particular importance is attached to their success. The jelly obstinately refused to clarify, and the blanc-mange was equally unwilling to congeal. The maccaroons having run in baking, had neither shape nor feature, the kisses declined rising, and the spongecake contradicted its name. Some of the things succeeded, but most were complete failures: probably because (as old Katy insisted) "there was a spell upon them." In a city these disasters could easily have been remedied (even at the eleventh hour) by sending to a confectioner's shop, but in the country there is no alternative. Some of these mischances might perhaps have been attributed to the volunteered assistance of a mantua-maker that had been sent for from the city to make new dresses for the occasion, and who on this busy day, being "one of the best creatures in the world," had declared her willingness to turn her hand to anything.

It was late in the afternoon before the papering was over, and then great indeed was the bustle in clearing away the litter, cleaning the floors, putting down the carpets, and replacing the furniture. In the midst of the confusion, and while the ladies were earnestly engaged in fixing the ornaments, Drusa came in to say that Dixon, the waiter that had been hired for the evening, had just arrived, and falling to work immediately he had poured all the blanc-mange down the sink, mistaking it for bonny-clabber.* This intelligence was almost too much to bear, and Mrs. Marsden could scarcely speak for vexation.

"Drusa," said Albina, "you are a raven that has done nothing all day but croak of disaster. Away and show your face no more, let what will happen."

Drusa departed, but in a few minutes she again put in her head at the parlour door and said, "Ma'am may I jist speak one time more."

"What now," exclaimed Mrs. Marsden.

"Oh! there's nothing else spiled or flung down the sink, jist now," said Drusa, "but something's at hand a heap worse than all. Missus's old Aunt Quimby has jist landed from the boat, and is coming up the road with baggage enough to last all summer."

"Aunt Quimby!" exclaimed Albina; "this indeed caps the climax!"

*Thick sour milk.

"Was there ever anything more provoking," said Mrs. Marsden. "When I lived in town she annoyed me sufficiently by coming every week to spend a day with me, and now she does not spend days but *weeks.* I would go to Alabama to get rid of her."

"And then," said Albina, "she would come and spend *months* with us. However, to do her justice, she is a very respectable woman."

"All bores are respectable people," replied Mrs. Marsden; "if they were otherwise, it would not be in their power to bore us, for we could cut them and cast them off at once. How very unlucky. What will Mrs. Washington Potts think of her—and the Montagues too, if they *should* come? Still we must not affront her, as you know she is rich."

"What can her riches signify to us," said Albina, "she has a married daughter."

"True," replied Mrs. Marsden, "but you know riches should always command a certain degree of respect, and there are such things as legacies."

"After all, according to the common saying, ''tis an ill wind that blows no good,' the parlours having been freshly papered, we can easily persuade Aunt Quimby that they are too damp for her to sit in, and so we can make her stay up stairs all the evening."

At this moment the old lady's voice was heard at the door, discharging the porter who had brought her baggage on his wheelbarrow; and the next minute she was in the front parlour. Mrs. Marsden and Albina were properly astonished, and properly delighted at seeing her; but each, after a pause of recollection, suddenly seized the old lady by the arms and conveyed her into the entry, exclaiming, "Oh! Aunt Quimby! Aunt Quimby! this is no place for you."

"What's the meaning of all this?" cried Mrs. Quimby, "why won't you let me stay in the parlour?"

"You'll get your death," answered Mrs. Marsden, "you'll get the rheumatism. Both parlours have been newly papered to-day, and the walls are quite wet!"

"That's a bad thing," said Mrs. Quimby, "a very bad thing. I wish you had put off your papering till next spring. Who'd have thought of your doing it this day of all days?"

"Oh! Aunt Quimby," said Albina, "why did you not let us know that you were coming?"

"Why, I wanted to give you an agreeable surprise," replied the old lady. "But tell me why the rooms are so decked out, with flowers hanging about the looking-glasses and lamps, and why the candles are drest with cut paper, or something that looks like it?"

"We are going to have a party to-night," said Albina.

"A party. I'm glad of it. Then I'm just come in the nick of time."

"I thought you had long since given up parties," said Mrs. Marsden, turning pale.

"No, indeed—why should I—I always go when I am asked—to be sure I can't make much figure at parties now, being in my seventy-fifth year. But Mrs. Howks and Mrs. Himes, and several others of my old friends always invite me to their daughters' parties, along with Mary; and I like to sit there and look about me and see people's new ways. Mary had a party herself last winter, and it went off very well, only that both the children came out that night with the measles; and one of the lamps leaked, and the oil ran all over the sideboard and streamed down on the carpet; and, it being the first time we ever had ice-cream in the house, Peter, the stupid black boy, not only brought saucers to eat it in, but cups and saucers both."

The old lady was now hurried up stairs, and she showed much dissatisfaction on being told that as the damp parlours would certainly give her her death, there was no alternative but for her to remain all the evening in the chamber allotted to her. This chamber, (the best furnished in the house) was also to be 'the ladies' room,' and Albina somewhat consoled Mrs. Quimby by telling her that as the ladies would come up there to take off their hoods and arrange their hair, she would have an opportunity of seeing them all before they went down stairs. And Mrs. Marsden promised to give orders that a portion of all the refreshments should be carried up to her, and that Miss Matson, the mantua-maker, should sit with her a great part of the evening.

It was now time for Albina and her mother to commence dressing, but Mrs. Marsden went down stairs again with 'more last words' to the servants, and Albina to make some change in the arrangement of the centre-table.

She was in a loose gown, her curls were pinned up, and to keep them close and safe she had tied over her head an old gauze handkerchief. While bending over the centre-table and marking with rose-leaves some of the most beautiful of Mrs. Hemans' poems, and opening two or three souvenirs at their finest plates, a knock was suddenly heard at the door, which proved to be the baker with the second plum-cake, it having been consigned to *his* oven. Albina desired him to bring it to her, and putting it on the silver waiter she determined to divide it herself into slices, being afraid to trust that business to any one else, lest it should be awkwardly cut or broken to pieces; it being quite warm.

The baker went out, leaving the front door open, and Albina, intent on her task of cutting the cake, did not look up till she heard the sound of footsteps in the parlour, and then what was her dismay on perceiving Mr. and Mrs. Montague and their daughter.

Albina's first impulse was to run away, but she saw that it was now too late; and pale with confusion and vexation she tried to summon sufficient self-command to enable her to pass off this *contre-tems* with something like address.

It was not yet dusk, the sun being scarcely down, and of all the persons invited to the party, it was natural to suppose that the English family would have come the latest.

Mr. Montague was a long-bodied short-legged man, with round grey eyes, that looked as if they had been put on the outside of his face, the sockets having no apparent concavity: a sort of eye that is rarely seen in an American. He had a long nose and a large heavy mouth with projecting under-teeth, and altogether an unusual quantity of face; which face was bordered round with whiskers, that began at his eyes and met under his chin, and resembled in texture the coarse wiry fur of a black bear. He kept his hat under his arm, and his whole dress seemed as if modelled from one of the caricature prints of a London dandy.

Mrs. Montague (evidently some years older than her husband) was a gigantic woman, with features that looked as if seen through a magnifying glass. She wore heavy piles of yellowish curls, and a crimson velvet tocque. Her daughter was a tall hard-faced girl of seventeen, meant for a child by her parents, but not meaning herself as such. She was drest in a white muslin frock and trowsers, and had a mass of black hair curling on her neck and shoulders.

They all fixed their large eyes directly upon her, and it was no wonder that Albina quailed beneath their glance, or rather their stare, particularly when Mrs. Montague surveyed her through her eye-glass. Mr. Montague spoke first. "Your note did not specify the hour—Miss—Miss Martin," said he, "and as you Americans are early people, we thought we were complying with the simplicity of republican manners by coming before dark. We suppose that in general you adhere to the primitive maxim of 'early to bed and early to rise.' I forget the remainder of the rhyme, but *you* know it undoubtedly."

Albina at that moment wished for the presence of Bromley Cheston. She saw from the significant looks that passed between the Montagues, that the unseasonable earliness of this visit did not arise from their ignorance of the customs of American society, but from premeditated impertinence. And she regretted still more having invited them, when Mr. Montague with impudent familiarity walked up to the cake (which she had nicely cut into slices without altering its form) and took one of them out.—"Miss Martin," said he, "your cake looks so inviting that I cannot refrain from helping myself to a piece. Mrs. Montague give me leave to present one to you. Miss Montague will you try a slice."

They sat down on the sofa, each with a piece of cake, and Albina saw that they could scarcely refrain from laughing openly, not only at her dishabille, but at her disconcerted countenance.

Just at this moment, Drusa appeared at the door, and called out, "Miss Albinar, the presarved squinches are all working. Missus found 'em so when she opened the jar." Albina could bear no more, but hastily darting out of the room, she ran up stairs almost crying with vexation.

Old Mrs. Quimby was loud in her invectives against Mr. Montague for spoiling the symmetry of the cake, and helping himself and his family so unceremoniously. "You may rely upon it," said she, "a man that will do such a thing in a strange house is no gentleman."

"On the contrary," observed Mrs. Marsden, "I have no doubt that in England these free and easy proceedings are high tone. Albina have not you read some such things in Vivian Grey?"

"I do not believe," said Mrs. Quimby, "that if this Englishman was in his own country, he would dare to go and take other people's cake without leave or license. But he thinks any sort of behaviour good enough for the Yankees, as they call us."

"I care not for the cake," said Albina, "although the pieces must now be put into baskets, I only think of the Montagues walking in without knocking, and catching me in complete dishabille: after I had kept poor Bromley Cheston waiting half an hour this morning rather than he should see me in my pink gingham gown and with my hair in pins."

"As sure as sixpence," remarked Mrs. Quimby, "this last shame has come upon you as a punishment for your pride to your own cousin."

Mrs. Marsden having gone into the adjoining room to dress, Albina remained in this, and placed herself before the glass for the same purpose. "Heigho!" said she, "how pale and jaded I look. What a fatiguing day I have had! I have been on my feet since five o'clock this morning, and I feel now more fit to go to bed than to add to my weariness by the task of dressing, and then playing the agreeable for four or five hours. I begin to think that parties (at least such parties as are now in vogue) should only be given by persons who have large houses, large purses, conveniences of every description, and servants enough to do all that is necessary."

"Albina is talking quite sensibly," said Aunt Quimby to Mrs. Marsden, who came in to see if her daughter required her assistance in dressing.

"Pho," said Mrs. Marsden, "think of the eclat of giving a party to Mrs. Washington Potts, and of having the Montagues among the guests. We shall find the advantage of it when we visit the city again."

"Albina," said Aunt Quimby, "now we are about dressing, just quit for a few moments and help me on with my long stays and my new black silk gown, and let me have the glass awhile; I am going to wear my lace cap with the white satin riband. This dark calico gown and plain muslin cap won't do at all to sit here in, before all the ladies that are coming up."

"Oh! no matter," replied Albina, who was unwilling to relinquish the glass or to occupy any of her time by assisting her aunt in dressing, (which was always a troublesome and tedious business with the old lady) and her mother had now gone down to be ready for the reception of the company, and to pay her compliments to the Montagues. "Oh! no matter," said Albina, "your present dress looks perfectly well, and the ladies will be too much engaged with themselves and their own dresses to remark anything else. No one will observe whether your gown is calico or silk, and whether your cap is muslin or lace. Elderly ladies are always privileged to wear what is most convenient to them."

Albina put on the new dress that the mantua-maker had made for her. When she had tried it on the preceding evening Miss Matson declared that "it fitted like wax." She now found that it was scarcely possible to get it on at all, and that one side of the forebody was larger than the other. Miss Matson was called up, and by dint of the pulling, stretching, and smoothing well known to mantua-makers, and still more by means of her pertinacious assurances that the dress had no fault whatever, Albina was obliged to acknowledge that she *could* wear it, and the redundancy of the large side was pinned down and pinned over. In sticking in her comb she broke it in half, and it was long before she could arrange her hair to her satisfaction without it. Before she had completed her toilette, several of the ladies arrived and came into the room, and Albina was obliged to snatch up her paraphernalia and make her escape into the next apartment.

At last she was drest—she went down stairs. The company arrived fast, and the party began.

Bromley Cheston had come early to assist in doing the honours, and as he led Albina to a seat, he saw that in spite of her smiles she looked weary and out of spirits, and he pitied her. "After all," thought he, "there is much that is interesting about Albina Marsden."

The party was *very* select, consisting of the elite of the village and its neighbourhood; but still, as is often the case, those whose presence was most desirable had sent excuses, and those who were not wanted had taken care to come. And Miss Boreham, (a young lady who having nothing else to recommend her, had been invited solely on account of the usual elegance of her attire, and whose dress was expected to add prodigiously to the effect of the rooms,) came most unaccountably in an old faded frock of last year's fashion, with her hair quite plain, and tucked behind her ears with two side-combs. Could she have had a suspicion of the reason for which she was generally invited, and have therefore perversely determined on a reaction?

The Montagues sat together in a corner, putting up their eye-glasses at every one that entered the room, and criticising the company in loud whispers to each other; poor Mrs. Marsden endeavouring to catch opportunities of paying her court to them.

About nine o'clock, appeared an immense cap of blond lace, gauze riband, and flowers; and under the cap was Mrs. Washington Potts, a little, thin, trifling looking woman with a whitish freckled face, small sharp features, and flaxen hair. She leaned on the arm of Mr. Washington Potts, who was nothing in company or anywhere else; and she led by the hand a little boy in a suit of scarlet, braided and frogged with blue: a pale rat-looking child, whose name she pronounced Laughy-yet, meaning La

Fayette; and who being the youngest scion of the house of Potts, always went to parties with his mother, because he would not stay at home.

Bromley Cheston, on being introduced to Mrs. Washington Potts was surprised at the insignificance of her figure and face. He had imagined her tall in stature, large in feature, loud in voice, and in short the very counterpart to Mrs. Montague. He found her, however, as he had supposed, replete with vanity, pride, ignorance and folly: to which she added a sickening affectation of sweetness and amiability, and a flimsy pretension to extraordinary powers of conversation, founded on a confused assemblage of incorrect and superficial ideas, which she mistook for a general knowledge of everything in the world.

Mrs. Potts was delighted with the handsome face and figure, and the very genteel appearance of the young lieutenant, and she bestowed upon him a large portion of her talk.

"I hear, sir," said she, "you have been in the Mediterranean Sea. A sweet pretty place, is it not?"

"Its shores," replied Cheston, "are certainly very beautiful."

"Yes, I should admire its chalky cliffs vastly," resumed Mrs. Potts, "they are quite poetical you know. Pray, sir, which do you prefer, Byron or Bonaparte. I dote upon Byron; and considering what sweet verses he wrote, 'tis a pity he was a corsair, and a vampyre pirate, and all such horrid things. As for Bonaparte, I never could endure him after I found that he had cut off poor old King George's head. Now, when we talk of great men, my husband is altogether for Washington. I laugh, and tell Mr. Potts it's because he and Washington are namesakes. How do you like La Fayette,"—(pronouncing the name a la canaille.)

"The man or the name?" inquired Cheston.

"Oh! both to be sure. You see we have called our youngest blossom after him. Come here Lafayette, stand forward my dear, hold up your head, and make a bow to the gentleman."

"I won't," screamed La Fayette. "I'll never make a bow when you tell me."

"Something of the spirit of his ancestors," said Mrs. Potts, affectedly smiling to Cheston and patting the urchin on the head.

"His ancestors!" thought Cheston. "Who could they possibly have been?"

"Perhaps the dear fellow may be a little, a very little spoiled," pursued Mrs. Potts. "But to make a comparison in the marine line, (quite in your way, you know,) it is as natural for a mother's heart to turn to her youngest darling as it is for the needle to point out the longitude. Now we talk of longitude, have you read Cooper's last novel, by the author of the Spy. It's a sweet book—Cooper is one of my pets. I saw him in dear delightful Paris. Are you musical, Mr. Cheston?—But, of course, you are. Our whole aristocracy is musical now. How do you like Paganini? You must have heard him in Europe. It's a very expensive thing to hear

Paganini.—Poor man! he is quite ghastly with his own playing. Well; as you have been in the Mediterranean, which do you prefer, the Greeks or the Poles?"

"The Poles, decidedly," answered Cheston, "from what I have heard of *them*, and seen of the Greeks."

"Well, for my part," resumed Mrs. Potts, "I confess I like the Greeks, as I have always been rather classical. They are so Grecian. Think of their beautiful statues and paintings by Reubens and Reynolds. Are you fond of paintings? At my house in the city, I can show you some very fine ones."

"By what artists?" asked Cheston.

"Oh! by my daughter Harriet. She did them at drawing-school with theorems. They are beautiful flower-pieces, all framed and hung up; they are almost worthy of Sir Benjamin West."*

In this manner Mrs. Potts ran on till the entrance of tea, and Cheston took that opportunity of escaping from her; while she imagined him deeply imbued with admiration of her fluency, vivacity and variety of information. But in reality, he was thinking of the strange depravity of taste that is sometimes found even in intelligent minds; for in no other way could he account for Albina's predilection for Mrs. Washington Potts. "And yet," thought he, "is a young and inexperienced girl more blameable for her blindness in friendship, (or what she imagines to be friendship) than an acute, sensible, talented man for his blindness in love. The master-spirits of the earth have almost proverbially married women of weak intellect, and almost as proverbially the children of such marriages resemble the mother rather than the father. A just punishment for choosing so absurdly. Albina I must know you better."

The party went on, much as parties generally do where there are four or five guests that are supposed to rank all the others. The patricians evidently despised the plebeians, and the plebeians were offended at being despised; for in no American assemblage is any real inferiority of rank ever felt or acknowledged. There was a general dullness, and a general restraint. Little was done, and little was said. La Fayette wandered about in every body's way; having been kept wide awake all the evening by two cups of strong coffee, which his mother allowed him to take because he would have them.

There was always a group round the centre-table, listlessly turning over the souvenirs, albums, &c. and picking at the flowers; and La Fayette ate plum-cake over Cheston's beautiful drawings.

Albina played an Italian song extremely well, but the Montagues exchanged glances at her music; and Mrs. Potts, to follow suit, hid her

---

*The author takes this occasion to remark that the illustrious artist to whom so many of his countrymen erroneously give the title of *Sir* Benjamin West, never in reality had the compliment of knighthood conferred on him. He lived and died *Mr.* West, as is well known to all who have any acquaintance with pictures and painters.

face behind her fan and simpered; though in truth she did not in reality know Italian from French, or a semibreve from a semiquaver. All this was a great annoyance to Cheston. At Albina's request, he led Miss Montague to the piano. She ran her fingers over the instrument as if to try it; gave a shudder, and declared it most shockingly out of tune, and then rose in horror from the music stool. This much surprised Mrs. Marsden, as a musician had been brought from the city only the day before for the express purpose of tuning this very instrument.

"No," whispered Miss Montague, as she resumed her seat beside her mother, "I will not condescend to play before people who are incapable of understanding my style."

At this juncture (to the great consternation of Mrs. Marsden and her daughter) who should make her appearance but Aunt Quimby in the calico gown which Albina now regretted having persuaded her to keep on. The old lady was wrapped in a small shawl and two large ones, and her head was secured from cold by a black silk handkerchief tied over her cap and under her chin. She smiled and nodded all round to the company, and said—"How do you do, good people; I hope you are all enjoying yourselves. I thought I *must* come down and have a peep at you. For after I had seen all the ladies take off their hoods, and had my tea, I found it pretty dull work sitting up stairs with the mantua-maker, who had no more manners than to fall asleep while I was talking."

Mrs. Marsden, much discomfited, led Aunt Quimby to a chair between two matrons who were among "the unavoidably invited," and whose pretensions to refinement were not very palpable. But the old lady had no idea of remaining stationary all the evening between Mrs. Johnson and Mrs. Jackson. She wisely thought "she could see more of the party," if she frequently changed her place, and being of what is called a sociable disposition, she never hesitated to talk to any one that was near her, however high or however low.

"Dear mother," said Albina in an under-voice, "what can be the reason that every one in tasting the ice-cream, immediately sets it aside as if it was not fit to eat. I am sure there is everything in it that ought to be."

"And something more than ought to be," replied Mrs. Marsden, after trying a spoonful—"the salt that was laid round the freezer has got into the cream, (I suppose by Dixon's carelessness) and it is *not* fit to eat."

"And now," said Albina starting, "I will show you a far worse mortification than the failure of the ice-cream. Only look—there sits Aunt Quimby between Mr. Montague and Mrs. Washington Potts."

"How in the world did she get there?" exclaimed Mrs. Marsden. "I dare say she walked up, and asked them to make room for her between them. There is nothing now to be done but to pass her off as well as we can, and to make the best of her. I will manage to get as near as possible, that I may hear what she is talking about, and take an opportunity of persuading her away."

As Mrs. Marsden approached within hearing distance; Mr. Montague was leaning across Aunt Quimby, and giving Mrs. Potts an account of something that had been said or done during a splendid entertainment at Devonshire House.—"Just at that moment," said he, "I was lounging into the room with Lady Augusta Fitzhenry on my arm (unquestionably the finest woman in England) and Mrs. Montague was a few steps in advance, leaning on my friend the Marquis of Elvington."

"Pray, sir," said Mrs. Quimby, "as you are from England, do you know anything of Betsey Dempsey's husband?"

"I have not the honour of being acquainted with that person," replied Mr. Montague, after a withering stare.

"Well, that's strange," pursued Aunt Quimby, "considering that he has been living in London at least eighteen years—or perhaps it is only seventeen. And yet I think it must be near eighteen, if not quite. May-be seventeen and a half. Well it's best to be on the safe side, so I'll say seventeen. Betsey Dempsey's mother was an old school-mate of mine. Her father kept the Black Horse tavern. She was the only acquaintance I ever had that married an Englishman. He was a grocer, and in very good business; but he never liked America, and was always finding fault with it, and so he went home, and was to send for Betsey. But he never sent for her at all; and for a very good reason; which was that he had another wife in England, as most of them have—no disparagement to you, Sir."

Mrs. Marsden now came up, and informed Mrs. Potts in a whisper that the good old lady beside her, was a distant relation or rather connexion of *Mr.* Marsden's, and that, though a little primitive in appearance and manner, she had considerable property in bank-stock. To Mrs. Marsden's proposal that she should exchange her seat for a very pleasant one in the other room next to her old friend Mrs. Willis, Aunt Quimby replied nothing but "Thank you, I'm doing very well here."

Mrs. and Miss Montague, apparently heeding no one else, had talked nearly the whole evening to each other, but loudly enough to be heard by all around them. The young lady, though dressed as a child, talked like a woman, and she and her mother were now engaged in an argument whether the flirtation of the Duke of Risingham with Lady Georgiana Melbury would end seriously or not.

"To my certain knowledge," said Miss Montague, "his Grace has never yet declared himself to Lady Georgiana, or to any one else."

"I'll lay you two to one," said Mrs. Montague, "that he is married to her before we return to England."

"No," replied the daughter, "like all others of his sex he delights in keeping the ladies in suspense."

"What you say Miss, is very true," said Aunt Quimby, leaning in her turn across Mr. Montague, "and considering how young you are you talk very sensibly. Men certainly have a way of keeping women in suspense, and an unwillingness to answer questions even when we ask them.

There's my son-in-law Billy Fairfowl, that I live with. He married my daughter Mary eleven years ago the 23d of last April. He's as good a man as ever breathed, and an excellent provider too. He always goes to market himself; and sometimes I can't help blaming him a little for his extravagance. But his greatest fault is his being so unsatisfactory. As far back as last March, as I was sitting at my knitting in the little front parlour with the door open, (for it was quite warm weather for the time of the year) Billy Fairfowl came home carrying in his hand a good sized shad; and I called out to him to ask what he gave for it, for it was the very beginning of the shad season; but he made not a word of answer; he just passed on, and left the shad in the kitchen, and then went to his store. At dinner we had the fish, and a very nice one it was; and I asked him again how much he gave for it, but he still avoided answering, and began to talk of something else; so I thought I'd let it rest awhile. A week or two after, I again asked him; so then he actually said he had forgotten all about it. And to this day I don't know the price of that shad."

The Montagues looked at each other—almost laughed aloud, and drew back their chairs as far from Aunt Quimby as possible. So also did Mrs. Potts. Mrs. Marsden came up in an agony of vexation, and reminded her aunt in a low voice of the risk of renewing her rheumatism by staying so long between the damp newly-papered walls. The old lady answered aloud—"Oh! you need not fear, I am well wrapped up on purpose. And indeed considering that the parlours were only papered to-day, I think the walls have dried wonderfully, (putting her hand on the paper)—I am sure nobody could find out the damp if they were not told."

"What!" exclaimed the Montagues; "only papered to-day—(starting up and testifying all that prudent fear of taking cold, so characteristic of the English). How barbarous to inveigle us into such a place!"

"I thought I felt strangely chilly all the evening," said Mrs. Potts, whose fan had scarcely been at rest five minutes.

The Montagues proposed going away immediately, and Mrs. Potts declared she was *most* apprehensive for poor little Lafayette. Mrs. Marsden who could not endure the idea of their departing till all the refreshments had been handed round, (the best being yet to come) took great pains to persuade them that there was no real cause of alarm, as she had had large fires all the afternoon. They held a whispered consultation, in which they agreed to stay for the oysters and chicken salad, and Mrs. Marsden went out to send them their shawls, with one for Lafayette.

By this time the secret of the newly-papered walls had spread round both rooms; the conversation now turned entirely on colds and rheumatisms; there was much shivering and considerable coughing, and the demand for shawls increased. However nobody actually went home in consequence.

"Papa," said Miss Montague, "let us all take French leave as soon as the oysters and chicken salad have gone round."

Albina now came up to Aunt Quimby (gladly perceiving that the old lady looked tired,) and proposed that she should return to her chamber, assuring her that the waiters should be punctually sent up to her—"I do not feel quite ready to go yet," replied Mrs. Quimby. "I am very well here. But you need not mind *me*. Go back to your company, and talk a little to those three poor girls in the yellow frocks that nobody has spoken to yet, except Bromley Cheston. When I am ready to go I shall take French leave, as these English people call it."

But Aunt Quimby's idea of French leave was very different from the usual acceptation of the term; for having always heard that the French were a very polite people, she concluded that their manner of taking leave must be particularly respectful and ceremonious. Therefore, having paid her parting compliments to Mrs. Potts and the Montagues, she walked all round the room, curtseying to every body and shaking hands, and telling them she had come to take French leave. To put an end to this ridiculous scene, Bromley Cheston (who had been on assiduous duty all the evening) now came forward and taking the old lady's arm in his, offered to escort her up stairs. Aunt Quimby was much flattered by this unexpected civility from the finest looking young man in the room, and she smilingly departed with him, complimenting him on his politeness, and assuring him that he was a real gentleman; trying also to make out the degree of relationship that existed between them.

"So much for Buckingham," said Cheston, as he ran down stairs after depositing the old lady at the door of her room. "Fools of all ranks and of all ages are to me equally intolerable. I never can marry into such a family."

The party went on.

"In the name of heaven, Mrs. Potts," said Mrs. Montague, "what induces you to patronize these people?"

"Why they are the only tolerable persons in the neighbourhood," answered Mrs. Potts, "and very kind and obliging in their way. I really think Albina a very sweet girl, very sweet indeed: and Mrs. Marsden is rather amiable too, quite amiable. And they are so grateful for any little notice I take of them, that it is really quite affecting. Poor things! how much trouble they have given themselves in getting up this party. They look as if they had had a hard day's work; and I have no doubt they will be obliged, in consequence, to pinch themselves for months to come; for I can assure you their means are very small, very small indeed. As to this intolerable old aunt, I never saw her before, and as there is something rather genteel about Mrs. Marsden and her daughter; rather so at least about Albina; I did not suppose they had any such relations belonging to them. I think, in future, I must confine myself entirely to the aristocracy."

"We deliberated to the last moment," said Mrs. Montague, "whether we should come. But as Mr. Montague is going to write his tour when we return to England, he thinks it expedient to make some sacrifices, for the sake of seeing the varieties of American society."

"Oh! these people are not in society," exclaimed Mrs. Potts eagerly. "I can assure you these Marsdens have not the slightest pretensions to society. Oh! no—I beg you not to suppose that Mrs. Marsden and her daughter are at all in society."

This conversation was overheard by Bromley Cheston, and it gave him more pain than he was willing to acknowledge, even to himself.

At length all the refreshments had gone their rounds, and the Montagues had taken real French leave; but Mrs. Washington Potts preferred a conspicuous departure, and therefore made her adieu with a view of producing great effect. This was the signal for the company to break up, and Mrs. Marsden gladly smiled them out, while Albina could have said with Gray's Prophetess—

> Now my weary lips I close,
> Leave me, leave me to repose."

But, according to Mrs. Marsden, the worst of all was the poet, the professedly eccentric Bewley Garvin Gandy, author of the World of Sorrow, Elegy on a Broken Heart, Lines on a Suppressed Sigh, Sonnet to a Hidden Tear, Stanzas to Faded Hopes, &c. &c. and who was just now engaged in a tale called "The Bewildered," and an Ode to the Waning Moon, which set him to wandering about the country, and "kept him out o'nights." The poet, not being a man of this world, did not make his appearance at the party till the moment of the bustle occasioned by the exit of Mrs. Washington Potts. He then darted suddenly into the room, and looked wild.

We will not insinuate that he bore any resemblance to Sandy Clark. He certainly wore no chapeau, and his coat was not in the least a la militaire, for it was a dusky brown frock. His collar was open, in the fashion attributed to Byron, and much affected by scribblers who are incapable of imitating the noble bard in anything but his follies. His hair looked as if he had just been tearing it, and his eyes seemed "in a fine frenzy rolling." He was on his return from one of his moonlight rambles on the banks of the river, and his pantaloons and coat-skirt showed evident marks of having been deep among the cat-tails and splatter-docks that grew in the mud on its margin.

Being a man that took no note of time, he wandered into Mrs. Marsden's house between eleven and twelve o'clock, and remained an hour after the company had gone; reclining at full length on a sofa, and discussing Barry Cornwall and Thomas Haynes Bayley, L. E. L. and Mrs. Cornwall Baron Wilson. After which he gradually became classical, and poured into the sleepy ears of Mrs. Marsden and Albina a parallel between Tibullus and Propertius, a dissertation on Alexus, and another on Menander.

Bromley Cheston who had been escorting home two sets of young ladies that lived "far as the poles asunder," passed Mrs. Marsden's house on returning to his hotel, and seeing the lights still gleaming, he went in to see what was the matter, and kindly relieved his Aunt and cousin by reminding the poet of the lateness of the hour, and "fairly carrying him off."

Aunt Quimby had long since been asleep. But before Mrs. Marsden and Albina could forget themselves in "tired nature's sweet restorer," they lay awake for an hour, discussing the fatigues and vexations of the day, and the mortifications of the evening. "After all," said Albina, "this party has cost us five times as much as it is worth, both in trouble and expense, and I really cannot tell what pleasure we have derived from it."

"No one expects pleasure at their own party," replied Mrs. Marsden. "But you may depend on it, this little compliment to Mrs. Washington Potts will prove highly advantageous to us hereafter. And then it is *something* to be the only family in the neighbourhood that could presume to do such a thing."

Next morning, Bromley Cheston received a letter which required his immediate presence in New York on business of importance. When he went to take leave of his aunt and cousin, he found them busily engaged in clearing away and putting in order; a task which is nearly equal to that of making the preparations for a party. They looked pale and spiritless, and Mrs. Washington Potts had just sent her three boys to spend the day with them.

When Cheston took Albina's hand at parting, he felt it tremble, and her eyes looked as if they were filling with tears. "After all," thought he, "she is a charming girl, and has both sense and sensibility."

"I am very nervous to-day," said Albina, "the party has been too much for me; and I have in prospect for to-morrow the pain of taking leave of Mrs. Washington Potts, who returns with all her family to Philadelphia."

"Strange infatuation," thought Cheston, as he dropped Albina's hand, and made his parting bow. "I must see more of this girl, before I can resolve to trust my happiness to her keeping; I cannot share her heart with Mrs. Washington Potts. When I return from New York I will talk to her seriously about that ridiculous woman, and I will also remonstrate with her mother on the folly of straining every nerve in the pursuit of what she calls a certain style."

In the afternoon, Mrs. Potts did Albina the honour to send for her to assist in the preparations for to-morrow's removal to town; and in the evening the three boys were all taken home sick, in consequence of having laid violent hands on the fragments of the feast: which fragments they had continued during the day to devour almost without intermission. Also Randolph had thrown Jefferson down stairs, and raised two green bumps on his forehead, and Jefferson had pinched La Fayette's fingers in the door till the blood came; not to mention various minor squabbles and hurts.

At parting, Mrs. Potts went so far as to kiss Albina, and made her promise to let her know immediately, whenever she or her mother came to the city.

In about two weeks, Aunt Quimby finished her visitation: and the day after her departure Mrs. Marsden and Albina went to town to make their purchases for the season, and also with a view towards a party which they knew Mrs. Potts had in contemplation. This time they did not as usual stay with their relations, but they took lodgings at a fashionable boarding-house where they could receive their "great woman," comme il faut.

On the morning after their arrival Mrs. Marsden and her daughter, in their most costly dresses, went to visit Mrs. Potts that she might be apprized of their arrival; and they found her in a spacious house, expensively and ostentatiously furnished. After they had waited till even *their* patience was nearly exhausted, Mrs. Potts came down stairs to them, but there was evidently a great abatement in her affability. She seemed uneasy, looked frequently towards the door, got up several times and went to the window, and appeared fidgety when the bell rung. At last there came in two very flaunting ladies, whom Mrs. Potts received as if she considered them people of consequence. They were not introduced to the Marsdens, who after the entrance of these new visitors sat awhile in the pitiable situation of cyphers, and then took their leave. "Strange," said Mrs. Marsden, "that she did not say a word of her party."

Three days after their visit, Mrs. Washington Potts left cards for Mrs. and Miss Marsden, without inquiring if they were at home. And they heard from report that her party was fixed for the week after next, and that it was expected to be very splendid, as it was to introduce her daughter who had just quitted boarding-school. The Marsdens had seen this young lady, who had spent the August holidays with her parents. She was as silly as her mother, and as dull as her father in the eyes of all who were not blindly determined to think her otherwise, or who did not consider it particularly expedient to uphold every one of the name of Potts.

At length they heard that the invitations were going out for Mrs. Potts's party, and that though very large it was not to be general; which meant that only one or two of the members were to be selected from each family with whom Mrs. Potts thought proper to acknowledge an acquaintance. From this moment Mrs. Marsden, who at the best of times had never really been treated with much respect by Mrs. Potts, gave up all hope of an invitation for herself; but she counted certainly on one for Albina, and every ring at the door was expected to bring it. There were many rings but no invitation; and poor Albina and her mother took turns in watching at the window.

At last Bogle was seen to come up the steps with a handful of notes and Albina, regardless of all rule, ran to the front-door herself. They were cards for a party, but not Mrs. Potts's, and were intended for two other ladies that lodged in the house.

Every time that Albina went out and came home, she inquired anxiously of all the servants if no note had been left for her. Still there was none. And her mother still insisted that the note *must* have come, but had been mislaid afterwards, or that Bogle had lost it in the street.

Wednesday, Thursday, Friday, and Saturday passed over, and still no invitation. Mrs. Marsden talked much of the carelessness of servants, and had no doubt of the habitual negligence of Messrs. Bogle, Shepherd, and other "fashionable party-men." Albina was almost sick with "hope deferred." At last, when she came home on Monday morning from Second street, her mother met her at the door with a delighted face, and showed her the long-desired note, which had just been brought by Mrs. Potts's own man. The party was to take place in two days: and so great was now Albina's happiness, that she scarcely felt the fatigue of searching the shops for articles of attire that were very elegant and yet not *too* expensive; and shopping with a limited purse is certainly no trifling exercise both of mind and body; so also is the task of going round among fashionable mantua-makers, in the hope of coaxing one of them to undertake a dress at a short notice.

Next morning, Mrs. Potts sent for Albina immediately after breakfast, and told her that as she knew her to be very clever at all sorts of things, she wanted her to stay that day and assist in the preparations for the next. Mrs. Potts, like many other people who live in showy houses and dress extravagantly, was very economical in servants. She gave such low wages that none would come to her who could get places anywhere else, and she kept them on such limited allowance that none would stay with her who were worth having.

Fools are seldom consistent in their expenditure. They generally (to use a homely expression) strain at gnats and swallow camels.

About noon Albina having occasion to consult Mrs. Potts concerning something that was to be done, found her in the front parlour with Mrs. and Miss Montague. After Albina had left the room, Mrs. Montague said to Mrs. Potts—"Is not that the girl who lives with her mother at the place on the river, I forget what you call it?—I mean the niece of the aunt."

"That is Albina Marsden," replied Mrs. Potts.

"Yes," pursued Mrs. Montague, "the people that made so great an exertion to give you a sort of party, and honoured Mr. and Miss Montague and myself with invitations."

"She's not to be here to-morrow night, I hope!" exclaimed Miss Montague.

"Really," replied Mrs. Potts, "I could do no less than ask her. The poor thing did her very best to be civil to us all last summer."

"Oh!" said Mrs. Montague, "in the country one is willing sometimes to take up with such company as we should be very sorry to acknowledge in town. You assured me that your party to-morrow night would be extremely *recherchée*. And as it is so early in the season, you know that it is necessary to be more particular now than at the close of the campaign, when every one is tired of parties, and unwilling to get new evening dresses lest they should be out of fashion before they are wanted again. Excuse me, I speak only from what I have heard of American customs."

"I am always particular about my parties," said Mrs. Potts.

"A word in your ear," continued Mrs. Montague. "Is it not impolite, or rather are you not afraid to bring forward so beautiful a girl as this Miss Martin on the very night of your own daughter's debut?"

Mrs. Potts looked alarmed for a moment, and then recovering herself said—"I have no fear of Miss Harriet Angelina Potts being thrown in the shade by a little country girl like this. Albina Marsden is pretty enough, to be sure—at least, rather pretty—but then there is a certain style—a certain air which she of course—in short, a certain style—"

"As to what you call a certain style," said Mrs. Montague, "I do not know exactly what you mean. If it signifies the air and manner of a lady, this Miss Martin has as much of it as any other American girl. To me they are all nearly alike. I cannot distinguish those minute shades of difference that you all make such a point of. In my unpracticed eyes the daughters of your mechanics and shopkeepers look as well and behave as well as the daughters of your lawyers and doctors, for I find your nobility is chiefly made up of these two professions, with the addition of a few merchants; and you call every one a merchant that does not sell his commodities by the single yard or the single quart."

"Mamma," whispered Miss Montague, "if that girl is to be here I don't wish to come. I can't endure her."

"Take my advice," continued Mrs. Montague to Mrs. Potts, "and put off this Miss Martin. If she was not so strikingly handsome, she might pass unnoticed in the crowd. But her beauty will attract general observation, and you will be obliged to tell exactly who she is, where you picked her up, and to give or to hear an account of her family and all her connexions; and from the specimen we have had in the old aunt, I doubt if they will bear a very minute scrutiny. So if she *is* invited, endeavour to uninvite her."

"I am sure I would willingly do that," replied Mrs. Potts, "but I can really think of no excuse."

"Oh! send her a note to-morrow," answered Mrs. Montague, carelessly, and rising to depart, "anything or nothing, so that you only signify to her that she is not to come."

All day Mrs. Potts was revolving in her mind the most feasible means of preventing Albina from appearing at her party; and her conscience smote her when she saw the unsuspecting girl so indefatigable in assisting with the preparations. Before Albina went home, Mrs. Potts had come to the conclusion to follow Mrs. Montague's advice, but she shrunk from the task of telling her so in person. She determined to send her next morning a concise note, politely requesting her not to come; and she intended afterwards to call on her and apologize, on the plea of her party being by no means general, but still so large that every inch of room was an object of importance; also that the selection consisted entirely of persons well known to each other and accustomed to meet in company, and that there was every reason to fear that her gentle and modest friend Albina would have been unable to enjoy herself among so many strangers, &c. &c. These excuses, she knew, were very flimsy, but she trusted to Albina's good nature, and she thought she could smooth off all by inviting both her and her mother to a sociable tea.

Next morning, Mrs. Potts, who was on no occasion very ready with her pen, considering that she professed to be *au fait* to everything, employed near an hour in manufacturing the following note to Albina.

"Mrs. Washington Potts' compliments to Miss Marsden, and she regrets being under the necessity of dispensing with Miss M.'s company to join the social circle at her mansion-house this evening. Mrs. W. P. will explain hereafter, hoping Mrs. and Miss M. are both well. Mr. W. P. requests his respects to both ladies, as well as Miss Potts, and their favourite little Lafayette desires his best love."

This billet arrived while Albina had gone to her mantua-maker to have her new dress fitted on for the last time. Her mother opened the note and read it; a liberty which no parent should take with the correspondence of a grown-up daughter. Mrs. Marsden was shocked at its contents, and at a loss to guess the motive of so strange an interdiction. At first her only emotion was resentment against Mrs. Potts. Then she thought of the disappointment and mortification of poor Albina, whom she pictured to herself passing a forlorn evening at home, perhaps crying in her own room. Next, she recollected the elegant new dress in which Albina would have looked so beautifully, and which would now be useless.

"Oh!" soliloquized Mrs. Marsden, "what a pity this unaccountable note was not dropped and lost in the street. But then, of course some one would have found and read it, and that would have been worse than all. How could Mrs. Potts be guilty of such abominable rudeness, as to desire poor Albina not to come, after she had been invited. But great people think they may do anything. I wish the note had fallen into the fire before it came to my hands; then Albina would have known nothing of it; she would have gone to the party, looking more charmingly than ever she did in her life; and she would be seen there, and admired, and make new acquaintances, and Mrs. Potts could do no otherwise than behave to her politely in her own house. Nobody would know of this vile billet, which perhaps after all is only a joke, and Mrs. Potts would suppose that of course Albina had not received it; besides I have no doubt that Mrs. Potts will send for her tomorrow, and make a satisfactory explanation. But then; to-night, if Albina could only get there to-night. What harm can possibly arrive from my not showing her the note till to-morrow? Why should the dear girl be deprived of all the pleasure she anticipated this evening? And even if she expected no enjoyment whatever, still how great will be the advantage of having her seen at Mrs. Washington Potts's select party; it will at once get her on in the world. Of course Mrs. Potts will conclude that the note miscarried, and will treat her as if it had never been sent. I am really most strongly tempted to suppress it, and let Albina go."

The more Mrs. Marsden thought of this project the less objectionable it appeared to her. When she saw Albina come home delighted with her new dress which fitted her exactly, and when she heard her impatiently wishing that evening was come, this weak and ill-judging mother could not resolve (as she afterwards said) to dash all her pleasant anticipations to the ground and demolish her castles in the air. "My daughter shall be happy to-night," thought she, "whatever may be the event of to-morrow." She hastily concealed the note, and kept her resolution of not mentioning it to Albina.

Evening came, and Albina's beautiful hair was arranged and decorated by a fashionable French barber. She was drest, and she looked charmingly.

Albina knew that Mrs. Potts had sent an invitation to the United States Hotel for Lieutenant Cheston, who was daily expected but had not yet returned from New York, and she regretted much that she could not go to the party under his escort. She knew no one else of the company, and she had no alternative but to send for a carriage, and proceeded thither by herself, after her mother had despatched repeated messages to the hotel to know if Mr. Cheston had yet arrived, for he was certainly expected back that evening.

As Albina drove to the house, she felt all the terrors of diffidence coming upon her, and already repented that she had ventured on this enterprise alone. On arriving, she did not go into the ladies' room but gave her hood and cloak at once to a servant, and tremulously requested another attendant to inform Mr. Potts that a lady wished to see him. Mr. Potts accordingly came out into the hall, and looked surprised at finding Albina there, for he had heard his wife and daughter talking of the note of interdiction. But concluding, as he often did, that it was in vain for him to try to comprehend the proceedings of women, he thought it best to say nothing.

On Albina requesting him to accompany her on her entrance, he gave her his arm in silence, and with a very perplexed face escorted her into the principal room. As he led her up to his wife, his countenance gradually changed from perplexity to something like fright. Albina paid her compliments to Mrs. Potts, who received her with evident amazement, and without replying. Mrs. Montague, who sat next to the lady of the mansion, opened still wider her immense eyes, and then, "to make assurance doubly sure" applied her opera-glass. Miss Montague first stared and then laughed.

Albina, much disconcerted, turned to look for a seat, Mr. Potts having withdrawn his arm. As she retired to the only vacant chair, she heard a half whisper running along the line of ladies, and though she could not distinguish the words so as to make any connected sense of them, she felt that they alluded to her.

"Can I believe my eyes?" said Mrs. Potts.

"The assurance of American girls is astonishing," said Mrs. Montague.

"She was forbidden to come," said Miss Montague to a young lady beside her. "Mrs. Potts herself forbade her to come."

"She was actually prohibited," resumed Mrs. Montague leaning over to Mrs. Jones.

"I sent her myself a note of prohibition," said Mrs. Potts leaning over to Mrs. Smith. "I had serious objections to having her here."

"I never saw such downright impudence," pursued Mrs. Montague. "This I suppose is one of the consequences of the liberty, and freedom and independence that you Americans are always talking about. I must tell Mr. Montague, for really this is too good to lose."

And beckoning her husband to come to her—"My dear," said she, "put down in your memorandum-book, that when American married ladies invite young ladies to parties, they on second thoughts forbid them to come, and that the said American young ladies boldly persist in coming in spite of the forbiddance."

And she then related to him the whole affair, at full length, and with numerous embellishments, looking all the time at poor Albina.

The story was soon circulated round the room in whispers and murmurs, and no one had candour or kindness to suggest the possibility of Miss Marsden's having never received the note.

Albina soon perceived herself to be an object of remark and animadversion, and she was sadly at a loss to divine the cause. The two ladies that were nearest to her, rose up and left their seats, while two others edged their chairs farther off. She knew no one, she was introduced to no one, but she saw that every one was looking at her as she sat by herself, alone, conspicuous, and abashed. Tea was waiting for a lady that came always last, and the whole company seemed to have leisure to gaze on poor Albina, and to whisper about her.

Her situation now became intolerable. She felt that there was nothing left for her but to go home. Unluckily she had ordered the carriage at eleven o'clock. At last she resolved on making a great effort, and on plea of a violent head-ache (a plea which by this time was literally true) to ask Mrs. Potts if she would allow a servant to bring a coach for her.

After several attempts, she rose for this purpose; but she saw at the same moment that all eyes were turned upon her. She tremblingly and with downcast looks advanced till she got into the middle of the room, and then all her courage deserted her at once, when she heard some one say, "I wonder what she is going to do next."

She stopped suddenly, and stood motionless, and she saw Miss Potts giggle, and heard her say to a schoolgirl near her—"I suppose she is going to speak a speech." She turned very pale, and felt as if she could gladly sink into the floor, when suddenly some one took her hand, and the voice of Bromley Cheston said to her—"Albina—Miss Marsden—I will conduct you wherever you wish to go"—and then, lowering his tone, he asked her—"Why this agitation—what has happened to distress you?"

Cheston had just arrived from New York, having been detained on the way by an accident that happened to one of the boats, and finding that Mrs. Marsden was in town, and had that day sent several messages for him, he repaired immediately to her lodgings. He had intended declining the invitation of Mrs. Potts, but when he found that Albina had gone thither, he hastily changed his dress and went to the party. When he entered, what was his amazement to see her standing alone in the centre of the room, and the company whispering and gazing at her.

Albina on hearing the voice of a friend, the voice of Bromley Cheston, was completely overcome, and she covered her face and burst into tears. "Albina," said Cheston, "I will not now ask an explanation; I see that, whatever may have happened, you had best go home."

"Oh! most gladly, most thankfully," she exclaimed in a voice almost inarticulate with sobs.

Cheston drew her arm within his and bowing to Mrs. Potts, he led Albina out of the apartment, and conducted her to the staircase, whence she went to the ladies' room to compose herself a little, and prepare for her departure.

Cheston then sent one servant for a carriage, and another to tell Mr. Potts that he desired to speak with him in the hall. Potts came out with a pale frightened face, and said—"Indeed, sir—indeed, I had nothing to do with it; ask the women. It was all them entirely. It was the women that laughed at Miss Albina and whispered about her."

"For what?" demanded the lieutenant. "I insist on knowing for what cause."

"Why sir," replied Potts, "she came here to my wife's party, after Mrs. Potts had sent her a note desiring her to stay away; which was certainly an odd thing for a young lady to do."

"There is some mistake," exclaimed Cheston, "I'll stake my life that she never saw the note. And now for what reason did Mrs. Potts write such a note? How did she dare—"

"Oh!" replied Potts stammering and hesitating, "women will have their notions; men are not half so particular about their company. Somehow, after Mrs. Potts had invited Miss Albina, she thought on farther consideration that poor Miss Albina was not quite genteel enough for her party. You know all the women now make a great point of being genteel. But indeed, sir, (observing the storm that was gathering on Cheston's brow) indeed, sir—*I* was not in the least to blame. It was altogether the fault of my wife."

The indignation of the lieutenant was so highly excited, that nothing could have checked it but the recollection that Potts was in his own house. At this moment Albina came down stairs, and Cheston took her hand and said to her, "Albina, did you receive a note from Mrs. Potts interdicting your presence at the party."—"Oh! no, indeed!" exclaimed Albina, amazed at the question. "Surely she did not send me such a note."—"Yes, she did though," said Potts quickly.—"Is it then necessary for me to say," said Albina indignantly, "that under those circumstances nothing could have induced me to enter this house, now or ever. I saw or heard nothing of this note. And is this the reason that I have been treated so rudely—so cruelly—"

Upon this Mr. Potts made his escape, and Cheston having put Albina into the carriage, desired the coachman to wait a few moments. He then returned to the drawing-room, and approached Mrs. Potts who was standing with half the company collected round her, and explaining with great volubility the whole history of Albina Marsden. On the appearance of Cheston she stopped short, and all her auditors looked foolish.

The young officer advanced into the centre of the circle, and first addressing Mrs. Potts, he said to her—"In justice to Miss Marsden, I have returned madam, to inform you that your note of interdiction, with which you have so kindly made all the company acquainted, was till this moment unknown to that young lady. But even had she come wilfully, and in the full knowledge of your prohibition, no circumstances whatever could justify the rudeness with which I find she has been treated. I have now only to say that if any gentleman presumes either here or hereafter to cast a reflection on the conduct of Miss Albina Marsden, in this or in any other instance, he must answer to me for the consequences. And if I find that any lady has invidiously misrepresented this occurrence, I shall insist on an atonement from her husband, her brother or her admirer."

He then bowed and departed, and the company looked still more foolish.

"This lesson," thought Cheston, "will have the salutary effect of curing Albina of her predominant follies. She is a lovely girl after all, and when withdrawn from the influence of her mother will make a charming woman and an excellent wife."

Before the carriage stopped at the residence of Mrs. Marsden, Cheston had made Albina an offer of his heart and hand, and the offer was not refused.

Mrs. Marsden was scarcely surprised at the earliness of Albina's return from the party, for she had a secret misgiving that all was not right, that the suppression of the note would not eventuate well, and she bitterly regretted having done it. When her daughter related to her the story of the evening, Mrs. Marsden was overwhelmed with compunction, and though Cheston was present, she could not refrain from acknowledging at once her culpability, for it certainly deserved no softer name. Cheston and Albina were shocked at this disclosure, but in compassion to Mrs. Marsden they forbore to add to her distress by a single comment. Cheston shortly after took his leave, saying to Albina as he departed, "I hope you are done for ever with Mrs. Washington Potts."

Next morning Cheston seriously but kindly expostulated with Albina and her mother on the folly and absurdity of sacrificing their comfort, their time, their money, and indeed their self-respect to the paltry distinction of being capriciously noticed by a few vain, silly, heartless people, inferior to themselves in everything but in wealth and in a slight tincture of soi-disant fashion; and who, after all, only took them on or threw them off as it suited their own convenience.

"What you say is very true, Bromley," replied Mrs. Marsden. "I begin to view these things in their proper light, and as Albina remarks, we ought to profit by this last lesson. To tell the exact truth, I have heard since I came to town that Mrs. Washington Potts is, after all, by no means in the first circle, and it is whispered that she and her husband are both of very low origin."

"No matter for her circle or her origin," said Cheston, "in our country the only acknowledged distinction should be that which is denoted by superiority of mind and manners."

Next day Lieutenant Cheston escorted Mrs. Marsden and Albina back to their own home—and a week afterwards he was sent unexpectedly on a cruise in the West Indies.

He returned in the spring, and found Mrs. Marsden more rational than he had ever known her, and Albina highly improved by a judicious course of reading which he had marked out for her, and still more by her intimacy with a truly genteel, highly talented, and very amiable family from the eastward, who had recently bought a house in the village, and in whose society she often wondered at the infatuation which had led her to fancy such a woman as Mrs. Washington Potts, with whom, of course, she never had any further communication.

A recent and very large bequest to Bromley Cheston from a distant relation, made it no longer necessary that the young lieutenant should wait for promotion before he married Albina; and accordingly their union took place immediately on his return.

Before the Montagues left Philadelphia to prosecute their journey to the south, there arrived an acquaintance of theirs from England, who injudiciously "told the secrets of his prison-house," and made known in whispers "not loud but deep," that Mr. Dudley Montague, of Normancourt Park, Hants, (alias Mr. John Wilkins of Lamb's Conduit Street,

Clerkenwell,) had long been well-known in London as a reporter for a newspaper; that he had recently married a widow, the ei-devant governess of a Somers Town Boarding school, who had drawn her ideas of fashionable life from the columns of the Morning Post, and who famished her pupils so much to her own profit that she had been able to retire on a sort of fortune. With the assistance of this fund, she and her daughter (the young lady was in reality the offspring of her mother's first marriage) had accompanied Mr. Wilkins across the Atlantic: all three assuming the lordly name of Montague, as one well calculated to strike the republicans with proper awe. The truth was, that for a suitable consideration proffered by a tory publisher, the soi-disant Mr. Montague had undertaken to add another octavo to the numerous volumes of gross misrepresentation and real ignorance that profess to contain an impartial account of the United States of America.

LYDIA SIGOURNEY
(1791–1865)

The Father

Sketches (Philadelphia: Key and Biddle), 1834.

Born in Norwich, Connecticut on September 1, 1791, the only child of Zerviah Wentworth and Ezekiel Huntley, Lydia Howard Huntley Sigourney received as her "first gift" from her parents the name of her father's first wife who died of tuberculosis before she had been married a year. Ezekiel Huntley was the hired man and gardener for Mrs. Daniel Lathrop, a well-to-do Norwich widow, who rented him half of her house as his residence. Left childless before she was thirty and in her seventies when Lydia was born, Mrs. Lathrop turned, according to Sigourney's own account, "the yearning tenderness of a heart which had continued to flow out toward the children of others . . . on the little one born in her house" (*Letters of Life*, p. 43). She frequently invited Lydia into her parlor and asked her to read aloud from such works as Young's "Night Thoughts." In addition to its educational benefits, which included access to a "dark mahogany bookcase" and an introduction to poetry, Mrs. Lathrop's friendship proved central to Sigourney's career; through her she met the Wadsworths, Mrs. Lathrop's wealthy Hartford relatives, who later became Sigourney's patrons. When, on Mrs. Lathrop's death in 1805, Sigourney was sent to Hartford to relieve her grief, the Wadsworths received her as her "mother" had hoped: "I remembered, too, that she had said, in her feebleness, 'I wish I might have taken you to Hartford. Then you would have been received as my child.' My heart said to her, 'See, I have been so received' " (*Letters of Life*, p. 84).

   In her biography, Sigourney claims that her "earliest promptings of ambition were, not to possess the trappings of wealth or the indulgences of luxury, but to keep a school" (*Letters of Life*, p. 186). Back in Nor-

105

wich, she made an unsuccessful attempt to start a school for girls in her own home. Then, in 1811, at the age of twenty, after spending some months in the best female seminaries of Hartford where "we devoted ourselves to the accomplishments of drawing, painting in water-colors, embroidery of various kinds, filigree, and other things too tedious to mention," she opened with a friend, Nancy Maria Hyde, a school for young ladies in Norwich (*Letters of Life,* p. 190). Three years later, Daniel Wadsworth invited her to head a school whose pupils were gathered from among the daughters of the first families of Hartford. It opened in 1814, nearly a decade before Catharine Beecher established her Hartford Female Seminary, and, to Sigourney's delight, her patron did not require her to pay any attention to the "ornamental branches" of female education.

According to Gordon Haight, Sigourney's biographer, "if Lydia had continued teaching it seems likely that her name would rank nearly as high as Emma Willard's in the history of education for women" (Haight, p. 10). She did not, however, continue to teach but instead gave up this career in 1819 to marry Charles Sigourney, a widower with three small children. Charles Sigourney, then a prosperous Hartford merchant and later a bank president, college trustee, and church warden, certainly fit the description of a "good" match and, when the gardener's daughter found herself established as mistress of a fine new house built by her husband from his own plans, she might well have felt that she was indeed Mrs. Lathrop's child.

When Sigourney married, she had already begun her career as a writer. With the encouragement, business advice, and editorial assistance of Daniel Wadsworth, she had published in 1815 *Moral Pieces in Prose and Verse.* Although she had no intention of ceasing to write after marriage, her husband evidently intended otherwise. There then followed more than a decade of negotiation around the issue of writing, during which Sigourney discontinued at least one work and published several others anonymously. She did, however, continue to sign some of the poetry that she sent to magazines and newspapers and she was under continuing pressure from various editors to publish a collection of these pieces acknowledging her authorship, since such a project would be economically advantageous to both parties. By the late 1820s money had, in fact, become an issue for Charles Sigourney's prosperity, somewhat exaggerated at the time of his marriage, had declined even further; their establishment was expensive and, in addition, Sigourney provided the sole support for her elderly parents. Sigourney faced a major dilemma in her desire to be at once a dutiful wife and a famous poet. The full extent of this dilemma can only be measured when we realize that, to be a famous poet in early nineteenth-century America, a woman had to appear before the public as a dutiful wife. Edgar Allan Poe, for example, remarked that "a woman will never be brought to admit a non-identity between herself and her book"; and Ann Stephens, a contemporary of Sigourney and herself a victim of this identification, makes the point even more emphatically in her pamphlet biography of Sigourney: "I write more of the woman than the authoress, because had the woman been less perfect, the author had never been reverenced as she is reverenced" (Haight, p. 99).

In 1833, Sigourney published *Letters to Young Ladies, by A Lady* at her own expense and with the copyright taken out in the name of Huntley. Naturally, her authorial identity was quickly "discovered" and from then on she abandoned anonymity and openly pursued a career in literature. Characterized by a sharp business sense, she became extraordinarily successful in terms of money, fame, and critical opinion. From 1840 to 1842, for example, Louis Godey paid her $500 a year simply to use her name on the title page of the *Lady's Book*, and Poe solicited her contributions for the *Southern Literary Messenger* and later for *Graham's Magazine*. For the American public of her day, according to Haight, Sigourney figured as a kind of female Ben Franklin, the poor girl who had made good: "Everyone knew of 'her romantic marriage with the wealthy and scholarly merchant, Mr. Sigourney'; pictures of their 'magnificent' house were often published with accounts of her career; her reception by 'the crowned heads of Europe' was evolved by a popular imagination, which delighted to represent Monarchy prostrate at the feet of Republican Genius" (Haight, p. 99).

Sigourney bore five children, three of whom died at birth. Of the two who lived past infancy, only her daughter Mary survived her. Her son, Andrew, died of tuberculosis in 1850, and his death and dying were memorialized in *The Faded Hope* (1853). Charles Sigourney died of apoplexy in 1854. No volume was written to memorialize his life or death. Indeed, it would seem significant for a writer best known for her responsiveness to the phenomena of death and bereavement, and often willing to write memorial and consolatory verses for strangers, that not one line exists to note the death of her husband. Sigourney herself died on June 10, 1865, in Hartford, at the age of seventy-three, and was buried there.

Sigourney is treated, when mentioned at all, in American literary histories or even in contemporary criticism, with almost universal contempt, but she was, like Sedgwick, a major event in the history of women and literature in nineteenth-century America. Preceding Henry Wadsworth Longfellow by a decade in the symbolic role of American poet laureate, she made poetry an acceptable and profitable profession for women. Indeed, her very success seems held against her. Certainly held against her is the identification she established between the poet, poetry, and the feminine. An intensely public figure, Sigourney made the career of poet to some degree an extension of the service role conventionally assigned to women. In *Letters of Life,* she lists over ten pages of *samples* of the requests she received from various individuals for original poems to commemorate some event in their lives. Unable to refuse such requests, she developed an annual correspondence of over two-thousand letters. Sigourney herself was well aware of the price she paid for this vision of the role of the poet: "If there is any kitchen in Parnassus, my Muse has surely officiated there as a woman of all work, and an aproned waiter" (*Letters of Life,* p. 376). Yet both the extent of the need readers expressed for her work and the volume of her response might suggest to us the potential significance of what Susan Glaspell in "A Jury of Her Peers" refers to as "kitchen things."

Although Sigourney was not primarily a writer of fiction, "The Father" exhibits an imaginative power rarely found in her poetry. Indeed, this story possesses that weird and haunting quality, even the image and the act (the violated tomb, the desperate struggle to recover some lost essential self), that one associates with the work of her major male contemporary, Poe.

Given the context set by Poe's observation that a woman will never admit "a non-identity between herself and her book," Sigourney's decision to use a male narrator might well have been liberating. Released somewhat from the autobiographical presumption and freed to some degree from the conventions governing the expression of a "feminine" sensibility, Sigourney may have thus gained access to the most forceful part of her imagination. Certainly the mechanism of a male narrator enables her to express in relative safety a considerable degree of hostility to male culture, for she can present her judgment as masculine self-criticism.

In "The Father," the masculine principle emerges as sterile, dependent, and ultimately impotent. Despite the apparent supremacy of masculine values, in the final context set by death, the feminine triumphs. Thus "The Father" is a kind of *tour de force* in that re-ordering of values which forms so large a part of the agenda of nineteenth-century women writers. The language of the opening paragraph prepares for the subsequent inversion. "I was in the full-tide of a laborious and absorbing profession," "unsparing discipline," "wealth and fame," "pursued," "determined," "distinction," "ambition's promptings," "career"—here is the world of men, its possibilities, its riches carefully catalogued. But immediately a warning note sounds; there is danger in this world, a peculiar kind of danger, the threat of becoming "indurated" (an example of Sigourney's often fatal attraction for Latin words). The overtones of this word, which means "to harden," are suggestively sexual. Indeed, as Ann Douglas points out, the father's behavior "is almost symbolic of an erection prolonged to the point of nightmare" (Douglas, p. 171). The only chance for release lies in the realm of "the domestic charities" wherein springs up a "fountain of living water . . . to allay thirst, and to renovate weariness." The superiority of the feminine, apparent by the second paragraph, is further conveyed, and explained, by the word "charities." Sufficient unto itself, the female world opens its doors to thirsting men as an act of kindness, a *noblesse oblige* by means of which the home becomes a sort of universal "female beneficient society" for the relief of "indurated" males.

Interestingly enough, the initial object of the narrator's fixation—his wife—plays no part in the story. Rather it is the daughter, who "resembled her mother," who experiences the full weight of masculine dependency. The narrator reveals his self-delusion, confirmed by the story's ending when he discovers that his friends and not himself have acted to protect his daughter, in his pronouncements on the father/

daughter relationship. Despite his claiming for this relationship a disin-
terest that distinguishes it from the father/son bond, the narrator
describes a connection in which he is thoroughly "interested."
Nameless, like her mother, the daughter exists to serve the narrator's
needs. Determined to mold her and make her after his will, he seems to
have accomplished his imperialist design when he can say, "It was *for
my sake*, that she strove to render herself the most graceful among
women,—*for my sake*, that she rejoiced in the effect of her attainments."
Service takes on sexual overtones in the incident that follows this testament to his success. Trained to believe that the "husbandman who had
labored, should be first partaker of the fruits," this daughter offers her
fruits at home: "A form of beauty was on the sofa, by my side, but I
regarded it not. Then my hand was softly clasped, breathed upon,—
pressed to ruby lips. It was enough. I took my daughter in my arms,
and my sorrow vanished." "Protection" is the claim of a daughter on a
father, but safety from this father's demands is not to be had, even in the
tomb.

Sigourney sacrifices the daughter in order to confront the father with
the limitations of his Pygmalion mythology and godlike self-concept,
for though "a father's love can conquer . . . it cannot create." In his
daughter's death, the father faces his own dependency, sterility, and
hunger. Significantly, the bereaved father cannot cry. Cut off from the
living fountain, he is himself incapable of generating a single drop of
water for his own relief. As frozen as the winter landscape through
whose "dreary and interminable" nights he haunts his daughter's tomb
and whose "blasts . . . through the leafless boughs" mockingly echo his
despair, he finally articulates the utter dead end to which his "full-tide"
has carried him: *"Give it to me,—Give it to me."* No succor lies in that
male world to which he returns with a vengeance after his daughter's
death, for he finds it "less than nothing, and vanity," composed of "jarring competitions and perpetual strifes," "duplicity," "subterfuges,"
"self-conceit," "chicanery," "empty honors," and "perishable dross"—a
litany that parallels, exposes, and reverses the initial catalogue of treasures.

The narrator finds relief only when he can cry, that is, when he can
himself become a "woman." He becomes "feminized," in turn, only
when he perceives the "feminization" of his friends. In their "tenderness," they have acted as mothers not fathers; they have sought to
protect, not to violate, the daughter, and to protect her and him from
the father in him. Thus the narrator's moment of revelation and awakening involves a transformation of identity. Returned to the state of a
child, "as powerless as the weaned infant," he is no longer the shaper
but the shaped. In the experience of subjection, he yields his imperialist
imagination and pays homage to the power of the feminine whose "tenderness" accomplishes, through its "still, small voice," what "the severity of Heaven had failed to produce."

In "The Father," Sigourney has written a powerful fable on the primacy of the feminine principle and the inadequacy of the masculine
principle. The story's power derives from the fact that it is written, not

from the relatively static point of view of the self-sustaining and self-contained female world, but rather from the point of view of the famished male outsider who frantically seeks entrance to that "tomb."

Yet, as the word "tomb" suggests, there is irony as well as energy in this choice. In a story that asserts the primacy of the feminine principle and enacts the "feminization" of men, the nameless mother and the nameless daughter never speak. Although Poe, in such stories as "The Fall of the House of Usher" and "Ligeia," could endow his women with will sufficient to burst living from the tomb to astonish, terrify, and destroy the men who have shut them living in it, Sigourney's women are thoroughly and permanently stilled. One is literally, the other symbolically, dead. Thus the assertion of female power occurs in a context that seems to deny its reality. It is difficult to determine to what degree Sigourney is conscious of this irony or what she intends by it. On the one hand, one can argue that, in choosing a male narrator, she becomes complicit in a culture that defines the "most exquisite of woman's perfections" as "a knowledge both *when* to be silent, and *where* to speak," for her narrator's voice effectively silences both wife and daughter. In this reading her strategy of reordering cultural values through asserting the primacy of feminine power appears spurious at best, for only men can experience this power; actual women have none of it. On the other hand, one can argue that her decision to create a male narrator engaged in a solipsistic monologue represents a highly subversive appropriation of "that most exquisite of women's perfections," for, understanding indeed both when to be silent and where to speak, she lets the father's speech expose the arrogant egotism behind his masculine assumptions. Reversing the sexual imperialism of traditional American fiction in which male writers inhabit and speak through female characters, Sigourney implants herself in her male character and forces him to speak for her. In this reading, the form of the story itself validates the assertion of female power. Yet, however one reads "The Father," one thing is certain; it provides a significant context for considering the connection between women, language, and power in early nineteenth-century American fiction.

Source:

The Young Ladies' Offering; or Gems of Prose and Poetry (Boston: Phillips, Sampson), 1849.

Selected Primary Works:

Moral Pieces, in Prose and Verse, 1815; *Traits of the Aborigines of America*, 1822; *Poems*, 1827; *Letters to Young Ladies*, 1833; *Sketches*, 1834; *Pocahontas, and Other Poems*, 1841; *Illustrated Poems*, 1849; *Letters to My Pupils: with Narrative and Biographical Sketches*, 1851; *The Faded Hope*, 1853; *Past Meridian*, 1854; *Letters of Life*, 1866.

Selected Secondary Works:

Ann Douglas (Wood), "Mrs. Sigourney and the Sensibility of the Inner Space," *New England Quarterly*, 45 (1972), 163–81; David Bonnell Green, "William Wordsworth and Lydia Huntley Sigourney," *New England Quarterly*, 37

(1964), 527–31; Gordon S. Haight, *Mrs. Sigourney: The Sweet Singer of Hartford* (New Haven: Yale University Press), 1930.

Contexts:

1833—Child, *An Appeal in Favor of that Class of Americans Called Africans;* Western Monthly Magazine
1834—*Southern Literary Messenger;* Bancroft, *History of the United States,* Vol. I

> "Yes,—I am he,—who look'd and saw decay
> Steal o'er the lov'd of earth,—the ador'd too much.
> It is a fearful thing, to love what Death may touch."
> Mrs. Hemans.

I WAS IN the full tide of a laborious and absorbing profession,—of one which imposes on intellect an unsparing discipline, but ultimately opens the avenues to wealth and fame. I pursued it, as one determined on distinction,—as one convinced that *mind* may assume a degree of omnipotence over matter and circumstance, and popular opinion. Ambition's promptings were strong within me, nor was its career unprosperous.—I had no reason to complain that its promises were deceptive, or its harvest tardy.

Yet as my path was among the competitions and asperities of men, a character combining strong elements might have been in danger of becoming indurated, had it not been softened and refined by the domestic charities. Conjugal love, early fixing on an object most amiable and beautiful, was as a fountain of living water, springing up to allay thirst, and to renovate weariness. I was anxious that my home should be the centre of intellectual and polished society, where the buddings of thought should expand unchilled, and those social feelings which are the life-blood of existence, flow forth, unfettered by heartless ceremony.—And it was so.

But my present purpose is to delineate a single, and simple principle of our nature,—the most deep-rooted and holy,—*the love of a father for a daughter.* My province has led me to analyze mankind; and in doing this, I have sometimes thrown their affections into the crucible. And the one of which I speak, has come forth most pure, most free from drossy admixture. Even the earth that combines with it, is not like other earth. It is what the foot of a seraph might rest upon, and contract no pollution. With the love of our sons, ambition mixes its spirit, till it becomes a fiery essence. We anticipate great things for them,—we covet honors,—we goad them on in the race of glory;—if they are victors, we too proudly exult,—if vanquished, we are prostrate and in bitterness. Perhaps we detect in them the same latent perverseness, with which we have waged warfare in our own breasts, or some imbecility of purpose with which we have no affinity; and then, from the very nature of our love, an impatience is generated, which they have no power to soothe, or we to control. A father loves his son, as he loves himself,—and in all selfishness, there is a bias to disorder and pain. But his love for his daughter is different and more disinterested; possibly he believes that it is called forth by a being of a higher and better order. It is based on the integral and immutable principles of his nature. It recognizes the sex in hearts, and from the very gentleness and mystery of womanhood, takes that coloring and zest which romance gathers from remote antiquity. It draws nutriment from circumstances which he may not fully comprehend, from the power which she possesses to awaken his sympathies, to soften his irritability, to sublimate his aspirations;—while the support and protection which she claims in return, elevate him with a consciousness of assimilation to the ministry of those benevolent and powerful spirits, who ever "bear us up in their hands, lest we dash our foot against a stone."

I should delight longer to dwell on this development of affection, for who can have known it more perfectly in its length and breadth, in its depth and height? I had a daughter, beautiful in infancy, to whom every year added some new charm to awaken admiration, or to rivet love. To me, it was of no slight import, that she resembled her mother, and that in grace and accomplishment, she early surpassed her contemporaries. I was desirous that her mind should be worthy of the splendid temple allotted for its habitation. I decided to render it familiar with the whole circle of the arts and sciences. I was not satisfied with the commendation of her teachers. I determined to take my seat in the sacred pavilion of intellect, and superintend what entered there. But how should one buried beneath the ponderous tomes and Sysiphean toils of jurisprudence, gain freedom, or undivided thought, for such minute supervision? A father's love can conquer, if it cannot create. I deprived myself of sleep: I sat till the day dawned, gathering materials for the lectures that I gave her. I explored the annals of architecture and sculpture, the recesses of literature and poetry, the labyrinthine and colossal treasure-houses of history,—I entered the ancient catacombs of the illustrious dead, traversed the regions of the dim and shadowy past, with no coward step,—ransacked earth and heaven, to add one gem to her casket. At stated periods, I required her to condense, to illustrate, to combine, what I had brought her. I listened, with wonder, to her intuitive eloquence: I gazed with intense delight upon the intellect that I thus embellished,—upon the Corinthian capital that I had erected and adorned. Not a single acanthus-leaf started forth, but I cherished and fostered it with the dews of a father's blessing.

Yet while the outpoured riches of a masculine understanding were thus incorporating themselves with her softer structure, I should not have been content, unless she had also borne the palm of female grace and loveliness. Was it therefore nothing to me, that she evinced in her bloom of youth, a dignity surpassing her sex, that in symmetry she restored the image of the Medicean Venus, that amid the circles of rank and fashion, she was the model—the cynosure? Still was she saved from that vanity which would have been the destroyer of all those charms, by the hallowed prevalence of her filial piety. It was *for my sake*, that she strove to render herself the most graceful among women,—*for my sake*, that she rejoiced in the effect of her attainments. Her gentle and just nature felt that the "husbandman who had labored, should be first partaker of the fruits." Returning from those scenes of splendor, where she was the object of every eye, the theme of every tongue, when the youthful bosom might be forgiven for inflation from the clouds of incense that had breathed upon it, to the inquiry of her mother, if she had been happy, the tender and sweet reply was, "Yes,—because I saw that my dear father was so."

Sometimes, I was conscious of gathering roughness from the continual conflict with passion and prejudice, and that the fine edge of the feelings could not ever be utterly proof against the corrosions of such an atmosphere. Then I sought my home, and called my bird of song, and listened to the warbling of her high, heaven-toned voice. The melody of that music fell upon my soul, like oil upon the troubled billows,—and all was tranquil. I wondered where my perturbations had fled, but still more, that I had ever indulged them. Sometimes, the turmoil and fluctuation of the world, threw a shade of dejection over me: then it was her pride to smooth my brow, and to restore its smile. Once, a sorrow of no common order had fallen upon me; it rankled in my breast, like a dagger's point; I came to my house, but I shunned all its inmates. I threw myself down, in solitude, that I might wrestle alone with my fate, and subdue it; a light footstep approached, but I heeded it not. A form of beauty was on the sofa, by my side, but I regarded it not. Then my hand was softly clasped, breathed upon,—pressed to ruby lips. It was enough. I took my daughter in my arms, and my sorrow vanished. Had she essayed the hackneyed expressions of sympathy, or even the usual epithets of endearment, I might have desired her to leave my presence. Had she uttered only a single word, it would have been too much, so wounded was my spirit within me. But the deed, the very poetry of tenderness, breathing, not speaking, melted "the winter of my discontent." Ever was she endued with that most exquisite of woman's perfections, a knowledge both *when* to be silent, and *where* to speak,—and *so* to speak, that the frosts might dissolve from around the heart she loved, and its discords be tuned to harmony.

Thus was she my comforter, and in every hour of our intercourse, was my devotion to her happiness richly repaid. Was it strange that I should gaze on the work of my own hands with ineffable delight? At twilight I quickened my homeward step, with the thought of that countenance, which was both my evening and morning star; as the bird nerves her wearied wing, when she hears from the still-distant forest, the chirpings of her own nest.

I sat in the house of God, in the silence of sabbath meditation, and tears of thrilling exultation moistened my eyes. I gazed upon my glorious creature, in the stainless blossom of unfolding youth, and my whole soul overflowed with a father's pride. I said, *What more can man desire?* I challenged the whole earth to add another drop to my cup of felicity. Did I forget to give glory to the Almighty, that his decree even then went forth, to smite down my idol?

I came from engrossing toil, and found her restless, with strange fire upon her cheek. Fever had lain rankling in her veins, and they had concealed it from me. I raved. I filled my house with physicians. I charged them wildly to restore her to health and to me. It was in vain. I saw that God claimed her. His will was written upon her brow. The paleness and damps of the tomb settled upon her.

I knelt by the bed of death, and gave her back to her Creator. Amid the tears and groans of mourners, I lifted up a firm voice. A fearful courage entered into me. I seemed to rush even upon the buckler of the Eternal. I likened myself unto him who, on Mount Moria, "stretched forth his hand, and took the knife to slay his son." The whole energy of my nature armed itself for the awful conflict. I gloried in my strength to suffer. With terrible sublimity, I stood forth, as the High Priest of my smitten and astonished household. I gave the lamb in sacrifice, with an unshrinking hand, though it was my own heart's blood, that steeped, and streamed over the altar.

It was over. She had gone. She stayed not for my embraces. She was permitted to give me no parting-token. The mind that I had adored, shrouded itself and fled. I knew that the seal upon those eyes must not be broken, till the trump of the Archangel.

Three days and nights, I sat by the dead. Beauty lingered there, in deep, and solemn, and sacred repose. I laid my head upon her pillow. I pressed my lips to hers, and their ice entered into my soul. I spoke to her of the angels, her companions. I talked long to the beautiful spirit, and methought, it answered me. Then I listened breathlessly, but "there was no voice, nor any that regarded." And still, I wept not.

The fatal day came, in which even that clay was to be no longer mine. The funeral knell, with its heavy, yet suppressed summons, came over me like the dividing of soul and body. There was a flood of weeping, when that form, once so replete with every youthful charm, so instinct with the joyous movement of the mysterious principle of life, was borne in marble stillness from its paternal halls. The eye of the mother that bore her, of the friend that had but casually beheld her, even of the poor menial that waited upon her, knew the luxury of tears. All were wet with that balm of sorrow, to overflowing—*all save mine.*

The open grave had a revolting aspect. I could not bear that the form which I had worshipped, should be left to its cold and hideous guardianship. At the hollow sound of the first falling clod, I would fain have leaped into the pit, and demanded her. But I ruled myself. I committed her to the frozen earth, without a tear. There was a tremendous majesty in such grief. I was a wonder to myself.

I returned to my desolated abode. The silence that reigned there was appalling. My spirit sank beneath it, as a stone goes down into the depths of ocean, bearing the everlasting burden of its fathomless tide. I sought the room where I had last seen her, arrayed in the vestments of the tomb. There lay the books which we had read together. Their pages bore the marks of her pencil. I covered my eyes from them, and turned away. I bowed down to inhale the fragrance of her flowers, and felt that they had no right to bloom so fair, when she, their culturer and their queen, was blighted. I pressed my fingers upon the keys of her piano, and started back at the mournful sound they made. I wandered to her own apartment. I threw myself on the couch where from infancy she had slumbered. I trusted to have wept there. But my grief was too mighty, to be thus unchained. It disdained the relief of tears. I seemed to rush as upon a drawn sword, and still it refused to pierce me.

Yet all this was when no eye saw me. In the presence of others, I was like Mount Atlas, bearing unmoved the stormy heavens upon his shoulders.

I went forth, amid the jarring competitions and perpetual strifes of men. I adjusted their opposing interests, while I despised them and their concerns. I unravelled their perplexities. I penetrated their subterfuges. I exposed their duplicity. I cut the Gordian knots of their self-conceit. I made the "crooked straight, and the rough places plain,"—with an energy that amazed them and myself. It was like that of a spirit, which has nothing to do with the flesh. I suffered the tumult of my soul to breathe itself out in bursts of stormy declamation. I exerted the strength of a giant, when it was not required. I scorned to balance power with necessity. The calculations of prudence, and the devices of cunning, seemed equally pitiful, and despicable. I put forth the same effort to crush an emmet, as to uproot the oak of a thousand centuries. It was sufficient for me always to triumph. While men marvelled at the zeal with which I served them, I was loathing them in my heart. I was sick of their chicanery, and their sabbathless rush after empty honors and perishable dross. The whole world seemed to me, "less than nothing, and vanity." Still, I was sensible of neither toil, nor fatigue, nor physical exhaustion. I was like one, who in his troubled dream of midnight, treads on air, and finds it strangely sustaining him.

But every night, I went to my daughter's grave. I laid me down there, in unutterable bitterness. While the stars looked coldly on me, I spoke to her fondly and earnestly, as one who could not be denied. I said,— "Angel! who art mine no longer, listen to me. Thou, who art raised above all tears, cause *one tear* to moisten my burning brow. Give it to me, as a token that thou hearest me, that thou hast not forgotten me." And the blasts of Winter, through the leafless boughs, mocking replied,—*"Give it to me,—Give it to me."* But I wept not. Ten days and nights passed over me,—and still I wept not.

My brain was heated to agony. The visual nerves were scorched and withered. My heart was parched and arid, as the Libyan desert. Then I knew that the throne of Grief was in *the heart:* that though her sceptre may reach the remotest nerve, and touch the minutest cell where the brain slumbers, and perplex every ethereal ambassador from spirit to sense,— yet the pavilion where her darkest dregs are wrung out, the laboratory where her consuming fires are compounded, is *the heart,—the heart.*

I have implied that my intellect faltered. Yet every morning I went to the scene of my labors. I put my shoulder to the wheel, caring not though it crushed me. I looked at men fixedly and haughtily with my red eye-balls. But I spoke no word to betray the flame feeding at my vitals. The heartstrings shrivelled and broke before it, yet the martyrdom was in silence.

Again, Night drew her sable curtain, and I sought my daughter's grave. Methought, its turf-covering was discomposed, and some half-rooted shrubs that shuddered and drooped when placed in that drear assemblage of the dead, had been trampled and broken. A horrible suspi-cion took possession of my mind. I rushed to the house of the sexton.— "Has any one troubled my daughter's grave?" Alarmed at my vehemence, he remained speechless and irresolute.

"Tell me," I exclaimed, in a voice of terror, "who has disturbed my daughter's grave." He evaded my adjuration, and murmured something about an injunction to secrecy. With the grasp of a maniac, I bore him to an inner apartment, and bade him satisfy my question. Trembling at my violence, he confessed that the grave had been watched for ten nights.

"Who has watched my daughter's grave?" Reluctantly he gave me the names of those friends,—names for ever graven upon my soul.

And so, for those ten long, wintry nights, so dreary and interminable, which I had cast away amid the tossings of profitless, delirious, despair-ing sorrow, they had been watching, that the repose of that unsullied clay might remain unbroken.

A new tide of emotion was awakened. I threw myself down, as pow-erless as the weaned infant. Torrents of tears flowed. The tenderness of man wrought what the severity of Heaven had failed to produce. It was not the earthquake, nor the thunder, nor the tempest, that subdued me. It was the still, small voice. I wept until the fountains of tears failed. The relief of that hour of weeping, can never be shadowed forth in language. The prison-house of passionate agony was unlocked. I said to God that he was merciful, and I loved him because my angel lived in his presence. Since then, it would seem, that my heart has been made better. Its aspira-tions are upward, whither she has ascended, and as I tread the devious path of my pilgrimage, both the sunbeam and the thorn point me as a suppliant to the Redeemer of Man, that I may be at last fitted to dwell with her for ever.

CAROLINE KIRKLAND

(1801–1864)

A New Home—Who'll Follow?

(New York: C. S. Francis), 1839.

Caroline Stansbury Kirkland was born in New York City on January 11, 1801, the eldest of eleven children and one of two daughters of Eliza Alexander and Samuel Stansbury. With the exception of a five year period between 1804 and 1809, when her family resided in Greenwich, Connecticut, Kirkland spent her childhood and adolescence in New York. Her father was not particularly successful in business (being alternately a clerk, an insurance agent, and a bookseller); the family environment, however, remained steadily middle-class. Her family valued education and literature; Kirkland's mother was herself a writer, and Kirkland revised and published some of her mother's work in the gift books she later edited. An aunt headed a series of schools distinguished for their academic curriculum. Caroline attended her aunt's schools in which she received an education superior to that available to most of her contemporaries. After completing her own education, she assisted her aunt and eventually began to teach, thus initiating a lifelong commitment to the education of women.

At the time Kirkland began teaching, her aunt's school was located in New Hartford, New York, near Clinton, the site of Hamilton College. Here, in 1819, Caroline met William Kirkland, a tutor in classics, whom she married in 1828. As their first joint venture, they opened a girls' school in Geneva, New York, where they both taught. But in 1835 they moved to Detroit, Michigan, for William, tired of teaching, had dreams of buying land and founding a "city" on the Michigan frontier. To that end, he took a job as principal of the Detroit Female Seminary, and Kirkland accepted a teaching position there. Within a year, William had purchased 800 acres of Michigan woodland and swamp 60 miles

117

northwest of Detroit, and, having invested his father's capital in an additional 500 acres, he controlled a territory sufficient to support his experiment in upward mobility. In the fall of 1837, the Kirkland family moved to the village of Pinckney to begin their experience in frontier living. It is this experience that Kirkland chronicles in *A New Home—Who'll Follow?* Not surprisingly, given the difficulties inherent in the effort to establish a settlement and given William's lack of entrepreneurial ability, after five years on the frontier, William emerged poorer than when he had started.

In 1843, at the age of forty-two, Kirkland returned with her family to New York City where she continued to pursue seriously her career as a writer. By this time, in addition to *A New Home,* she had written a full-length sequel to it, *Forest Life* (1842), and had published several regional sketches and essays in various magazines, most notable of which, perhaps, was "The Bee Tree," published in *The Gift* of 1840. In contrast to many of the writers represented in this anthology, Kirkland chose to write carefully and deliberately and to resist the pressure exerted by publishers for more and new work. Writing in 1843 to the editors of *The Gift,* she commented that she found their "present demand somewhat astonishing. It will not be easy to furnish another long story for the same volume, and still preserve the air of variety so necessary for an Annual. . . . I am already engaged to furnish a story for [another] magazine" (Osborne, p. 27). In the opening chapter of *Forest Life,* Kirkland observes, simply, that "people write because they cannot help it." Perhaps Kirkland was able to make, and live by, the decision to write less rather than more and to maintain a consistently high quality in all of her work because she located her literary impulse in the realm of personal preference rather than in that of economic necessity or public service.

In 1846, however, William Kirkland drowned and, at forty-five, Kirkland became the sole support for herself and four children. She responded by becoming a full-time professional, alternating between teaching—during the next few years she ran several girls' schools herself and taught in several others—and literature. In 1847, she became editor of the *Union Magazine of Literature and Art.* As editor, a position she occupied for eighteen months, Kirkland evinced a firm commitment to realism in the materials she accepted for publication; in addition, she demonstrated considerable critical skill, providing, for example, enthusiastic reviews of Melville's early books.

Until the end of her life, Kirkland continued to write essays, reviews, stories, and sketches for magazine publication. Many of these pieces were later collected in the various gift books that she edited, gift books deservedly popular as they provided a higher quality of intellectual and aesthetic fare than many similar offerings. And Kirkland continued to demonstrate a serious interest in the profession of literature as practised by women. In her long review essay of Susan Warner's *The Wide, Wide World* (1851) and *Queechy* (1852), and Anna Warner's *Dollars and Cents* (1852), published in the *North American Review* in 1853, she provides, in addition to the detailed analysis of the strengths and weaknesses of these books, a survey of the state of the art of the novel in America with particular reference to women writers. In "Literary Women," an essay collected in *A Book for the Home Circle* (1853), she satirizes the conventional attitudes toward women writers and exposes their inherent contradictions, concluding that women should only be educated after they reach the age of forty and advocating "a heavier fine on selling to a female under forty, unaccompanied by parent or guardian, a card of Joseph Gillot's pens, than for allowing a paper of poison to go from the shop unlabelled." Kirkland was herself part of the social and professional friendship network of mid-nineteenth-century women writers. Her home frequently functioned as a literary salon, where she entertained such figures as Lydia Maria Child, Catharine Sedgwick, Lydia Sigourney, and Ann Stephens.

Kirkland died in New York on April 6, 1864, at the age of sixty-three, and was buried in Greenwood Cemetery in Brooklyn. After her death, her son, Joseph Kirkland, published three of her articles in his newspaper, *The Prairie Chicken;* one of these, "Essay on Works of Fiction: Written as a Preface to an Unpublished Novel," suggests that Kirkland contemplated writing a full-length work of fiction. We can only regret that she did not, in fact, do so, since to know whether she could have or would have transposed her particular point of view and its attendant stylistic virtues into the genre of women's fiction would tell us a good deal about the limitations and flexibilities of that form.

A New Home—Who'll Follow? was published in 1839 under the pseudonymn of Mary Clavers. Contemporary reviews were uniformly enthusiastic, and later acts of criticism, such as Rufus W. Griswold's inclusion of her in *The Prose Writers of America* (1846) and her appearance in Evert and George Duyckinck's *Cyclopedia of American Literature* (1855), reiterated those initial judgments. Margaret Fuller commented favorably on Kirkland in "American Literature" (*Papers on Literature and Art*, 1846). In "The Literati of New York City" (1846), Edgar Allan Poe wrote: "Unquestionably, she is one of our best writers, has a province of her own, and in that province has few equals. Her most noticeable trait is a certain *freshness* of style, seemingly drawn, as her subjects in general, from the west."

A New Home—Who'll Follow? records the experience of a white relatively well-educated middle-class woman transported to the American frontier by impulses not her own. The fact of "following" is central to Kirkland's stance; she defines her role as that of an observer and takes advantage of the accident of her presence on the Michigan frontier to become a recorder of American social history. The voice she develops for this role is remarkably authoritative and free. Despite her awareness of "women's sphere," Kirkland does not write as one restricted or curtailed.

A commitment to realism provides the essential impetus for Kirkland's work. Consciously defining herself against the romanticism of previous western chroniclers, such as Charles Fenno Hoffman and James Hall, Kirkland asserts at the outset that she will write what is "valuable only for its truth." Thus much of the structure of *A New Home* derives from a contrast, implicit or explicit, between expectations and reality. Yet Kirkland's realism does not exclude an appreciation of the "beautiful"; she waxes poetic over Michigan wild flowers and is even willing to be "a little sentimental" at times. A sense of proportion, balance, and complexity ensure a realism that is not itself a distortion.

Choosing the course of realism presents a challenge: how can one make a "story" out of events valuable only for their truth? what can one say if she has "never seen a cougar—nor been bitten by a rattlesnake"? In meeting this challenge, Kirkland recognizes that she is doing something new in American literature.

At the heart of her enterprise is the education of her readers to the significance of the American frontier. For Kirkland, the frontier is a true text, revealing both the individual and the national character. The obsession of Americans with the issue of class forms a primary theme of the frontier text. In Kirkland's reading, the greatest danger that the new settler faces comes not from the cougar or the rattlesnake, but rather from the envy and hostility of neighbors. If they see one as "putting on airs" and pretending to be better than other folks, then there is sure to be trouble. The pressure toward "levelling downwards" derives its intensity from the fact that upward mobility is the prevailing motive for western emigration. Thus settlers who have come to Michigan to improve their class status wish no reminders of the class system they think they have left behind. If such reminders occur, then they must reckon with the fact that their experiment has failed—an outcome that, as Kirkland realizes in her description of the Titmouses, is far more common than success.

There are, however, other features of the frontier experience that assist in this process of leveling downwards. Unable to readily find in the wilderness anyone who is willing to "chore round," that is, do housework for someone else, Kirkland herself is leveled downward. Furthermore, in this context, she comes to recognize the absurdity and contingency of much of the basis for class structure in America. Unpacking in the backwoods produces a great infusion of common sense on the subject, for what seems in the city to be "absolutely essential" here appears "ridiculously superfluous," "gimcracks" useful only for kindling. The conversion of cupboard into corn crib aptly symbolizes the inevitable readjustment of values attendant on frontier life. After only fourteen days in Montacute, Kirkland's "ideas of comfort" have been reduced to "a well-swept room with a bed in one corner." In addition, the inevitable interdependence of frontier life promotes and supports the leveling process: "What can be more absurd than a feeling of proud distinction, where a stray spark of fire, a sudden illness, or a day's contre-temps, may throw you entirely upon the kindness of your humblest neighbor? If I treat Mrs. Timson with neglect to-day can I with any face borrow her broom tomorrow?" (chapter 17, section not reprinted).

Kirkland's attitudes on the subject of class are complex, and her final position is perhaps more practical than theoretical. Aware that her material possessions and her position as wife of the owner of Montacute

make her inherently suspect, she seeks to accommodate herself to frontier pride, "that most terrific bugbear of the woods," product of the
national obsession with class. Toward her friend, Mrs. Rivers, a genuine
eastern snob, "easily shocked by those sins against Chesterfield, which
one encounters here at every turn," Kirkland assumes the role of mentor, seeking to persuade her that "her true happiness lay in making
friends of her neighbors." (chapter 17, section not reprinted). Kirkland
is admirably suited for this role, for she has learned how to negotiate
her territory through the practically, if not theoretically, sound art of
"wearing round": "It did not require a very long residence in Michigan,
to convince me that it is unwise to attempt to stem directly the current
of society, even in the wilderness, but I have since learned many ways of
wearing round which give me the opportunity of living very much after
my own fashion, without offending, very seriously, any body's preju-
dices" (chapter 14, not reprinted).

Kirkland's Mrs. Clavers learns to negotiate her world far better than
Mr. Clavers learns to negotiate his. Indeed, as a follower, Kirkland oc-
cupies an excellent vantage point from which to view the nature of those
masculine impulses that have brought her to the frontier. While Mrs.
Clavers concern as a woman is how to establish a community with her
neighbors, the desire to make money at the expense of one's neighbors
dominates the male world that Mr. Clavers must manage. Essentially
unambitious and anything but "an enterprising man," Clavers is no
match for the confidence artist "factotum" who offers to build Montacute for him and who clears out after having gotten rich on his money.
Nor are the poor farmers any match for those "enterprising" men who
designed the "General Banking Law," a piece of legislation that resulted
in a series of "Wild Cat" banks. The inevitable failure of these banks left
the officers rich and the farmers in "indescribable" distress, cursing "the
soul-less wretches who had thus drained their best blood for the fur-
therance of their own schemes of low ambition" (chapter 32, not reprinted). If Mrs. Jenkins does not effect the "thorough reformation" of
Simeon, similar schemes will no doubt ensue from his presence in the
"arena of public life." Nothing escapes the scythe of masculine ambition
if it can be made profitable. A forest bridle path remains "for the special
delight of those who can discern glory and splendor in grass and wild-
flowers" because, "as no money was likely to flow in upon us from that
direction," it will never be turned into a road (chapter 37, not reprinted).

Kirkland's detachment from the Michigan "madness" does not blind
her to the degree to which this madness shapes her life. Unable to save
the trees, she is granted only the symbolic power of naming the venture
to be erected on their stumps. But her detachment does enable her to
focus on the lives of women and to recognize that the experience of
those who follow is not necessarily the experience of those who lead. In
Kirkland's eyes, "man and wife" are not a single person and, as she
separates them from each other, she articulates the unique experience of
women on the American frontier. Although Kirkland herself has never
been bitten by a rattlesnake, she soon discovers that frontier women
think nothing of killing them: "'I han't seen but two this spring, and

them was here in the garden, and I killed 'em both.' '*You* killed them!' 'Why, law, yes!—Betsey come in one night after tea and told me on 'em, and we went out, and she held the candle while I killed them. But I tell you we had a real chase after them!' " (chapter 5, not reprinted). In the Michigan backwoods, a woman need not feel ashamed of being able to kill snakes; indeed the "killing of a rattle-snake is peculiarly appropriate to constitute a Michigan heroine" (chapter 16, not reprinted).

This extension of the realm of acceptable female behavior, which is part of the frontier experience for women, has some consequences that Kirkland finds repugnant. The visit of Cleory Jenkins disintegrates abruptly when "the sallow damsel" begins to smoke and spit. Obviously, the fetters of class still bind Kirkland's imagination, constricting not only what she sees but how she sees it. Middle-class women occupy the major share of her attention and their dilemmas form her primary subject. Eloise Fidler is a case in point. Her sentimental excesses, absurd posturings, and unreal relation to life are the product of Eloise's eastern education designed to socialize her into conventional femininity. In Kirkland's eyes, the Michigan frontier has the capacity to undermine such socialization and replace it with values less damaging to women. Eloise is better off in Michigan than in New York, for the West neither encourages nor permits that uselessness that is the hallmark of eastern femininity and that the unredeemed Eloise displays so abundantly. On the frontier, Kirkland herself is neither useless nor imprisoned but, waiting not for "escort," walks out at night to assist sick neighbors, loaded with a sack of flour and prepared to try to milk a cow.

Yet Kirkland sees the negative aspects of frontier life for women as well. Although her "sphere" may be enlarged, woman's world is still primarily the home. Kirkland devotes much of her text to describing the physical and material hardship of housekeeping in the wilderness: "The inexorable dinner hour, which is passed *sub silentio* in imaginary forests, always recurs, in real woods, with distressing iteration, once in twenty-four hours, as I found to my cost" (chapter 13, not reprinted). Far more serious, however, is the emotional trauma that often attended the westward move for women. Assigned the task of home-making and committed to the values associated with the home, women nevertheless frequently experienced homelessness on the frontier. Since the westering impulse originates in the masculine agenda of upward mobility, men have little incentive to make homes; rather they view their land as counters in the status game, and they are prepared to sell out and move on at the first good offer: "The possession of a large number of acres is esteemed a great good, though it makes but little difference in the owner's mode of living. Comforts do not seem to abound in proportion to landed increase, but often on the contrary, are really diminished for the sake of it; and the habit of selling out so frequently makes that *home*-feeling, which is so large an ingredient in happiness elsewhere, almost a nonentity in Michigan" (chapter 6, not reprinted).

It is women, of course, who pay the hidden costs of this game:

> Woman's little world is overclouded for lack of the old familiar means and appliances. The husband goes to his work with the same axe or

hoe which fitted his hand in his old woods and fields, he tills the same
soil, or perhaps a far richer and more hopeful one—he gazes on the
same book of nature which he has read from his infancy, and sees
only a fresher and more glowing page; and he returns to his home
with the sun, strong in heart and full of self-gratulation on the favorable change in his lot. But he finds the home-bird drooping and disconsolate. *She* has been looking in vain for the reflection of any of the
cherished features of her own dear fire-side. She has found a thousand
deficiencies which her rougher mate can scarce be taught to feel as
evils (chapter 36, not reprinted).

A New Home—Who'll Follow? signals a realism in American fiction designed not simply to counter previous romanticism; it is designed
equally to counter that masculine "realism" that believes the whole story
has been told when the man's story has been told.

As the portrait of Eloise Fidler indicates, Kirkland, like Sedgwick,
understood the conventional assumptions about women and writing
and, again like Sedgwick, was determined to engage them and to define,
even police, her own literary territory. Eloise Fidler precedes Emmeline
Grangerford of Mark Twain's *Adventures of Huckleberry Finn* by almost fifty years, a fact that testifies not only to the endurance of the
phenomenon thus satirized but also to the accuracy of women's sense of
danger in the prominence accorded this version of the female artist.
Kirkland's strategy for self-protection and self-definition does not lie in
fleeing association with the feminine. Indeed, she delights in drawing
attention to her sex and thus insisting that her readers recognize they are
reading the work of a woman: "and with such brief salvo, I make my
humble curtsey"; "so I may as well cut short my mazy dance and resume at once my proper position as a 'wall flower,' with an unceremoni-
ous adieu to the kind and courteous reader." Rather her strategy
involves frequent references to these assumptions, couched in a tone of
ironic playfulness that reveals their bias and requires the reader to consider the possibility that the female style may have its own unique virtues and value: "I know this rambling gossiping style, this going back to
take up dropped stitches, is not the orthodox way of telling one's story;
and if I thought I could do any better, I would certainly go back and
begin at the very beginning; but I feel conscious that the truly feminine
sin of talking 'about it and about it,' the unconquerable partiality for
wandering wordiness would cleave to me still; so I proceed . . ."; and,
again, "But I think I have discovered that the bent of my genius is altogether towards digression. Association leads me like a Will-o'-the-
wisp. I can no more resist following a new train of thought, than a
coquette the encouraging of a new lover, at the expense of all the old
ones, though often equally conscious that the old are most valuable"
(chapters 21, 45, not reprinted). Here, for example, Kirkland parodies
the assumption that women's art has no form because women have no
wills, and she suggests instead that one consider the special "genius" of
digression. Through her reference at the end of her preface, to Mary
Russell Mitford, whose sketches of English village life were published in
five volumes between 1824 and 1832, Kirkland implies that she has
studied this genius and sees herself as part of a female literary tradition.

A New Home—Who'll Follow amply testifies to the value of following that tradition.

Source:

A New Home—Who'll Follow? (New York: C. S. Francis), 1839.

Selected Primary Works:

Forest Life, 1842; *Western Clearings,* 1845; *The Evening Book; or, Fireside Talk on Morals and Manners, with Sketches of Western Life,* 1852; *A Book for the Home Circle; or, Familiar Thoughts on Various Topics, Literary, Moral, and Social,* 1853; *Autumn Hours, and Fireside Reading,* 1854.

Selected Secondary Works:

Langley C. Keyes, "Caroline M. Kirkland: A Pioneer in Realism" (Ph.D. dissertation, Harvard University) 1936; Annette Kolodny, *The Land Before Her* (Chapel Hill: University of North Carolina Press), 1984; Thomas Ollive Mabbott, "Mrs. Kirkland's 'Essay on Fiction,'" *Bulletin of the New York Public Library,* 64 (1960), 395–97; John C. McCloskey, "Back-Country Folkways in Mrs. Kirkland's *A New Home—Who'll Follow?" Michigan History,* 40 (1956), 297–308; ———, "Land Speculation in Michigan in 1835–36 as Described in Mrs. Kirkland's *A New Home—Who'll Follow?" Michigan History,* 42 (1958), 26–34; ———, "Jacksonian Democracy in Mrs. Kirkland's *A New Home—Who'll Follow?" Michigan History,* 45 (1961), 347–52; William S. Osborne, *Caroline M. Kirkland* (New York: Twayne), 1972; Daniel G. Riordan, "The Concept of Simplicity in the Works of Caroline M. Kirkland" (Ph.D. dissertation, University of North Carolina), 1974; Audrey Roberts, "The Letters of Caroline M. Kirkland" (Ph.D. dissertation, University of Wisconsin), 1976; James B. Stronks, "Author Rejects Publisher: Caroline Kirkland and *The Gift,*" *Bulletin of the New York Public Library,* 64 (1960), 548–50.

Contexts:

1835—Child, *The History of the Condition of Women;* Holmes, *Poems*
1836—Child, *Philothea;* Emerson, *Nature*
1837—Emerson, "The American Scholar"; Hawthorne, *Twice-Told Tales; United States Magazine and Democratic Review;* Sarah Josepha Hale becomes editor of *Godey's Lady's Book;* Mt. Holyoke founded
1838—Emerson, "The Divinity School Address"; Grimké, *Letters on the Equality of the Sexes;* Poe, *The Narrative of Arthur Gordon Pym;* Whittier, *Ballads and Anti-Slavery Poems*
1839—Longfellow, *Hyperion, Voices of the Night;* Margaret Fuller's conversations

---

PREFACE

I AM GLAD to be told by those who live in the world, that it has lately become fashionable to read prefaces. I wished to say a few words, by way of introduction, to a work which may be deemed too slight to need a preface, but which will doubtless be acknowledged to require some recommendation.

I claim for these straggling and cloudy crayon-sketches of life and manners in the remoter parts of Michigan, the merit of general truth of outline. Beyond this I venture not to aspire. I felt somewhat tempted to set forth my little book as being entirely, what it is very nearly—a veritable history; an unimpeachable transcript of reality; a rough picture, in detached parts, but pentagraphed from the life; a sort of "Emigrant's Guide:"—considering with myself that these my adventurous journeyings and tarryings beyond the confines of civilization, might fairly be held to confer the traveller's privilege. But conscience prevailed, and I must honestly confess, that there be glosses, and colourings, and lights, if not shadows, for which the author is alone accountable. Journals published entire and unaltered, should be Parthian darts, sent abroad only when one's back is turned. To throw them in the teeth of one's every-day associates might diminish one's popularity rather inconveniently. I would desire the courteous reader to bear in mind, however, that whatever is quite unnatural, or absolutely incredible, in the few incidents which diversify the following pages, is to be received as literally true. It is only in the most commonplace parts (if there be comparisons) that I have any leasing-making to answer for.

It will of course be observed that Miss Mitford's charming sketches of village life must have suggested the form of my rude attempt. I dare not flatter myself that any one will be led to accuse me of further imitation of a deservedly popular writer. And with such brief salvo, I make my humble curtsey.

M.C.

CHAPTER I

> Here are seen
> No traces of man's pomp and pride; no silks
> Rustle, nor jewels shine, nor envious eyes
> Encounter *   *   *   *   *
> Oh, there is not lost
> One of earth's charms; upon her bosom yet
> After the flight of untold centuries
> The freshness of her far beginning lies.
>
> Bryant.

Our friends in the "settlements" have expressed so much interest in such of our letters to them, as happened to convey any account of the peculiar features of western life, and have asked so many questions, touching particulars which we had not thought worthy of mention, that I have been for some time past contemplating the possibility of something like a detailed account of our experiences. And I have determined to give them to the world, in a form not very different from that in which they were originally recorded for our private delectation; nothing doubting, that a veracious history of actual occurrences, an unvarnished transcript of real characters, and an impartial record of every-day forms of speech (taken down in many cases from the lips of the speaker) will be pronounced "graphic," by at least a fair proportion of the journalists of the day.

'Tis true there are but meagre materials for anything which might be called a story. I have never seen a cougar—nor been bitten by a rattlesnake. The reader who has patience to go with me to the close of my desultory sketches, must expect nothing beyond a meandering recital of common-place occurrences—mere gossip about every-day people, little enhanced in value by any fancy or ingenuity of the writer; in short, a very ordinary pen-drawing; which, deriving no interest from colouring, can be valuable only for its truth.

A home on the outskirts of civilization—habits of society which allow the maid and her mistress to do the honours in complete equality, and to make the social tea visit in loving conjunction—such a distribution of the duties of life as compels all, without distinction, to rise with the sun or before him—to breakfast with the chickens—then,

"Count the slow clock and dine exact at noon"—

to be ready for tea at four, and for bed at eight—may certainly be expected to furnish some curious particulars for the consideration of those whose daily course almost reverses this primitive arrangement—who "call night day and day night," and who are apt occasionally to forget, when speaking of a particular class, that "those creatures" are partakers with themselves of a common nature.

I can only wish, like other modest chroniclers, my respected prototypes, that so fertile a theme had fallen into worthier hands. If Miss Mitford, who has given us such charming glimpses of Aberleigh, Hilton Cross and the Loddon, had by some happy chance been translated to Michigan, what would she not have made of such materials as Tinkerville, Montacute, and the Turnip?

When my husband purchased two hundred acres of wild land on the banks of this to-be-celebrated stream, and drew with a piece of chalk on the bar-room table at Danforth's the plan of a village, I little thought I was destined to make myself famous by handing down to posterity a faithful record of the advancing fortunes of that favoured spot.

"The madness of the people" in those days of golden dreams took more commonly the form of city-building; but there were a few who contented themselves with planning villages, on the banks of streams which certainly never could be expected to bear navies, but which might yet be turned to account in the more homely way of grinding or sawing—

operations which must necessarily be performed somewhere for the well-being of those very cities. It is of one of these humble attempts that it is my lot to speak, and I make my confession at the outset, warning any fashionable reader who may have taken up my book, that I intend to be "decidedly low."

Whether the purchaser of *our* village would have been moderate under all possible circumstances, I am not prepared to say, since, never having enjoyed a situation under government, his resources have not been unlimited;—and for this reason any remark which may be hazarded in the course of these my lucubrations touching the more magnificent plans of wealthier aspirants, must be received with some grains of allowance. "Il est plus aisé d'être sage pour les autres, que de l'être pour soi-même."

When I made my first visit to these remote and lonely regions, the scattered woods through which we rode for many miles were gay in their first gosling-green suit of half-opened leaves, and the forest odours which exhaled with the dews of morning and evening, were beyond measure delicious to one "long in populous cities pent." I desired much to be a little sentimental at the time, and feel tempted to indulge to some small extent even here—but I forbear; and shall adhere closely to matters more in keeping with my subject.

I think, to be precise, the time was the last, the very last of April, and I recollect well that even at that early season, by availing myself with sedulous application, of those times when I was fain to quit the vehicle through fear of the perilous mud-holes, or still more perilous half-bridged marshes, I picked upwards of twenty varieties of wild-flowers—some of them of rare and delicate beauty;—and sure I am, that if I had succeeded in inspiring my companion with one spark of my own floral enthusiasm, one hundred miles of travel would have occupied a week's time.

The wild flowers of Michigan deserve a poet of their own. Shelley, who sang so quaintly of "the pied wind-flowers and the tulip tall," would have found many a fanciful comparison and deep-drawn meaning for the thousand gems of the road-side. Charles Lamb could have written charming volumes about the humblest among them. Bulwer would find means to associate the common three-leaved white lily so closely with the Past, the Present, and the Future—the Wind, the stars, and the tripod of Delphos, that all future botanists, and eke all future philosophers, might fail to unravel the "linked sweetness." We must have a poet of our own.

Since I have casually alluded to a Michigan mud-hole, I may as well enter into a detailed memoir on the subject, for the benefit of future travellers, who, flying over the soil on rail-roads, may look slightingly back upon the achievements of their predecessors. In the "settlements," a mud-hole is considered as apt to occasion an unpleasant jolt—a breaking of the thread of one's reverie—or in extreme cases, a temporary standstill or even an overturn of the rash or the unwary. Here, on approaching one of these characteristic features of the "West"—(How much does that expression mean to include? I never have been able to discover its limits)—the driver stops—alights—walks up to the dark gulf—and around it if he can get round it. He then seeks a long pole and sounds it, measures it across to ascertain how its width compares with the length of his wagon—tries whether its sides are perpendicular, as is usually the case if the road is much used. If he find it not more than three feet deep, he remounts cheerily, encourages his team, and in they go, with a plunge and a shock rather apt to damp the courage of the inexperienced. If the hole be narrow the hinder wheels will be quite lifted off the ground by the depression of their precedents, and so remain until by unwearied chirruping and some judicious touches of "the string" the horses are induced to struggle as for their lives; and if the fates are propitious they generally emerge on the opposite side, dragging the vehicle, or at least the fore wheels after them. When I first "penetrated the interior" (to use an indigenous phrase) all I knew of the wilds was from Hoffman's tour or Captain Hall's "graphic" delineations: I had some floating idea of "driving a barouche-and-four anywhere through the oak-openings"—and seeing "the murdered Banquos of the forest" haunting the scenes of their departed strength and beauty. But I confess, these pictures, touched by the glowing pencil of fancy, gave me but incorrect notions of a real journey through Michigan.

Our vehicle was not perhaps very judiciously chosen;—at least we have since thought so. It was a light high-hung carriage—of the description commonly known as a buggy or shandrydan—names of which I would be glad to learn the etymology. I seriously advise any of my friends who are about flitting to Wisconsin or Oregon, to prefer a heavy lumber-waggon, even for the use of the ladies of the family; very little aid or consolation being derived from making a "genteel" appearance in such cases.

At the first encounter of such a mud-hole as I have attempted to describe, we stopped in utter despair. My companion indeed would fain have persuaded me that the many wheel tracks which passed through the formidable gulf were proof positive that it might be forded. I insisted with all a woman's obstinancy that I could not and would not make the attempt, and alighted accordingly, and tried to find a path on one side or the other. But in vain, even putting out of the question my paper-soled shoes—sensible things for the woods. The ditch on each side was filled with water and quite too wide to jump over; and we were actually contemplating a return, when a man in an immense bear-skin cap and a suit of deer's hide, sprang from behind a stump just within the edge of the forest. He "poled" himself over the ditch in a moment, and stood beside us, rifle in hand, as wild and rough a specimen of humanity as one would wish to encounter in a strange and lonely road, just at the shadowy dusk of the evening. I did *not* scream, though I own I was prodigiously frightened. But our stranger said immediately, in a gentle tone and with a French accent, "Me watch deer—you want to cross?" On receiving an answer in the affirmative, he ran in search of a rail which he threw over the terrific mudhole—aided me to walk across by the help of his pole—showed my husband where to plunge—waited till he had gone safely through and "slow circles dimpled o'er the quaking mud"—then took himself off by the way he came, declining any compensation with a most polite "rien, rien!" This instance of true and genuine and generous politeness I record for the benefit of all bearskin caps, leathern jerkins and cowhide boots, which ladies from the eastward world may hereafter encounter in Michigan.

Our journey was marked by no incident more alarming than the one I have related, though one night passed in a wretched inn, deep in the "timbered land"—as all woods are called in Michigan—was not without its terrors, owing to the horrible drunkenness of the master of the house, whose wife and children were in constant fear of their lives, from his insane fury. I can never forget the countenance of that desolate woman, sitting trembling and with white, compressed lips in the midst of her children. The father raving all night, and coming through our sleeping apartment with the earliest ray of morning, in search of more of the poison already boiling in his veins. The poor wife could not forbear telling me her story—her change of lot—from a well-stored and comfortable home in Connecticut to this wretched den in the wilderness—herself and children worn almost to shadows with the ague, and her husband such as I have described him. I may mention here that not very long after I heard of this man in prison in Detroit, for stabbing a neighbour in a drunken brawl, and ere the year was out he died of delirium tremens, leaving his family destitute. So much for turning our fields of golden grain into "fire water"—a branch of business in which Michigan is fast improving.

Our ride being a deliberate one, I felt, after the third day, a little wearied, and began to complain of the sameness of the oak-openings and to wish we were fairly at our journey's end. We were crossing a broad expanse of what seemed at a little distance a smooth shaven lawn of the most brilliant green, but which proved on trial little better than a quaking bog—embracing within its ridgy circumference all possible varieties of

"Muirs, and mosses, slaps and styles"—

I had just indulged in something like a yawn, and wished that I could see our hotel. At the word, my companion's face assumed rather a comical expression, and I was preparing to inquire somewhat testily what there was so laughable—I was getting tired and cross, reader—when down came our good horse to the very chin in a bog-hole, green as Erin on the top, but giving away on a touch, and seeming deep enough to have engulphed us entirely if its width had been proportionate. Down came the horse—and this was not all—down came the driver; and I could not do less than follow, though at a little distance—our good steed kicking and floundering—covering us with hieroglyphics, which would be readily decyphered by any Wolverine we should meet, though perchance strange to the eyes of our friends at home. This mishap was soon amended. Tufts of long marsh grass served to assoilize our habiliments a little, and a clear stream which rippled through the marsh aided in removing the eclipse from our faces. We journeyed on cheerily, watching the splendid changes in the west, but keeping a bright look-out for bog-holes.

Chapter III.

The greatness of an estate, in bulk and territory doth fall under measure; and the greatness of finances and revenue doth fall under computation.*** By all means it is to be procured, that the trunk of Nebuchadnezzar's tree of monarchy be great enough to bear the branches and the boughs.

Bacon.

The morning passed in viewing and reviewing the village site and the "Mill privilege," under the condescending guidance of a regular land speculator, into whose clutches—but I anticipate.

The public square, the water lots, the value *per foot* of this undulating surface, clothed as it then was with burr-oaks, and haunted by the red deer; these were almost too much for my gravity. I gave my views, however, as to the location of the grand esplanade, and particularly requested that the fine oaks which now graced it might be spared when the clearing process commenced.

"Oh, certainly, mem!" said our Dousterswivel, "a place that's designed for a public promenade must not be divested of shade trees!" Yet I believe these very trees were the first "Banquos" at Montacute. The water lots, which were too valuable to sell save by the foot, are still in the market, and will probably remain there for the present.

This factotum, this Mr. Mazard, was an odd-looking creature, with "diverse ocular foci," and a form gaunt enough to personify Grahamism. His words sometimes flowed in measured softness, and sometimes tumbled over each other, in his anxiety to convince, to persuade, to inspire. His air of earnest conviction, of sincere anxiety for your interest, and, above all, of entire forgetfulness of his own, was irresistible. People who did not know him always believed every word he said; at least so I have since been informed.

This gentleman had kindly undertaken to lay out our village, to build a mill, a tavern, a store, a blacksmith's shop; houses for cooper, miller, &c. &c., to purchase the large tracts which would be required for the mill-pond, a part of which land was already improved; and all this,

although sure to cost Mr. Clavers an immense sum, *he*, from his experience of the country, his large dealings with saw-mills, &c., would be able
to accomplish at a very moderate cost. The mill, for instance, was to be a
story and a half high, and to cost perhaps twenty-five hundred dollars at
the utmost. The tavern, a cheap building of moderate size, built on the
most popular plan, and connected with a store, just large enough for the
infant needs of the village, reserving our strength for a splendid one, (I
quote Mr. Mazard) to be built out of the profits in about three years. All
these points being thus satisfactorily arranged, Mr. Mazard received *carte
blanche* for the purchase of the lands which were to be flowed, which he
had ascertained might be had for a mere trifle.

The principal care now was to find a name—a title at once simple and
dignified—striking and euphonious—recherché and yet unpretending.
Mr. Mazard was for naming it after the proprietor. It was a proper opportunity, he thought, of immortalizing one's-self. But he failed in convincing the proprietor, who relished not this form of fame, and who referred
the matter entirely to me. Here was a responsibility! I begged for time,
but the matter must be decided at once. The village plot was to be drawn
instanter—lithographed and circulated through the United States, and, to
cap the climax, printed in gold, splendidly framed, and hung up in Detroit, in the place "where merchants most do congregate."

I tried for an aboriginal designation, as most characteristic and un-
worn. I recollected a young lady speaking with enthusiastic admiration of
our Indian names, and quoting *Ypsilanti* as a specimen. But I was not
fortunate in my choice; for to each of the few which I could recollect, Mr.
Mazard found some insuperable objection. One was too long, another
signified *Slippery Eel,* another *Big Bubble;* and these would be so inappropriate! I began to be very tired. I tried romantic names; but these
again did not suit any of us. At length I decided by lot, writing ten of the
most sounding names I could muster from my novel reading stores, on
slips of paper, which were mingled in a *shako,* and out came—Montacute.
How many matters of greater importance are thus decided.

Chapter XII

> The ripeness or unripeness of the occasion must ever be well
> weighed; and generally, it is good to commit the beginnings of
> all great actions to Argus with his hundred eyes, and the ends to
> Briareus with his hundred hands.
>
> Bacon

> Trust not yourself; but your defects to know
> Make use of every friend.
>
> Pope

The log-house, which was to be our temporary home, was tenanted at
this time; and we were obliged to wait while the incumbent could build a
framed one; the materials for which had been growing in the woods not

long before; I was told it would take but a short time, as it was already framed.

What was my surprise, on walking that way to ascertain the progress of things, to find the materials still scattered on the ground, and the place quite solitary.

"Did not Mr. Ketchum say Green's house was framed?" said I to the *dame du palais*, on my return; "the timbers are all lying on the ground, and nobody at work."

"Why, la! so they be all framed, and Green's gone to ____ for the sash. They'll be ready to raise tomorrow."

It took me some time to understand that *framing* was nothing more than cutting the tenons and mortices ready for putting the timbers together, and that these must be *raised* before there could be a frame. And that "sash," which I in my ignorance supposed could be but for one window, was a *generic* term.

The "raising" took place the following afternoon, and was quite an amusing scene to us cockneys, until one man's thumb was frightfully mashed, and another had a severe blow upon the head. A jug of whiskey was pointed out by those who understood the matter, as the true cause of these disasters, although the Fates got the blame.

"Jem White always has such bad luck!" said Mr. Ketchum, on his return from the raising, "and word spake never more," for that night at least; for he disappeared behind the mysterious curtain, and soon snored most sonorously.

The many raisings which have been accomplished at Montacute, without that ruinous ally, strong drink, since the days of which I speak, have been free from accidents of any sort; Jem White having carried his "bad luck" to a distant county, and left his wife and children to be taken care of by the public.

Our cottage bore about the same proportion to the articles we had expected to put into it, that the "lytell hole" did to the fiend whom Virgilius cajoled into its narrow compass; and the more we reflected, the more certain we became that without the magic powers of necromancy, one half of our moveables at least must remain in the open air. To avoid such necessity, Mr. Clavers was obliged to return to Detroit and provide storage for sundry unwieldy boxes which could by no art of ours be conjured into our cot.

While he was absent, Green had enclosed his new house; that is to say put on the roof and the siding, and laid one floor, and forthwith he removed thither without door, window or chimney, a course by no means unusual in Michigan.

As I was by this time, truth to speak, very nearly starved, I was anxious to go as soon as possible to a place where I could feel a little more at home; and so completely had my nine days at Ketchum's brought down my ideas, that I anticipated real satisfaction in a removal to this hut in the wilderness. I would not wait for Mr. Clavers's return; but insisted on setting up for myself at once.

But I should in vain attempt to convey to those who know nothing of the woods, any idea of the difficulties in my way. If one's courage did not increase, and one's invention brighten under the stimulus of such occasions, I should have given up at the outset, as I have often done with far less cause.

It was no easy matter to get a "lady" to clean the place, and ne'er had place more need of the tutelary aid of the goddess of scrubbing brushes. Then this lady must be provided with the necessary utensils, and here arose dilemma upon dilemma. Mrs. Ketchum rendered what aid she could, but there was little superfluous in her house.

And then, such racing and chasing, such messages and requisitions! Mrs. Jennings "couldn't do nothin' without a mop," and I had not thought of such a thing and was obliged to sacrifice on the spot sundry nice towels, a necessity which made all the housekeeping blood in my veins tingle.

After one day's experience of this sort, I decided to go myself to the scene of action, so as to be at hand for these trying occasions; and I induced Mr. Ketchum to procure a waggon and carry to our new home the various articles which we had piled in a hovel on his premises.

Behold me then seated on a box, in the midst of as anomalous a congregation of household goods as ever met under one roof in the backwoods, engaged in the seemingly hopeless task of calling order out of chaos, attempting occasionally to throw out a hint for the instruction of Mrs. Jennings, who uniformly replied by requesting me not to fret, as she knew what she was about.

Mr. Jennings, with the aid of his sons, undertook the release of the pent up myriads of articles which crammed the boxes, many of which though ranked when they were put in as absolutely essential, seemed ridiculously superfluous when they came out. The many observations made by the spectators as each new wonder made its appearance, though at first rather amusing, became after a while quite vexatious; for the truth began to dawn upon me that the common sense was all on their side.

"What on airth's them gimcracks for?" said my lady, as a nest of delicate japanned tables were set out upon the uneven floor.

I tried to explain to her the various convenient uses to which they were applicable; but she looked very scornfully after all and said "I guess they'll do better for kindlin's than any thing else, here." And I began to cast a disrespectful glance upon them myself, and forthwith ordered them up stairs, wondering in my own mind how I could have thought a log house would afford space for such superfluities.

All this time there was a blazing fire in the chimney to accommodate Mrs. Jennings in her operations, and while the doors and windows were open we were not sensible of much discomfort from it. Supper was prepared and eaten—beds spread on the floor, and the children stowed away. Mrs. Jennings and our other "helps" had departed, and I prepared to rest from my unutterable weariness, when I began to be sensible of the suffocating heat of the place. I tried to think it would grow cooler in a little while, but it was absolutely insufferable to the children as well as myself, and I was fain to set both doors open, and in this exposed situation passed the first night in my western home, alone with my children and far from any neighbour.

If I could live a century, I think, that night will never fade from my memory. Excessive fatigue made it impossible to avoid falling asleep, yet the fear of being devoured by wild beasts, or poisoned by rattlesnakes, caused me to start up after every nap with sensations of horror and alarm, which could hardly have been increased by the actual occurrence of all I dreaded. Many wretched hours passed in this manner. At length sleep fairly overcame fear, and we were awakened only by a wild storm of wind and rain which drove in upon us and completely wetted every thing within reach.

A doleful morning was this—no fire on the hearth—streams of water on the floor, and three hungry children to get breakfast for. I tried to kindle a blaze with matches, but alas! even the straw from the packing-boxes was soaked with the cruel rain; and I was distributing bread to the hungry, hopeless of anything more, when Mr. Jennings made his appearance.

"I was thinking you'd begin to be sick o' your bargain by this time," said the good man, "and so I thought I'd come and help you a spell. I reckon you'd ha' done better to have waited till the old man got back."

"What old man?" asked I, in perfect astonishment.

"Why, *your* old man to be sure," said he laughing. I had yet to learn that in Michigan, as soon as a man marries he becomes "th' old man," though he may be yet in his minority. Not long since I gave a young bride the how d' ye do in passing, and the reply was, "I'm pretty well, but my old man's sick a-bed."

But to return, Mr. Jennings kindled a fire which I took care should be a very moderate one; and I managed to make a cup of tea to dip our bread in, and then proceeded to find places for the various articles which strewed the floor. Some auger-holes bored in the logs received large and long pegs, and these served to support boards which were to answer the purpose of shelves. It was soon found that the multiplicity of articles which were to be accommodated on these shelves would fill them a dozen times.

"Now to my thinkin'," said my good genius, Mr. Jennings, "that 'ere soup-t'reen, as you call it, and them little ones, and these here great glass-dishes, and all *sich*, might jist as well go up chamber for all the good they'll ever do you here."

This could not be gainsaid; and the good man proceeded to exalt them to another set of extempore shelves in the upper story; and so many articles were included in the same category, that I began to congratulate myself on the increase of clear space below, and to fancy we should soon begin to look very comfortable.

My ideas of comfort were by this time narrowed down to a well-swept room with a bed in one corner, and cooking-apparatus in another—and this in some fourteen days from the city! I can scarcely, myself, credit the reality of the change.

It was not till I had occasion to mount the ladder that I realized that all I had gained on the confusion below was most hopelessly added to the confusion above, and I came down with such a sad and thoughtful brow, that my good aid-de-camp perceived my perplexity.

"Had n't I better go and try to get one of the neighbour's *gals* to come and help you for a few days?" said he.

I was delighted with the offer, and gave him carte-blanche as to terms, which I afterwards found was a mistake, for, where sharp bargains are the grand aim of every body, those who express anything like indifference on the subject, are set down at once as having more money than they know what to do with; and as this was far from being my case, I found reason to regret having given room for the conclusion.

The damsel made her appearance before a great while—a neat looking girl with "scarlet hair and belt to match;" and she immediately set about "reconciling" as she called it, with a good degree of energy and ingenuity. I was forced to confess that she knew much better than I how to make a log-house comfortable.

She began by turning out of doors the tall cup-board, which had puzzled me all the morning, observing very justly, "Where there ain't no room for a thing, why, there ain't;" and this decision cut the Gordian knot of all my plans and failures in the disposal of the ungainly convenience. It did yeoman's service long afterwards as a corn-crib.

When the bedsteads were to be put up, the key was among the missing; and after we had sent far and wide and borrowed a key, or the substitute for one, no screws could be found, and we were reduced to the dire necessity of trying to keep the refractory posts in their places by means of ropes. Then there were candles, but no candle-sticks. This seemed at first rather inconvenient, but when Mr. Jennings had furnished blocks of wood with auger-holes bored in them for sockets, we could do nothing but praise the ingenuity of the substitute.

My rosy-haired Phillida who rejoiced in the euphonius appellation of Angeline, made herself entirely at home, looking into my trunks, &c., and asking the price of various parts of my dress. She wondered why I had not my hair cut off, and said she reckoned I would before long, as it was all the fashion about here.

"When d' ye expect *Him?*" said the damsel, with an air of sisterly sympathy, and ere I could reply becomingly, a shout of "tiny joy" told me that Papa had come.

I did not cry for sorrow this time.

Chapter XV.

Honester men have stretch'd a rope, or the law has been
sadly cheated. But this unhappy business of yours? Can nothing be done? Let me see the charge.

He took the papers, and as he read them, his countenance
grew hopelessly dark and disconsolate.

Antiquary.

A strange fish! Were I in England now, and had but this fish
painted, not a holiday fool there but would give me a piece of
silver.

Shakspeare.—*Tempest.*

Sorrow chang'd to solace, and solace mixed with sorrow.

The Passionate Pilgrim.

SEVERAL lots had already been purchased in Montacute and some
improvement marked each succeeding day. The mill had grown to its full
stature, the dam was nearly completed; the tavern began to exhibit promise of its present ugliness, and all seemed prosperous as our best dreams,
when certain rumours were set afloat touching the solvency of our disinterested friend Mr. Mazard. After two or three days' whispering, a tall
black-browed man who "happened in" from Gullsborough, the place
which had for some time been honoured as the residence of the Dousterswivel of Montacute, stated boldly that Mr. Mazard had absconded; or, in
Western language "cleared." It seemed passing strange that he should run
away from the large house which was going on under his auspices; the
materials all on the ground and the work in full progress. Still more
unaccountable did it appear to us that his workmen should go on so
quietly, without so much as expressing any anxiety about their pay.

Mr. Clavers had just been telling me of these things, when the long
genius above mentioned, presented himself at the door of the loggery. His
abord was a singular mixture of coarseness, and an attempt at being civil;
and he sat for some minutes looking round and asking various questions
before he touched the mainspring of his visit.

At length, after some fumbling in his pocket, he produced a dingy
sheet of paper, which he handed to Mr. Clavers.

"There; I want you to read that, and tell me what you think of it."

I did not look at the paper, but at my husband's face, which was black
enough. He walked away with the tall man, "and I saw no more of them
at that time."

Mr. Clavers did not return until late in the evening, and it was then I
learned that Mr. Mazard had been getting large quantities of lumber and
other materials on his account, and as his agent; and that the money
which had been placed in the agent's hands, for the purchase of certain
lands to be flowed by the mill-pond, had gone into government coffers in
payment for sundry eighty acre lots, which were intended for his, Mr.

Mazard's, private behoof and benefit. These items present but a sample of our amiable friends trifling mistakes. I will not fatigue the reader by dwelling on the subject. The results of all this were most unpleasant to us. Mr. Clavers found himself involved to a large amount; and his only remedy seemed to prosecute Mr. Mazard. A consultation with his lawyer, however, convinced him, that even by this most disagreeable mode, redress was out of the question, since he had through inadvertence rendered himself liable for whatever that gentleman chose to buy or engage in his name. All that could be done, was to get out of the affair with as little loss as possible, and to take warning against land sharks in future.

An immediate journey to Detroit became necessary, and I was once more left alone, and in no overflowing spirits. I sat,

"Revolving in *my* altered soul
The various turns of fate below,"

when a tall damsel, of perhaps twenty-eight or thirty came in to make a visit. She was tastefully attired in a blue gingham dress, with broad cuffs of black morocco, and a black cambric apron edged with orange worsted lace. Her oily black locks were cut quite short round the ears, and confined close to her head by a black ribbon, from one side of which depended, almost in her eye, two very long tassels of black silk, intended to do duty as curls. Prunelle slippers with high heels, and a cotton handkerchief tied under the chin, finished the costume, which I have been thus particular in describing, because I have observed so many that were nearly similar.

The lady greeted me in the usual style, with a familiar nod, and seated herself at once in a chair near the door.

"Well, how do like Michig*an*?"

This question received the most polite answer which my conscience afforded; and I asked the lady in my turn, if she was one of my neighbours?

"Why, massy, yes!" she replied; "do n't you know me? I tho't every body know'd me. Why, I'm the school ma'am, Simeon Jenkins' sister, Cleory Jenkins."

Thus introduced, I put all my civility in requisition to entertain my guest, but she seemed quite independent, finding amusement for herself, and asking questions on every possible theme.

"You're doing your own work now, a'n't ye?"

This might not be denied; and I asked if she did not know of a girl whom I might be likely to get.

"Well, I do n't know; I'm looking for a place where I can board and do chores myself. I have a good deal of time before school, and after I get back; and I did n't know but I might suit ye for a while."

I was pondering on this proffer, when the sallow damsel arose from her seat, took a short pipe from her bosom, (not "Pan's reedy pipe," reader) filled it with tobacco, which she carried in her "work-pocket," and reseating herself, began to smoke with the greatest gusto, turning ever and anon to spit at the hearth.

Incredible again? alas, would it were not true! I have since known a girl of seventeen, who was attending a neighbour's sick infant, smoke the live-long day, and take snuff besides; and I can vouch for it, that a large proportion of the married women in the interior of Michigan use tobacco in some form, usually that of the odious pipe.

I took the earliest decent opportunity to decline the offered help, telling the school-ma'am plainly, that an inmate who smoked would make the house uncomfortable to me.

"Why, law!" said she, laughing; "that's nothing but pride now: folks is often too proud to take comfort. For my part, I could n't do without my pipe to please nobody."

Mr. Simeon Jenkins, the brother of this independent young lady now made his appearance on some trifling errand; and his sister repeated to him what I had said.

Mr. Jenkins took his inch of cigar from his mouth, and asked if I really disliked tobacco-smoke, seeming to think it scarcely possible.

"Do n't your old man smoke?" said he.

"No, indeed," said I, with more than my usual energy; "I should hope he never would."

"Well," said neighbour Jenkins, "I tell you what, I'm *boss* at home; and if my old woman was to stick up that fashion, I'd keep the house so blue she could n't see to snuff the candle."

His sister laughed long and loud at this sally, which was uttered rather angrily, and with an air of most manful bravery; and, Mr. Jenkins, picking up his end of cigar from the floor, walked off with an air evidently intended to be as expressive as the celebrated and oft-quoted nod of Lord Burleigh in the Critic.

CHAPTER XVII.

The house's form within was rude and strong,
    Like an huge cave hewn out of rocky clift;
From whose rough vault the ragged breaches hung:—
        *   *   *   *   *   *   *   *

And over them Arachne high did lift
    Her cunning web, and spread her subtle net,
Enwrapped in foul smoke, and clouds more black than jet.
                        SPENCER.—*Faery Queene.*

It were good that men, in their innovations, would follow the example of time itself, which, indeed, innovateth greatly, but quietly, and by degrees scarce to be perceived.—BACON.

It was on one of our superlatively doleful ague days, when a cold drizzling rain had sent mildew into our unfortunate bones; and I lay in bed, burning with fever, while my stronger half sat by the fire, taking his chill with his great-coat, hat, and boots on, that Mr. Rivers came to introduce his young daughter-in-law. I shall never forget the utterly disconsolate air, which, in spite of the fair lady's politeness, would make itself visible in the pauses of our conversation. She *did* try not to cast a curious glance round the room. She fixed her eyes on the fire-place—but there were the clay-filled sticks, instead of a chimney-piece—the half-consumed wooden *crane,* which had, more than once, let our dinner fall—the Rocky-Mountain hearth, and the reflector, baking biscuits for tea—so she thought it hardly polite to appear to dwell too long there. She turned towards the window: there were the shelves, with our remaining crockery, a grotesque assortment! and, just beneath, the unnameable iron and tin affairs, that are reckoned among the indispensables, even of the half-civilized state. She tried the other side, but there was the ladder, the flour-barrel, and a host of other things—rather odd parlour furniture—and she cast her eyes on the floor, with its gaping cracks, wide enough to admit a massasauga from below, and its inequalities, which might trip any but a sylph. The poor thing looked absolutely confounded, and I exerted all the energy my fever had left me, to try to say something a little encouraging.

"Come to-morrow morning, Mrs. Rivers," said I, "and you shall see the aspect of things quite changed; and I shall be able to tell you a great deal in favour of this wild life."

She smiled faintly, and tried not to look miserable, but I saw plainly that she was sadly depressed, and I could not feel surprised that she should be so. Mr. Rivers spoke very kindly to her, and filled up all the pauses in our forced talk with such cheering observations as he could muster.

He had found lodgings, he said, in a farm-house, not far from us, and his son's house would, ere long, be completed, when we should be quite near neighbours.

I saw tears swelling in the poor girl's eyes, as she took leave, and I longed to be well for her sake. In this newly-formed world, the earlier settler has a feeling of hostess-ship toward the new comer. I speak only of women—men look upon each one, newly arrived, merely as an additional business-automaton—a somebody more with whom to try the race of enterprize, i.e., money-making.

The next day Mrs. Rivers came again, and this time her husband was with her. Then I saw at a glance why it was that life in the wilderness looked so peculiarly gloomy to her. Her husband's face shewed but too plainly the marks of early excess; and there was at intervals, in spite of an evident effort to play the agreeable, an appearance of absence, of indifference, which spoke volumes of domestic history. He made innumerable inquiries, touching the hunting and fishing facilities of the country around us, expressed himself enthusiastically fond of those sports, and said the country was a living death without them, regretting much that Mr. Clavers was not of the same mind.

Meanwhile, I had begun to take quite an interest in his little wife. I found that she was as fond of novels and poetry, as her husband was of field-sports. Some of her flights of sentiment went quite beyond my sobered-down views. But I saw we should get on admirably, and so we have done ever since. I did not mistake that pleasant smile, and that soft sweet voice. They are even now as attractive as ever. And I had a neighbour.

Chapter XXVII.

> Smelling so sweetly (all musk,) and so rushling, I warrant
> you, in silk and gold; and in such alligant terms.
> > Shakspeare.—*Merry Wives of Windsor.*

> Art thou not Romeo, and a Montague?
> > Shakspeare.

> My brain 's in a fever, my pulses beat quick
> I shall die, or at least be exceedingly sick!
> Oh what do you think! after all my romancing
> My visions of glory, my sighing, my glancing—
> > Miss Biddy Fudge.

An addition to our Montacute first circle had lately appeared in the person of Miss Eloise Fidler, an elder sister of Mrs. Rivers, who was to spend some months "in this peaceful retreat,"—to borrow one of her favourite expressions.

This young lady was not as handsome as she would fain have been, if I may judge by the cataracts of ash-coloured ringlets which shaded her cheeks, and the exceeding straitness of the stays which restrained her somewhat exuberant proportions. Her age was at a stand; but I could never discover exactly where, for this point proved an exception to the general communicativeness of her disposition. I guessed it at eight-and-twenty; but perhaps she would have judged this uncharitable, so I wll not insist. Certain it is that it must have taken a good while to read as many novels and commit to memory as much poetry, as lined the head and exalted the sensibilities of our fair visitant.

Her dress was in the height of fashion, and all her accoutrements *point de vice.* A gold pencil-case of the most delicate proportions was suspended by a kindred chain round a neck which might be called whity-brown; and a note-book of corresponding lady-like-ness was peeping from the pocket of her highly-useful apron of blue silk—ever ready to secure a passing thought or an elegant quotation. Her album—she was just the person to have an album—was resplendent in gold and satin, and the verses which meandered over its emblazoned pages were of the most unexceptionable quality, overlaid with flowers and gems—love and despair. To find any degree of appropriateness in these various offerings, one must allow the fortunate possessor of the purple volume, at least all the various perfections of an Admirable Crichton, allayed in some small measure by the trifling faults of coldness, fickleness, and deceit; and to judge of Miss Fidler's friends by their hand-writing, they must have been able to offer an edifying variety of bumps to the fingers of the phrenologist. But here is the very book itself at my elbow, waiting these three months, I blush to say, for a contribution which has yet to be pumped up from my unwilling brains; and I have a mind to steal a few specimens from its already loaded pages, for the benefit of the distressed, who may, like myself, be at their wits' end for something to put in just such a book.

The first page, rich with embossed lilies, bears the invocation, written in a great black spattering hand, and wearing the air of a defiance. It runs thus:

> If among the names of the stainless few
>   Thine own hath maintain'd a place,
> Come dip thy pen in the sable dew
>   And with it this volume grace.
>
> But oh! if thy soul e'er encouraged a thought
>   Which purity's self might blame,
> Close quickly the volume, and venture not
>   To sully its snows with thy name.

Then we come to a wreath of flowers of gorgeous hues, within whose circle appears in a *miminee piminee* hand, evidently a young lady's—

THE WREATH OF SLEEP.

> Oh let me twine this glowing wreath
>   Amid those rings of golden hair,
> 'T will soothe thee with its odorous breath
>   To sweet forgetfulness of care.
>
> 'T is form'd of every scented flower
>   That flings its fragrance o'er the night;
> And gifted with a fairy power
>   To fill thy dreams with forms of light.
>
> 'T was braided by an angel boy
>   When fresh from Paradise he came
> To fill our earth-born hearts with joy—
>   Ah! need I tell the cherub's name?

This contributor I have settled in my own mind to be a descendant of Anna Matilda, the high-priestess of the Della Cruscan order. The next blazon is an interesting view of a young lady, combing her hair. As she seems not to have been long out of bed, the lines which follow are rather appropriate, though I feel quite sure they come from the expert fingers of a merchant's clerk—from the finished elegance, and very sweeping tails of the chirography.

MORNING.

Awake! arise! art thou slumbering still?
When the sun is above the mapled hill,
And the shadows are flitting fast away,
And the dews are diamond beneath his ray,
And every bird in our vine-roofed bower
Is waked into song by the joyous hour;
Come, banish sleep from thy gentle eyes,
Sister! sweet sister! awake! arise!

Yet I love to gaze on thy lids of pearl,
And to mark the wave of the single curl
That shades in its beauty thy brow of snow,
And the cheek that lies like a rose below;
And to list to the murmuring notes that fall
From thy lips, like music in fairy hall.
But it must not be—the sweet morning flies
Ere thou hast enjoyed it; awake! arise!

There is balm on the wings of this freshen'd air;
'T will make thine eye brighter, thy brow more fair,
And a deep, deep rose on thy cheek shall be
The meed of an early walk with me.
We will seek the shade by the green hill side,
Or follow the clear brook's whispering tide;
And brush the dew from the violet's eyes—
Sister! sweet sister! awake! arise!

This I transcribe for the good advice which it contains. And what have we here? It is tastefully headed by an engraving of Hero and Ursula in the "pleached bower," and Beatrice running "like a lap-wing" in the background. It begins ominously.

TO ___.

Oh, look upon this pallid brow!
   Say, canst thou there discern one trace
Of that proud soul which oft ere now
   Thou'st sworn shed radiance o'er my face?
Chill'd is that soul—its darling themes,
   Thy manly honour, virtue, truth
Prove now to be but fleeting dreams,
   Like other lovely thoughts of youth.

Meet, if thy coward spirit dare,
   This sunken eye; say, dost thou see

> The rays thou saidst were sparkling there
>> When first its gaze was turn'd on thee?
> That eye's young light is quench'd forever;
>> No change its radiance can repair:
> Will Joy's keen touch relume it? Never!
>> It gleams the watch-light of Despair.

I find myself growing hoarse by sympathy, and I shall venture only a single extract more, and this because Miss Fidler declares it, without exception, the sweetest thing she ever read. It is written with a crow-quill, and has other marks of femininity. Its vignette is a little girl and boy playing at battle-door.

BALLAD.

The deadly strife was over, and across the field of fame,
With anguish in his haughty eye, the Moor Almanzor came;
He prick'd his fiery courser on among the scatter'd dead,
Till he came at last to what he sought, a sever'd human head.

It might have seem'd a maiden's, so pale it was, and fair;
But the lip and chin were shaded till they match'd the raven hair.
There lingered yet upon the brow a spirit bold and high,
And the stroke of death had scarcely closed the piercing eagle eye.

Almanzor grasp'd the flowing locks, and he staid not in his flight,
Till he reach'd a lonely castle's gate where stood a lady bright.
"Inez! behold thy paramour!" he loud and sternly cried,
And threw his ghastly burden down, close at the lady's side.

"I sought thy bower at even-tide, thou syren, false as fair!"
"And, would that I had rather died! I found yon stripling there.
"I turn'd me from the hated spot, but I swore by yon dread Heaven,
"To know no rest until my sword the traitor's life had riven."

The lady stood like stone until he turn'd to ride away,
And then she oped her marble lips, and wildly thus did say:
"Alas, alas! thou cruel Moor, what is it thou hast done!
"This was my brother Rodriguez, my father's only son."

And then before his frenzied eyes, like a crush'd lily bell,
Lifeless upon the bleeding head, the gentle Inez fell.
He drew his glittering ataghan—he sheath'd it in his side—
And for his Spanish ladye-love the Moor Almanzor died.

This is not a very novel incident, but young ladies like stories of love and murder, and Miss Fidler's tastes were peculiarly young-lady-like. She praised Ainsworth and James, but thought Bulwer's works "very immoral," though I never could discover that she had more than skimmed the story from any of them. Cooper she found "pretty;" Miss Sedgwick, "pretty well, only her characters are such common sort of people."

Miss Fidler wrote her own poetry, so that she had ample employment for her time while with us in the woods. It was unfortunate that she could not walk out much on account of her shoes. She was obliged to make out with diluted inspiration. The nearest approach she usually made to the study of Nature, was to sit on the wood-pile, under a girdled tree, and there, with her gold pencil in hand, and her "eyne, grey as glas," rolled upwards, poefy by the hour. Several people, and especially one marriage-able lady of a certain age, felt afraid Miss Fidler was "kind o' crazy."

And, standing marvel of Montacute, no guest at morning or night ever found the fair Eloise ungloved. Think of it! In the very wilds to be always like a cat in nutshells, alone useless where all are so busy! I do not wonder our good neighbours thought the damsel a little touched. And then her shoes! "Saint Crispin Crispianus" never had so self-sacrificing a votary. No shoemaker this side of New-York could make a sole papery enough; no tannery out of France could produce materials for this piece of exquisite feminine foppery. Eternal imprisonment within doors, except in the warmest and driest weather, was indeed somewhat of a price to pay, but it was ungrudged. The sofa and its footstool, finery and novels, *would* have made a delicious world for Miss Eloise Fidler, *if*——

But alas! "all this availeth me nothing," has been ever the song of poor human nature. The mention of that unfortunate name includes the only real, personal, pungent distress which had as yet shaded the lot of my interesting heroine. Fidler! In the mortification adhering to so unpoetical, so unromantic, so inelegant a surname—a name irredeemable even by the highly classical elegance of the Eloise, or as the fair lady herself pro-nounced it, "Elovees;" in this lay all her wo; and the grand study of her life had been to sink this hated cognomen in one more congenial to her taste. Perhaps this very anxiety had defeated itself; at any rate, here she was at——I did not mean to touch on the ungrateful guess again, but at least at mateable years; neither married, nor particularly likely to be married.

Mrs. Rivers was the object of absolute envy to the pining Eloise. "Anna had been so fortunate," she said; "Rivers was the sweetest name! and Harley was such an elegant fellow!"

We thought poor Anna had been any thing but fortunate. She might better have been Fidler or Fiddlestring all her life than to have taken the name of an indifferent and dissipated husband. But not so thought Miss Fidler. It was not long after the arrival of the elegant Eloise, that the Montacute Lyceum held its first meeting in Mr. Simeon Jenkins's shop, lighted by three candles, supported by candelabra of scooped potatoes; Mr. Jenkins himself sitting on the head of a barrel, as president. At first the debates of the institute were held with closed doors; but after the youthful or less practised speakers had tried their powers for a few eve-nings, the Lyceum was thrown open to the world every Tuesday evening, at six o'clock. The list of members was not very select as to age, character, or standing; and it soon included the entire gentility of the town, and some who scarce claimed rank elsewhere. The attendance of the ladies was particularly requested; and the whole fair sex of Montacute made a point of showing occasionally the interest they undoubtedly felt in the gallant knights who tilted in this field of honour.

But I must not be too diffuse—I was speaking of Miss Fidler. One evening—I hope that beginning prepares the reader for something highly interesting—one evening the question to be debated was the equally novel and striking one which regards the comparative mental capacity of the sexes; and as it was expected that some of the best speakers on both sides would be drawn out by the interesting nature of the subject, every body was anxious to attend.

Among the rest was Miss Fidler, much to the surprise of her sister and myself, who had hitherto been so unfashionable as to deny ourselves this gratification.

"What new whim possesses you, Eloise?" said Mrs. Rivers; "you who never go out in the day-time."

"Oh, just *per passy le tong*," said the young lady, who was a great French scholar; and go she would and did.

The debate was interesting to absolute breathlessness, both of speakers and hearers, and was gallantly decided in favour of the fair by a youthful member who occupied the barrel as president for the evening. He gave it as his decided opinion, that if the natural and social disadvantages under which woman laboured and must ever continue to labour, could be removed; if their education could be entirely different, and their position in society the reverse of what it is at present, they would be very nearly, if not quite, equal to the nobler sex, in all but strength of mind, in which very useful quality it was his opinion that man would still have the advantage, especially in those communities whose energies were developed by the aid of debating societies.

This decision was hailed with acclamations, and as soon as the question for the ensuing debate, "which is the more useful animal the ox or the ass?" was announced, Miss Eloise Fidler returned home to rave of the elegant young man who sat on the barrel, whom she had decided to be one of "Nature's aristocracy," and whom she had discovered to bear the splendid appellative of Dacre. "Edward Dacre," said she, "for I heard the rude creature Jenkins call him Ed."

The next morning witnessed another departure from Miss Fidler's usual habits. She proposed a walk; and observed that she had never yet bought an article at the store, and really felt as if she ought to purchase something. Mrs. Rivers chancing to be somewhat occupied, Miss Fidler did me the honour of a call, as she could not think of walking without a chaperon.

Behind the counter at Skinner's I saw for the first time a spruce clerk, a really well-looking young man, who made his very best bow to Miss

Fidler, and served us with much assiduity. The young lady's purchases occupied some time, and I was obliged gently to hint home-affairs before she could decide between two pieces of muslin, which she declared to be so nearly alike, that it was almost impossible to say which was the best.

When we were at length on our return, I was closely questioned as to my knowledge of "that gentleman," and on my observing that he seemed to be a very decent young man, Miss Fidler warmly justified him from any such opinion, and after a glowing eulogium on his firm countenance, his elegant manners and his grace as a debater, concluded by informing me, as if to cap the climax, that his name was Edward Dacre.

I had thought no more of the matter for some time, though I knew Mr. Dacre had become a frequent visitor at Mr. Rivers', when Mrs. Rivers came to me one morning with a perplexed brow, and confided to me her sisterly fears that Eloise was about to make a fool of herself, as she had done more than once before.

"My father," she said, "hoped in this remote corner of creation Eloise might forget her nonsense and act like other people; but I verily believe she is bent upon encouraging this low fellow, whose principal charm in her bewildered eyes is his name.

"His name?" said I, "pray explain;" for I had not then learned all the boundless absurdity of this new Cherubina's fancies.

"Edward Dacre?" said my friend, "this is what enchants my sister, who is absolutely mad on the subject of her own homely appellation."

"Oh, is that all?" said I, "send her to me, then; and I engage to dismiss her cured."

And Miss Fidler came to spend the day. We talked of all novels without exception, and all poetry of all magazines, and Miss Fidler asked me if I had read the "Young Duke." Upon my confessing as much, she asked my opinion of the heroine, and then if I had ever heard so sweet a name. "May Dacre—May Dacre," she repeated, as if to solace her delighted ears.

"Only think how such names are murdered in this country," said I, tossing carelessly before her an account of Mr. Skinner's which bore, "Edkins Daker" below the receipt. I never saw a change equal to that which seemed to "come o'er the spirit of her dream." I went on with my citations of murdered names, telling how Rogers was turned into Rudgers, Conway into Coniway, and Montague into Montaig, but poor Miss Fidler was no longer in talking mood; and, long before the day was out, she complained of a head-ache and returned to her sister's. Mr. Daker found her "not at home" that evening; and when I called next morning, the young lady was in bed, steeping her long ringlets in tears, real tears.

To hasten to the catastrophe: it was discovered ere long that Mr. Edkins Daker's handsome face, and really pleasant manners, had fairly vanquished Miss Fidler's romance, and she had responded to his professions of attachment with a truth and sincerity, which while it vexed her family inexpressibly, seemed to me to atone for all her follies. Mr. Daker's prospects were by no means despicable, since a small capital employed in merchandize in Michigan, is very apt to confer upon the industrious and fortunate possessor that crowning charm, without which handsome faces, and even handsome names, are quite worthless in our Western eyes.

Some little disparity of age existed between Miss Fidler and her adorer; but this was conceded by all to be abundantly made up by the superabounding gentility of the lady; and when Mr. Daker returned from New-York with his new stock of goods and his stylish bride, I thought I had seldom seen a happier or better mated couple. And at this present writing, I do not believe Eloise, with all her whims, would exchange her very nice Edkins for the proudest Dacre of the British Peerage.

Chapter XXX.

Qu'ay je oublié? dere is some simples in my closet, dat I vill not for de varld I shall leave behind.

    ✳   ✳   ✳   ✳   ✳   ✳   ✳

Shal. The Council shall hear it: it is a riot.

Evans. It is petter that friends is the sword, and end it; and there is another device in my prain which, peradventure, prings goot discretions with it. . . . We will afterwards 'ork upon the cause with as great discreetly as we can.

                          Shakspeare.—*Merry Wives of Windsor.*

"Ah! who can tell how hard it is to" *say*—any thing about an unpretending village like ours, in terms suited to the delicate organization of "ears polite." How can one hope to find anything of interest about such common-place people? Where is the aristocratic distinction which makes the kind visit of the great lady at the sick-bed of suffering indigence so great a favour, that all the inmates of the cottage behave picturesquely out of gratitude—form themselves into *tableaux*, and make speeches worth recording? Here are neither great ladies nor humble cottagers. I cannot bring to my aid either the exquisite boudoir of the one class, with its captivating *bijouterie*—its velvet couches and its draperies of rose-coloured satin, so becoming to the complexions of one's young-lady characters—nor yet the cot of the other more simple but not less elegant, surrounded with clustering eglantine and clematis, and inhabited by goodness, grace, and beauty. These materials are denied me; but yet I must try to describe something of Michigan cottage life, taking care to avail myself of such delicate periphrasis as may best veil the true homeliness of my subject.

Moonlight and the ague are, however, the same every where. At least I meet with no description in any of the poets of my acquaintance which might not be applied, without reservation, to Michigan moonlight; and as for the ague, did not great Cæsar shake "when the fit was on him?"

T'is true, this god did shake:
His coward lips did from their colour fly—

And in this important particular poor Lorenzo Titmouse was just like the
inventor of the laurel crown. We—Mrs. Rivers and I—went to his
father's, at his urgent request, on just such a night as is usually chosen for
romantic walks by a certain class of lovers. We waited not for escort,
although the night had already fallen, and there was a narrow strip of
forest to pass in our way; but leaving word whither we had gone, we
accompanied the poor shivering boy, each carrying what we could. And
what does the gentle reader think we carried? A custard or a glass of jelly
each, perhaps; and a nice sponge-cake, or something equally delicate, and
likely to tempt the faint appetite of the invalid. No such thing. We had
learned better than to offer such nick-nacks to people who "a'n't us'd to
sweetnin'." My companion was "doubly arm'd:" a small tin pail of cran-
berry sauce in one hand, a bottle of vinegar in the other. I carried a
modicum of "hop 'east," and a little bag of crackers; a scrap of Hyson,
and a box of quinine pills. Odd enough; but we had been at such places
before.

We had a delicious walk; though poor Lorenzo, who had a bag of
flour on his shoulders, was fain to rest often. This was his "well day," to
be sure; but he had had some eight or ten fits of ague, enough to wither
any body's pith and marrow, as those will say who have tried it. That
innate politeness which young rustics, out of books as well as in them, are
apt to exhibit when they are in good humour, made Lorenzo decline,
most vehemently, our offers of assistance. But we at length fairly took his
bag from him, and passing a stick through the string, carried it between
us; while the boy disposed of our various small articles by the aid of his
capacious pockets. And a short half mile from the bridge brought us to
his father's.

It was an ordinary log house, but quite old and dilapidated: the great
open chimney occupying most of one end of the single apartment, and
two double-beds with a trundle-bed, the other. In one of the large beds
lay the father and the eldest son; in the other, the mother and two little
daughters, all ill with ague, and all sad and silent, save my friend Mrs.
Titmouse, whose untameable tongue was too much even for the ague.
Mrs. Titmouse is one of those fortunate beings who can talk all day
without saying any thing. She is the only person whom I have met in
these regions who appears to have paid her devoirs at Castle Blarney.

"How d'ye do, ladies,—how d'ye do? Bless my soul! if ever I thought
to be catch'd in sitch a condition, and by sich grand ladies too! Not a
chair for you to sit down on. I often tell Titmouse that we live jist like the
pigs; but he ha'n't no ambition. I'm sure I'm under a thousand compliments to ye for coming to see me. We're expecting a mother of his'n to
come and stay with us, but she ha'n't come yet—and I in sitch a condi-

tion; can't show ye no civility. Do sit down, ladies, if you *can* sit upon a chest—ladies like you. I'm sure I'm under a thousand compliments—" and so the poor soul ran on till she was fairly out of breath, in spite of our efforts to out-talk her with our assurances that we could accommodate ourselves very well, and could stay but a few minutes.

"And now, Mrs. Titmouse," said Mrs. Rivers, in her sweet, pleasant voice, "tell us what we can do for you."

"Do for me! Oh, massy! Oh, nothing, I thank ye. There a' n't nothing that ladies like you can do for me. We make out very well, and—"

"What do you say so for!" growled her husband from the other bed. "You know we ha'n't tasted a mouthful since morning, nor had n't it, and I sent Lorenzo myself—"

"Well, I never!" responded his help-mate; "you're always doing just so; troubling people. You never had no ambition, Titmouse; you know I always said so. To be sure, we ha'n't had no tea this good while, and tea *does* taste dreadful good when a body's got the agur; and my bread is gone, and I ha'n't been able to set no emptins; but——"

Here we told what we had brought, and prepared at once to make some bread; but Mrs. Titmouse seemed quite horrified, and insisted upon getting out of bed, though she staggered, and would have fallen if we had not supported her to a seat.

"Now tell *me* where the water is, and I will get it myself," said Mrs. Rivers, "and do you sit still and see how soon I will make a loaf."

"Water!" said the poor soul; "I'm afraid we have not water enough to make a loaf. Mr. Grimes brought us a barrel day before yesterday, and we've been dreadful careful of it, but the agur is so dreadful thirsty—I'm afraid there a' n't none."

"Have you no spring?"

"No, ma'am; but we have always got plenty of water down by the *mash* till this dry summer."

"I should think that was enough to give you the ague. Do n't you think the marsh water unwholesome?"

"Well, I do n't know but it is; but you see *he* was always a-going to dig a well; but he ha' n't no ambition, nor never had, and I always told him so. And as to the agur, if you've got to have it, why you can't get clear of it."

There was, fortunately, water enough left in the barrel to set the bread and half-fill the tea-kettle; and we soon made a little blaze with sticks, which served to boil the kettle to make that luxury of the woods, a cup of green tea.

Mrs. Titmouse did not need the tea to help her talking powers, for she was an independent talker, whose gush of words knew no ebb nor exhaustion.

> Alike to her was tide or time,
> Moonless midnight or matin prime.

Her few remaining teeth chattered no faster when she had the ague than at any other time. The stream flowed on

In one weak, washy, everlasting flood.

When we had done what little we could, and were about to depart, glad to escape her overwhelming protestations of eternal gratitude, her husband reminded her that the cow had not been milked since the evening before, when "Miss Grimes" had been there. Here was a dilemma! How we regretted our defective education, which prevented our rendering so simple yet so necessary a service to the sick poor.

We remembered the gentleman who did not know whether he could read Greek, as he had never tried; and set ourselves resolutely at work to ascertain our powers in the milking line.

But alas! the "milky mother of the herd" had small respect for timid and useless town ladies.

Crummie kick'd, and Crummie flounced,
And Crummie whisk'd her tail.

In vain did Mrs. Rivers hold the pain with both hands, while I essayed the arduous task. So sure as I succeeded in bringing ever so tiny a stream, the ill-mannered beast would almost put out my eyes with her tail, and oblige us both to jump up and run away; and after a protracted strug-gle,the cow gained the victory, as might have been expected, and we were fain to retreat into the house.

The next expedient was to support Mrs. Titmouse on the little bench, while she tried to accomplish the mighty work; and having been partially successful in this, we at length took our leave, promising aid for the morrow, and hearing the poor woman's tongue at intervals till we were far in the wood.

"Lord bless ye! I'm sure I'm under an everlastin' compliment to ye; I wish I know'd how I could pay ye. Such ladies to be a waitin' on the likes of me; I'm sure I never see nothing like it," &c. &c.

And now we began to wonder how long it would be before we should see our respected spouses, as poor Lorenzo had fallen exhausted on the bed, and was in no condition to see us even a part of the way home. The wood was very dark, though we could see glimpses of the mill-pond lying like liquid diamonds in the moonlight.

We had advanced near the brow of the hill which descends toward the pond, when strange sounds met our ears. Strange sounds for our peaceful village! Shouts and howling—eldrich screams—Indian yells—the braying of tin horns, and the violent clashing of various noisy articles.

We hurried on, and soon came in sight of a crowd of persons, who seemed coming from the village to the pond. And now loud talking, threats—"Duck him! duck the impudent rascal!" what could it be?

Here was a mob! a Montacute mob! and the cause? I believe all mobs pretend to have causes. Could the choice spirits have caught an abolitionist? which they thought, as I had heard, meant nothing less than a monster.

But now I recollected having heard that a ventriloquist, which I believe most of our citizens considered a beast of the same nature, had sent notices of an exhibition for the evening; and the truth flashed upon us at once.

"In with him! in with him!" they shouted as they approached the water, just as we began to descend the hill. And then the clear fine voice of the dealer in voice was distinctly audible above the hideous din—

"Gentlemen, I have warned you; I possess the means of defending myself, you will force me to use them."

"Stop his mouth," shouted a well-known bully, "he lies; he ha' n't got nothing! in with him!" and a violent struggle followed, some few of our sober citizens striving to protect the stranger.

One word to Mrs. Rivers, and we set up a united shriek, a screech like an army of sea-gulls. "Help! help!" and we stopped on the hill-side, our white dresses distinctly visible in the clear, dazzling moonlight.

We "stinted not nor staid" till a diversion was fairly effected. A dozen forms seceded at once from the crowd, and the spirit of the thing was at an end.

We waited on the spot where our artifice began, certain of knowing every individual who should approach; and the very first proved those we most wished to see. And now came the very awkward business of explaining our *ruse*, and Mrs. Rivers was rather sharply reproved for *her* part of it. Harley Rivers was not the man to object to any thing like a *lark*, and he had only attempted to effect the release of the ventriloquist, after Mr. Clavers had joined him on the way to Mr. Titmouse's. The boobies who had been most active in the outrage, would fain have renewed the sport; but the ventriloquist had wisely taken advantage of our diversion in his favour, and was no where to be found. The person at whose house he had put up told afterwards that he had gone out with loaded pistols in his pocket; so even a woman's shrieks, hated of gods and men, may sometimes be of service.

Montacute is far above mobbing now. This was the first and last exhibition of the spirit of the age. The most mobbish of our neighbours have flitted westward, seeking more congenial association. I trust they may be so well satisfied that they will not think of returning; for it is not pleasant to find a dead pig in one's well, or a favourite dog hung up at the gate-post; to say nothing of cows milked on the marshes, hen-roosts rifled, or melon-patches cleared in the course of the night.

We learned afterwards the "head and front" of the ventriloquist's offence. He had asked twenty-five cents a-head for the admission of the sovereign people.

CHAPTER XLIII.

On ne doit pas juger du merite d'un homme par ses grandes
qualités, mais par l'usage qu'il en sait faire.
       . Rochefoucault.

Des mots longs d'une toise,
De grands mots qui tiendroient d'ici jusqu' à Pontoise
       Racine.—*Les Plaideurs.*

But what he chiefly valued himself on, was his knowledge of
metaphysics, in which, having once upon a time ventured too
deeply, he came well nigh being smothered in a slough of unintelligible learning.
       W. Irving.—*Knickerbocker.*

MR. SIMEON JENKINS entered at an early stage of his career upon the
arena of public life, having been employed by his honoured mother to
dispose of a basket full of hard-boiled eggs, on election day, before he was
eight years old. He often dwells with much unction upon this his debût;
and declares that even at that dawning period, he had cut his eye-teeth.

"There was n't a feller there," Mr. Jenkins often says, "that could find
out which side I was on, for all they tried hard enough. They thought I
was soft, but I let 'em know I was as much baked as any on 'em. 'Be you a
dimocrat?' says one. Buy some eggs and I'll tell ye, says I; and by the
time he'd bought his eggs, I could tell well enough which side *he* belonged to, and I'd hand him out a ticket according, for I had blue ones in
one end o' my basket, and white ones in the other, and when night come,
and I got off the stump to go home, I had eighteen shillin' and four pence
in my pocket."

From this auspicious commencement may be dated Mr. Jenkins' glowing desire to serve the public. Each successive election day saw him at his
post. From eggs he advanced to pies, from pies to almanacs, whiskey,
powder and shot, foot-balls, playing-cards, and at length, for ambition
ever "did grow with what it fed on," he brought into the field a large
turkey, which was tied to a post and stoned to death at twenty-five cents a
throw. By this time the still youthful aspirant had become quite the man
of the world; could smoke twenty four cigars per diem, if any body else
would pay for them; play cards, in old Hurler's shop, from noon till daybreak, and rise winner; and all this with suitable trimmings of gin and
hard words. But he never lost sight of the main chance. He had made up
his mind to serve his country, and he was all this time convincing his
fellow-citizens of the disinterested purity of his sentiments.

"Patriotism," he would say, "patriotism is the thing! any man that's
too proud to serve his country aint fit to live. Some thinks so much o'
themselves, that if they can't have just what they think they're fit for, they
wont take nothing; but for my part, *I* call myself an American citizen;
and any office that's in the gift o' the people will suit *me*. I'm up to any

thing. And as there aint no other man about here,—no suitable man, I mean—that's got a horse, why I'd be willing to be constable, if the people's a mind to, though it would be a dead loss to me in my business, to be sure; but I could do any thing for my country. Hurra for patriotism! them's my sentiments."

It can scarcely be doubted that Mr. Jenkins became a very popular citizen, or that he usually played a conspicuous part at the polls. Offices began to fall to his share, and though they were generally such as brought more honour than profit, office is office, and Mr. Jenkins did not grumble. Things were going on admirably.

> The spoils of office glitter in his eyes,
> He climbs, he pants, he grasps them—

Or thought he was just going to grasp them, when, presto! he found himself in the minority; the wheel of fortune turned, and Mr. Jenkins and his party were left undermost. Here was a dilemma! His zeal in the public service was ardent as ever, but how could he get a chance to show it unless his party was in power? His resolution was soon taken. He called his friends together, mounted a stump, which had fortunately been left standing not far from the door of his shop, and then and there gave "reasons for my ratting" in terms sublime enough for any meridian.

"My friends and feller-citizens," said this self-sacrificing patriot, "I find myself conglomerated in sich a way, that my feelin's suffers severely. I'm sitivated in a peculiar sitivation. O' one side, I see my dear friends, pussonal friends—friends, that's stuck to me like wax, through thick and thin, never shinnyin' off and on, but up to the scratch, and no mistake. O' t' other side I behold my country, my bleedin' country, the land that fetch'd me into this world o' trouble. Now, sence things be as they be, and can't be no otherways as I see, I feel kind o' screwed into an au-gerhold to know what to do. If I hunt over the history of the universal world from the creation of man to the present day, I see that men has always had difficulties; and that some has took one way to get shut of 'em, and some another. My candid and unrefragable opinion is, that rather than remain useless, buckled down to the shop, and indulging in selfishness, it is my solemn dooty to change my ticket. It is severe, my friends, but dooty is dooty. And now, if any man calls me a turn-coat," continued the orator, gently spitting in his hands, rubbing them together, and rolling his eyes round the assembly, "all I say is, let him say it so that I can hear him."

The last argument was irresistible, if even the others might have brooked discussion, for Mr. Jenkins stands six feet two in his stockings, when he wears any, and gesticulates with a pair of arms as long and muscular as Rob Roy's. So, though the audience did not cheer him, they contented themselves with dropping off one by one, without calling in question the patriotism of the rising statesman.

The very next election saw Mr. Jenkins justice of the peace, and it was in this honourable capacity that I have made most of my acquaintance with him, though we began with threatenings of a storm. He called to take the acknowledgement of a deed, and I, anxious for my country's honour, for I too am something of a patriot in my own way, took the liberty of pointing out to his notice a trifling slip of the pen; videlicet, "Justas of Piece," which manner of writing those words I informed him had gone out of fashion.

He reddened, looked at me very sharp for a moment, and then said he thanked me; but subjoined,

"Book-learning is a good thing enough where there aint too much of it. For my part, I've seen a good many that know'd books that did n't know much else. The proper cultivation and edication of the human intellect, has been the comprehen*sive* study of the human understanding from the original creation of the universal world to the present day, and there has been a good many ways tried besides book-learning. Not but what that's very well in its place."

And the justice took his leave with somewhat of a swelling air. But we are excellent friends, notwithstanding this hard rub; and Mr. Jenkins favours me now and then with half an hour's conversation, when he has had leisure to read up for the occasion in an odd volume of the Cyclopedia, which holds an honoured place in the corner of his shop. He ought, in fairness, to give me previous notice, that I might study the dictionary a little, for the hard words with which he arms himself for these "keen encounters," often push me to the very limits of my English.

I ought to add, that Mr. Jenkins has long since left off gambling, drinking, and all other vices of that class, except smoking; in this point he professes to be incorrigible. But as his wife, who is one of the nicest women in the world, and manages him admirably, pretends to like the smell of tobacco, and takes care never to look at him when he disfigures her well-scoured floor, I am not without hopes of his thorough reformation.

CHAPTER XLVI.

> Go with speed
> To some forlorn and naked hermitage,
> Remote from all the pleasures of the world;
> There stay until the twelve celestial signs
> Have brought about their annual reckoning.
> If this austere, insociable life—
> If frosts and fasts, hard lodging and thin weeds
> Nip not the gaudy blossoms of your *pride*—
>
> *Love's Labour Lost.*

> They wear themselves in the cap of time there; do muster
> true gait, eat, speak, and move, under the influence of the most
> received star; and though the devil lead the measure, such are to
> be followed.—*All's well that ends well.*

One must come quite away from the conveniences and refined indulgences of civilized life to know any thing about them. To be always inundated with comforts, is but too apt to make us proud, selfish, and ungrateful. The mind's health, as well as the body's, is promoted by occasional privation or abstinence. Many a sour-faced grumbler I wot of, would be marvellously transformed by a year's residence in the woods, or even in a Michigan village of as high pretensions as Montacute. If it were not for casting a sort of dishonour on a country life, turning into a magnificent "beterinhaus" these

> "Haunts of deer,
> And lanes in which the primrose ere her time
> Peeps through the moss."

I should be disposed to recommend a course of Michigan to the Sybarites, the puny exquisites, the world-worn and sated Epicureans of our cities. If I mistake not, they would make surprising advances in philosophy in the course of a few months' training. I should not be severe either. I should not require them to come in their strictly natural condition as featherless bipeds. I would allow them to bring many a comfort—nay, even some real luxuries; books, for instance, and a reasonable supply of New-York Safety-Fund notes, the most tempting form which "world's gear" can possibly assume for our western, wild-cat wearied eyes. I would grant to each Neophyte a ready-made loggery, a garden fenced with tamarack poles, and every facility and convenience which is now enjoyed by the better class of our settlers, yet I think I might after all hope to send home a reasonable proportion of my subjects completely cured, sane for life.

I have in the course of these detached and desultory chapters, hinted at various deficiencies and peculiarities, which strike, with rather unpleasant force, the new resident in the back-woods; but it would require volumes to enumerate all the cases in which the fastidiousness, the taste, the pride, the self-esteem of the refined child of civilization, must be wounded by a familiar intercourse with the persons among whom he will find himself thrown, in the ordinary course of rural life. He is continually reminded in how great a variety of particulars his necessities, his materials for comfort, and his sources of pain, are precisely those of the humblest of his neighbours. The humblest, did I say? He will find that he has no humble neighbours. He will very soon discover, that in his new sphere, no act of kindness, no offer of aid, will be considered as any thing short of insult, if the least suspicion of *condescension* peep out. Equality, perfect and practical, is the *sine qua non;* and any appearance of a desire to avoid this rather trying fraternization, is invariably met by a fierce and indignant resistance. The spirit in which was conceived the motto of the French revolution, "La fraternité ou la mort," exists in full force among us, though modified as to results. In cities we bestow charity—in the country we can only exchange kind offices, nominally at least. If you are perfectly well aware that your nearest neighbour has not tasted meat in a month, nor found in his pocket the semblance of a shilling to purchase it, you must not be surprised, when you have sent him a piece, to receive for reply,

"Oh! your pa wants to *change,* does he? Well, you may put it down." And this without the remotest idea that the time for repayment ever will arrive, but merely to avoid saying, "I thank you," a phrase especially eschewed, so far as I have had opportunity to observe.

This same republican spirit is evinced rather amusingly, in the reluctance to admire, or even to approve, any thing like luxury or convenience which is not in common use among the settlers. Your carpets are spoken of as "*one* way to hide dirt;" your mahogany tables, as "dreadful plaguy to scour;" your kitchen conveniences, as "lumberin' up the house for nothin';" and so on to the end of the chapter. One lady informed me, that if she had such a pantry full of "dishes," under which general term is included every variety of china, glass and earthenware, she should set up store, and "sell them off pretty quick," for she would not "be plagued with them." Another, giving a slighting glance at a French mirror of rather unusual dimensions, larger by two-thirds, I verily believe, than she had ever seen, remarked, "that would be quite a nice glass, if the frame was done over."

Others take up the matter reprovingly. They "do n't think it right to spend money so;" they think too, that "pride never did nobody no good;" and some will go so far as to suggest modes of disposing of your superfluities.

"Any body that's got so many dresses, might afford to give away half on 'em;" or, "I should think you'd got so much land, you might give a poor man a lot, and never miss it." A store of any thing, however simple or necessary, is, as I have elsewhere observed, a subject of reproach, if you decline supplying whomsoever may be deficient.

This simplification of life, this bringing down the transactions of daily intercourse to the original principles of society, is neither very eagerly adopted, nor very keenly relished, by those who have been accustomed to the politer atmospheres. They rebel most determinedly, at first. They perceive that the operation of the golden rule, in circumstances where it is all *give* on one side, and all *take* on the other, must necessarily be rather severe; and they declare manfully against all impertinent intrusiveness. But, sooth to say, there are in the country so many ways of being made uncomfortable by one's most insignificant enemy, that it is soon discovered that warfare is even more costly than submission.

And all this forms part of the schooling which I propose for my spoiled child of refined civilization. And although many of these remarks and requisitions of our unpolished neighbours are unreasonable and absurd enough, yet some of them commend themselves to our better feelings in such a sort, that we find ourselves ashamed to refuse what it seemed at first impertinent to ask; and after the barriers of pride and prejudice are once broken, we discover a certain satisfaction in this homely fellowship with our kind, which goes far towards repaying whatever sacrifices or concessions we may have been induced to make. This has its limits of course; and one cannot help observing that "levelling upwards" is much more congenial to "human natur'," than levelling downwards. The man who thinks you ought to spare him a piece of ground for a garden, because you have more than he thinks you need, would be far from sharing with his poorer neighbour the superior advantages of his lot. He would tell him to work for them as *he* had done.

But then there are, in the one case, some absolute and evident superfluities, according to the primitive estimate of these regions; in the other, none. The doll of Fortune, who may cast a languid eye on this homely page, from the luxurious depths of a velvet-cushioned library-chair, can scarce be expected to conceive how natural it may be, for those who possess nothing beyond the absolute requisites of existence, to look with a certain degree of envy on the extra comforts which seem to cluster round the path of another; and to feel as if a little might well be spared, where so much would still be left. To the tenant of a log-cabin whose family, whatever be its numbers, must burrow in a single room, while a bed or two, a chest, a table, and a wretched handful of cooking utensils, form the chief materials of comfort, an ordinary house, small and plain it may be, yet amply supplied, looks like the very home of luxury. The woman who owns but a suit a-piece for herself and her children, considers the possession of an abundant though simple and inexpensive wardrobe, as needless extravagance; and we must scarcely blame her too severely, if she should be disposed to condemn as penurious, any reluctance to supply her pressing need, though she may have no shadow of claim on us beyond that which arises from her being a daughter of Eve. We look at the matter from opposite points of view. *Her* light shows her very plainly, as she thinks, what is *our* Christian duty; we must take care that ours does not exhibit too exclusively her envy and her impertinence.

The inequalities in the distribution of the gifts of fortune are not greater in the country than in town, but the contrary; yet circumstances render them more offensive to the less-favoured class. The denizens of the crowded alleys and swarming lofts of our great cities see, it is true, the lofty mansions, the splendid equipages of the wealthy—but they are seldom or never brought into contact or collision with the owners of these glittering advantages. And the extreme width of the great gulf between, is almost a barrier, even to all-reaching envy. But in the ruder stages of society, where no one has yet begun to expend any thing for show, the difference lies chiefly in the ordinary requisites of comfort; and this comes home at once "to men's business and bosoms." The keenness of their appreciation, and the strength of their envy, bear a direct proportion to the *real* value of the objects of their desire; and when they are in habits of entire equality and daily familiarity with those who own ten or twenty times as much of the *matériel* of earthly enjoyment as themselves, it is surely natural, however provoking, that they should not be studious to veil their longings after a share of the good, which has been so bounteously showered upon their neighbours.

I am only making a sort of apology for the foibles of my rustic friends. I cannot say that I feel much respect for any thing which looks like a willingness to live at others' cost, save as a matter of the last necessity.

I was adverting to a certain unreservedness of communication on these points, as often bringing wholesome and much-needed instruction home to those whom prosperity and indulgence may have rendered unsympathizing, or neglectful of the kindly feelings which are among the best ornaments of our nature.

But I am aware that I have already been adventurous, far beyond the bounds of prudence. To hint that it may be better not to cultivate *too* far that haughty spirit of exclusiveness which is the glory of the fashionable world, is, I know, hazardous in the extreme. I have not so far forgotten the rules of the sublime *clique* as not to realize, that in acknowledging even a leaning toward the "vulgar" side, I place myself forever beyond its pale. But I am now a denizen of the wild woods—in my view, "no mean city" to own as one's home; and I feel no ambition to aid in the formation of a Montacute aristocracy, for which an ample field is now open, and all the proper materials are at hand. What lack we? Several of us have as many as three cows; some few, carpets and shanty-kitchens; and one or two, piano-fortes and silver tea-sets. I myself, as *dame de la seigneurie*, have had secret thoughts of an astral lamp! but even if I should go so far, I am resolved not to be either vain-glorious or over-bearing, although this kind of superiority forms the usual ground for exclusiveness. I shall visit my neighbours just as usual, and take care not to say a single word about dipped candles, if I can possibly help it.

LYDIA MARIA CHILD

(1802–1880)

Letters from New York

(New York: C. S. Francis), 1843.

Lydia Maria Francis Child, the youngest of the six children of Susanna
Rand and David Convers Francis, was born in Medford, Massachusetts,
on February 11, 1802. Her father was a baker, and of her mother, according to Thomas Wentworth Higginson, "it is only recorded that she
had a simple, loving heart, and a spirit busy in doing good' " (Higginson, p. 39). Child's early formal education consisted of attendance at a
local dame school, followed by one year at a local female seminary. Her
far more influential informal education included conversation and, later,
correspondence with her older brother, Convers Francis, who entered
Harvard when Child was still quite young. In 1814, Child's mother
died. Bored with the education offered by the female seminary and
lonely at home, Child accepted an invitation to live with an older married sister in Norridgewock, Maine. Here she had access to her brother-
in-law's library and she enrolled in the local academy, staffed by
students on leave from Bowdoin.

   Although, like Catharine Sedgwick, she worried about her lack of
system in reading and complained to Convers that she had "quickness of
perception, without profoundness of thought," Child nevertheless felt
sufficiently accomplished to move out of her sister's home in 1820 and
begin teaching school in Gardiner, Maine. The desire for independence
that motivated this act characterized Child throughout her life and
would prove the source of severe tensions between herself and an im-
practical husband.

   In 1824, her brother Convers, by then a Unitarian minister and just
recently married, invited Child to make her home with him in Watertown, Massachusetts, an offer that she gladly accepted, delighted with

159

the opportunities for intellectual stimulation provided by nearby Cambridge and Boston. Here she decided to be baptized in her brother's church and to take a new name for herself, adding Maria to the original Lydia. And here, in 1824 at the age of twenty-two, she wrote her first novel, *Hobomok, A Tale of Early Times.* In an old issue of the *North American Review* (April 1821), discovered in her brother's study, Child read a review of *Yamoyden,* a narrative poem about an Indian man married to a white woman and set in the period of King Philip's War (1675–76). The reviewer praised the poem for having demonstrated "the unequalled fitness of our early history for the purposes of a work of fiction," and went on to predict that "whoever in this country first attains the rank of a first rate writer of fiction . . . will lay his scene here." Inspired by the implicit challenge and practically given much of the material for her novel, Child finished the book quickly and signed it "By an American." Although primarily a study of puritan culture, *Hobomok* marks a significant moment in the history of American women's writing; appearing three years before Sedgwick's *Hope Leslie,* it represents an early expression of an ongoing concern for the situation of Native Americans.

At least one reviewer found *Hobomok* to be in very bad taste because of its presentation of an interracial marriage, but on the whole the book was a popular and critical success and Child became a local celebrity. Acquisition of library privileges at the all-male Boston Athenaeum testified to her achievement. A second novel, *The Rebels, or Boston before the Revolution,* followed in 1825, but unable to make a living by her writing and still desirous of economic independence, she opened a school for girls in Watertown. Even more indicative of Child's energy, imagination, and determination, however, was her decision to produce the *Juvenile Miscellany,* the first periodical for children in the United States. The first issue appeared in September, 1826; most of its ninety pages were written by Child herself.

In 1828, despite the reservations of family and friends, Maria Francis married David Child, a Harvard graduate who had taught at the Boston Latin School, served as secretary of the American legation in Lisbon, fought briefly on the side of the Spanish revolutionary army against the French invasion in 1823, and returned to the United States to study law with an uncle in Watertown. To Maria, David's idealism made him a "knight," but to her "family and friends, Child appeared a latter-day Quixote who rushed ineffectually from one enthusiasm to the next. . . . His effect on business problems, Maria's family warned her, was about equal to 'cutting stones with a razor' " (Jeffrey, p. 114). In less than a year, the family judgment proved accurate; the Childs were in debt and Maria, reduced to a "state little short of insanity," was writing from painful personal experience books of practical advice for women such as *The Frugal Housewife* (1830). Designed as educational and economic aids for her readers, such works also offered Child the possibility of a significant and stable income by which to support herself and her husband.

Access to the library of the Boston Athenaeum gave Child the opportunity to pursue another educational scheme, this one also directed to women. The *Ladies' Family Library,* conceived primarily as a series of biographies of women, was intended to provide the contemporary reader with both information and exempla. Between 1832 and 1835, Child completed four volumes of the projected series, including the panoramic *History of the Condition of Women, in Various Ages and Nations* (1835), the source for much of Sarah Grimké's material in *Letters on the Equality of the Sexes* (1838). When her publishers went bankrupt, she dropped the project. By this time, however, her interest had taken a different direction. According to a later account, Child's meeting with William Lloyd Garrison changed her life: "He got hold of the strings of my conscience, and pulled me into Reforms. It is of no use to imagine what might have been, if I had never met him. Old dreams vanished, old associates departed, and all things became new" (Meltzer and Holland, p. 558). As a result of her connection with Garrison, Child, using the resources of the Athenaeum, researched and wrote *An Appeal in Favor of That Class of Americans Called Africans.* Published in 1833, it was one of the first American antislavery books and played a major role in converting others to the cause of abolition. It also converted Child into a "radical," whose works were no longer suitable for proper people to read. The Athenaeum revoked her library privileges, the sales of her books dwindled, and, in 1834, one year after publication of the *Appeal,* the *Juvenile Miscellany* failed for lack of subscribers.

During the next few years Child's commitment to the cause of abolition was sorely tried from another direction. In 1836, David left for a year abroad to study European methods of farming sugar beets. After his return, in the spring of 1838, the Childs moved to Northampton, Massachusetts to begin the experiment of farming beets in the North as a substitute for the cane sugar produced by slave labor in the South. According to all accounts, the years Child spent in Northampton were among the bleakest in her life. Cut off from Boston's social and intellectual life, isolated from the political world of the abolitionist movement, overwhelmed by the physical drudgery of farm work and housework, harassed by lack of money, she was understandably depressed. The opportunity to edit the *National Anti-Slavery Standard,* the weekly newspaper of the American Anti-Slavery Society, must have seemed an acceptable way out of a nearly intolerable situation. With David serving as assistant editor and sending articles from Northampton, Child moved to New York in May, 1841. The first issue of the *Standard* under her editorship appeared on May 21, 1841.

Letters from New York were written during Child's tenure as editor of the *Standard.* Originally designed for the *Boston Courier* and conceived as a source of income, Child was soon publishing her "letters" concurrently in the *Standard* and seeing them widely reprinted in other newspapers throughout the country. In 1843, Child published a selection of these "letters" in book form and at her own expense, because the firm that had originally agreed to publish them backed out at the last minute, fearing that the book's content would "prove offensive to the South" (Karcher, p. 21). Nevertheless, *Letters from New York* quickly sold out its first printing. In addition, critical response was positive; writing in the *Dial* for January, 1844, Margaret Fuller called the *Letters* "really, a contribution to *American* literature, recording in generous spirit, and with lively truth, the pulsations in one great centre of the national existence."

Child resigned as editor of the *Standard* in May of 1843. Tired of the internal struggles and sectarian nature of the abolitionist movement, she declared in her final editorial, "I am too distinctly and decidedly an individual, to edit the organ of any association." Henceforth she determined to devote herself to "the attainment of literary excellence," and to rebuilding her literary reputation. *Letters from New York* was intended to serve as her "letter of [re] introduction to the literary world" and thus she put considerable time and effort into the process of editing, revising, and selecting the material for this volume (Karcher, p. 10). She also determined to accomplish her goal of economic independence. Realizing that she could support herself by writing, she also realized that she could never be economically independent as long as her financial affairs were involved with David's. In June of 1843, she wrote to her financial advisor and manager, asking him to separate her income from her husband's and further declaring her intention of establishing her own residence in New York. David Child concurred in both of these decisions, and during the next few years they lived essentially apart. Child's literary career flourished during this period. In addition to numerous articles and stories for magazines and newspapers, she published a second series of *Letters from New York* (1845) and began work on her monumental *The Progress of Religious Ideas Through Successive Ages*, eventually published in 1855.

In the fall of 1849, David visited Maria in New York. The visit lasted several months, and, by the spring of 1850, they had decided to reunite. Returning to Massachusetts, the Childs lived first in West Newton on a farm owned by friends and, then, in 1853, they moved to Wayland to live with Maria's father. When he died in 1856, Child inherited the house and for the first time since the earliest days of her marriage she had a home of her own with some possibility of permanence. The Childs lived the remainder of their lives in Wayland.

The issue of slavery continued to break into Child's life and to shape her literary activity. After John Brown's raid on Harper's Ferry in 1859 and his subsequent arrest, Child wrote to Brown offering to nurse him in prison. She also wrote to the governor of Virginia, Henry Wise, requesting his permission to visit Brown. On November 12, without Child's knowledge, her correspondence with Governor Wise appeared in the *New York Tribune*. The publicity and controversy that attended this event inspired Child to further abolitionist writing, including the pamphlet, "The Right Way, The Safe Way" (1860), which urged immediate emancipation. In 1861, Child edited and arranged for the publication of Harriet Jacobs's *Incidents in the Life of a Slave Girl*. During this time she also organized relief projects to aid the "contrabands" (slaves fleeing the South into Union army camps), and she watched with particular interest the experiment at Port Royal, South Carolina, in which Charlotte Forten Grimké participated. In 1865, she published, primarily at her own expense, *The Freedmen's Book*, an anthology of poems, essays, and biographical sketches by and about black people. Designed for use as a reader in schools for the newly-freed slaves, Child meant it to offer encouragement through "this true record of what colored men have accomplished, under great disadvantages." Included among the selections were excerpts from Jacobs's *Incidents* and Grimké's "Life on the Sea Islands." Child donated the proceeds of this book, as well as those from her relatively successful *Looking Toward Sunset* (1865), to the relief of the "freedmen."

David Child died in 1874, and Child spent the rest of her life in Boston and Wayland. She died in Wayland on October 20, 1880, at the age of seventy-eight, and was buried there. A woman with a radical imagination, Child possessed as well extraordinary personal courage in acting on the dictates of that imagination. Her correspondence, as impressive a "work" as anything else she wrote, reveals a person who, while fully aware of the disability of being female in her culture, firmly believed she had both the right and the capacity to evaluate and effect the major events of her time. Writing late in life about Catharine Sedgwick, she indirectly defined herself: "I thank you for Miss Sedgwick's Memoirs. I will return the volume when read, as it is not a kind of book I care to keep. . . . She sincerely wished well to the negroes, but she could not bear to *contend* for them, or for anything else. She was afraid of the subject. She was very deficient in moral *courage*" (Meltzer and Holland, p. 506).

In *Letters from New York*, Child confronts the mid-nineteenth-century's eastern urban frontier, just as Caroline Kirkland in *A New Home* confronted its western rural frontier. Working in the same genre as Kirkland—that of the relatively informal "letter home"—Child developed a voice that was personal, conversational, and frank. She freely shares with the reader the full range of responses that "this great Babylon" evokes from her and shares as well her own internal conflicts as to what the city means. Frequently based on her rambles through the city, the letters themselves often duplicate these rambles. Exploiting the informality and consequent organizational looseness of the form she has chosen, Child is free to let her pen follow her mind and eye. In this context, digression becomes a meaningless concept, and coherence, integration, unity result from the developing perspective through which Child views the multiplicity of experience.

In *Letters from New York*, Child aligns herself with New York and identifies a preference for its Battery over the Boston Common. In New York, Child finds not only those traces of the Infinite so common to transcendental Boston thought, but also that density of detail that promises to ground her theory firmly in the practical and the real. Further, Child suggests that New York, not Boston, constitutes the essential fact that any theory of American character or of human nature must reckon with. In her first letter, she indicates the central perceptions that structure her response to New York: the violent contrasts between rich and poor, which reflect the greed and cruelty of human nature, "the World's contract with the Devil"; and the presence within the "noisy discord" of Babylon of moments of beauty (the musical cadence of a feminine voice, the poetry of the street cry), which reveal the Infinite behind the finite. The tension between these different perceptions produces pieces of varying tones. The form Child has chosen for communicating her vision enables her to modulate between tones with relative ease and protects her from a commitment to one extreme or another. Thus, when the "lines" threaten to cut too deep, she can draw back to her promise of "an airy unfinished sketch"; and when the promise to keep the "disagreeables" out of sight threatens to create a transcendental fantasy unattached to fact, she willingly breaks it "to speak of the dog-killers."

In the second letter, Child identifies more clearly the position from which she writes. Humorously aware that there are many points "on which most American juries would be prone to convict me of insanity," she establishes herself as an outsider to, as well as a participant in, her culture. Both critic and lover, she alternately endorses and despairs of her "great" nineteenth century. In reflecting on the Washington Temperance Society, Child articulates a position to which she will recur throughout the *Letters,* a position that might well draw a verdict of insanity from many American juries. For Child, the distinction between criminal and noncriminal disintegrates on analysis because she perceives that the very behavior that is rewarded in the rich and successful is punished in the poor and powerless. Furthermore, she rejects the notion of the "naturally" vicious and contends instead that whatever may be truly criminal is the product of society, not of individual human nature. In Letter 29 (not reprinted), which describes her visit to the prison on Blackwell's Island, she validates the "criminals'" perception that they are victims of chance, not justice, and asserts that they are right in feeling wronged:

> Of two young men nurtured under such influences, one becomes a successful merchant; five thousand dollars are borrowed of him; he takes a mortgage on a house worth twenty thousand dollars; in the absence of the owner, when sales are very dull, he offers the house for sale, to pay his mortgage; he bids it in himself, for four thousand dollars; and afterwards persecutes and imprisons his debtor for the remaining thousand. Society calls him a shrewd business man, and pronounces his dinners excellent; the chance is, he will be a magistrate before he dies. The other young man is unsuccessful; his necessities are great; he borrows some money from his employer's drawer, perhaps resolving to restore the same; the loss is discovered before he has a chance to refund it; and society sends him to Blackwell's Island, to hammer stone with highway robbers. Society made both these men thieves; but punished the one, while she rewarded the other.

Against the "Law of Chance," Child sets the "Law of Love," for her the only intelligent answer to the perversity of trying to overcome evil with evil and the only power capable of resolving the contradictions of nineteenth-century America. In the Washington Temperance Society, Child finds an example of this law in action and thus a source of optimism, for it may be able "to teach society that it *makes its own criminals.*"

Child misses the presence of women and children in the temperance parade because "without something to represent the genial influence of domestic life, the circle of joy and hope is ever incomplete." But in other letters, Child recognizes the fact that women could play a different role in the temperance tableau than that of the redemptive influence of domestic life. Female alcoholics also exist; in Letter 14, their misery constitutes a major chord in "the voice of human wo . . . destined to follow me through the whole of that unblest day." Her record of that day describes her effort to handle, indeed simply to survive, her anguished response to the sheer mass of human misery that a "crazy" like herself encounters at every corner. Setting out "for exercise merely," without much hope of finding a trace of that natural world that for her is "home," overwhelmed by the alienation and loneliness that characterize urban life and that both cause and aggravate the misery of the scene, she is soon driven back from this minor relief by the fact of human suffering, "hungry eyes . . . at last gone mute in still despair," the "frightful masks" through which the human soul looks forth, "leering, peeping, and defying." With no solution in sight beyond the individual dole, which Child's own relative poverty makes even more pitiful, the temptation to return, stay in, not see, and so not suffer is severe: "I wish I could walk abroad without having misery forced on my notice, which I have no power to relieve. . . . At times, I almost fancy I can feel myself turning to stone by inches" (Letter 28, not reprinted). No sentimentalist, however, Child readily perceives that there is no escape from her dilemma. The way of retreat is paved with pain, and even home itself offers no shelter. Although profoundly isolated by urban life, Child retains her sense of community with "strangers"; thus visions of despair will always await her on the streets of New York.

After the testimony of such unblessed days, we are not perhaps surprised to find Child responding almost positively to the experience of a "great fire." Child's fascination with the fire derives from her sense of its power to accomplish rapid and massive transformations. Her longing for such a transformation is clearly engendered by the experiences of her daily rambles and constitutes an alternate response and a possible solution to the horrors she has witnessed. As an emblem of transforming force, the first holds out the lure of a New York cleaned out, opened up, and ready for a fresh start on different and better principles. Child also construes the fire as an instrument for clarifying values. It can force people to identify the nature and source of true wealth, and it can force them to invest in realities, not abstractions. The fire itself is a great fact, and has thus a great beauty. Clarification of values is central to Child's enterprise in the *Letters*. In Letter 13 (not reprinted), she describes walking past a theatre that announces, in misspelled French, the performance of a comedy, "Valley de Sham," and she queries: "Is not that comedy New-York? Nay, is not the whole world a Valley of Sham? Are

not you, and I, and every other mortal, the 'valet' of some 'sham' or
other?"

Possibly the idea of progress is the biggest sham of all and the one
whose valet Child might most readily recognize herself to be. In Letter
31, Child records an event that tests the limits of her philosophy of the
"law of love" and shatters the possibility of any simple belief in the
myth of human progress. Indeed, "the savage customs of my time," in
this case, the spectacle of a public execution, specimens of which should
be "kept, as relics of a barbarous age," have "made me ashamed of belonging to the human species; and were it not that I struggled hard
against it, and prayed earnestly for a spirit of forgiveness, they would
have made me hate my race" (Letter 32, not reprinted). This appalling
event threatens to corrupt even Child herself who is "by nature tender-
hearted" and to pull her into the orbit of its own "infernal" emotions.
She can find no relief from this threat in the conventional assumption
that women are by nature exempt from such corruption, for this experience makes clear that women "can be taught murder by as short a lesson
as any man." Implicitly, Child exposes here the sham of nineteenth-century sexism; male "chivalry," equally an object of attack in Letter 34,
amounts, in this context, to nothing more than the refusal to allow
women to vent their blood lust as freely as men. This exposure fittingly
precedes her fuller discussion of "Women's Rights," for throughout the
Letters, Child's observant eye has consistently recorded how equal
women are before the law of chance.

Child ends this first volume of her Letters on a lighter note, though
even in the comedy of May Day moving she finds a fitting emblem of
her age, that nineteenth-century that alternately delights and plagues
her. Making a final effort to reconcile her ambivalent feelings, she concludes with her own vision of "manifold" destiny. The sources for
Child's final, if qualified, optimism can perhaps best be found in a
figure like Julia Pell, who commands Child's full respect and who mani-
fests the presence of that inward spirit in response to which the outward
world eventually will have to change. A black, a woman, and an artist—
emblematic of Child's vision of herself: "I have spoken in a language
which few understand, and none can teach or learn"—Julia Pell contains
the promise of that better future for which Child longs and works.

Source:

Letters from New York, third edition (New York: C. S. Francis), 1845.

Selected Primary Works:

Hobomok, 1824; The Frugal Housewife, 1830; An Appeal in Favor of That Class of
    Americans Called Africans, 1833; The History of the Condition of Women, in
    Various Ages and Nations, 1835; Philothea, 1836; Letters from New York,
    second series, 1845; The Progress of Religious Ideas through Successive Ages,
    1855; The Freedmen's Book, 1865.

Selected Secondary Works:

Helene G. Baer, The Heart is Like Heaven (Philadelphia: University of Pennsyl-
    vania Press), 1964; T. W. Higginson, "Lydia Maria Child," Eminent Women

of the Age (Hartford: S. M. Betts), 1868; Patricia G. Holland, "Lydia Maria Child as a Nineteenth-Century Professional Author," *Studies in the American Renaissance* (1981), 157–67; Kirk Jeffrey, "Marriage, Career, and Feminine Ideology in Nineteenth-Century America: Reconstructing the Marital Experience of Lydia Maria Child, 1828–1874," *Feminist Studies,* 2 (1974–75), 113–30; Carolyn Karcher, "Censorship, American Style: The Case of Lydia Maria Child," paper delivered at American Studies Association, Philadelphia, 1983; Milton Meltzer, *Tongue of Flame* (New York: Thomas Y. Crowell), 1965; *Lydia Maria Child: Selected Letters, 1817–1880,* ed. Milton Meltzer and Patricia G. Holland (Amherst: University of Massachusetts Press), 1982; William Osborne, *Lydia Maria Child* (Boston: Twayne), 1980; Lloyd C. Taylor, Jr., "Lydia Maria Child: Biographer," *New England Quarterly,* 34 (1961), 211–27; Ethel K. Ware, "Lydia Maria Child and Anti-Slavery," *Boston Public Library Quarterly,* 3 (1951), 251–75, and 4 (1952), 34–49; *Letters of Lydia Maria Child,* ed. John Greenleaf Whittier (Boston: Houghton, Mifflin), 1883.

Contexts:

1840—Cooper, *The Pathfinder;* Dana, *Two Years Before the Mast;* Poe, *Tales of the Grotesque and Arabesque; Dial; Lowell Offering; National Anti-Slavery Standard*

1841—Beecher, *A Treatise on Domestic Economy;* Cooper, *The Deerslayer;* Emerson, *Essays,* first series; Sigourney, *Pocahantas and Other Poems;* Brook Farm

1842—Hawthorne, *Twice-Told Tales;* Griswold, *The Poets and Poetry of America;* Kirkland, *Forest Life*

1843—Fuller, "The Great Lawsuit"; Prescott, *The Conquest of Mexico;* Smith, "The Sinless Child"; Stephens, *High Life in New York;* Stowe, *The Mayflower: or, Sketches of Scenes and Characters among the Descendants of the Puritans*

1844—Emerson, *Essays,* second series; Fuller, *Summer on The Lakes*

1845—Douglass, *Narrative of The Life of Frederick Douglass;* Fuller, *Woman in the Nineteenth Century;* Kirkland, *Western Clearings;* Poe, *The Raven and Other Poems, Tales*

LETTER I.

August 19, 1841.

YOU ASK WHAT is now my opinion of this great Babylon; and playfully remind me of former philippics, and a long string of vituperative alliterations, such as magnificence and mud, finery and filth, diamonds and dirt, bullion and brass-tape, &c. &c. Nor do you forget my first impression of the city, when we arrived at early dawn, amid fog and drizzling rain, the expiring lamps adding their smoke to the impure air, and close beside us a boat called the 'Fairy Queen,' laden with dead hogs.

Well, Babylon remains the same as then. The din of crowded life, and the eager chase for gain, still run through its streets, like the perpetual murmur of a hive. Wealth dozes on French couches, thrice piled, and canopied with damask, while Poverty camps on the dirty pavement, or sleeps off its wretchedness in the watch-house. There, amid the splendour of Broadway, sits the blind negro beggar, with horny hand and tattered garments, while opposite to him stands the stately mansion of the slave trader, still plying his bloody trade, and laughing to scorn the cobweb laws, through which the strong can break so easily.

In Wall-street, and elsewhere, Mammon, as usual, coolly calculates his chance of extracting a penny from war, pestilence, and famine; and Commerce, with her loaded drays, and jaded skeletons of horses, is busy as ever fulfilling the 'World's contract with the Devil.' The noisy discord of the street-cries gives the ear no rest; and the weak voice of weary childhood often makes the heart ache for the poor little wanderer, prolonging his task far into the hours of night. Sometimes, the harsh sounds are pleasantly varied by some feminine voice, proclaiming in musical cadence, 'Hot corn! hot corn!' with the poetic addition of 'Lily white corn! Buy my lily white corn!' When this sweet, wandering voice salutes my ear, my heart replies—

> 'Tis a glancing gleam o' the gift of song—
> And the soul that speaks hath suffered wrong.

There *was* a time when all these things would have passed by me like the flitting figures of the magic lantern, or the changing scenery of a theatre, sufficient for the amusement of an hour. But now, I have lost the power of looking merely on the surface. Every thing seems to me to come from the Infinite, to be filled with the Infinite, to be tending toward the Infinite. Do I see crowds of men hastening to extinguish a fire? I see not merely uncouth garbs, and fantastic flickering lights of lurid hue, like a tramping troop of gnomes,—but straightway my mind is filled with thoughts about mutual helpfulness, human sympathy, the common bond of brotherhood, and the mysteriously deep foundations on which society rests; or rather, on which it now reels and totters.

But I am cutting the lines deep, when I meant only to give you an airy, unfinished sketch. I will answer your question, by saying, that though New-York remains the same, I like it better. This is partly because I am like the Lady's Delight, ever prone to take root, and look up with a smile, in whatever soil you place it; and partly because bloated disease, and black gutters, and pigs uglier than their ugly kind, no longer constitute the foreground in my picture of New-York. I have become more familiar with the pretty parks, dotted here and there; with the shaded alcoves of the various public gardens; with blooming nooks, and 'sunny spots of greenery.' I am fast inclining to the belief, that the Battery rivals our beautiful Boston Common. The fine old trees are indeed wanting; but the newly-planted groves offer the light, flexile gracefulness of youth, to compete with their matured majesty of age. In extent, and variety of surface, this noble promenade is greatly inferior to ours; but there is

> 'The sea, the sea, the open sea;
> The fresh, the bright, the ever free.

Most fitting symbol of the Infinite, this trackless pathway of a world! heaving and stretching to meet the sky it never reaches—like the eager, unsatisfied aspirations of the human soul. The most beautiful landscape is imperfect without this feature. In the eloquent language of Lamartine— 'The sea is to the scenes of nature what the eye is to a fine countenance; it illuminates them, it imparts to them that radiant physiognomy, which makes them live, speak, enchant, and fascinate the attention of those who contemplate them.'

If you deem me heretical in preferring the Battery to the Common, consecrated by so many pleasant associations of my youth, I know you will forgive me, if you will go there in the silence of midnight, to meet the breeze on your cheek, like the kiss of a friend; to hear the continual plashing of the sea, like the cool sound of oriental fountains; to see the moon look lovingly on the sea-nymphs, and throw down wealth of jewels on their shining hair; to look on the ships in their dim and distant beauty, each containing within itself, a little world of human thought, and human passion. Or go, when 'night, with her thousand eyes, looks down into the heart, making it also great'—when she floats above us, dark and solemn, and scarcely sees her image in the black mirror of the ocean. The city lamps surround you, like a shining belt of descended constellations, fit for the zone of Urania; while the pure bright stars peep through the dancing foliage, and speak to the soul of thoughtful shepherds on the ancient plains of Chaldea. And there, like mimic Fancy, playing fantastic freaks in the very presence of heavenly Imagination, stands Castle Garden—with its gay perspective of coloured lamps, like a fairy grotto, where imprisoned fire-spirits send up sparkling wreaths, or rockets laden with glittering ear-drops, caught by the floating sea-nymphs, as they fall.

But if you would see the Battery in *all* its glory, look at it when, through the misty mantle of retreating dawn, is seen the golden light of the rising sun! Look at the horizon, where earth, sea, and sky, kiss each other, in robes of reflected glory! The ships stretch their sails to the coming breeze, and glide masjestically along—fit and graceful emblems of the Past; steered by Necessity; the Will constrained by outward Force. Quick as a flash, the steamboat passes them by—its rapidly revolving wheel made golden by the sunlight, and dropping diamonds to the laughing Nereides, profusely as pearls from Prince Esterhazy's embroidered coat. In that steamer, see you not an appropriate type of the busy, powerful, self-conscious Present? Of man's Will conquering outward Force; and thus making the elements his servants?

From this southern extremity of the city, anciently called 'The Wall of the Half-Moon,' you may, if you like, pass along the Bowery to Bloomingdale, on the north. What a combination of flowery sounds to take captive the imagination! It is a pleasant road, much used for fashionable drives; but the lovely names scarcely keep the promise they give the ear; especially to one accustomed to the beautiful environs of Boston.

During your ramble, you may meet wandering musicians. Perhaps a poor Tyrolese with his street-organ, or a Scotch lad, with shrill bag-pipe, decorated with tartan ribbons. Let them who will, despise their humble calling. Small skill, indeed, is needed to grind forth that machinery of sounds; but my heart salutes them with its benison, in common with all things that cheer this weary world. I have little sympathy with the severe morality that drove these tuneful idlers from the streets of Boston. They are to the drudging city, what Spring birds are to the country. This world has passed from its youthful, Troubadour Age, into the thinking, toiling Age of Reform. This we may not regret, because it needs must be. But welcome, most welcome all that brings back reminiscences of its childhood, in the cheering voice of poetry and song.

Therefore blame me not, if I turn wearily aside from the dusty road of reforming duty, to gather flowers in sheltered nooks, or play with gems in hidden grottoes. The Practical has striven hard to suffocate the Ideal within me; but it is immortal, and cannot die. It needs but a glance of Beauty from earth or sky, and it starts into blooming life, like the aloe touched by fairy wand.

LETTER II.

August 21, 1841.

You think my praises of the Battery exaggerated: perhaps they are so; but there are three points on which I am crazy—music, moonlight, and the sea. There are other points, greatly differing from these, on which most American juries would be prone to convict me of insanity. You know a New-York lawyer defined insanity to be 'a differing in opinion from the mass of mankind.' By this rule, I am as mad as a March hare; though, as Andrew Fairservice said, 'why a hare should be more mad in March than at Michaelmas, is more than I ken.'

I admit that Boston, in her extensive and airy Common, possesses a blessing unrivalled by any other city; but I am not the less disposed to be thankful for the circumscribed, but well-shaded, limits of the Washington Parade Ground, and Union Park, with its nicely-trimmed circle of hedge, its well-rolled gravel walks, and its velvet greensward, shaven as smooth as a Quaker beau. The exact order of its arrangement would be offensive in the country; and even here, the eye of taste would prefer variations, and undulation of outline; but trimness seems more in place in a city, than amid the graceful confusion of nature; and neatness has a charm in New-

York, by reason of its exceeding rarity. St. John's Park, though not with-out pretensions to beauty, never strikes my eye agreeably, because it is shut up from the people; the key being kept by a few genteel families in the vicinity. You know I am an enemy to monopolies; wishing all Heaven's good gifts to man to be as free as the wind, and as universal as the sunshine.

I like the various small gardens in New-York, with their shaded al-coves of lattice-work, where one can eat an ice-cream, shaded from the sun. You have none such in Boston; and they would probably be objected to, as open to the vulgar and the vicious. I do not walk through the world with such fear of soiling my garments. Let science, literature, music, flowers, all things that tend to cultivate the intellect, or humanize the heart, be open to 'Tom, Dick, and Harry;' and thus, in process of time, they will become Mr. Thomas, Richard, and Henry. In all these things, the refined should think of what they can *impart*, not of what they can *receive*.

As for the vicious, they excite in me more of compassion than dislike. The Great Searcher of Hearts alone knows whether I should not have been as they are, with the same neglected childhood, the same vicious examples, the same overpowering temptation of misery and want. If they will but pay to virtue the outward homage of decorum, God forbid that I should wish to exclude them from the healthful breeze, and the shaded promenade. Wretched enough are they in their utter degradation; nor is society so guiltless of their ruin, as to justify any of its members in unpitying scorn.

And this reminds me that in this vast emporium of poverty and crime, there are, *morally* speaking, some flowery nooks, and 'sunny spots of greenery.' I used to say, I knew not where were the ten righteous men to save the city; but I have found them now. Since then, the Washington Temperance Society has been organized, and active in good works. Apart from the physical purity, the triumph of soul over sense, implied in abstinence from stimulating liquors, these societies have peculiarly inter-ested me, because they are based on the Law of Love. The Pure is inlaid in the Holy, like a pearl set in fine gold. Here is no 'fifteen-gallon-law,' no attendance upon the lobbies of legislatures, none of the bustle or manoeuvres of political party; measures as useless in the moral world, as machines to force water above its level are in the physical world. Serenely above all these, stands this new Genius of Temperance; her trust in Heaven, her hold on the human heart. To the fallen and the perishing she throws a silken cord, and gently draws him within the golden circle of human brotherhood. She has learned that persuasion is mightier than coercion, that the voice of encouragement finds an echo in the heart deeper, far deeper, than the thunder of reproof.

The blessing of the perishing, and of the merciful God, who cares for them, will rest upon the Washington Temperance Society. A short time since, one of its members found an old acquaintance lying asleep in a dirty alley, scarcely covered with filthy rags, pinned and tied together. Being waked, the poor fellow exclaimed, in piteous tones, 'O, don't take me to the Police Office—Please don't take me there.' 'O, no,' replied the missionary of mercy; 'you shall have shoes to your feet, and a decent coat on your back, and be a Man again! We have better work for you to do, than to lie in prison. You will be a Temperance preacher yet.'

He was comfortably clothed, kindly encouraged, and employment procured for him at the printing office of the Washington Society. He now works steadily all day, and preaches temperance in the evening. Every week I hear of similar instances. Are not these men enough to save a city? This Society is one among several powerful agencies now at work, to teach society that it *makes its own criminals,* and then, at prodigious loss of time, money, and morals, punishes its own work.

The other day, I stood by the wayside while a Washingtonian procession, two miles long, passed by. All classes and trades were represented, with appropriate music and banners. Troops of boys carried little wells and pumps; and on many of the banners were flowing fountains and running brooks. One represented a wife kneeling in gratitude for a husband restored to her and himself; on another, a group of children were joyfully embracing the knees of a reformed father. Fire companies were there with badges and engines; and military companies, with gaudy colours and tinsel trappings. Toward the close, came two barouches, containing the men who first started a Temperance Society on the Washingtonian plan. These six individuals were a carpenter, a coach-maker, a tailor, a blacksmith, a wheelwright, and a silver-plater. They held their meetings in a carpenter's shop, in Baltimore, before any other person took an active part in the reform. My heart paid them reverence, as they passed. It was a beautiful pageant, and but one thing was wanting to make it complete; there should have been carts drawn by garlanded oxen, filled with women and little children, bearing a banner, on which was inscribed, WE ARE HAPPY NOW! I missed the women and the children; for without something to represent the genial influence of domestic life, the circle of joy and hope is ever incomplete.

But the absent ones were present to my mind; and the pressure of many thoughts brought tears to my eyes. I seemed to see John the Baptist preparing a pathway through the wilderness for the coming of the Holiest; for like unto his is this mission of temperance. Clean senses are fitting vessels for pure affections and lofty thoughts.

Within the outward form I saw, as usual, spiritual significance. As the bodies of men were becoming weaned from stimulating drinks, so were their souls beginning to approach those pure fountains of living water, which refresh and strengthen, but never intoxicate. The music, too, was revealed to me in fulness of meaning. Much of it was of a military character, and cheered onward to combat and to victory. Everything about war I loathe and detest, except its music. My heart leaps at the trumpet-call, and marches with the drum. Because I cannot ever hate it, I know that it is the utterance of something good, perverted to a ministry of sin. It is the voice of resistance to evil, of combat with the false; therefore the brave soul springs forward at the warlike tone, for in it is heard a call to its appointed mission. Whoso does not see that genuine life is a battle and a march, has poorly read his origin and his destiny. Let the trumpet sound, and the drums roll! Glory to resistance! for through its agency men become angels. The instinct awakened by martial music is noble and true; and therefore its voice will not pass away; but it will cease to represent war with carnal weapons, and remain a type of that spiritual combat, whereby the soul is purified. It is right noble to fight with wickedness and wrong; the mistake is in supposing that spiritual evil can be overcome by physical means.

Would that Force were banished to the unholy region, whence it came, and that men would learn to trust more fully in the law of kindness. I think of this, every time I pass a dozing old woman, who, from time immemorial, has sat behind a fruit stall at the corner of St. Paul's Church. Half the time she is asleep, and the wonder is that any fruit remains upon her board; but in this wicked city very many of the boys deposit a cent, as they take an apple: for *they have not the heart to wrong one who trusts them.*

A sea-captain of my acquaintance, lately returned from China, told me that the Americans and English were much more trusted by the natives, than their own countrymen; that the fact of belonging to those nations was generally considered good security in a bargain. I expressed surprise at this; not supposing the Yankees, or their ancestors, were peculiarly distinguished for generosity in trade. He replied, that they were more so in China than at home; because, in the absence of adequate laws, and legal penalties, they had acquired the habit of *trusting in each other's honour and honesty;* and this formed a bond so sacred, that few were willing to break it. I saw deep significance in the fact.

Speaking of St. Paul's Church, near the Astor House, reminds me of the fault so often found by foreigners with our light grey stone as a material for Gothic edifices. Though the church is not Gothic, I now understand why such buildings contrast disadvantageously with the dark-coloured cathedrals of Europe. St. Paul's has lately been covered with a cement of dark, reddish-brown sand. Some complain that it looks 'like gingerbread;' but for myself, I greatly like the depth of colour. Its steeple now stands relieved against the sky, with a sombre grandeur which would be in admirable keeping with the massive proportions of Gothic architecture. Grey and slate colour appropriately belong to lighter styles of building; applied to the Gothic they become like tragic *thoughts* uttered in mirthful *tones.*

The disagreeables of New-York, I deliberately mean to keep out of

sight, when I write to you. By contemplating beauty, the character becomes beautiful; and in this wearisome world, I deem it a duty to speak
genial words, and wear cheerful looks.

Yet for once, I will depart from this rule, to speak of the dog-killers.
Twelve or fifteen hundred of these animals have been killed this summer;
in the hottest of the weather at the rate of three hundred a day. The safety
of the city doubtless requires their expulsion; but the *manner* of it strikes
me as exceedingly cruel and demoralizing. The poor creatures are
knocked down on the pavement, and beat to death. Sometimes they are
horribly maimed, and run howling and limping away. The company of
dog-killers themselves are a frightful sight, with their bloody clubs, and
spattered garments. I always run from the window when I hear them; for
they remind me of the Reign of Terror. Whether such brutal scenes do not
prepare the minds of the young to take part in bloody riots and revolutions is a serious question.

You promised to take my letters as they happened to come—fanciful,
gay, or serious. I am in autumnal mood to-day, therefore forgive the
sobriety of my strain.

LETTER XI.

December 9, 1841.

A friend passing by the Methodist church in Elizabeth street, heard
such loud and earnest noises issuing therefrom, that he stepped in to
ascertain the cause. A coloured woman was preaching to a full audience,
and in a manner so remarkable that his attention was at once rivetted. The
account he gave excited my curiosity, and I sought an interview with the
woman, whom I ascertained to be Julia Pell, of Philadelphia. I learned
from her that her father was one of the innumerable tribe of fugitives
from slavery, assisted by that indefatigable friend of the oppressed,
Isaac T. Hopper. This was quite a pleasant surprise to the benevolent old
gentleman, for he was not aware that any of Zeek's descendants were
living; and it was highly interesting to him to find one of them in the
person of this female Whitfield. Julia never knew her father by the name
of Zeek; for that was his appellation in slavery, and she had known him
only as a freeman. Zeek, it seems, had been 'sold running,' as the term is;
that is, a purchaser had given a very small part of his original value, taking
the risk of not catching him. In Philadelphia a coloured man, named
Samuel Johnson, heard a gentleman making inquiries concerning a slave
called Zeek, whom he had 'bought running.' 'I know him very well,' said
Samuel; 'as well as I do myself; he's a good-for-nothing chap; and you'll
be better without him than with him.' 'Do you think so?' 'Yes; if you
gave what you say for him, it was a bite—that's all. He's a lazy, good-for-
nothing dog; and you'd better sell your right in him the first chance you
get.' After some further talk, Samuel acknowledged that Zeek was his

brother. The gentleman advised him to buy him; but Samuel protested that he was such a lazy, vicious dog, that he wanted nothing to do with him. The gentleman began to have so bad an opinion of his bargain, that he offered to sell the fugitive for sixty dollars. Samuel, with great apparent indifference, accepted the terms, and the necessary papers were drawn. Isaac T. Hopper was in the room during the whole transaction; and the coloured man requested him to examine the papers to see that all was right. Being assured that every thing was in due form, he inquired, 'And is Zeek now free?' 'Yes, entirely free.' 'Suppose I was Zeek, and that was the man that bought me; couldn't he take me?' 'Not any more than he could take me,' said Isaac. As soon as Samuel received this assurance, he made a low bow to the gentleman, and, with additional fun in a face always roguish, said, 'Your servant, sir; I am Zeek!" The roguishness characteristic of her father is reflected in some degree in Julia's intelligent face; but imagination, uncultivated, yet highly poetic, is her leading characteristic.

Some have the idea that our destiny is prophesied in early presentiments: thus, Hannah More, when a little child, used to play, 'Go up to London and see the bishops'—an object for which she afterwards sacrificed a large portion of her own moral independence and freedom of thought. In Julia Pell's case, 'coming events cast their shadows before.' I asked her when she thought she first 'experienced religion.' She replied, 'When I was a little girl, father and mother used to go away to meetings on Sundays, and leave me and my brothers at home all day. So, I thought I'd hold class-meetings as the Methodists did. The children all round in the neighbourhood used to come to hear me preach. The neighbours complained that we made such a noise, shouting and singing; and every Monday father gave us a whipping. At last, he said to mother, 'I'm tired of beating these poor children every week to satisfy our neighbours. I'll send for my sister to come, and she will stay at home on Sundays, and keep them out of mischief.' So my aunt was brought to take care of us; and the next Sunday, when the children came thronging to hear me preach, they were greatly disappointed indeed to hear me say, in a mournful way, 'We can't have any more meetings now; because aunt's come, and she won't let us.' When my aunt heard this, she seemed to pity me and the children; and she said if we would get through before the folks came home, we might hold a meeting; for she should like to see for herself what it was we did, that made such a fuss among the neighbours. Then we had a grand meeting. My aunt's heart was taken hold of that very day; and when we all began to sing, 'Come to the Saviour, poor sinner, come!' she cried, and I cried; and when we had done crying, the whole of us broke out singing 'Come to the Saviour.' That very instant I felt my heart leap up, as if a great load had been taken right off of it! That was the beginning of my getting religion; and for many years after that, I saw all the time a blue smoke rising before my eyes—the whole time a blue smoke rising, rising.' As she spoke, she imitated the ascent of smoke, by a graceful, undulating motion of her hand.

'What do you suppose was the meaning of the blue smoke?' said I.

'I don't know, indeed, ma'am; but I always supposed it was my sins rising before me, from the bottomless pit.'

She told me that when her mother died, some years after, she called her to her bed-side, and said, 'Julia, the work of grace is only begun in you. You haven't got religion yet. When you can freely forgive all your enemies, and love to do them good, then you may know that the true work is completed within you.' I thought the wisest schools of theology could not have established a better test.

I asked Julia, if she had ever tried to learn to read. She replied, 'Yes, ma'am, I tried once; because I thought it would be such a convenience, if I could read the Bible for myself. I made good progress, and in a short time could spell B-a-k-e-r, as well as anybody. But it dragged my mind *down*. It dragged it *down*. When I tried to think, every thing scattered away like smoke, and I could do nothing but spell. Once I got up in an evening meeting to speak; and when I wanted to say, 'Behold the days come' I began 'B-a—.' I was dreadfully ashamed, and concluded I'd give up trying to learn to read.'

These, and several other particulars I learned of Julia, at the house of Isaac T. Hopper. When about to leave us, she said she felt moved to pray. Accordingly, we all remained in silence, while she poured forth a brief, but very impressive prayer for her venerable host; of whom she spoke as 'that good old man, whom thou, O Lord, hast raised up to do such a blessed work for my down-trodden people.'

Julia's quiet, dignified, and even lady-like deportment in the parlour, did not seem at all in keeping with what I had been told of her in the pulpit, with a voice like a sailor at mast-head, and muscular action like Garrick in Mad Tom. On the Sunday following, I went to hear her for myself; and in good truth, I consider the event as an era in my life never to be forgotten. Such an odd jumbling together of all sorts of things in Scripture, such wild fancies, beautiful, sublime, or grotesque, such vehemence of gesture, such dramatic attitudes, I never before heard and witnessed. I verily thought she would have leaped over the pulpit; and if she had, I was almost prepared to have seen her poise herself on unseen wings, above the wondering congregation.

I know not whether her dress was of her own choosing; but it was tastefully appropriate. A black silk gown, with plain, white cuffs; a white muslin kerchief, folded neatly over the breast, and crossed by a broad black scarf, like that which bishops wear over the surplice.

She began with great moderation, gradually rising in her tones, until she arrived at the shouting pitch, common with Methodists. This she sustained for an incredible time, without taking breath, and with a huskiness of effort, that produced a painful sympathy in my own lungs.

Imagine the following, thus uttered; that is, spoken without punctuation: 'Silence in Heaven! The Lord said to Gabriel, bid all the angels keep silence. Go up into the third heavens, and tell the archangels to hush their golden harps. Let the mountains be filled with silence. Let the sea stop its roaring, and the earth be still. What's the matter now? Why, man has sinned, and who shall save him? Let there be silence, while God makes search for a Messiah. Go down to the earth; make haste, Gabriel, and inquire if any there are worthy; and Gabriel returned and said, No, not one. Go search among the angels, Gabriel, and inquire if any there are worthy; make haste, Gabriel; and Gabriel returned and said, No, not one. But don't be discouraged. Don't be discouraged, fellow-sinners. God arose in his majesty, and he pointed to his own right hand, and said to Gabriel, Behold the Lion of the tribe of Judah; he alone is worthy. He shall redeem my people.'

You will observe it was purely her own idea, that silence reigned on earth and in heaven, while search was made for a Messiah. It was a beautifully poetic conception not unworthy of Milton.

Her description of the resurrection and the day of judgment, must have been terrific to most of her audience, and was highly exciting even to me, whose religious sympathies could never be roused by fear. Her figure looked strangely fantastic, and even supernatural, as she loomed up above the pulpit, to represent the spirits rising from their graves. So powerful was her rude eloquence, that it continually impressed me with grandeur, and once only excited a smile; that was when she described a saint striving to rise, 'buried perhaps twenty feet deep, with three or four sinners a top of him.'

This reminded me of a verse in Dr. Nettleton's Village Hymns:

> 'Oh how the resurrection light
> Will *clarify* believers' sight,
> How joyful will the saints arise,
> And *rub the dust* from off their eyes.'

With a power of imagination singularly strong and vivid, she described the resurrection of a young girl, who had died a sinner. Her body came from the grave, and her soul from the pit, where it had been tormented for many years. 'The guilty spirit came up with the flames all around it—rolling—rolling—rolling.' She suited the action to the word, as Siddons herself might have done. Then she described the body wailing and shrieking, 'O Lord! must I take that ghost again? Must I be tormented with that burning ghost for ever?'

Luckily for the excited feelings of her audience, she changed the scene, and brought before us the gospel ship, laden with saints, and bound for the heavenly shore. The majestic motion of a vessel on the heaving sea, and the fluttering of its pennon in the breeze, was imitated with wild gracefulness by the motion of her hands. 'It touched the strand. Oh! it was a pretty morning! and at the first tap of Heaven's bell, the angels came crowding round, to bid them welcome. There you and I shall meet, my beloved fellow-travellers. Farewell—Farewell—I have it in my temporal feelings that I shall never set foot in this New-York again. Farewell on earth, but I shall meet you there,' pointing reverently upward. 'May we all be aboard that blessed ship!' Shouts throughout the audience, 'We will! We will!' Stirred by such responses, Julia broke out with redoubled fervour. 'Farewell—farewell. Let the world say what they will of me, I shall surely meet you in Heaven's broad bay. Hell clutched me, but it hadn't energy enough to hold me. Farewell on earth. I shall meet you in the morning.' Again and again she tossed her arms abroad, and uttered her wild 'farewell;' responded to by the loud farewell of a whole congregation, like the shouts of an excited populace. Her last words were the poetic phrase, *'I shall meet you in the morning!'*

Her audience were wrought up to the highest pitch of enthusiasm I ever witnessed. 'That's God's truth!' 'Glory!' 'Amen!' 'Hallelujah!' resounded throughout the crowded house. Emotion vented itself in murmuring, stamping, shouting, singing, and wailing. It was like the uproar of a sea lashed by the winds.

You know that religion has always come to me in stillness; and that the machinery of theological excitement has ever been as powerless over my soul, as would be the exorcisms of a wizard. You are likewise aware of my tendency to *generalize;* to look at truth as *universal,* not merely in its particular relations; to observe human nature as a *whole,* and not in fragments. This propensity, greatly strengthened by the education of circumstances, has taught me to look calmly on all forms of religious opinion—not with the indifference, or the scorn, of unbelief; but with a friendly wish to discover everywhere the great central ideas common to all religious souls, though often re-appearing in the strangest disguises, and lisping or jabbering in the most untranslated tones.

Yet combined as my religious character is, of quiet mysticism, and the coolest rationality, will you believe me, I could scarcely refrain from shouting Hurrah for that heaven-bound ship! and the tears rolled down my cheeks, as that dusky priestess of eloquence reiterated her wild and solemn farewell.

If she gained such power over my spirit, there is no cause to marvel at the tremendous excitement throughout an audience so ignorant, and so keenly susceptible to outward impressions. I knew not how the high-wrought enthusiasm would be let down in safety. The shouts died away, and returned in shrill fragments of echoes, like the trembling vibrations of a harp, swept with a strong hand, to the powerful music of a war-song. Had I remembered a lively Methodist tune, as well as I recollected the words, I should have broke forth:

'The gospel ship is sailing by!
The Ark of safety now is nigh;
Come, sinners, unto Jesus fly,
Improve the day of grace.
Oh, there'll be glory, hallelujah,
When we all arrive at home!'

The same instinct that guided me, impelled the audience to seek rest in music, for their panting spirits and quivering nerves. All joined spontaneously in singing an old familiar tune, more quiet than the bounding, billowing tones of my favourite Gospel Ship. Blessings on music! Like a gurgling brook to feverish lips are sweet sounds to the heated and weary soul.

Everybody round me could sing; and the tones were soft and melodious. The gift of song is universal with Africans; and the fact is a prophetic one. Sculpture blossomed into its fullest perfection in a Physical Age, on which dawned the intellectual; Painting blossomed in an Intellectual Age, warmed by the rising sun of moral sentiment; and now Music goes forward to its culmination in the coming Spiritual Age. Now is the time that Ethiopia begins 'to stretch forth her hands.' Her soul, so long silenced, will yet utter itself in music's highest harmony.

When the audience paused, Mr. Matthews, their pastor, rose to address them. He is a religious-minded man, to whose good influence Julia owes, under God, her present state of mind. She always calls him 'father,' and speaks of him with the most affectionate and grateful reverence. At one period of her life, it seems that she was led astray by temptations, which peculiarly infest the path of coloured women in large cities; but ever since her 'conversion to God,' she has been strictly exemplary in her walk and conversation. In her own expressive language, 'Hell clutched her, but hadn't energy enough to hold her.' The missteps of her youth are now eagerly recalled by those who love to stir polluted waters; and they are brought forward as reasons why she ought not to be allowed to preach. I was surprised to learn that to this prejudice was added another, against women's preaching. This seemed a strange idea for Methodists, some of whose brightest ornaments have been women preachers. As far back as Adam Clarke's time, his objections were met by the answer, 'If an *ass* reproved Balaam, and a *barn-door fowl* reproved Peter, why shouldn't a *woman* reprove sin?'

This classification with donkeys and fowls is certainly not very complimentary. The first comparison I heard most wittily replied to, by a coloured woman who had once been a slave. 'Maybe a speaking woman *is* like an Ass,' said she; 'but I can tell you one thing—the Ass saw the angel, when Balaam didn't.'

Father Matthews, after apologizing for various misquotations of Scripture, on the ground of Julia's inability to read, added:—'But the

Lord has evidently called this woman to a great work. He has made her mighty to the salvation of many souls, as a cloud of witnesses can testify. Some say she ought not to preach, because she is a woman. But I say, 'Let the Lord send by whom he *will* send.' Let everybody that has a message, deliver it—whether man or woman, white or coloured! Some say women mustn't preach, because they were first in the transgression; but it seems to me hard that if they helped us *into* sin, they shouldn't be suffered to help us *out*. I say, 'Let the Lord send by whom he *will* send;' and my pulpit shall be always open.'

Thus did the good man instil a free principle into those uneducated minds, like gleams of light through chinks in a prison-wall. Who can foretell its manifold and ever-increasing results in the history of that long-crippled race? Verily great is the Advent of a true Idea, made manifest to men; and great are the miracles of works—making the blind to see, and the lame to walk.

LETTER XIV.

February 17, 1842.

I was always eager for the spring-time, but never so much as now!

Patience yet a little longer! and I shall find delicate bells of the trailing arbutus, fragrant as an infant's breath, hidden deep, under their coverlid of autumn leaves, like modest worth in this pretending world. My spirit is weary for rural rambles. It is sad walking in the city. The streets shut out the sky, even as commerce comes between the soul and heaven. The busy throng, passing and repassing, fetter freedom, while they offer no sympathy. The loneliness of the soul is deeper, and far more restless, than in the solitude of the mighty forest. Wherever are woods and fields I find a home; each tinted leaf and shining pebble is to me a friend; and wherever I spy a wild flower, I am ready to leap up, clap my hands, and exclaim, 'Cocatoo! he know me very well!" as did the poor New Zealander, when he recognised a bird of his native clime, in the menageries of London.

But amid these magnificent masses of sparkling marble, hewn *in prison*, I am alone. For eight weary months, I have met in the crowded streets but two faces I had ever seen before. Of some, I would I could say that I should never see them again; but they haunt me in my sleep, and come between me and the morning. Beseeching looks, begging the comfort and the hope I have no power to give. Hungry eyes, that look as if they had pleaded long for sympathy, and at last gone mute in still despair. Through what woful, what frightful masks, does the human soul look forth, leering, peeping, and defying, in this thoroughfare of nations. Yet in each and all lie the capacities of an archangel; as the majestic oak lies enfolded in the acorn that we tread carelessly under foot, and which decays, perchance, for want of soil to root in.

The other day, I went forth for exercise merely, without other hope of enjoyment than a farewell to the setting sun, on the now deserted Battery, and a fresh kiss from the breezes of the sea, ere they passed through the polluted city, bearing healing on their wings. I had not gone far, when I met a little ragged urchin, about four years old, with a heap of news-papers, 'more big as he could carry,' under his little arm, and another clenched in his small, red fist. The sweet voice of childhood was prema-turely cracked into shrillness, by screaming street cries, at the top of his lungs; and he looked blue, cold, and disconsolate. May the angels guard him! How I wanted to warm him in my heart. I stood looking after him, as he went shivering along. Imagination followed him to the miserable cellar where he probably slept on dirty straw; I saw him flogged, after his day of cheerless toil, because he had failed to bring home pence enough for his parents grog; I saw wicked ones come muttering and beckoning between his young soul and heaven; they tempted him to steal to avoid the dreaded beating. I saw him, years after, bewildered and frightened, in the police-office, surrounded by hard faces. Their law-jargon conveyed no meaning to his ear, awakened no slumbering moral sense, taught him no clear distinction between right and wrong; but from their cold, harsh tones, and heartless merriment, he drew the inference that they were enemies; and, as such, he hated them. At that moment, one tone like a mother's voice might have wholly changed his earthly destiny; one kind word of friendly counsel might have saved him—as if an angel, standing in the genial sunlight, had thrown to him one end of a garland, and gently diminishing the distance between them, had drawn him safely out of the deep and tangled labyrinth, where false echoes and winding paths con-spired to make him lose his way.

But watchmen and constables were around him, and they have small fellowship with angels. The strong impulses that might have become overwhelming love for his race, are perverted to the bitterest hatred. He tries the universal resort of weakness against force; if they are too strong for *him,* he will be too cunning for *them. Their* cunning is roused to detect *his* cunning: and thus the gallows-game is played, with interludes of damnable merriment from police reports, whereat the heedless mul-titude laugh; while angels weep over the slow murder of a human soul.

When, O when, will men learn that society makes and cherishes the very crimes it so fiercely punishes, and *in* punishing reproduces?

> 'The key of knowledge first ye take away,
> And then, because ye've robbed him, ye enslave;
> Ye shut out from him the sweet light of day,
> And then, because he's in the dark, ye pave
> The road, that leads him to his wished-for grave,
> With stones of stumbling: then, if he but tread
> Darkling and slow, ye call him 'fool' and 'knave;'—
> Doom him to toil, and yet deny him bread:
> Chains round his limbs ye throw, and curses on his head.'

God grant the little shivering carrier-boy a brighter destiny than I have foreseen for him.

A little further on, I encountered two young boys fighting furiously for some coppers, that had been given them and had fallen on the pavement. They had matted black hair, large, lustrous eyes, and an olive complexion. They were evidently foreign children, from the sunny clime of Italy or Spain, and nature had made them subjects for an artist's dream. Near by on the cold stone steps, sat a ragged, emaciated woman, whom I conjectured, from the resemblance of her large dark eyes, might be their mother; but she looked on their fight with languid indifference, as if seeing, she saw it not. I spoke to her, and she shook her head in a mournful way, that told me she did not understand my language. Poor, forlorn wanderer! would I could place thee and thy beautiful boys under shelter of sun-ripened vines, surrounded by the music of thy motherland! Pence I will give thee, though political economy reprove the deed. They can but appease the hunger of the body; they cannot soothe the hunger of thy heart; that I obey the kindly impulse may make the world none the better—perchance some iota the worse; yet I must needs follow it—I cannot otherwise.

I raised my eyes above the woman's weather-beaten head, and saw, behind the window of clear, plate glass, large vases of gold and silver, curiously wrought. They spoke significantly of the sad contrasts in this disordered world; and excited in my mind whole volumes, not of political, but of angelic economy. 'Truly,' said I, 'if the Law of Love prevailed, vases of gold and silver might even more abound—but no homeless outcast would sit shivering beneath their glittering mockery. All would be richer, and no man the poorer. When will the world learn its best wisdom? When will the mighty discord come into heavenly harmony?' I looked at the huge stone structures of commercial wealth, and they gave an answer that chilled my heart. Weary of city walks, I would have turned homeward; but nature, ever true and harmonious, beckoned to me from the Battery, and the glowing twilight gave me friendly welcome. It seemed as if the dancing Spring Hours had thrown their rosy mantles on old silvery winter in the lavishness of youthful love.

I opened my heart to the gladsome influence, and forgot that earth was not a mirror of the heavens. It was but for a moment; for there, under the leafless trees, lay two ragged little boys, asleep in each other's arms. I remembered having read in the police reports, the day before, that two little children, thus found, had been taken up as vagabonds. They told, with simple pathos, how both their mothers had been dead for months; how they had formed an intimate friendship, had begged together, ate together, hungered together, and together slept uncovered beneath the steel-cold stars.

The twilight seemed no longer warm; and brushing away a tear, I walked hastily homeward. As I turned into the street where God has provided me with a friendly shelter, something lay across my path. It was a woman, apparently dead; with garments all draggled in New-York gutters, blacker than waves of the infernal rivers. Those who gathered around, said she had fallen in intoxication, and was rendered senseless by the force of the blow. They carried her to the watch-house, and the doctor promised she should be well attended. But, alas, for watch-house charities to a breaking heart! I could not bring myself to think otherwise than that hers *was* a breaking heart! Could she but give a full revelation of early emotions checked in their full and kindly flow, of affections repressed, of hopes blighted, and energies misemployed through ignorance, the heart would kindle and melt, as it does when genius stirs its deepest recesses.

It seemed as if the voice of human wo was destined to follow me through the whole of that unblest day. Late in the night I heard the sound of voices in the street, and raising the window, saw a poor, staggering woman in the hands of a watchman. My ear caught the words, 'Thank you kindly, sir. I should *like* to go home.' The sad and humble accents in which the simple phrase was uttered, the dreary image of the watch-house, which that poor wretch dreamed was her *home,* proved too much for my overloaded sympathies. I hid my face in the pillow, and wept; for 'my heart was almost breaking with the misery of my kind.'

I thought, then, that I would walk no more abroad, till the fields were green. But my mind and body grow alike impatient of being inclosed within walls; both ask for the free breeze, and the wide, blue dome that overarches and embraces *all.* Again I rambled forth under the February sun, as mild and genial as the breath of June. Heart, mind, and frame grew glad and strong, as we wandered on, past the old Stuyvesant church, which a few years agone was surrounded by fields and Dutch farm-houses, but now stands in the midst of peopled streets;—and past the trim, new houses, with their green verandahs, in the airy suburbs. Following the railroad, which lay far beneath our feet, as we wound our way over the hills, we came to the burying-ground of the poor. Weeds and brambles grew along the sides, and the stubble of last year's grass waved over it, like dreary memories of the past; but the sun smiled on it, like God's love on the desolate soul. It was inexpressibly touching to see the frail memorials of affection, placed there by hearts crushed under the weight of poverty. In one place was a small rude cross of wood, with the initials J.S. cut with a penknife, and apparently filled with ink. In another a small hoop had been bent into the form of a heart, painted green, and nailed on a stick at the head of the grave. On one upright shingle was painted only 'MUTTER;' the German word for MOTHER. On another was scrawled, as if with charcoal, *So ruhe wohl, du unser liebes kind.'* (Rest well, our beloved child.) One recorded life's brief history thus: 'H.G. born in Bavaria; died in New-York.' Another short epitaph, in French, told that the sleeper came from the banks of the Seine.

The predominance of foreign epitaphs affected me deeply. Who could now tell with what high hopes those departed ones had left the heart-homes of Germany, the sunny hills of Spain, the laughing skies of Italy, or the wild beauty of Switzerland? Would not the friends they had left in their childhood's home, weep scalding tears to find them in a pauper's grave, with their initials rudely carved on a fragile shingle? Some had not even these frail memorials. It seemed there was none to care whether they lived or died. A wide, deep trench was open; and there I could see piles of unpainted coffins heaped one upon the other, left uncovered with earth, till the yawning cavity was filled with its hundred tenants.

Returning homeward, we passed a Catholic burying-ground. It belonged to the upper classes, and was filled with marble monuments, covered with long inscriptions. But none of them touched my heart like that rude shingle, with the simple word 'Mutter' inscribed thereon. The gate was open, and hundreds of Irish, in their best Sunday clothes, were stepping reverently among the graves, and kissing the very sods. Tenderness for the dead is one of the loveliest features of their nation and their church.

The evening was closing in, as we returned, thoughtful, but not gloomy. Bright lights shone through crimson, blue, and green, in the apothecaries' windows, and were reflected in prismatic beauty from the dirty pools in the street. It was like poetic thoughts in the minds of the poor and ignorant; like the memory of pure aspirations in the vicious; like a rainbow of promise, that God's spirit never leaves even the most degraded soul. I smiled, as my spirit gratefully accepted this love-token from the outward; and I thanked our heavenly Father for a world beyond this.

LETTER XVI.

August 7, 1842.

Were you ever near enough to a great fire to be in immediate danger? If you were not, you have missed one form of keen excitement, and awful beauty. Last week, we had here one of the most disastrous conflagrations that have occurred for a long time. It caught, as is supposed, by a spark from a furnace, falling on the roof of a wheelwright's shop. A single bucket of water, thrown on immediately, would have extinguished it; but it was not instantly perceived, roofs were dry, and the wind was blowing a perfect March gale. Like slavery in our government, it was not put out in the day of small beginnings, and so went on increasing in its rage, making a great deal of hot and disagreeable work.

It began at the corner of Chrystie-street, not far from our dwelling; and the blazing shingles that came flying through the air, like a storm in the infernal regions, soon kindled our roof. We thought to avert the danger by buckets of water, until the block opposite us was one sheet of fire, and the heat like that of the furnace which tried Shadrach, Meshach and Abednego. Then we began to pack our goods, and run with them in all haste to places of safety; an effort more easily described than done—for the streets all round were filled with a dense mass of living beings, each eager in playing the engines, or saving the *lares* of his own hearth-stone.

Nothing surprised me so much as the rapidity of the work of destruction. At three o'clock in the afternoon, there stood before us a close neighbourhood of houses, inhabited by those whose faces were familiar, though their names were mostly unknown; at five the whole was a pile of sinking ruins. The humble tenement of Jane Plato, the coloured woman, of whose neatly-kept garden and white-washed fences I wrote you last summer, has passed away forever. The purple iris, and yellow daffodils, and variegated sweet-williams, were all trampled down under heaps of red-hot mortar. I feel a deeper sympathy for the destruction of Jane's little garden, than I do for those who have lost whole blocks of houses; for I have known and loved flowers, like the voice of a friend—but with houses and lands I was never cumbered. In truth, I am ashamed to say how much I grieve for that little flowery oasis in a desert of bricks and stone. My beautiful trees, too—the Ailanthus, whose graceful blossoms, changing their hue from month to month, blessed me the live-long summer; and the glossy young Catalpa, over which it threw its arms so lovingly and free—there they stand, scorched and blackened; and I know not whether nature, with her mighty healing power, can ever make them live again.

The utilitarian and the moralist will rebuke this trifling record, and remind me that one hundred houses were burned, and not less than two thousand persons deprived of shelter for the night. Pardon my childish lamentations. Most gladly would I give a home to all the destitute; but I cannot love two thousand persons; and I *loved* my trees. Insurance stocks are to me an abstraction; but stock gilliflowers a most pleasant reality.

Will your kind heart be shocked that I seem to sympathize more with Jane Plato for the destruction of her little garden-patch, than I do with others for loss of houses and furniture?

Do not misunderstand me. It is simply my way of saying that money is not wealth. I know the universal opinion of mankind is to the contrary; but it is nevertheless a mistake. Our real losses are those in which the *heart* is concerned. An autograph letter from Napoleon Bonaparte might sell for fifty dollars; but if I possessed such a rare document, would I save it from the fire, in preference to a letter from a beloved and deceased husband, filled with dear little household phrases? Which would a mother value most, the price of the most elegant pair of Parisian slippers, or a little worn-out shoe, once filled with a precious infant foot, now walking with the angels?

Jane Plato's garden might not be worth much in dollars and cents; but it was to her the endeared companion of many a pleasant hour. After her daily toil, she might be seen, till twilight deepened into evening, digging round the roots, pruning branches, and training vines. I know by experience how very dear inanimate objects become under such circumstances. I have dearly loved the house in which I *lived,* but I could not love the one I merely *owned.* The one in which the *purse* had interest might be ten times more valuable in the market; but let me calculate as I would, I should mourn most for the one in which the *heart* had invested stock. The common wild-flower that I have brought to my garden, and nursed, and petted, till it has lost all home-sickness for its native woods, is *really* more valuable than the costly exotic, purchased in full bloom from the conservatory. Men of princely fortunes never know what wealth of happiness there is in a garden.

'The rich man in his garden walks,
    Beneath his garden trees;
Wrapped in a dream of other things,
    He seems to take his ease.

One moment he beholds his flowers.
    The next they are forgot;
He eateth of his rarest fruits,
    As though he ate them not.

It is not with the poor man so;
    He knows each inch of ground,
And every single plant and flower,
    That grows within its bound.

And though his garden-plot is small,
    Him doth it satisfy;
For there's no inch of all his ground,
    That does not fill his eye.

It is not with the rich man thus;
    For though his grounds are wide,
He looks beyond, and yet beyond,
    With soul unsatisfied.

Yes, in the poor man's garden grow
    Far more than herbs and flowers;
Kind thoughts, contentment, peace of mind,
    And joy for weary hours.

The reason of this difference is easily explained

'The rich man has his gardeners—
    His gardeners young and old:
He never takes a spade in hand,
    Nor worketh in the mould.

It is not with the poor man so—
    Wealth, servants, he has none;

And all the work that's done for him,
Must by *himself* be done.'

I have said this much to prove that money is *not* wealth, and that *God's* gifts are equal; though joint-stock companies and corporations do their worst to prevent it.

And all the highest *truths*, as well as the genuine *good*, are universal. Doctrinal dogmas may be hammered out on theological anvils, and appropriated to spiritual corporations, called sects. But those high and holy truths, which make the soul at one with God and the neighbour, are by their very nature universal—open to all who wish to receive. Outward forms are always in harmonious correspondence with inward realities; therefore the material types of highest truths defy man's efforts to monopolize. Who can bottle up the sunlight, to sell at retail? or issue dividends of the ocean and the breeze?

This great fire, like all calamities, public or private, has its bright side. A portion of New-York, and that not a small one, is for once thoroughly cleaned; a wide space is opened for our vision, and the free passage of the air. True, it looks desolate enough now; like a battle-field, when waving banners and rushing steeds, and fife and trumpet all are gone; and the dead alone remain. But the dreary sight ever brings up images of those hundred volcanoes spouting flame, and of the scene at midnight, so fearful in its beauty. Where houses so lately stood, and welcome feet passed over the threshold, and friendly voices cheered the fireside, there arose the lurid gleam of mouldering fires, with rolling masses of smoke, as if watched by giants from the nether world; and between them all lay the thick darkness. It was strikingly like Martin's pictures. The resemblance renewed my old impression, that if the arts are cultivated in the infernal regions, of such are their galleries formed; not without a startling beauty, which impresses, while it disturbs the mind, because it embodies the idea of Power, and its discords bear harmonious relation to each other.

If you wanted to see the real, unqualified beauty of fire, you should have stood with me, in the darkness of evening, to gaze at a burning house nearly opposite. Four long hours it sent forth flame in every variety. Now it poured forth from the windows, like a broad banner on the wind; then it wound round the door-posts like a brilliant wreath; and from the open roof there ever went up a fountain of sparks that fell like a shower of gems. I watched it for hours, and could not turn away from it. In my mind there insensibly grew up a respect for that house; because it defied the power of the elements, so bravely and so long. It must have been built of sound timber, well-jointed; and as the houses round it had fallen, its conflagration was not hastened by excessive heat, as the others had been. It was one o'clock at night when the last tongue of flame flickered and died reluctantly. The next day, men came by order of the city authorities, to pull down the walls. This, too, the brave building resisted to the utmost. Ropes were fastened to it with grappling irons, and a hundred men tugged, and tugged at it, in vain. My respect for it increased, till it seemed to me like an heroic friend. I could not bear that it should fall. It seemed to me, if it did, I should no longer feel sure that John Quincy Adams and Joshua R. Giddings would stand on their feet against Southern Aggression. I sent up a joyful shout when the irons came out, bringing away only a few bricks, and the men fell backward from the force of the shock. But at last the walls reeled, and came down with a thundering crash. Nevertheless, I will trust Adams and Giddings, tug at them as they may.

By the blessing of heaven on the energy and presence of mind of those who came to our help, our walls stand unscathed, and nothing was destroyed in the tumult; but our hearts are aching; for all round us comes a voice of wailing from the houseless and the impoverished.

LETTER XXXI.

November 19, 1842

To-day, I cannot write of beauty; for I am sad and troubled. Heart, head, and conscience, are all in battle-array against the savage customs of my time. By and by, the law of love, like oil upon the waters, will calm my surging sympathies, and make the current flow more calmly, though none the less deep or strong. But to-day do not ask me to love governor, sheriff or constable, or any man who defends capital punishment. I ought to do it; for genuine love enfolds even murderers with its blessing. By to-morrow, I think I can remember them without bitterness; but to-day, I cannot love them; on my soul, I cannot.

We were to have had an execution yesterday; but the wretched prisoner avoided it by suicide. The gallows had been erected for several hours, and with a cool refinement of cruelty, was hoisted before the window of the condemned; the hangman was all ready to cut the cord; marshals paced back and forth, smoking and whistling; spectators were waiting impatiently to see whether he would 'die game.' Printed circulars had been handed abroad to summon the number of witnesses required by law:—'You are respectfully invited to witness the execution of John C. Colt.' I trust some of them are preserved for museums. Specimens should be kept, as relics of a barbarous age, for succeeding generations to wonder at. They might be hung up in a frame; and the portrait of a New Zealand Chief, picking the bones of an enemy of his tribe, would be an appropriate pendant.

This bloody insult was thrust into the hands of *some* citizens, who carried hearts under their vests, and they threw it in tattered fragments to the dogs and swine, as more fitting witnesses than human beings. It was cheering to those who have faith in human progress, to see how many viewed the subject in this light. But as a general thing, the very spirit of murder was rife among the dense crowd, which thronged the place of execution. They were swelling with revenge, and eager for blood. One man came all the way from New Hampshire, on purpose to witness the entertainment; thereby showing himself a likely subject for the gallows, whoever he may be. *Women* deemed themselves not treated with becoming gallantry, because tickets of admittance were denied *them;* and I think it showed injudicious partiality; for many of them can be taught murder by as short a lesson as any man, and sustain it by arguments from Scripture, as ably as any theologian. However *they* were not admitted to this edifying exhibition in the great school of public morals; and had only the slim comfort of standing outside, in a keen November wind, to catch the first toll of the bell, which would announce that a human brother had been sent struggling into eternity by the hand of violence. But while the multitude stood with open watches, and strained ears to catch the sound, and the marshals smoked and whistled, and the hangman walked up and down, waiting for his prey, lo! word was brought that the criminal was found dead in his bed! He had asked one half hour alone to prepare his mind for departure; and at the end of that brief interval, he was found with a dagger thrust into his heart. The tidings were received with fierce mutterings of disappointed rage. The throng beyond the walls were furious to see him with their own eyes, to be sure that he was dead. But when the welcome news met *my* ear a tremendous load was taken from my heart. I had no chance to analyze right and wrong; for over all thought and feeling flowed impulsive joy that this 'Christian' community were cheated of a hanging. They who had assembled to commit legalized murder, in cold blood, with strange confusion of ideas, were unmindful of their own guilt, while they talked of his suicide as a crime equal to that for which he was condemned. I am willing to leave it between him and his God. For myself, I would rather have the burden of it on my own soul, than take the guilt of those who would have executed a fellow-creature. *He* was driven to a fearful extremity of agony and desperation. He was precisely in the situation of a man on board a burning ship, who being *compelled* to face death, jumps into the waves, as the least painful mode of the two. But they, who thus drove him 'to walk the plank,' made cool, deliberate preparations to take life, and with inventive cruelty sought to add every bitter drop that *could* be added to the dreadful cup of vengeance.

To me, human life seems so sacred a thing, that its violent termination always fills me with horror, whether perpetrated by an individual or a crowd; whether done contrary to law and custom, or according to law and custom. Why John C. Colt should be condemned to an ignominious death for an act of resentment altogether unpremeditated, while men, who deliberately, and with malice aforethought, go out to murder another for some insulting word, are judges and senators in the land, and favourite candidates for the President's chair, is more than I can comprehend. There is, to say the least, a strange inconsistency in our customs.

At the same moment that I was informed of the death of the prisoner,

I heard that the prison was on fire. It was soon extinguished, but the remarkable coincidence added not a little to the convulsive excitement of the hour. I went with a friend to look at the beautiful spectacle; for it was exceedingly beautiful. The fire had kindled at the very top of the cupola, the wind was high, and the flames rushed upward, as if the angry spirits below had escaped on fiery wings. Heaven forgive the feelings that, for a moment mingled with my admiration of that beautiful conflagration! Society had kindled all around me a bad excitement, and one of the infernal sparks fell into my own heart. If this was the effect produced on me, who am by nature tender-hearted, by principle opposed to all retalia-tion, and by social position secluded from contact with evil, what must it have been on the minds of rowdies and desperadoes? The effect of execu-tions on *all* brought within their influence is evil, and nothing but evil. For a fortnight past, this whole city has been kept in a state of corroding excitement, either of hope or fear. The stern pride of the prisoner left little in his peculiar case to appeal to the sympathies of society; yet the instincts of our common nature rose up against the sanguinary spirit manifested toward him. The public were, moreover, divided in opinion with regard to the legal construction of his crime; and in the keen discussion of *legal* distinctions, *moral* distinctions became wofully confused. Each day hope and fear alternated; the natural effect of all this, was to have the whole thing regarded as a game, in which the criminal might, or might not, become the winner; and every experiment of this kind shakes public respect for the laws, from centre to circumference. Worse than all this was the horrible amount of diabolical passion excited. The hearts of men were filled with murder; they gloated over the thoughts of vengeance, and were rabid to witness a fellow-creature's agony. They complained loudly that he was not to be hung high enough for the crowd to *see* him. 'What a pity!' exclaimed a woman, who stood near me, gazing at the burning tower; 'they will have to give him two hours more to live.' 'Would you feel so, if he were your *son?*' said I. Her countenance changed instantly. She had not before realized that every criminal was *somebody's* son.

As we walked homeward, we encountered a deputy sheriff; not the most promising material, certainly, for lessons on humanity; but to him we spoke of the crowd of savage faces, and the tones of hatred, as obvious proofs of the bad influence of capital punishment. 'I know that,' said he; 'but I don't see how we could dispense with it. Now suppose we had fifty murderers shut up in prison for life, instead of hanging 'em; and suppose there should come a revolution; what an awful thing it would be to have fifty murderers inside the prison, to be let loose upon the community!' 'There is another side to that proposition,' we answered; 'for every crimi-nal you execute, you make a hundred murderers *outside* the prison, each as dangerous as would be the one inside.' He said perhaps it was so, and went his way.

As for the punishment and the terror of such doings, they fall most keenly on the best hearts in the community. Thousands of men, as well as women, had broken and startled sleep for several nights preceding that dreadful day. Executions always excite a universal shudder among the innocent, the humane, and the wise-hearted. It is the voice of God, crying aloud within us against the wickedness of this savage custom. Else why is it that the instinct is so universal?

The last conversation I had with the late William Ladd made a strong impression upon my mind. While he was a sea-captain, he occasionally visited Spain, and once witnessed an execution there. He said that no man, however low and despicable, would consent to perform the office of hangman; and whoever should dare to suggest such a thing to a decent man, would be likely to have his brains blown out. This feeling was so strong, and so universal, that the only way they could procure an executioner, was to offer a condemned criminal his own life, if he would consent to perform the vile and hateful office on another. Sometimes executions were postponed for months, because there was no condemned criminal to perform the office of hangman. A fee was allotted by law to the wretch who did perform it, but no one would run the risk of touching his polluted hand by giving it to him; therefore, the priest threw the purse as far as possible; the odious being ran to pick it up, and hastened to escape from the shuddering execrations of all who had known him as a hangman. Even the poor animal that carried the criminal and his coffin in a cart to the foot of the gallows, was an object of universal loathing. He was cropped and marked, that he might be known as the 'Hangman's Donkey.' No man, however great his needs, would use this beast, either for pleasure or labour; and the peasants were so averse to having him pollute their fields with his footsteps, that when he was seen approaching, the boys hastened to open the gates, and drive him off with hisses, sticks and stones. Thus does the human heart cry out aloud against this wicked practice!

A tacit acknowledgement of the demoralizing influence of executions is generally made, in the fact that they are forbidden to be *public,* as formerly. The scene is now in a prison yard, instead of open fields, and no spectators are admitted but officers of the law, and those especially invited. Yet a favourite argument in favour of capital punishment has been the terror that the spectacle inspires in the breast of evil doers. I trust the two or three hundred, singled out from the mass of New-York population, by particular invitation, especially the judges and civil officers, will feel the full weight of the compliment. During the French Revolution, public executions seemed too slow, and Fouquier proposed to put the guillotine under cover, where batches of a hundred might be despatched with few spectators. 'Wilt thou *demoralize the guillotine?*' asked Callot, reproachfully.

That bloody guillotine was an instrument of *law,* as well as our gallows; and what, in the name of all that is villainous, has *not* been established by law? Nations, clans, and classes, engaged in fierce struggles of selfishness and hatred, made laws to strengthen each other's power, and revenge each other's aggressions. By slow degrees, always timidly and reluctantly, society emerges out of the barbarisms with which it thus became entangled. It is but a short time ago that men were hung in this country for stealing. The last human brother who suffered under this law, in Massachusetts, was so wretchedly poor, that when he hung on the gallows, his rags fluttered in the wind. What think you was the comparative guilt, in the eye of God, between him and those who hung him? Yet, it was *according to law;* and men cried out as vociferously then as they now do, that it was not *safe* to have the law changed. Judge McKean, governor of Pennsylvania, was strongly opposed to the abolition of death for stealing, and the disuse of the pillory and whipping-post. He was a very humane man, but had the common fear of changing old customs. 'It will not do to abolish these salutary restraints,' said the old gentleman; 'it will break up the foundations of society.' Those relics of barbarism were banished long ago; but the foundations of society are in nowise injured thereby.

The testimony from all parts of the world is invariable and conclusive, that crime diminishes in proportion to the mildness of the laws. The *real* danger is in having laws on the statute-book at variance with universal instincts of the human heart, and thus tempting men to continual evasion. The *evasion,* even of a bad law, is attended with many mischievous results; its *abolition* is always safe.

In looking at Capital Punishment in its practical bearings on the operation of justice, an observing mind is at once struck with the extreme *uncertainty* attending it. The balance swings hither and thither, and settles, as it were, by chance. The strong instincts of the heart teach juries extreme reluctance to convict for capital offences. They will avail themselves of every loophole in the evidence, to avoid the bloody responsibility imposed upon them. In this way, undoubted criminals escape all punishment, until society becomes alarmed for its own safety, and insists that the next victim *shall* be sacrificed. It was the misfortune of John C. Colt, to be arrested at the time when the popular wave of indignation had been swelling higher and higher, in consequence of the impunity with which Robinson, White, and Jewell, had escaped. The wrath and jealousy which they had excited was visited upon him, and his chance for a merciful verdict was greatly diminished. The scale now turns the other way; and the next offender will probably receive very lenient treatment, though he should not have half so many extenuating circumstances in his favour.

Another thought which forces itself upon the mind in consideration of this subject is the danger of convicting the innocent. Murder is a crime which must of course be committed in secret, and therefore the proof must be mainly circumstantial. This kind of evidence is in its nature so precarious, that men have learned great timidity in trusting to it. In Scotland, it led to so many terrible mistakes, that they long ago refused to convict any man of a capital offence, upon circumstantial evidence.

A few years ago, a poor German came to New-York, and took lodgings, where he was allowed to do his cooking in the same room with the family. The husband and wife lived in a perpetual quarrel. One day the German came into the kitchen with a clasp knife and a pan of potatoes, and began to pare them for his dinner. The quarrelsome couple were in a more violent altercation than usual; but he sat with his back toward them, and being ignorant of their language, felt in no danger of being involved in their disputes. But the woman, with a sudden and unexpected movement, snatched the knife from his hand, and plunged it in her husband's heart. She had sufficient presence of mind to rush into the street, and scream murder. The poor foreigner, in the meanwhile, seeing the wounded man reel, sprang forward to catch him in his arms, and drew out the knife. People from the street crowded in, and found him with the dying man in his arms, the knife in his hand, and blood upon his clothes. The wicked woman swore, in the most positive terms, that he had been fighting with her husband, and had stabbed him with a knife he always carried. The unfortunate German knew too little English to understand her accusation, or to tell his own story. He was dragged off to prison, and the true state of the case was made known through an interpreter; but it was not believed. Circumstantial evidence was exceedingly strong against the accused, and the real criminal swore unhesitatingly that she saw him commit the murder. He was executed, notwithstanding the most persevering efforts of his lawyer, John Anthon, Esq., whose convictions of the man's innocence were so painfully strong, that from that day to this, he has refused to have any connection with a capital case. Some years after this tragic event, the woman died, and, on her death-bed, confessed her agency in the diabolical transaction; but her poor victim could receive no benefit from this tardy repentance; society had wantonly thrown away its power to atone for the grievous wrong.

Many of my readers will doubtless recollect the tragical fate of Burton, in Missouri, on which a novel was founded, which still circulates in the libraries. A young lady, belonging to a genteel and very proud family, in Missouri, was beloved by a young man named Burton; but unfortunately, her affections were fixed on another less worthy. He left her with a tarnished reputation. She was by nature energetic and high-spirited, her family were proud, and she lived in the midst of a society which considered revenge a virtue, and named it honour. Misled by this false popular sentiment, and her own excited feelings, she resolved to repay her lover's treachery with death. But she kept her secret so well, that no one suspected her purpose, though she purchased pistols, and practised with them daily. Mr. Burton gave evidence of his strong attachment by renewing his attentions when the world looked most coldly upon her. His generous kindness won her bleeding heart, but the softening influence of love did not lead her to forego the dreadful purpose she had formed. She watched for a favourable opportunity, and shot her betrayer, when no one was near, to witness the horrible deed. Some little incident excited the suspicion of Burton, and he induced her to confess to him the whole transaction. It was obvious enough that suspicion would naturally fasten upon him, the well-known lover of her who had been so deeply injured. He was arrested, but succeeded in persuading her that he was in no danger. Circumstantial evidence was fearfully against him, and he soon saw that his chance was doubtful; but with affectionate magnanimity, he concealed this from her. He was convicted and condemned. A short time before the execution, he endeavoured to cut his throat; but his life was saved for the cruel purpose of taking it away according to the cold-blooded barbarism of the law. Pale and wounded, he was hoisted to the gallows before the gaze of a *Christian* community.

The guilty cause of all this was almost frantic, when she found that he had thus sacrificed himself to save her. She immediately published the whole history of her wrongs, and her revenge. Her keen sense of wounded honour was in accordance with public sentiment, her wrongs excited indignation and compassion, and the knowledge that an innocent and magnanimous man had been so brutally treated, excited a general revulsion of popular feeling. No one wished for another victim, and she was left unpunished, save by the dreadful records of her memory.

Few know how numerous are the cases where it has subsequently been discovered that the innocent suffered instead of the guilty. Yet one such case in an age is surely enough to make legislators pause before they cast a vote against the abolition of Capital Punishment.

But many say, 'the Old Testament requires blood for blood.' So it requires that a woman should be put to death for adultery; and men for doing work on the Sabbath; and children for cursing their parents; and 'If an ox were to push with his horn, in time past, and it hath been testified to his owner, and he hath not kept him in, but that he hath killed a man or a woman, the ox shall be stoned, and his owner also shall be put to death.' The commands given to the Jews, in the old dispensation, do not form the basis of any legal code in Christendom. They *could* not form the basis of any civilized code. If one command is binding on our consciences, *all* are binding; for they all rest on the same authority. They who feel bound to advocate capital punishment for murder, on account of the law given to Moses, ought, for the same reason, to insist that children should be executed for striking or cursing their parents.

'It was said by them of *old* time, an eye for an eye, and a tooth for a tooth; but *I* say unto you, resist not evil.' If our 'eyes were lifted up,' we should see not Moses and Elias, but *Jesus only.*

LETTER XXXIV.

Jan. 1843.

You ask what are my opinions about 'Women's Rights.' I confess, a strong distaste to the subject, as it has been generally treated. On no other theme probably has there been uttered so much of false, mawkish sentiment, shallow philosophy, and sputtering, farthing-candle wit. If the style of its advocates has often been offensive to taste, and unacceptable to reason, assuredly that of its opponents have been still more so. College boys have amused themselves with writing dreams, in which they saw women in hotels, with their feet hoisted, and chairs tilted back, or growling and bickering at each other in legislative halls, or fighting at the polls, with eyes blackened by fisticuffs. But it never seems to have occurred to these facetious writers, that the proceedings which appear so ludicrous and improper in *women*, are also ridiculous and disgraceful in *men*. It were well that *men* should learn not to hoist their feet above their heads, and tilt their chairs backward, nor to growl and snap in the halls of legislation, nor give each other black eyes at the polls.

Maria Edgeworth says, 'We are disgusted when we see a woman's mind overwhelmed with a torrent of learning: that the tide of literature has passed over it should be betrayed only by its fertility.' This is beautiful and true; but is it not likewise applicable to man? The truly great never seek to display themselves. If they carry their heads high above the crowd, it is only made manifest to others by accidental revelations of their extended vision. 'Human duties and proprieties do not lie so very far apart,' said Harriet Martineau; 'if they did, there would be two gospels and two teachers, one for man and another for woman.'

It would seem indeed, as if men were willing to give women the exclusive benefit of gospel-teaching. '*Women* should be gentle,' say the advocates of subordination; but when Christ said, 'Blessed are the meek,' did he preach to women only? '*Girls* should be modest,' is the language of common teaching, continually uttered in words and customs. Would it not be an improvement for men also to be scrupulously pure in manners, conversation and life? Books addressed to young married people abound with advice to the *wife*, to control her temper, and never to utter wearisome complaints, or vexatious words when the husband comes home fretful and unreasonable from his out-of-door conflicts with the world. Would not the advice be as excellent and appropriate, if the husband were advised to conquer *his* fretfulness, and forbear *his* complaints, in consideration of his wife's ill-health, fatiguing cares, and the thousand disheartening influences of domestic routine? In short, whatsoever can be named as loveliest, best, and most graceful in woman, would likewise be good and graceful in man. You will perhaps remind me of courage. If you use the word in its highest signification, I answer, that woman, above others, has abundant need of it in her pilgrimage: and the true woman wears it with a quiet grace. If you mean mere animal courage, *that* is not mentioned in the Sermon on the Mount, among those qualities which enable us to inherit the earth, or become the children of God. That the feminine ideal approaches much nearer to the gospel standard, than the prevalent idea of manhood, is shown by the universal tendency to represent the Saviour and his most beloved disciple with mild, meek expression, and feminine beauty. None speak of the bravery, the might, or the intellect of Jesus; but the devil is always imagined as a being of acute intellect, political cunning, and the fiercest courage. These universal and instinctive tendencies of the human mind reveal much.

That the present position of women in society is the result of physical force, is obvious enough; whosoever doubts it, let her reflect why she is afraid to go out in the evening without the protection of a man. What constitutes the danger of aggression? Superior physical strength, uncontrolled by the moral sentiments. If physical strength were in complete subjection to moral influence, there would be no need of outward protection. That animal instinct and brute force now govern the world, is painfully apparent in the condition of women everywhere; from the Morduan Tartars, whose ceremony of marriage consists in placing the bride on a mat, and consigning her to the bridegroom, with the words, 'Here, wolf, take thy lamb,'—to the German remark, that 'stiff ale, stinging tobacco, and a girl in her smart dress, are the best things.' The same thing, softened by the refinements of civilization, peeps out in Stephens's remark, that 'woman never looks so interesting, as when leaning on the arm of a soldier;' and in Hazlitt's complaint that 'it is not easy to keep up a conversation with women in company. It is thought a piece of rudeness to differ from them; it is not quite fair to ask them a *reason* for what they say.'

This sort of politeness to women is what men call gallantry; an odious word to every sensible woman, because she sees that it is merely the flimsy veil which foppery throws over sensuality, to conceal its grossness. So far is it from indicating sincere esteem and affection for women, that the profligacy of a nation may, in general, be fairly measured by its gallantry. This taking away *rights,* and *condescending* to grant *privileges,* is an old trick of the physical-force principle; and with the immense majority, who only look on the surface of things, this mask effectually disguises an ugliness, which would otherwise be abhorred. The most inveterate slave-holders are probably those who take most pride in dressing their household servants handsomely, and who would be most ashamed to have the name of being *unnecessarily* cruel. And profligates, who form the lowest and most sensual estimate of women, are the very ones to treat them with an excess of outward deference.

There are few books which I can read through, without feeling insulted as a woman; but this insult is almost universally conveyed through that which was intended for praise. Just imagine, for a moment, what impression it would make on men, if women authors should write about *their* 'rosy lips,' and 'melting eyes,' and 'voluptuous forms,' as they write about *us!* That women in general do not feel this kind of flattery to be an insult, I readily admit; for, in the first place, they do not perceive the gross chattel-principle, of which it is the utterance; moreover, they have, from long habit, become accustomed to consider themselves as household conveniences, or gilded toys. Hence, they consider it feminine and pretty to abjure all such use of their faculties, as would make them co-workers with man in the advancement of those great principles, on which the progress of society depends. 'There is perhaps no *animal,*' says Hannah More, 'so much indebted to subordination, for its good behaviour, as woman.' Alas, for the animal age, in which such utterance could be tolerated by public sentiment!

Martha More, sister of Hannah, describing a very impressive scene at the funeral of one of her Charity School teachers, says: 'The spirit within seemed struggling to speak, and I was in a sort of agony; but I recollected that I had heard, somewhere, a woman must not speak in the *church.* Oh, had she been buried in the church-*yard,* a messenger from Mr. Pitt himself should not have restrained me; for I seemed to have received a message from a higher Master within.'

This application of theological teaching carries its own commentary.

I have said enough to show that I consider prevalent opinions and customs highly unfavourable to the moral and intellectual development of women: and I need not say, that, in proportion to their true culture, women will be more useful and happy, and domestic life more perfected. True culture, in them, as in men, consists in the full and free development of individual character, regulated by their *own* perceptions of what is true, and their *own* love of what is good.

This individual responsibility is rarely acknowledged, even by the most refined, as necessary to the spiritual progress of women. I once heard a very beautiful lecture from R. W. Emerson, on Being and Seeming. In the course of many remarks, as true as they were graceful, he urged women to *be,* rather than *seem.* He told them that all their laboured education of forms, strict observance of genteel etiquette, tasteful arrangement of the toilette, &c., all this *seeming* would not *gain hearts* like *being* truly what God made them; that earnest simplicity, the sincerity of nature, would kindle the eye, light up the countenance, and give an inexpressible charm to the plainest features.

The advice was excellent, but the motive, by which it was urged, brought a flush of indignation over my face. *Men* were exhorted to *be,* rather than to *seem,* that they might fulfil the sacred mission for which their souls were embodied; that they might, in God's freedom, grow up into the full stature of spiritual manhood; but *women* were urged to simplicity and truthfulness, that they might become more *pleasing.*

Are we not all immortal beings? Is not each one responsible for himself and herself? There is no measuring the mischief done by the prevailing tendency to teach women to be virtuous as a duty to *man* rather than to *God*—for the sake of pleasing the creature, rather than the Creator.

'*God* is thy law, *thou* mine,' said Eve to Adam. May Milton be forgiven for sending that thought 'out into everlasting time' in such a jewelled setting. What weakness, vanity, frivolity, infirmity of moral purpose, sinful flexibility of principle—in a word, what soul-stifling, has been the result of thus putting man in the place of God.

But while I see plainly that society is on a false foundation, and that prevailing views concerning women indicate the want of wisdom and purity, which they serve to perpetuate—still, I must acknowledge that much of the talk about Women's Rights offends both my reason and my taste. I am not of those who maintain there is no sex in souls; nor do I like the results deducible from that doctrine. Kinmont, in his admirable book, called the Natural History of Man, speaking of the warlike courage of the ancient German women, and of their being respectfully consulted on important public affairs, says: 'You ask me if I consider all this right, and deserving of approbation? or that women were here engaged in their appropriate tasks? I answer, yes; it is just *as* right that they should take this interest in the honour of their country, as the other sex. Of course, I do not think that women were *made* for war and battle; neither do I believe that *men* were. But since the fashion of the times had made it so, and settled it that war was a necessary element of greatness, and that no safety was to be procured without it, I argue that it shows a healthful state of feeling in other respects, that the feelings of both sexes were *equally* enlisted in the cause: that there was no *division* in the house, or the state; and that the serious pursuits and objects of the one were also the serious pursuits and objects of the other.'

The nearer society approaches to divine order, the less separation will there be in the characters, duties, and pursuits of men and women. Women will not become less gentle and graceful, but men will become more so. Women will not neglect the care and education of their children, but men will find themselves ennobled and refined by sharing those duties with them; and will receive, in return, co-operation and sympathy in the discharge of various other duties, now deemed inappropriate to women. The more women become rational companions, partners in business and in thought, as well as in affection and amusement, the more highly will men appreciate *home*—that blessed word, which opens to the human heart the most perfect glimpse of Heaven, and helps to carry it thither, as on an angel's wings.

'Domestic bliss,
That can, the world eluding, be itself
A world enjoyed; that wants no witnesses
But its own sharers and approving heaven;
That, like a flower deep hid in rocky cleft,
Smiles, though 'tis looking only at the sky.'

Alas, for these days of Astor houses and Tremonts, and Albions! where families exchange comfort for costliness, fireside retirement for flirtation and flaunting, and the simple, healthful, cozy meal, for gravies and gout, dainties and dyspepsia. There is no characteristic of my countrymen, which I regret so deeply as their slight degree of adhesiveness to home. Closely intertwined with this instinct, is the religion of a nation. The Home and the Church bear a near relation to each other. The French have no such word as home in their language, and I believe they are the least reverential and religious of all the Christian nations. A Frenchman had been in the habit of visiting a lady constantly for several years, and being alarmed at a report that she was sought in marriage, he was asked why he did not marry her himself. '*Marry* her!' exclaimed he,—'Good heavens! *where should I spend my evenings?*' The idea of domestic happiness was altogether a foreign idea to his soul, like a word that conveyed no meaning. Religious sentiment in France leads the same roving life as the domestic affections; breakfasting at one restaurateur's and supping at another's. When some wag in Boston reported that Louis Philippe had sent over for Dr. Channing to manufacture a religion for the French people, the witty significance of the joke was generally appreciated.

There is a deep spiritual reason why all that relates to the domestic affections should ever be found in close proximity with religious faith. The age of chivalry was likewise one of unquestioning veneration, which led to the crusade for the holy sepulchre. The French revolution, which tore down churches, and voted that there was no God, likewise annulled marriage; and the doctrine, that there is no sex in souls, has usually been urged by those of infidel tendencies. Carlyle says, 'But what feeling it was in the ancient, devout, deep soul, which of marriage made a *sacrament,* this, of all things in the world, is what Diderot will think of for æons without discovering; unless perhaps it were to increase the *vestry fees.*'

The conviction that woman's present position in society is a false one, and therefore re-acts disastrously on the happiness and improvement of man, is pressing by slow degrees on the common consciousness, through all the obstacles of bigotry, sensuality, and selfishness. As man approaches to the truest life, he will perceive more and more that there is no separation or discord in their mutual duties. They will be one; but it will be as affection and thought are one; the treble and bass of the same harmonious tune.

LETTER XL.

May 1, 1843.

The first of May! How the phrase is twined all round with violets; and clumps of the small Housitania (which remind me of a 'sylvania phalanx' of babies,) and slight anemones, nodding gracefully as blooming maidens, under the old moss-grown trees! How it brings up visions of fair young floral queens, and garlanded May-poles, and door-posts wreathed with flowers, and juvenile choirs hymning the return of the swallows, in the ancient time! The old French word *Mes,* signifies a garden; and in Loraine, *Mai* still has that meaning; from which, perhaps, the word *maiden*. In Britanny, *Mae* signifies green, flourishing; the Dutch *Mooy*, means beautiful, agreeable; the Swedish *Mio* is small, pretty and pleasant; and the East India *Maya* is Goddess of Nature. Thus have men shown their love of this genial month by connecting its name with images of youth and loveliness.

In our climate, it happens frequently, that 'Winter, lingering, chills the lap of May,' and we are often tantalized with promises unfulfilled. But though our Northern Indians name June 'the month of flowers,' yet, with all her abundant beauty, I doubt whether she commends herself to the heart, like May, with her scanty love-tokens from the grave of the frosty past. They are like infancy, like resurrection, like everything new and fresh, and full of hopefulness and promise.

The *First*, and the *Last!* Ah, in all human things, how does one idea forever follow the other, like its shadow! The circling year oppresses me with its fulness of meaning. Youth, manhood, and old age, are its most external significance. It is symbolical of things far deeper, as every soul knows, that is travelling over steep hills, and through quiet valleys, unto the palace called Beautiful, like Bunyan's world-renowned Pilgrim. Human life, in its forever-repeating circle, like Nature, in her perpetual self-restoring beauty, tells us that from the burial place of Winter young Spring shall come forth to preach resurrection; and thus it must be in the outward and symbolical, because thus it is in the inward, spiritual progression of the soul.

> 'Two children in two neighbour villages,
> Playing mad pranks along the heathy leas;
> Two strangers meeting at a festival;
> Two lovers whispering by an orchard wall;
> Two lives bound fast in one, with golden ease;
> Two graves grass-green beside a grey church-tower,
> Washed with still rains, and daisy-blossomed;
> Two children in one hamlet, born and bred;
> So runs the round of life from hour to hour.'

Blessings on the Spring-time, when Nature stands like young children hand in hand, in prophecy of future marriage!

May-day in New-York is the saddest thing, to one who has been used to hunting mosses by the brook, and paddling in its waters. Brick walls, instead of budding trees, and rattling wheels in lieu of singing birds, are bad enough; but to make the matter worse, all New-York *moves* on the first of May; not only moves about, as usual, in the everlasting hurry-scurry of business, but one house empties itself into another, all over the city. The streets are full of loaded drays, on which tables are dancing, and carpets rolling to and fro. Small chairs, which bring up such pretty, cozy images of rollypooly mannikins and maidens, eating supper from tilted porringers, and spilling the milk on their night-gowns—these go ricketing along on the tops of beds and bureaus, and not unfrequently pitch into the street, and so fall asunder. Children are driving hither and yon, one with a flower-pot in his hand, another with work-box, band-box, or oil-canakin; each so intent upon his important mission, that all the world seems to him (as it does to many a theologian,) safely locked up within the walls *he* carries. Luckily, both boy and bigot are mistaken, or mankind would be in a bad box, sure enough. The dogs seem bewildered with this universal transmigration of bodies; and as for the cats, they sit on the door-steps, mewing piteously, that they were not born in the middle ages, or at least in the quiet old portion of the world. And I, who have almost as strong a love of localities as poor puss, turn away from the windows, with a suppressed anathema on the nineteenth century, with its perpetual changes. Do you want an appropriate emblem of this country, and this age? Then stand on the side-walks of New-York, and watch the universal transit on the first of May. The facility and speed with which our people change politics, and move from sect to sect, and from theory to theory, is comparatively slow and moss-grown; unless, indeed, one except the Rev. O. A. Brownson, who seems to stay in any spiritual habitation a much shorter time than the New-Yorkers do in their houses. It is the custom here for those who move out to leave the accumulated dust and dirt of the year, for them who enter to clear up. I apprehend it is somewhat so with all the ecclesiastical and civil establishments, which have so long been let out to tenants in rotation. Those who enter them must make a great sweeping and scrubbing, if they would have a clean residence.

That people should move so *often* in this city, is generally a matter of their own volition. Aspirations after the infinite, lead them to perpetual change, in the restless hope of finding something better and better still. But they would not raise the price of drays, and subject themselves to great inconvenience, by moving *all on one day,* were it not that the law compels everybody who intends to move at all, to quit his premises before twelve o'clock, on May morning. Failing to do this, the police will put him and his goods into the street, where they will fare much like a boy beside an upset hornet's nest. This regulation, handed down from old Dutch times, proves very convenient in arranging the Directory with promptness and accuracy; and as theologians, and some reformers, can perceive no higher mission for human souls, than to arrange themselves rank and file in sectarian platoons, so perhaps the civil authorities may imagine there is nothing more important to a citizen than to have his name set in a well-ordered Directory.

However, human beings are such creatures of habit and imitation, that what is necessity soon becomes fashion, and each one wishes to do what everybody else is doing. A lady in the neighbourhood closed all her blinds and shutters, on May-day; being asked by her acquaintance whether she had been in the country, she answered, 'I was *ashamed* not to be moving on the first of May; and so I shut up the house that the neighbours might not know it.' One could not well imagine a fact more characteristic of the despotic sway of custom and public opinion, in the United States, and the nineteenth century. Elias Hicks' remark, that it takes '*live* fish to swim *up* stream,' is emphatically true of this age and country, in which liberty-caps abound, but no one is allowed to wear them.

I am by temperament averse to frequent changes, either in my spiritual or material abode. I think I was made for a German; and that my soul in coming down to earth, got drifted away by some sidewind, and so was wafted into the United States, to take up its abode in New-York. Jean Paul, speaking of the quiet habits of the Germans, says he does not believe they turn in their beds so often as the French do. O, for one of those old German homes, where the same stork, with his children and grandchildren, builds on the same roof, generation after generation; where each family knows its own particular stork, and each stork knows the family from all the world beside. Oh, for a quiet nook in good old Nuremberg, where still flourishes the lime tree, planted seven hundred years ago, by Empress Cunegunde; where the same family inhabits the same mansion for five centuries; where cards are still sold in the same house where cards were first manufactured; and where the great-grandson makes watches in the same shop that was occupied by his watch-making great-grandfather.

But after all, this is a foolish, whining complaint. A stork's nest is very pleasant, but there are better things. Man is moving to his highest destiny through manifold revolutions of spirit; and the outward must change with the inward.

It is selfish and unwise to quarrel with this spiritual truth or its ultimate results, however inconvenient they may be. The old fisherman, who would have exterminated steam-boats, because they frightened the fish away from the waters where he had baited them for years, was by no means profound in his social views, or of expansive benevolence.

If the world were filled with different tribes of Nurembergers, with their storks, what strangers should we brethren of the human household be to each other! Thanks to Carlyle, who has brought England and America into such close companionship with the mind of Germany. Thanks to Mary Howitt, who has introduced Frederika Bremer into our homes, like a sunbeam of spring, and thus changed Sweden from a snowy abstraction to a beautiful and healthy reality. It is so pleasant to look into the hearts and eyes of those Northern brothers! To be conveyed to their firesides by a process so much swifter than steam!

Do you fear that the patriot will be lost in the cosmopolite! Never fear. We shall not love our own household less, because we love others more. In the beautiful words of Frederika: 'The human heart is like Heaven; the more angels, the more room.'

ELIZABETH STUART PHELPS

(1815–1852)

The Angel Over The Right Shoulder

(Andover: Warren F. Draper), 1852.

The career of Elizabeth Stuart Phelps offers a fit emblem of the degree to which the talent and the life of the mid-nineteenth-century American woman of genius were sacrificed by and to a culture that had no place for the woman artist. *The Angel Over The Right Shoulder* articulates and documents this sacrifice. Originally, Phelps wished to paint. Yet writing had a more obvious social utility and writing was "easier" to integrate into the life of wife and mother. In *The Story of Avis* (1877), Phelps's daughter, who after her mother's death took her mother's name and called herself Elizabeth Stuart Phelps, recognized and paid tribute to her mother's passion for painting and gave her in fiction the artistic self-expression she never had in life. Equally suggestive of the degree to which convention warped talent, Phelps, of a disposition inherently gloomy and imaginatively dominated throughout childhood by the fear of her mother's death, forced herself as a woman and a Christian to write of and from "the sunny side." That "power of blackness" which Herman Melville recognized in Nathaniel Hawthorne as the sign of genius was, in fact, a masculine prerogative.

Phelps was born on August 13, 1815, in Andover, Massachusetts, the second of five daughters and fifth of nine children of Abigail Clark and Moses Stuart. Her mother was an invalid and her father a prominent professor at Andover Theological Seminary. The severe self-discipline of the latter, combined with the nervous exhaustion that resulted from his frequent insomnia, made a powerful impression on Phelps as a child. To win the approval of this father became a central motive for Phelps, the writer, and her husband records, "It is doubtful whether any subsequent success ever gave her keener pleasure, than she felt when she first received from his lips the hearty 'Well done,' after the publication of one of her simple stories" ("Memorial," p. 19). At the age of ten, Phelps began writing stories for the amusement of her younger sisters and of the family servants and their friends. Throughout her life, her writing continued to have a domestic cast and to be directed to the "family circle."

Educated initially at Abbott Academy in Andover, Phelps left home at the age of sixteen and moved to Boston where she attended the Mount Vernon school and lived with the family of Jacob Abbott, director of the school and later author of the Rollo books for children. Here she first wrote for publication, contributing brief articles signed H. Trusta (an anagram of Stuart) to a religious magazine that Abbott edited. At the same time, she entered on a period of intense religious inquiry that culminated in 1834 in a public profession of faith and a decision to renounce all literary work as not sufficiently "useful":

> My days were all given up to the "solid and useful," as the world would say. I felt, as everyone feels, a sort of happiness in making a sacrifice with a good motive. . . . Yet, I was not happy. My soul did thirst for the beautiful and the true. Suppressed longings, and unsatisfied tastes, and despised capacities, at length took their revenge. They fretted, and chafed, and wore upon the delicate framework that enclosed them, until it gave way. Then followed four long, dreary years ("Memorial," p. 37).

At the end of this period, Phelps renounced her renunciation and, "what is the result? Why, from the very first half hour in which I broke down the barriers of my old system, and took up my pencil, I said, 'Good bye to doctors.' I have been happier, I have been better, every way" ("Memorial," p. 38). Illness had forced Phelps's return to Andover in 1834 and, although the decision to resume her artistic life brought with it physical recovery, she was never again for any length of time free from sickness.

In 1842, at the age of twenty-seven, Elizabeth Stuart married Austin Phelps, a student at Andover who had accepted a pastorate in Boston. The next six years of residence in Boston were by far the happiest period in Phelps's life. Boston provided a welcome change from the atmosphere of Andover: "It introduced her to new varieties of human nature and to new modes of life. She was brought by it more constantly than before into contact with life—with men, women, and children, as they are in a busy, and on the whole a happy, world. It added to the lessons of seclusion, those of society, and to the discipline of study, that of action" ("Memorial," p. 53).

In 1848, when her husband decided to accept a faculty position at Andover, Phelps experienced an overwhelming sense of despair. The return to Andover cast a "black shadow" over her, "like a pall"; it foreshadowed, and in part caused, her death, which occurred only four years later. Elizabeth, however, was a "good" wife. The conventions governing the definition of a "good" wife insured that her needs, if they conflicted with her husband's, would not form a part of the decision-making process. Austin based his decision to leave the pulpit and accept a chair at Andover on his assessment of his own health; an assessment of Elizabeth's health did not figure in his decision, for she, "with her usual generosity, concealed in great measure the foreboding with which she anticipated the change, lest his decision should be unduly influenced by a knowledge of her feelings. When the change was made, it was for a long time the almost hourly struggle of her life to resist the depression that weighed upon her mind" ("Memorial," p. 74).

Phelps died at Andover on November 29, 1852, at the height of her artistic power, her mind full of ideas for future work. She was thirty-seven years old. In her autobiography, *Chapters from a Life* (1896), Elizabeth Stuart Phelps, the daughter, describes the situation that killed her mother:

> Her last book and her last baby came together, and killed her. She lived one of those rich and piteous lives such as only gifted women know; torn by the civil war of the dual nature which can be given to women only. . . . Now she sits correcting proof-sheets, and now she is painting apostles for the baby's first Bible lesson. Now she is writing her new book, and now she is dyeing things canary-yellow in the white-oak dye—for the professor's salary is small, and a crushing economy was in those days one of the conditions of faculty life on Andover Hill. . . . Now she is a popular writer, incredulous of her first success, with her future flashing before her; and now she is a tired, tender mother, crooning to a sick child, while the M.S. lies unprinted on the table, and the publishers are wishing their professor's wife were a free woman, childless and solitary, able to send copy as fast as it is wanted. The struggle killed her, but she fought till she fell.

The publication in 1851 of *The Sunny Side; or, The Country Minister's Wife* brought Phelps international recognition. Previously she had written and published anonymously articles for newspapers and magazines and numerous children's books. The following incident, recorded by her husband, suggests the formulaic nature of these stories and describes the gap between self and text that often characterized the nineteenth-century woman writer: "She herself was often unable to recognize with confidence her own volumes, after years had passed since she wrote them. She has several times been seen bending over the counter of a bookstore, in perplexity as to the authorship of some little book which she held in her hand, seeming to detect some familiar traces of her former self, and yet unable at last to decide whether she were the author of it or not" ("Memorial," p. 58).

No such ambiguity attended her later work, which was marked by her commitment to her own distinctive style of realism. Her husband describes in detail the realist at work:

> She took great delight in her daily rambles through the metropolis. The hours thus spent were her most *studious* hours. She would go out of her way to walk in the thoroughfare, where she could see life in its greatest variety. She would often pause in the street to watch the

sports of a group of children. She could draw a picture of the young
girl she saw behind the counter, or the trio she met at a confectionery.
She could characterize and caricature, with pen or crayon, the motley
company she encountered in an omnibus. The busy hum of voices
continually dropped something which her quick ear appropriated,
storing together the aphorism of gray-haired wisdom with the prattle
of a child at a toy-shop window, and the harangue of a truck man to
his horses. She would pay a street-beggar for a five minutes' conversation; and a talk with an apple-woman on Boston Common, was a
treat for the day ("Memorial," p. 60).

As might be expected, Phelps's self-doubt and self-deprecation kept
pace with her achievement. In a passage written only one year before
her death, she reflects on her success and concludes: "I work in the
dark. Everything lies in chaos before me. My life is a riddle to me; the
past is all I can read. *I cannot tell a letter of the future*" ("Memorial,"
p. 90).

Although Phelps herself made composition a daily habit, reserving
"two hours each day—no more, no less—for her writing table" and
becoming "unhappy, and even desponding . . . if her mind were long
deprived of its customary gratification," she paid an enormous physical
and psychological price for this gratification ("Memorial," pp. 66, 59).
In *The Angel Over The Right Shoulder*, she records both the struggle
and the cost, and reveals, despite those two hours she managed to get
each day, her essential sense of failure. The story posits a different solution to the conflict than the one Phelps herself chose, but it is no less
deadly. In this story, Phelps attempts to resolve the conflict by allowing
her protagonist to substitute the role of object for that of subject, the
role of character for that of author. Imagining herself in her dream as a
character in a divine text, Mrs. James gives over to God the power of
authorship, the task of making pattern and meaning out of the chaos of
her life. In the emphatic and reiterated reference to the angel who
"wrote it down," we sense Mrs. James's, and Phelps's, relief at relin-
quishing the pen to someone else and with this gesture giving up the
effort to become the author of her own life.
    The opening scene defines Mrs. James's dilemma. Clearly, writing
stories constitutes no part of that "woman's work" which is never done.
But why is a woman's work never done? What assumptions determine
that she, not he, will get up and fix the lamp and how do those assumptions ensure that the wife will never get time for what she defines as her
work? Implicit in this opening scene is an analysis of the nature of
housework—unpaid labor, which, because it is unpaid, is often not recognized as work at all but is rather seen as service and thus has no
limitations on it. Implicit also is an understanding of how the marriage
contract contains and enforces these assumptions about women and
work. "A woman's place is in the home" produces a worker who can
never leave the work place and who can therefore never stop working.
The political function of the domestic iconography so central to mid-
nineteenth-century American culture surfaces here as well, for reference
to that "group upon the floor," composed of father and children, has

power to stifle the wife's instinctively affirmative response to her husband's "good-natured" rhetorical question: "Don't you wish you had never been married?"

Phelps's own "good-natured" irony turns on Mr. James, for she perceives the role that individual men play, unwittingly and wittingly, in the creation of women's dilemmas. While Mrs. James fixes the lamp, Mr. James spends the "half hour" meditating on how his wife's want of "system" keeps her from having time for herself. Yet systems govern the life of Mrs. James—both the system she devises to accomplish that work which is never done and the system which puts her in this position. To change this situation would require a "genius" beyond the imagination, or interest, of Mr. James for, as Phelps lets us discover, he likes his system.

Mr. James's response to his wife's brief, and no doubt unusual, expression of frustration places the burden for her predicament squarely on her shoulders, while at the same time his "advice" indicates his assumption that she neither understands nor can solve her own problems. Although she knows that he does not know what he is talking about, she is nevertheless forced to promise that she will follow his advice. Since his plan is based on contradictory premises—you are responsible, you are not responsible; you are free to act and command your time, I must act for and command you—and since it is generated, not only in complete ignorance of the conditions it proposes to solve but also from an unarticulated and presumably unconscious commitment to maintaining those very conditions, it is obviously doomed to failure. Predictably, Mr. James plays a large role in this failure; indeed, his system ensures it for, after all, a man "cannot go down town without a shirt-bosom" nor can a man be expected to remember the marketing. Thus his syntax, "I am anxious to have you try the month out faithfully," rings particularly false. The wife's dream stems directly from the psychological anguish produced by the radical disparity between formulation and fact. She must seek her solution in dreams because her situation makes it impossible for her to articulate directly her own feelings, her own perceptions, her own truths. She can never say to her husband, "*I* am anxious for *you* to try *my* plan"; she can never insist that he promise to "follow me around for one day, and see what I have to do."

Significantly, Mrs. James contacts the truth of her own experience only in the presence of her daughter. For her son who will inherit his father's kingdom of "good natured" laughs, she has no worries; in her sleeping daughter, hugging her doll, she recognizes herself and the need to find answers to give this daughter overwhelms her. The pain of mothering when the child is a daughter forces her to confront her situation. The solution she dreams up may not finally help her daughter, but the commitment evident in the effort has an empowering potential.

Although able to pose her dilemma only in the form of questions, this woman clearly seeks that sense of mastery, self-determination, and authorship that the role of wife and mother conspires to deny her. Unable, in fact, despite her genius, to create and enforce a "system" that would reconcile the identity of wife and mother with that of artist, she seeks a solution that will recognize the reality of her situation, validate her sense of her own powerlessness, and at the same time provide a context within which her life makes sense. Tired of being asked to write her own text, while denied all real possibility of doing so, she willingly relinquishes that responsibility in return for a script she can trust. She herself will never write a book, but someone else is making a text of her life; all the trivial details, the "disjointed effort," the meaningless fragments of her life that to her as author appear "nothing . . . worthy of such careful record"—"these duties and cares acquired a dignity from the strokes of that golden pen." Thus, ironically, this woman's art (for the dream is itself a story) provides the means for disburdening herself of the identity of author and accepting instead the identity of character. After this dream, Mrs. James can give up her struggle to author herself because such self-directing "diligence" constitutes material for a sinister text.

Not surprisingly, the ending of *The Angel Over the Right Shoulder* is weak and unconvincing. The invocation of domestic iconography— "wish you a happy new year, mamma"—carries even less conviction after our exposure to its cost. And the proposition that Mrs. James can choose both self and family is belied by the structure of her dream, which dramatizes the incompatibility of these alternatives and sharply distinguishes between their respective moral value. And, finally, though the dream may provide temporary relief, for continued effectiveness it requires a set of impossible conditions, not the least of which is a constant backward glance to make sure the angels are still there and still writing.

The "real" end of the story occurs somewhat earlier. It indicates the degree to which the dream has, in fact, evaded rather than confronted the reality of the dreamer's life and registers the alienation from self inherent in its "solution": "Eager to warn the traveller of what she had seen, she touched her. The traveller turned, and she recognized or seemed to recognize *herself.* Startled and alarmed, she awoke in tears." Privileged during her dream to be among, indeed behind, the angel authors, Mrs. James's tears signal her despair at resigning herself to the role of character. It is her best, perhaps her only, solution, but it will take a lot of dreaming to keep her on the sunny side of this particular grave.

Source:

The Angel Over The Right Shoulder, twelfth edition (Andover: Warren F. Draper), 1868.

Selected Primary Works:

The Sunny Side; or, The Country Minister's Wife, 1851; *A Peep at "Number Five"; or, A Chapter in the Life of a City Pastor,* 1852; *The Last Leaf from Sunny Side,* 1853; *The Tell-Tale; or, Home Secrets Told by Old Travellers,* 1853.

Selected Secondary Works:

Margo Culley, "The Career/Marriage Conflict in Some Fictions by American Women," Proceedings of the Spring 1974 Conference of the Michigan Women's Studies Association, supplement to the *University of Michigan Papers in Women's Studies* (1974), 35–43; ———, "Vain Dreams: The Dream

Convention and Women's Fiction," *Frontiers,* 1 (1976) 94–102; Carol Farley Kessler, "A Literary Legacy: Elizabeth Stuart Phelps, Mother and Daughter," *Frontiers,* 3 (1980), 28–33; ———, *Elizabeth Stuart Phelps* (Boston: Twayne), 1982; Austin Phelps, "Memorial," in *The Last Leaf from Sunny Side* (Boston: Phillips, Sampson), 1853; Elizabeth Stuart Phelps, *Chapters from a Life* (Boston: Houghton, Mifflin), 1896.

Contexts:

1846—Emerson, *Poems;* Griswold, *The Prose Writers of America;* Hawthorne, *Mosses from an Old Manse;* Judson, *Alderbrook;* Melville, *Typee*

1847—Longfellow, *Evangeline;* Melville, *Omoo;* American Medical Association founded; *The National Era*

1848—Griswold, *The Female Poets of America;* May, *The American Female Poets;* Read, *The Female Poets of America;* gold discovered in California; New York Married Women's Property Act

1849—Alice and Phoebe Cary, *Poems;* Melville, *Mardi, Redburn;* Parkman, *The Oregon Trail;* Sigourney, *Illustrated Poems;* Southworth, *Retribution;* Thoreau, *A Week on the Concord and Merrimack Rivers;* Whittier, *Voices of Freedom*

1850—Emerson, *Representative Men;* Hawthorne, *The Scarlet Letter;* Lippincott, *Greenwood Leaves;* Melville, *White Jacket,* "Hawthorne and His Mosses"; Mitchell, *Reveries of a Bachelor;* Whittier, "Ichabod"; *Harper's New Monthly Magazine;* Fugitive Slave Law

---

"THERE! a woman's work is never done," said Mrs. James. "I thought, for once, I was through; but just look at that lamp, now! it will not burn, and I must go and spend half an hour over it."

"Don't you wish you had never been married?" said Mr. James, with a good-natured laugh.

"Yes"—rose to her lips, but was checked by a glance at the group upon the floor where her husband was stretched out, and two little urchins with sparkling eyes and glowing cheeks were climbing and tumbling over him, as if they found in this play the very essence of fun.

She did say, "I should like the good, without the evil, if I could have it."

"You have no evils to endure," replied her husband.

"That is just all you gentlemen know about it. What would you think, if you could not get an uninterrupted half hour to yourself, from morning till night? I believe you would give up trying to do anything."

"There is no need of that; all you want, is *system.* If you arranged your work systematically, you would find that you could command your time."

"Well," was the reply, "all I wish is, that you could just follow me around for one day, and see what I have to do. If you could reduce it all to system, I think you would show yourself a genius."

When the lamp was trimmed, the conversation was resumed. Mr. James had employed the "half hour," in meditating on this subject.

"Wife," said he, as she came in, "I have a plan to propose to you, and I wish you to promise me beforehand, that you will accede to it. It is to be an experiment, I acknowledge, but I wish it to have a fair trial. Now to please me, will you promise?"

Mrs. James hesitated. She felt almost sure that his plan would be quite impracticable, for what does a man know of a woman's work? Yet she promised.

"Now I wish you," said he, "to set apart two hours of every day for your own private use. Make a point of going to your room, and locking yourself in; and also make up your mind to let the work which is not done, go undone, if it must. Spend this time on just those things which will be most profitable to yourself. I shall bind you to your promise for one month—then, if it has proved a total failure, we will devise something else."

"When shall I begin?"

"To-morrow."

The morrow came. Mrs. James had chosen the two hours before dinner as being, on the whole, the most convenient and the least liable to interruption. They dined at one o'clock. She wished to finish her morning work, get dressed for the day, and enter her room at eleven.

Hearty as were her efforts to accomplish this, the hour of eleven found her with her work but half done; yet, true to her promise, she left all, retired to her room and locked the door.

With some interest and hope, she immediately marked out a course of reading and study, for these two precious hours: then arranging her table, her books, pen and paper, she commenced a schedule of her work with much enthusiasm. Scarcely had she dipped her pen in ink, when she heard the tramping of little feet along the hall, and then a pounding at her door.

"Mamma! mamma! I cannot find my mittens, and Hannah is going to slide without me."

"Go to Amy, my dear; mamma is busy."

"So Amy busy too; she say she can't leave baby."

The child began to cry, still standing close to the fastened door. Mrs. James knew the easiest, and indeed the only way of settling the trouble, was to go herself and hunt up the missing mittens. Then a parley must be held with Frank, to induce him to wait for his sister, and the child's tears must be dried, and little hearts must be all set right before the children went out to play; and so favorable an opportunity must not be suffered to slip, without impressing on young minds the importance of having a "place for everything, and everything in its place." This took time; and when Mrs. James returned to her study, her watch told her that *half* her portion had gone. Quietly resuming her work, she was endeavoring to mend her broken train of thought, when heavier steps were heard in the hall, and the fastened door was once more besieged. Now, Mr. James must be admitted.

"Mary," said he, "cannot you come and sew a string on for me? I do believe there is not a bosom in my drawer in order, and I am in a great hurry. I ought to have been down town an hour ago."

The schedule was thrown aside, the work-basket taken, and Mrs. James followed him. She soon sewed on the tape, but then a button needed fastening; and, at last, a rip in his glove was to be mended. As Mrs. James stitched away on the glove, a smile lurked in the corners of her mouth, which her husband observed.

"What are you laughing at?" asked he.

"To think how famously your plan works."

"I declare!" said he, "is this your study hour? I am sorry, but what can a man do? He cannot go down town without a shirt-bosom!"

"Certainly not," said his wife, quietly.

When her liege lord was fairly equipped and off, Mrs. James returned to her room. A half an hour yet remained to her, and of this she determined to make the most. But scarcely had she resumed her pen, when there was another disturbance in the entry. Amy had returned from walking out with the baby, and she entered the nursery with him, that she might get him to sleep. Now it happened that the only room in the house which Mrs. James could have to herself with a fire, was the one adjoining the nursery. She had become so accustomed to the ordinary noise of the children, that it did not disturb her; but the very extraordinary noise which master Charley sometimes felt called upon to make, when he was fairly on his back in the cradle, did disturb the unity of her thoughts. The words which she was reading rose and fell with the screams and lulls of the child, and she felt obliged to close her book, until the storm was over. When quiet was restored in the cradle, the children came in from sliding, crying with cold fingers; and just as she was going to them, the dinner-bell rang.

"How did your new plan work this morning?" inquired Mr. James.

"Famously," was the reply; "I read about seventy pages of German, and as many more in French."

"I am sure *I* did not hinder you long."

"No—yours was only one of a dozen interruptions."

"O, well! you must not get discouraged. Nothing succeeds well the first time. Persist in your arrangement, and by and by the family will learn that if they want anything of you, they must wait until after dinner."

"But what can a man do?" replied his wife; "he cannot go down town without a shirt-bosom."

"I was in a bad case," replied Mr. James, "it may not happen again. I am anxious to have you try the month out faithfully, and then we will see what has come of it."

The second day of trial was a stormy one. As the morning was dark, Bridget overslept, and consequently breakfast was too late by an hour. This lost hour Mrs. James could not recover. When the clock struck eleven, she seemed but to have commenced her morning's work, so much remained to be done. With mind disturbed and spirits depressed, she left her household matters "in the suds," as they were, and punctually retired to her study. She soon found, however, that she could not fix her attention upon any intellectual pursuit. Neglected duties haunted her, like ghosts around the guilty conscience. Perceiving that she was doing nothing with her books, and not wishing to lose the morning wholly, she commenced writing a letter. Bridget interrupted her before she had proceeded far on the first page.

"What, ma'am, shall we have for dinner? No marketing ha'n't come."

"Have some steaks, then."

"We ha'n't got none, ma'am."

"I will send out for some, directly."

Now there was no one to send but Amy, and Mrs. James knew it. With a sigh, she put down her letter and went into the nursery.

"Amy, Mr. James has forgotten our marketing. I should like to have you run over to the provision store, and order some beef-steaks; I will stay with the baby."

Amy was not much pleased to be sent out on this errand. She remarked, that she "must change her dress first."

"Be as quick as possible," said Mrs. James, "for I am particularly engaged at this hour."

Amy neither obeyed, nor disobeyed, but managed to take her own time, without any very deliberate intention to do so. Mrs. James, hoping to get along with a sentence or two, took her German book into the nursery. But this arrangement was not to master Charley's mind. A fig did he care for German, but "the kitties" he must have, whether or no—and kitties he would find in that particular book—so he turned its leaves over in great haste. Half of the time on the second day of trial had gone when Amy returned, and Mrs. James, with a sigh, left the nursery. Before one o'clock, she was twice called into the kitchen to superintend some important dinner arrangement, and thus it turned out that she did not finish one page of her letter.

On the third morning the sun shone, and Mrs. James rose early, made every provision which she deemed necessary for dinner, and for the comfort of her family; and then, elated by her success, in good spirits, and with good courage, she entered her study precisely at eleven o'clock, and locked her door. Her books were opened, and the challenge given to a hard German lesson. Scarcely had she made the first onset, when the door-bell was heard to ring, and soon Bridget, coming nearer and nearer,—then, tapping at the door.

"Somebodies wants to see you in the parlor, ma'am."

"Tell them I am engaged, Bridget."

"I told 'em you were to home, ma'am, and they sent up their names, but I ha'n't got 'em, jist."

There was no help for it—Mrs. James must go down to receive her callers. She had to smile when she felt little like it—to be sociable when her thoughts were busy with her task. Her friends made a long call—they had nothing else to do with their time, and when they went, others came. In very unsatisfactory chit-chat, her morning slipped away.

On the next day, Mr. James invited company to tea, and her morning was devoted to preparing for it; she did not enter her study. On the day following, a sick-head-ache confined her to bed; and on Saturday, the care of the baby devolved upon her, as Amy had extra work to do. Thus passed the first week.

True to her promise, Mrs. James patiently persevered for a month, in her efforts to secure for herself this little fragment of her broken time, but with what success, the first week's history can tell. With its close, closed the month of December.

On the last day of the old year, she was so much occupied in her preparations for the morrow's festival, that the last hour of the day was approaching, before she made her good night's call in the nursery. She first went to the crib and looked at the baby. There he lay in his innocence and beauty, fast asleep. She softly stroked his golden hair—she kissed gently his rosy cheek—she pressed the little dimpled hand in hers; and then carefully drawing the coverlet over it, tucked it in,—and stealing yet another kiss, she left him to his peaceful dreams,—and sat down on her daughter's bed. She also slept sweetly, with her dolly hugged to her bosom. At this her mother smiled, but soon grave thoughts entered her mind, and these deepened into sad ones. She thought of her disappointment and the failure of her plans. To her, not only the past month but the whole past year, seemed to have been one of fruitless effort—all broken and disjointed—even her hours of religious duty had been encroached upon, and disturbed. She had accomplished nothing, that she could see, but to keep her house and family in order, and even this, to her saddened mind, seemed to have been but indifferently done. She was conscious of yearnings for a more earnest life than this. Unsatisfied longings for something which she had not attained, often clouded what, otherwise, would have been a bright day to her; and yet the causes of these feelings seemed to lie in a dim and misty region, which her eye could not penetrate.

What then did she need? To see some *results* from her life's work? To know that a golden cord bound her life-threads together into *unity* of purpose—notwithstanding they seemed, so often, single and broken?

She was quite sure that she felt no desire to shrink from duty, however humble, but she sighed for some comforting assurance of what *was duty.* Her employments, conflicting as they did with her tastes, seemed to her frivolous and useless. It seemed to her that there was some better way of living, which she, from deficiency in energy of character, or of principle, had failed to discover. As she leaned over her child, her tears fell fast upon its young brow.

Most earnestly did she wish, that she could shield that child from the disappointments and mistakes and self-reproach from which the mother was then suffering; that the little one might take up life where she could give it to her—all mended by her own experience. It would have been a comfort to have felt that, in fighting the battle, she had fought for both; yet she knew that so it could not be—that for ourselves must we all learn what are those things which "make for our peace."

The tears were in her eyes, as she gave the good-night to her sleeping daughter; then, with soft steps, she entered an adjoining room, and there fairly kissed out the old year on another chubby cheek, which nestled among the pillows. At length she sought her own rest.

Soon she found herself in a singular place. She was traversing a vast plain. No trees were visible, save those which skirted the distant horizon, and on their broad tops rested wreaths of golden clouds. Before her was a female, who was journeying towards that region of light. Little children were about her, now in her arms, now running by her side, and as they travelled, she occupied herself in caring for them. She taught them how to place their little feet; she gave them timely warnings of the pit-falls; she gently lifted them over the stumbling-blocks. When they were weary, she soothed them by singing of that brighter land, which she kept ever in view, and towards which she seemed hastening with her little flock. But what was most remarkable was, that, all unknown to her, she was constantly watched by two angels, who reposed on two golden clouds which floated above her. Before each was a golden book, and a pen of gold. One angel, with mild and loving eyes, peered constantly over her right shoulder; another, kept as strict watch over her left. Not a deed, not a word, not a look, escaped their notice. When a good deed, word, look, went from her, the angel over the right shoulder, with a glad smile, wrote it down in his book; when an evil, however trivial, the angel over the left shoulder recorded it in his book,—then, with sorrowful eyes, followed the pilgrim until he observed penitence for the wrong, upon which he dropped a tear on the record, and blotted it out, and both angels rejoiced.

To the looker-on, it seemed that the traveller did nothing which was worthy of such careful record.

Sometimes, she did but bathe the weary feet of her little children, but the angel over the *right shoulder*—wrote it down. Sometimes, she did but patiently wait to lure back a little truant who had turned his face away from the distant light, but the angel over the *right shoulder*—wrote it down. Sometimes, she did but soothe an angry feeling or raise a drooping eyelid, or kiss away a little grief; but the angel over the right shoulder— *wrote it down.*

Sometimes, her eye was fixed so intently on that golden horizon, and she became so eager to make progress thither, that the little ones, missing her care, did languish or stray. Then it was that the angel over the *left shoulder,* lifted his golden pen, and made the entry, and followed her with sorrowful eyes, until he could blot it out. Sometimes, she seemed to advance rapidly, but in her haste the little ones had fallen back, and it was the sorrowing angel who recorded her progress. Sometimes, so intent was she to gird up her loins, and have her lamp trimmed and burning, that the little children wandered away quite into forbidden paths, and it was the angel over the *left shoulder* who recorded her diligence.

Now the observer as she looked, felt that this was a faithful and true record, and was to be kept to that journey's end. The strong clasps of gold on those golden books, also impressed her with the conviction that, when they were closed, it would only be for a future opening.

Her sympathies were warmly enlisted for the gentle traveller, and with a beating heart she quickened her steps that she might overtake her. She wished to tell her of the angels keeping watch above her—to entreat her to be faithful and patient to the end—for her life's work was all written down—every item of it—and the *results* would be known when those golden books should be unclasped. She wished to beg of her to think no duty trivial which must be done, for over her right shoulder and over her left were recording angels, who would surely take note of all!

Eager to warn the traveller of what she had seen, she touched her. The traveller turned, and she recognized or seemed to recognize *herself.* Startled and alarmed, she awoke in tears. The gray light of morning struggled through the half-open shutter, the door was ajar, and merry faces were peeping in.

"Wish you a happy new year, mama"!—"Wish you a *Happy new Year!*"—"A happy noo ear!"

She returned the merry greeting most heartily. It seemed to her as if she had entered upon a new existence. She had found her way through the thicket in which she had been entangled, and a light was now about her path. The *Angel over the Right Shoulder* whom she had seen in her dream, would bind up in his golden book her life's work, if it were but well done. He required of her no great deeds, but faithfulness and patience to the end of the race which was set before her. Now she could see, plainly enough, that, though it was right and important for her to cultivate her own mind and heart, it was equally right and equally important, to meet and perform faithfully all those little household cares and duties on which the comfort and virtue of her family depended; for into these things the angels carefully looked—and these duties and cares acquired a dignity from the strokes of that golden pen—they could not be neglected without danger.

Sad thoughts and sadder misgivings—undefined yearnings and ungratified longings seemed to have taken their flight with the Old Year, and it was with fresh resolution and cheerful hope, and a happy heart, she welcomed the *Glad* New Year. The *Angel over the Right Shoulder* would go with her, and if she were found faithful, would strengthen and comfort her to its close.

ALICE CARY

(1820–1871)

Uncle William's

Clovernook; or,
Recollections of Our Neighborhood in the West,
second series (New York: Redfield), 1853.

A visitor to the Cary Cottage, located on the property of the Clover-nook Home and School for the Blind in North College Hill near Cincinnati, Ohio, will find carefully maintained evidence of the regard that nineteenth-century readers had for Alice Cary, and her sister Phoebe (1824–71). The Cary Cottage, however, is not the "brown house, 'low and small' " of Alice Cary's birth or childhood, the house which, according to Mary Clemmer Ames, her friend and biographer, "appeared and reappeared in the verse of both sisters, till their last lines were written" and for which they had both a "deep and life-long" affection (Ames, p. 1). Although no longer on the original site, this house is also still standing and can be seen by the visitor, if only from the outside. In this house, on what was then a farm eight miles north of Cincinnati, Alice Cary was born on April 26, 1820. She was the fourth of nine children born to Elizabeth Jessup and Robert Cary.

Hard work, little leisure, and less education defined for Alice Cary the circumstances of her early years, leaving her with a permanent sense of disadvantage:

> I don't like to think how much we are robbed of in this world by just
> the conditions of our life. How much better work I should have
> done, how much more success I might have won, if I had had a better
> opportunity in my youth. But for the first fourteen years of my life, it
> seemed as if there was actually nothing in existence but work. . . . We
> hungered and thirsted for knowledge; but there were not a dozen
> books on our family shelf, not a library within our reach. There was
> little time to study, and had there been more, there was no chance to
> learn but in the district school-house, down the road (Ames, p. 19).

In her memorial tribute to Alice, Phoebe Cary lists the few books available to them in their youth: "On a small shelf of the cottage lay all the literary treasures of the family. These consisted of a Bible, hymn-book, The History of the Jews, Lewis and Clarke's Travels, Pope's Essays, and Charlotte Temple, 'a romance, founded on fact.'" Nevertheless, Cary's parents, though with little time to pursue such interests, were both literate and literary. According to Phoebe, Robert Cary "was very fond of reading, especially romance and poetry." Elizabeth Cary read poetry "but cared little for fictitious literature," preferring instead "history, politics, moral essays, biography, and works of religious controversy." In addition, the Cary parents were among the first converts to Universalism and their enthusiasm brought into the household the *Trumpet*, a Universalist newspaper. This paper, according to Phoebe, had a poet's corner that provided early "food" for Alice's "fancy."

More substantial nourishment for Cary's imagination apparently came, however, from the companionship of her older sister, Rhoda, whom Alice always considered the most gifted of the family with a genius for telling stories. On the way to and from school, Rhoda would tell her sister "wonderful" stories and "when we saw the house in sight, we would often sit down under a tree, that she might have more time to finish the story" (Ames, p. 17). The death of this sister in 1833, shortly after the family moved to their new house (the current Cary Cottage), marked the beginning of a series of losses that included Cary's younger sister, Lucy, also in 1833, and in 1835 her mother. According to Phoebe, Alice Cary never completely recovered from the effect of these deaths.

In 1837, Robert Cary remarried. His new wife had no use for literature and when Cary began to write seriously, joined by Phoebe, she received neither encouragement nor assistance from her stepmother. Required to do housework during the day, Cary proceeded to read and write at night, giving early evidence of her extraordinary sense of purpose, determination, and will. Denied candles, Alice and Phoebe "used a saucer of lard with a rag wick for light. . . . They hid their manuscripts in the 'manuscript closet' under the narrow stairway leading from the front hall to the second floor" (Pulsifer, p. 13).

Cary's career as a published poet began when she was eighteen and the Cincinnati *Sentinel*, another Universalist paper, published "The Child of Sorrow." Although for several years Cary published primarily in the *Sentinel*, other local papers and religious periodicals accepted her early work, as did such national magazines as *Graham's*. Rufus Griswold, indefatigable anthologizer and always on the lookout for new poets to include in his collections, noticed Cary's poetry in his researches through western newspapers and printed selections from Alice, and Phoebe, in *The Female Poets of America* (1848). Griswold also assisted Alice in arranging the publication of her first book, *Poems of Alice and Phoebe Cary* (1849).

When Cincinnatian Gamaliel Bailey moved to Washington, D.C. in 1847 to publish the abolitionist weekly, *The National Era*, Cary, now in her late twenties, was sufficiently established to write regularly for its columns. For the *Era*, Cary first tried her hand at prose, publishing a series of sketches entitled "Recollections of Country Life" under the pseudonym of Patty Lee. From Bailey she received the first money she ever earned by writing. Through her work for the *Era*, Cary also attracted the attention of John Greenleaf Whittier, corresponding editor for the paper from 1847 to 1860. Whittier offered Cary early and public recognition, a gift to which Cary assigned considerable value. In a letter to Whittier, dated September 22, 1847, she comments on how difficult it is for the "nameless . . . to obtain a fair public hearing" and thanks him for his "kind notice and encouragement" (Pulsifer, p. 18).

In the summer of 1850, Alice and Phoebe made a trip to Boston, New York City, and Amesbury, Massachusetts, where Whittier lived. After this trip, Cary determined to make her permanent home in New York and to earn there her own living and that of her sister Phoebe. In November, 1850, at the age of thirty, she moved east; in the spring of 1851 she was joined by Phoebe. Commenting on the enormity of Cary's decision, Horace Greeley, whose friendship with the Carys began when he visited them in Ohio in the summer of 1849, noted: "I do not know at whose suggestion they resolved to migrate to this city, and attempt to live here by literary labor; it surely was not mine. If my judgment was ever invoked, I am sure I must have responded that the hazard seemed to me too great, the inducements inadequate" (Ames, p. 31). More tough-minded in the pursuit of her own self-interest than Greeley could imagine, Cary based her decision on a realistic assessment of the "inducements" New York offered to the professional writer. Although her fictional imagination was essentially rural, Cary realized that access to that imagination depended on obtaining the economic and cultural advantages of urban New York.

In 1856, Cary purchased a house on East Twentieth Street. Here she and Phoebe lived until their deaths in 1871. The Carys soon established a household known as a center for New York literary and social life and they created a domestic life based quite literally on sisterhood. On Alice, however, fell the burden not only of economic support, but also of household management. Ames's description of the sisters' daily routine portrays Alice as working to live and living to work: "I have never known any other woman so systematically and persistently industrious as Alice Cary. . . . Her pleasure was her labor. Of rest, recreation, amusement, as other women sought these, she knew almost nothing" (Ames, p. 39). Unlike Phoebe, who took vacations during the summer and once stopped writing for eight years, Alice remained in New York City year after year, permanently destroying her health in the process.

Although both an abolitionist and a feminist, Cary was personally reserved and shy and resisted public involvement in either cause. Once she allowed herself to be pressured into accepting a public role—the first presidency of Sorosis, one of New York City's pioneer women's clubs. Jane Croly, the club's founder, first approached Sara Parton (Fanny Fern); unsuccessful here, she turned to Alice Cary:

> Desirous of having a literary club, with the name of a distinguished literary woman, I begged Alice Cary to accept the position. She found

it difficult to refuse my urgent entreaties, but did so, until I rose in great agitation, saying, "Alice Cary, think what faith, reverence, and affection thousands of women have given to you, and you will not even give to them your name." I left the house hastily, and went back to my office, concealing hot tears of grief and disappointment behind my veil. A moment after I arrived there, to my astonishment she came in, sank down in a chair, breathless with her haste, and said, "If my name is worth anything to women, I have come to tell you to take it" (Ames, pp. 76–77).

During her lifetime, Cary published five volumes of poetry. Her poetry was always a popular success, but it received a mixed critical response. She also published three volumes of short fiction. Her first collection of Clovernook sketches (1852) received positive notice both at home and abroad; the later *Pictures of Country Life* (1859) was praised in a long review in the London *Literary Gazette,* a magazine "not accustomed to flatter American authors" (Greely, p. 169).

In addition, Cary published three novels: *Hagar, A Story of To-day* (1852); *Married, Not Mated* (1856); and *The Bishop's Son* (1867). At her death she left one completed novel in manuscript and one half-finished, "The Born Thrall," designed for serial publication in the *Revolution,* the radical feminist paper established by Susan B. Anthony and Elizabeth Cady Stanton. In this novel, "which was to deal with the sorrows and the wrongs of woman . . . a work dear to her heart, which was especially drawn out toward her own sex," Cary hoped, according to Phoebe, "to do herself greater credit in . . . fiction." Cary's novels are her weakest work. In her evaluation of the novels, Ames calls them Cary's "rudest work" and finds in them material "often unworthy of her" (Ames, pp. 122, 123).

Alice Cary died on February 12, 1871, at the age of fifty, at her home in New York. She was buried in Greenwood Cemetery in Brooklyn. During her last illness, she suffered, in Phoebe's words, "in body all that it seemed possible for mortality to suffer and yet survive, and, from the condition of her nerves, such mental torture, such fear of shapeless and nameless terrors as few souls, let us hope, are ever called upon to endure." Phoebe, who after Alice's death found no reason to live and who followed into death the "cord that stretches from Alice's heart to mine," concludes her tribute to her sister, written shortly before her own death in July, 1871, simply: "Life was to Alice Cary no holiday."

The stories in the first and second Clovernook series and in *Pictures of Country Life* constitute a remarkable piece of American literature. Like so many of the writers represented in this anthology, Cary did her best work in a genre less obviously "literary" and hence less affected by those conventions of plot, character, language, and tone that predetermined the form and content of her novels. In her short fiction, Cary's imagination had free play.

Formal innovation and imaginative freedom are evident in the story reprinted here. "Uncle William's" has no particular beginning, middle, or end. Although Delia and Edward eventually get married, this event is

not an ending, for the courtship of Delia and Edward has not provided
the story's plot; indeed, the process of courtship, central to so many of
the longer fictions, appears here as one of several events set into and
contained within a different narrative structure. The story actually
"ends" in a mode that reflects its lack of conventional structure: "A year
after my visit I heard, by chance, that Mrs. Hevelyn was dead, and the
fragment of her life and love that I have written, is all I know." In
describing her narrative as a "fragment" of life, the narrator/author rejects those preconceived patterns that produced the plots of so many
women's novels, and implies instead that the fragmentary nature of life
determines her form.

This predilection for the fragmentary commits Cary to the mode of
realism. The narrator introduces herself as one bound by the attractions
of "a simple statement of facts" and aware that any attempt at "a flight
in the realms of fancy" would only land her back at the Clovernook
hotel. In the description of the stagecoach journey, which brings the
narrator to her Uncle William's, we reap the rewards of her attractions.
Here, Cary captures with remarkable accuracy that fragmentary quality
of life experienced acutely when people whom we have never seen before and will never see again enter our lives, become temporarily engrossing, and then disappear forever, leaving us full of questions that
will never be answered: "Whether the aforesaid Polly was his wife, and,
if she was, whether she was mad as a hornet, are matters of which to
this day I am profoundly ignorant; but I have hoped that if Polly were
wife to the little merchant, she was pacified with a new dress, and that
the poor beast soon get the better of the lameness."

The strategy of a journey, so successful in conveying the fragmentary
nature of experience, offers Cary in addition the occasion for her narrator to observe a wide range of human characters. Indeed, Cary
realized early what Sarah Orne Jewett would realize later—namely, that
one can solve to some degree the problems that plot presents for women
writers, problems admirably articulated in Joanna Russ's "What Can A
Heroine Do? or, Why Women Can't Write" (1972) and demonstrated in
Harriet Beecher Stowe's *The Pearl of Orr's Island,* by subordinating
plot to character rather than character to plot. So, for example, if Mrs.
Widdleton's "meddling" did not accomplish the marriage of Delia and
Edward, the meaning of "Uncle William's" would not be significantly
altered, for our attention is focused on Mrs. Widdleton's character as a
"meddler," not on its consequences. A commitment to character rather
than plot, then, dominates and shapes Cary's short fiction and is a
major source of her artistic success in the genre.

Cary's narrator has no particular message to convey, no doubt because she has no predetermined story to tell. Structural openness facili-
tates interpretive openness and thus Cary avoids the didacticism that
frequently afflicted her novels as an apparently inevitable concomitant
of plot. Although the fragments of life that the narrator records are
obviously suggestive and are obviously chosen for their suggestiveness,
no authorial, or narrative, voice emerges over our right shoulder to tell
us what they mean. In Elizabeth Stuart Phelps's *The Angel Over The*

Right Shoulder, the narrator's need to interpret detracts from the power of the text. In "Uncle William's," Cary's narrator rarely steps out of her role as observer and recorder.

Cary's idea for her story is simple but it enables her to explore her interest in formal and interpretive openness. She calls the story "Uncle William's" and in it her narrator describes nothing more, nor less, than a visit, of undetermined length, to the home of this Uncle William. We are never told why this visit occurs; more significantly, we never feel the need to be told. As resistant to interpreting her own behavior (for example, her sudden change of mood on the eve of her departure) as that of others, the narrator simply records the facts: "the fat man smiled, and everyone else smiled"; "it would be hard to tell why, but all the coach passengers looked with interest at the various fields, and woods, and pens, where the drover's hogs had rested on their fatal journey toward the city"; "'I wish I could see the one that discovered him,' the woman said, trying to pull down the window"; "and as he spoke he lifted the child from her knees, unbuttoned his brown coat, and folded him warmly beneath it, resting his chin on the boy's hair, informing him that at home he had a little boy just about his size, and asking him if he would like to go home with him and be his little boy."

Some behaviors, however, are given more context than others. In the description of the woman with the child, for example, we feel her disaffection from and even hostility toward her charge. From the description of the gentleman next to Nelly, we realize his resistance to her dependence on him. In Nelly's response, we recognize both shame and powerlessness, the consequences, as we later learn, of her loss of chastity and compulsory marriage. And in the interminable flow of Mrs. Widdleton's speech, joyfully released when she finds an appropriate pretense, we recognize a woman who thinks of herself as an authority with something to say about everything of interest to everyone.

Yet these contexts are themselves still shrouded in mystery. We never learn, for example, why Nelly capitulated or why John married her. When we consider the nature of these mysteries, however, we discover that inexplicability itself makes Cary's point. November melancholy sets the tone for Cary's fictional world. A sense of sadness and loss, of possibilities wasted, of individual human life as insignificant and contingent, determined not by free will or even personal malice but by accident and indifference, inform her work. Here on this very ordinary and unassuming coach ride we casually encounter madness, suicide, deformity, child-abuse, and wife-abuse. Cumulatively, these encounters make a statement about the nature of the human condition. The absence of any narrative need to explain the reasons for these events makes an equally powerful statement. Suicide, madness, death require no explanation; there is sufficient material in any human life to craze or kill.

Arrival at Uncle William's brings no new set of norms. Although we might reasonably assume that the narrator is visiting her female cousins, and particularly her younger cousin, as much as she is visiting her uncle, nevertheless, without explanation or comment, Delia gets on the coach as the narrator steps off and, assisted by the gentleman whose gallantry extends only to the unseduced, departs for an unidentified destination for an undetermined length of time, leaving the narrator to "enjoy" the "society" of Uncle William and Cousin Jane. In the figure of Uncle William, we see how human life can be reduced to a minimum of action and interest and still continue. The narrator's observant stance here provides an admirable technique for registering her own experience; the description of one day, which is every day, in the life of Uncle William captures more powerfully the boredom that afflicts her than any attempt to describe her own reaction directly could do. Significantly enough, Uncle William himself shows no trace of boredom. Here, as elsewhere in her fiction, Cary records the extraordinary ability of men to find in the petty details and repetitious routines of their own lives objects of consuming interest.

Not all women can, like Cousin Jane, so readily shrink their lives to fit the narrow compass described by the dominant male. In Cary's fictional world, women are often bored, and, since boredom breeds either meddling or narration, women are for her the natural storytellers. Cary's narrator takes her seat at the window where she can watch the movements of her neighbors. The neighbors who most interest her are the women. No single view of women's estate emerges from Cary's short fiction; nor is this fiction informed by any theories about "woman's nature." Her stories are singularly free from that prescriptive tyranny that required so much of women's literature to define the right way for the true woman to be. Cousin Jane is neither better nor worse than Mrs. Hevelyn; and the instance of Mrs. Widdleton indicates that not all husbands are "Johns." Nevertheless, the story is titled "Uncle William's" and the example of Nelly carries considerable weight. Delia and Edward may manage to be happy, but the relative powerlessness of women is conveyed through the fate of Mrs. Hevelyn. Loss of chastity has made her morally subject to the man forced to marry her, and moral subjection has increased her psychological vulnerability. Economic dependence seals her doom, placing her life completely in the hands of a husband whose indifference is slowly killing her. That she is frantic with joy at the chance to rejoin him makes sufficient comment on the nature of women's experience. In such a context, perhaps only the fragmentary is capable of realism.

Source:

Clovernook; or, Recollections of Our Neighborhood in the West, second series (New York: Redfield), 1853

Selected Primary Works:

Poems of Alice and Phoebe Cary, 1849; Clovernook; or, Recollections of Our Neighborhood in the West, 1852; Hagar: A Story for Today, 1852; Married, Not Mated; or, How They Lived at Woodside and Throckmorton Hall, 1856; Pictures of Country Life, 1859; Ballads, Lyrics, and Hymns, 1866; A Lover's Diary, 1868.

Selected Secondary Works:

Mary Clemmer Ames, A Memorial of Alice and Phoebe Cary, with Some of Their Later Poems (New York: Hurd and Houghton), 1873; M. F. Armstrong,

"Alice and Phoebe Cary—A Remembrance," *Woman's Journal* (September 9), 1871; Phoebe Cary, "Alice Cary," *Woman's Journal* (August 5), 1871; James C. Derby, *Fifty Years among Authors, Books, and Publishers* (New York: G. W. Carleton), 1884; Horace Greeley, "Alice and Phebe [*sic*] Cary," *Eminent Women of the Age* (Hartford: S. M. Betts), 1868; Annette Kolodny, *The Land Before Her* (Chapel Hill: University of North Carolina Press), 1984; Janice G. Pulsifer, "Alice and Phoebe Cary, Whittier's Sweet Singers of the West," *Essex Institute Historical Collections*, 109 (1973), 9–59; W. H. Venable, *Beginnings of Literary Culture in the Ohio Valley* (Cincinnati: Robert Clarke), 1891.

Contexts:

1851—Hart, *The Female Prose Writers of America;* Hawthorne, *The House of Seven Gables;* Melville, *Moby Dick;* Mitchell, *Dream Life;* Phelps, *The Sunny Side; or, The Country Minister's Wife;* Smith, *Woman and Her Needs;* Warner, *The Wide, Wide World*

1852—Hawthorne, *The Blithedale Romance;* Melville, *Pierre;* Phelps, *A Peep at "Number Five"; or, A Chapter in the Life of a City Pastor;* Stowe, *Uncle Tom's Cabin;* Warner, *Queechy*

1853—Brown, *Clotel;* Melville, "Bartleby, The Scrivener"; *The Una; Putnam's Monthly Magazine*

I.

No MATTER HOW ingeniously probabilities may be woven, how cunning are plots, or effective situations, the fictitious narrative has rarely the attractive interest of a simple statement of facts; and every one seems to have that quick instinct which detects the most elaborate imitations of truth, so that all the skill of the novelist fails to win a single tribute not due merely to his art. I cannot tell what I might be tempted to essay if I possessed more imagination or fancy, but with a brain so unfruitful of invention, and a heart bound as with spells to the past, I should find myself, even if attempting a flight in the realms of fancy, but recalling some half forgotten experience, and making Puck or Titania discourse after the manner of our landlord at the Clovernook Hotel, or the young women whose histories I began to mark when we were girls together in the district school.

It is, perhaps, seven or eight years ago—ah me, how soon we grow old enough to look back to seven, and eight, and ten years, as to yesterday!—since I went to spend the winter with my cousins, Delia and Jane Peters. They lived in the neighborhood of Elm Ridge. It is an obscure and was to me a lonesome place, though they said they had society enough all around them; and indeed the village meeting-house and tavern-sign were within view, and the window lights of Abner Widdleton, the nearest neighbor, shone across the door-yard.

The happiest occasions, if they bring change with them, are sad; and I remember that I could not sleep well the night previous to my setting out, though I had been for weeks talking of the pleasure I should have in visiting uncle William's family. The last collar was ruffled, the last strings and hooks and eyes adjusted, my trunk packed, and my bonnet, with the green veil pinned fast, laid on the bed, and but a night lay between me and my little journey. Then it was, when all was ready, that a sorrowful, half-regretful feeling came over me. I stood at the window and looked on the way the stage-coach would come in the morning; watched the cows as they crouched with petty rifts of snow along their backs, and their faces from the wind; and the chickens, as they flew into the cherry-tree, cackling their discomfort as they settled themselves on the smoothly worn boughs; for it was a blustery night, and these commonplaces seemed to have in them a solemn import, all because I was to be a dozen miles away for a few weeks!

A dozen times I said to little Dillie, with whom I slept, "Are you awake?" before I could sleep. But I was wearied out at last, and but imperfectly heard the speckled cock telling his mates of midnight when a blessed wave of oblivion came between me and Elm Ridge, and I woke not till a hand rested lightly on my shoulder, and a familiar voice said, "I guess it's time." I needed no second call, but was dressed and waiting in a few minutes. It did not require much time for breakfast, I think. There seemed nothing for us to say as we watched the coming of the coach, while my baggage was carried toward the gate that I might occasion no detention. A few repetitions of what had been already said, a few exchanges of smiles that faded into sighs, and the well-known rumble of the approaching vehicle arrested our make-believe conversation.

My little baggage was hoisted to the top. I was afraid I should never see it again. A portly gentleman, having a round red face and pale blue eyes, reached out one hand—it was freckled and fat, I remember—to assist me in; "All ready?" cried the driver, and we were off. I looked back presently, and saw them all standing just as I had left them, except little Dillie, who had climbed on the fence, and was gazing after us very earnestly. The coach jolted and rolled from side to side, for the road was rough and frozen; and the plethoric individual, who wore a tightly buttoned brown overcoat, leaned his double chin on his round hands, which were crossed over the gold head of a crooked but highly polished walkingstick, and conversed with the gentleman opposite, in an easy and complacent way that indicated a state of satisfaction with the world and with himself. His companion was exceedingly diminutive, having the delicate hands and feet of a child; a mouth in which a shilling might scarcely be slipped; a little long head, bald about the crown, and with thin brown hair hanging far over his coat-collar, which was glazed with such contact to the depth of half an inch, as it seemed. I soon learned their respective homes and avocations: the fat man proved to be a pork merchant, homeward bound from a profitable sale; and his little fellow traveller a tailor and small merchant of one of the western states. "There," said he, smiling, and pointing to a huge wagon of several tons burden, drawn by six stout horses, wearing bells on their collars, "there goes a little buggy that's got a budget or two of mine aboard."

The fat man smiled, and every one else smiled, as they saw the six horses straining with all their ability, slowly to drag along the ponderous load; for the great wagon-body was heaped and overheaped with bags, bales, and baskets, crocks, cradles, and calicoes, in fact with all sorts of family and household utensils, from a plow to a teapot, and with wearing apparel from buckram and ducks to cambrics and laces.

"Two or three times a year I buy up such a little bunch as that," he said; and he smiled again, and so did every body else.

"That bay cretur on the off side," he resumed, letting down the window and looking back, "is fallen lame, I believe my heart. Polly will be as mad as a hornet about it; it's her riding nag, d' ye see—that ere bay." And as long as we could hear the bells he continued to gaze back, tying a silk handkerchief over his head as he did so, to protect it from the cold. Whether the aforesaid Polly was his wife, and, if she was, whether she was mad as a hornet, are matters of which to this day I am profoundly ignorant; but I have hoped that if Polly were wife to the little merchant, she was pacified with a new dress, and that the poor beast soon got the better of the lameness.

The fat man pointed out all the places in which the hogs he had just sold had rested of nights, and each time he concluded with, "Well, they'll never root any more." It would be hard to tell why, but all the coach passengers looked with interest at the various fields, and woods, and pens, where the drover's hogs had rested on their fatal journey toward the city. "Just on this knoll, or that rise," he would say, "a fat fellow gave out, and we let him have a ride the rest of the way, or treated him to a hot bath." He occupied more than his share of room, to the very evident annoyance of the woman who was on the seat with him; for she had much less than half for herself and her child, a deformed and forlorn-looking little boy of perhaps six years of age. He was scantily, even meanly dressed, his bare feet hanging quite below his cotton frock, and his stiff fur hat so large as to fall over his eyes, which were remarkably black and large. I could not but notice that the mother, as I supposed her to be, wrapped her shawl more carefully about herself than the child, who kept all the time moaning and fretting, sometimes crying out bitterly. She made no effort to soothe him, except that she now and then turned his face from one direction to another. Once or twice she held it close against her—I thought not fondly, but crushingly—and more than once or twice she dashed his head against the fat man's side, partly by way of jostling him, as I thought, and partly to punish the child for crying. He rubbed his eyes till his little hands were wet with tears; but never did she warm them in her bosom or dry them with kisses. Indeed, she seemed no more concerned than as if she had held on her lap a bundle of sticks. A sudden cry of evident pain drew all eyes to her. In one of the dabs at the fat man she had scratched the boy's face with a pin sticking in his sleeve.

"Poor little beauty!" whispered a pale, lady-like looking woman to the person beside her, a black-whiskered, well-fed sort of man: "poor little beauty! I wish I had it."

"Really, Nelly," he answered, in a half kind, half mocking way, "you *are* benevolent;" and in a lower voice he added, "considering the circumstances."

I occupied the middle seat, with the merchant, and she who had spoken so kindly sat directly behind me, but I turned involuntarily when I heard her voice, and saw, as I have said, that she looked pale and delicate, and that she dropped her veil and blushed at the gentle reproval of her companion.

With this couple sat a rosy-cheeked, middle-aged woman, who had hitherto kept her lips compressed, but, as it appeared to me, with difficulty. She now leaned across the lap of the gentleman, and asked the invalid traveller if she had any children of her own, and if she was married or single; saying she wondered she should feel such sympathy for that "ornary child," for that nobody but a mother could have the feelings of a mother. "Now I," she added, "have left a little one at home—six months old it was the fourteenth of last month—and I'm just fairly crazy, though I have n't been gone a day, as you may say, for it was three o'clock yesterday when I started; the baby was asleep then; I expect maybe he cried when he waked up and missed me, but it seemed necessary for me to go away. I had to go, in fact, as you may say. Nobody drove me to be sure, but then we wanted a good many things about the house that, as you may say, nobody could get but myself, and I thought I might as well go now as ever. I knew the baby would be taken good care of by Liddy— that's my oldest girl; but it seemed like I could n't get my own consent, and I went without it at last, as you may say. Do you live in town?" she inquired; and, without pausing for a reply, continued, "A body sees a heap of pretty things that a body would like to have, do n't they, if they only had plenty of money? This is a tea-pot," she said, holding up a carefully wrapped parcel; "it's a new fashion, they told me; but I think it's a new-fashioned old fashion; for I remember, when I was a girl, we used to have one just a'most like it." And she kindly tore off a bit of the envelope, telling the lady she could see the color, and that she had a set of things in a basket on the top of the coach, the same color, and the make of the same man, she supposed. "Dear sakes! I hope none of them will get broken, and won't I be glad to see my baby!" Having settled herself in her place, she leaned forward again to say, "Just hear that fat man! he talks about his affairs as if he thought every body as much interested in them as himself."

I could not help but smile at her innocent simplicity. How quick we are to detect the faults of others—how slow to "see ourselves as others see us."

"Do you see that old tree with the fork split off and hanging down?" It was the fat man who asked this question—of nobody in particular—but every body tried to see, and most of us did see. "One of my fellows hung himself there last week. He was well the day before. At supper—we slept at a tavern not half a mile away—I noticed that he did n't eat, and seemed down-hearted like; but I did n't say nothing to him; I wish now I had; and in the morning he could n't be found, high nor low. Finally, we gave up the search, and got our drovers started-along later than common. I stopped a bit after the rest, settling with the landlord, who said to me, in a joking way like, that he guessed he'd have to charge me for his wife's clothes-line; that she said she was as certain as she was alive that it hung on a particular peg the last night, and she thought the missing drover knew something about it; he looked wild out of his eyes, she said. Just that way he spoke about it; and I laughs at him, mounts my horse, and rides away. I had just come in sight of the drove when one of my fellers—that's the one whose legs you see," and he pointed to a pair of muddy boots hanging against the window from the outside of the coach,—"came toward me running on the full jump, and told me they had discovered Jake hung on a tree, and swinging in the wind, stiff as a poker."

"Good gracious me!" exclaimed the woman with the sick child, and giving the fat man as much room as possible, "how did he look, and what did you do with him?"

"Look! he looked like a dead man; and as for doing with him, we cut him down, and put him underground by the side of an old black log."

"I wish I could see the one that discovered him," the woman said, trying to pull down the window; "is he any kin to the man that hung himself, and had he taken the clothes-line?"

"He had taken the clothes-line, but the landlady on its being returned to her, said it would bring bad luck to the house, and so threw it in the fire."

The poor child was not thrust against him any more; but it kept crying and moaning, and rubbing its eyes and the scratch on its face, which smarted as the tears rolled over it.

"What ails your child?" asked the fat man, who seemed not to have noticed its crying till he turned to answer the nurse's question.

"Nothing, only he's ugly and cross," she answered.

"I guess any of us would feel bad," said the rosy-cheeked woman with the new tea-pot, "if our bare feet hung dangling about like his 'n, to say nothing of that scratch on his face. Wont you be good enough, sir, to take that pin out of your sleeve?"

"Certainly, ma'am; I was not aware"—he did n't finish the sentence to her, for she had leaned across the coach, and was saying to the pale lady that she never could see what a man wanted to have pins sticking about him for.

"Naughty pin, was n't it!" said the fat man to the baby, taking from his sleeve the offending instrument and throwing it from the window; and he continued, putting the child's feet in one of his mittens, "Tell him murrur she must wrap him in her shawl."

"You need n't look at me," she replied, "I am not his mother by a great sight; she's in a mad-house; they just took her this morning. It was a dreadful sight—she a raving, and the children screaming and carrying on at a dreadful rate. They say she is past all cure, and I s'pose she is. She liked to have pulled all the hair out of my head when she saw I was going to take the baby. I am only a distant relation, but it's not always near of kin that are the best to orphans. Sit up!" she exclaimed, giving the child a rough jerk; "do n't lean against the gentleman as heavy as a bag of mush." The fat man had become a lion in her estimation since she learned that one of his drovers had hanged himself.

"He does n't disturb me in the least," said he; and taking off the child's hat, he smoothed its hair with his great hand.

"I guess he is a right nice man," said the rosy-cheeked woman, leaning toward her of the pale cheek, who was untying a fur cape from her neck. "Put it round the little boy, my good woman," she said, reaching it toward her.

"Really, Nelly," said the gentleman beside her, and he looked at her with evident displeasure.

But the woman returned the cape, saying, "He's got to take the world as he can get it; there is no use of wrapping him in a fine fur cape for an hour."

"That fellow up there," said the fat man, "could give more particulars than I can about the wretched suicide I was telling of."

"Wretched what?" inquired the woman.

"The fellow that was so fond of swinging;" and as he spoke he lifted the child from her knees, unbuttoned his brown coat, and folded him warmly beneath it, resting his chin on the boy's hair, informing him that at home he had a little boy just about his size, and asking him if he would like to go home with him and be his little boy.

The coach now rattled along at a lively rate, and, soothed by the warmth and kindliness of the drover's tone, the poor little fellow was soon fast asleep.

I noticed that the lady in the corner looked weary; and that once when she laid her head on the shoulder of the man beside her, he moved uneasily, as if the weight burdened him, and that she lifted herself up again, though she seemed scarcely able to do so.

"That's my house," said the rosy-cheeked woman, "right fernent William Peters's; and I guess I am as glad to get home as they will be to see me—the dear knows I did n't want to go. I would have paid anybody, and been very much obliged to them besides, if they could have done my errands for me."

At the gate of her house an obedient-looking man stood in waiting for her; and as the crockery was handed down, the good-natured owner gathered her sundry little parcels together; shook hands with the pale lady, saying she hoped she would soon get the better of the ill turn she seemed to have; uncovered the baby's face, and kissed it, dropping a tear on its clasped hands, as she did so, and saying "Just to think if it was mine!" I suppose by way of apology for what the world considers a weakness; and, smiling a sort of benediction on us all, she descended the side of the coach. I followed, for my destination was also reached.

"*You* going to stop here? Well now, if that do n't beat all! I suppose you are Mr. Peters's niece that I've heard so much tell of. And as I am alive, if there aint Delia, just going away! Poor girl, I guess she leaves her heart behind her." This suspicion she imparted in a whisper; and having said I must come in and see her, she flew rather than walked toward the house, for Jane was coming to meet her with the baby. I could only shake hands an instant with my cousin Delia, who seemed to anticipate little happiness from her journey, as I judged from tear-blind eyes and quivering lips. I thought she whispered to her father something about remaining at home, now that I was come.

"Oh, no, Dillie, I do n't think it's worth while," he said; "she will stay here all winter, and you will be back in a month, at furthest."

The companion of the pale lady assisted Delia into the coach with much gallantry; the driver's whip-lash made a circuit in the air; the jaded horses sprang forward as though fresh for the race; and the poor little child, with its bare feet and red hands, was lost to me forever. May the good Shepherd have tempered the winds to its needs, and strengthened it against temptations, in all its career in this hard and so often uncharitable world.

II.

"How glad I am you have come," said uncle William, when we were in the house; "but it seems kind a lonesome for all."

Jane was ten years older than Delia—not so pretty nor stylish, but very good, motherly, and considerate. They had no mother, and lived with their father in the old house where they were brought up. Delia was about sixteen at the time of my visit; handsome, captivating, and considered quite the belle of the village and neighborhood.

We were a small and quiet family at uncle William's. He himself did little but tend the parlor fire, read the newspaper, and consult the almanac and his watch, which things made up his world. He knew all the phases of the moon, and what the weather would be likely to be for a month in advance; he knew what his favorite editor said, and believed it; in fact, there was no other paper; its contents seemed designed more especially for him than for anybody else; and to this day I can not rid myself of the impression that uncle William's newspaper was altogether the most excellent thing of its kind in the world. When the sun came up, he took from beneath the parlor looking-glass, where it hung of nights, the great silver chronometer that had been his father's and his grandfather's, turned the key a few times, held it to his ear, consulted the almanac, and compared the sunrise with his time, as if to see that the sun were punctual to its appointment. He then mended the fire, and took up the "Republican," and when it was read through once he began again, more studiously to examine, and thoughtfully to digest its most noticeable contents. It always had something good in it, he said, and it would do him no harm to read some of the pieces a dozen times. When the sunlight slanted through the south window, he carefully folded the paper, and again consulted his watch. At sunset another comparison was made of time authorities, and the almanac again resorted to, and then began the evening reading.

Uncle William never indulged in what is termed frivolous conversation; the only thing in the way of fun I ever heard him say was that the editor of his paper was a man that had a head. But he was less morose, and far more genial, than another of my relations, uncle Christopher, with whom he held no intercourse whatever, but of whom I shall have something to relate in these reminiscences of Clovernook history.

Jane had little more to say than her father. She never read, and had never been from home; and so, of course, she was not very wise; and as she never talked of things that did not concern her, there was not much for her to discuss. In all ways she was strictly proper; so much so that ordinary mortals found it more difficult to love her than they would have done had she possessed more of the common human infirmities. Our conversation was mostly of the weather, with which, however, she was always contented; so that if the storm beat never so tempestuously, I scarcely dared yawn, or say even that "I wish it would clear off."

I should have been happier if the house had been left in some disorder on Delia's departure, so that we might have employed ourselves by setting it to rights; but everything was in its place; so we of necessity sat down by the fire, and the little we did say was in whispers, that we might not disturb uncle William, who forever sat by, reading in a monotonous mutter, neither aloud nor in silence. Sometimes he would invite me to read, for the benefit of himself, who had read it twenty times previously, Jane, who did n't care a straw for reading, and the sixteen cats that dozed about the hearth, some "piece" which he thought of remarkable interest or beauty.

"Will Delia be gone long?" I inquired after my arrival; for I had previously learned that she was gone two or three hundred miles from Elm Ridge, to a small city which I had never known uncle William's folks to visit, and I was curious to know the why and wherefore. Jane stitched a little faster, I thought; the twilight was deepening so much that I could not have seen to stitch at all; but she only answered that her sister's stay was uncertain.

"I did n't know you had friends there," I said, for I did not like to ask more directly.

"Did n't you?" answered Jane, stitching as before.

I was not discouraged, and remembering what the rosy-cheeked woman had said about Delia's having left her heart behind her, I continued, "She has grown very pretty since I saw her; she must be very much admired."

"Our preacher's wife gave her a book," she said, "at Christmas, and our singing master—old Mr. White—offered to teach her for nothing." And these were all the evidences of the admiration she received which Propriety Jane thought fit to disclose for me.

"Who lives opposite?" I asked; for the house looked so cheerful, with its lights moving about, the chimneys sending up their blue smoke, and the bustling in and out of doors, that I could not help wishing myself there, since not a candle was lighted in our house, and there was no supper in preparation, nor any cheerful talk to enliven the time.

"Mr. Widdleton's folks," replied Jane, and rising from her chair, she stood close against the window, that she might see to stitch a little longer.

"What sort of people are they?"

"Oh, very nice people."

"It must have been Mrs. Widdleton with whom I came up in the coach: a rosy-cheeked, good-natured woman, who seems fond of talking."

"Yes, it was she."

"Well," said I, "she bought a new teapot, with a variety of other things, as she was good enough to inform us all."

Jane made no reply whatever, nor by smile or gesture indicated that Mrs. Widdleton had been communicative in any unusual degree.

The snow was falling dismally, the fire was low, and the coming on of night seemed gloomy enough. Uncle William was splitting pine boards into kindling, and though all day I had wished he would afford us by his absence a little opportunity for conversation, I now heartily wished he would return, and tell us when the moon would change.

As I listened to the winds, and wondered what kept my uncle and cousin alive, there was a low and what seemed to me a very timid rap at the door. Jane opened it; and though her tone evinced neither surprise nor pleasure, it was not uncivil, as she received the visitor. He seemed—for he was a young man—not to feel at liberty to sit down, though Jane invited him so to do; but, having made some commonplace observations relative to the weather, he inquired whether Miss Delia were at home.

"No," answered Jane; and she gave no intimation as to where her sister was gone, or when she would return, or whether she would ever do so.

"I will then bid you good evening," he said, "and do myself the pleasure of calling again."

When he was gone, Jane left the room, having made no reply to the young gentleman's intimation.

On his entrance, I had stirred the coals to make a little light, but it was so faint that I saw him but imperfectly, though with enough distinctness to warrant me in believing him a very handsome man, of not more than twenty-two or three years of age. Besides, his voice was so soft and musical as, together with his fair looks, to leave a most agreeable impression. Who he was or whence he came I could not know, but somehow I was interested in him, and pressing my face to the window, looked eagerly through the snow to see in what direction he went. At the gate he paused, thrust his hands into his pockets, and seemed to muse for a moment, looking one way and then another, as if in doubt what to do; but presently he lighted a cigar with a match, and, turning in the direction of a tavern, was quickly lost from my observation.

"Who was that young person?" I asked, when Jane returned to the parlor.

"Edward Courtney."

"Does he live in the village?"

"No."

"I noticed that he went in that direction."

Jane lighted the candle and took up her work.

"Very handsome, is n't he?" I said.

"Yes."

"What is his occupation?"

"His father, with whom he lives, is a farmer, but lately come to our neighborhood."

"Well, I wish he had passed the evening with us, and not been so exclusively devoted to Miss Delia."

Jane said nothing, and I inquired when he would be likely to come again.

"I do n't know."

"Really, Jane," I said, "you are provoking; for once in your life tell me something I wish to find out. What is it, that his name is Edward Courtney, and that his father is a farmer; he may be a scapegrace for all that. Pray, what do you know about him, and why do you not like him? for I am sure you do not."

"Why, yes, I like him well enough," she answered; "but I know nothing about him to tell; he is rather a wild young man, I think."

"What wild thing has he done?"

"Oh, I do n't know: I do n't know as he is wild.'

And holding out one foot, she asked me how I liked her shoes, saying they were made out of dog-skin; she thought they were as pretty as morocco, and her father said he thought they would last all winter.

"S'cat!" exclaimed uncle William, at this moment making his way through a dozen of the feline tribe; and having mended the fire, he said he believed the moon quartered that night, and proceeded to examine the almanac.

To me the evening seemed setting in very lonesomely, and it was a most agreeable surprise when one of Mrs. Widdleton's children came in to ask cousin Jane and myself to pass it with her. To my disappointment, however, Jane did not feel like going; she was afraid of getting the tooth-ache, and believed she could not go very well.

"You go, any how," said the boy who had asked us; "Mother says if you ain't acquainted, come and get acquainted."

I hesitated, for it seemed awkward to go alone into a stranger's house, but the urgency of the lad and my own inclination prevailed; and I was already aware that the social customs of Elm Ridge were not trammeled by oppressive conventional restrictions.

On my arrival, I saw, to my surprise, the whiskered gentleman whom I have mentioned as the companion of the pale lady in the coach.

"Really, madam," he said, "I do hope, if it will not be a serious inconvenience, that I can prevail upon you—not so much on my own account as for my wife's sake. She is *pious,* and does n't like being at the hotel, where Sunday is pretty nearly as good as any other day."

"And are you not pious?" asked Mrs. Widdleton, looking at him in innocent astonishment.

He smiled and shook his head, but made no other answer.

"Well, I do n't know what to say. I liked the little woman"—

"Yes, I like her too," interrupted the man, with a peculiar smile, intended perhaps as an expression of humor.

"Did you ever!" exclaimed Mrs. Widdleton, and she went on to say that she feared their plain way of living would not suit a fine lady, who had been used to servants, and like enough never had to wet her hands. She would see what Abner thought.

"By all means."

And the gentleman seated himself, and caressed one leg, while she withdrew, for a consultation, to the kitchen, where a hammering seemed to indicate the going forward of some active business.

"Just have it your own way, mother," I heard him say. "If you are a mind to do more and have more, why you can; but seems to me you have enough to do; though I do n't care. Do just as you please; but I hate to have you make a slave of yourself, mother."

"Well, Abner," she answered, "one or two more in the family do n't seem to make much difference; and if they are not suited, why they can find another place, may be."

When the gentleman had taken leave, which he did very politely, Mrs.

Widdleton informed me that his name was Hevelyn; that he was a southern man, lately married, and had come north for the sake of his wife's health. This she had learned during her late interview with him. She also informed me she was going to board them awhile; that she wanted to get a few things for Liddy, more than she could spare the money to buy—not that Abner would be unwilling to give it to her, but then he had so many uses for his money.

Mrs. Widdleton was one of those bustling, active women, who never seem in their right sphere except with hands full and overflowing. Everybody was active about her—Mr. Widdleton mending her washing-tub, Liddy making a new gown, one of the children rocking the cradle, and all at something. As for what she did during the evening in the way of mending and making, I can not recount it, but the cradle was heaped, and so were all the chairs about her, with the work she did. We had cakes, and apples, and cider, and nuts, besides a constant flow of talking, in which Mr. Widdleton, having finished his tub, participated. I felt, I remember, a wish that everybody might be just as contented as they, and have just as bright a fire.

But Mrs. Widdleton—ah me, I do n't like to write that *"but"*—was a little given to talking of things that did not concern her, as well as of things that did; and when the children were gone to bed, and while Abner had ground the coffee for breakfast—"he is so handy about the house," said Mrs. Widdleton—we drew close to the embers, and the good woman glided naturally from her own tea-set to the tea-sets of her neighbors, and thence the transition to her neighbors themselves was almost imperceptible. A number of interesting little family affairs came to my knowledge that night; but I will not attempt a report of all her disclosures—only of some intimations that more immediately interested me. Uncle William and Jane had put their heads together, she said, and sent off Delia, the dear knows where, to prevent her keeping the company of Edward Courtney; and for her part she thought, though she did n't want to say anything one way or the other, and it was very seldom she did speak at all, that Delia or any other girl might go further and fare worse, for Edward Courtney was just as nice a young man, apparently, as ever she set eyes on, and she would just as soon a daughter of hers married him as to marry some persons that some persons thought a good deal better, or to live at home till she was forty years old, and nurse the cats. Jane, she confessed, was just as good a girl as ever was, and uncle William was just as good a man as ever was, but they would think it very hard to be made to marry somebody they did n't like; and, for her part, she thought it was just as bad to be kept from marrying whom you did like. "It's one thing to marry," said Mrs. Widdleton, "and another thing to love the man you marry; and, for my part, I would have Abner or I would have nobody. I was always averse to match-making, but I have a great mind as ever I had in my life"—she suddenly paused, and added, "No, I do n't know as I will, either; but I hate to see folks as cool as a cucumber about such things, and think nobody has any feeling more than themselves. Poor Delia! Yes, I have the greatest mind—no—I do n't know as I will—I might reflect on myself if it did n't all come out right." And she vigorously trotted her baby, long after he was asleep; and I have always thought that then and there she settled the knotty point, for she said at last, with a smile, that if she should tell Edward where Delia was, it would n't be telling him to go there and marry her; but even if she should give him a piece of her mind to that effect, she did n't know as they could take her up and hang her. Before I returned to uncle William's that night, she concluded she would call on Mrs. Courtney in a day or two; she wanted to borrow a dress pattern of her; perhaps she would see Edward, and perhaps not; and she did n't know as she would say anything about Delia if she did see him; it was the pattern she wanted. But notwithstanding this conclusion, I felt assured that she would give Edward the "piece of her mind" with which she had first proposed to endow him.

The following day I related to Jane the incidents of the evening: how Mr. Widdleton had mended a tub, and his wife had darned and mended; in fact, whatever had been done or said that could interest her, not omitting the conversation about Edward and Delia—for I was determined to find out something in reference to the affair, as I persuaded myself I had a perfect right to do, considering our relationship; and Delia's pale face haunted me; her supplicating appeal for permission to remain at home I felt assured was not on my account; I saw pots of her flowers standing about, dying from neglect, and I could not help thinking her thoughts had been otherwise. So, as I said, I told Jane that Mrs. Widdleton thought Delia and Edward would make a fine match, and that she was sorry it was likely not to take place; for I did not choose to repeat her precise words. My very proper cousin colored slightly, and said, that if Mrs. Widdleton had not so many excellent qualities, she would be a busybody. This was the only reproach of any one I ever heard from her. I confess to greater imperfection; the affairs of other people interest me, and I am apt sometimes to say what I think of their conduct and character.

I used to take my seat at the window, and there being neither conversation nor reading within, I naturally looked out for amusement, and found it in the movements of our neighbors; for humanity is more to us than everything else, as those who have passed a winter in an isolated country place can very easily believe. The evening after this visit, I saw a light in the front chamber of Mr. Widdleton's house, where I had never seen a light before, and supposed the Hevelyns were there. The following morning I saw Mrs. Widdleton set out, bright and early, in the direction of Mr. Courtney's house. She walked against the north wind with a straightforward and energetic step, and I wondered whether there were any purpose in her movements that did not concern the pattern. It was nearly noon when she returned, accompanied by young Mr. Courtney. They paused at the gate, and seemed in earnest conversation for a long time. Liddy came to the door and looked earnestly toward her mother several times; the baby was fretting, I knew; but as often as they seemed about to separate they drew nearer again, till it seemed their conversation would never have an end. Seated on the outside of the evening coach that day I noticed a young man who, I thought, resembled Courtney, and I was the more convinced of its being him from the graceful way in which he recognized Mrs. Widdleton, as he passed. A red scarf about his neck concealed, in part, his face, so that I could not be positive it was he. "But if it is," thought I, "he may have a thousand objects in view besides Delia. I have no right to think anything about it." Still I did think about it.

Often in the course of the days I saw Mrs. Hevelyn, wrapt in a shawl which seemed of a very rich and costly pattern, standing or sitting by the chamber window. Sometimes I observed her wipe her eyes, and always her movements indicated sadness and dejection. Occasionally when the sun shone in the middle of the day, she walked about the yard, examined the dead flowers, and looked up and down the lonesome road, returning to the house with a languid and heavy step. When the evening coach came rattling over the near hill, I saw her either raise the sash or step out into the yard, and watch it eagerly, as though in expectation of some one; and when it passed she would sometimes return with her handkerchief to her eyes, and sometimes, sinking at once on the frozen ground, sit, as though powerless to go in, for an hour or more. One sunshiny day I went out into the yard to see if the flags were sprouting or the daffodils coming through the grass, for I had seen a blue-bird twittering in the lilac and picking its feathers that morning. "How d' you do?" called a voice that seemed not altogether unfamiliar, and looking up, I saw Mrs. Widdleton leaning over her yard-fence, with the evident intention of having a little chat.

"What is the news," she asked, "at your house?"

"Oh nothing; what is the news with you?"

"How does uncle William (for she called Mr. Peters uncle William when she spoke to me of him) seem to take it?"

"Take what?" said I.

"Why, about Edward and Delia."

"And what about them?"

"Why, they say he's gone off to B——." Here she lowered her voice, and, saying that walls had ears sometimes, crossed from her yard-fence to ours. "He's gone off to B——," she continued, "and they say it's to get married."

"Is it possible!"

"Yes; and old Mr. Courtney is going back to the city to live, and they say Edward and Delia are going right into the old house; and from the way things seem to begin and go on, I think they will do well."

I said I thought so too, though what things she had seen beginning and going on I was not in the least advised, however shrewdly I might guess.

If they should be married, and come and live in the old place, and do right well, as she hoped and believed they would, she thought Miss Jane and "uncle William" would be ashamed of themselves.

III.

As often as I met the ever busy and good natured Mrs. Widdleton, she had much to say about poor Mrs. Hevelyn. Her husband went away, she said, the very day he brought her there and right among strangers so, it seemed as if the poor thing would cry her eyes out. "Often of evenings," said Mrs. Widdleton, "I go up into her room to have a cheerful chat. You know a body must talk or they won't say anything—and I find her lying on the bed, her face all smothered in the pillow, and her heart ready to break." She informed me further, that Mr. Hevelyn had written only once, and then barely a few lines, since he went away.

Two or three days went by, when, at nightfall, I observed an unusual stir about Mr. Widdleton's house; lights moved busily from cellar to chamber; a strange woman, in a high white cap, appeared from time to time; and presently the two little girls came over to pass the evening, saying their mother had given them leave to stay all night if they wished to. The next morning the chamber-windows were closed, and Mrs. Widdleton herself came in soon after breakfast to take her children home, and informed them that somebody had brought Mrs. Hevelyn "the sweetest little baby!" Tidings were despatched to the absent husband, and day after day the young mother exerted herself beyond her ability to make her little darling look pretty, that the heart of the expected father might be rejoiced the more; and day after day the coach went by, and the sun went down, and he did not come. At length, one day, in answer to Mrs. Widdleton's urgent entreaties, and with a hope of giving the poor lady some comfort, I went in to sit for an hour with her, taking my sewing. I found her a sweet and lovable creature, indeed—not possessed of very strong mind or marked characteristics, but gentle, confiding, and amiable. She had put back her curls in motherly fashion, and her cheek was thin and pale; but she was beautiful, and her large eyes had in them a pathos and power which drew one toward her, as if by a spell. She seemed pleased with my praise of the child; said she had named him John, for his father; and added, "He wants to see the darling so much! and nothing but the most pressing necessity keeps him away—poor John!" It was a new illustration of the difficulty of dispossessing a faithful heart of its confidence: she would be the last to learn how little that father merited her affection.

"Do you think my little beauty is going to have red hair?" she said, pressing her lips against his head. Her own was a deep auburn. She looked at me, as if she wanted me to say no; but I could not, conscientiously, and so replied evasively, "Why, do n't you like that color?"

"I do n't care," she said; "it would be pretty to me, no matter what color it was; but John thinks red hair so ugly."

"Perhaps it will be the color of yours, and that will please him."

"He used to call mine pretty," she said; and, taking it down, laid it on the baby's head, and compared it, with the greatest apparent interest. While thus engaged, the coach drew up at the gate. "Oh, it is he!—it is he!" she cried; and, placing the baby in my arms, wound back her long hair, and flew to meet him, as though the heavens were opening before her.

"Why, Nell," I heard him say, as he assisted her up stairs, "you have grown old and ugly since I left."

The tone was playful, but she replied, "Oh, John!" in a reproachful accent that indicated a deeply felt meaning.

"And where did you learn this style of arranging your hair? Is it by good mother Widdleton's suggestion? Really, it is not becoming—it is positively shocking; and red hair requires the most careful dressing to make it endurable."

She tried to laugh as she entered the room, and said to me, "Do n't you think John is finding fault with me already! but, never mind, I'll find fault with him one of these days."

"I dare say, my dear, you will have cause," he answered, half seriously, half laughingly; and, putting her arms about his neck, she kissed him as fondly as though he had said she was looking young and beautiful. "Oh, the baby!" she suddenly exclaimed. "Why, John, you have n't seen him!"

"Do n't, my dear, make yourself ridiculous," he whispered, "but introduce the lady, and then go and arrange your hair: there is time enough to see the baby."

I rose to go, as I would have done sooner but for my little charge; but the Hevelyns insisted so much on my remaining, that I was forced to sit down. The mother kept smiling, but tears seemed ready to fall; and I placed the child in the father's arms, and said, "See, how like you he is!"

"Good gracious!" he exclaimed, turning away his eyes, "you do n't mean to say I look like this thing!"

"No, not quite," I said, laughing; "not so well."

"And you call this boy mine, do you?" he said to his wife; "red hair, and blue eyes, and ugly in every way. Why, his hand is as big as a woodchopper's." And he held up his own, which was delicate and beautiful.

"Now, John, dear, he does look like you, and Mrs. Widdleton, too, says he does." And to prove the resemblance she brought a picture of her husband, saying I might trace the resemblance more readily from that.

"Ah, Nelly," he said, putting it aside, "that never looked like me."

And to me he added, "You see it was painted when I found that I had to marry Nell; and no wonder I looked woebegone!"

I took up a book of engravings, and, laying down the child, he turned over the leaves for me.

"I am so faint!" said the wife, putting her hand to her forehead. "What shall I do, John?"

"Oh, I do n't know," he answered, without looking toward her; "get some water, or lie down, or something."

I gave her some water, and, seating her in the arm-chair, returned to the book, that I might not appear to notice her emotion. She turned her back toward us with a pretence of rocking the cradle, but, in reality, to conceal inevitable tears. Mr. Hevelyn saw it, his conscience smote him, and, stooping over her, he kissed her forehead, and smoothed her hair, saying, with real or affected fondness, "You know, dear, I was only jesting." And she was pacified, and smiled again. The next morning the strange gentleman took the coach; he could not stay longer, the wife said; and other lonesome days came and went.

One wild March morning, when the snow blew blindingly against the windows, little Peter Widdleton came running in with great haste. Mrs. Hevelyn's baby was very sick, and she wanted me to come. I found, on arriving at her room, that it had not seemed well for several days, and that the previous night it had grown seriously worse, and that then the most alarming symptoms were visible. She had written every day to her husband, she told me, and as he neither came nor wrote, she was terrified on his account, though it was possible her letters might have been miscarried. Dear, credulous soul! The morning coach went by, and the evening coach went by, and he came not; and all the while the child grew worse. Mrs. Widdleton's skill was baffled; and as the mother rocked the little sufferer on her bosom, and said, "What shall I do! oh, what shall I do!" I forgot all the words of comfort I had ever known.

Poor baby! its little hands clinging tightly to the mother's, it lay all day; but at nightfall it sunk into slumber, and, though its mother kissed it a thousand times, it did not wake any more. It was piteous to see her grief when we put it down in the snow, and left it with the March winds making its lullaby.

After the burial, Mrs. Hevelyn lost the little energy that had kept her up before, and sat without speaking all the day. She seemed to have lost every interest in life.

We were sitting around the fire one night, eight or ten days after the baby died, when Mrs. Widdleton came bustling in to tell us that Mrs. Hevelyn was gone; that her husband had written her to join him without a moment's delay; that he had not sent her one cent of money, nor in any way made provision for her to go. "But for all that," said our neighbor, "she was nearly crazy to go, and the letter really made her a deal better. She gave my Liddy most of her clothes, partly by way of paying, I suppose—for you see she had no money—all but her weddingdress; that, she said, she should need before long;" and the kind woman, taking up one of the cats, hugged it close by way of keeping down her emotion. "Ah well," she added, presently, "she has n't much to care to live for, I am afraid."

IV.

When our excellent neighbor had completed the narrative respecting her late guest, and bestowed fit tributes on the respective characters of the wife and the husband, she sat a moment in profound silence, and then, as if she had said Be gone! to all gloomy recollections, her face resumed its wonted glow, and her eyes sparkled with secrets until now suppressed, and at the thoughts of surprise and consternation she was likely to introduce into my uncle's family—surprise and consternation in no degree associated with real evil, or the good woman would have been the last being in the world to feel a satisfaction in their creation or anticipation. Suddenly interrupting the third perusal of the leading article in the week's "Republican," she said, "Did you know, Old Mr. and Mrs. Courtney move to town to-day."

"Do tell," said uncle William, looking very much pleased, "I wonder what they are going to do with their house?"

"Well, I hardly know," replied Mrs. Widdleton, looking slyly at me; "some say one thing and some say another; but I have my own thoughts. I do n't think Edward Courtney went to B—— for nothing; and I do n't think he will come back without a certain little woman, whose name begins with Delia, for a wife."

Cousin Jane dropped half the stitches off one needle, and uncle William opened the paper so suddenly that he tore it, which he said he would not have done for a fip; and he forgot what quarter the moon was in, and, on being questioned, said he did n't know as he cared.

Mrs. Widdleton was right; for the next evening I went with her to call on the bride, my friend carrying with her a custard-pie and a loaf of plum-cake. We found the happy pair taking tea at a little table, with their faces glowing with sympathetic devotion; and when last I saw them they were as happy as then—lovers yet, though they had been married a dozen years.

A year after my visit I heard, by chance, that Mrs. Hevelyn was dead, and the fragment of her life and love that I have written, is all I know.

SARA WILLIS PARTON
[FANNY FERN]
(1811–1872)

Fern Leaves from Fanny's Portfolio

(Auburn, New York: Derby and Miller), 1853.

In his introduction to the selections from her work in *The Female Prose Writers of America* (revised edition, 1854), John S. Hart describes the birth of "Fanny Fern":

> But suddenly a bolt fell. Death came. The husband and father was smitten down. The widowed mother and the half-orphan children were left to fight the battle of life alone. Adversity succeeded adversity. Poverty followed in the dismal train, and illness and want had the afflicted family at their mercy. The mother struggled on as best she could; but we all know how hard it is for a lady to find employment which will enable her to obtain a livelihood even for herself, much less for a family of children. The female teacher generally receives only a meagre salary; the copyist pursues an uncertain calling; the seamstress can at best earn but a miserable pittance. And so, at last, after bitter years, the widowed mother, from sheer desperation, took to her pen; and another and a bright star was added to our literary galaxy.

As Ann Douglas has pointed out in "The 'Scribbling Women' and Fanny Fern," the mid-nineteenth-century literary establishment found this version of how women came to write comforting for it removed from women all taint of self-consciousness, self-assertion, and personal ambition. Fanny Fern herself contributed substantially to this view of her career through her autobiographical novel, *Ruth Hall* (1855), which told essentially the same story, though with considerably more anger. Whether Sara Parton would ever have become a professional writer if her first husband had not died is, of course, a moot point. What both

241

biographical and autobiographical portraits omit, however, is the context that made this decision less accidental and more self-determined. For, in fact, Parton came from a relatively literary background and had begun to write long before the "bolt fell."

Born Grata Payson Willis (the first name was soon changed to Sara) on July 9, 1811, in Portland, Maine, she was the fifth of the nine children of Hannah Parker and Nathaniel Willis. Her paternal grandfather, also named Nathaniel Willis, edited a Whig newspaper in Boston during the Revolutionary War and her father, while still in Portland, published an anti-Federalist paper called the *Eastern Argus*. Moving to Boston in 1812, he opened a printing business and in 1816 began publishing the Boston *Recorder,* one of America's first religious newspapers. In 1827, he founded the *Youth's Companion,* whose editor he remained until 1862.

Of her mother, Parton wrote: "Had my mother's time not been so constantly engrossed by a fast-increasing family, had she found time for literary pursuits, I am confident she would have distinguished herself. Her hurried letters, written with one foot upon the cradle, give ample evidence of this" (*Fanny Fern: A Memorial Volume,* p. 96). She further attributed to her mother "all the capability for writing which I possess" and declared, "I shall never be 'weaned,' never! . . . Even now, I *want* her, every day and hour" (Grace Greenwood, p. 67). In a gesture similar to that of Elizabeth Stuart Phelps, the daughter, Parton chose for the second half of her pen name an object that symbolized her mother: "when a child, and walking with my mother in the country, she always used to pluck a leaf of [fern] to place in her bosom, for its sweet odor" (*Memorial,* p. 92).

James Parton, in his memorial volume, remarks on the literary ambience in which the Willis children were raised: "Facility in composition was too common among them to be remarked, and they took to pen and ink as to a native element. They were brought up among newspapers and books, and the father and mother shared the universal ambition of New England parents to give their children the best advantages of education" (*Memorial,* p. 32). Of the nine Willis children, three, in addition to Sara, distinguished themselves in the fields of literature and journalism. Her older brother, Nathaniel Parker Willis, widely known as a writer of prose and poetry, was, in addition, an editor of the *New York Mirror* and later founder and editor of the *Home Journal.* A younger brother, Richard Storrs Willis, was a poet, composer, and editor of the *Musical World and Times* and *Once A Week.* A sister, Julia Dean Willis, served for many years on the staff of her brother's *Home Journal.*

Parton herself began to write while in attendance at Catharine Beecher's seminary in Hartford, Connecticut, where Harriet Beecher was also a pupil and teacher. According to her granddaughter, Ethel Parton, her compositions caught the attention of a local editor, who occasionally asked to print excerpts from them in his paper. A humorous essay, "Suggestions on Arithmetic," read at the Annual Exhibition of 1829, so impressed one of her schoolmates that she preserved it for forty-three years, sending a copy to Parton only shortly before the latter's death. On her return to Boston after completing her education, which included, in addition to her time at Beecher's seminary, attendance at other high quality institutions, Parton continued to write, contributing pieces to her father's *Youth's Companion.* In her remarks to "Literary Aspirants" (reprinted in *Ginger Snaps*), describing the difficulties of breaking into the writing business, Parton characterizes herself as relatively well-prepared for the struggle. She had "the advantages of a good education"; she knew not only how to write but how to spell, punctuate, and capitalize so as to produce a "properly prepared MS."; and she had undergone "the initiation 'of reading proof'—for my father, who was an editor, when I was not more than twelve years old."

In 1837, when she was twenty-five, Sara Willis married Charles Eldredge. By all accounts, this marriage was a happy one. In 1846, however, Eldredge died and his wife found herself reduced from relative affluence to relative poverty. Neither her husband's family nor her own (her mother had died in 1844) offered Parton adequate support at this crucial point in her life. Yet why, given her background and previous experience, she did not immediately turn to writing as the most likely means of support for herself and her two children is a puzzling question. Mary Kelley, in *Private Woman, Public Stage*, argues that the milieu in which Parton grew up provided no connection between her youthful experiments and the status of professional writer and, indeed, that Fanny Fern was never "supposed to have happened" (Kelley, p. 139). Still, by the late 1840s there were several examples of American women who earned their living by the pen and who considered themselves to be professional writers. Nevertheless, Parton first tried to earn a living by sewing and then by teaching, and when these failed to support her, she chose the traditional recourse of marriage. In 1849 she married a Boston merchant named Samuel P. Farrington. This attempt to solve her economic dilemma proved disastrous, however; after two years the couple separated and after two more they were divorced.

With the dissolution of her second marriage, Parton turned to writing. In 1851, at the age of forty, she began publishing pieces in various minor Boston magazines. Discovering that these pieces were being reprinted, not only in Boston papers but elsewhere, she began to develop an estimate of the potential economic value of her work. She wrote to her brother, enclosing some of her pieces and asking him to help her find a market in New York. Although noted for his support of other women writers, Willis was disinterested in and even hostile to his sister's career. At one point, he ordered his editorial assistant, James Parton, to accept no more work for the *Home Journal* from the writer called Fanny Fern. Undaunted, despite her brother's refusal of assistance, Parton secured a contract, through skillful use of competing offers, for a weekly column in the Boston *True Flag*, thus becoming one of America's first women columnists. In 1853, she negotiated with the publisher, James C. Derby, for a volume of selections from her columns; rejecting, according to Derby, the offer of $1000 outright, she accepted instead a royalty of 10¢ per copy. Within a year, the book had sold over

80,000 copies and earned for its author $8000. *Fern Leaves from Fanny's Portfolio* was followed in 1854 by a second series and by a collection for young readers, *Little Ferns for Fanny's Little Friends.* Together, these books sold over 62,000 copies and pushed Parton's royalties for the two year period well beyond $10,000.

Parton moved to New York in 1854. Here she attracted the attention of Robert Bonner, owner of the *New York Ledger* and legendary for his flamboyant, and successful, advertising schemes. To build up the reputation, and thus the circulation of his paper, Bonner paid sensational prices for contributions from well-known authors (for example, $3000 for Longfellow's "The Hanging of the Crane"). On June 9, 1855, the *New York Ledger* carried a lead story by Fanny Fern, for which Bonner paid the enormous and well-advertised sum of $100 per column. This figure represented a substantial increase over the $25 initially offered. Bonner's generosity in this instance, however, proved a good investment for it secured Parton's loyalty. For the next sixteen years, still paid $100 for her weekly column, "Fresh Leaves," she wrote only for the *Ledger,* never missing an issue until a month before her death.

In 1855, Parton published *Ruth Hall.* According to Susan Geary, the idea for the novel began not with its author but with its publisher. Desirous of capitalizing on the new advertising strategies of the 1850s, and believing that a long fiction from the pen of the notorious Fanny Fern would produce the biggest commercial success to date, the New York firm of Mason Brothers approached Parton and engaged her in a contract to produce such a book. Geary's claim provides an important context for evaluating the sensational and autobiographical elements of this book. Not only did the publishers "commission a novel with the express intent of turning it into a best seller via an elaborate and multifaceted advertising campaign but they may also have pressured the author into fabricating a work that would lend itself to sensational advertising. That is to say, the novel may have been tailored to their sales strategy rather than the strategy to the book" (Geary, p. 383).

Although not as big a commercial success as its publishers had anticipated or promised in their contract with Parton, *Ruth Hall* nevertheless created a predictable stir in a literary community devoted, as Grace Greenwood put it, to the idea that "true feminine genius is ever timid, doubtful, and clingingly dependent, a perpetual childhood," and committed to the principle that women's writing should be characterized by "piety, lack of energy and resolute disregard of conflict" (Douglas, pp. 5, 7). Attacked by many critics for its lack of feminine qualities and eliciting at least one vicious response advertised as exposing the "true" character and situation of its author but designed in fact to capitalize on her success (*The Life and Beauties of Fanny Fern,* 1855), *Ruth Hall* received a positive comment from Nathaniel Hawthorne. In 1855 he wrote to his publisher, William Ticknor, requesting information on its author:

> In my last, I recollect, I bestowed some vituperation on female authors. I have since been reading *Ruth Hall*; and I must say I enjoyed it a good deal. The woman writes as if the Devil was in her; and that

is the only condition under which a woman ever writes anything worth reading. Generally women write like emasculated men, and are only to be distinguished from male authors by greater feebleness and folly; but when they throw off the restraints of decency and come before the public stark naked, as it were—then their books are sure to possess character and value.

Approaching the book from a different perspective, Elizabeth Cady Stanton, in a review for *The Una* of February, 1855, spoke with equal enthusiasm, describing *Ruth Hall* as "a slave narrative" and declaring that it should be read as if one were hearing "the words of a Frederick Douglass" (Susan Conrad, *Perish The Thought*, p. 173).

Despite the "effect" of her novel, a tribute to its emotional force and cultural significance, Parton's strength did not lie in the direction of the long fiction. Her *forte* was the short piece, the weekly column, which comprised the bulk of her work. In these columns, she addressed herself to a wide variety of contemporary issues—women's rights, birth control, housekeeping, money, husbands, childrearing, women's fashions. More radical in thought than in act, Parton never joined any of the movements designed to solve the various problems she identified. She assisted in the founding of Sorosis, the New York City woman's club begun in 1868; this was as close as she came to direct political action. Nor was she part of any friendship network of women writers, such as those that provided a context for the work of, for example, Lydia Sigourney, Caroline Kirkland, Harriet Spofford, and Gail Hamilton.

From the perspective of conventional American literary history, one of Parton's most significant pieces appeared in the *Ledger* on May 10, 1856; to Walt Whitman's *Leaves of Grass* she gave a positive, even enthusiastic, review. Like Whitman, Parton could recognize and express, albeit obliquely, the existence of sexual attraction between women and men. In addition, she could, like Whitman, recognize the existence of sexual attraction and behavior between members of the same sex. In a piece entitled "Women Lovers" and reprinted in *Caper-Sauce* (1872), she declares, "Perhaps you don't know it, but there are women that fall in love with each other. Woe be to the unfortunate she who *does the courting!*"

In 1856, at the age of forty-four, Sara Eldredge married James Parton, a man eleven years younger than herself and a noted journalist, essayist, and biographer. By the terms of their marriage agreement, Parton retained control over her own income and capital "as fully and absolutely as if she were a feme sole" (Kelley, p. 158). She died on October 1, 1872, at sixty-one, after a six year struggle with cancer. She was buried in Mt. Auburn Cemetery, Cambridge; her monument, provided by Robert Bonner, bears as identification only the name "Fanny Fern."

Exploiting the arena created by the publishing developments of mid-nineteenth-century America, Parton created a unique literary form and created a voice to inhabit that form that was remarkably "fresh." In identifying that voice as of the "Devil," Hawthorne may have intended to align Fanny Fern with the best of her male contemporaries—a cate-

gory that would certainly have included Hawthorne himself, who called
The Scarlet Letter a "hell-fired" book, and Herman Melville, who dedicated *Moby Dick* to Hawthorne in tribute to his "blackness." Certainly
Parton evinces little anxiety about angels hovering over the right or the
left shoulder, and she equally defies the pressure to write of and from
the "sunny side." Yet the "devil" in her work is, in fact, her willingness
to articulate that women's point of view conventionally ignored or suppressed, like the "yes" that rises to the lips of Mrs. James in *The Angel
Over The Right Shoulder.* Many of her pieces begin with examples of
the dominant masculine voice taken from her own reading of contemporary books, newspapers, and magazines. This masculine voice is often
overtly misogynistic (see, for example, the epigraph to "Important for
Married Men," reprinted below); it is always advisory, and it is relent-
lessly one-sided. Even in the so-called sentimental pieces, Fanny Fern's
goal is to interject into the complacent hegemony established by and
reflected in this voice, a good dose of the "devil," and thus to create
space for a more honest expression of women's perspective.

Her sense of authority in this enterprise has several roots. In part, it
derives from her presentation of herself as speaking, not simply indi-
vidually, but as a woman for women; as articulating a perspective
neither personal nor unique but communal. In speaking communally,
she invokes the authority of women's collective experience—that authority which Phelps's Mrs. James is unable or unwilling to claim and
which comes from confronting the facts of one's life, despite men's
tendency to ignore or redefine these facts. Her authority stems as well
from her willingness to contact and express the emotions generated by
the facts of women's lives. Unlike many other nineteenth-century
women writers, Fanny Fern refuses to suppress or revise her feelings to
conform to the conventionally acceptable view of the feminine—bland,
unassuming, unambitious, and never, never angry. Her power comes
from being in touch with her own emotional reality, an emotional reality that, in turn, she presents as representative.

The form Parton developed for her work is admirably suited to accomplishing its intention. Although her attempts at long fictions proved
an aesthetic failure, this failure may well reveal more about the limitations of the novel form as a vehicle for expressing women's perspective
than it does about Parton's artistic ability. As the poetry of Emily Dickinson might suggest, the articulation of a woman's point of view, so
long suppressed, is potentially explosive; initially it may require the intensity and concentration that only a short form can provide. The brev-
ity of Fanny Fern implies that the truth she has touched is too hot to
handle for very long.

The pieces included in this anthology provide an appropriate sample
of the range of characters, issues, tones, and techniques that characterize
the work of Fanny Fern. Present in all of them is a current of anger;
indeed, anger provides the connective tissue that links pieces of apparently different tones. The barely concealed rage at the economic dependence of women that informs a piece like "Dark Days" can easily turn
into the bite that defines "The Tear of a Wife." And, similarly, the
humorous sarcasm of a piece like "The Invalid Wife" can readily shift

into the more emotionally direct, serious, even sentimental tone of "The Ball-Room and The Nursery," which deals with the same subject—the powerlessness of women to control their environment and their lives. Anger at men, whether thickly or thinly veiled, constitutes one of the primary facts of women's lives that Fanny Fern both contacts and articulates.

The pieces included here are representative as well of Parton's techniques for organizing her material. Some of them can be described as brief narratives, depending for their intelligibility and their effect on the assumption that they are emblematic of longer stories that are themselves representative and even generic. Fanny Fern has no interest in developing character; her emphasis is rather on situation. Thus, for example, "The Flirt; or, the Unfaithful Lover" invokes, as is clear from its title, a set of types that symbolize a familiar and frequently repeated situation. She is then free to manipulate the various responses possible to the woman who finds herself in this situation. In a piece like "Dark Days," she compresses much of the material elaborated less effectively in *Ruth Hall;* sharply juxtaposing a series of emblematic vignettes, she increases the emotional impact of her generic situation.

Other pieces, like "The Invalid Wife" and "The Model Stepmother," have little or no narrative structure. Rather, they take off from a cultural stereotype and go on to express a radically different reality. The voices and views heard in these pieces are those of persons who, traditionally, are to be seen but not heard. Imagining what they might say if they were enabled to speak provides the generative formal germ from which many of these pieces grow. Thus, both Fanny Fern's energy and her form derive from a tension between her perspective and that embodied in cultural conventions and stereotypes.

Ironically enough, and a salutary reminder of the considerable complexity of the mid-nineteenth-century literary situation for women, Parton's articulation of a conventionally suppressed point of view constituted a significant portion of her popular success. In "Important for Married Men," she calls attention to men's consuming desire to hear what women have to say when they are "alone"—that is, without men and talking to each other. Despite the myth, promoted in the literature of American men, that men must evade those "civilizing" women who try to make them stay home, women's reality, according to Fanny Fern, reveals a rather different tale. For women, the problem is how to get men out of the house so that they can talk freely to each other. Although the misogynistic comment from which the piece takes off implies that men would gladly poison women to shut them up, Fanny Fern presents an alternate hypothesis: men enjoy women's texts; indeed, they often find them more interesting than their own.

Simple curiosity may be part of the source of this interest—what do women say to each other and how do they say it? Self-protection may provide another motive—what are women saying about men? what secrets for survival or dominance are they sharing? what plots are they hatching? A quasi-sexual voyeurism may also be at issue. Consider, in this context, the language Hawthorne chooses for praising women writers: "when they throw off the restraints of decency and come before the public stark naked. . . ." In sum, then, if men want to overhear women talking as if men were not present, Fanny Fern gives them the illusion of this experience.

Parton's extraordinary success, however, may also reflect an underlying conservatism in her work. Although her pieces present unconventional, and on occasion even radical, positions, they finally argue for nothing beyond the opportunity for expression. In "The Tear of a Wife," for example, she does not propose any change in the marriage "contract"; she only insists that women be given the chance to cry once they have signed on. The conclusion of "Aunt Hetty on Matrimony" can serve as an appropriate example of her conservatism. After detailing the numerous reasons why marriage is for women "the hardest way on earth of getting a living," she concludes by resigning herself to the "facts" of human "nature"; girls, after all, will be girls and it is in the nature of girls to succumb to the "bewitchment" of marriage the first chance they get. Like the tears she demands as a woman's right, Parton's work provided her readers with a safety valve. But since the hunger for such safety valves reflected women's discontent and indicated serious problems in women's condition, Parton's work also contained evidence of the need for a more radical solution. It was, no doubt, Parton's skillful combination of the radical and the conservative that made her so successful.

Source:

Fern Leaves from Fanny's Portfolio (Auburn, N.Y.: Derby and Miller), 1853.

Selected Primary Works:

Fern Leaves from Fanny's Portfolio, second series, 1854; *Ruth Hall*, 1855; *Rose Clark*, 1856; *Fresh Leaves*, 1857; *Folly as It Flies*, 1859; *Ginger-Snaps*, 1870; *Caper-Sauce*, 1872; *Fanny Fern: A Memorial Volume*, ed. James Parton, 1873.

Selected Secondary Works:

Florence Bannard Adams, *Fanny Fern, or A Pair of Flaming Shoes* (West Trenton, N.J.: Hermitage Press), 1966; James C. Derby, *Fifty Years Among Authors, Books and Publishers* (New York: G. W. Carleton), 1884; Ann Douglas (Wood), "The 'Scribbling Women' and Fanny Fern: Why Women Wrote," *American Quarterly*, 23 (1971), 3–24; Susan Geary, "The Domestic Novel as a Commercial Commodity: Making a Best Seller in the 1850's," *Papers of the Bibliographical Society of America*, 70 (1976), 365–93; Grace Greenwood, "Fanny Fern—Mrs. Parton," *Eminent Women of the Age* (Hartford: S. M. Betts), 1868; Mary Kelley, *Private Woman, Public Stage* (New York: Oxford University Press), 1984; Elizabeth Bancroft Schlesinger, "Fanny Fern: Our Grandmothers' Mentor," *New York Historical Society Quarterly*, 38 (1954), 501–19.

THE BALL-ROOM AND THE NURSERY

"YOU ARE QUITE beautiful to-night," said Frank Fearing to his young wife, as she entered the drawing-room dressed for a ball; "I shall fall in love with you over again. What! not a smile for your lover-husband? and a tear in your eye, too! What does this mean, dearest?"

Mary leaned her beautiful head upon her husband's shoulder, and turned pale as she said:

"Frank, I feel a strange, sad presentiment of some impending evil; from whence, I cannot tell. I have striven to banish it, but it will not go away. I had not meant to speak of it to you, lest you should think me weak or superstitious; and, Frank," said his sweet wife, in pleading tones, "this is a frivolous life we lead. We are all the world to each other,—why frequent such scenes as these? A fearful shadow lies across my path. Stay at home with me, dearest; I dare not go to-night."

Frank looked at her thoughtfully a moment, then, gayly kissing her, he said,

"This vile east wind has given you the blues; the more reason you should not give yourself time to think of them; beside, do you think me such a Blue Beard as to turn the key on so bright a jewel as yourself? No, no, Mary, I would have others see it sparkle and shine, and envy me its possession; so throw on your cloak, little wife, and let us away."

"Stop a moment, then," said Mary, with a smile and a sigh, "let me kiss little Walter before I go; he lies in his little bed so rosy and so bright. Come with me, Frank, and look at him."

With kisses on lip, brow and cheek, the child slumbered on, and the carriage rolled away from the door to the ball.

It was a brilliant scene; that ball-room!—Necks and arms, that shamed for whiteness the snowy robes that floated around them; eyes rivalling the diamond's light; tresses whose hue was borrowed from the sun; manhood's peerless form and noble brow; odorous garlands, flashing lights, music to make the young blood race more swiftly through the veins; all—all—were there, to intoxicate and bewilder.

Peerless in the midst—queen of hearts and of the dance—stood the young wife of Frank Fearing. Accepting the offered hand of an acquaintance, she took her place among the waltzers. She made a few turns upon the floor, then, pale as death, she turned to her husband, saying,

"O, Frank, I cannot,—I feel such an oppression here, here;" and she placed her hand on heart and brow.

Frank looked annoyed; he was very proud of his wife; her beauty was the admiration of the room. She had never looked lovelier than to-night. Whispering in her ear, "For my sake, Mary, conquer this weakness," he led her again to the dancers. With a smile of gratified pride he followed her with his eyes, as her fairy form floated past him, excitement and exercise lending again to her cheek its loveliest glow, while on all sides murmurs of "Beautiful,—most beautiful!" fell on his ear. "And that bright vision is mine," said Frank to himself; "I have won her from hearts that were breaking for her."

When the dance was over, following her to the window, he arranged her scarf about her neck, with a fond care; and with a "Thank you, dearest," was leaving her, when she again laid her hand upon his arm, saying, with a wild brilliancy in her eye, "Frank! something has happened to Walter! take me home now."

"Pshaw! Mary, dear; you looked so radiant, I thought you had danced the vapors away. One more, dearest, and then, if you say so, we will go."

Suffering herself to be persuaded, again those tiny feet were seen spurning the floor; towards the close, her face grew so deadly pale, that her husband, in alarm, flew to her side.

"The effort costs you too much, Mary," said Frank; "let us go home." He wrapped her cloak carefully about her. She was still, and cold as a marble statue.

As the carriage stopped at their door, she rushed past him with the swiftness of an antelope, and gaining her boy's chamber, Frank heard her exclaim, as she fell senseless to the floor, "I knew it, I told you so!" The child was dead.

The servant in whose care it had been left,—following the example of her mistress,—had joined some friends in a dance in the hall. That terrible scourge of children, the croup, had attacked him, and alone, in the still darkness, the fair boy wrestled with the "King of Terrors."

From whence came the sad presentiment that clouded the fair brow of the mother; or the mysterious magnetism drawing her so irresistibly back to her dying child? Who shall tell?

For months she lay vibrating between life and death.

> "Yet the Healer was there, who had smitten her heart,
>   And taken her treasure away;
> To allure her to Heaven, he has placed it on high,
>   And the mourner will sweetly obey."
>
> "There had whispered a voice,—'t was the voice of her God,—
> "I love thee! I love thee! pass under the rod!'"
>
> *   *   *   *   *   *   *   *

Other fair children now call her "mother;" but never again, with flying feet, has she chased the midnight hours away. Nightly, as they return, they find her within the quiet circle of home—within call of helpless childhood. Dearer than the admiration of the gay throng,— sweeter to her than viol or harp,—is the music of their young voices, and tenderly she leads their little feet "into the green pastures and unto the still waters of salvation;" blest with the smile of the Good Shepherd, who saith, "Suffer the little children to come unto me, and forbid them not."

The Invalid Wife

"Every wife needs a good stock of love to start with."

Don't she?—You are upon a sick bed; a little, feeble thing lies upon your arm, that you might crush with one hand. You take those little velvet fingers in yours, close your eyes, and turn your head languidly to the pillow. Little brothers and sisters,—Carry, and Harry, and Fanny, and Frank, and Willy, and Mary, and Kitty,—half a score,—come tiptoeing into the room, "to see the new baby." It is quite an old story to "nurse," who sits there like an automaton, while they give vent to their enthusiastic admiration of its wee toes and fingers, and make profound inquiries, which nobody thinks best to hear. You look on with a languid smile, and they pass out, asking, "Why they can't stay with dear mamma, and why they mus n't play puss in the corner," as usual? You wonder if your little croupy boy tied his tippet on when he went to school, and whether Betty will see that your husband's flannel is aired, and if Peggy has cleaned the silver, and washed off the front-door steps, and what your blessed husband is about, that he don't come home to dinner. There sits old nurse, keeping up that dreadful tread-mill trotting, "to quiet the baby," till you could fly through the keyhole in desperation. The odor of dinner begins to creep up stairs. You wonder if your husband's pudding will be made right, and if Betty will remember to put wine in the sauce, as he likes it; and then the perspiration starts out on your forehead, as you hear a thumping on the stairs, and a child's suppressed scream; and nurse swathes the baby up in flannel to the tip of its nose, dumps it down in the easy-chair, and tells you to "leave the family to her, and go to sleep." By and by she comes in,—after staying down long enough to get a refreshing cup of coffee,—and walks up to the bed with a bowl of gruel, tasting it, and then putting the spoon back into the bowl. In the first place, you hate gruel; in the next, you couldn't eat it, if she held a pistol to your head, after that spoon has been in her mouth; so you meekly suggest that it be set on the table to cool—hoping, by some providential interposition, it may get tipped over. Well, she moves round your room with a pair of creaking shoes, and a bran-new gingham gown, that rattles like a paper window-curtain, at every step and smoothes her hair with your nice little head-brush, and opens a drawer by mistake (?), "thinking it was the baby's drawer." Then you hear little nails scratching on the door; and Charley whispers through the key hole, "Mamma, Charley's tired; please let Charley come in." Nurse scowls, and says no; but you intercede— poor Charley, he's only a baby himself. Well, he leans his little head wearily against the pillow, and looks suspiciously at that little, moving bundle of flannel in nurse's lap. It's clear he's had a hard time of it, what with tears and molasses! The little shining curls, that you have so often rolled over your fingers, are a tangled mass; and you long to take him, and make him comfortable, and cosset him a little; and, then, the baby cries again, and you turn your head to the pillow with a smothered sigh. Nurse hears it, and Charley is taken struggling from the room. You take your watch from under the pillow, to see if husband won't be home soon, and then look at nurse, who takes a pinch of snuff over your bowl of gruel, and sits down nodding drowsily, with the baby in alarming proximity to the fire. Now you hear a dear step on the stairs. It's your

Charley! How bright he looks! and what nice fresh air he brings with him from out doors! He parts the bed-curtains, looks in, and pats you on the cheek. You just want to lay your head on his shoulder, and have such a splendid cry! but there sits that old Gorgon of a nurse,—she don't believe in husbands, she don't! You make Charley a free-mason sign to send her down stairs for something. He says,—right out loud,—men are so stupid!—"What did you say, dear?" Of course, you protest you did n't say a word,—never thought of such a thing—and cuddle your head down to your ruffled pillows, and cry because you don't know what else to do, and because you are weak and weary, and full of care for your family, and don't want to see anybody but "Charley." Nurse says "she shall have you sick," and tells your husband "he'd better go down, and let you go to sleep." Off he goes, wondering what on earth ails you, to cry!—wishes he had nothing to do but lie still, and be waited upon! After dinner he comes in to bid you good-by before he goes to his office,—whistles "Nelly Bly" loud enough to wake up the baby, whom he calls "a comical little concern,"—and puts his dear, thoughtless head down to your pillow, at a signal from you, to hear what you have to say. Well, there's no help for it, you cry again, and only say "Dear Charley;" and he laughs, and settles his dickey, and says you are "a nervous little puss," gives you a kiss, lights his cigar at the fire, half strangles the new baby with the first whiff, and takes your heart off with him down street!

And you lie there and eat that gruel! and pick the fuzz all off the blanket, and make faces at the nurse, under the sheet, and wish Eve had never ate that apple,—Genesis 3:16,—or that you were "Abel" to "Cain" her for doing it!

DARK DAYS.

> "DYING! How can you ever struggle through the world alone? Who will care for you, Janie, when I am dead?"

"Have you rooms to let?" said a lady in sable to a hard-featured person.

"Rooms? Why—yes—we have rooms;" surveying Mrs. Grey very deliberately. "You are a widow, I suppose? Thought so by the length of your veil. Been in the city long? How long has your husband been dead? What was the matter of him? Take in sewing or anything? Got any reference? How old is that child of yours?"

"I hardly think the situation will suit," said Mrs. Grey, faintly, as she rose to go.

"Don't cry, mamma," said Charley, as they gained the street. "Won't God take care of us?"

"Put another stick of wood on the fire, Charley; my fingers are quite benumbed, and I've a long while to work yet."

"There's not even a chip left," said the boy, mournfully, rubbing his little purple hands. "It seems as though I should never grow a big man, so that I could help you!"

"Hist! there's a rap." "Work done?" said a rough voice; "cause, if you ain't up to the mark, you can't have any more. 'No fire, and cold fingers.' Same old story. Business is business; I've no time to talk about your affairs. Women never can look at a thing in a commercial p'int of view. What I want to know is in a nutshell. Is them shirts done or not, young woman?"

"Indeed, there is only one finished, though I have done my best," said Mrs. Grey.

"Well, hand it along; you won't get any more; and sit up to-night and finish the rest, d' ye hear?"

"Have you vests that you wish embroidered, sir?"

"Y-e-s," said the gentleman (?) addressed, casting a look of admiration at Mrs. Grey.—"Here, James, run out with this money to the bank.—Wish it for yourself, madam?" said he blandly. "Possible? Pity to spoil those blue eyes over such drudgery."

A moment, and he was alone.

"He's a very sick child," said the doctor, "and there's very little chance for him to get well here;" drawing his furred coat to his ears, as the wind whistled through the cracks. "Have you no friends in the city, where he could be better provided for?"

Mrs. Grey shook her head mournfully.

"Well, I'll send him some medicine to-night, and to-morrow we will see what can be done for him."

"To-morrow!" All the long night the storm raged fearfully. The driving sleet sifted in through the loose windows, that rattled, and trembled, and shook. Mrs. Grey hushed her breath, as she watched the little, waxen face, and saw that look creep over it that comes but once. The sands of life were fast ebbing. The little taper flickered and flashed—and then—went out forever!

It was in the "poor man's lot" that Harry Grey's pet boy was buried. There were no carriages, no mourners, no hearse. Mrs. Grey shuddered, as the wagon jolted over the rough stones to the old burying-place. She uttered a faint scream, as the sexton hit the coffin against the wagon in lifting it out. Again and again she stayed his hand, when he would have fastened down the lid; she heard with fearful distinctness the first heavy clod that fell upon her boy's breast; she looked on with a dreadful fascination, while he filled up the grave; she saw the last shovelful of earth stamped down over him, and when the sexton touched her arm, and pointed to the wagon, she followed him mechanically, and made no objection, when he said "he guessed he'd drive a little faster, now that the lad was out." He looked at her once or twice, and thought it very odd that she did n't cry; but he did n't profess to understand women folks. So, when it was quite dusk, they came back again to the old wooden house; and there he left her, with the still night and her crushing sorrow.

"Who will care for you, Janie, when I am dead?"

THE FLIRT;
OR, THE UNFAITHFUL LOVER.

Kate Stanley was a brilliant, sparkling brunette. Woe to the rash youth who exposed his heart to her fascinations! If he were not annihilated by the witching glance of her bright eye, he would be sure to be caught by the dancing dimple that played "hide-and-seek" so roguishly in her rosy cheek, or the little, rounded waist that supported her faultless bust, or the tiny feet that crept, mice-like, in and out from under the sweeping folds of her silken robe.

I am sorry to say Miss Kitty was an arrant coquette. She angled for hearts with the skill of a practised sportsman, and was never satisfied till she saw them quivering and bleeding at her feet; then, they might flounce and flutter, and twist and writhe at their leisure,—it was no further concern of hers. She was off for a new subject.

One fine morning she sat listlessly in her boudoir, tapping one little foot upon the floor, and sighing for a new sensation, when a note was handed her. It ran thus:

"DEAR KITTY:—Our little cottage home is looking lovely, this 'leafy June.' Are you not weary of city life? Come and spend a month with us, and refresh heart and body. You will find nothing artificial here, save yourself!
"Yours,
"NELLY."

"Just the thing," said Kitty. "But the girl must be crazy, or intolerably vain, to bring me into such close contact with her handsome lover. I might as well try to stop breathing as to stop flirting; and the country, of all places, for a flirtation! The girl must be *non compos*. However, it's her own affair, not mine;" and she glanced triumphantly at her beautiful face, and threaded her jewelled fingers through her long ringlets, and conquered him—in imagination!

"When do you expect your friend?" said a laughing young girl to Nelly. "From the descriptions I have had of her, your bringing her here will be something akin to the introduction of Satan into Paradise. You would not find me guilty of such a folly, were I engaged to your handsome Fitz. Now you know, Nelly dear, that although you are fascinating and intellectual, you have no pretensions to beauty, and there are few men who prize a gem, unless it is handsomely set, however great its value. Now be warned in time, and send him off on a pilgrimage, till her visit is over. I won't bet on his constancy!"

"On the contrary," said Nelly, as she rose slowly from the little couch where she was reclining, and her small figure grew erect, and her large eyes lustrous, "I would marry no man who could not pass through such an ordeal and remain true to me. I am, as you see, hopelessly plain and ungraceful; yet, from my earliest childhood, I have been a passionate worshipper of beauty. I never expected to win love; I never expected to marry; and when Fitz, with all his glorious beauty, sued for my hand, I could not convince myself that it was not all a bewildering dream. It was such a temptation to a heart so isolated as mine; and eloquently it pleaded for itself! When I drank in the music of his voice, I said, 'Surely I must be lovely in his eyes; else why has he sought me?' Then, in my solitary moments, I said, sadly, 'There are none to dispute the prize with me here. He is deceiving himself. He has mistaken his own heart.' Then, again, I would ask myself, 'Can nothing but beauty win a noble heart? Are all my intellectual gifts valueless?' And still, Fitz, unable to understand my contradictory moods, passionately urged his suit. It needed not that waste of eloquence; my heart was already captive. And now, by the intensity of that happiness of which I know myself to be capable, I will prove him. Kate's beauty,—Kate's witchery, shall be the test! If his heart remains loyal to me, I am his. If not,"—and her cheek grew pale, and large tears gathered slowly in her eyes,—"I have saved myself a deeper misery!"

Fitz Allan had "travelled;" and that is generally understood to mean to go abroad and remain a period of time long enough to grow a fierce beard, and fiercer moustache, and cultivate a thorough contempt for everything in your own country. This was not true of Fitz Allan. It had only bound him the more closely to home and friends. His splendid person and cultivated manners had been a letter of recommendation to him in cultivated society. He was no fop, and yet he was fully aware of these personal advantages. What handsome man is not? He had trophies of all kinds, to attest his skilful generalship; such as dainty satin slippers, tiny kid gloves, faded roses, ringlets of all colors, ebony, flaxen and auburn, and *bijouterie* without limit.

Happy Fitz! What spell bound him to the plain, but lovable Nelly? A nature essentially feminine; a refined, cultivated taste; a warm, passionate heart. Did he remember, when he listened to that most musical of musical voices, and sat hour after hour, magnetized by its rare witchery, as it glanced gracefully and skilfully from one topic to another, that its possessor had not the grace and beauty of a Hebe or a Venus?

It was a bright, moonlight evening. Fitz and Nelly were seated in the little rustic parlor, opening upon the piazza. The moon shone full upon

Kate, as she stood in the low doorway. Her simple white dress was confined at the waist by a plain silken cord. Her fair white shoulders rose gracefully from the snowy robe. Her white arms, as they were crossed upon her breast, or raised above her head to catch playfully the long tendrils of the woodbine, as the wind swept them past her forehead, gleamed fair in the moonlight; and each and all had their bewildering charm. She seated herself upon the low door-step. Song after song was borne upon the air. Her eyes now flashing with the enthusiasm of an improvisatrice; then, soft, and lustrous, and liquid, and—dangerous! Nelly's heart beat quick; a deep crimson spot glowed upon her cheek, and, for once, *she* was beautiful.

Kate, apparently, took but little notice of the lovers; but not an expression that flitted across the fine face of Fitz Allan passed unnoticed by her. And she said, proudly, to herself, "I have conquered him!"

And so the bright summer month passed by, and they rambled through the cool woods, and rode through the winding paths, and sang to the quiet stars in the dim, dewy evening.

*   *   *   *   *   *

"Fie, Mr. Fitz Allan! What would Nelly say, to see you kneeling here at my feet? You forget," said the gay beauty, mockingly curling her rosy lip, "that you are an affianced lover, when you address such flattering language to me!"

"I only know that you are beautiful as a dream!" said the bewildered Fitz, as he passionately kissed the jewelled hand that lay unresistingly in his own.

That night, Fitz might be seen pacing his room with rapid strides, crushing in his hands a delicate note, from Nelly, containing these words:

> " 'The moon looks on many brooks;
>   The brook sees but one moon.'

"Farewell!

                                                              "NELLY."

LETA.

A SKETCH FROM LIFE.

"Be careful, dear father," said Leta, as she smoothed the old man's gray locks, and placed a little basket in his hand. "Mind the crossings,— you are so hard of hearing, and the streets are so crowded. If you would but wait till I get this work done."

"Never fear," said the old man, taking his staff from the corner; "I shall be back before you hardly know I'm gone. These old limbs won't carry me far. My work is most done, Leta. I shall have my six feet of earth before long, and that's all the richest man in the land can hold at the last."

Hurry, drive and bustle; coaches, wheelbarrows, carts and omnibuses, dogs and children, ladies and shop-girls, apprentices and masters, each one at tip-top speed, as if they were going to sign a quit-claim to life the next minute. Everybody looking out for number one, and caring little who jostled past, if their rights were not infringed. Very gay the ladies looked in their rainbow dresses; the little children's cheeks, pale with the close air of the heated school-room, flushed with delight at their temporary emancipation, and their little owners were trying the strength of their respective lungs in a way that made the old man's deafness a very questionable affliction. The overtasked sempstress, in her shabby little bonnet, looked on hopelessly at the moving panorama. She had become habituated to brick pavements and Babel sounds, an aching side, weary eyes and a dull, dead weight at her heart; and so she creeps home from her daily task,—home to her gloomy attic, to look at the patch of blue sky from her roof window. Now and then a blade of grass, that has forced its way through the brick pavements, brings to her mind the fragrant hay-field, and sunny meadow, and dim old woods of her country home and she wonders if the little wild-flowers still grow in their favorite nook; and if the little brook, where she bathed her feet, goes babbling on as musically as ever; and if the golden moss blossoms out on the rock clefts; and if the wind makes sweet leaf-music in the tall tree-tops; and if the bright sunset clouds still rest like a glory on the mountain-brow; and if the little lake lies like a sheet of silver in the clear moonbeams; and if her old father sits in the honeysuckle porch, that the wind may lift the silver hairs from his heated temples; and if her little brother and sister still sit under the old shady oak, making tea-sets of acorns.

Hurry, bustle and drive!—on they go, and the little sempstress disappears around the corner with the crowd.

A shriek, a shout! Poor, old man!—there he lies under the horses' hoofs, his gray hairs trampled in the dust, struggling, with what strength he may, for the remnant of his poor life. The coachman "was not to blame." Nobody is ever "to blame," now-a-days! So he swore as he dismounted, and dragging the old man, covered with dust and blood, to the side-walk, jumped on his coachbox, cracked his whip, and thanked his stars it was "nothing but an old beggar-man, whom nobody cared for." And the young physician, whose maiden sign was that morning hung out the door, popped his head out the window, took a professional bird's-eye view of the case,—sighed, as he returned to his cigar, that accidents always seemed to happen, now-a-days, to people from whom one could not get a fee. It was a case he did not feel called upon to notice. His net was spread for golden fish.

THE MODEL STEP-MOTHER.

Gratifies every childish desire, how injurious soever, or unreasonable, and yet maintains the most perfect government;—is perfectly willing her step-children's relatives should feed them to surfeiting, with pickles, pre-serves, and sugar,—meekly holding herself in readiness for a two months' siege by a sick-bed rather than venture a remonstrance;—has no objection to their being stopped on the way to school, by a self-appointed commit-tee of Paul Prys in petticoats, to pass an examination as to the fitness of their shoestrings, pinafores and satchels;—always lets "the children" take papa's two hands going to church, and walks behind herself, if the neigh-bors think best;—is quite charmed to welcome a stage-load of their rela-tives, who come on a foraging expedition, to see "how the dear children are treated;"—looks as sweet as a June morning, when she finds them in the kitchen, lifting the covers off pots and kettles, peeping into tea-caddies, and punching their knuckles into the bread, "to see if it has riz;"—goes through the catechism, without flinching, from the price of brown soap and the wages of her cook, to the straw mat in the entry, and the trimming on her Sunday gown;—is perfectly willing to see them holding little, private caucuses with the juveniles, who are keen enough to see which way they are *expected* to answer;—shuts her own children up in a dark room, if they make any objection to being used for a pincush-ion, or to being scalped, one hair at a time, by the strange brood;—after wearing herself to a skeleton trying to please everybody, has the satisfac-tion of hearing herself called "a cruel, hard-hearted step-mother!"

The Tear of a Wife

> "The tear of a loving girl is like a dew-drop on a rose; but on the cheek of a wife, is a drop of poison to her husband."

It is "an ill wind that blows nobody any good." Papas will be happy to hear that twenty-five dollar pocket-handkerchiefs can be dispensed with now, in the bridal *trousseau*. Their "occupation's gone"! Matrimonial tears "are poison." There is no knowing what you will do, girls, with that escape-valve shut off; but that is no more to the point, than—whether you have anything to smile at or not; one thing is settled—you must not cry! Never mind back-aches, and side-aches, and head-aches, and drop-sical complaints, and smoky chimneys, and old coats, and young babies! Smile! It flatters your husband. He wants to be considered the source of your happiness, whether he was baptized Nero or Moses! Your mind never being supposed to be occupied with any other subject than himself, of course a tear is a tacit reproach. Besides, you miserable little whim-perer! what have you to cry for? A-i-n-t y-o-u m-a-r-r-i-e-d? Is n't that the *summum bonum*,—the height of feminine ambition? You can't get beyond that! It is the jumping-off place! You've arriv!—got to the end of your journey! Stage puts up there! You have nothing to do but retire on your laurels, and spend the rest of your life endeavoring to be thankful that you are Mrs. John Smith! "Smile!" you simpleton!

Important for Married Men.

> "The Budget says, that a lady lost the use of her tongue for nearly a week the other day, from eating too many tomatoes. The price of this indispensable vegetable will, no doubt, rise in consequence."

No it won't! There is nothing in this world—with one exception—that gentlemen love so well as to hear women talk to each other. You are sitting *tête-à-tête* with Moses, at your domestic fireside. A lady friend comes in; she is bright, and witty, and agreeable. You have both a tremendous budget of feminine *"bon mots"* and good things to share with each other. The question is, how to get rid of Moses. You hint that there is a great political meeting at Tammany Hall, on which occasion Cass, or whoever is god of your husband's political idolatry, is going to speak. He don't stir a peg. Then you adroitly raise the window-curtain, and speak of the beauty of the night, and how many gentlemen are out with cigars in their mouths. It dont "end in—smoke!" Then you ask him "if he has carried the morning's paper over to his mother?" He is as deaf as a "post!" Finally, in despair, you get into the remotest corner of the room, and commence operations, leaving Moses to his corner and his book, for fear of disturbing (?) him.

Kitty tells you a most excruciating story, and you tell her another; and you laugh till the tears start. Well, now you just creep slily round Moses' chair, and take a peep at him. St. Cecilia! if that book is not upside down, and his mouth stretched from ear to ear! He has swallowed every word with the avidity of a cat over her first mouse banquet; and yet, if you did not face him up with that upside down book, he would persist he had been reading the funniest book alive! And so he has, but it was not bound in "calf" or "sheep-skin!"

Aunt Hetty on Matrimony.

"Now girls," said Aunt Hetty, "put down your embroidery and worsted work; do something sensible, and stop building air-castles, and talking of lovers and honeymoons. It makes me sick; it is perfectly antimonial. Love is a farce; matrimony is a humbug; husbands are domestic Napoleons, Neroes, Alexanders,—sighing for other hearts to conquer, after they are sure of yours. The honey-moon is as short-lived as a lucifer-match; after that you may wear your wedding-dress at breakfast, and your night-cap to meeting, and your husband would n't know it. You may pick up your own pocket-handerchief, help yourself to a chair, and split your gown across the back reaching over the table to get a piece of butter, while he is laying in his breakfast as if it was the last meal he should eat in this world. When he gets through he will aid your digestion,—while you are sipping your first cup of coffee,—by inquiring what you'll have for dinner; whether the cold lamb was all ate yesterday; if the charcoal is all out, and what you gave for the last green tea you bought. Then he gets up from the table lights his cigar with the last evening's paper, that you have not had a chance to read; gives two or three whiffs of smoke,—which are sure to give you a headache for the afternoon,—and, just as his coattail is vanishing through the door, apologizes for not doing 'that errand' for you yesterday,—thinks it doubtful if he can to-day,—'so pressed with business.' Hear of him at eleven o'clock, taking an ice-cream with some ladies at a confectioner's, while you are at home new-lining his coat-sleeves. Children by the ears all day; can't get out to take the air; feel as crazy as a fly in a drum. Husband comes home at night; nods a 'How d'ye do, Fan?' boxes Charley's ears, stands little Fanny in the corner; sits down in the easiest chair in the warmest nook; puts his feet up over the grate, shutting out all the fire, while the baby's little pug nose grows blue with the cold; reads the newspaper all to himself; solaces his inner man with a cup of tea, and, just as you are laboring under the hallucination that he will ask you to take a mouthful of fresh air with him, he puts on his dressing-gown and slippers, and begins to reckon up the family expenses; after which he lies down on the sofa, and you keep time with your needle, while he sleeps till nine o'clock. Next morning, ask him to leave you a 'little money,' he looks at you as if to be sure that you are in your right mind, draws a sigh long enough and strong enough to inflate a pair of bellows, and asks you 'what you want with it, and if a half-a-dollar won't do?' Gracious king! as if those little shoes, and stockings, and petticoats could be had for half-a-dollar! O, girls! set your affections on cats, poodles, parrots or lap-dogs; but let matrimony alone. It's the hardest way on earth of getting a living. You never know when your work is done. Think of carrying eight or nine children through the measles, chicken-pox, rash, mumps, and scarlet fever,—some of them twice over. It makes my head ache to think of it. O, you may scrimp and save, and twist and turn, and dig and delve, and economize and die; and your husband will marry again, and take what you have saved to dress his second wife with; and she'll take your portrait for a fire-board!

"But, what's the use of talking? I'll warrant every one of you ll try it the first chance you get; for, somehow, there's a sort of bewitchment about it. I wish one half the world were not fools, and the other half idiots."

HARRIET PRESCOTT SPOFFORD

(1835–1921)

Circumstance

Atlantic Monthly, 5 (May), 1860.

Harriet Prescott Spofford was born on April 3, 1835, in Calais, Maine, the oldest of the five children and four daughters of Sarah Bridges and Joseph Prescott. Her family, in New England for over two hundred years, was conventionally distinguished in its social, military, and economic history. Her shipowning grandfather Prescott, however, lost his fortune in the War of 1812, and economic difficulty continued to plague his children. Spofford's father, a lumber merchant, failed in 1834, the year before Harriet was born. He was never again financially stable. Indeed, economic pressures played a large part in Spofford's decision to become a professional writer. During her years in Calais, Spofford attended, whenever family finances permitted, a private school taught by a Miss Porter. Here she first began to write, composing original essays in response to traditional school assignments.

In 1849, Spofford's mother moved with her children to Newburyport, Massachusetts, to live with a married sister while her husband went West to Oregon, presumably to seek his fortune in that new world. The move to Newburyport not only brought Spofford within range of the heart of literary New England; it also offered her the opportunity to attend the already famous Putnam Free School, founded in 1848 in Newburyport. Entrance exams were required for admission since the curriculum of the school was intellectually ambitious. The school encouraged reading and provided Spofford with a community of friends who shared her literary interests. The school also published its own paper, called "The Experiment," which offered a forum for those students with literary inclinations and ambitions. In addition, it had anniversary exercises each year, whose prime feature was a dramatic dialogue. For three years, Spofford wrote the dialogue for these exercises. In Newburyport, Spofford met Thomas Wentworth Higginson, with whom she formed a lifelong friendship and whose influence she relied on in the early stages of her career. Higginson sponsored a series of prizes for the best compositions in poetry and prose written by the youth of the town. At the age of sixteen, Spofford won a prize with an essay on Hamlet. Higginson also organized poetry study groups that Spofford attended and reading groups for factory "girls" in whose instruction Spofford and her friends assisted.

In 1853, the Prescott family, still primarily female—her father remained in Oregon—moved to Derry, New Hampshire where Harriet completed her formal education at the Pinkerton Academy, another prestigious New England school founded in 1815. Although women were readmitted to the school in 1853 (they had been formally excluded in 1821), there were no regular courses of study for girls and no formal certificate was issued to them in recognition of their attendance. Nevertheless, Spofford received a good education at Pinkerton; indeed, she is noteworthy as a nineteenth-century American woman writer with a relatively high level of formal schooling. Spofford's first printed work, a poem entitled "Life" and published as a broadside, dates from this period.

In 1856, Spofford's father returned from the West. He had not recovered his fortunes by this venture; indeed, he had only added ill health to his burdens. Soon after his return, her mother also became an invalid. This set of circumstances led Spofford to attempt to support herself and her family through writing. In the late 1850s, she began publishing anonymous pulp fiction in various Boston papers. Sometimes writing as much as fifteen hours a day, with an arm and hand swollen from excessive use—she wrote over one hundred tales in three years for one periodical alone—she nevertheless earned from her labor only a modest income. Out of a desire to improve her economic situation and perhaps also out of a desire to become something more than a hack writer, Spofford submitted in 1858, at the age of twenty-three, a story to the *Atlantic Monthly*. "In A Cellar" was published in February of 1859, and, after Higginson had vouched to the editors for its authorship ("I had to be called in to satisfy them that a demure little Yankee girl could have written it"), Spofford's entrance into the realm of literature and literary circles was assured. An invitation to the *Atlantic* dinner given in July, 1859, to honor Harriet Beecher Stowe testified to her accomplishment.

In 1860, Spofford published her first novel, *Sir Rohan's Ghost;* in 1863, she published *The Amber Gods and Other Stories,* a collection of stories previously published, with one exception, in the *Atlantic;* in 1864, she published a second novel, *Azarian.* With these three volumes, Spofford was fairly started on a literary career that lasted for sixty years and was characterized by a productivity extraordinary even for a woman writer of her day. She wrote poems, short stories, novels, novellas, children's books, literary essays, essays and books on domestic issues, travel books, and personal reminiscences. Spofford's early work reflects considerable imaginative power, but she had difficulty finding a form that could control and give shape to that power. Indeed, only the genre of short fiction provided such a form, and thus her collections of short fiction constitute her strongest claim to literary fame. In her short fiction, Spofford's gift for creating atmosphere through vivid descriptions, her ability to use setting and object to capture character, and her fascination with the passionate and often amoral aspects of human behavior receive full play.

Spofford's ability to realize her aesthetic power was no doubt vitiated by her excessive productivity. Her experience with pulp fiction set early patterns of easy writing. In addition, she suffered, according to Higginson, from "that fatal cheapness of immediate reputation which stunts most of our young writers, making the rudiments of fame so easy to acquire, and fame itself so difficult—which dwarfs our female writers so especially" (Anna Mary Wells, *Dear Preceptor: The Life and Times of Thomas Wentworth Higginson* [Boston: Houghton, Mifflin, 1963], p. 194). Unfortunately, she also had friends like Mary Louise Booth, who, as editor of *Harper's Bazar* from 1867 to 1889, made it simple for Spofford to find ready publication for anything she wrote, regardless of its quality. Although, by the turn of the century, Spofford was one of the most popular women writers in America, her critical reputation steadily worsened and did not revive until the publication in 1920 of *The Elder's People,* her major effort in the direction of the New England regional tale. Spofford also suffered from the changing literary tastes of post–Civil War America. While many of the writers in this volume could be called realists at a time when romance was the dominant form, at least among the aesthetically committed male American writers, Spofford might be called a romanticist who began to write at a time when the literary establishment was moving in the direction of realism. Henry James, who reviewed both *The Amber Gods* and *Azarian* for the *North American Review,* severely criticized the latter work for its lack of realism and urged the writer to cultivate the actual, not the fantastic. Spofford lacked the courage of her own convictions. Instead of cultivating her strength, she tried to embrace realism in response to changing demands. Writing in later years to Fred Lewis Pattee, she addressed this issue: "You wonder why I did not continue in the vein of 'The Amber Gods.' I suppose because the public taste changed. With the coming of Mr. Howells as editor of the *Atlantic,* and his influence, the realistic arrived. I doubt if anything I wrote in those days would be accepted by any magazine now" (Halbeisen, p. 122).

In 1865, at the age of thirty, Harriet Prescott married Richard Spofford, to whom she had dedicated *The Amber Gods.* A lawyer and poet, Richard Spofford consistently devoted himself to his wife's career, reading her manuscripts critically and planning trips to stimulate her imagination. During the first ten years of marriage, the Spoffords lived alternately in Washington, D.C. and Newburyport where Richard was professionally active. In 1874, they bought Deer Island in the Merrimack River. Here they established the home that became central to Spofford's literary and social life, and was famous for its hospitality and

the extended visits of friends; "In the midst of this circle, Harriet Spofford carried on her literary work. It was her habit to write in the drawing-room to the left of the wide entrance hall with its curious open
stairway. Here where the view is that of the west curve she sat, rarely at
the desk, but with pad on knee, a large bottle of ink on the floor beside
her. Now and then she stopped to join the conversation" (Halbeisen,
pp. 114–15). An excellent hostess and housekeeper (she wrote both essays and books on the subject), Spofford was often held up as a model
of behavior for other"lady authors." One child was born of this marriage, a son who died in infancy.

Richard Spofford died in 1888, when Harriet was fifty-three. After
his death, her friends became more than ever the center of Spofford's
emotional, social, and intellectual life. During the decade of the 1890s,
when Spofford was dividing her time between Deer Island and Boston,
she became part of a Boston circle of women writers, which included,
among others, Louise Chandler Moulton, Annie Fields, Gail Hamilton,
Celia Thaxter, Rose Terry Cooke, Sarah Orne Jewett, and Alice Brown.
In *A Little Book of Friends* (1916), Spofford pays tribute to these
women and to her friendships with them. Spofford died on August 14,
1921, at Deer Island, at the age of eighty-six. She was buried in Newburyport.

"I read Miss Prescott's 'Circumstance,' but it followed me in the
Dark—so I avoided her." So wrote Emily Dickinson to Thomas Wentworth Higginson on April 25, 1862. To her sister-in-law, Sue Gilbert
Dickinson, she wrote, "Sue, it is the only thing I ever read in my life
that I didn't think I could have imagined myself," and, despite her comment to Higginson, she begged Sue to "send me everything she writes"
(Martha Dickinson Bianchi, *Emily Dickinson Face to Face.* [Boston:
Houghton, Mifflin, 1932], p. 28). Clearly Dickinson was impressed. A
recent article in *Dickinson Studies* suggests that she was sufficiently impressed to write a poem, " 'Twas like a Maelstrom, with a notch," ap-
propriating Spofford's imagery and vocabulary and identifying the
experience of "Circumstance" as her own. As a woman writer, Dickinson might well have been appalled by "Circumstance," for in this story
Spofford presents an extraordinary, compelling, and harsh vision of the
circumstances of the woman artist.

The story, based on an incident that actually happened to Spofford's
maternal great-grandmother, describes the experience of a woman who
spends an entire winter night pinned motionless in a tree by a panther,
known as the "Indian Devil." Like her prototype, Scheherazade, this
woman's life literally depends on her art. Singing to "soothe the savage
beast," she is singing for her life. But although her song is her lifeline,
the circumstances of her performance are hardly self-determined or free.
She does not choose to begin and she dare not choose to stop. Her
choice of song grows out of a frantic effort to determine what will
please and placate the beast: "franticly she darted from tune to tune; his
restless movements followed her." In striking contrast to her frenzy, she
imagines her husband at home deciding to amuse himself by fiddliing

while he waits for her return, "playing lightly with his head inclined, playing while she sang, while she sang for her life to an Indian Devil." Although some personal and aesthetic power resides in the fact that this woman saves her life through song and lives to tell the tale, the primary imagery of the story conveys a far less optimistic point: "How appalling the thought that with her voice ceased her existence." Only when she accepts her death as inevitable is she free to concentrate on her art. For Dickinson, the sense of violation and vulnerability in this set of circumstances must have struck a shuddering response. Nathaniel Hawthorne wanted women's literature to exhibit women's bodies, naked, without the restraint of decency; "Circumstance" expresses the violence behind that desire. Made to sing to please the beast, for whom the pleasure has a distinctly sexual connotation, this woman experiences a sense of shame and loathing at such enforced and public exposure.

The protagonist of "Circumstance" is nameless. In Lydia Sigourney's "The Father," the namelessness of mother and daughter indicates the degree to which they are functions of the father. In "Circumstance," the same device serves to give the character and situation of the protagonist a symbolic and even representative cast. A frontier woman, she has lived a life of "reality" and "hard fact." (We are perhaps reminded here of Caroline Kirkland's analysis of the frontier as offering women an escape from conventional definitions of the "feminine.") Although spiritually receptive and open to visions, she has no "flimsy habit of mind." Rather, living on the edge of civilization, she has clothed her mind in the garb of self-reliance. She has gone alone to assist a sick neighbor and alone she will return. Domestic in her affections and interests, this woman is not domesticated. The path through the woods leads from house to home, but while she is on it she is out in what men define as the "world." Indeed, much of the strength of "Circumstance" derives from Spofford's success in finding a mechanism for presenting a woman outside the home. As if to emphasize her strategy, Spofford presents in detail her protagonist's visions of her husband, safe at home, tending the hearth, soothing the child. He, not she, is domestic, and she, not he, is out in the world, exposed to the hard fact of real danger.

And, yet, beneath the surface of this story may well lie paradoxes by means of which safety and danger are radically redefined, as they are in the Dickinson poem. At the end of the story, the protagonist discovers that her visions of the home as safe were false: "Desolation and death were indeed there, and beneficence and life in the forest." Earlier in the story, the appearance of the domestic has been associated with both physical and spiritual danger. When husband and child arrive on the scene, the woman loses her voice and her vision. To what degree, then, do these paradoxes inform the rest of the story? "You have no evils to endure," says Mr. James and Mrs. James in *The Angel Over The Right Shoulder.* The idea of home as safe, as Elizabeth Stuart Phelps points out, serves Mr. James, not Mrs. James. In "Circumstance," danger, tangible and visible, ratifies the woman's sense of herself as threatened. But what is the nature of the danger that confronts the woman in Spofford's story?

After a single flourish of the supernatural—"a swift shadow, like the fabulous flying-dragon"—the descriptions of the panther become graphically real. These descriptions focus on specific physical features—his "foetid breath," "flaming balls," sharp claws, snarling hiss, and again and again his tongue: "his rasping tongue," "the rough, sharp, and multiplied stings of his tongue," "the long red tongue," "once he scored her cheek with his tongue, savage caresses that hurt like wounds." The panther uses the power of his body to hold the woman subject to his attentions and to enforce physical contact on her: "the beast moved again, but only to lay the disengaged paw across her with heavy satisfaction"; "he settled himself composedly on the bough, still clasping her with invincible pressure to his rough, ravenous breast." The experience described is that of physical violation; its overtones are clearly sexual. When we examine the nature of the woman's response to this sudden attack in the night from one whom she is powerless to resist and can only hope to placate, the sexual context is intensified. A "quivering disgust" far worse than physical pain or fear of death defines this woman's nightmare. Her revulsion derives from her idea of the beast: a "living lump of appetites," "the strength of our lower natures let loose," possessed of the hideous "vitality" of "foaming chops" and "slaver." In the context of mid-nineteenth-century America, this language constitutes a familiar code for referring to unrestrained male sexuality, that lower nature often let loose on the bodies of women. The woman's experience can be read, then, as an experience of "rape," a nightmare as likely to occur in the home as in the woods.

This reading is reinforced by another aspect of the beast. Clearly in control and most demanding—he will not stand for repetitions, each tune must be different—the beast can nevertheless be reached. While the woman's shrieks arouse him only to more violence, her singing stirs in him a different element of his nature. Like Lydia Sigourney's "The Father" and Harriet Beecher Stowe's The Pearl of Orr's Island, "Circumstance" dramatizes the nineteenth-century conviction that men, despite their lower nature, have a spiritual component that responds to women and by means of which women can tame their beast and raise them to a higher level. At the beginning of "Circumstance," we learn that the protagonist is open to the spiritual realm. "Receptive of every influence," she has visions from the world beyond the flesh, the world of God.

For "Circumstance" also describes a religious experience. In the woods, alone and in danger, the protagonist undergoes a test of faith. When first assaulted, she calls, not on God, but on her husband, for "it seemed to her that she had but one friend in the world; that was he." As the night drags on and her husband fails to appear, she realizes her mistake, perhaps her "sin," and, then, "without being aware of it, her voice forsook the songs of suffering and sorrow for old Covenanting hymns,—hymns with which her mother had lulled her. . . ." For the first time she forgets her circumstance and thinks only of her song and its subject; "He is the Lord our God; his judgments are in all the earth." She asks for neither rescue nor reprieve, but resigns herself to God's will. At the end of the story, her faith is vindicated and the wisdom of God made plain. She has come through her test of faith triumphant and, though ejected from Eden, perhaps through her sin, perhaps only through her husband's, she has reaffirmed her spiritual nature. And she has been the instrument of her husband's salvation as well; drawn by her voice he has left the doomed settlement and found safety in the woods.

Although the husband's bullet kills the beast and frees the woman, his role as rescuer is distinctly underplayed. In part, this results from the religious dimension of the story that insists that God, not man, is the true "savior." In part, it reflects the message encoded in the concluding paradox and implicit in the descriptions of the panther—namely, that home is often where the beasts are. Yet while the story stops short of the conventional simplicities of helpless maiden, heroic knight, deadly dragon, and miraculous rescue, it also stops well short of any direct identification of husband with beast. Instead, it identifies the beast with those other men who cannot be the woman's husband. In the very first paragraph of "Circumstance," Spofford makes a connection between literal beast and human beast ("stealthy native or deadly panther tribes") and identifies these human beasts as "savages"—red men who must be carefully distinguished from the white men who inhabit the "civilization" of the settlement. When the beast makes its spring, we learn that hunters know it as the "Indian Devil"; at the end of the story, we learn that this "Indian Devil" is less deadly than the actual Indians whose "tomahawk and scalpingknife, descending during that night, had left behind them only this work of their accomplished hatred and one subtle foot-print in the snow." By the end of the story, we know how to interpret the spectral invocation, "The Lord have mercy on the people." For "people," we read "whites," and for "mercy," we read protection against the Indians who are not people but devils, capable of every atrocity, including rape.

Although many of the women represented in this anthology made a sincere and serious effort to combat racism in themselves and in their world, it would of course be a mistake to assume that, as a group, nineteenth-century white American women writers were free from racist thinking. "Circumstance" exemplifies the insidiousness and pervasiveness of the racist imagination in white American literature. Subtle, deadly, and ultimately self-serving, racist assumptions appear in such texts in part because they are so readily available and so easy to invoke, particularly in circumstances in which hostility must be accomplished by stealth.

Source:

The Amber Gods and Other Stories (Boston: Ticknor and Fields), 1863.

Selected Primary Works:

Sir Rohan's Ghost: A Romance, 1860; Azarian: An Episode, 1864; A Scarlet Poppy, and Other Stories, 1894; Old Madame, and Other Tragedies, 1900; Four Days of God, 1905; A Little Book of Friends, 1916; The Elder's People, 1920.

Selected Secondary Works:

Rose Terry Cooke, "Harriet Prescott Spofford," *Our Famous Women* (Hartford, Worthington), 1884; Maryanne M. Garbowsky, "A Maternal Muse for Emily Dickinson," *Dickinson Studies,* no. 41 (1981), 12–17; Elizabeth K. Halbeisen, *Harriet Prescott Spofford: A Romantic Survival* (Philadelphia: University of Pennsylvania Press), 1935; Arthur Hobson Quinn, *American Fiction* (New York: D. Appleton-Century), 1936.

Contexts:

1854—Cummins, *The Lamplighter;* Thoreau, *Walden;* Kansas-Nebraska Act
1855—Duyckinck, *Cyclopedia of American Literature;* Fanny Fern, *Ruth Hall;* Longfellow, *Hiawatha;* Melville, "Benito Cereno," "The Paradise of Bachelors"; Whitman, *Leaves of Grass; Frank Leslie's Illustrated Newspaper;* New York *Ledger*
1856—Hentz, *Ernest Linwood;* Melville, *The Piazza Tales;* Stowe, *Dred;* Whitcher, *The Widow Bedott Papers*
1857—Cooke, "Sally Parsons's Duty"; Cummins, *Mabel Vaughan;* Melville, *The Confidence Man;* Sedgwick, *Married or Single?;* Webb, *The Garies and Their Friends;* Whittier, *Collected Poems; Atlantic Monthly;* Dred Scott decision; *Harper's Weekly*
1858—Holmes, *The Autocrat of the Breakfast Table*

SHE HAD REMAINED, during all that day, with a sick neighbor,—those eastern wilds of Maine in that epoch frequently making neighbors and miles synonymous,—and so busy had she been with care and sympathy that she did not at first observe the approaching night. But finally the level rays, reddening the snow, threw their gleam upon the wall, and, hastily donning cloak and hood, she bade her friends farewell and sallied forth on her return. Home lay some three miles distant, across a copse, a meadow, and a piece of woods,—the woods being a fringe on the skirts of the great forests that stretch far away into the North. That home was one of a dozen log-houses lying a few furlongs apart from each other, with their half-cleared demesnes separating them at the rear from a wilderness untrodden save by stealthy native or deadly panther tribes.

She was in a nowise exalted frame of spirit,—on the contrary, rather depressed by the pain she had witnessed and the fatigue she had endured; but in certain temperaments such a condition throws open the mental pores, so to speak, and renders one receptive of every influence. Through the little copse she walked slowly, with her cloak folded about her, lingering to imbibe the sense of shelter, the sunset filtered in purple through the mist of woven spray and twig, the companionship of growth not sufficiently dense to band against her, the sweet homefeeling of a young and tender wintry wood. It was therefore just on the edge of the evening that she emerged from the place and began to cross the meadowland. At one hand lay the forest to which her path wound; at the other the evening star hung over a tide of failing orange that slowly slipped down the earth's broad side to sadden other hemispheres with sweet regret. Walking rapidly now, and with her eyes wide-open, she distinctly saw in the air before her what was not there a moment ago, a winding-sheet,—cold, white, and ghastly, waved by the likeness of four wan hands,—that rose with a long inflation, and fell in rigid folds, while a voice, shaping itself from the hollowness above, spectral and melancholy, sighed,—"The Lord have mercy on the people! The Lord have mercy on the people!" Three times the sheet with its corpse-covering outline waved beneath the pale hands, and the voice, awful in its solemn and mysterious depth, sighed, "The Lord have mercy on the people!" Then all was gone, the place was clear again, the gray sky was obstructed by no deathly blot; she looked about her, shook her shoulders decidedly, and, pulling on her hood, went forward once more.

She might have been a little frightened by such an apparition, if she had led a life of less reality than frontier settlers are apt to lead; but dealing with hard fact does not engender a flimsy habit of mind, and this woman was too sincere and earnest in her character, and too happy in her situation, to be thrown by antagonism, merely, upon superstitious fancies and chimeras of the second-sight. She did not even believe herself subject to an hallucination, but smiled simply, a little vexed that her thought could have framed such a glamour from the day's occurences, and not sorry to lift the bough of the warder of the woods and enter and disappear in their sombre path. If she had been imaginative, she would have hesitated at her first step into a region whose dangers were not visionary; but I suppose that the thought of a little child at home would conquer that propensity in the most habituated. So, biting a bit of spicy birch, she went along. Now and then she came to a gap where the trees had been partially felled, and here she found that the lingering twilight was explained by that peculiar and perhaps electric film which sometimes sheaths the sky in diffused light for many hours before a brilliant aurora. Suddenly, a swift shadow, like the fabulous flying-dragon, writhed through the air before her, and she felt herself instantly seized and borne aloft. It was that wild beast—the most savage and serpentine and subtle and fearless of our latitudes—known by hunters as the Indian Devil, and he held her in his clutches on the broad floor of a swinging fir-bough. His long sharp claws were caught in her clothing, he worried them sagaciously a little, then, finding that ineffectual to free them, he commenced licking her bare arm with his rasping tongue and pouring over her the wide streams of his hot, foetid breath. So quick had this flashing action been that the woman had had no time for alarm; moreover, she was not of the screaming kind: but now, as she felt him endeavoring to disentangle his claws, and the horrid sense of her fate smote her, and she saw instinctively the fierce plunge of those weapons, the long strips of living flesh torn from her bones, the agony, the quivering disgust, itself a worse agony,—while by her side, and holding her in his great lithe embrace, the monster crouched, his white tusks whetting and gnashing, his eyes glaring through all the darkness like balls of red fire,—a shriek, that rang in every forest hollow, that startled every winter-housed thing, that stirred and woke the least needle of the tasselled pines, tore through her lips. A moment afterward, the beast left the arm, once white, now crimson, and looked up alertly.

She did not think at this instant to call upon God. She called upon her husband. It seemed to her that she had but one friend in the world; that was he; and again the cry, loud, clear, prolonged, echoed through the woods. It was not the shriek that disturbed the creature at his relish; he was not born in the woods to be scared of an owl, you know; what then? It must have been the echo, most musical, most resonant, repeated and yet repeated, dying with long sighs of sweet sound, vibrated from rock to river and back again from depth to depth of cave and cliff. Her thought flew after it; she knew, that, even if her husband heard it, he yet could not reach her in time; she saw that while the beast listened he would not gnaw,—and this she *felt* directly, when the rough, sharp, and multiplied stings of his tongue retouched her arm. Again her lips opened by instinct, but the sound that issued thence came by reason. She had heard that music charmed wild beasts,—just this point between life and death intensified every faculty,—and when she opened her lips the third time, it was not for shrieking, but for singing.

A little thread of melody stole out, a rill of tremulous motion; it was the cradle-song with which she rocked her baby;—how could she sing that? And then she remembered the baby sleeping rosily on the long settee before the fire,—the father cleaning his gun, with on foot on the green wooden rundle,—the merry light from the chimney dancing out and through the room, on the rafters of the ceiling with their tassels of onions and herbs, on the log walls painted with lichens and festooned with apples, on the king's-arm slung across the shelf with the old pirate's-cutlass, on the snow-pile of the bed, and on the great brass clock,—dancing, too, and lingering on the baby, with his fringed-gentian eyes, his chubby fists clenched on the pillow, and his fine breezy hair fanning with the motion of his father's foot. All this struck her in one, and made a sob of her breath, and she ceased.

Immediately the long red tongue thrust forth again. Before it touched, a song sprang to her lips, a wild sea-song, such as some sailor might be singing far out on trackless blue water that night, the shrouds whistling with frost and the sheets glued in ice,—a song with the wind in its burden and the spray in its chorus. The monster raised his head and flared the fiery eyeballs upon her, then fretted the imprisoned claws a moment and was quiet; only the breath like the vapor from some hell-pit still swathed her. Her voice, at first faint and fearful, gradually lost its quaver, grew under her control and subject to her modulation; it rose on long swells, it fell in subtile cadences, now and then its tones pealed out like bells from distant belfries on fresh sonorous mornings. She sung the song through, and, wondering lest his name of Indian Devil were not his true name, and if he would not detect her, she repeated it. Once or twice now, indeed, the beast stirred uneasily, turned, and made the bough sway at his movement. As she ended, he snapped his jaws together, and tore away the fettered member, curling it under him with a snarl,—when she burst into the gayest reel that ever answered a fiddle-bow. How many a time she had heard her husband play it on the homely fiddle made by himself from birch and cherrywood! how many a time she had seen it danced on the floor of their one room, to the patter of wooden clogs and the rustle of homespun petticoat! how many a time she had danced it herself!—and did she not remember once, as they joined clasps for eight-hands-round, how it had lent its gay, bright measure to her life? And here she was singing it alone, in the forest, at midnight, to a wild beast! As she sent her voice trilling up and down its quick oscillations between joy and pain, the creature who grasped her uncurled his paw and scratched the bark from the bough; she must vary the spell; and her voice spun leaping along the projecting points of tune of a hornpipe. Still singing, she felt herself twisted about with a low growl and a lifting of the red lip from the glittering teeth; she broke the hornpipe's thread, and commenced unravelling a lighter, livelier thing, an Irish jig. Up and down and round about her voice flew, the beast threw back his head so that the diabolical face fronted hers, and the torrent of his breath prepared her for his feast as the anaconda slimes his prey. Franticly she darted from tune to tune; his restless movements followed her. She tired herself with dancing and vivid national airs, growing feverish and singing spasmodically as she felt her horrid tomb yawning wider. Touching in this manner all the slogan and keen clan cries, the beast moved again, but only to lay the disengaged paw across her with heavy satisfaction. She did not dare to pause; through the clear cold air, the frosty starlight, she sang. If there were yet any tremor in the tone, it was not fear,—she had learned the secret of sound at last; nor could it be chill,—far too high a fever throbbed her pulses; it was nothing but the thought of the log-house and of what might be passing within it. She fancied the baby stirring in his sleep and moving his pretty lips,—her husband rising and opening the door, looking out after her, and wondering at her absence. She fancied the light pouring through the chink and then shut in again with all the safety and comfort and joy, her husband taking down the fiddle and playing lightly with his head inclined, playing while she sang, while she sang for her life to an Indian Devil. Then she knew he was fumbling for and finding some shining fragment and scoring it down the yellowing hair, and unconsciously her voice forsook the wild wartunes and drifted into the half-gay, half-melancholy Rosin the Bow.

Suddenly she woke pierced with a pang, and the daggered tooth pene-
trating her flesh;—dreaming of safety, she had ceased singing and lost it.
The beast had regained the use of all his limbs, and now, standing and
raising his back, bristling and foaming, with sounds that would have been
like hisses but for their deep and fearful sonority, he withdrew step by
step toward the trunk of the tree, still with his flaming balls upon her. She
was all at once free, on one end of the bough, twenty feet from the
ground. She did not measure the distance, but rose to drop herself down,
careless of any death, so that it were not this. Instantly, as if he scanned
her thoughts, the creature bounded forward with a yell and caught her
again in his dreadful hold. It might be that he was not greatly famished;
for, as she suddenly flung up her voice again, he settled himself composedly on the bough, still clasping her with invincible pressure to his
rough, ravenous breast, and listening in a fascination to the sad, strange
U-la-lu that now moaned forth in loud, hollow tones above him. He half
closed his eyes, and sleepily reopened and shut them again.

What rending pains were close at hand! Death! and what a death!
worse than any other that is to be named! Water, be it cold or warm, that
which buoys up blue icefields, or which bathes tropical coasts with cur-
rents of balmy bliss, is yet a gentle conqueror, kisses as it kills, and draws
you down gently through darkening fathoms to its heart. Death at the
sword is the festival of trumpet and bugle and banner, with glory ringing
out around you and distant hearts thrilling through yours. No gnawing
disease can bring such hideous end as this; for that is a fiend bred of your
own flesh, and this—is it a fiend, this living lump of appetites? What
dread comes with the thought of perishing in flames! but fire, let it leap
and hiss never so hotly, is something too remote, too alien, to inspire us
with such loathly horror as a wild beast; if it have a life, that life is too
utterly beyond our comprehension. Fire is not half ourselves; as it de-
vours, arouses neither hatred nor disgust; is not to be known by the
strength of our lower natures let loose; does not drip our blood into our
faces with foaming chaps, nor mouth nor slaver above us with vitality.
Let us be ended by fire, and we are ashes, for the winds to bear, the leaves
to cover; let us be ended by wild beasts, and the base, cursed thing howls
with us forever through the forest. All this she felt as she charmed him,
and what force it lent to her song God knows. If her voice should fail! If
the damp and cold should give her any fatal hoarseness! If all the silent
powers of the forest did not conspire to help her! The dark, hollow night
rose indifferently over her; the wide, cold air breathed rudely past her,
lifted her wet hair and blew it down again; the great boughs swung with a
ponderous strength, now and then clashed their iron lengths together and
shook off a sparkle of icy spears or some long-lain weight of snow from
their heavy shadows. The green depths were utterly cold and silent and
stern. These beautiful haunts that all the summer were hers and rejoiced
to share with her their bounty, these heavens that had yielded their

largess, these stems that had thrust their blossoms into her hands, all these friends of three moons ago forgot her now and knew her no longer.

Feeling her desolation, wild, melancholy, forsaken songs rose thereon from that frightful aerie,—weeping, wailing tunes, that sob among the people from age to age, and overflow with otherwise unexpressed sadness,—all rude, mournful ballads,—old tearful strains, that Shake-speare heard the vagrants sing, and that rise and fall like the wind and tide,—sailor-songs, to be heard only in lone mid-watches beneath the moon and stars,—ghastly rhyming romances, such as that famous one of the Lady Margaret, when

> "She slipped on her gown of green
> A piece below the knee,—
> And 't was all a long cold winter's night
> A dead corse followed she."

Still the beast lay with closed eyes, yet never relaxing his grasp. Once a half-whine of enjoyment escaped him,—he fawned his fearful head upon her; once he scored her cheek with his tongue—savage caresses that hurt like wounds. How weary she was! and yet how terribly awake! How fuller and fuller of dismay grew the knowledge that she was only pro-longing her anguish and playing with death! How appalling the thought that with her voice ceased her existence! Yet she could not sing forever; her throat was dry and hard; her very breath was a pain; her mouth was hotter than any desert-worn pilgrim's;—if she could but drop upon her burning tongue one atom of the ice that glittered about her!—but both of her arms were pinioned in the giant's vice. She remembered the winding-sheet, and for the first time in her life shivered with spiritual fear. Was it hers? She asked herself, as she sang, what sins she had committed, what life she had led, to find her punishment so soon and in these pangs,—and then she sought eagerly for some reason why her husband was not up and abroad to find her. He failed her,—her one sole hope in life; and without being aware of it, her voice forsook the songs of suffering and sorrow for old Covenanting hymns,—hymns with which her mother had lulled her, which the class-leader pitched in the chimney-corners,—grand and sweet Methodist hymns, brimming with melody and with all fantastic involu-tions of tune to suit that ecstatic worship,—hymns full of the beauty of holiness, steadfast, relying, sanctified by the salvation they had lent to those in worse extremity than hers,—for they had found themselves in the grasp of hell, while she was but in the jaws of death. Out of this strange music, peculiar to one character of faith, and than which there is none more beautiful in its degree nor owning a more potent sway of sound, her voice soared into the glorified chants of churches. What to her was death by cold or famine or wild beasts? "Though He slay me, yet will I trust in him," she sang. High and clear through the frore fair night, the level moonbeams splintering in the wood, the scarce glints of stars in the shadowy roof of branches, these sacred anthems rose,—rose as a hope from despair, as some snowy spray of flower-bells from blackest mould. Was she not in God's hands? Did not the world swing at his will? If this were in his great plan of providence, was it not best, and should she not accept it?

"He is the Lord our God; his judgments are in all the earth."

Oh, sublime faith of our fathers, where utter self-sacrifice alone was true love, the fragrance of whose unrequired subjection was pleasanter than that of golden censers swung in purple-vapored chancels!

Never ceasing in the rhythm of her thoughts, articulated in music as they thronged, the memory of her first communion flashed over her. Again she was in that distant place on that sweet spring morning. Again the congregation rustled out, and the few remained, and she trembled to find herself among them. How well she remembered the devout, quiet faces, too accustomed to the sacred feast to glow with their inner joy! how well the snowy linen at the altar, the silver vessels slowly and silently shifting! and as the cup approached and passed, how the sense of delicious perfume stole in and heightened the transport of her prayer, and she had seemed, looking up through the windows where the sky soared blue in constant freshness, to feel all heaven's balms dripping from the portals, and to scent the lilies of eternal peace! Perhaps another would not have felt so much ecstasy as satisfaction on that occasion; but it is a true, if a later disciple, who has said, "The Lord bestoweth his blessings there, where he findeth the vessels empty."

"And does it need the walls of a church to renew my communion?" she asked. "Does not every moment stand a temple four-square to God? And in that morning, with its buoyant sunlight, was I any dearer to the Heart of the World than now?—'My beloved is mine, and I am his,'" she sang over and over again, with all varied inflection and profuse tune. How gently all the winter-wrapt things bent toward her then! into what relation with her had they grown! how this common dependence was the spell of their intimacy! how at one with Nature had she become! how all the night and the silence and the forest seemed to hold its breath, and to send its soul up to God in her singing! It was no longer despondency, that singing. It was neither prayer nor petition. She had left imploring, "How long wilt thou forget me, O Lord? Lighten mine eyes, lest I sleep the sleep of death! For in death there is no remembrance of thee,"—with countless other such fragments of supplication. She cried rather, "Yea, though I walk through the valley of the shadow of death, I will fear no evil: for thou art with me; thy rod and thy staff, they comfort me,"—and lingered, and repeated, and sang again, "I shall be satisfied, when I awake, with thy likeness."

Then she thought of the Great Deliverance, when he drew her up out of many waters, and the flashing old psalm pealed forth triumphantly:—

"The Lord descended from above,
    and bow'd the heavens hie:
And underneath his feet he cast
    the darknesse of the skie.
On cherubs and on cherubins
    full royally he road:
And on the wings of all the winds
    came flying all abroad."

She forgot how recently, and with what a strange pity for her own shapeless form that was to be, she had quaintly sung,—

"O lovely appearance of death!
    What sight upon earth is so fair?
Not all the gay pageants that breathe,
    Can with a dead body compare!"

She remembered instead,—"In thy presence is fulness of joy; at thy right hand there are pleasures forevermore. God will redeem my soul from the power of the grave: for he shall receive me. He will swallow up death in victory." Not once now did she say, "Lord, how long wilt thou look on; rescue my soul from their destructions, my darling from the lions,"—for she knew that the young lions roar after their prey and seek their meat from God. "O Lord, thou preservest man and beast!" she said.

She had no comfort or consolation in this season, such as sustained the Christian martyrs in the amphitheatre. She was not dying for her faith; there were no palms in heaven for her to wave; but how many a time had she declared,—"I had rather be a doorkeeper in the house of my God, than to dwell in the tents of wickedness!" And as the broad rays here and there broke through the dense covert of shade and lay in rivers of lustre on crystal sheathing and frozen fretting of trunk and limb and on the great spaces of refraction, they builded up visibly that house, the shining city on the hill, and singing, "Beautiful for situation, the joy of the whole earth, is Mount Zion, on the sides of the North, the city of the Great King," her vision climbed to that higher picture where the angel shows the dazzling thing, the holy Jerusalem descending out of heaven from God, with its splendid battlements and gates of pearls, and its foundations, the eleventh a jacinth, the twelfth an amethyst,—with its great white throne, and the rainbow round about it, in sight like unto an emerald: "And there shall be no night there,—for the Lord God giveth them light," she sang.

What whisper of dawn now rustled through the wilderness? How the night was passing? And still the beast crouched upon the bough, changing only the posture of his head, that again he might command her with those charmed eyes;—half their fire was gone; she could almost have released herself from his custody; yet, had she stirred, no one knows what malevolent instinct might have dominated anew. But of that she did not dream; long ago stripped of any expectation, she was experiencing in her divine rapture how mystically true it is that "he that dwelleth in the secret place of the Most High shall abide under the shadow of the Almighty."

Slow clarion cries now wound from the distance as the cocks caught the intelligence of day and re-echoed it faintly from farm to farm,—sleepy sentinels of night, sounding the foe's invasion, and translating that dim intuition to ringing notes of warning. Still she chanted on. A remote crash of brushwood told of some other beast on his depredations, or some night-belated traveller groping his way through the narrow path. Still she chanted on. The far, faint echoes of the chanticleers died into distance, the crashing of the branches grew nearer. No wild beast that, but a man's step,—a man's form in the moonlight, stalwart and strong,—on one arm slept a little child, in the other hand he held his gun. Still she chanted on.

Perhaps, when her husband last looked forth, he was half ashamed to find what a fear he felt for her. He knew she would never leave the child so long but for some direst need,—and yet he may have laughed at himself, as he lifted and wrapped it with awkward care, and, loading his gun and strapping on his horn, opened the door again and closed it behind him, going out and plunging into the darkness and dangers of the forest. He was more singularly alarmed than he would have been willing to acknowledge; as he had sat with his bow hovering over the strings, he had half believed to hear her voice mingling gayly with the instrument, till he paused and listened if she were not about to lift the latch and enter. As he drew nearer the heart of the forest, that intimation of melody seemed to grow more actual, to take body and breath, to come and go on long swells and ebbs of the night-breeze, to increase with tune and words, till a strange shrill singing grew ever clearer, and, as he stepped into an open space of moonbeams, far up in the branches, rocked by the wind, and singing, "How beautiful upon the mountains are the feet of him that bringeth good tidings, that publisheth peace," he saw his wife,—his wife,—but, great God in heaven! how? Some mad exclamation escaped him, but without diverting her. The child knew the singing voice, though never heard before in that unearthly key, and turned toward it through the veiling dreams. With a celerity almost instantaneous, it lay, in the twinkling of an eye, on the ground at the father's feet, while his gun was raised to his shoulder and levelled at the monster covering his wife with shaggy form and flaming gaze,—his wife so ghastly white, so rigid, so stained with blood, her eyes so fixedly bent above, and her lips, that had indurated into the chiselled pallor of marble, parted only with that flood of solemn song.

I do not know if it were the mother-instinct that for a moment lowered her eyes,—those eyes, so lately riveted on heaven, now suddenly seeing all life-long bliss possible. A thrill of joy pierced and shivered through her like a weapon, her voice trembled in its course, her glance lost its steady strength, fever-flushes chased each other over her face, yet she never once ceased chanting. She was quite aware, that, if her husband shot now, the ball must pierce her body before reaching any vital part of the beast,—and yet better that death, by his hand, than the other. But this her husband also knew, and he remained motionless, just covering the creature with the sight. He dared not fire, lest some wound not mortal should break the spell exercised by her voice, and the beast, enraged with pain, should rend her in atoms; moreover, the light was too uncertain for his aim. So he waited. Now and then he examined his gun to see if the damp were injuring its charge, now and then he wiped the great drops from his forehead. Again the cocks crowed with the passing hour,—the last time they were heard on that night. Cheerful home sound then, how full of safety and all comfort and rest it seemed! what sweet morning incidents of sparkling fire and sunshine, of gay household bustle, shining dresser, and cooing baby, of steaming cattle in the yard, and brimming milk-pails at the door! what pleasant voices! what laughter! what security! and here—

Now, as she sang on in the slow, endless, infinite moments, the fervent vision of God's peace was gone. Just as the grave had lost its sting, she was snatched back again to the arms of earthly hope. In vain she tried to sing, "There remaineth a rest for the people of God,"—her eyes trembled on her husband's, and she could only think of him, and of the child, and of happiness that yet might be, but with what a dreadful gulf of doubt between! She shuddered now in the suspense; all calm forsook her; she was tortured with dissolving heats or frozen with icy blasts; her face contracted, growing small and pinched; her voice was hoarse and sharp,—every tone cut like a knife,—the notes became heavy to lift,—withheld by some hostile pressure,—impossible. One gasp, a convulsive effort, and there was silence,—she had lost her voice.

The beast made a sluggish movement,—stretched and fawned like one awaking,—then, as if he would have yet more of the enchantment, stirred her slightly with his muzzle. As he did so, a sidelong hint of the man standing below with the raised gun smote him; he sprung round furiously, and, seizing his prey, was about to leap into some unknown airy den of the topmost branches now waving to the slow dawn. The late moon had rounded through the sky so that her gleam at last fell full upon the bough with fairy frosting; the wintry morning light did not yet penetrate the gloom. The woman, suspended in mid-air an instant, cast only one agonized glance beneath,—but across and through it, ere the lids could fall, shot a withering sheet of flame,—a rifle-crack, half-heard, was lost in the terrible yell of desperation that bounded after it and filled her ears with savage echoes, and in the wide arc of some eternal descent she was falling;—but the beast fell under her.

I think that the moment following must have been too sacred for us, and perhaps the three have no special interest again till they issue from the shadows of the wilderness upon the white hills that skirt their home. The father carries the child hushed again into slumber, the mother follows with no such feeble step as might be anticipated. It is not time for reaction,—the tension not yet relaxed, the nerves still vibrant, she seems to herself like some one newly made; the night was a dream; the present stamped upon her in deep satisfaction, neither weighed nor compared with the past; if she has the careful tricks of former habit, it is as an automaton; and as they slowly climb the steep under the clear gray vault and the paling morning star, and as she stops to gather a spray of the red-rose berries or a feathery tuft of dead grasses for the chimney-piece of the log-house, or a handful of brown cones for the child's play,—of these quiet, happy folk you would scarcely dream how lately they had stolen from under the banner and encampment of the great King Death. The husband proceeds a step or two in advance; the wife lingers over a singular foot-print in the snow, stoops and examines it, then looks up with a hurried word. Her husband stands alone on the hill, his arms folded across the babe, his gun fallen,—stands defined as a silhouette against the pallid sky. What is there in their home, lying below and yellowing in the light, to fix him with such a stare? She springs to his side. There is no home there. The log-house, the barns, the neighboring farms, the fences, are all blotted out and mingled in one smoking ruin. Desolation and death were indeed there, and beneficence and life in the forest. Tomahawk and scalping-knife, descending during that night, had left behind them only this work of their accomplished hatred and one subtle foot-print in the snow.

For the rest,—the world was all before them, where to choose.

HARRIET JACOBS

(CA. 1815–1897)

Incidents in the Life of a Slave Girl

(Boston: Published for the Author), 1861.

According to Jean Fagan Yellin, currently the primary source of biographical information on Harriet Jacobs (Jacobs appears in neither of the
basic reference works used in the preparation of this anthology), no
major discrepancies exist between Jacobs's presentation of her life in *Incidents in the Life of a Slave Girl* and the primary documents that have
thus far been uncovered. Therefore, the best source of information
about Jacobs's life prior to 1861 is her autobiography, portions of which
are excerpted below.

In a recent article in *American Literature,* Yellin summarizes what is
known of Jacobs's life.

> She was born near Edenton, North Carolina, about 1815. . . . her
> parents died while she was a child, and . . . at the death of her beloved
> mistress (who had taught her to read and spell) she was sent to a
> licentious master. He subjected her to unrelenting sexual harassment.
> In her teens she bore two children to another white man. When her
> jealous master threatened her with concubinage, Jacobs ran away.
> Aided by sympathetic black and white neighbors, she was sheltered
> by her family and for years remained hidden in the home of her
> grandmother, a freed slave. During this time the father of her chil-
> dren, who had bought them from her master, allowed them to live
> with her grandmother. Although later he took their little girl to a free
> state, he failed to keep his promise to emancipate the children. About
> 1842, Harriet Jacobs finally escaped North, contacted her daughter,
> was joined by her son, and found work in New York City.

The work Jacobs found was that of nurse to the infant daughter of
Nathaniel P. Willis, brother of Sara Willis Parton (Fanny Fern). Jacobs

viewed Willis as proslavery, and therefore, according to Yellin, "although she repeatedly sought help to win the time and privacy to write, and even requested introductions to public figures in hope that they would effect the publication of her book—Jacobs consistently refused to ask for Willis' aid. She did not even want him to know that she was writing. For years, while living under his roof, she worked on her book secretly and at night."

In 1849, Yellin writes, Jacobs

> moved to Rochester, New York, where the Women's Rights Convention had recently met and where Frederick Douglass' *North Star* was being published each week. With her brother, a fugitive active in the abolitionist movement, she ran an antislavery reading room and met other reformers. Jacobs made the Rochester Quaker Amy Post, a feminist and abolitionist, her confidante; her letters to Post date from this period. In September 1850 Jacobs returned to New York and resumed work in the Willis household. When she was again hounded by her owner, she and her children were purchased and manumitted by Willis.
>
> It was following this—between 1853 and 1858—that Jacobs acquiesced to Post's urgings [to write the story of her life] ; after a brush with Harriet Beecher Stowe, she wrote out the story of her life by herself. With the help of the black abolitionist writer William C. Nell and white abolitionist woman of letters L. Maria Child (whose correspondence, too, corroborates Jacobs'), her narrative was finally published early in 1861. As the national crisis deepened, Jacobs attempted to swell sentiment for Emancipation by publicizing and circulating her book. During the Civil War she went to Washington, D.C., to nurse black troops; she later returned South to help the freedmen.

Further information from Yellin extends our knowledge of Jacobs's activities during and after the Civil War. In 1863 and 1864, Jacobs worked, apparently as a representative of the Philadelphia Quakers, among the refugees at Alexandria, Virginia, distributing clothing, establishing and teaching in schools, organizing essential medical care. In 1865, she became a representative of the New York Quakers among the newly freed blacks of Savannah, Georgia, where, assisted by her daughter, she engaged directly in relief work.

Jacobs died in Washington, D.C., in 1897. At the time of her death, she was eulogized by the Reverend Francis J. Grimké, nephew of Angelina and Sarah Grimké and husband of Charlotte Forten Grimké.

Incidents in the Life of a Slave Girl carried on its title page a testament to its authenticity: "Written By Herself." In her introduction, Lydia Maria Child carefully describes her role in revising Jacobs's manuscript: "such changes as I have made have been mainly for purposes of condensation and orderly arrangement. I have not added any thing to the incidents, or changed the import of her very pertinent remarks." Nevertheless, the authenticity of Jacobs's narrative has been questioned and even denied, and its significance blunted by efforts to trivialize its content, first, by identifying it as a work of fiction, and, second, by identifying it as the fiction of a white woman, Child herself. In establishing, through an investigation of primary sources, the truth of Jacobs's claim to have written her narrative "by herself," Yellin has performed a service of inestimable value to the field of nineteenth-century American women's literature. *Incidents in the Life of a Slave Girl* constitutes a major text in this tradition and provides a remarkable and unique forum for exploring the intersections and distinctions between the thematic concerns and stylistic commitments of black and white women writers in mid-nineteenth-century America.

Despite the fact that many women as well as men escaped from slavery (see, for example, the information contained in William Still's *The Underground Railroad,* [Philadelphia: Porter and Coates], 1872), the genre of the slave narrative, to which *Incidents in the Life of a Slave Girl* properly belongs, is overwhelmingly male. A brief glance at the bibliography contained in Charles Nichols's *Many Thousand Gone* will confirm this fact, as will reference to the critical discussion of this material. Although an awareness of the particular difficulties that afflicted female slaves, and in particular of the sexual exploitation of black women by white men, appears frequently in the narratives written by men, in none of them is this experience made central. In contrast, the narrative of Harriet Jacobs centers on the perception, articulated at the birth of her daughter, that "slavery is terrible for men; but it is far more terrible for women."

The text that results from Jacobs's choice of focus differs from those produced by male narrators. Image patterns provide one of the more striking aspects of this difference. Images of flight, of movement—getting out by running away—dominate the narratives by men and provide a primary structural principle for them. In contrast is Jacobs's "loophole of retreat," a tiny crawl space nine feet long, seven feet wide, and three feet tall at its highest point, in which she spends seven years within blocks of the master from whom she is "running" and within earshot of her children and grandmother. While Jacobs is confined to her loophole, her brother William is taken as a servant by his master, who is also Jacobs's lover, to Washington, D.C.; from here he escapes with relative ease. Earlier in her narrative, Jacobs describes the escape, considerably more difficult than William's but nevertheless successful, of her uncle Benjamin. In the notoriety accorded Henry "Box" Brown, who gained his freedom by being shipped to Philadelphia in a box, we can measure the disjunction between the idea of confinement and the dominant imagery of escape. The fact of women's greater immobility, so central to Jacobs's narrative, produces a text whose imagery may remind us as much of the literature written by nineteenth-century white women as it does of the literature written by nineteenth-century black men.

Jacobs knew that in choosing to focus on the "wrongs, and sufferings, and mortifications peculiarly their own" of black women in slavery she was taking on a difficult task. For a woman to write openly of her sexual history in itself constituted a violation of powerful nineteenth-century conventions. But the particular content of Jacobs's sexual history placed her even further outside the bounds of what was conventionally acceptable to her primarily white and primarily female audience. Jacobs's response to this situation was multiple. On the one hand, she engaged the issue directly, pointing out the absurdity and the injustice of expecting black slave women to live by the moral and behavioral code applied to free white women. On the other hand, she emphasized those aspects of her experience that were congruent with the value system of her audience and thus to lessen the distance between them.

Jacobs's primary concern in *Incidents in the Life of a Slave Girl*, and her reason for wishing to establish a context in which she can be heard, is to record the sexual exploitation of black women in the slave South and thus to expose the actual nature of southern culture. Early in her text, Jacobs identifies the source of white wealth. A silver candelabra, which will be handed down in the family, from generation to generation, has, in fact, been purchased by money stolen from her grandmother. The particular reference serves as a metaphor for the pervasive theft of black body and black soul that forms the foundation of southern society. Yet that southern culture is based more specifically on the theft of the bodies and souls of black women, that it is based on rape, constitutes a much more explosive proposition. Jacobs first encounters the physical torture endemic to slavery when she overhears the terrible punishment given a male slave who has dared to accuse his master of being the father of his wife's child. At an early age, Jacobs witnesses the consequences of speaking out on sexual abuse. After this incident, she understands the depths of the southern commitment to silence on this issue. Later, she understands equally well the degree of northern complicity in this conspiracy of silence, for northerners "are not only willing, but proud, to give their daughters in marriage to slaveholders," deeming insignificant their sexual exploitation of black women. Determined to break this silence and to force the issue of sexual slavery into consciousness and significance, Jacobs focuses her narrative on her struggle to escape rape.

For Jacobs to resist successfully requires extraordinary measures—nights spent in a swamp crawling with snakes and swarming with mosquitoes ("In an hour's time they had so poisoned my flesh that I was a pitiful sight to behold"); years spent in an attic crawl space. That she must go to such lengths tells us, clearly and succinctly, how central rape is to the system of slavery. Dr. Flint's obsession makes the same point. Since under slavery all black women are fair game for white men and since many are easier to bag than "Linda," Flint's insistence on getting "Linda" identifies the issue as one of power. "Dr. Flint loved money but he loved power more," and Jacobs leaves no doubt in our minds that for Dr. Flint rape is a primary form of "nigger breaking": "My master met me at every turn, reminding me that I belonged to him, and swearing by heaven and earth that he would compel me to submit to him" (chapter 5, not reprinted). In his narrative, Frederick Douglass equates his freedom from slavery and his acquisition of humanity with the moment when he decides to physically resist his particular "nigger breaker."

Jacobs similarly locates her identity and her humanity in her resistance to Dr. Flint's physical dominance of her: "When he told me that I was made for his use, made to obey his command in *every* thing; that I was nothing but a slave, whose will must and should surrender to his, never before had my puny arm felt half so strong" (chapter 4, not reprinted).

Amazingly enough, Jacobs's narrative records a story of successful resistance. This success must be attributed at least in part to the presence in her life of a strong "mother" capable of nourishing her. Jacobs's maternal grandmother is a woman defined by her struggle to protect and maintain her family. This grandmother, "much praised for her cooking" and her famous crackers, keeps Jacobs from literal as well as emotional starvation. Jacobs perceives at an early age the role of starvation in maintaining the system of slavery. In the hands of the white master, food becomes a primary instrument of torture and control. Mrs. Flint spits in the cooking pots to make sure her slaves remain hungry. Dr. Flint forces the cook to eat to the point of nausea. More significantly, under slavery black women themselves become a form of food over which the white master maintains control, denying them thus not only humanity but also the possibility and power of feeding their own children: "in fact, my mother had been weaned at three months old, that the babe of the mistress might obtain sufficient food." In this context we can understand the triumph that her grandmother's success in feeding Jacobs represents.

Jacobs's success in resisting, however, does not blunt her indictment of southern slavery or of the white men and women who run it. As telling in this indictment as the obsession of Dr. Flint is the softer touch of her "lover," Mr. Sands. In describing this "perilous passage in the slave girl's life," Jacobs exposes the essential identity of the best and the worst of white men under slavery. In her analysis, the "good" white man's concern for what the "bad" white man does to the black woman amounts to little more than his seducing her into giving him what the other man tries to take by force. Mr. Sands's "protection" is just a subtler version of Dr. Flint's rape.

Just as radical and explosive as her exposure of the sexual exploitation of black slave women, however, is Jacobs's exploration of the consequences of this exploitation for the relations between black and white women in the South. Slavery pits white women against black women, undermining what ought to be, in Jacobs's view, a natural alliance: "The mistress, who ought to protect the helpless victim, has no other feelings towards her but those of jealousy and rage" (chapter 5, not reprinted). Early in her narrative, Jacobs presents a chilling image of this enmity: a white mistress fiendishly taunts a dying slave who has just given birth to a child nearly white. Equally chilling is Jacobs's description of waking up in the middle of the night to find Mrs. Flint bending over her, listening for an incriminating response to lewdness whispered in her husband's voice. Although Jacobs at last begins to be fearful for her life at the hands of this jealous mistress, she observes: "Yet I, whom she detested so bitterly, had far more pity for her than he had, whose duty it was to make her life happy. I never wronged her, or wished to wrong her; and one word of kindness from her would have brought me to her feet."

The black slave's pity for her white mistress stems in part from her perception that the mistress is herself a kind of slave. In significant ways, Mrs. Flint's experience in marriage parallels Jacobs's own experience. The sexual power of white men defines the lives of both women. In relation to her husband, Mrs. Flint is as helpless as "Linda." Yet slavery gives Mrs. Flint power over "Linda" and thus ensures that the anger of white women will be deflected away from the white man and onto his other victim. When Mrs. Flint takes out on "Linda" the rage she feels at her husband, she, unwittingly or not, participates in her own oppression as well as that of her black "sister."

In her narrative, Jacobs attempts to reverse this pattern of enmity and to forge an alliance between black and white women. To do this, she must, on the one hand, identify the essential similarity of their situations and, on the other, stress the radical difference. Chapter 10 provides a prime example of the art with which Jacobs accomplishes this task. In this chapter, Jacobs establishes that she shares the value system of her white northern female reader. It would be difficult to imagine a stronger commitment to chastity than that which Jacobs demonstrates in her resistance to Dr. Flint. Nevertheless, Jacobs also insists that it is unfair, and even immoral, to demand that black women be chaste when slavery makes chastity impossible for them. Thus, she forces her reader to reconsider the monolithic application of a moral code that by definition excludes black women from sisterhood. If Jacobs can succeed in producing such a reconsideration, she will have achieved a triumph second only to her successful resistance of Dr. Flint; she will have created the possibility for an alliance between black and white women capable of threatening the dual slavery of racism and sexism.

Demythologizing the black woman, fighting her reader's tendency to view the black woman as a stereotype of the licentious, bestial, and inherently degraded, is not, however, the sum of Jacobs's battle. Demythologizing the white southern woman presents an equally important challenge, for no genuine alliance can occur until white women see not only black women but themselves clearly. *Incidents in the Life of a Slave Girl* contains no Eva St. Clair. Rather, Jacobs treats the white southern woman with both realism and complexity. From her various portraits, the white southern woman emerges neither as saint nor as sinner, but instead as someone capable of both cruelty and kindness. In achieving such a balanced presentation, Jacobs clearly worked against a strong tradition of adulation and mystification. In the following anecdote, Rebecca Harding Davis describes the almost mythological status frequently accorded the southern "belle." With this context in mind, we can more readily grasp the dimension of Jacobs's task and the significance of her achievement.

I was once in a southern town when one of these famous beauties passed through on her way to the Virginia Springs. She remained all day with her escort in the little village inn, and all day a closely packed mass of men waited patiently outside to see her. Probably every man in the town was there. When the young girl was brought out at last to enter her coach, every head was uncovered. There was not a sound nor a whisper. With a deference that was almost reverent they gazed at her beauty and blushes, and stood bareheaded and still silent until she was out of sight (*Bits of Gossip,* p. 225).

Source:

Incidents in the Life of a Slave Girl: Written By Herself (Boston: Published for the Author), 1861.

Selected Secondary Works:

H. Bruce Franklin, *The Victim as Criminal and Artist* (New York: Oxford University Press), 1978; Charles H. Nichols, *Many Thousand Gone* (Leiden: E. J. Brill), 1963; Kenny J. Williams, *They Also Spoke: An Essay on Negro Literature in America, 1787–1930* (Nashville, Tenn: Townsend Press), 1970; Jean Fagan Yellin, "Written By Herself: *Harriet Jacobs' Slave Narrative,*" *American Literature,* 53 (1981), 479–86.

Contexts:

1859—Cary, *Pictures of Country Life;* Southworth, *The Hidden Hand;* Stowe, *The Minister's Wooing; Anglo-African Magazine;* John Brown's raid on Harper's Ferry
1860—Grimké, "Glimpses of New England"; Hawthorne, *The Marble Faun;* Stephens, *Malaeska*
1861—Cooke, *Poems*

PREFACE BY THE AUTHOR.

READER, BE ASSURED this narrative is no fiction. I am aware that some of my adventures may seem incredible; but they are, nevertheless, strictly true. I have not exaggerated the wrongs inflicted by Slavery; on the contrary, my descriptions fall far short of the facts. I have concealed the names of places, and given persons fictitious names. I had no motive for secrecy on my own account, but I deemed it kind and considerate towards others to pursue this course.

I wish I were more competent to the task I have undertaken. But I trust my readers will excuse deficiencies in consideration of circumstances. I was born and reared in Slavery; and I remained in a Slave State twenty-seven years. Since I have been at the North, it has been necessary for me to work diligently for my own support, and the education of my children. This has not left me much leisure to make up for the loss of early opportunities to improve myself; and it has compelled me to write these pages at irregular intervals, whenever I could snatch an hour from household duties.

When I first arrived in Philadelphia, Bishop Paine advised me to publish a sketch of my life, but I told him I was altogether incompetent to such an undertaking. Though I have improved my mind somewhat since that time, I still remain of the same opinion; but I trust my motives will excuse what might otherwise seem presumptuous. I have not written my experiences in order to attract attention to myself; on the contrary, it would have been more pleasant to me to have been silent about my own history. Neither do I care to excite sympathy for my own sufferings. But I do earnestly desire to arouse the women of the North to a realizing sense of the condition of two millions of women at the South, still in bondage, suffering what I suffered, and most of them far worse. I want to add my testimony to that of abler pens to convince the people of the Free States what Slavery really is. Only by experience can any one realize how deep, and dark, and foul is that pit of abominations. May the blessing of God rest on this imperfect effort in behalf of my persecuted people!

LINDA BRENT.

INTRODUCTION BY THE EDITOR.

The author of the following autobiography is personally known to me, and her conversation and manners inspire me with confidence. During the last seventeen years, she has lived the greater part of the time with a distinguished family in New York, and has so deported herself as to be highly esteemed by them. This fact is sufficient, without further credentials of her character. I believe those who know her will not be disposed to doubt her veracity, though some incidents in her story are more romantic than fiction.

At her request, I have revised her manuscript; but such changes as I have made have been mainly for purposes of condensation and orderly arrangement. I have not added any thing to the incidents, or changed the import of her very pertinent remarks. With trifling exceptions, both the ideas and the language are her own. I pruned excrescences a little, but otherwise I had no reason for changing her lively and dramatic way of telling her own story. The names of both persons and places are known to me; but for good reasons I suppress them.

It will naturally excite surprise that a woman reared in Slavery should be able to write so well. But circumstances will explain this. In the first place, nature endowed her with quick perceptions. Secondly, the mistress, with whom she lived till she was twelve years old, was a kind, considerate friend, who taught her to read and spell. Thirdly, she was placed in favorable circumstances after she came to the North; having frequent intercourse with intelligent persons, who felt a friendly interest in her welfare, and were disposed to give her opportunities for self-improvement.

I am well aware that many will accuse me of indecorum for presenting these pages to the public; for the experiences of this intelligent and much-injured woman belong to a class which some call delicate subjects, and others indelicate. This peculiar phase of Slavery has generally been kept veiled; but the public ought to be made acquainted with its monstrous features, and I willingly take the responsibility of presenting them with the veil withdrawn. I do this for the sake of my sisters in bondage, who are suffering wrongs so foul, that our ears are too delicate to listen to them. I do it with the hope of arousing conscientious and reflecting women at the North to a sense of their duty in the exertion of moral influence on the question of Slavery, on all possible occasions. I do it with the hope that every man who reads this narrative will swear solemnly before God that, so far as he has power to prevent it, no fugitive from Slavery shall ever be sent back to suffer in that loathsome den of corruption and cruelty.

L. Maria Child.

I. Childhood.

I was born a slave; but I never knew it till six years of happy childhood had passed away. My father was a carpenter, and considered so intelligent and skilful in his trade, that, when buildings out of the common line were to be erected, he was sent for from long distances, to be head workman. On condition of paying his mistress two hundred dollars a year, and supporting himself, he was allowed to work at his trade, and manage his own affairs. His strongest wish was to purchase his children; but, though he several times offered his hard earnings for that purpose, he never succeeded. In complexion my parents were a light shade of brownish yellow, and were termed mulattoes. They lived together in a comfortable home; and, though we were all slaves, I was so fondly shielded that I never dreamed I was a piece of merchandise, trusted to them for safe keeping, and liable to be demanded of them at any moment. I had one brother, William, who was two years younger than myself—a bright, affectionate child. I had also a great treasure in my maternal grandmother, who was a remarkable woman in many respects. She was the daughter of a planter in South Carolina, who, at his death, left her mother and his three children free, with money to go to St. Augustine, where they had relatives. It was during the Revolutionary War; and they were captured on their passage, carried back, and sold to different purchasers. Such was the story my grandmother used to tell me; but I do not remember all the particulars. She was a little girl when she was captured and sold to the keeper of a large hotel. I have often heard her tell how hard she fared during childhood. But as she grew older she evinced so much intelligence, and was so faithful, that her master and mistress could not help seeing it was for their interest to take care of such a valuable piece of property. She became an indispensable personage in the household, officiating in all capacities, from cook and wet nurse to seamstress. She was much praised for her cooking; and her nice crackers became so famous in the neighborhood that many people were desirous of obtaining them. In consequence of numerous requests of this kind, she asked permission of her mistress to bake crackers at night, after all the household work was done; and she obtained leave to do it, provided she would clothe herself and her children from the profits. Upon these terms, after working hard all day for her mistress, she began her midnight bakings, assisted by her two oldest children. The business proved profitable; and each year she laid by a little, which was saved for a fund to purchase her children. Her master died, and the property was divided among his heirs. The widow had her dower in the hotel, which she continued to keep open. My grandmother remained in her service as a slave; but her children were divided among her master's children. As she had five, Benjamin, the youngest one, was sold, in order that each heir might have an equal portion of dollars and cents. There was so little difference in our ages that he seemed more like my brother than my uncle. He was a bright, handsome lad, nearly white; for he inherited the complexion my grandmother had derived from Anglo-Saxon ancestors. Though only ten years old, seven hundred and twenty dollars were paid for him. His sale was a terrible blow to my grandmother; but she was naturally hopeful, and she went to work with renewed energy, trusting in time to be able to purchase some of her children. She had laid up three hundred dollars, which her mistress one day begged as a loan, promising to pay her soon. The reader probably knows that no promise or writing given to a slave is legally binding; for, according to Southern laws, a slave, *being* property, can *hold* no property. When my grandmother lent her hard earnings to her mistress, she trusted solely to her honor. The honor of a slaveholder to a slave!

To this good grandmother I was indebted for many comforts. My brother Willie and I often received portions of the crackers, cakes, and preserves, she made to sell; and after we ceased to be children we were indebted to her for many more important services.

Such were the unusually fortunate circumstances of my early childhood. When I was six years old, my mother died; and then, for the first time, I learned, by the talk around me, that I was a slave. My mother's mistress was the daughter of my grandmother's mistress. She was the foster sister of my mother; they were both nourished at my grandmother's breast. In fact, my mother had been weaned at three months old, that the babe of the mistress might obtain sufficient food. They played together as children; and, when they became women, my mother was a most faithful servant to her whiter foster sister. On her death-bed her mistress promised that her children should never suffer for any thing; and during her lifetime she kept her word. They all spoke kindly of my dead mother, who had been a slave merely in name, but in nature was noble and womanly. I grieved for her, and my young mind was troubled with the thought who would now take care of me and my little brother. I was told that my home was now to be with her mistress; and I found it a happy one. No toilsome or disagreeable duties were imposed upon me. My mistress was so kind to me that I was always glad to do her bidding, and proud to labor for her as much as my young years would permit. I would sit by her side for hours, sewing diligently, with a heart as free from care as that of any free-born white child. When she thought I was tired, she would send me out to run and jump; and away I bounded, to gather berries or flowers to decorate her room. Those were happy days— too happy to last. The slave child had no thought for the morrow; but there came that blight, which too surely waits on every human being born to be a chattel.

When I was nearly twelve years old, my kind mistress sickened and died. As I saw the cheek grow pale and the eye more glassy, how earnestly I prayed in my heart that she might live! I loved her; for she had been almost like a mother to me. My prayers were not answered. She died, and they buried her in the little churchyard, where, day after day, my tears fell upon her grave.

I was sent to spend a week with my grandmother. I was now old enough to begin to think of the future; and again and again I asked myself what they would do with me. I felt sure I should never find another mistress so kind as the one who was gone. She had promised my dying mother that her children should never suffer for any thing; and when I remembered that, and recalled her many proofs of attachment to me, I could not help having some hopes that she had left me free. My friends were almost certain it would be so. They thought she would be sure to do it, on account of my mother's love and faithful service. But, alas! we all know that the memory of a faithful slave does not avail much to save her children from the auction block.

After a brief period of suspense, the will of my mistress was read, and we learned that she had bequeathed me to her sister's daughter, a child of five years old. So vanished our hopes. My mistress had taught me the precepts of God's Word: "Thou shalt love thy neighbor as thyself." "Whatsoever ye would that men should do unto you, do ye even so unto them." But I was her slave, and I suppose she did not recognize me as her neighbor. I would give much to blot out from my memory that one great wrong. As a child, I loved my mistress; and, looking back on the happy days I spent with her, I try to think with less bitterness of this act of injustice. While I was with her, she taught me to read and spell; and for this privilege, which so rarely falls to the lot of a slave, I bless her memory.

She possessed but few slaves; and at her death those were all distributed among her relatives. Five of them were my grandmother's children, and had shared the same milk that nourished her mother's children. Notwithstanding my grandmother's long and faithful service to her owners, not one of her children escaped the auction block. These God-breathing machines are no more, in the sight of their masters, than the cotton they plant, or the horses they tend.

II. The New Master and Mistress.

Dr. Flint, a physician in the neighborhood, had married the sister of my mistress, and I was now the property of their little daughter. It was not without murmuring that I prepared for my new home; and what added to my unhappiness, was the fact that my brother William was purchased by the same family. My father, by his nature, as well as by the habit of transacting business as a skilful mechanic, had more of the feelings of a freeman than is common among slaves. My brother was a spirited boy; and being brought up under such influences, he early detested the name of master and mistress. One day, when his father and his mistress both happened to call him at the same time, he hesitated between the two; being perplexed to know which had the strongest claim upon his obedience. He finally concluded to go to his mistress. When my father reproved him for it, he said, "You both called me, and I didn't know which I ought to go to first."

"You are *my* child," replied our father, "and when I call you, you should come immediately, if you have to pass through fire and water."

Poor Willie! He was now to learn his first lesson of obedience to a master. Grandmother tried to cheer us with hopeful words, and they found an echo in the credulous hearts of youth.

When we entered our new home we encountered cold looks, cold words, and cold treatment. We were glad when the night came. On my narrow bed I moaned and wept, I felt so desolate and alone.

I had been there nearly a year, when a dear little friend of mine was buried. I heard her mother sob, as the clods fell on the coffin of her only child, and I turned away from the grave, feeling thankful that I still had something left to love. I met my grandmother, who said, "Come with me, Linda;" and from her tone I knew that something sad had happened. She led me apart from the people, and then said, "My child, your father is dead." Dead! How could I believe it? He had died so suddenly I had not even heard that he was sick. I went home with my grandmother. My heart rebelled against God, who had taken from me mother, father, mistress, and friend. The good grandmother tried to comfort me. "Who knows the ways of God?" said she. "Perhaps they have been kindly taken from the evil days to come." Years afterwards I often thought of this. She promised to be a mother to her grandchildren, so far as she might be permitted to do so; and strengthened by her love, I returned to my master's. I thought I should be allowed to go to my father's house the next morning; but I was ordered to go for flowers, that my mistress's house might be decorated for an evening party. I spent the day gathering flowers and weaving them into festoons, while the dead body of my father was lying within a mile of me. What cared my owners for that? he was merely a piece of property. Moreover, they thought he had spoiled his children, by teaching them to feel that they were human beings. This was blasphemous doctrine for a slave to teach; presumptuous in him, and dangerous to the masters.

The next day I followed his remains to a humble grave beside that of my dear mother. There were those who knew my father's worth, and respected his memory.

My home now seemed more dreary than ever. The laugh of the little slave children sounded harsh and cruel. It was selfish to feel so about the joy of others. My brother moved about with a very grave face. I tried to comfort him, by saying, "Take courage, Willie; brighter days will come by and by."

"You don't know any thing about it, Linda," he replied. "We shall have to stay here all our days; we shall never be free."

I argued that we were growing older and stronger, and that perhaps we might, before long, be allowed to hire our own time, and then we could earn money to buy our freedom. William declared this was much easier to say than to do; moreover, he did not intend to *buy* his freedom. We held daily controversies upon this subject.

Little attention was paid to the slaves' meals in Dr. Flint's house. If they could catch a bit of food while it was going, well and good. I gave myself no trouble on that score, for on my various errands I passed my grandmother's house, where there was always something to spare for me. I was frequently threatened with punishment if I stopped there; and my grandmother, to avoid detaining me, often stood at the gate with something for my breakfast or dinner. I was indebted to *her* for all my comforts, spiritual or temporal. It was *her* labor that supplied my scanty wardrobe. I have a vivid recollection of the linsey-woolsey dress given me every winter by Mrs. Flint. How I hated it! It was one of the badges of slavery.

While my grandmother was thus helping to support me from her hard earnings, the three hundred dollars she had lent her mistress were never repaid. When her mistress died, her son-in-law, Dr. Flint, was appointed executor. When grandmother applied to him for payment, he said the estate was insolvent, and the law prohibited payment. It did not, however, prohibit him from retaining the silver candelabra, which had been purchased with that money. I presume they will be handed down in the family, from generation to generation.

My grandmother's mistress had always promised her that, at her death, she should be free; and it was said that in her will she made good the promise. But when the estate was settled, Dr. Flint told the faithful old servant that, under existing circumstances, it was necessary she should be sold.

On the appointed day, the customary advertisement was posted up, proclaiming that there would be a "public sale of negroes, horses, &c." Dr. Flint called to tell my grandmother that he was unwilling to wound her feelings by putting her up at auction, and that he would prefer to dispose of her at private sale. My grandmother saw through his hypocrisy; she understood very well that he was ashamed of the job. She was a very spirited woman, and if he was base enough to sell her, when her mistress intended she should be free, she was determined the public should know it. She had for a long time supplied many families with crackers and preserves; consequently, "Aunt Marthy," as she was called, was generally known, and every body who knew her respected her intelligence and good character. Her long and faithful service in the family was also well known, and the intention of her mistress to leave her free. When the day of sale came, she took her place among the chattels, and at the first call she sprang upon the auction-block. Many voices called out, "Shame! Shame! Who is going to sell *you*, aunt Marthy? Don't stand there! That is no place for *you*." Without saying a word, she quietly awaited her fate. No one bid for her. At last, a feeble voice said, "Fifty dollars." It came from a maiden lady, seventy years old, the sister of my grandmother's deceased mistress. She had lived forty years under the same roof with my grandmother; she knew how faithfully she had served her owners, and how cruelly she had been defrauded of her rights; and she resolved to protect her. The auctioneer waited for a higher bid; but her wishes were respected; no one bid above her. She could neither read nor write; and when the bill of sale was made out, she signed it with a cross. But what consequence was that, when she had a big heart overflowing with human kindness? She gave the old servant her freedom.

At that time, my grandmother was just fifty years old. Laborious years had passed since then; and now my brother and I were slaves to the man who had defrauded her of her money, and tried to defraud her of her freedom. One of my mother's sisters, called Aunt Nancy, was also a slave in his family. She was a kind, good aunt to me; and supplied the place of both housekeeper and waiting maid to her mistress. She was, in fact, at the beginning and end of every thing.

Mrs. Flint, like many southern women, was totally deficient in energy. She had not strength to superintend her household affairs; but her nerves were so strong, that she could sit in her easy chair and see a woman whipped, till the blood trickled from every stroke of the lash. She was a member of the church; but partaking of the Lord's supper did not seem to put her in a Christian frame of mind. If dinner was not served at the exact time on that particular Sunday, she would station herself in the kitchen, and wait till it was dished, and then spit in all the kettles and pans that had been used for cooking. She did this to prevent the cook and her children from eking out their meagre fare with the remains of the gravy and other scrapings. The slaves could get nothing to eat except what she chose to give them. Provisions were weighed out by the pound and ounce, three times a day. I can assure you she gave them no chance to eat wheat bread from her flour barrel. She knew how many biscuits a quart of flour would make, and exactly what size they ought to be.

Dr. Flint was an epicure. The cook never sent a dinner to his table without fear and trembling; for if there happened to be a dish not to his liking, he would either order her to be whipped, or compel her to eat every mouthful of it in his presence. The poor, hungry crature might not have objected to eating it; but she did object to having her master cram it down her throat till she choked.

They had a pet dog, that was a nuisance in the house. The cook was ordered to make some Indian mush for him. He refused to eat, and when his head was held over it, the froth flowed from his mouth into the basin. He died a few minutes after. When Dr. Flint came in, he said the mush had not been well cooked, and that was the reason the animal would not eat it. He sent for the cook, and compelled her to eat it. He thought that the woman's stomach was stronger than the dog's; but her sufferings afterwards proved that he was mistaken. The poor woman endured many cruelties from her master and mistress; sometimes she was locked up, away from her nursing baby, for a whole day and night.

When I had been in the family a few weeks, one of the plantation slaves was brought to town, by order of his master. It was near night when he arrived, and Dr. Flint ordered him to be taken to the work house, and tied up to the joist, so that his feet would just escape the ground. In that situation he was to wait till the doctor had taken his tea. I shall never forget that night. Never before, in my life, had I heard hundreds of blows fall, in succession, on a human being. His piteous groans, and his "O, pray don't, massa," rang in my ear for months afterwards. There were many conjectures as to the cause of this terrible punishment. Some said master accused him of stealng corn; others said the slave had quarrelled with his wife, in presence of the overseer, and had accused his master of being the father of her child. They were both black, and the child was very fair.

I went into the work house next morning, and saw the cowhide still wet with blood, and the boards all covered with gore. The poor man lived, and continued to quarrel with his wife. A few months afterwards Dr. Flint handed them both over to a slavetrader. The guilty man put their value into his pocket, and had the satisfaction of knowing that they were out of sight and hearing. When the mother was delivered into the trader's hands, she said, "You *promised* to treat me well." To which he replied, "You have let your tongue run too far; damn you!" She had forgotten that it was a crime for a slave to tell who was the father of her child.

From others than the master persecution also comes in such cases. I once saw a young slave girl dying soon after the birth of a child nearly white. In her agony she cried out, "O Lord, come and take me!" Her mistress stood by, and mocked at her like an incarnate fiend. "You suffer, do you?" she exclaimed. "I am glad of it. You deserve it all, and more too."

The girl's mother said, "The baby is dead, thank God; and I hope my poor child will soon be in heaven, too."

"Heaven!" retorted the mistress. "There is no such place for the like of her and her bastard."

The poor mother turned away, sobbing. Her dying daughter called her, feebly, and as she bent over her, I heard her say, "Don't grieve so, mother; God knows all about it; and HE will have mercy upon me."

Her sufferings, afterwards, became so intense, that her mistress felt unable to stay; but when she left the room, the scornful smile was still on her lips. Seven children called her mother. The poor black woman had but the one child, whose eyes she saw closing in death, while she thanked God for taking her away from the greater bitterness of life.

VI. The Jealous Mistress.

I would ten thousand times rather that my children should be the half-starved paupers of Ireland than to be the most pampered among the slaves of America. I would rather drudge out my life on a cotton plantation, till the grave opened to give me rest, than to live with an unprincipled master and a jealous mistress. The felon's home in a penitentiary is preferable. He may repent, and turn from the error of his ways, and so find peace; but it is not so with a favorite slave. She is not allowed to have any pride of character. It is deemed a crime in her to wish to be virtuous.

Mrs. Flint possessed the key to her husband's character before I was born. She might have used this knowledge to counsel and to screen the young and the innocent among her slaves; but for them she had no sympathy. They were the objects of her constant suspicion and malevolence. She watched her husband with unceasing vigilance; but he was well practised in means to evade it. What he could not find opportunity to say in words he manifested in signs. He invented more than were ever thought of in a deaf and dumb asylum. I let them pass, as if I did not understand what he meant; and many were the curses and threats bestowed on me for my stupidity. One day he caught me teaching myself to write. He frowned, as if he was not well pleased; but I suppose he came to the conclusion that such an accomplishment might help to advance his favorite scheme. Before long, notes were often slipped into my hand. I would return them, saying, "I can't read them, sir." "Can't you?" he replied; "then I must read them to you." He always finished the reading by asking, "Do you understand?" Sometimes he would complain of the heat of the tea room, and order his supper to be placed on a small table in the piazza. He would seat himself there with a well-satisfied smile, and tell me to stand by and brush away the flies. He would eat very slowly, pausing between the mouthfuls. Those intervals were employed in describing the happiness I was so foolishly throwing away, and in threatening me with the penalty that finally awaited my stubborn disobedience. He boasted much of the forbearance he had exercised towards me, and reminded me that there was a limit to his patience. When I succeeded in avoiding opportunities for him to talk to me at home, I was ordered to come to his office, to do some errand. When there, I was obliged to stand and listen to such language as he saw fit to address to me. Sometimes I so openly expressed my contempt for him that he would become violently enraged, and I wondered why he did not strike me. Circumstanced as he was, he probably thought it was better policy to be forbearing. But the state of things grew worse and worse daily. In desperation I told him that I must and would apply to my grandmother for protection. He threatened me with death, and worse than death, if I made any complaint to her. Strange to say, I did not despair. I was naturally of a buoyant disposition, and always I had a hope of somehow getting out of his clutches. Like many a poor, simple slave before me, I trusted that some threads of joy would yet be woven into my dark destiny.

I had entered my sixteenth year, and every day it became more apparent that my presence was intolerable to Mrs. Flint. Angry words frequently passed between her and her husband. He had never punished me himself, and he would not allow any body else to punish me. In that respect, she was never satisfied; but, in her angry moods, no terms were too vile for her to bestow upon me. Yet I, whom she detested so bitterly, had far more pity for her than he had, whose duty it was to make her life happy. I never wronged her, or wished to wrong her; and one word of kindness from her would have brought me to her feet.

After repeated quarrels between the doctor and his wife, he announced his intention to take his youngest daughter, then four years old, to sleep in his apartment. It was necessary that a servant should sleep in the same room, to be on hand if the child stirred. I was selected for that office, and informed for what purpose that arrangement had been made. By managing to keep within sight of people, as much as possible, during the day time, I had hitherto succeeded in eluding my master, though a razor was often held to my throat to force me to change this line of policy. At night I slept by the side of my great aunt, where I felt safe. He was too prudent to come into her room. She was an old woman, and had been in the family many years. Moreover, as a married man, and a professional man, he deemed it necessary to save appearances in some degree. But he resolved to remove the obstacle in the way of his scheme; and he thought he had planned it so that he should evade suspicion. He was well aware how much I prized my refuge by the side of my old aunt, and he determined to dispossess me of it. The first night the doctor had the little child in his room alone. The next morning, I was ordered to take my station as nurse the following night. A kind Providence interposed in my favor. During the day Mrs. Flint heard of this new arrangement, and a storm followed. I rejoiced to hear it rage.

After a while my mistress sent for me to come to her room. Her first question was, "Did you know you were to sleep in the doctor's room?"

"Yes, ma'am."

"Who told you?"

"My master."

"Will you answer truly all the questions I ask?"

"Yes, ma'am."

"Tell me, then, as you hope to be forgiven, are you innocent of what I have accused you?"

"I am."

She handed me a Bible, and said, "Lay your hand on your heart, kiss this holy book, and swear before God that you tell me the truth."

I took the oath she required, and I did it with a clear conscience.

"You have taken God's holy word to testify your innocence," said she. "If you have deceived me, beware! Now take this stool, sit down, look me directly in the face, and tell me all that has passed between your master and you."

I did as she ordered. As I went on with my account her color changed frequently, she wept, and sometimes groaned. She spoke in tones so sad, that I was touched by her grief. The tears came to my eyes; but I was soon convinced that her emotions arose from anger and wounded pride. She felt that her marriage vows were desecrated, her dignity insulted; but she had no compassion for the poor victim of her husband's perfidy. She pitied herself as a martyr; but she was incapable of feeling for the condition of shame and misery in which her unfortunate, helpless slave was placed.

Yet perhaps she had some touch of feeling for me; for when the conference was ended, she spoke kindly, and promised to protect me. I should have been much comforted by this assurance if I could have had confidence in it; but my experiences in slavery had filled me with distrust. She was not a very refined woman, and had not much control over her passions. I was an object of her jealousy, and, consequently, of her hatred; and I knew I could not expect kindness or confidence from her under the circumstances in which I was placed. I could not blame her. Slaveholders' wives feel as other women would under similar circumstances. The fire of her temper kindled from small sparks, and now the flame became so intense that the doctor was obliged to give up his intended arrangement.

I knew I had ignited the torch, and I expected to suffer for it afterwards; but I felt too thankful to my mistress for the timely aid she rendered me to care much about that. She now took me to sleep in a room adjoining her own. There I was an object of her especial care, though not of her especial comfort, for she spent many a sleepless night to watch over me. Sometimes I woke up, and found her bending over me. At other times she whispered in my ear, as though it was her husband who was speaking to me, and listened to hear what I would answer. If she startled me, on such occasions, she would glide stealthily away; and the next morning she would tell me I had been talking in my sleep, and ask who I was talking to. At last, I began to be fearful for my life. It had been often threatened; and you can imagine, better than I can describe, what an unpleasant sensation it must produce to wake up in the dead of night and find a jealous woman bending over you. Terrible as this experience was, I had fears that it would give place to one more terrible.

My mistress grew weary of her vigils; they did not prove satisfactory. She changed her tactics. She now tried the trick of accusing my master of crime, in my presence, and gave my name as the author of the accusation. To my utter astonishment, he replied, "I don't believe it; but if she did acknowledge it, you tortured her into exposing me." Tortured into exposing him! Truly, Satan had no difficulty in distinguishing the color of his soul! I understood his object in making this false representation. It was to show me that I gained nothing by seeking the protection of my mistress; that the power was still all in his own hands. I pitied Mrs. Flint. She was a second wife, many years the junior of her husband; and the hoary-headed miscreant was enough to try the patience of a wiser and better woman. She was completely foiled, and knew not how to proceed. She would gladly have had me flogged for my supposed false oath; but, as I have already stated, the doctor never allowed any one to whip me. The old sinner was politic. The application of the lash might have led to remarks that would have exposed him in the eyes of his children and grandchildren. How often did I rejoice that I lived in a town where all the inhabitants knew each other! If I had been on a remote plantation, or lost among the multitude of a crowded city, I should not be a living woman at this day.

The secrets of slavery are concealed like those of the Inquisition. My master was, to my knowledge, the father of eleven slaves. But did the mothers dare to tell who was the father of their children? Did the other slaves dare to allude to it, except in whispers among themselves? No, indeed! They knew too well the terrible consequences.

My grandmother could not avoid seeing things which excited her suspicions. She was uneasy about me, and tried various ways to buy me; but the neverchanging answer was always repeated: "Linda does not belong to *me*. She is my daughter's property, and I have no legal right to sell her." The conscientious man! He was too scrupulous to *sell* me; but he had no scruples whatever about committing a much greater wrong against the helpless young girl placed under his guardianship, as his daughter's property. Sometimes my persecutor would ask me whether I would like to be sold. I told him I would rather be sold to any body than to lead such a life as I did. On such occasions he would assume the air of a very injured individual, and reproach me for my ingratitude. "Did I not take you into the house and make you the companion of my own children?" he would say. "Have I ever treated you like a negro? I have never allowed you to be punished, not even to please your mistress. And this is the recompense I get, you ungrateful girl!" I answered that he had reasons of his own for screening me from punishment, and that the course he pursued made my mistress hate me and persecute me. If I wept, he would say, "Poor child! Don't cry! don't cry! I will make peace for you with your mistress. Only let me arrange matters in my own way. Poor, foolish girl! you don't know what is for your own good. I would cherish you. I would make a lady of you. Now go, and think of all I have promised you."

I did think of it.

Reader, I draw no imaginary pictures of southern homes. I am telling you the plain truth. Yet when victims make their escape from this wild beast of Slavery, northerners consent to act the part of bloodhounds, and hunt the poor fugitive back into his den, "full of dead men's bones, and all uncleanness." Nay, more, they are not only willing, but proud, to give their daughters in marriage to slaveholders. The poor girls have romantic notions of a sunny clime, and of the flowering vines that all the year round shade a happy home. To what disappointments are they destined! The young wife soon learns that the husband in whose hands she has placed her happiness pays no regard to his marriage vows. Children of every shade of complexion play with her own fair babies, and too well she knows that they are born unto him of his own household. Jealousy and hatred enter the flowery home, and it is ravaged of its loveliness.

Southern women often marry a man knowing that he is the father of many little slaves. They do not trouble themselves about it. They regard such children as property, as marketable as the pigs on the plantation; and it is seldom that they do not make them aware of this by passing them into the slavetrader's hands as soon as possible, and thus getting them out of their sight. I am glad to say there are some honorable exceptions.

I have myself known two southern wives who exhorted their husbands to free those slaves towards whom they stood in a "parental relation;" and their request was granted. These husbands blushed before the superior nobleness of their wives natures. Though they had only counselled them to do that which it was their duty to do, it commanded their respect, and rendered their conduct more exemplary. Concealment was at an end, and confidence took the place of distrust.

Though this bad institution deadens the moral sense, even in white women, to a fearful extent, it is not altogether extinct. I have heard southern ladies say of Mr. Such a one, "He not only thinks it no disgrace to be the father of those little niggers, but he is not ashamed to call himself their master. I declare, such things ought not to be tolerated in any decent society!"

X. A Perilous Passage in the Slave Girl's Life.

After my lover went away, Dr. Flint contrived a new plan. He seemed to have an idea that my fear of my mistress was his greatest obstacle. In the blandest tones, he told me that he was going to build a small house for me, in a secluded place, four miles away from the town. I shuddered; but I was constrained to listen, while he talked of his intention to give me a home of my own, and to make a lady of me. Hitherto, I had escaped my dreaded fate, by being in the midst of people. My grandmother had already had high words with my master about me. She had told him pretty plainly what she thought of his character, and there was considerable gossip in the neighborhood about our affairs, to which the open-mouthed jealousy of Mrs. Flint contributed not a little. When my master said he was going to build a house for me, and that he could do it with little trouble and expense, I was in hopes something would happen to frustrate his scheme; but I soon heard that the house was actually begun. I vowed before my Maker that I would never enter it. I had rather toil on the plantation from dawn till dark; I had rather live and die in jail, than drag on, from day to day, through such a living death. I was determined that the master, whom I so hated and loathed, who had blighted the prospects of my youth, and made my life a desert, should not, after my long struggle with him, succeed at last in trampling his victim under his feet. I would do any thing, every thing, for the sake of defeating him. What *could* I do? I thought and thought, till I became desperate, and made a plunge into the abyss.

And now, reader, I come to a period in my unhappy life, which I would gladly forget if I could. The remembrance fills me with sorrow and shame. It pains me to tell you of it; but I have promised to tell you the truth, and I will do it honestly, let it cost me what it may. I will not try to screen myself behind the plea of compulsion from a master; for it was not so. Neither can I plead ignorance or thoughtlessness. For years, my master had done his utmost to pollute my mind with foul images, and to destroy the pure principles inculcated by my grandmother, and the good mistress of my childhood. The influences of slavery had had the same effect on me that they had on other young girls; they had made me prematurely knowing, concerning the evil ways of the world. I knew what I did, and I did it with deliberate calculation.

But, O, ye happy women, whose purity has been sheltered from childhood, who have been free to choose the objects of your affection, whose homes are protected by law, do not judge the poor desolate slave girl too severely! If slavery had been abolished, I, also, could have married the man of my choice; I could have had a home shielded by the laws; and I should have been spared the painful task of confessing what I am now about to relate; but all my prospects had been blighted by slavery. I wanted to keep myself pure; and, under the most adverse circumstances,

I tried hard to preserve my self-respect; but I was struggling alone in the powerful grasp of the demon Slavery; and the monster proved too strong for me. I felt as if I was forsaken by God and man; as if all my efforts must be frustrated; and I became reckless in my despair.

I have told you that Dr. Flint's persecutions and his wife's jealousy had given rise to some gossip in the neighborhood. Among others, it chanced that a white unmarried gentleman had obtained some knowledge of the circumstances in which I was placed. He knew my grandmother, and often spoke to me in the street. He became interested for me, and asked questions about my master, which I answered in part. He expressed a great deal of sympathy, and a wish to aid me. He constantly sought opportunities to see me, and wrote to me frequently. I was a poor slave girl, only fifteen years old.

So much attention from a superior person was, of course, flattering; for human nature is the same in all. I also felt grateful for his sympathy, and encouraged by his kind words. It seemed to me a great thing to have such a friend. By degrees, a more tender feeling crept into my heart. He was an educated and eloquent gentleman; too eloquent, alas, for the poor slave girl who trusted in him. Of course I saw whither all this was tending. I knew the impassable gulf between us; but to be an object of interest to a man who is not married, and who is not her master, is agreeable to the pride and feelings of a slave, if her miserable situation has left her any pride or sentiment. It seems less degrading to give one's self, than to submit to compulsion. There is something akin to freedom in having a lover who has no control over you, except that which he gains by kindness and attachment. A master may treat you as rudely as he pleases, and you dare not speak; moreover, the wrong does not seem so great with an unmarried man, as with one who has a wife to be made unhappy. There may be sophistry in all this; but the condition of a slave confuses all principles of morality, and, in fact, renders the practice of them impossible.

When I found that my master had actually begun to build the lonely cottage, other feelings mixed with those I have described. Revenge, and calculations of interest, were added to flattered vanity and sincere gratitude for kindness. I knew nothing would enrage Dr. Flint so much as to know that I favored another; and it was something to triumph over my tyrant even in that small way. I thought he would revenge himself by selling me, and I was sure my friend, Mr. Sands, would buy me. He was a man of more generosity and feeling than my master, and I thought my freedom could be easily obtained from him. The crisis of my fate now came so near that I was desperate. I shuddered to think of being the mother of children that should be owned by my old tyrant. I knew that as soon as a new fancy took him, his victims were sold far off to get rid of them; especially if they had children. I had seen several women sold, with his babies at the breast. He never allowed his offspring by slaves to remain long in sight of himself and his wife. Of a man who was not my master I could ask to have my children well supported; and in this case, I felt confident I should obtain the boon. I also felt quite sure that they would be made free. With all these thoughts revolving in my mind, and seeing no other way of escaping the doom I so much dreaded, I made a headlong plunge. Pity me, and pardon me, O virtuous reader! You never knew what it is to be a slave; to be entirely unprotected by law or custom; to have the laws reduce you to the condition of a chattel, entirely subject to the will of another. You never exhausted your ingenuity in avoiding the snares, and eluding the power of a hated tyrant; you never shuddered at the sound of his footsteps, and trembled within hearing of his voice. I know I did wrong. No one can feel it more sensibly than I do. The painful and humiliating memory will haunt me to my dying day. Still, in looking back, calmly, on the events of my life, I feel that the slave woman ought not to be judged by the same standard as others.

The months passed on. I had many unhappy hours. I secretly mourned over the sorrow I was bringing on my grandmother, who had so tried to shield me from harm. I knew that I was the greatest comfort of her old age, and that it was a source of pride to her that I had not degraded myself, like most of the slaves. I wanted to confess to her that I was no longer worthy of her love; but I could not utter the dreaded words.

As for Dr. Flint, I had a feeling of satisfaction and triumph in the thought of telling *him*. From time to time he told me of his intended arrangements, and I was silent. At last, he came and told me the cottage was completed, and ordered me to go to it. I told him I would never enter it. He said, "I have heard enough of such talk as that. You shall go, if you are carried by force; and you shall remain there."

I replied, "I will never go there. In a few months I shall be a mother."

He stood and looked at me in dumb amazement, and left the house without a word. I thought I should be happy in my triumph over him. But now that the truth was out, and my relatives would hear of it, I felt wretched. Humble as were their circumstances, they had pride in my good character. Now, how could I look them in the face? My self-respect was gone! I had resolved that I would be virtuous, though I was a slave. I had said, "Let the storm beat! I will brave it till I die." And now, how humiliated I felt!

I went to my grandmother. My lips moved to make confession, but the words stuck in my throat. I sat down in the shade of a tree at her door and began to sew. I think she saw something unusual was the matter with me. The mother of slaves is very watchful. She knows there is no security for her children. After they have entered their teens she lives in daily expectation of trouble. This leads to many questions. If the girl is of a sensitive nature, timidity keeps her from answering truthfully, and this well-meant course has a tendency to drive her from maternal counsels. Presently, in came my mistress, like a mad woman, and accused me concerning her husband. My grandmother, whose suspicions had been previously awakened, believed what she said. She exclaimed, "O Linda! has it come to this? I had rather see you dead than to see you as you now are. You are a disgrace to your dead mother." She tore from my fingers my mother's wedding ring and her silver thimble. "Go away!" she exclaimed, "and never come to my house, again." Her reproaches fell so hot and heavy, that they left me no chance to answer. Bitter tears, such as the eyes never shed but once, were my only answer. I rose from my seat, but fell back again, sobbing. She did not speak to me; but the tears were running down her furrowed cheeks, and they scorched me like fire. She had always been so kind to me! *So* kind! How I longed to throw myself at her feet, and tell her all the truth! But she had ordered me to go, and never to come there again. After a few minutes, I mustered strength, and started to obey her. With what feelings did I now close that little gate, which I used to open with such an eager hand in my childhood! It closed upon me with a sound I never heard before.

Where could I go? I was afraid to return to my master's. I walked on recklessly, not caring where I went, or what would become of me. When I had gone four or five miles, fatigue compelled me to stop. I sat down on the stump of an old tree. The stars were shining through the boughs above me. How they mocked me, with their bright, calm light! The hours passed by, and as I sat there alone a chilliness and deadly sickness came over me. I sank on the ground. My mind was full of horrid thoughts. I prayed to die; but the prayer was not answered. At last, with great effort I roused myself, and walked some distance further, to the house of a woman who had been a friend of my mother. When I told her why I was there, she spoke soothingly to me; but I could not be comforted. I thought I could bear my shame if I could only be reconciled to my grandmother. I longed to open my heart to her. I thought if she could know the real state of the case, and all I had been bearing for years, she would perhaps judge me less harshly. My friend advised me to send for her. I did so; but days of agonizing suspense passed before she came. Had she utterly forsaken me? No. She came at last. I knelt before her, and told her the things that had poisoned my life; how long I had been persecuted; that I saw no way of escape; and in an hour of extremity I had become desperate. She listened in silence. I told her I would bear any thing and do any thing, if in time I had hopes of obtaining her forgiveness. I begged of her to pity me, for my dead mother's sake. And she did pity me. She did not say, "I forgive you;" but she looked at me lovingly, with her eyes full of tears. She laid her old hand gently on my head, and murmured, "Poor child! Poor child!"

XXI. The Loophole of Retreat

A small shed had been added to my grandmother's house years ago. Some boards were laid across the joists at the top, and between these boards and the roof was a very small garret, never occupied by any thing but rats and mice. It was a pent roof, covered with nothing but shingles, according to the southern custom for such buildings. The garret was only nine feet long and seven wide. The highest part was three feet high, and sloped down abruptly to the loose board floor. There was no admission for either light or air. My uncle Philip, who was a carpenter, had very skilfully made a concealed trap-door, which communicated with the storeroom. He had been doing this while I was waiting in the swamp. The storeroom opened upon a piazza. To this hole I was conveyed as soon as I entered the house. The air was stifling; the darkness total. A bed had been spread on the floor. I could sleep quite comfortably on one side; but the slope was so sudden that I could not turn on the other without hitting the roof. The rats and mice ran over my bed; but I was weary, and I slept such sleep as the wretched may, when a tempest has passed over them. Morning came. I knew it only by the noises I heard; for in my small den day and night were all the same. I suffered for air even more than for light. But I was not comfortless. I heard the voices of my children. There was joy and there was sadness in the sound. It made my tears flow. How I longed to speak to them! I was eager to look on their faces; but there was no hole, no crack, through which I could peep. This continued darkness was oppressive. It seemed horrible to sit or lie in a cramped position day after day, without one gleam of light. Yet I would have chosen this, rather than my lot as a slave, though white people considered it an easy one; and it was so compared with the fate of others. I was never cruelly over-worked; I was never lacerated with the whip from head to foot; I was never so beaten and bruised that I could not turn from one side to the other; I never had my heel-strings cut to prevent my running away; I was never chained to a log and forced to drag it about, while I toiled in the fields from morning till night; I was never branded with hot iron, or torn by bloodhounds. On the contrary, I had always been kindly treated, and tenderly cared for, until I came into the hands of Dr. Flint. I had never wished for freedom till then. But though my life in slavery was comparatively devoid of hardships, God pity the woman who is compelled to lead such a life!

My food was passed up to me through the trap-door my uncle had contrived; and my grandmother, my uncle Phillip, and aunt Nancy would seize such opportunities as they could, to mount up there and chat with me at the opening. But of course this was not safe in the daytime. It must all be done in darkness. It was impossible for me to move in an erect position, but I crawled about my den for exercise. One day I hit my head against something, and found it was a gimlet. My uncle had left it sticking there when he made the trap-door. I was as rejoiced as Robinson Crusoe could have been at finding such a treasure. It put a lucky thought into my head. I said to myself, "Now I will have some light. Now I will see my children." I did not dare to begin my work during the daytime, for fear of attracting attention. But I groped round; and having found the side next the street, where I could frequently see my children, I stuck the gimlet in and waited for evening. I bored three rows of holes, one above another; then I bored out the interstices between. I thus succeeded in making one hole about an inch long and an inch broad. I sat by it till late into the night, to enjoy the little whiff of air that floated in. In the morning I watched for my children. The first person I saw in the street was Dr. Flint. I had a shuddering, superstitious feeling that it was a bad omen. Several familiar faces passed by. At last I heard the merry laugh of children, and presently two sweet little faces were looking up at me, as though they knew I was there, and were conscious of the joy they imparted. How I longed to *tell* them I was there!

My condition was now a little improved. But for weeks I was tormented by hundreds of little red insects, fine as a needle's point, that pierced through my skin, and produced an intolerable burning. The good grandmother gave me herb teas and cooling medicines, and finally I got rid of them. The heat of my den was intense, for nothing but thin shingles protected me from the scorching summer's sun. But I had my consolations. Through my peeping-hole I could watch the children, and when they were near enough, I could hear their talk. Aunt Nancy brought me all the news she could hear at Dr. Flint's. From her I learned that the doctor had written to New York to a colored woman, who had been born and raised in our neighborhood, and had breathed his contaminating atmosphere. He offered her a reward if she could find out any thing about me. I know not what was the nature of her reply; but he soon after started for New York in haste, saying to his family that he had business of importance to transact. I peeped at him as he passed on his way to the steamboat. It was a satisfaction to have miles of land and water between us, even for a little while; and it was a still greater satisfaction to know that he believed me to be in the Free States. My little den seemed less dreary than it had done. He returned, as he did from his former journey to New York, without obtaining any satisfactory information. When he passed our house next morning, Benny was standing at the gate. He had heard them say that he had gone to find me, and he called out, "Dr. Flint, did you bring my mother home? I want to see her." The doctor stamped his foot at him in a rage, and exclaimed, "Get out of the way, you little damned rascal! If you don't, I'll cut off your head."

Benny ran terrified into the house, saying, "You can't put me in jail again. I don't belong to you now." It was well that the wind carried the words away from the doctor's ear. I told my grandmother of it, when we had our next conference at the trap-door; and begged of her not to allow the children to be impertinent to the irascible old man.

Autumn came, with a pleasant abatement of heat. My eyes had become accustomed to the dim light, and by holding my book or work in a certain position near the aperture I contrived to read and sew. That was a great relief to the tedious monotony of my life. But when winter came, the cold penetrated through the thin shingle roof, and I was dreadfully chilled. The winters there are not so long, or so severe, as in northern latitudes; but the houses are not built to shelter from cold, and my little den was peculiarly comfortless. The kind grandmother brought me bed-clothes and warm drinks. Often I was obliged to lie in bed all day to keep comfortable; but with all my precautions, my shoulders and feet were frostbitten. O, those long, gloomy days, with no object for my eye to rest upon, and no thoughts to occupy my mind, except the dreary past and the uncertain future! I was thankful when there came a day sufficiently mild for me to wrap myself up and sit at the loophole to watch the passers by. Southerners have the habit of stopping and talking in the streets, and I heard many conversations not intended to meet my ears. I heard slave-hunters planning how to catch some poor fugitive. Several times I heard allusions to Dr. Flint, myself, and the history of my children, who, perhaps, were playing near the gate. One would say, "I wouldn't move my little finger to catch her, as old Flint's property." Another would say, "I'll catch *any* nigger for the reward. A man ought to have what belongs to him, if he *is* a damned brute." The opinion was often expressed that I was in the Free States. Very rarely did any one suggest that I might be in the vicinity. Had the least suspicion rested on my grandmother's house, it would have been burned to the ground. But it was the last place they thought of. Yet there was no place, where slavery existed, that could have afforded me so good a place of concealment.

Dr. Flint and his family repeatedly tried to coax and bribe my children to tell something they had heard said about me. One day the doctor took them into a shop, and offered them some bright little silver pieces and gay handkerchiefs if they would tell where their mother was. Ellen shrank away from him, and would not speak; but Benny spoke up, and said, "Dr. Flint, I don't know where my mother is. I guess she's in New York; and when you go there again, I wish you'd ask her to come home, for I want to see her; but if you put her in jail, or tell her you'll cut her head off, I'll tell her to go right back."

REBECCA HARDING DAVIS

(1831–1910)

Life in the Iron Mills

Atlantic Monthly, 7 (April), 1861.

Rebecca Harding Davis was born on June 24, 1831, in Washington, Pennsylvania, the first of the five children of Rachel Leet and Richard Harding. At the time of her birth, her family was living in Huntsville, Alabama, but her mother returned to her parents' home in Pennsylvania for the birth of her first child. When Davis was about five years old, the family returned to the North and the formative years of her life were spent in what was then Wheeling, Virginia. Davis's early education took place at home. She was taught first by her mother, of whom she later wrote. "She was the most accurate historian and grammarian I ever have known, and had enough knowledge to fit out half a dozen modern college bred women" (Langford, p. 4); and then by various tutors. When she was fourteen, she entered the Washington Female Seminary in Washington, Pennsylvania; during her three years of formal schooling, she lived in the home of her mother's sister. In 1848, she graduated with the highest honors in her class, delivered the valedictory address, and returned home to help her mother run the household and manage the younger children. She continued her education through her younger brother, Wilson, who entered Washington College in 1850, studying with him those subjects she had not encountered at the Female Seminary.

In her memories of childhood, Davis recalls her first encounter with Nathaniel Hawthorne when, at age twelve, in the cherry-tree house built for her by her nurse Barbara and distinguished by the fact that "not a boy had ever heard of it," she read

> two or three unsigned stories . . . over so often that I almost know
> every line of them by heart now. One was a story told by a town

pump, and another the account of the rambles of a little girl like myself, and still another a description of a Sunday morning in a quiet
town like our sleepy village. There was no talk of enchantment in
them. But in these papers the commonplace folk and things which I
saw every day took on a sudden mystery and charm, and, for the first
time, I found that they, too, belonged to the magic world of knights
and pilgrims and fiends (*Bits of Gossip*, pp. 28, 30).

We know almost nothing about Davis's life from the time she completed her formal schooling until the publication of "Life in the Iron
Mills." And, as Tillie Olsen comments, "there is scarcely a word" of
what was most singular about those years—how she "developed an ear,
a discipline, made of herself a writer, *against the prevalent, found her
own subject*" (Olsen, p. 80). That Davis wrote and published during this
period is apparent from a letter, dated January 26, 1861, to James T.
Fields, editor of the *Atlantic Monthly*, to whom she had sent "Life in
the Iron Mills": "I have written but little, hitherto, and then anonymously;—principally—reviews of new books. A few verses and stories,
impelled by the necessity or whim of the moment" (Grayburn, pp. 75–
76). No manuscripts or copies of this early work have as yet been discovered.

In April, 1861, two months before Davis's thirtieth birthday, the
Atlantic published "Life in the Iron Mills." Fields, impressed by both its
subject matter and its art, sent her a check for fifty dollars and asked for
more material. In return, Davis sent a manuscript that was serialized in
the *Atlantic* from October, 1861 to March, 1862 as *A Story of To-day*
(later published as the book *Margret Howth*). Here Davis first encountered those pressures, both external and internal, that would undermine
her vision and compromise the talent so clearly evident in "Life in the
Iron Mills." Fields initially returned the manuscript, complaining that it
"assembled the gloom" too depressingly. Davis agreed to try to be
"more cheerful." If the life and death of one character were allowed to
remain a "dark thread" ("I cannot give up all, you see"), then she would
be willing to let "the rest of the picture be steeped in warm healthy
light" (Grayburn, pp. 158, 159). Davis evidently rewrote the ending to
make it "happy" and the resultant work was artistically flawed and unconvincing. Obviously, a decade had done little to dispel the pressure on
women to write of and from the "sunny side."

In the summer of 1862, Davis made a trip East, stopping first in
Boston, to visit Fields and his wife, Annie; she had already begun to
correspond with Annie and they were to be lifelong friends. In Concord, she stayed with Hawthorne, for whom she felt, as he for her, a
basic affinity. Here she also met Ralph Waldo Emerson and Bronson
Alcott, for whom she felt no affinity. Alcott she disliked intensely. She
thought his attitude toward the war was thoroughly sentimental. A
daily witness to its "filthy spewings," she had attempted to record this
reality in two pieces, both published in the *Atlantic:* "John Lamar"
(April, 1862) and "David Gaunt" (September and October, 1862). As
Alcott "chanted paeans to the war, the 'armed angel which was waken-
ing the nation to a lofty life unknown before,'" Davis remembered "the

political jobbery in Union and Confederate camps; the malignant personal hatreds wearing patriotic masks, and glutted by burning homes and outraged women; the chances in it, well improved on both sides, for brutish men to grow more brutish, and for honorable gentlemen to degenerate in to thieves and sots" (*Bits of Gossip*, pp. 33, 34).

On her way home from Boston, Rebecca stopped in Philadelphia to meet the L. Clarke Davis who had been corresponding with her since the publication of "Life in the Iron Mills." The meeting resulted in an engagement and Rebecca Harding and Clarke Davis were married in March of 1863. Three years younger than his wife, Clarke Davis was at the time of his marriage a relatively poor apprentice-lawyer supporting himself by a series of odd jobs, including those of journalist and editor. Although obviously attracted to those qualities in Davis that made her different and extraordinary—at thirty-two she was both an artist and a "spinster"—Clarke was evidently incapable of, or uninterested in, counteracting the processes by which marriage would undermine that difference and distinction.

Clarke's literary tastes and connections also exerted a negative influence on Davis's career. A friend of the publisher of Philadelphia's *Peterson's Magazine,* Clarke solicited from Davis, shortly after meeting her, a contribution to that magazine which paid far better for its "potboilers" than the *Atlantic* did for its stories. Aware that, after marriage, she would need to supplement Clarke's income through writing, Davis began what Gerald Langford calls "two separate literary careers, one artistic and the other strictly commercial" (Langford, p. 29). Davis had agreed by this time to write exclusively for the *Atlantic,* but she evidently felt no conflict between this commitment and her anonymous contributions to *Peterson's.* This somewhat schizophrenic sleight of hand became public in the summer of 1865 when the *Atlantic* published an article by Davis based on the same material that she had used two years earlier for a story in *Peterson's.* Accused of plagiarism, Davis had to explain that she herself had written the earlier piece. Shortly after this, Davis began signing her contributions to *Peterson's.*

Letters written to Annie Fields during the first year and a half of Davis's marriage, a period that coincided with her first pregnancy and the birth of her first child, Richard Harding Davis, on April 18, 1864, reveal that Davis experienced some form of mental breakdown at this time. In addition to the strain of living with in-laws and of separating from her own mother and father, Davis must have encountered the conflict between what was required of a wife and what was necessary for the artist. In July 1864, she published in the *Atlantic* a frightening account of this conflict and a frightening solution to it. The protagonist of "The Wife's Story" leaves her husband and child to pursue a career in the opera. On the opening night of the opera, which she has written herself and in which she sings the lead role, she discovers that her husband is in the audience. The opera and her performance prove a total failure; she is jeered and hissed by the audience. Worse yet, however, her husband has died of a heart attack brought on by the "excitement" of her performance. The wife determines to drown herself but at this point, luckily, she "wakes up" and discovers that her dream of a career has been in fact a fever-induced nightmare. Safely at home with husband and child, she realizes that "a woman has no better work in life than . . . to make herself a visible Providence to her husband and child." Unlike Elizabeth Stuart Phelps, Davis evidently lived out the terms of her fictional "solution" to the conflict between wife and artist. When she was first married and living in Philadelphia, the Philadelphia Public Library, in recognition of her literary distinction and in support of her career outside the home, gave her desk space to use for her work. In later years, in letters filled with references to the comings and goings of her husband and son, Davis makes virtually no reference to going anywhere herself.

In 1870, Clarke bought a town house in Philadelphia. The Davises called this house "the Centre of the Universe," and she apparently stayed there. In 1870, Clarke also gave up his law practice to become managing editor of the Philadelphia *Inquirer,* and from then on he pursued a full-time career in journalism. Davis devoted her energies to supporting his career and then, later, to supporting the career of her famous, globe-trotting son, Richard Harding Davis. Her obituary in the *New York Times* listed her as the mother of Richard Harding Davis. She died on September 29, 1910, at the age of seventy-nine, and was buried in Philadelphia in the same grave as her husband. The stone over the grave bears the name, L. Clarke Davis. Below it, and partially concealed are the words, "And His Wife" (Grayburn, p. 72).

Davis was a prolific writer; her complete bibliography contains literally hundreds of items. As contributing editor to the *New York Tribune,* a position she assumed in 1869 and retained for twenty years, she wrote essays on contemporary issues; for the *North American Review, Harper's Bazar,* the *Independent,* and the *Outlook,* she wrote articles; for the *Youth's Companion* and *St. Nicholas* she wrote children's stories and historical essays; for *Peterson's,* she wrote gothic thrillers and potboiling romances; in addition, there are travel sketches, regional fiction, short stories, and novels.

Davis's most serious literary efforts after her marriage were *Waiting for the Verdict,* published serially in the *Galaxy* in 1867 and in book form in 1868, and *John Andross,* published serially in *Hearth and Home* from December 13, 1873 to May 2, 1874 and as a book in 1874. *Waiting for the Verdict* addresses issues that other American writers of the time were resolutely evading, in particular the fate of black people after the Civil War in a nation still dominated by racism. Although negatively reviewed at the time—Henry James writing for the *Nation* called it sentimental, unreal, and impossible to read—and informed by an intention beyond her ability to fulfill, the novel contains unmistakable evidence of Davis's artistic skill and imaginative power. Arthur Hobson Quinn contends that *Waiting for the Verdict,* "if it had not been overloaded with propaganda, would have been a great" novel; "even as it is, [it] ranks with the best of this period" (Quinn, p. 185).

Yet in the aggregate, Davis's career does not reflect a realization of the talent apparent in "Life in the Iron Mills." The circumstances of her

life, like those of her fictional protagonist, were against it. He was imprisoned in the industrial iron mill; she was buried alive in the "Centre
of the Universe."

Although usually acclaimed as an early example of American literary
realism, "Life in the Iron Mills" shares, as Walter Hesford has indicated,
a primary affinity with the romance as shaped by Hawthorne and other
mid-nineteenth-century male American writers. Davis took her first
literary lessons from Hawthorne. In her tree house, as a child, reading
Hawthorne's early tales she could have learned "that the phenomena
which fall within our daily observation and experience have moral, historic, and imaginative significance, and participate in an on-going mystery and revelation"; and she might also have learned from Hawthorne
"a sense of the power and responsibility of those engaged in what is,
though seemingly performed in an unassuming manner, a radical task"
(Hesford, pp. 71–72). There is, however, nothing unassuming about
Davis's manner. Her narrative language insistently claims for her material the imaginative significance of an on going mystery and revelation.
The complex image patterns, primarily visual and spatial, by which she
structures her text carry an equally symbolic weight. Blood and moonlight, white hand and ruby ring, the infernal fires of the Dantean mills
and the ghostly white of the Korl woman; prison cell, upstairs room,
basement hovel, and the opening out of evening sky, green hills, and
"clover-crimsoned meadows," claim for her text a mythic dimension.
    In "Life in the Iron Mills," Davis exposes her readers to experience
not only foreign to them but potentially distasteful and even threatening. Her self-appointed role of exposer and interpreter seems to require
the development of a relatively obtrusive narrative voice capable of engaging in a dialogue with the reader. As readers, we are rarely allowed
to forget the presence of this narrative voice or to escape from the pressure it places on us to realign our vision and our values. Much of the
energy of the text centers on this implicit dialogue between narrator and
readers. Since Davis's readers, if not belonging to, presumably identify
with the class that owns the mills and for whom the workers are a
"presence they soon forgot entirely," the narrator's task is to make her
readers see what is currently invisible to them. Hence the reiterated emphasis on visual images and imperatives.
    The narrator, who belongs to the same class as the reader, defines her
own position in visual terms: "I open the window, and, looking out, can
scarcely see . . ." While the narrator plays a major role in the text, an air
of mystery surrounds her relation to her material. We do not know how
she has come to see differently from the majority of her class. Nor do
we know how she has come to know the lives of those about whom she
writes. The origins of both her story and her authority are obscure. Her
efforts to explain simply raise more questions. How has she come to be
in a house where mill hands once lived? How has she come to possess
the figure of the korl woman? Why is the story set thirty years ago
when everything in it points to its contemporaneity? This slippage between narrator and story, addressed obliquely in the text ("I cannot tell

why I choose the half-forgotten story of this Wolfe more than that of myriads of these furnace-hands. Perhaps . . . or perhaps . . ."), makes for an awkward transition from the philosophic introduction to the specific narrative beginning. "One rainy night, about eleven o'clock" jars against "Christ's charity."

Despite the degree of mystery surrounding the story's provenance and despite a similar degree of mystery cast over the story's meaning ("I dare not put this secret into words"; "I dare make my meaning no clearer"), the question posed by the story we are told is clear enough: why are some people rich and others poor? why is life for some people "an altogether serious thing," while, for others, it is "a drunken jest, a joke"? The significance of "Life in the Iron Mills" rests to a considerable degree on the fact that it presents the issue of class as a primary instance of human injustice rather than as a logistical difficulty that the middle class must negotiate, often with the help of the middle-class author. The middle-class point of view is represented by the group of men who come to tour the iron mill, observing its inhabitants as a variety of "local color." Each of these men views the issue of class as a tactical problem, but Davis carefully distinguishes among their different modes of solving the problem. The cumulative weight of their respective behaviors, however, presents a sweeping indictment of the ethical poverty of the middle class.

The overseer, Clarke, in the midst of a heat that they all find "intolerable," talks obsessively of profits. Kirby, son of the owner, orders the men to make seats for the company; he finds them dangerous when he is "unarmed," he sneers at Wolfe's attempts to explain his sculpture, but, as he leaves, he speaks kindly and throws money. The Doctor, patronizing, smug, complacent, parades his empty rhetoric with obvious self-satisfaction until brought up short by Wolfe's request for help. Later, his thin veneer of concern cracks quickly against the fact of money: "Scoundrel! Serves him right! After all our kindness that night!" On the surface, Mitchell might appear the best of the lot. He has contempt for Kirby's sneer and for the Doctor's self-serving sentimental gestures. He recognizes Wolfe as the sculptor; his affinity for both artist and work draws Wolfe into obeisance and dialogue. Yet, for all his understanding, his final position is essentially no different from Kirby's brutally clear *"ce n'est pas mon affaire."* When his money is stolen, he prosecutes.

It is easy for Kirby to imagine himself as god; his race, sex, and class conspire to foster this illusion, and so he can fantasize, "If I had the making of men, these men who do the lowest part of the world's work should be machines,—nothing more,—hands. It would be kindness." Still, it is not possible for him to effect his "kindness," and so he decides "not to think at all." Ironically, he thus relinquishes his claim to deity and identifies himself instead, as Mitchell is quick to point out, with the Christ-killing Pilate. Hugh Wolfe, the hand whose mind Kirby would like to remove, has more deity in him than his masters have. His hand shapes his thought and that shape, so different from what the masters imagine, startles and frightens them: "Mitchell started back, half-frightened, as, suddenly turning a corner, the white figure of a woman faced him in the darkness,—a woman, white, of giant proportions, crouching on the ground, her arms flung out in some wild gesture of warning."

This figure, made of the refuse that the industrial machine has rejected, is a truly extraordinary image to encounter in the pages of nineteenth-century American fiction. Female, nude, muscular, "grown coarse with labor," without "one line of beauty or grace," the korl woman bears no resemblance to the conventional images of the feminine found in either male or female texts. Here instead is a woman's body imagined as an expression of power and longing in a context that is neither erotic nor maternal. Indeed, here is a woman's body imagined as a symbol for the human experience of spiritual hunger. In "Life in the Iron Mills," a male artist finds in a woman's flesh the analogue for his inner wolf.

When we consider how conventionally Davis handles gender elsewhere in her text, we can appreciate more fully the significance of the korl woman. Creating this figure is an act of power, not simply for Hugh Wolfe but for Rebecca Davis as well. In "Life in the Iron Mills," Davis articulates the issue of class as a problem for men. She does not follow Deborah to her work in the cotton mill, but focuses instead on the male world of the iron mill where Deborah is merely an interloper. Since the environment she chooses to explore is male, the experience contained in that environment is also male: "If you could go into this mill where Deborah lay, and drag out from the hearts of these men the terrible tragedy of their lives, taking it as a symptom of the disease of their class, no ghost Horror would terrify you more."

Even more conventional, however, is Davis's treatment of Deborah. Hugh hungers for self-expression; Deborah hungers for Hugh. Derivative rather than primary, Deborah is different from Hugh: "Wolfe, while Deborah watched him as a spaniel its master, bent over the furnace with his iron pole, unconscious of her scrutiny, only stopping to receive orders." In the context of Deborah and Hugh, Davis gives the term "master" a different meaning from the one it takes in the context of Wolfe and Kirby.

With Deborah, Davis works within the constrictions, both internal and external, of what she can imagine as a woman's story. Not surprisingly, Deborah figures more as a reader than a text. She recognizes the existence of Hugh's text, and, unlike the middle-class men, she can interpret that text even though it hurts her: "She knew, that, down under all the vileness and coarseness of his life, there was a groping passion for whatever was beautiful and pure,—that his soul sickened with disgust at her deformity, even when his words were kindest." But it never occurs to Hugh to recognize Deborah as a text or to "read" her: "If anything like this were hidden beneath the pale, bleared eyes, and dull, washed-out-looking face, no one had ever taken the trouble to read its faint signs; not the half-clothed furnace-tender, Wolfe, certainly." Although the narrator can recognize a text in Deborah, she can only make of it the most traditional of women's stories, that of frustrated love and hopeless self-abnegation. Deborah acts—it is she, not Hugh, who steals the purse—but she acts for Hugh. In Deborah's story, there are no ironic changes rung on the theme of godhood. Hugh roams the streets all night, locked in a fierce struggle that defines him as larger than the men who own him. Deborah takes without thinking and she offers her prize with equal simplicity: "But it is hur right to keep it." Apparently, his "rights" relieve her of the burden of potential godhood.

Deborah shares her story with women of other classes: "One sees that dead, vacant look steal sometimes over the rarest, finest of women's faces,—in the very midst, it may be, of their warmest summer's day; and then one can guess at the secret of intolerable solitude that lies hid beneath the delicate laces and brilliant smile." In a story designed to document and expose the tragedy of class in America, Davis presents the unspoken premise that women are exempt from this tragedy. Women's hunger for love may be denied or fed, but whether their life turns tragic or joyous bears no relation to their class; whether men's hunger for godhood be denied or fed, however, depends entirely on the accident of class. Thus the frustrated artist, not the frustrated lover, is a tragedy of class.

Yet the korl figure is female. Davis's frustrated artist imagines his hunger in the form of a woman who is "the very type of her class." Does this suggest, then, that Davis can, in fact, conceive of the issue of class as transcending that of gender? Or does it suggest another complication in the intersection of gender and class? If Hugh Wolfe can project himself as female, might not Davis project herself as male? In the figure of Wolfe, Davis perhaps forged a self-image as powerful and compelling as that which her character creates from his korl. One of the "girl-men," whose *sobriquet* is "Molly," Hugh has distinctly feminine overtones. Indeed, one might argue that his experience makes more sense when seen as that of a white middle-class woman than as that of a lower-class immigrant man. His burning question, "What made the difference between them? That was the mystery of his life," is perhaps finally more intelligible as the cry of the woman of genius who finds no visible sign in dirt, poverty, stupefaction, or illiteracy to explain the mystery of her exclusion from the world of her brother.

In the imagery that frames the story, we can find further evidence of the implicit connection between character and author. The story opens with the narrator looking out her window; it ends with Hugh looking out the window of his prison cell. Both narrator and character are imprisoned. With a piece of tin not fit for cutting korl, Hugh slits his wrists; a waste product of the industrial system, he turns his hand against himself. Davis, too, chose a form of suicide; artistic compromise turned her pen against herself.

Source:

Atlantic Monthly, 7 (April), 1861.

Selected Primary Works:

Margret Howth, 1862; "John Lamar," 1862; "David Gaunt," 1862; "The Wife's Story," 1864; Waiting for the Verdict, 1868; "Earthen Pitchers," 1873–74; John Andross, 1874; Silhouettes of American Life, 1892; Bits of Gossip, 1904.

Selected Secondary Works:

Philip B. Eppard, "Rebecca Harding Davis: A Misattribution," *Papers of the Bibliographical Society of America*, 69 (1975), 265–67; William F. Grayburn, "The Major Fiction of Rebecca Harding Davis" (Ph.D. dissertation, Pennsylvania State University), 1965; Walter Hesford, "Literary Contexts of 'Life in the Iron Mills,'" *American Literature*, 49 (1977), 70–85; Gerald Langford, *The Richard Harding Davis Years: A Biography of A Mother and Son* (New York: Holt, Rinehart, and Winston), 1961; Tillie Olsen, "A Biographical Interpretation," *Life in the Iron Mills* (Old Westbury, N.Y.: Feminist Press), 1972; Jean Pfaelzer, "Rebecca Harding Davis: Domesticity, Social Order, and the Industrial Novel," *International Journal of Women's Studies*, 4 (1981), 234–44; Arthur Hobson Quinn, *American Fiction* (New York: D. Appleton-Century), 1936; Helen Woodward Sheaffer, "Rebecca Harding Davis, Pioneer Realist" (Ph.D. dissertation, University of Pennsylvania), 1947.

> "Is this the end?
> O Life, as futile, then, as frail!
> What hope of answer of redress?"

A CLOUDY DAY: do you know what that is in a town of iron-works? The sky sank down before dawn, muddy, flat, immovable. The air is thick, clammy with the breath of crowded human beings. It stifles me. I open the window, and, looking out, can scarcely see through the rain the grocer's shop opposite, where a crowd of drunken Irishmen are puffing Lynchburg tobacco in their pipes. I can detect the scent through all the foul smells ranging loose in the air.

The idiosyncrasy of this town is smoke. It rolls sullenly in slow folds from the great chimneys of the iron-foundries, and settles down in black, slimy pools on the muddy streets. Smoke on the wharves, smoke on the dingy boats, on the yellow river,—clinging in a coating of greasy soot to the house-front, the two faded poplars, the faces of the passers-by. The long train of mules, dragging masses of pig-iron through the narrow street, have a foul vapor hanging to their reeking sides. Here, inside, is a little broken figure of an angel pointing upward from the mantel-shelf; but even its wings are covered with smoke, clotted and black. Smoke everywhere! A dirty canary chirps desolately in a cage beside me. Its dream of green fields and sunshine is a very old dream,—almost worn out, I think.

From the back-window I can see a narrow brick-yard sloping down to the river-side, strewed with rain-butts and tubs. The river, dull and tawny-colored, *(la belle rivière!)* drags itself sluggishly along, tired of the heavy weight of boats and coal-barges. What wonder? When I was a child, I used to fancy a look of weary, dumb appeal upon the face of the negro-like river slavishly bearing its burden day after day. Something of the same idle notion comes to me to-day, when from the street-window I look on the slow stream of human life creeping past, night and morning, to the great mills. Masses of men, with dull, besotted faces bent to the ground, sharpened here and there by pain or cunning; skin and muscle and flesh begrimed with smoke and ashes; stooping all night over boiling caldrons of metal, laired by day in dens of drunkenness and infamy; breathing from infancy to death an air saturated with fog and grease and soot, vileness for soul and body. What do you make of a case like that, amateur psychologist? You call it an altogether serious thing to be alive: to these men it is a drunken jest, a joke,—horrible to angels perhaps, to them commonplace enough. My fancy about the river was an idle one: it is no type of such a life. What if it be stagnant and slimy here? It knows that beyond there waits for it odorous sunlight,—quaint old gardens, dusky with soft, green foliage of apple-trees, and flushing crimson with roses,—air, and fields, and mountains. The future of the Welsh puddler passing just now is not so pleasant. To be stowed away, after his grimy work is done, in a hole in the muddy graveyard, and after that,—*not* air, nor green fields, nor curious roses.

Can you see how foggy the day is? As I stand here, idly tapping the window-pane, and looking out through the rain at the dirty back-yard and the coal-boats below, fragments of an old story float up before me,— a story of this old house into which I happened to come to-day. You may think it a tiresome story enough, as foggy as the day, sharpened by no sudden flashes of pain or pleasure.—I know: only the outline of a dull life, that long since, with thousands of dull lives like its own, was vainly lived and lost: thousands of them,—massed, vile, slimy lives, like those of the torpid lizards in yonder stagnant water-butt.—Lost? There is a curi- ous point for you to settle, my friend, who study psychology in a lazy, *dilettante* way. Stop a moment. I am going to be honest. This is what I want you to do. I want you to hide your disgust, take no heed to your clean clothes, and come right down with me,—here, into the thickest of the fog and mud and foul effluvia. I want you to hear this story. There is a secret down here, in this nightmare fog, that has lain dumb for centuries: I want to make it a real thing to you. You, Egoist, or Pantheist, or Arminian, busy in making straight paths for your feet on the hills, do not see it clearly,—this terrible question which men here have gone mad and died trying to answer. I dare not put this secret into words. I told you it was dumb. These men, going by with drunken faces and brains full of unawakened power, do not ask it of Society or of God. Their lives ask it; their deaths ask it. There is no reply. I will tell you plainly that I have a great hope; and I bring it to you to be tested. It is this: that this terrible dumb question is its own reply; that it is not the sentence of death we think it, but, from the very extremity of its darkness, the most solemn prophecy which the world has known of the Hope to come. I dare make my meaning no clearer, but will only tell my story. It will, perhaps, seem to you as foul and dark as this thick vapor about us, and as pregnant with death; but if your eyes are free as mine are to look deeper, no perfume-tinted dawn will be so fair with promise of the day that shall surely come.

My story is very simple,—only what I remember of the life of one of these men,—a furnace-tender in one of Kirby & John's rolling-mills,— Hugh Wolfe. You know the mills? They took the great order for the Lower Virginia railroads there last winter; run usually with about a thousand men. I cannot tell why I choose the half-forgotten story of this Wolfe more than than of myriads of these furnace-hands. Perhaps because there is a secret underlying sympathy between that story and this day with its impure fog and thwarted sunshine,—or perhaps simply for the reason that this house is the one where the Wolfes lived. There were the father and son,—both hands, as I said, in one of Kirby & John's mills for making railroad-iron,—and Deborah, their cousin, a picker in some of the cotton-mills. The house was rented then to half a dozen families. The Wolfes had two of the cellar-rooms. The old man, like many of the puddlers and feeders of the mills, was Welsh,—had spent half of his life in the Cornish tin-mines. You may pick the Welsh emigrants, Cornish miners, out of the throng passing the windows, any day. They are a trifle more filthy; their muscles are not so brawny; they stoop more. When they are drunk, they neither yell, nor shout, nor stagger, but skulk along like beaten hounds. A pure, unmixed blood, I fancy: shows itself in the slight angular bodies and sharply-cut facial lines. It is nearly thirty years since the Wolfes lived here. Their lives were like those of their class: incessant labor, sleeping in kennel-like rooms, eating rank pork and molasses, drinking—God and the distillers only know what; with an occasional night in jail, to atone for some drunken excess. Is that all of their lives?—of the portion given to them and these their duplicates swarming the streets to-day?—nothing beneath?—all? So many a political reformer will tell you,—and many a private reformer, too, who has gone among them with a heart tender with Christ's charity, and come out outraged, hardened.

One rainy night, about eleven o'clock, a crowd of half-clothed women stopped outside of the cellar-door. They were going home from the cotton-mill.

"Good-night, Deb," said one, a mulatto, steadying herself against the gas-post. She needed the post to steady her. So did more than one of them.

"Dah's a ball to Miss Potts' to-night. Ye'd best come."

"Inteet, Deb, if hur'll come, hur'll hef fun," said a shrill Welsh voice in the crowd.

Two or three dirty hands were thrust out to catch the gown of the woman, who was groping for the latch of the door.

"No."

"No? Where's Kit Small, then?"

"Begorra! on the spools. Alleys behint, though we helped her, we dud. An wid ye! Let Deb alone! It's ondacent frettin' a quite body. Be the powers, an' we'll have a night of it! there'll be lashin's o' drink,—the Vargent be blessed and praised for 't!"

They went on, the mulatto inclining for a moment to show fight, and drag the woman Wolfe off with them; but, being pacified, she staggered away.

Deborah groped her way into the cellar, and, after considerable stumbling, kindled a match, and lighted a tallow dip, that sent a yellow glimmer over the room. It was low, damp,—the earthen floor covered with a green, slimy moss,—a fetid air smothering the breath. Old Wolfe lay asleep on a heap of straw, wrapped in a torn horse-blanket. He was a pale, meek little man, with a white face and red rabbit-eyes. The woman Deborah was like him; only her face was even more ghastly, her lips bluer, her eyes more watery. She wore a faded cotton gown and a slouching bonnet. When she walked, one could see that she was deformed, almost a hunchback. She trod softly, so as not to waken him, and went through into the room beyond. There she found by the half-extinguished fire an iron saucepan filled with cold boiled potatoes, which she put upon a broken chair with a pint-cup of ale. Placing the old candlestick beside this dainty repast, she untied her bonnet, which hung limp and wet over her face, and prepared to eat her supper. It was the first food that had touched her lips since morning. There was enough of it, however: there is not always. She was hungry,—one could see that easily enough,—and not drunk, as most of her companions would have been found at this hour. She did not drink, this woman,—her face told that, too,—nothing stronger than ale. Perhaps the weak, flaccid wretch had some stimulant in her pale life to keep her up,—some love or hope, it might be, or urgent need. When that stimulant was gone, she would take to whiskey. Man cannot live by work alone. While she was skinning the potatoes, and munching them, a noise behind her made her stop.

"Janey!" she called, lifting the candle and peering into the darkness. "Janey, are you there?"

A heap of ragged coats was heaved up, and the face of a young girl emerged, staring sleepily at the woman.

"Deborah," she said, at last, "I'm here the night."

"Yes, child, Hur's welcome," she said, quietly eating on.

The girl's face was haggard and sickly; her eyes were heavy with sleep and hunger: real Milesian eyes they were, dark, delicate blue, glooming out from black shadows with a pitiful fright.

"I was alone," she said, timidly.

"Where's the father?" asked Deborah, holding out a potato, which the girl greedily seized.

"He's beyant,—wid Haley,—in the stone house." (Did you ever hear the word *jail* from an Irish mouth?) "I came here. Hugh told me never to stay me-lone."

"Hugh?"

"Yes."

A vexed frown crossed her face. The girl saw it, and added quickly,—

"I have not seen Hugh the day, Deb. The old man says his watch lasts till the mornin'."

The woman sprang up, and hastily began to arrange some bread and flitch in a tin pail, and to pour her own measure of ale into a bottle. Tying on her bonnet, she blew out the candle.

"Lay ye down, Janey dear," she said, gently, covering her with the old rags. "Hur can eat the potatoes, if hur's hungry."

"Where are ye goin', Deb? The rain's sharp."

"To the mill, with Hugh's supper."

"Let him bide till th' morn. Sit ye down."

"No, no,"—sharply pushing her off. "The boy'll starve."

She hurried from the cellar, while the child wearily coiled herself up for sleep. The rain was falling heavily, as the woman, pail in hand, emerged from the mouth of the alley, and turned down the narrow street, that stretched out, long and black, miles before her. Here and there a flicker of gas lighted an uncertain space of muddy footwalk and gutter; the long rows of houses, except an occasional lager-bier shop, were closed; now and then she met a band of mill-hands skulking to or from their work.

Not many even of the inhabitants of a manufacturing town know the vast machinery of system by which the bodies of workmen are governed, that goes on unceasingly from year to year. The hands of each mill are divided into watches that relieve each other as regularly as the sentinels of an army. By night and day the work goes on, the unsleeping engines groan and shriek, the fiery pools of metal boil and surge. Only for a day in the week, in half-courtesy to public censure, the fires are partially veiled; but as soon as the clock strikes midnight, the great furnaces break forth with renewed fury, the clamor begins with fresh, breathless vigor, the engines sob and shriek like "gods in pain."

As Deborah hurried down through the heavy rain, the noise of these thousand engines sounded through the sleep and shadow of the city like far-off thunder. The mill to which she was going lay on the river, a mile below the city-limits. It was far, and she was weak, aching from standing twelve hours at the spools. Yet it was her almost nightly walk to take this man his supper, though at every square she sat down to rest, and she knew she should receive small word of thanks.

Perhaps, if she had possessed an artist's eye, the picturesque oddity of the scene might have made her step stagger less, and the path seem shorter; but to her the mills were only "summat deilish to look at by night."

The road leading to the mills had been quarried from the solid rock, which rose abrupt and bare on one side of the cinder-covered road, while the river, sluggish and black, crept past on the other. The mills for rolling iron are simply immense tent-like roofs, covering acres of ground, open on every side. Beneath these roofs Deborah looked in on a city of fires, that burned hot and fiercely in the night. Fire in every horrible form: pits of flame waving in the wind; liquid metal-flames writhing in tortuous streams through the sand; wide caldrons filled with boiling fire, over which bent ghastly wretches stirring the strange brewing; and through all, crowds of half-clad men, looking like revengeful ghosts in the red light, hurried, throwing masses of glittering fire. It was like a street in Hell. Even Deborah muttered, as she crept through, "'T looks like t' Devil's place!" It did,—in more ways than one.

She found the man she was looking for, at last, heaping coal on a furnace. He had not time to eat his supper; so she went behind the furnace, and waited. Only a few men were with him, and they noticed her only by a "Hyur comes t' hunchback, Wolfe."

Deborah was stupid with sleep; her back pained her sharply; and her teeth chattered with cold, with the rain that soaked her clothes and dripped from her at every step. She stood, however, patiently holding the pail, and waiting.

"Hout, woman! ye look like a drowned cat. Come near to the fire,"— said one of the men, approaching to scrape away the ashes.

She shook her head. Wolfe had forgotten her. He turned, hearing the man, and came closer.

"I did no' think; gi' me my supper, woman."

She watched him eat with a painful eagerness. With a woman's quick instinct, she saw that he was not hungry,—was eating to please her. Her pale, watery eyes began to gather a strange light.

"Is't good, Hugh? T'ale was a bit sour, I feared."

"No, good enough." He hesitated a moment. "Ye're tired, poor lass! Bide here till I go. Lay down there on that heap of ash, and go to sleep."

He threw her an old coat for a pillow, and turned to his work. The heap was the refuse of the burnt iron, and was not a hard bed; the half-smothered warmth, too, penetrated her limbs, dulling their pain and cold shiver.

Miserable enough she looked, lying there on the ashes like a limp, dirty rag,—yet not an unfitting figure to crown the scene of hopeless discomfort and veiled crime: more fitting, if one looked deeper into the heart of things,—at her thwarted woman's form, her colorless life, her waking stupor that smothered pain and hunger,—even more fit to be a type of her class. Deeper yet if one could look, was there nothing worth reading in this wet, faded thing, half-covered with ashes? no story of a soul filled with groping passionate love, heroic unselfishness, fierce jealousy? of years of weary trying to please the one human being whom she loved, to gain one look of real heart-kindness from him? If anything like this were hidden beneath the pale, bleared eyes, and dull, washed-out-looking face, no one had ever taken the trouble to read its faint signs: not the half-clothed furnace-tender, Wolfe, certainly. Yet he was kind to her: it was his nature to be kind, even to the very rats that swarmed in the cellar; kind to her in just the same way. She knew that. And it might be that very knowledge had given to her face its apathy and vacancy more than her low, torpid life. One sees that dead, vacant look steal sometimes over the rarest, finest of women's faces,—in the very midst, it may be, of their warmest summer's day; and then one can guess at the secret of intolerable solitude that lies hid beneath the delicate laces and brilliant smile. There was no warmth, no brilliancy, no summer for this woman; so the stupor and vacancy had time to gnaw into her face perpetually. She was young, too, though no one guessed it; so the gnawing was the fiercer.

She lay quiet in the dark corner, listening, through the monotonous din and uncertain glare of the works, to the dull plash of the rain in the far distance,—shrinking back whenever the man Wolfe happened to look towards her. She knew, in spite of all his kindness, that there was that in her face and form which made him loathe the sight of her. She felt by instinct, although she could not comprehend it, the finer nature of the man, which made him among his fellow-workmen something unique, set apart. She knew, that, down under all the vileness and coarseness of his life, there was a groping passion for whatever was beautiful and pure,— that his soul sickened with disgust at her deformity, even when his words were kindest. Through this dull consciousness, which never left her, came, like a sting, the recollection of the dark blue eyes and lithe figure of the little Irish girl she had left in the cellar. The recollection struck through even her stupid intellect with a vivid glow of beauty and of grace. Little Janey, timid, helpless, clinging to Hugh as her only friend: that was the sharp thought, the bitter thought, that drove into the glazed eyes a fierce light of pain. You laugh at it? Are pain and jealousy less savage realities down here in this place I am taking you to than in your own house or your own heart,—your heart, which they clutch at sometimes? The note is the same, I fancy, be the octave high or low.

If you could go into this mill where Deborah lay, and drag out from the hearts of these men the terrible tragedy of their lives, taking it as a symptom of the disease of their class, no ghost Horror would terrify you more. A reality of soul-starvation, of living death, that meets you every day under the besotted faces on the street,—I can paint nothing of this, only give you the outside outlines of a night, a crisis in the life of one man: whatever muddy depth of soul-history lies beneath you can read according to the eyes God has given you.

Wolfe, while Deborah watched him as a spaniel its master, bent over the furnace with his iron pole, unconscious of her scrutiny, only stopping to receive orders. Physically, Nature had promised the man but little. He had already lost the strength and instinct vigor of a man, his muscles were thin, his nerves weak, his face (a meek, woman's face) haggard, yellow with consumption. In the mill he was known as one of the girl-men: "Molly Wolfe" was his *sobriquet.* He was never seen in the cockpit, did not own a terrier, drank but seldom; when he did, desperately. He fought sometimes, but was always thrashed, pommelled to a jelly. The man was game enough, when his blood was up: but he was no favorite in the mill; he had the taint of school-learning on him,—not to a dangerous extent, only a quarter or so in the free-school in fact, but enough to ruin him as a good hand in a fight.

For other reasons, too, he was not popular. Not one of themselves, they felt that, though outwardly as filthy and ash-covered; silent, with foreign thoughts and longings breaking out through his quietness in innumerable curious ways: this one, for instance. In the neighboring furnace-buildings lay great heaps of the refuse from the ore after the pig-metal is run. *Korl* we call it here: a light, porous substance, of a delicate, waxen, flesh-colored tinge. Out of the blocks of this korl, Wolfe, in his off-hours from the furnace, had a habit of chipping and moulding figures,—hideous, fantastic enough, but sometimes strangely beautiful: even the mill-men saw that, while they jeered at him. It was a curious fancy in the man, almost a passion. The few hours for rest he spent hewing and hacking with his blunt knife, never speaking, until his watch came again,—working at one figure for months, and, when it was finished, breaking it to pieces perhaps, in a fit of disappointment. A morbid, gloomy man, untaught, unled, left to feed his soul in grossness and crime, and hard, grinding labor.

I want you to come down and look at this Wolfe, standing there among the lowest of his kind, and see him just as he is, that you may judge him justly when you hear the story of this night. I want you to look back, as he does every day, at his birth in vice, his starved infancy; to remember the heavy years he has groped through as boy and man,—the slow, heavy years of constant, hot work. So long ago he began, that he thinks sometimes he has worked there for ages. There is no hope that it will ever end. Think that God put into this man's soul a fierce thirst for beauty,—to know it, to create it; to *be*—something, he knows not what,—other than he is. There are moments when a passing cloud, the sun glinting on the purple thistles, a kindly smile, a child's face, will rouse him to a passion of pain,—when his nature starts up with a mad cry of rage against God, man, whoever it is that has forced this vile, slimy life upon him. With all this groping, this mad desire, a great blind intellect stumbling through wrong, a loving poet's heart, the man was by habit only a coarse, vulgar laborer, familiar with sights and words you would blush to name. Be just: when I tell you about this night, see him as he is. Be just,—not like man's law, which seizes on one isolated fact, but like God's judging angel, whose clear, sad eye saw all the countless cankering days of this man's life, all the countless nights, when, sick with starving, his soul fainted in him, before it judged him for this night, the saddest of all.

I called this night the crisis of his life. If it was, it stole on him unawares. These great turning-days of life cast no shadow before, slip by unconsciously. Only a trifle, a little turn of the rudder, and the ship goes to heaven or hell.

Wolfe, while Deborah watched him, dug into the furnace of melting iron with his pole, dully thinking only how many rails the lump would yield. It was late,—nearly Sunday morning; another hour, and the heavy work would be done,—only the furnaces to replenish and cover for the next day. The workmen were growing more noisy, shouting, as they had to do, to be heard over the deep clamor of the mills. Suddenly they grew less boisterous,—at the far end, entirely silent. Something unusual had happened. After a moment, the silence came nearer; the men stopped their jeers and drunken choruses. Deborah, stupidly lifting up her head, saw the cause of the quiet. A group of five or six men were slowly approaching, stopping to examine each furnace as they came. Visitors often came to see the mills after night: except by growing less noisy, the men took no notice of them. The furnace where Wolfe worked was near the bounds of the works; they halted there hot and tired: a walk over one of these great foundries is no trifling task. The woman, drawing out of sight, turned over to sleep. Wolfe, seeing them stop, suddenly roused from his indifferent stupor, and watched them keenly. He knew some of them: the overseer, Clarke,—a son of Kirby, one of the millowners,—and a Doctor May, one of the town-physicians. The other two were strangers. Wolfe came closer. He seized eagerly every chance that brought him into contact with this mysterious class that shone down on him perpetually with the glamour of another order of being. What made the difference between them? That was the mystery of his life. He had a vague notion that perhaps to-night he could find it out. One of the strangers sat down on a pile of bricks, and beckoned young Kirby to his side.

"This *is* hot, with a vengeance. A match, please?"—lighting his cigar. "But the walk is worth the trouble. If it were not that you must have heard it so often, Kirby, I would tell you that your works look like Dante's Inferno."

Kirby laughed.

"Yes. Yonder is Farinata himself in the burning tomb,"—pointing to some figure in the shimmering shadows.

"Judging from some of the faces of your men," said the other, "they bid fair to try the reality of Dante's vision, some day."

Young Kirby looked curiously around, as if seeing the faces of his hands for the first time.

"They're bad enough, that's true. A desperate set, I fancy. Eh, Clarke?"

The overseer did not hear him. He was talking of net profits just then,—giving, in fact, a schedule of the annual business of the firm to a sharp peering little Yankee, who jotted down notes on a paper laid on the crown of his hat: a reporter for one of the city-papers getting up a series of reviews of the leading manufactories. The other gentlemen had accompanied them merely for amusement. They were silent until the notes were finished, drying their feet at the furnaces, and sheltering their faces from the intolerable heat. At last the overseer concluded with—

"I believe that is a pretty fair estimate, Captain."

"Here, some of you men!" said Kirby, "bring up those boards. We may as well sit down, gentlemen, until the rain is over. It cannot last much longer at this rate."

"Pig-metal,"—mumbled the reporter,—"um!—coal facilities,—um!—hands employed, twelve hundred,—bitumen,—um!—all right, I believe, Mr. Clarke;—sinking-fund,—what did you say was your sinking-fund?"

"Twelve hundred hands?" said the stranger, the young man who had first spoken. "Do you control their votes, Kirby?"

"Control? No." The young man smiled complacently. "But my father brought seven hundred votes to the polls for his candidate last November. No force-work, you understand,—only a speech or two, a hint to form themselves into a society, and a bit of red and blue bunting to make them a flag. The Invincible Roughs,—I believe that is their name. I forget the motto: 'Our country's hope,' I think."

There was a laugh. The young man talking to Kirby sat with an amused light in his cool gray eye, surveying critically the half-clothed figures of the puddlers, and the slow swing of their brawny muscles. He was a stranger in the city,—spending a couple of months in the borders of a Slave State, to study the institutions of the South,—a brother-in-law of Kirby's,—Mitchell. He was an amateur gymnast,—hence his anatomical eye; a patron, in a *blasé* way, of the prize-ring; a man who sucked the essence out of a science or philosophy in an indifferent, gentlemanly way; who took Kant, Novalis, Humboldt, for what they were worth in his own scales; accepting all, despising nothing, in heaven, earth, or hell, but one-idead men; with a temper yielding and brilliant as summer water, until his Self was touched, when it was ice, though brilliant still. Such men are not rare in the States.

As he knocked the ashes from his cigar, Wolfe caught with a quick pleasure the contour of the white hand, the blood-glow of a red ring he wore. His voice, too, and that of Kirby's, touched him like music,—low, even, with chording cadences. About this man Mitchell hung the impalpable atmosphere belonging to the thoroughbred gentleman. Wolfe, scraping away the ashes beside him, was conscious of it, did obeisance to it with his artist sense, unconscious that he did so.

The rain did not cease. Clarke and the reporter left the mills; the others, comfortably seated near the furnace, lingered, smoking and talking in a desultory way. Greek would not have been more unintelligible to the furnace-tenders, whose presence they soon forgot entirely. Kirby drew out a newspaper from his pocket and read aloud some article, which they discussed eagerly. At every sentence, Wolfe listened more and more like a dumb, hopeless animal, with a duller, more stolid look creeping over his face, glancing now and then at Mitchell, marking acutely every smallest sign of refinement, then back to himself, seeing as in a mirror his filthy body, his more stained soul.

Never! He had no words for such a thought, but he knew now, in all the sharpness of the bitter certainty, that between them there was a great gulf never to be passed. Never!

The bells of the mills rang for midnight. Sunday morning had dawned. Whatever hidden message lay in the tolling bells floated past these men unknown. Yet it was there. Veiled in the solemn music ushering the risen saviour was a key-note to solve the darkest secrets of a world gone wrong,—even this social riddle which the brain of the grimy puddler grappled with madly to-night.

The men began to withdraw the metal from the caldrons. The mills were deserted on Sundays, except by the hands who fed the fires, and those who had no lodgings and slept usually on the ash-heaps. The three strangers sat still during the next hour, watching the men cover the furnaces, laughing now and then at some jest of Kirby's.

"Do you know," said Mitchell, "I like this view of the works better than when the glare was fiercest? These heavy shadows and the amphitheatre of smothered fires are ghostly, unreal. One could fancy these red smouldering lights to be the half-shut eyes of wild beasts, and the spectral figures their victims in the den."

Kirby laughed. "You are fanciful. Come, let us get out of the den. The spectral figures, as you call them, are a little too real for me to fancy a close proximity in the darkness,—unarmed, too."

The others rose, buttoning their over-coats, and lighting cigars.

"Raining, still," said Doctor May, "and hard. Where did we leave the coach, Mitchell?"

"At the other side of the works.—Kirby, what's that?"

Mitchell started back, half-frightened, as, suddenly turning a corner, the white figure of a woman faced him in the darkness,—a woman, white, of giant proportions, crouching on the ground, her arms flung out in some wild gesture of warning.

"Stop! Make that fire burn there!" cried Kirby, stopping short.

The flame burst out, flashing the gaunt figure into bold relief. Mitchell drew a long breath.

"I thought it was alive," he said, going up curiously.

The others followed.

"Not marble, eh?" asked Kirby, touching it.

One of the lower overseers stopped.

"Korl, Sir."

"Who did it?"

"Can't say. Some of the hands; chipped it out in off-hours."

"Chipped to some purpose, I should say. What a flesh-tint the stuff has! Do you see, Mitchell?"

"I see."

He had stepped aside where the light fell boldest on the figure, looking at it in silence. There was not one line of beauty or grace in it: a nude woman's form, muscular, grown coarse with labor, the powerful limbs instinct with some one poignant longing. One idea: there it was in the tense, rigid muscles, the clutching hands, the wild, eager face, like that of a starving wolf's. Kirby and Doctor May walked around it, critical, curious. Mitchell stood aloof, silent. The figure touched him strangely.

"Not badly done," said Doctor May. "Where did the fellow learn that sweep of the muscles in the arm and hand? Look at them! They are groping,—do you see?—clutching: the peculiar action of a man dying of thirst."

"They have ample facilities for studying anatomy," sneered Kirby, glancing at the half-naked figures.

"Look," continued the Doctor, "at this bony wrist, and the strained sinews of the instep! A working woman,—the very type of her class."

"God forbid!" muttered Mitchell.

"Why?" demanded May. "What does the fellow intend by the figure? I cannot catch the meaning."

"Ask him," said the other, dryly. "There he stands,"—pointing to Wolfe, who stood with a group of men, leaning on his ash-rake.

The Doctor beckoned him with the affable smile which kind-hearted men put on, when talking with these people.

"Mr. Mitchell has picked you out as the man who did this,—I'm sure I don't know why. But what did you mean by it?"

"She be hungry."

Wolfe's eyes answered Mitchell, not the Doctor.

"Oh-h! But what a mistake you have made, my fine fellow! You have given no sign of starvation to the body. It is strong,—terribly strong. It has the mad, half-despairing gesture of drowning."

Wolfe stammered, glanced appealingly at Mitchell, who saw the soul of the thing, he knew. But the cool, probing eyes were turned on himself now,—mocking, cruel, relentless.

"Not hungry for meat," the furnace-tender said at last.

"What then? Whiskey?" jeered Kirby, with a coarse laugh.

Wolfe was silent a moment, thinking.

"I dunno," he said, with a bewildered look. "It mebbe. Summat to make her live, I think,—like you. Whiskey ull do it, in a way."

The young man laughed again. Mitchell flashed a look of disgust somewhere,—not at Wolfe.

"May," he broke out impatiently, "are you blind? Look at that woman's face! It asks questions of God, and says, 'I have a right to know.' Good God, how hungry it is!"

They looked a moment; then May turned to the mill-owner:—

"Have you many such hands as this? What are you going to do with them? Keep them at puddling iron?"

Kirby shrugged his shoulders. Mitchell's look had irritated him.

"*Ce n'est pas mon affaire.* I have no fancy for nursing infant geniuses. I suppose there are some stray gleams of mind and soul among these wretches. The Lord will take care of his own; or else they can work out their own salvation. I have heard you call our American system a ladder which any man can scale. Do you doubt it? Or perhaps you want to banish all social ladders, and put us all on a flat table-land,—eh, May?"

The Doctor looked vexed, puzzled. Some terrible problem lay hid in this woman's face, and troubled these men. Kirby waited for an answer, and, receiving none, went on, warming with his subject.

"I tell you, there's something wrong that no talk of '*Liberté*' or '*Égalité*' will do away. If I had the making of men, these men who do the lowest part of the world's work should be machines,—nothing more,—hands. It would be kindness. God help them! What are taste, reason, to creatures who must live such lives as that?" He pointed to Deborah, sleeping on the ash-heap. "So many nerves to sting them to pain. What if God had put your brain, with all its agony of touch, into your fingers, and bid you work and strike with that?"

"You think you could govern the world better?" laughed the Doctor.

"I do not think at all."

"That is true philosophy. Drift with the stream, because you cannot dive deep enough to find bottom, eh?"

"Exactly," rejoined Kirby. "I do not think. I wash my hands of all social problems,—slavery, caste, white or black. My duty to my operatives has a narrow limit,—the pay-hour on Saturday night. Outside of that, if they cut korl, or cut each other's throats, (the more popular amusement of the two,) I am not responsible."

The Doctor sighed,—a good honest sigh, from the depths of his stomach.

"God help us! Who is responsible?"

"Not I, I tell you," said Kirby, testily. "What has the man who pays them money to do with their souls' concerns, more than the grocer or butcher who takes it?"

"And yet," said Mitchell's cynical voice, "look at her! How hungry she is!"

Kirby tapped his boot with his cane. No one spoke. Only the dumb face of the rough image looking into their faces with the awful question, "What shall we do to be saved?" Only Wolfe's face, with its heavy weight of brain, its weak, uncertain mouth, its desperate eyes, out of which looked the soul of his class,—only Wolfe's face turned towards Kirby's. Mitchell laughed,—a cool, musical laugh.

"Money has spoken!" he said, seating himself lightly on a stone with the air of an amused spectator at a play. "Are you answered?"—turning to Wolfe his clear, magnetic face.

Bright and deep and cold as Arctic air, the soul of the man lay tranquil beneath. He looked at the furnace-tender as he had looked at a rare mosaic in the morning; only the man was the more amusing study of the two.

"Are you answered? Why, May, look at him! *'De profundis clamavi.'* Or, to quote in English, 'Hungry and thirsty, his soul faints in him.' And so Money sends back its answer into the depths through you, Kirby! Very clear the answer, too!—I think I remember reading the same words somewhere:—washing your hands in Eau de Cologne, and saying, 'I am innocent of the blood of this man. See ye to it!'"

Kirby flushed angrily.

"You quote Scripture freely."

"Do I not quote correctly? I think I remember another line, which may amend my meaning: 'Inasmuch as ye did it unto one of the least of these, ye did it unto me.' Deist? Bless you, man, I was raised on the milk of the Word. Now, Doctor, the pocket of the world having uttered its voice, what has the heart to say? You are a philanthropist, in a small way,—*n'est ce pas?* Here, boy, this gentleman can show you how to cut korl better,—or your destiny. Go on, May!"

"I think a mocking devil possesses you to-night," rejoined the Doctor, seriously.

He went to Wolfe and put his hand kindly on his arm. Something of a vague idea possessed the Doctor's brain that much good was to be done here by a friendly word or two: a latent genius to be warmed into life by a waited-for sun-beam. Here it was: he had brought it. So he went on complacently:—

"Do you know, boy, you have it in you to be a great sculptor, a great man?—do you understand?" (talking down to the capacity of his hearer: it is a way people have with children, and men like Wolfe,)—"to live a better, stronger life than I, or Mr. Kirby here? A man may make himself anything he chooses. God has given you stronger powers than many men,—me, for instance."

May stopped, heated, glowing with his own magnanimity. And it was magnanimous. The puddler had drunk in every word, looking through the Doctor's flurry, and generous heat, and self-approval, into his will, with those slow, absorbing eyes of his.

"Make yourself what you will. It is your right."

"I know," quietly. "Will you help me?"

Mitchell laughed again. The Doctor turned now, in a passion,—

"You know, Mitchell, I have not the means. You know, if I had, it is in my heart to take this boy and educate him for"—

"The glory of God, and the glory of John May."

May did not speak for a moment; then, controlled, he said,—

"Why should one be raised, when myriads are left?—I have not the money, boy," to Wolfe, shortly.

"Money?" He said it over slowly, as one repeats the guessed answer to a riddle, doubtfully. "That is it? Money?"

"Yes, money,—that is it," said Mitchell, rising, and drawing his furred coat about him. "You've found the cure for all the world's diseases.— Come, May, find your good-humor, and come home. This damp wind chills my very bones. Come and preach your Saint-Simonian doctrines to-morrow to Kirby's hands. Let them have a clear idea of the rights of the soul, and I'll venture next week they'll strike for higher wages. That will be the end of it."

"Will you send the coach-driver to this side of the mills?" asked Kirby, turning to Wolfe.

He spoke kindly: it was his habit to do so. Deborah, seeing the puddler go, crept after him. The three men waited outside. Doctor May walked up and down, chafed. Suddenly he stopped.

"Go back, Mitchell! You say the pocket and the heart of the world speak without meaning to these people. What has its head to say? Taste, culture, refinement? Go!"

Mitchell was leaning against a brick wall. He turned his head indolently, and looked into the mills. There hung about the place a thick, unclean odor. The slightest motion of his hand marked that he perceived it, and his insufferable disgust. That was all. May said nothing, only quickened his angry tramp.

"Besides," added Mitchell, giving a corollary to his answer, "it would be of no use. I am not one of them."

"You do not mean"—said May, facing him.

"Yes, I mean just that. Reform is born of need, not pity. No vital movement of the people's has worked down, for good or evil; fermented, instead, carried up the heaving, cloggy mass. Think back through history, and you will know it. What will this lowest deep—thieves, Magdalens, negroes—do with the light filtered through ponderous Church creeds, Baconian theories, Goethe schemes? Some day, out of their bitter need will be thrown up their own light-bringer,—their Jean Paul, their Cromwell, their Messiah."

"Bah!" was the Doctor's inward criticism. However, in practice, he adopted the theory; for, when, night and morning, afterwards, he prayed that power might be given these degraded souls to rise, he glowed at heart, recognizing an accomplished duty.

Wolfe and the woman had stood in the shadow of the works as the coach drove off. The Doctor had held out his hand in a frank, generous way, telling him to "take care of himself, and to remember it was his right to rise." Mitchell had simply touched his hat, as to an equal, with a quiet look of thorough recognition. Kirby had thrown Deborah some money, which she found, and clutched eagerly enough. They were gone now, all of them. The man sat down on the cinder-road, looking up into the murky sky.

"'T be late, Hugh. Wunnot hur come?"

He shook his head doggedly, and the woman crouched out of his sight against the wall. Do you remember rare moments when a sudden light flashed over yourself, your world, God? when you stood on a mountain-peak, seeing your life as it might have been, as it is? one quick instant, when custom lost its force and every-day usage? when your friend, wife, brother, stood in a new light? your soul was bared, and the grave,—a foretaste of the nakedness of the Judgment-Day? So it came before him, his life, that night. The slow tides of pain he had borne gathered themselves up and surged against his soul. His squalid daily life, the brutal coarseness eating into his brain, as the ashes into his skin: before, these things had been a dull aching into his consciousness; to-night, they were reality. He gripped the filthy red shirt that clung, stiff with soot, about him, and tore it savagely from his arm. The flesh beneath was muddy with grease and ashes,—and the heart beneath that! And the soul? God knows.

Then flashed before his vivid poetic sense the man who had left him,—the pure face, the delicate, sinewy limbs, in harmony with all he knew of beauty or truth. In his cloudy fancy he had pictured a Something like this. He had found it in this Mitchell, even when he idly scoffed at his pain: a Man all-knowing, all-seeing, crowned by Nature, reigning,—the keen glance of his eye falling like a sceptre on other men. And yet his instinct taught him that he too—He! He looked at himself with sudden loathing, sick, wrung his hands with a cry, and then was silent. With all the phantoms of his heated, ignorant fancy, Wolfe had not been vague in his ambitions. They were practical, slowly built up before him out of his knowledge of what he could do. Through years he had day by day made this hope a real thing to himself,—a clear, projected figure of himself, as he might become.

Able to speak, to know what was best, to raise these men and women working at his side up with him: sometimes he forgot this defined hope in the frantic anguish to escape,—only to escape,—out of the wet, the pain, the ashes, somewhere, anywhere,—only for one moment of free air on a hill-side, to lie down and let his sick soul throb itself out in the sunshine. But to-night he panted for life. The savage strength of his nature was roused; his cry was fierce to God for justice.

"Look at me!" he said to Deborah, with a low, bitter laugh, striking his puny chest savagely. "What am I worth, Deb? Is it my fault that I am no better? My fault? My fault?"

He stopped, stung with a sudden remorse, seeing her hunchback shape writhing with sobs. For Deborah was crying thankless tears, according to the fashion of women.

"God forgi' me, woman! Things go harder wi' you nor me. It's a worse share."

He got up and helped her to rise; and they went doggedly down the muddy street, side by side.

"It's all wrong," he muttered, slowly,—"all wrong! I dunnot understan'. But it'll end some day."

"Come home, Hugh!" she said, coaxingly; for he had stopped, looking around bewildered.

"Home,—and back to the mill!" He went on saying this over to himself, as if he would mutter down every pain in this dull despair.

She followed him through the fog, her blue lips chattering with cold. They reached the cellar at last. Old Wolfe had been drinking since she went out, and had crept nearer the door. The girl Janey slept heavily in the corner. He went up to her, touching softly the worn white arm with his fingers. Some bitterer thought stung him, as he stood there. He wiped the drops from his forehead, and went into the room beyond, livid, trembling. A hope, trifling, perhaps, but very dear, had died just then out of the poor puddler's life, as he looked at the sleeping, innocent girl,—some plan for the future, in which she had borne a part. He gave it up that moment, then and forever. Only a trifle, perhaps, to us: his face grew a shade paler,—that was all. But, somehow, the man's soul, as God and the angels looked down on it, never was the same afterwards.

Deborah followed him into the inner room. She carried a candle, which she placed on the floor, closing the door after her. She had seen the look on his face, as he turned away: her own grew deadly. Yet, as she came up to him her eyes glowed. He was seated on an old chest, quiet, holding his face in his hands.

"Hugh!" she said, softly.

He did not speak.

"Hugh, did hur hear what the man said,—him with the clear voice? Did hur hear? Money, money,—that it wud do all?"

He pushed her away,—gently, but he was worn out; her rasping tone fretted him.

"Hugh!"

The candle flared a pale yellow light over the cobwebbed brick walls, and the woman standing there. He looked at her. She was young, in deadly earnest; her faded eyes, and wet, ragged figure caught from their frantic eagerness a power akin to beauty.

"Hugh, it is true! Money ull do it! Oh, Hugh, boy, listen till me! He said it true! It is money!"

"I know. Go back! I do not want you here."

"Hugh, it is t' last time. I'll never worrit hur again."

There were tears in her voice now, but she choked them back.

"Hear till me only to-night! If one of t' witch people wud come, them we heard of t' home, and gif hur all hur wants, what then? Say, Hugh!"

"What do you mean?"

"I mean money."

Her whisper shrilled through his brain.

"If one of t' witch dwarfs wud come from t' lane moors to-night, and gif hur money, to go out,—*out,* I say,—out, lad, where t' sun shines, and t' heath grows, and t' ladies walk in silken gownds, and God stays all t' time,—where t' man lives that talked to us to-night,—Hugh knows,— Hugh could walk there like a king!"

He thought the woman mad, tried to check her, but she went on, fierce in her eager haste.

"If I were t' witch dwarf, if I had t' money, wud hur thank me? Wud hur take me out o' this place wid hur and Janey? I wud not come into the gran' house hur wud build, to vex hur wid t' hunch,—only at night, when t' shadows were dark, stand far off to see hur."

Mad? Yes! Are many of us mad in this way?

"Poor Deb! poor Deb!" he said, soothingly.

"It is here," she said, suddenly jerking into his hand a small roll. "I took it! I did it! Me, me!—not hur! I shall be hanged, I shall be burnt in hell, if anybody knows I took it! Out of his pocket, as he leaned against t' bricks. Hur knows?"

She thrust it into his hand, and then, her errand done, began to gather chips together to make a fire, choking down hysteric sobs.

"Has it come to this?"

That was all he said. The Welsh Wolfe blood was honest. The roll was a small green pocket-book containing one or two gold pieces, and a check for an incredible amount, as it seemed to the poor puddler. He laid it down, hiding his face again in his hands.

"Hugh, don't be angry wud me! It's only poor Deb,—hur knows?"

He took the long skinny fingers kindly in his.

"Angry? God help me, no! Let me sleep. I am tired."

He threw himself heavily down on the wooden bench, stunned with pain and weariness. She brought some old rags to cover him.

It was late on Sunday evening before he awoke. I tell God's truth, when I say he had then no thought of keeping this money. Deborah had hid it in his pocket. He found it there. She watched him eagerly, as he took it out.

"I must gif it to him," he said, reading her face.

"Hur knows," she said with a bitter sigh of disappointment. "But it is hur right to keep it."

His right! The word struck him. Doctor May had used the same. He washed himself, and went out to find this man Mitchell. His right! Why did this chance word cling to him so obstinately? Do you hear the fierce devils whisper in his ear, as he went slowly down the darkening street?

The evening came on, slow and calm. He seated himself at the end of an alley leading into one of the larger streets. His brain was clear to-night, keen, intent, mastering, It would not start back, cowardly, from any hellish temptation, but meet it face to face. Therefore the great temptation of his life came to him veiled by no sophistry, but bold, defiant, owning its own vile name, trusting to one bold blow for victory.

He did not deceive himself. Theft! That was it. At first the word sickened him; then he grappled with it. Sitting there on a broken cartwheel, the fading day, the noisy groups, the church-bells' tolling passed before him like a panorama, while the sharp struggle went on within. This money! He took it out, and looked at it. If he gave it back, what then? He was going to be cool about it.

People going by to church saw only a sickly mill-boy watching them quietly at the alley's mouth. They did not know that he was mad, or they would not have gone by so quietly: mad with hunger; stretching out his hands to the world, that had given so much to them, for leave to live the life God meant him to live. His soul within him was smothering to death; he wanted so much, thought so much, and *knew*—nothing. There was nothing of which he was certain, except the mill and things there. Of God and heaven he had heard so little, that they were to him what fairy-land is to a child: something real, but not here; very far off. His brain, greedy, dwarfed, full of thwarted energy and unused powers, questioned these men and women going by, coldly, bitterly, that night. Was it not his right to live as they,—a pure life, a good, true-hearted life, full of beauty and kind words? He only wanted to know how to use the strength within him. His heart warmed, as he thought of it. He suffered himself to think of it longer. If he took the money?

Then he saw himself as he might be, strong, helpful, kindly. The night crept on, as this one image slowly evolved itself from the crowd of other thoughts and stood triumphant. He looked at it. As he might be! What wonder, if it blinded him to delirium,—the madness that underlies all revolution, all progress, and all fall?

You laugh at the shallow temptation? You see the error underlying its argument so clearly,—that to him a true life was one of full development rather than self-restraint? that he was deaf to the higher tone in a cry of voluntary suffering for truth's sake than in the fullest flow of spontaneous harmony? I do not plead his cause. I only want to show you the mote in my brother's eye: then you can see clearly to take it out.

The money,—there it lay on his knee, a little blotted slip of paper, nothing in itself; used to raise him out of the pit; something straight from God's hand. A thief! Well, what was it to be a thief? He met the question at last, face to face, wiping the clammy drops of sweat from his forehead.

God made this money—the fresh air, too—for his children's use. He never made the difference between poor and rich. The Something who looked down on him that moment through the cool gray sky had a kindly face, he knew,—loved his children alike. Oh, he knew that!

There were times when the soft floods of color in the crimson and purple flames, or the clear depth of amber in the water below the bridge, had somehow given him a glimpse of another world than this,—of an infinite depth of beauty and of quiet somewhere,—somewhere,—a depth of quiet and rest and love. Looking up now, it became strangely real. The sun had sunk quite below the hills, but his last rays struck upward, touching the zenith. The fog had risen, and the town and river were steeped in its thick, gray damp; but overhead, the sun-touched smoke-clouds opened like a cleft ocean,—shifting, rolling seas of crimson mist, waves of billowy silver veined with blood-scarlet, inner depths unfathomable of glancing light. Wolfe's artist-eye grew drunk with color. The gates of that other world! Fading, flashing before him now! What, in that world of Beauty, Content, and Right, were the petty laws, the mine and thine, of mill-owners and mill-hands?

A consciousness of power stirred within him. He stood up. A man,—he thought, stretching out his hands,—free to work, to live, to love! Free! His right! He folded the scrap of paper in his hand. As his nervous fingers took it in, limp and blotted, so his soul took in the mean temptation, lapped it in fancied rights, in dreams of improved existences, drifting and endless as the cloud-seas of color. Clutching it, as if the tightness of his hold would strengthen his sense of possession, he went aimlessly down the street. It was his watch at the mill. He need not go, need never go again, thank God!—shaking off the thought with unspeakable loathing.

Shall I go over the history of the hours of that night? how the man wandered from one to another of his old haunts, with a half-consciousness of bidding them farewell,—lanes and alleys and back-yards where the mill-hands lodged,—noting, with a new eagerness, the filth and drunkenness, the pig-pens, the ash-heaps covered with potato-skins, the bloated, pimpled women at the doors,—with a new disgust, a new sense of sudden triumph, and, under all, a new, vague dread, unknown before, smothered down, kept under, but still there? It left him but once during the night, when, for the second time in his life, he entered a church. It was a sombre Gothic pile, where the stained light lost itself in far-retreating arches; built to meet the requirements and sympathies of a far other class than Wolfe's. Yet it touched, moved him uncontrollably. The distances, the shadows, the still, marble figures, the mass of silent kneeling worshippers, the mysterious music, thrilled, lifted his soul with a wonderful pain. Wolfe forgot himself, forgot the new life he was going to live, the mean terror gnawing underneath. The voice of the speaker strengthened the charm; it was clear, feeling, full, strong. An old man, who had lived much, suffered much; whose brain was keenly alive, dominant; whose heart was summer-warm with charity. He taught it to-night. He held up Humanity in its grand total; showed the great world-cancer to his people. Who could show it better? He was a Christian reformer; he had studied the age thoroughly; his outlook at man had been free, world-wide, over all time. His faith stood sublime upon the Rock of Ages; his fiery zeal guided vast schemes by which the gospel was to be preached to all nations. How did he preach it to-night? In burning, light-laden words he painted the incarnate Life, Love, the universal Man: words that became reality in the lives of these people,—that lived again in beautiful words and actions, trifling, but heroic. Sin, as he defined it, was a real foe to them; their trials, temptations, were his. His words passed far over the furnace-tender's grasp, toned to suit another class of culture; they sounded in his ears a very pleasant song in an unknown tongue. He meant to cure this world-cancer with a steady eye that had never glared with hunger, and a hand that neither poverty nor strychnine-whiskey had taught to shake. In this morbid, distorted heart of the Welsh puddler he had failed.

Wolfe rose at last, and turned from the church down the street. He looked up; the night had come on foggy, damp; the golden mists had vanished, and the sky lay dull and ash-colored. He wandered again aimlessly down the street, idly wondering what had become of the cloud-sea of crimson and scarlet. The trial-day of this man's life was over, and he had lost the victory. What followed was mere drifting circumstance,—a quicker walking over the path,—that was all. Do you want to hear the end of it? You wish me to make a tragic story out of it? Why, in the police-reports of the morning paper you can find a dozen such tragedies: hints of shipwrecks unlike any that ever befell on the high seas; hints that here a power was lost to heaven,—that there a soul went down where no tide can ebb or flow. Commonplace enough the hints are,—jocose sometimes, done up in rhyme.

Doctor May, a month after the night I have told you of, was reading to his wife at breakfast from this fourth column of the morning-paper: an unusual thing,—these police-reports not being, in general, choice reading for ladies; but it was only one item he read.

"Oh, my dear! You remember that man I told you of, that we saw at Kirby's mill?—that was arrested for robbing Mitchell? Here he is; just listen:—'Circuit Court. Judge Day. Hugh Wolfe, operative in Kirby & John's Loudon Mills. Charge, grand larceny. Sentence, nineteen years hard labor in penitentiary.'—Scoundrel! Serves him right! After all our kindness that night! Picking Mitchell's pocket at the very time!"

His wife said something about the ingratitude of that kind of people, and then they began to talk of something else.

Nineteen years! How easy that was to read! What a simple word for Judge Day to utter! Nineteen years! Half a lifetime!

Hugh Wolfe sat on the window-ledge of his cell, looking out. His ankles were ironed. Not usual in such cases; but he had made two desperate efforts to escape. "Well," as Haley, the jailer, said, "small blame to him! Nineteen years' imprisonment was not a pleasant thing to look forward to." Haley was very good-natured about it, though Wolfe had fought him savagely.

"When he was first caught," the jailer said afterwards, in telling the story, "before the trial, the fellow was cut down at once,—laid there on that pallet like a dead man, with his hands over his eyes. Never saw a man so cut down in my life. Time of the trial, too, came the queerest dodge of any customer I ever had. Would choose no lawyer. Judge gave him one, of course. Gibson it was. He tried to prove the fellow crazy; but it wouldn't go. Thing was plain as day-light: money found on him. 'Twas a hard sentence,—all the law allows; but it was for 'xample's sake. These mill-hands are gettin' onbearable. When the sentence was read, he just looked up, and said the money was his by rights, and that all the world had gone wrong. That night, after the trial, a gentleman came to see him here, name of Mitchell,—him as he stole from. Talked to him for an hour. Thought he came for curiosity, like. After he was gone, thought Wolfe was remarkable quiet, and went into his cell. Found him very low; bed all bloody. Doctor said he had been bleeding at the lungs. He was as weak as a cat; yet, if ye'll b'lieve me, he tried to get a-past me and get out. I just carried him like a baby, and threw him on the pallet. Three days after, he tried it again: that time reached the wall. Lord help you! he fought like a tiger,—giv' some terrible blows. Fightin' for life, you see; for he can't live long, shut up in the stone crib down yonder. Got a death-cough now. 'T took two of us to bring him down that day; so I just put the irons on his feet. There he sits, in there. Goin' to-morrow, with a batch more of 'em. That woman, hunchback, tried with him,—you remember?—she's only got three years. 'Complice. But *she's* a woman, you know. He's been quiet ever since I put on irons: giv' up, I suppose. Looks white, sick-lookin'. It acts different on 'em, bein' sentenced. Most of 'em gets reckless, devilish-like. Some prays awful, and sings them vile songs of the mills, all in a breath. That woman, now, she's desper't'. Been beggin' to see Hugh, as she calls him, for three days. I'm a-goin' to let her in. She don't go with him. Here she is in this next cell. I'm a-goin' now to let her in."

He let her in. Wolfe did not see her. She crept into a corner of the cell, and stood watching him. He was scratching the iron bars of the window with a piece of tin which he had picked up, with an idle, uncertain, vacant stare, just as a child or idiot would do.

"Tryin' to get out, old boy?" laughed Haley. "Them irons will need a crow-bar beside your tin, before you can open 'em."

Wolfe laughed, too, in a senseless way.

"I think I'll get out," he said.

"I believe his brain's touched," said Haley, when he came out.

The puddler scraped away with the tin for half an hour. Still Deborah did not speak. At last she ventured nearer, and touched his arm.

"Blood?" she said, looking at some spots on his coat with a shudder.

He looked up at her. "Why, Deb!" he said, smiling,—such a bright, boyish smile, that it went to poor Deborah's heart directly, and she sobbed and cried out loud.

"Oh, Hugh, lad! Hugh! dunnot look at me, when it wur my fault! To think I brought hur to it! And I loved hur so! Oh, lad, I dud!"

The confession, even in this wretch, came with the woman's blush through the sharp cry.

He did not seem to hear her,—scraping away diligently at the bars with the bit of tin.

Was he going mad? She peered closely into his face. Something she saw there made her draw suddenly back,—something which Haley had not seen, that lay beneath the pinched, vacant look it had caught since the trial, or the curious gray shadow that rested on it. That gray shadow,— yes, she knew what that meant. She had often seen it creeping over women's faces for months, who died at last of slow hunger or consumption. That meant death, distant, lingering: but this—Whatever it was the woman saw, or thought she saw, used as she was to crime and misery, seemed to make her sick with a new horror. Forgetting her fear of him, she caught his shoulders, and looked keenly, steadily, into his eyes.

"Hugh!" she cried, in a desperate whisper,—"oh, boy, not that! for God's sake, not *that!*"

The vacant laugh went off his face, and he answered her in a muttered word or two that drove her away. Yet the words were kindly enough. Sitting there on his pallet, she cried silently a hopeless sort of tears, but did not speak again. The man looked up furtively at her now and then. Whatever his own trouble was, her distress vexed him with a momentary sting.

It was market-day. The narrow window of the jail looked down directly on the carts and wagons drawn up in a long line, where they had unloaded. He could see, too, and hear distinctly the clink of money as it changed hands, the busy crowd of whites and blacks shoving, pushing one another, and the chaffering and swearing at the stalls. Somehow, the sound, more than anything else had done, wakened him up,—made the whole real to him. He was done with the world and the business of it. He let the tin fall, and looked out, pressing his face close to the rusty bars. How they crowded and pushed! And he,—he should never walk that pavement again! There came Neff Sanders, one of the feeders at the mill, with a basket on his arm. Sure enough, Neff was married the other week. He whistled, hoping he would look up; but he did not. He wondered if Neff remembered he was there,—if any of the boys thought of him up there, and thought that he never was to go down that old cinder-road again. Never again! He had not quite understood it before; but now he did. Not for days or years, but never!—that was it.

How clear the light fell on that stall in front of the market! and how like a picture it was, the dark-green heaps of corn, and the crimson beets, and golden melons! There was another with game: how the light flickered on that pheasant's breast, with the purplish blood dripping over the brown feathers! He could see the red shining of the drops, it was so near. In one minute he could be down there. It was just a step. So easy, as it seemed, so natural to go! Yet it could never be—not in all the thousands of years to come—that he should put his foot on the street again! He thought of himself with a sorrowful pity, as of some one else. There was a dog down in the market, walking after his master with such a stately, grave look!—only a dog, yet he could go backwards and forwards just as he pleased: he had good luck! Why, the very vilest cur, yelping there in the gutter, had not lived his life, had been free to act out whatever thought God had put into his brain; while he—No, he would not think of that! He tried to put the thought away, and to listen to a dispute between a countryman and a woman about some meat; but it would come back. He, what had he done to bear this?

Then came the sudden picture of what might have been, and now. He knew what it was to be in the penitentiary,—how it went with men there. He knew how in these long years he should slowly die, but not until soul and body had become corrupt and rotten,—how, when he came out, if he lived to come, even the lowest of the mill-hands would jeer him,—how his hands would be weak, and his brain senseless and stupid. He believed he was almost that now. He put his hand to his head, with a puzzled, weary look. It ached, his head, with thinking. He tried to quiet himself. It was only right, perhaps; he had done wrong. But was there right or wrong for such as he? What was right? And who had ever taught him? He thrust the whole matter away. A dark, cold quiet crept through his brain. It was all wrong; but let it be! It was nothing to him more than the others. Let it be!

The door grated, as Haley opened it.

"Come, my woman! Must lock up for t' night. Come, stir yerself!"

She went up and took Hugh's hand.

"Good-night, Deb," he said, carelessly.

She had not hoped he would say more; but the tired pain on her mouth just then was bitterer than death. She took his passive hand and kissed it.

"Hur'll never see Deb again!" she ventured, her lips growing colder and more bloodless.

What did she say that for? Did he not know it? Yet he would not be impatient with poor old Deb. She had trouble of her own, as well as he.

"No, never again," he said, trying to be cheerful.

She stood just a moment, looking at him. Do you laugh at her, standing there, with her hunchback, her rags, her bleared, withered face, and the great despised love tugging at her heart?

"Come, you!" called Haley, impatiently.

She did not move.

"Hugh!" she whispered.

It was to be her last word. What was it?

"Hugh, boy, not THAT!"

He did not answer. She wrung her hands, trying to be silent, looking in his face in an agony of entreaty. He smiled again, kindly.

"It is best, Deb. I cannot bear to be hurted any more."

"Hur knows," she said, humbly.

"Tell my father good-bye; and—and kiss little Janey."

She nodded, saying nothing, looked in his face again, and went out of the door. As she went, she staggered.

"Drinkin' to-day?" broke out Haley, pushing her before him. "Where the Devil did you get it? Here, in with ye!" and he shoved her into her cell, next to Wolfe's, and shut the door.

Along the wall of her cell there was a crack low down by the floor, through which she could see the light from Wolfe's. She had discovered it days before. She hurried in now, and, kneeling down by it, listened, hoping to hear some sound. Nothing but the rasping of the tin on the bars. He was at his old amusement again. Something in the noise jarred on her ear, for she shivered as she heard it. Hugh rasped away at the bars. A dull old bit of tin, not fit to cut korl with.

He looked out of the window again. People were leaving the market now. A tall mulatto girl, following her mistress, her basket on her head, crossed the street just below, and looked up. She was laughing; but, when she caught sight of the haggard face peering out through the bars, suddenly grew grave, and hurried by. A free, firm step, a clear-cut olive face, with a scarlet turban tied on one side, dark, shining eyes, and on the head the basket poised, filled with fruit and flowers, under which the scarlet turban and bright eyes looked out half-shadowed. The picture caught his eye. It was good to see a face like that. He would try to-morrow, and cut one like it. *To-morrow!* He threw down the tin, trembling, and covered his face with his hands. When he looked up again, the daylight was gone.

Deborah, crouching near by on the other side of the wall, heard no noise. He sat on the side of the low pallet, thinking. Whatever was the mystery which the woman had seen on his face, it came out now slowly, in the dark there, and became fixed,—a something never seen on his face before. The evening was darkening fast. The market had been over for an hour; the rumbling of the carts over the pavement grew more infrequent: he listened to each, as it passed, because he thought it was to be for the last time. For the same reason, it was, I suppose, that he strained his eyes to catch a glimpse of each passer-by, wondering who they were, what kind of homes they were going to, if they had children,—listening eagerly to every chance word in the street, as if—(God be merciful to the man! what strange fancy was this?)—as if he never should hear human voices again.

It was quite dark at last. The street was a lonely one. The last passenger, he thought, was gone. No,—there was a quick step: Joe Hill, lighting the lamps. Joe was a good old chap; never passed a fellow without some joke or other. He remembered once seeing the place where he lived with his wife. "Granny Hill" the boys called her. Bedridden she was; but so kind as Joe was to her! kept the room so clean!—and the old woman, when he was there, was laughing at "some of t' lad's foolishness." The step was far down the street; but he could see him place the ladder, run up, and light the gas. A longing seized him to be spoken to once more.

"Joe!" he called, out of the grating. "Good-bye, Joe!"

The old man stopped a moment, listening uncertainly; then hurried on. The prisoner thrust his hand out of the window, and called again, louder; but Joe was too far down the street. It was a little thing; but it hurt him,—this disappointment.

"Good-bye, Joe!" he called, sorrowfully enough.

"Be quiet!" said one of the jailers, passing the door, striking on it with his club.

Oh, that was the last, was it?

There was an inexpressible bitterness on his face, as he lay down on the bed, taking the bit of tin, which he had rasped to a tolerable degree of sharpness, in his hand,—to play with, it may be. He bared his arms, looking intently at their corded veins and sinews. Deborah, listening in the next cell, heard a slight clicking sound, often repeated. She shut her lips tightly, that she might not scream, the cold drops of sweat broke over her, in her dumb agony.

"Hur knows best," she muttered at last, fiercely clutching the boards where she lay.

If she could have seen Wolfe, there was nothing about him to frighten her. He lay quite still, his arms outstretched, looking at the pearly stream of moonlight coming into the window. I think in that one hour that came then he lived back over all the years that had gone before. I think that all the low, vile life, all his wrongs, all his starved hopes, came then, and stung him with a farewell poison that made him sick unto death. He made neither moan nor cry, only turned his worn face now and then to the pure light, that seemed so far off, as one that said, "How long, O Lord? how long?"

The hour was over at last. The moon, passing over her nightly path, slowly came nearer, and threw the light across his bed on his feet. He watched it steadily, as it crept up, inch by inch, slowly. It seemed to him to carry with it a great silence. He had been so hot and tired there always in the mills! The years had been so fierce and cruel! There was coming now quiet and coolness and sleep. His tense limbs relaxed, and settled in a calm languor. The blood ran fainter and slow from his heart. He did not think now with a savage anger of what might be and was not; he was conscious only of deep stillness creeping over him. At first he saw a sea of faces: the mill-men,—women he had known, drunken and bloated,—Janeys timid and pitiful,—poor old Debs: then they floated together like a mist, and faded away, leaving only the clear, pearly moonlight.

Whether, as the pure light crept up the stretched-out figure, it brought with it calm and peace, who shall say? His dumb soul was alone with God in judgment. A Voice may have spoken for it from far-off Calvary, "Father, forgive them, for they know not what they do!" Who dare say? Fainter and fainter the heart rose and fell, slower and slower the moon floated from behind a cloud, until, when at last its full tide of white splendor swept over the cell, it seemed to wrap and fold into a deeper stillness the dead figure that never should move again. Silence deeper than the Night! Nothing that moved, save the black nauseous stream of blood dripping slowly from the pallet to the floor!

There was outcry and crowd enough in the cell the next day. The coroner and his jury, the local editors, Kirby himself, and boys with their hands thrust knowingly into their pockets and heads on one side, jammed into the corners. Coming and going all day. Only one woman. She came late, and outstayed them all. A Quaker, or Friend, as they call themselves. I think this woman was known by that name in heaven. A homely body, coarsely dressed in gray and white. Deborah (for Haley had let her in) took notice of her. She watched them all—sitting on the end of the pallet, holding his head in her arms—with the ferocity of a watch-dog, if any of them touched the body. There was no meekness, or sorrow, in her face; the stuff out of which murderers are made, instead. All the time Haley and the woman were laying straight the limbs and cleaning the cell, Deborah sat still, keenly watching the Quaker's face. Of all the crowd there that day, this woman alone had not spoken to her,—only once or twice had put some cordial to her lips. After they all were gone, the woman, in the same still, gentle way, brought a vase of wood-leaves and berries, and placed it by the pallet, then opened the narrow window. The fresh air blew in, and swept the woody fragrance over the dead face. Deborah looked up with a quick wonder.

"Did hur know my boy wud like it? Did hur know Hugh?"

"I know Hugh now."

The white fingers passed in a slow, pitiful way over the dead, worn face. There was a heavy shadow in the quiet eyes.

"Did hur know where they'll bury Hugh?" said Deborah in a shrill tone, catching her arm.

This had been the question hanging on her lips all day.

"In t' town-yard? Under t' mud and ash? T' lad'll smother, woman! He wur born on t' lane moor, where t' air is frick and strong. Take hur out, for God's sake, take hur out where t' air blows!"

The Quaker hesitated, but only for a moment. She put her strong arm around Deborah and led her to the window.

"Thee sees the hills, friend, over the river? Thee sees how the light lies warm there, and the winds of God blow all the day? I live there,—where the blue smoke is, by the trees. Look at me." She turned Deborah's face to her own, clear and earnest. "Thee will believe me? I will take Hugh and bury him there to-morrow."

Deborah did not doubt her. As the evening wore on, she leaned against the iron bars, looking at the hills that rose far off, through the thick sodden clouds, like a bright, unattainable calm. As she looked, a shadow of their solemn repose fell on her face: its fierce discontent faded into a pitiful, humble quiet. Slow, solemn tears gathered in her eyes: the poor weak eyes turned so hopelessly to the place where Hugh was to rest, the grave heights looking higher and brighter and more solemn than ever before. The Quaker watched her keenly. She came to her at last, and touched her arm.

"When thee comes back," she said, in a low, sorrowful tone, like one who speaks from a strong heart deeply moved with remorse or pity, "thee shall begin thy life again,—there on the hills. I came too late; but not for thee,—by God's help, it may be."

Not too late. Three years after, the Quaker began her work. I end my story here. At evening-time it was light. There is no need to tire you with the long years of sunshine, and fresh air, and slow, patient Christ-love, needed to make healthy and hopeful this impure body and soul. There is a homely pine house, on one of these hills, whose windows overlook broad, wooded slopes and clover-crimsoned meadows,—niched into the very place where the light is warmest, the air freest. It is the Friends' meeting-house. Once a week they sit there, in their grave, earnest way, waiting for the Spirit of Love to speak, opening their simple hearts to receive His words. There is a woman, old, deformed, who takes a humble place among them: waiting like them: in her gray dress, her worn face, pure and meek, turned now and then to the sky. A woman much loved by these silent, restful people; more silent than they, more humble, more loving. Waiting: with her eyes turned to hills higher and purer than these on which she lives,—dim and far off now, but to be reached some day. There may be in her heart some latent hope to meet there the love denied her here,—that she shall find him whom she lost, and that then she will not be all-unworthy. Who blames her? Something is lost in the passage of every soul from one eternity to the other,—something pure and beautiful, which might have been and was not: a hope, a talent, a love, over which the soul mourns, like Esau deprived of his birthright. What blame to the meek Quaker, if she took her lost hope to make the hills of heaven more fair?

Nothing remains to tell that the poor Welsh puddler once lived, but this figure of the mill-woman cut in korl. I have it here in a corner of my library. I keep it hid behind a curtain,—it is such a rough, ungainly thing.

Yet there are about it touches, grand sweeps of outline, that show a master's hand. Sometimes,—to-night, for instance,—the curtain is accidentally drawn back, and I see a bare arm stretched out imploringly in the darkness, and an eager, wolfish face watching mine: a wan, woful face, through which the spirit of the dead korl-cutter looks out, with its thwarted life, its mighty hunger, its unfinished work. Its pale, vague lips seem to tremble with a terrible question. "Is this the End?" they say,— "nothing beyond?—no more?" Why, you tell me you have seen that look in the eyes of dumb brutes,—horses dying under the lash. I know.

The deep of the night is passing while I write. The gas-light wakens from the shadows here and there the objects which lie scattered through the room: only faintly, though; for they belong to the open sunlight. As I glance at them, they each recall some task or pleasure of the coming day. A half-moulded child's head; Aphrodite; a bough of forest-leaves; music; work; homely fragments, in which lie the secrets of all eternal truth and beauty. Prophetic all! Only this dumb, woful face seems to belong to and end with the night. I turn to look at it. Has the power of its desperate need commanded the darkness away? While the room is yet steeped in heavy shadow, a cool, gray light suddenly touches its head like a blessing hand, and its groping arm points through the broken cloud to the far East, where, in the flickering, nebulous crimson, God has set the promise of the Dawn.

ROSE TERRY COOKE
(1827–1892)

Miss Lucinda

Atlantic Monthly, 8 (August), 1861.

Rose Terry Cooke was born on February 17, 1827, on a farm six miles
west of Hartford, Connecticut, the older of the two daughters of Anne
Wright Hurlbut and Henry Wadsworth Terry. Both her mother and her
father came from socially distinguished Connecticut families. When
Cooke was six, the family moved to Hartford to live with her paternal
grandmother, sister of the Daniel Wadsworth who had earlier befriended
Lydia Sigourney. Serious illness and delicate health marked Cooke's
childhood. As a result, she spent much time outdoors with her father
who taught her a love of nature and a knowledge of gardening. Her
mother, who, according to Harriet Prescott Spofford, had been Sigourney's pupil, educated her daughter at home and gave her the training to
which Cooke later credited her ability to write. Each day she had to
learn a page of the dictionary by rote and to record the events of her life
in a copybook. Cooke later attended the Hartford Female Seminary,
founded by Catharine Beecher; at the age of sixteen she graduated, prepared for a career of teaching. That same year she experienced a religious conversion and joined the Congregational church.

In 1843, she took a teaching position in Burlington, New Jersey. She
lived in the home of a local clergyman, William Van Rensselaer, and
supplemented her salary by serving as governess to his family. Four
years later, she returned to Hartford where she continued teaching until,
in 1848, at the age of twenty-one, she received a legacy on the death of
her great uncle, Daniel. Economic independence enabled her to give up
teaching, settle permanently in Hartford, and devote herself to writing.

Interested in writing from an early age, at thirteen Cooke published
in a local paper an elegiac poem on the death of a public figure. During

her days at the Hartford Female Seminary, she wrote poems and dramas for the entertainment of herself and her friends. Although she no doubt continued to publish poetry locally throughout the decade of the 1840s, none of her work appeared nationally until the 1850s. On April 26, 1851, "Trailing Arbutus" appeared in the *New York Daily Tribune;* Cooke signed it A.W.H. for Anne Wright Hurlbut, initials chosen, according to Spofford, "because her mother was so dear to her that she wished to associate her with all she did" (*A Little Book of Friends,* p. 153). During her lifetime, Cooke published two volumes of poems, one in 1861 and another in 1888. Like Alice Cary, she thought of herself primarily as a poet. Yet, like Cary, her real achievement was in prose and particularly in the genre of short fiction. Even the resolutely congratulatory Spofford admitted that "she was finer and greater in her best prose, and I enjoyed her prose more. I never told her so, for I would far rather have let truth go by than have hurt her feelings" (*A Little Book,* pp. 153–54). More significantly, Spofford attributes Cooke's power as a role model for later women writers to her prose: "and as story followed story, each better than the other, she kindled the ambition and had the felicitation of every other young woman who turned the pages throughout the country,—for most of us felt as if all girlhood were honored in her who carried her light before men with such proud strength and beauty" (*Our Famous Women,* p. 175).

According to Jean Downey, Cooke's primary biographer, it is not easy to determine precisely when Cooke began writing and publishing fiction. A clear record begins only with the publication in 1855 in *Putnam's* of "The Mormon's Wife." Between 1855 and 1857, eight of Cooke's stories were published in *Putnam's;* in 1856, she began contributing to *Harper's,* and in 1857 the editor of the prestigious new *Atlantic Monthly* invited her to provide a story for the magazine's initial issue. "Sally Parsons's Duty" was the first of over twenty sketches that Cooke published in the *Atlantic.*

Afflicted with ill health, Cooke wrote little during the decade of the 1860s; nevertheless, according to Downey, this "was artistically her greatest period of steady and unusual growth" (Downey, p. 59). By 1866, Cooke had moved to Collinsville, Connecticut, where she lived with her younger sister who had married in 1856. In 1872, Cooke's mother died and a year later, at the age of forty-six, she married. Rollin Cooke was a man sixteen years her junior and a widower with two daughters. With him she moved to Winsted, Connecticut, where he worked at the time as a clerk in a bank. Evidently Cooke's family disapproved of her marriage; her brother-in-law enforced an estrangement that kept Cooke from seeing her sister and her nieces.

Long accustomed to economic independence, Cooke found her financial situation drastically altered after marriage. Her husband never worked regularly and, when he did work, his income was insufficient to support the household. In addition, Cooke's father-in-law used her money for his business ventures and, when he failed in 1885, Cooke, now in her late fifties, "lost about a third of all I possess, indeed all my profitable property, for houses don't rent now" (Downey, pp. 97–98).

Cooke's writing suffered predictably from these changes in her economic situation. Under pressure to make money, she diverted her attention from her serious work in regional fiction and turned instead to those genres—didactic potboilers and stories for children—that sold most readily, sending her material to the newspapers that paid the highest prices for it: the *Christian Union*, the *Independent*, and the *Youth's Companion*. Simultaneously, her contributions to such periodicals as *Harper's* and the *Atlantic Monthly* decreased. Downey contends, however, that in the juvenile fiction written during this period, much of which was collected in the posthumous *Little Foxes* (1904), Cooke maintained the quality of her work.

In 1887, Cooke moved to Pittsfield, Massachusetts, following her husband as he attempted a fresh start in business. In 1889, at the age of sixty-two, she wrote her publisher and friend, Benjamin H. Ticknor, asking for work:

> I write to ask you if you think I could get anything to do in Boston in literary matters, any sort of hack-work that would bring in daily bread. Writing stories and poems is so precarious and payment so delayed that I want some steadier business. The reason for this is that Mr. Cooke has not succeeded in his business here, and the small property I owned has all gone in his failure, so that now I shall be homeless and penniless unless I can get work (Downey, p. 123).

In her essay on Harriet Prescott Spofford, published in *Our Famous Women*, Cooke indicates the effect that financial need had on her own life and art, and pays tribute to a sister writer's freedom from such pressure:

> "Work! Work! Work!" is not only the "Song of the Shirt," but the song of the Woman, and under that stringent cry we reel off pages of fiction, overridden by the dreamy facts of need, like the spider, spinning not only our dwellings, but our grave-clothes from our own breasts. Happy is she who need not so outwear heart and brain in the effort to live, dying daily; who is not forced to encounter that publicity and comment from which every true woman shrinks with real pain, but who can lay down her weapons of war, enter upon her rest and peace in this world, intrenched in "Honor, love, obedience, troops of friends," and dwell while life lasts in the dignities and felicities of home, like Harriet Prescott Spofford.

Cooke's last significant story, "A Town Mouse and A Country Mouse," appeared in the *Atlantic Monthly* in June, 1891; it was good enough to be included in a collection of stories published the same year, *Huckleberries Gathered from New England Hills*. Indeed, the quality of work in this late volume indicates the persistence of Cooke's commitment to her talent despite the years of writing for money. Cooke died in Pittsfield on July 18, 1892, at the age of sixty-five; she was buried in Collinsville.

Unquestionably, Cooke worked best in the genre of the regional sketch or tale. Much of this fiction is grimly realistic and much of it

documents the consequences for women of living within a world
defined by masculine values and masculine institutions. Capable of writing sentimental love stories with marriage as the happy ending and didactic homilies that extol and idealize the virtues of female self-sacrifice,
Cooke also wrote powerful stories exposing the economic and psychological consequences for women of marriage, often in terms more severe
than those of the later, and better known, New England regionalists—
Sarah Orne Jewett, Mary E. Wilkins Freeman, Alice Brown. In "Mrs.
Flint's Married Experience," (1880), for example, a second marriage entered into to avoid being a burden on the children, concludes in the
woman's death, a result of psychological abuse, overwork, and even
starvation. Furthermore, Cooke shows that Deacon Flint's "murder" of
his wife is condoned and even facilitated by the basic institutions of
New England village life, particularly the church. Cooke also confronts
directly the masculine psychology that results from a life lived within
such institutions. In "Freedom Wheeler's Controversy with Providence"
(1877), she links the infamous New England will with this psychology
and sees in it a raw and unmediated expression of male dominance, determined to have its way at whatever cost to the women who must serve
it.

Much of Cooke's best work, including the story selected for this
anthology, is characterized by humor. She frequently presents her
characters in comic situations, and views them through a comic perspective; many of these characters served as models for later writers in the
development of regional types. In addition, Cooke pioneered in the
serious use of vernacular speech in fiction. Her dialogue is eminently
readable and her characters speak "in a lively succession of metaphors
and similes" drawn "from New England language with abrupt accuracy"
(Toth, p. 125). Finally, Cooke's work is noteworthy for its use of realistic detail, detail that creates authentic settings and backgrounds for
both character and action.

Perhaps because of the unevenness of her work as a whole, and perhaps because of her own ambivalence toward the culture she exposes
and critiques, an ambivalence apparent even in her best work, Cooke's
reputation has never been as high as that of her successors in the genre
of regionalism. Yet, as a record of post–Civil War New England culture
and, in particular, as a record of the lives of women lived within that
culture, Cooke's work is invaluable. Moreover, her best work certainly
ranks with that of Jewett, her great contemporary.

"Miss Lucinda" demonstrates Cooke's strengths as a writer: her
natural gift for telling a story, her mastery of the comic perspective, her
capacity to create authentic vernacular characters, and her ability to provide a richly detailed background for both characters and story. "Miss
Lucinda" equally reveals the aesthetic values that produced Cooke's best
work. In language reminiscent of Caroline Kirkland, Cooke opens with
an "apology" for a story that is "nowise tragic" or "high" but is rather
committed to the commonplace. And, in the figure of "a woman who
could not be a heroine," "Miss Lucinda" reveals Cooke's determination

to make the commonplace an object of interest, sympathy, and respect. Consciously displacing the subject matter of the "hard times" of "war times," Cooke substitutes instead a re-evaluation of the figure of the "old maid," suggesting thus that the commonplace that commands her attention may well be different from that of some of her contemporaries.

Details, pages of them, establish the character of Miss Lucinda and describe the texture of the world she has fashioned for herself. We learn the accent with which she speaks French; we know the number of scissors necessary to her happiness, and the number of legs to her tables. The larger world within which she has established her domain is equally authentic. This world contains boys who shave the tail of her generic yellow dog; it produces piglet runts who innocently present themselves as perfect pets, incapable of the domestic tyranny practised by dogs and cats; there is, of all things, a dancing school in Dalton with a French dancing master; and a census taker, who arrives in the midst of Miss Lucinda's efforts to confine piggy to a pen long since outgrown, and elicits from her the fact of her age.

Although Israel Slater may nearly die of laughing at Miss Lucinda's naiveté on the subject of her piggy's fate, Cooke does not make fun of her. Explicitly excluded from the realm of the heroic, she is subtly aligned with an alternate category—the "modern and private" saint. Though unwilling to "associate familiarly with people who put their teaspoons into the sugar bowl" (shades of Kirkland's Mrs. Clavers), Miss Lucinda's "warm, kind heart made her a blessing to the poor and sick" and "no neighbor of hers, local or scriptural, fell ill, without an immediate offer of aid from her." When there is danger of her becoming an object of public ridicule, Jean Leclerc explicitly invokes the concept of sainthood to intercept the ridicule and correctly interpret her to the world: "I like to teach you the dance; but she could teach you the saints' ways, which are better. I think you will no more to laugh."

While she presents Miss Lucinda as a saint and not a joke, Cooke is hardly sentimental about her character. Instead, she maintains both distance and perspective. She perceives the humor in Miss Lucinda's mode of dancing and she raises questions about the limitations of one who lavishes attention on cats and dogs "while little morsels of flesh and blood, ragged, hungry, and immortal, wandered up and down the streets." Yet her tone toward her character is consistently loving, and even respectful, and, as testament to her essential approbation, Cooke endows Miss Lucinda with both happiness and self-delight. In her own eyes, Miss Lucinda does not have "idiosyncrasies." If she is different from her neighbors, it is *she* who feels *their* difference, evidenced in their deviations from those manners by which she lives and which she perceives as the norm. The dancing lesson amply tests the tenacity of her positive self-image. It is not she who must wrestle with "the little serpents of the ridiculous" and it is not she who terminates her lessons. Thoroughly comfortable with her youthful companions, she exhibits neither self-consciousness nor inhibition but leaps and skips in shortish dress on longish feet to her heart's content. Only in the realm of love

does Miss Lucinda evince self-doubt—"but how can you like *me*?" Perhaps merely the feminine demurral conventionally expected from
women, Miss Lucinda's response may also be based, not on self-deprecation, but on an accurate perception of reality. After all, Jean Leclerc's
motives for marrying her are hardly romantic.

Miss Lucinda has remained single, not through any objection to
"domestic tyranny" in the shape of man, but because she has never met
a man "who did not offend her sense of propriety, and shock her taste";
she has never met a man capable of displacing the paternal ideal set by
breeches, knee-buckles, white stockings, and supernatural legs. On the
surface, then, "Miss Lucinda," unlike, for example, Freeman's later "A
New England Nun," contains no critique of marriage; perhaps for this
reason Cooke, in contrast to Freeman, can treat the figure of the "old
maid" without ambiguity. Indeed, in this story, Cooke explicitly declares her conservatism on the issue of women's rights and aligns herself
with those women who recognize that they are "quite unable to do
without some masculine help." In Cooke's text, the "sublime theories of
the strong-minded sisters" collapse before the sublime fact of masculine
muscle. When Miss Lucinda, unable on her own to get piggy back in his
pen, dashes out into the street to find anything in the shape of a man,
she presumably proves this point.

Yet what follows Miss Lucinda's desperate dash into the streets, in
fact, subverts the theory of complementary opposites, which Cooke
presents as the irrefutable argument for the anti–women's rights position. The man whom Miss Lucinda finds to help her is no brawny specimen of superior masculine physique. Instead, he is an elderly dancing
master who proves to be little more of a match for the pig than Miss
Lucinda herself and whose strength in the struggle, such as it is, derives
from his brains not his brawn. In his effort to subdue the beast, he
breaks his leg and must lie helplessly by while the woman nails up the
bars "stronger than ever." The courtship that ensues from this encounter
continues the subversion of the theory that opposites attract, for what
draws Miss Lucinda to Monsieur Jean is not his difference from her, but
his similarity to her and his difference from other men. A foreigner, and
French at that; a dancing teacher—hardly a masculine profession; a de-
votee of the beautiful and the delicate; a lover of flowers and an excellent cook with a decided preference for the economical and the savory,
Jean Leclerc is firmly identified with feminine values. Further, as an exiled *valet-de-chambre* who is socially and politically marginal in Dalton,
he shares the status of women. In a word, Jean Leclerc is a male Lucinda
Manners, and the relationship flourishes by virtue of their similarity, not
their difference.

Nevertheless, there are some questions posed by Cooke's use of the
traditional comic ending of marriage. How spurious, for example, do
we find the reasoning of Israel Slater who, in his role as Cupid, functions to help his fellow man to a cushy situation by arguing that
" 'twould be jest as much for her good as yourn"? How sinister is the
hint of the mastery that will ensue from this change in Miss Lucinda's
status? "It occurred to Monsieur Leclerc, that, if they were married, she

would take no more lessons." And to what extent does Cooke connect the marriage of her heroine with Israel's willingness to use her as a joke to "entertain a few favored auditors"? Do women become foolish in, not out of, marriage? The potential ambiguity of her material has, however, no effect on Cooke's own narrative stance. In this story, the narrative voice retains control of the material and remains at ease with the act of telling. From ghostly legs to table legs to piggy legs to broken leg to dancing legs, "Miss Lucinda" proves its teller's art.

Source:

Sombody's Neighbors (Boston: Houghton, Mifflin), 1896.

Selected Primary Works:

Poems, 1861; Somebody's Neighbors, 1881; Root-Bound and Other Sketches, 1885; The Sphinx's Children, 1886; Happy Dodd, 1887; Poems, 1888; Huckleberries Gathered from New England Hills, 1891.

Selected Secondary Works:

Josephine Donovan, New England Local Color Literature: A Woman's Tradition (New York: Frederick Ungar), 1983; Jean Downey, "Rose Terry Cooke: A Bibliography," Bulletin of Bibliography, 21 (1955), 159–63, 191–92; ———, "A Biographical and Critical Study of Rose Terry Cooke" (Ph.D. dissertation, University of Ottawa), 1956; ———, "Three Unpublished Letters: Howells—Cooke," American Literature, 32 (1960–61), 463–65; Katherine Jobes, "The Resolution of Solitude: A Study of Four Writers of the New England Decline" (Ph.D. dissertation, Yale University), 1960; Babette Levy, "Mutations in New England Local Color," New England Quarterly, 19 (1946), 338–58; Evelyn Newlyn, "Rose Terry Cooke and the Children of the Sphinx," Regionalism and the Female Imagination, 4 (1979), 49–57; Harriet Prescott Spofford, "Rose Terry Cooke," Our Famous Women (Hartford; Worthington), 1884; ———, A Little Book of Friends (Boston: Little, Brown), 1916; Susan Allen Toth, "More Than Local Color: A Reappraisal of Rose Terry Cooke, Mary Wilkins Freeman and Alice Brown" (Ph.D. dissertation, University of Minnesota), 1969; ———, "Rose Terry Cooke," American Literary Realism, 4 (1971), 170–76; Perry Westbrook, Acres of Flint: Writers of Rural New England, 1870–1900 (Washington, D.C.: Scarecrow), 1951, revised 1981.

BUT THAT SOLOMON is out of fashion, I should quote him here and now, to the effect that there is a time for all things; but Solomon is obsolete, and never—no, never—will I dare to quote a dead language, "for raisons I have," as the exiles of Erin say. Yet, in spite of Solomon and Horace, I may express my own less concise opinion, that even in hard times, and dull times, and war times, there is yet a little time to laugh, a brief hour to smile and love and pity; just as through this dreary easterly storm, bringing clouds and rain, sobbing against casement and door with the inarticulate wail of tempests, there comes now and then the soft shine of a sun behind it all, a fleeting glitter, an evanescent aspect of what has been.

But if I apologize for a story that is nowise tragic, nor fitted to "the fashion of these times," possibly somebody will say at its end that I should also have apologized for its subject, since it is as easy for an author to treat his readers to high themes as vulgar ones, and velvet can be thrown into a portrait as cheaply as calico; but of this apology I wash my hands. I believe nothing in place or circumstance makes romance. I have the same quick sympathy for Biddy's sorrows with Patrick that I have for the Empress of France and her august but rather grim lord and master. I think words are often no harder to bear than "a blue bating;" and I have a reverence for poor old maids as great as for the nine Muses. Commonplace people are only commonplace from character, and no position affects that. So forgive me once more, patient reader, if I offer to you no tragedy in high life, no sentimental history of fashion and wealth, but only a little story about a woman who could not be a heroine.

Miss Lucinda Jane Ann Manners was a lady of unknown age, who lived in a place I call Dalton, in a State of these Disuniting States, which I do not mention for good cause. I have already had so many unconscious personalities visited on my devoted head, that, but for lucidity, I should never mention persons or places, inconvenient as it would be. However, Miss Lucinda did live, and lived by the aid of "means," which in the vernacular is money. Not a great deal, it is true,—five thousand dollars at lawful interest, and a little wooden house, do not imply many luxuries even to a single woman; and it is also true that a little fine sewing taken in helped Miss Manners to provide herself with a few small indulgences otherwise beyond her reach. She had one or two idiosyncrasies, as they are politely called, that were her delight. Plenty of dish-towels were necessary to her peace of mind; without five pair of scissors she could not be happy; and Tricopherous was essential to her well-being: indeed, she often said she would rather give up coffee than Tricopherous, for her hair was black and wiry and curly, and caps she abhorred; so that, of a winter's day, her head presented the most irrelevant and volatile aspect, each particular hair taking a twist on its own responsibility, and improvising a wild halo about her unsaintly face, unless subdued into propriety by the aforesaid fluid.

I said Miss Lucinda's face was unsaintly; I mean unlike ancient saints as depicted by contemporary artists: modern and private saints are after another fashion. I met one yesterday, whose green eyes, great nose, thick lips, and sallow-wrinkles, under a bonnet of fifteen years' standing, further clothed upon by a scant merino cloak and cat-skin tippet, would have cut a sorry figure in the gallery of the Vatican or the Louvre, and put the tranquil Madonna of San Sisto into a state of stunning antithesis. But if St. Agnes or St. Catharine was half as good as my saint, I am glad of it.

No, there was nothing sublime and dolorous about Miss Manners.

Her face was round, cheery, and slightly puckered, with two little black eyes sparkling and shining under dark brows, a nose she unblushingly called pug, and a big mouth, with eminently white and regular teeth, which she said were such a comfort, for they never ached, and never would to the end of time. Add to this physiognomy a small and rather spare figure, dressed in the cleanest of calicoes, always made in one style, and rigidly scorning hoops, without a symptom of a collar, in whose place (or it may be over which) she wore a white cambric handkerchief knotted about her throat, and the two ends brought into subjection by means of a little angular-headed gold pin, her sole ornament, and a relic of her old father's days of widowhood, when buttons were precarious tenures. So much for her aspect. Her character was even more quaint.

She was the daughter of a clergyman, one of the old school, the last whose breeches and knee-buckles adorned the profession, who never "outlived his usefulness," nor lost his godly simplicity. Parson Manners held rule over an obscure and quiet village in the wilds of Vermont, where hard-handed farmers wrestled with rocks and forests for their daily bread, and looked forward to heaven as a land of green pastures and still waters, where agriculture should be a pastime, and winter impossible. Heavy freshets from the mountains, that swelled their rushing brooks into annual torrents, and snow-drifts that covered five-rail fences a foot above the posts, and blocked up the turnpike-road for weeks, caused this congregation fully to appreciate Parson Manners's favorite hymns,—

"There is a land of pure delight,"

and

"On Jordan's stormy banks I stand."

Indeed, one irreverent but "pretty smart feller," who lived on the top of a hill known as Drift Hill, where certain adventurous farmers dwelt for the sake of its smooth sheep-pastures, was heard to say, after a mighty sermon by Parson Manners about the seventimes heated furnaces of judgment reserved for the wicked, that "parson hadn't better try to skeer Drift-Hillers with a hot place: 'twouldn't more'n jest warm 'em through down there, arter a real snappin' winter."

In this out-of-the-way nook was Lucinda Jane Ann born and bred. Her mother was like her in many things,—just such a cheery, round-faced little body, but with no more mind than found ample scope for itself in superintending the affairs of house and farm, and vigorously "seeing to" her husband and child. So, while Mrs. Manners baked, and washed and ironed, and sewed and knit, and set the sweetest example of quiet goodness and industry to all her flock, without knowing she *could* set an example, or be followed as one, the parson amused himself, between sermons of powerful doctrine and parochial duties of a more human interest, with educating Lucinda, whose intellect was more like his own than her mother's. A strange training it was for a young girl,—mathematics, metaphysics, Latin, theology of the dryest sort; and after an utter failure at Greek and Hebrew, though she had toiled patiently through seven books of the "Æneid," Parson Manners mildly sniffed at the inferiority of the female mind, and betook himself to teaching her French, which she learned rapidly, and spoke with a pure American accent, perhaps as pleasing to a Parisian ear as the hiss of Piedmont or the gutterals of Switzerland. Moreover, the minister had been brought up himself in the most scrupulous refinement of manner: his mother was a widow, the last of an "old family;" and her dainty, delicate observances were inbred, as it were, in her only son. This sort of elegance is perhaps the most delicate test of training and descent, and all these things Lucinda was taught from the grateful recollection of a son who never forgot his mother through all the solitary labors and studies of a long life. So it came to pass, that, after her mother died, Lucinda grew more and more like her father; and, as she became a woman, these rare refinements separated her more and more from those about her, and made her necessarily solitary. As for marriage, the possibility of such a thing never crossed her mind: there was not a man in the parish who did not offend her sense of propriety, and shock her taste, whenever she met one; and though her warm, kind heart made her a blessing to the poor and sick, her mother was yet bitterly regretted at quiltings and tea-drinkings, where she had been so "sociablelike."

It is rather unfortunate for such a position as Lucinda's, that, as deacon Stowell one day remarked to her father, "Natur' will be natur' as much on Drift Hill as down to Bosting;" and when she began to feel that "strong necessity of loving," that sooner or later assails every woman's heart, there was nothing for it to overflow on when her father had taken his share. Now, Lucinda loved the parson most devoutly. Ever since the time when she could just remember watching through the dusk his white stockings as they glimmered across the road to evening meeting, and looked like a supernatural pair of legs taking a walk on their own responsibility, twilight concealing the black breeches and coat from mortal view, Lucinda had regarded her father with a certain pleasing awe. His long abstractions, his profound knowledge, his grave, benign manners, and the thousand daily refinements of speech and act that seemed to put him far above the sphere of his pastorate,—all these things inspired as much reverence as affection; and when she wished with all her heart and soul she had a sister or a brother to tend and kiss and pet, it never once occurred to her that any of these tender familiarities could be expended on her father. She would as soon have thought of caressing any of the goodly angels, whose stout legs, flowing curls, and impossible draperies, sprawled among the pictures in the big Bible, and who excited her wonder as much by their garments as their turkey-wings and brandishing arms. So she betook herself to pets, and growing up to the old maiden-hood of thirty-five before her father fell asleep, was by that time the centre of a little world of her own,—hens, chickens, squirrels, cats, dogs, lambs, and sundry transient guests of stranger kind; so that when she left her old home, and removed to the little house in Dalton that had been left her by her mother's aunt, and had found her small property safely in-vested by means of an old friend of her father's, Miss Manners made one more journey to Vermont to bring in safety to their future dwelling a cat and three kittens, an old blind crow, a yellow dog of the true cur breed, and a rooster with three hens, "real creepers," as she often said, "none of your long-legged, screaming creatures."

Lucinda missed her father, and mourned him as constantly and faith-fully as ever a daughter could. But her temperament was more cheerful and buoyant than his; and when once she was quietly settled in her little house, her garden and her pets gave her such full occupation that she sometimes blamed herself for not feeling more lonely and unhappy. A little longer life, or a little more experience, would have taught her better: power to be happy is the last thing to regret. Besides, it would have been hard to be cheerless in that sunny little house, with its queer old furniture of three-legged tables, high-backed chairs, and chintz curtains, where red mandarins winked at blue pagodas on a deep yellow ground, and birds of insane ornithology pecked at insects that never could have been hatched, or perched themselves on blossoms totally unknown to any mortal flora. Old engravings of Bartolozzi, from the stiff elegances of Angelica Kauf-man and the mythologies of Reynolds, adorned the shelf; and the carpet in the parlor was of veritable English make, older than Lucinda herself, but as bright in its fading, and as firm in its usefulness, as she. Up stairs the tiny chambers were decked with spotless white dimity, and rush-bottomed chairs stood in each window, with a strip of the same old carpet by either bedside; and in the kitchen the blue settle that had stood by the Vermont fireside now defended this lesser hearth from the draught of the door, and held under the seat thereof sundry ironing-sheets, the blanket belonging to them, and good store of ticking and worsted holders. A half-gone set of egg-shell china stood in the parlor-closet,—cups and teapot rimmed with brown and gold in a square pattern, and a shield without blazon on the side; the quaint tea-caddy with its stopper stood over against the pursy little creampot; and the three-legged sugar-bowl held amid its lumps of sparkling sugar the oddest sugar tongs, also a family relic; beside this, six small spoons, three large ones, and a little silver porringer comprised all the "plate" belonging to Miss Manners, so that no fear of burglars haunted her, and, but for her pets, she would have led a life of profound and monotonous tranquillity. But this was a vast exception: in her life her pets were the great item now; her cat had its own chair in the parlor and kitchen; her dog, a rug and a basket never to be meddled with by man or beast; her old crow, its special nest of flannel and cotton, where it feebly croaked as soon as Miss Lucinda began to spread the little table for her meals; and the three kittens had their own play-things and their own saucer as punctiliously as if they had been children. In fact, Miss Manners had a greater share of kindness for beasts than for mankind. A strange compound of learning and unworldliness, of queer simplicity, native penetration, and common sense, she had read enough books to despise human nature as it develops itself in history and the-ology, and she had not known enough people to love it in its personal development. She had a general idea that all men were liars, and that she must be on her guard against their propensity to cheat and annoy a lonely and helpless woman; for, to tell the truth, in her good father's over-anxiety to defend her from the snares of evil men after his death, his teachings had given her opinion this bias, and he had forgotten to tell her how kindly and how true he had found many of his own parishioners, how few inclined to harm or pain him. So Miss Lucinda made her en-trance into life at Dalton, distrustful, but not suspicious; and, after a few attempts on the part of the women who were her neighbors to be friendly or intimate, they gave her up as impracticable: not because she was impo-lite or unkind; they did not themselves know why they failed, though she could have told them; for old maid as she was, poor and plain and queer, she could not bring herself to associate familiarly with people who put their teaspoons into the sugar-bowl, helped themselves with their own knives and forks, gathered up bits of uneaten butter and returned them to the plate for next time, or replaced on the dish pieces of cake half eaten, or cut with the knives they had just introduced into their mouths. Miss Lucinda's code of minor morals would have forbidden her to drink from the same cup with a queen, and have considered a pitchfork as suitable as a knife to eat with; nor would she have offered to a servant the least thing she had touched with her own lips or her own implements of eating; and she was too delicately bred to look on in comfort where such things were practised. Of course these women were not ladies; and, though many of them had kind hearts and warm impulses of goodness, yet that did not make up to her for their social misdemeanors; and she drew herself more into her own little shell, and cared more for her garden and her chickens, her cats and her dog, than for all the humanity of Dalton put together.

Miss Manners held her flowers next dearest to her pets, and treated them accordingly. Her garden was the most brilliant bit of ground possi-ble. It was big enough to hold one flourishing peach-tree, one Siberian crab, and a solitary egg-plum; while under these fruitful boughs bloomed moss-roses in profusion, of the dear old-fashioned kind, every deep pink bud, with its clinging garment of green, breathing out the richest odor. Close by, the real white rose, which fashion has banished to country towns, unfolded its cups of pearl, flushed with yellow sunrise, to the heart; and by its side its damask sister waved long sprays of bloom and perfume. Tulips, dark-purple and cream-color, burning scarlet and deep maroon, held their gay chalices up to catch the dew; hyacinths, blue, white, and pink, hung heavy bells beneath them; spiced carnations of rose and garnet crowded their bed in July and August; heart's-ease fringed the walks; May honeysuckles clambered over the board-fence; and monthly honeysuckles overgrew the porch at the back-door, making perpetual fragrance from their moth-like horns of crimson and ivory. Nothing inhabited those beds that was not sweet and fair and old-fashioned. Gray-lavender-bushes sent up purple spikes in the middle of the garden, and were duly housed in winter; but these were the sole tender plants admitted, and they pleaded their own cause in the breath of the linen-press and the bureau-drawers that held Miss Lucinda's clothes. Beyond the flowers, utility blossomed in a row of beanpoles, a hedge of currant-bushes against the farther fence, carefully tended cauliflowers, and onions enough to tell of their use as sparing as their number. A few deep-red beets and golden carrots were all the vegetables beside. Miss Lucinda never ate potatoes or pork.

Her housekeeping, but for her pets, would have been the proper housewifery for a fairy. Out of her fruit she annually conserved miracles of flavor and transparence,—great plums like those in Aladdin's garden, of shining topaz; peaches tinged with the odorous bitter of their pits, and clear as amber; crimson crabs floating in their own ruby sirup, or transmuted into jelly crystal clear, yet breaking with a grain; and jelly from the acid currants to garnish her dinnertable, or refresh the fevered lips of a sick neighbor. It was a study to visit her tiny pantry, where all these "lucent sirops" stood in tempting array, where spices and sugar and tea in their small jars flanked the sweetmeats, and a jar of glass showed its store of whitest honey, and another stood filled with crisp cakes. Here always a loaf or two of home-made bread lay rolled in a snowy cloth, and another was spread over a dish of butter. Pies were not in favor here, nor milk,—save for the cats. Salt fish Miss Manners never could abide: her savory taste allowed only a bit of rich old cheese, or thin scraps of hung beef, with her bread and butter. Sauces and spices were few in her repertory; but she cooked as only a lady can cook, and might have asked Sóyer himself to dinner. For verily, after much meditation and experience, I have divined that it takes as much sense and refinement and talent to cook a dinner, wash and wipe a dish, make a bed as it should be made, and dust a room as it should be dusted, as goes to the writing of a novel, or shining in high society.

But because Miss Lucinda Manners was reserved and "unsociable," as the neighbors pronounced her, I did not, therefore, mean to imply that she was inhuman. No neighbor of hers, local or scriptural, fell ill, without an immediate offer of aid from her. She made the best gruel known to Dalton invalids, sent the ripest fruit and the sweetest flowers; and if she could not watch with the sick because it interfered with her duties at home in an unpleasant and inconvenient way, she would sit with them hour after hour in the day-time, and wait on all their caprices with the patient tenderness of a mother. Children she always eyed with strange wistfulness, as if she longed to kiss them, but didn't know how; yet no child was ever invited across her threshold, for the yellow cur hated to be played with, and children always torment kittens.

So Miss Lucinda wore on happily toward the farther side of the middle ages. One after another of her pets passed away, and was replaced; the yellow cur barked his last currish signal; the cat died, and her kittens came to various ends of time or casualty; the crow fell away to dust, and was too old to stuff; and the garden bloomed and faded ten times over, before Miss Manners found herself to be forty-six years old, which she heroically acknowledged one fine day to the census-taker. But it was not this consciousness, nor its confession, that drew the dark brows so low over Miss Lucinda's eyes that day: it was quite another trouble, and one that wore heavily on her mind, as we shall proceed to explain. For Miss Manners, being, like all the rest of her sex, quite unable to do without some masculine help, had employed for some seven years an old man by the name of Israel Slater to do her "chores," as the vernacular hath it. It is a mortifying thing, and one that strikes at the roots of women's rights terribly sharp blows, but I must even own it, that one might as well try to live without one's bread and butter as without the aid of the dominant sex. When I see women split wood, unload coal-carts, move wash-tubs, and roll barrels of flour and apples handily down cellar-ways or up into carts, then I shall believe in the sublime theories of the strong-minded sisters; but as long as I see before me my own forlorn little hands, and sit down on the top stair to recover breath, and try in vain to lift the water-pitcher at table, just so long I shall be glad and thankful that there are men in the world, and that half a dozen of them are my kindest and best friends. It was rather an affliction to Miss Lucinda to feel this innate dependence; and at first she resolved to employ only small boys, and never any one of them more than a week or two. She had an unshaped theory that an old maid was a match for a small boy, but that a man would cheat and domineer over her. Experience sadly put to flight these notions; for a succession of boys in this cabinet ministry for the first three years of her stay in Dalton would have driven her into a Presbyterian convent, had there been one at hand. Boy Number One caught the yellow cur out of bounds one day, and shaved his plumy tail to a bare stick, and Miss Lucinda fairly shed tears of grief and rage when Pink appeared at the door with the denuded appendage tucked between his little legs, and his funny yellow eyes casting sidelong looks of apprehension at his mistress. Boy Number One was despatched directly. Number Two did pretty well for a month; but his integrity and his appetite conflicted, and Miss Lucinda found him one moonlight night perched in her plum-tree devouring the half-ripe fruit. She shook him down with as little ceremony as if he had been an apple; and, though he lay at death's door for a week with result-ing choleramorbus, she relented not. So the experiment went on, till a list of casualties that numbered in it fatal accidents to three kittens, two hens, and a rooster, and at last Pink himself, who was sent into a decline by repeated drenchings from the watering-pot, put an end to her forbear-ance, and she instituted in her viziership the old man who had now kept his office so long,—a queer, withered, slow, humorous old creature, who did "chores" for some six or seven other households, and got a living by sundry "jobs" of wood-sawing, hoeing corn, and other like works of labor, if not of skill. Israel was a great comfort to Miss Lucinda: he was efficient counsel in the maladies of all her pets, had a soverign cure for the gapes in chickens, and could stop a cat's fit with the greatest ease; he kept the tiny garden in perfect order, and was very honest, and Miss Manners favored him accordingly. She compounded liniment for his rheumatism, herb-sirup for his colds, presented him with a set of flannel shirts, and knit him a comforter; so that Israel expressed himself strongly in favor of "Miss Lucindy," and she said to herself he really was "quite good for a man."

But just now, in her forty-seventh year, Miss Lucinda had come to grief, and all on account of Israel, and his attempts to please her. About six months before this census-taking era, the old man had stepped into Miss Manners's kitchen with an unusual radiance on his wrinkles and in his eyes, and began, without his usual morning greeting,—

"I've got so'thin' for you naow, Miss Lucindy. You're a master-hand for pets; but I'll bet a red cent you ha'n't an idee what I've got for ye naow!"

"I'm sure I can't tell, Israel," said she: "you'll have to let me see it."

"Well," said he, lifting up his coat, and looking carefully behind him as he sat down on the settle, lest a stray kitten or chicken should pre-occupy the bench, "you see I was down to Orrin's abaout a week back, and he hed a litter o' pigs,—eleven on 'em. Well, he couldn't raise the hull on 'em,—'t a'n't good to raise more'n nine,—an' so he said ef I'd 'a' had a place o' my own, I could 'a' had one on 'em; but as 'twas he guessed he'd hev to send one to market for a roaster. I went daown to the barn to see 'em; an' there was one, the cutest little critter I ever sot eyes on,—an' I've seen more'n four pigs in my day,—'twas a little black-spotted one, as spry as an ant, and the dreffullest knowin' look out of its eyes. I fellowshipped it right off; and I said, says I, 'Orrin, ef you'll let me hev that 'ere little spotted feller, I'll git a place for him, for I do take to him consarnedly.' So he said I could, and I fetched him hum; and Miss Slater and me we kinder fed him up for a few days back, till he got sorter wonted, and I'm a-goin' to fetch him to you."

"But, Israel, I haven't any place to put him in."

"Well, that a'n't nothin' to hender. I'll jest fetch out them old boards out of the wood-shed, and knock up a little sty right off, daown by the end o' the shed, and you ken keep your swill that I've hed before, and it'll come handy."

"But pigs are so dirty!"

"I don't know as they be. They ha'n't no great conveniences for washin' ginerally; but I never heerd as they was dirtier'n other critters where they run wild. An' beside, that a'n't goin' to hender, nuther. I calculate to make it one o' the chores to take keer of him; 't won't cost no more to you, and I ha'n't no great opportunities to do things for folks that's allers a-doin' for me: so 't you needn't be afeard, Miss Lucindy: I love to."

Miss Lucinda's heart got the better of her judgment. A nature that could feel so tenderly for its inferiors in the scale could not be deaf to the tiny voices of humanity when they reached her solitude; and she thanked Israel for the pig so heartily, that the old man's face brightened still more, and his voice softened from its cracked harshness, as he said, clicking up and down the latch of the back-door,—

"Well, I'm sure you're as welcome as you are obleeged, and I'll knock up that 'ere pen right off. He sha'n't pester ye any, that's a fact."

Strange to say, yet perhaps it might have been expected from her proclivities, Miss Lucinda took an astonishing fancy to the pig. Very few people know how intelligent an animal a pig is; but, when one is regarded merely as pork and hams, one's intellect is apt to fall into neglect,—a moral sentiment which applies out of pigdom. This creature would not have passed muster at a county fair; no Suffolk blood compacted and rounded him: he belonged to the "racers," and skipped about his pen with the alacrity of a large flea, wiggling his curly tail as expressively as a dog's, and "all but speakin'," as Israel said. He was always glad to see Miss Lucinda, and established a firm friendship with her dog Fun,—a pretty, sentimental German spaniel. Besides, he kept tolerably clean by dint of Israel's care, and thrust his long nose between the rails of his pen for grass or fruit, or carrot and beet tops, with a knowing look out of his deep-set eyes, that was never to be resisted by the soft-hearted spinster. Indeed, Miss Lucinda enjoyed the possession of one pet who could not tyrannize over her. Pink's place was more than filled by Fun, who was so oppressively affectionate, that he never could leave his mistress alone. If she lay down on her bed, he leaped up and unlatched the door, and stretched himself on the white counterpane beside her with a grunt of satisfaction; if she sat down to knit or sew, he laid his head and shoulders across her lap, or curled himself up on her knees; if she was cooking, he whined and coaxed round her till she hardly knew whether she fried or broiled her steak; and if she turned him out, and buttoned the door, his cries were so pitiful, she could never be resolute enough to keep him in exile five minutes for it was a prominent article in her creed that animals have feelings that are easily wounded, and are of "like passions" with men, only incapable of expression. Indeed, Miss Lucinda considered it the duty of human beings to atone to animals for the Lord's injustice in making them dumb and four-legged. She would have been rather startled at such an enunciation of her practice, but she was devoted to it as a practice. She would give her own chair to the cat, and sit on the settle herself; get up at midnight if a mew or a bark called her, though the thermometer was below zero; the tenderloin of her steak, or the liver of her chicken, was saved for a pining kitten or an ancient and toothless cat; and no disease or wound daunted her faithful nursing, or disgusted her devoted tenderness. It was rather hard on humanity, and rather reversive of Providence, that all this care and pains should be lavished on cats and dogs, while little morsels of flesh and blood, ragged, hungry, and immortal, wandered up and down the streets. Perhaps that they were immortal was their defense from Miss Lucinda. One might have hoped that her "other-worldliness" accepted that fact as enough to outweigh present pangs, if she had not openly declared, to Israel Slater's immense amusement and astonishment, that *she* believed creatures had souls,—little ones perhaps, but souls, after all, and she did expect to see Pink again some time or other.

"Well, I hope he's got his tail feathered out ag'in," said Israel dryly. "I do'no' but what hair'd grow as well as feathers in a speretooal state, and I never see a picture of an angel but what hed consider'ble many feathers."

Miss Lucinda looked rather confounded. But humanity had one little revenge on her in the shape of her cat,—a beautiful Maltese with great yellow eyes, fur as soft as velvet, and silvery paws as lovely to look at as they were thistly to touch. Toby certainly pleaded hard for Miss Lucinda's theory of a soul: but his was no good one; some tricksy and malign little spirit had lent him his share of intellect, and he used it to the entire subjugation of Miss Lucinda. When he was hungry, he was as well-mannered and as amiable as a good child; he would coax and purr, and lick her fingers with his pretty red tongue, like a "perfect love:" but when he had his fill, and needed no more, then came Miss Lucinda's time of torment. If she attempted to caress him, he bit and scratched like a young tiger: he sprang at her from the floor, and fastened on her arm with real fury. If he cried at the window and was not directly let in, as soon as he had achieved entrance his first manœuvre was to dash at her ankles, and bite them if he could, as punishment for her tardiness. This skirmishing was his favorite mode of attack. If he was turned out of the closet, or off the pillow up stairs, he retreated under the bed, and made frantic sallies at her feet, till the poor woman got actually nervous, and if he was in the room made a flying leap as far as she could to her bed, to escape those keen claws. Indeed, old Israel found her more than once sitting in the middle of the kitchen-floor, with Toby crouched for a spring, under the table, his poor mistress afraid to move for fear of her unlucky ankles. And this literally cat-ridden woman was hazed about and ruled over by her feline tyrant to that extent that he occupied the easiest chair, the softest cushion, the middle of the bed, and the front of the fire, not only undisturbed, but caressed. This is a veritable history, beloved reader, and I offer it as a warning and an example. If you will be an old maid, or if you can't help it, take to petting children, or donkeys, or even a respectable cow, but beware of domestic tyranny in any shape but man's.

No wonder Miss Lucinda took kindly to the pig, who had a house of his own, and a servant as it were, to the avoidance of all trouble on her part,—the pig who capered for joy when she or Fun approached, and had so much expression in his physiognomy that one almost expected to see him smile. Many a sympathizing conference Miss Lucinda held with Israel over the perfections of piggy, as he leaned against the sty, and looked over at his favorite after this last chore was accomplished.

"I say for 't," exclaimed the old man one day, "I b'lieve that cre'tur' knows enough to be professor in a college. Why, he talks! he re'lly doos; a leetle through his nose, maybe, but no more'n Dr. Colton allers does,— 'n' I declare he appears to have abaout as much sense. I never see the equal of him. I thought he'd 'a' larfed right out yesterday when I gin him that mess o' corn. He got up onto his forelegs on the trough, an' he winked them knowin' eyes o' his'n, an' waggled his tail, an' then he set off an' capered round till he come bunt up ag'inst the boards. I tell *you*, that sorter sobered him. He gin a growlin' grunt, an' shook his ears, an' looked sideways at me; and then he put to and eet up that corn as sober as a judge. I swan! he doos beat the Dutch!"

But there was one calculation forgotten, both by Miss Lucinda and Israel: the pig would grow, and in consequence, as I said before, Miss Lucinda came to grief; for, when the census-taker tinkled her sharp little door-bell, it called her from a laborious occupation at the sty,—no more and no less than trying to nail up a board that piggy had torn down in struggling to get out of his durance. He had grown so large, that Miss Lucinda was afraid of him; his long legs and their vivacious motion added to the shrewd intelligence of his eyes; and his nose seemed as formidable to this poor little woman as the tusk of a rhinoceros: but what should she do with him? One might as well have proposed to her to kill and cut up Israel as to consign piggy to the "fate of race." She could not turn him into the street to starve, for she loved him; and the old maid suffered from a constancy that might have made some good man happy, but only emharrassed her with the pig. She could not keep him forever, that was evident. She knew enough to be aware that time would increase his disabilities as a pet; and he was an expensive one now, for the corn-swallowing capacities of a pig, one of the "racer" breed, are almost incredible, and nothing about Miss Lucinda wanted for food, even to fatness. Besides, he was getting too big for his pen; and so "cute" an animal could not be debarred from all out-door pleasures, and tantalized by the sight of a green and growing garden before his eyes continually, without making an effort to partake of its delights. So, when Miss Lucinda endued herself with her brown linen sack and sun-bonnet to go and weed her carrot-patch, she was arrested on the way by a loud grunting and scrambling in piggy's quarter, and found, to her distress, that he had contrived to knock off the upper board from his pen. She had no hammer at hand: so she seized a large stone that lay near by, and pounded at the board till the twice-tinkling bell recalled her to the house; and, as soon as she had made confession to the census-taker, she went back—alas, too late! Piggy had redoubled his efforts, another board had yielded, and he was free. What a thing freedom is!—how objectionable in practice! how splendid in theory! More people than Miss Lucinda have been put to their wits' end when "hoggie" burst his bonds, and became rampant instead of couchant. But he enjoyed it. He made the tour of the garden on a delightful canter, brandishing his tail with an air of defiance that daunted his mistress at once, and regarding her with his small bright eyes as if he would before long taste her, and see if she was as crisp as she looked. She retreated forthwith to the shed, and caught up a broom, with which she courageously charged upon piggy, and was routed entirely; for, being no way alarmed by her demonstration, the creature capered directly at her, knocked her down, knocked the broom out of her hand, and capered away again to the young carrot-patch.

"Oh, dear!" said Miss Manners, gathering herself up from the ground, "if there only was a man here!"

Suddenly she betook herself to her heels; for the animal looked at her, and stopped eating: that was enough to drive Miss Lucinda off the field. And now, quite desperate, she rushed through the house, and out of the front-door, actually in search of a man. Just down the street she saw one. Had she been composed, she might have noticed the threadbare cleanliness of his dress, the odd cap that crowned his iron-gray locks, and the peculiar manner of his walk; for our little old maid had stumbled upon no less a person than Monsieur Jean Leclerc, the dancing-master of Dalton. Not that this accomplishment was much in vogue in the embryo city; but still there were a few who liked to fit themselves for firemen's balls and sleighing-party frolics, and quite a large class of children were learning betimes such graces as children in New England receive more easily than their elders. Monsieur Leclerc had just enough scholars to keep his coat threadbare, and restrict him to necessities; but he lived, and was independent. All this Miss Lucinda was ignorant of: she only saw a man; and, with the instinct of the sex in trouble or danger, she appealed to him at once.

"O sir! won't you step in and help me? My pig has got out, and I can't catch him, and he is ruining my garden!"

"Madame, I shall!" replied the Frenchman, bowing low, and assuming the first position.

So Monsieur Leclerc followed Miss Manners, and supplied himself

with a mop that was hanging in the shed as his best weapon. Dire was the
battle between the pig and the Frenchman. They skipped past each other
and back again as if they were practising for a cotillon. Piggy had four
legs, which gave him a certain advantage; but the Frenchman had most
brain, and in the long-run brain gets the better of legs. A weary dance
they led each other; but after a while the pet was hemmed in a corner, and
Miss Lucinda had run for a rope to tie him, when, just as she returned,
the beast made a desperate charge, upset his opponent, and giving a leap
in the wrong direction, to his manifest astonishment landed in his own
sty. Miss Lucinda's courage rose: she forgot her prostrate friend in need,
and, running to the pen, caught up hammer and nail-box on her way, and
with unusual energy nailed up the bars stronger than ever, and then
bethought herself to thank the stranger. But there he lay quite still and
pale.

"Dear me!" said Miss Manners. "I hope you haven't hurt yourself,
sir."

"I have fear that I am hurt, madame," said he, trying to smile. "I
cannot to move but it pains me."

"Where is it? Is it your leg, or your arm? Try and move one at a time,"
said Miss Lucinda promptly.

The left leg was helpless, it could not answer to the effort; and the
stranger lay back on the ground, pale with the pain. Miss Lucinda took
her lavender-bottle out of her pocket, and softly bathed his head and face;
then she took off her sack, and folded it up under his head, and put the
lavender beside him. She was good at an emergency, and she showed it.

"You must lie quite still," said she. "You must not try to move till I
come back with help, or your leg will be hurt more."

With that she went away, and presently returned with two strong men
and the long shutter of a shopwindow. To this extempore litter she carefully moved the Frenchman; and then her neighbors lifted him, and carried him into the parlor, where Miss Lucinda's chintz lounge was already
spread with a tight-pinned sheet to receive the poor man; and, while her
helpers put him to bed, she put on her bonnet, and ran for the doctor.

Dr. Colton did his best for his patient, but pronounced it an impossi-
bility to remove him till the bone should be joined firmly, as a thorough
cure was all-essential to his professional prospects. And now, indeed,
Miss Lucinda had her hands full. A nurse could not be afforded; but
Monsieur Leclerc was added to the list of old Israel's "chores," and what
other nursing he needed Miss Lucinda was glad to do; for her kind heart
was full of self-reproaches to think it was her pig that had knocked down
the poor man, and her mop-handle that had twisted itself across and
under his leg, and aided, if not caused, its breakage. So Israel came in four
or five times a day to do what he could, and Miss Lucinda played nurse at
other times to the best of her ability. Such flavorous gruels and porridges
as she concocted! such *tisanes* after her guest's instructions! such dainty

soups and sweetbreads and cutlets, served with such neatness! After his experience of a second-rate boarding-house, Monsieur Leclerc thought himself in a gastronomic paradise. Moreover, these tiny meals were garnished with flowers, which his French taste for color and decoration appreciated,—two or three stems of lilies-of-the-valley in their folded green leaves, cool and fragrant; a moss-rosebud and a spire of purple-gray lavender bound together with ribbon-grass; or three carnations set in glittering myrtle-sprays, the last acquisition of the garden.

Miss Lucinda enjoyed nursing thoroughly, and a kindlier patient no woman ever had. Her bright needle flew faster than ever through the cold linen and flaccid cambric of the shirts and cravats she fashioned, while he told her, in his odd idioms, stories of his life in France, and the curious customs, both of society and *cuisinerie,* with which last he showed a surprising acquaintance. Truth to tell, when Monsieur Leclerc said he had been a member of the Duc de Montmorenci's household, he withheld the other half of this truth,—that he had been his *valet-de-chambre;* but it was an hereditary service, and seemed to him as different a thing from common servitude as a peer's office in the bed chamber differs from a lackey's. Indeed, Monsieur Leclerc was a gentleman in his own way, not of blood, but of breeding; and while he had faithfully served the "aristocrats," as his father had done before him, he did not limit that service to their prosperity, but in their greatest need descended to menial offices, and forgot that he could dance and ride and fence almost as well as his young master. But a bullet from a barricade put an end to his duty there; and he hated utterly the democratic rule that had overturned for him both past and future: so he escaped, and came to America, the grand resort of refugees, where he had labored, as he best knew how, for his own support, and kept to himself his disgust at the manners and customs of the barbarians. Now, for the first time, he was at home and happy. Miss Lucinda's delicate fashions suited him exactly. He adored her taste for the beautiful, which she was unconscious of. He enjoyed her cookery; and though he groaned within himself at the amount of debt he was incurring, yet he took courage from her kindness, to believe she would not be a hard creditor, and, being naturally cheerful, put aside his anxieties, and amused himself, as well as her, with his stories, his quavering songs, his recipes for *pot-au-feu, tisane,* and *pâtés,* at once economical and savory. Never had a leg of lamb or a piece of roast beef gone so far in her domestic experience. A chicken seemed almost to outlive its usefulness in its various forms of re-appearance; and the salads he devised were as wonderful as the omelets he superintended, or the gay dances he played on his beloved violin, as soon as he could sit up enough to manage it. Moreover,—I should say *mostover,* if the word were admissible,— Monsieur Leclerc lifted a great weight before long from Miss Lucinda's mind. He began by subduing Fun to his proper place by a mild determination that completely won the dog's heart. "Women and spaniels," the world knows, "like kicking;" and, though kicks were no part of the good man's Rareyfaction of Fun, he certainly used a certain amount of coercion, and the dog's lawful owner admired the skill of the teacher, and enjoyed the better manners of the pupil thoroughly. She could do twice as much sewing now, and never were her nights disturbed by a bark; for the dog crouched by his new friend's bed in the parlor, and lay quiet there. Toby was next undertaken, and proved less amenable to discipline. He stood in some slight awe of the man who tried to teach him, but still continued to sally out at Miss Lucinda's feet, to spring at her caressing hand when he felt ill-humored, and to claw Fun's patient nose and his approaching paws, when his misplaced sentimentality led him to caress the cat. But, after a while, a few well-timed slaps, administered with vigor, cured Toby of his worst tricks: though every blow made Miss Lucinda wince, and almost shook her good opinion of Monsieur Leclerc; for in those long weeks he had wrought out a good opinion of himself in her mind, much to her own surprise. She could not have believed a man could be so polite, so gentle, so patient, and, above all, so capable of ruling without tyranny. Miss Lucinda was puzzled.

One day, as Monsieur Leclerc was getting better, just able to go about on crutches, Israel came into the kitchen, and Miss Manners went out to see him. She left the door open; and along with the odor of a pot of raspberry-jam scalding over the fire, sending its steams of leaf-and-insect fragrance through the little house, there came in also the following conversation.

"Israel," said Miss Lucinda, in a hesitating and rather forlorn tone, "I have been thinking,—I don't know what to do with Piggy. He is quite too big for me to keep. I'm afraid of him, if he gets out; and he eats up the garden."

"Well, that *is* a consider'ble swaller for a pig, Miss Lucindy; but I b'lieve you're abaout right abaout keepin' on him. He *is* too big, that's a fact; but he's so like a human cre'tur', I'd jest abaout as lieves slarter Orrin. I declare, I don't know no more'n a taown-house goose what to do with him!"

"If I gave him away, I suppose he would be fatted and killed, of course?"

"I guess he'd be killed, likely; but, as for fattenin' on him, I'd jest as soon undertake to fatten a salt codfish. He's one o' the racers, an' they're as holler as hogsheads. You can fill 'em up to their noses, ef you're a mind to spend your corn, and they'll caper it all off their bones in twenty-four haours. I b'lieve, ef they was tied neck an' heels, an' stuffed, they'd wiggle thin betwixt feedin-times. Why, Orrin, he raised nine on 'em, and every darned critter's as poor as Job's turkey to'day. They a'n't no good. I'd as lieves ha' had nine chestnut-rails, an' a little lieveser'; cause they don't eat nothin'."

"You don't know of any poor person who'd like to have a pig, do you?" said Miss Lucinda wistfully.

"Well, the poorer they was, the quicker they'd eat him up, I guess,—ef they could eat such a razorback."

"Oh, I don't like to think of his being eaten! I wish he could be got rid of some other way. Don't you think he might be killed in his sleep, Israel?"

This was a little too much for Israel. An irresistible flicker of laughter twitched his wrinkles, and bubbled in his throat.

"I think it's likely 'twould wake him up," said he demurely. "Killin's killin', and a cre'tur' can't sleep over its though 'twas the stomach-ache. I guess he'd kick some, ef he *was* asleep—and screech some too!"

"Dear me!" said Miss Lucinda, horrified at the idea. "I wish he could be sent out to run in the woods. Are there any good woods near here, Israel?"

"I don't know but what he'd as lieves be slartered to once as to starve, an' be hunted down out in the lots. Besides, there a'n't nobody as I knows of would like a hog to be a-rootin' round amongst their turnips and young wheat."

"Well, what I shall do with him I don't know!" despairingly exclaimed Miss Lucinda. "He was such a dear little thing when you brought him, Israel! Do you remember how pink his pretty little nose was,—just like a rose-bud,—and how bright his eyes looked, and his cunning legs? And now he's grown so big and fierce! But I can't help liking him, either."

"He's a cute critter, that's sartain; but he does too much rootin' to have a pink nose now, I expect: there's consider'ble on't, so I guess it looks as well to have it gray. But I don't know no more'n you do what to do abaout it."

"If I could only get rid of him without knowing what became of him!" exclaimed Miss Lucinda, squeezing her forefinger with great earnestness, and looking both puzzled and pained.

"If Mees Lucinda would pairmit?" said a voice behind her.

She turned round to see Monsieur Leclerc on his crutches, just in the parlor-door.

"I shall, mees, myself dispose of piggee, if it please. I can. I shall have no sound: he shall to go away like a silent snow, to trouble you no more, never!"

"O sir, if you could! But I don't see how."

"If mees was to see, it would not be to save her pain. I shall have him to go by *magique* to fiery land."

Fairy-land probably. But Miss Lucinda did not perceive the *équivoque*.

"Nor yet shall I trouble Meester Israyel. I shall have the aid of myself and one good friend that I have; and some night, when you rise of the morning, he shall not be there."

Miss Lucinda breathed a deep sigh of relief.

"I am greatly obliged,—I shall be, I mean," said she.

"Well, I'm glad enough to wash my hands on't," said Israel. "I shall hanker arter the critter some, but he's a-gettin' too big to be handy; 'n' it's one comfort abaout critters, you ken get rid on 'em somehaow when they're more plague than profit. But folks has got to be let alone, excep' the Lord takes 'em; an' he don't allers see fit."

What added point and weight to these final remarks of old Israel was the well-known fact that he suffered at home from the most pecking and worrying of wives, and had been heard to say, in some moment of unusual frankness, that he "didn't see how 't could be sinful to wish Miss Slater was in heaven, for she'd be lots better off, and other folks too."

Miss Lucinda never knew what befell her pig one fine September night: she did not even guess that a visit paid to monsieur by one of his pupils, a farmer's daughter just out of Dalton, had any thing to do with this *enlèvement.* She was sound asleep in her bed up stairs, when her guest shod his crutches with old gloves, and limped out to the garden-gate by dawn, where he and the farmer tolled the animal out of his sty, and far down the street, by tempting red apples, and then Farmer Steele took possession of him, and he was seen no more. No, the first thing Miss Lucinda knew of her riddance was when Israel put his head into the back-door that same morning, some four hours afterward, and said with a significant nod,—

"He's gone!"

After all his other chores were done, Israel had a conference with Monsieur Leclerc; and the two sallied into the garden, and in an hour had dismantled the low dwelling, cleared away the wreck, levelled and smoothed its site, and monsieur, having previously provided himself with an Isabella grape-vine, planted it on this forsaken spot, and trained it carefully against the end of the shed: strange to say, though it was against all precedent to transplant a grape in September, it lived and flourished. Miss Lucinda's gratitude to Monsieur Leclerc was altogether disproportioned as he thought, to his slight service. He could not understand fully her devotion to her pets; but he respected it, and aided it whenever he could, though he never surmised the motive that adorned Miss Lucinda's table with such delicate superabundance after the late departure, and laid bundles of lavender-flowers in his tiny portmanteau till the very leather seemed to gather fragrance.

Before long Monsieur Leclerc was well enough to resume his classes, and return to his boarding-house; but the latter was filled, and only offered a prospect of vacancy in some three weeks after his application: so he returned home somewhat dejected; and as he sat by the little parlor-fire after tea, he said to his hostess in a reluctant tone,—

"Mees Lucinda, you have been of the kindest to the poor alien. I have it in my mind to relieve you of this care very rapidly, but it is not in the Fates that I do. I have gone to my house of lodgings, and they cannot to give me a chamber as yet. I have fear that I must yet rely me on your goodness for some time more, if you can to entertain me so much more of time?"

"Why, I shall like to, sir," replied the kindly, simple-hearted old maid. "I'm sure you are not a mite of trouble, and I never can forget what you did for my pig."

A smile flitted across the Frenchman's thin dark face, and he watched her glittering needles a few minutes in silence before he spoke again.

"But I have other things to say of the most unpleasant to me, Mees Lucinda. I have a great debt for the goodness and care you to me have lavished. To the angels of the good God we must submit to be debtors; but there are also of mortal obligations. I have lodged in your mansion for more of ten weeks, and to you I pay yet no silver; but it is that I have it not at present. I must ask of your goodness to wait."

The old maid's shining black eyes grew soft as she looked at him.

"Why," said she, "I don't think you owe me much of any thing, Mr. Leclerc. I never knew things last as they have since you came. I really think you brought a blessing. I wish you would please to think you don't owe me any thing."

The Frenchman's great brown eyes shone with suspicious dew.

"I cannot to forget that I owe to you far more than any silver of man repays; but I should not think to forget that I also owe to you silver, or I should not be worthy of a man's name. No, mees! I have two hands and legs. I will not let a woman most solitary spend for me her good self."

"Well," said Miss Lucinda, "if you will be uneasy till you pay me, I would rather have another kind of pay than money. I should like to know how to dance. I never did learn when I was a girl, and I think it would be good exercise."

Miss Lucinda supported this pious fiction through with a simplicity that quite deceived the Frenchman. He did not think it so incongruous as it was. He had seen women of sixty, rouged and jewelled and furbelowed, foot it deftly in the halls of the Faubourg St. Germain in his earliest youth; and this cheery, healthy woman, with lingering blooms on either cheek, and uncapped head of curly black hair but slightly strewn with silver, seemed quite as fit a subject for the accomplishment. Besides, he was poor; and this offered so easy a way of paying the debt he had so dreaded! Well said Solomon, "The destruction of the poor is their poverty." For whose moral sense, delicate sensitiveness, generous longings, will not sometimes give way to the stringent need of food and clothing, the gall of indebtedness, and the sinking consciousness of an empty purse and threatening possibilities?

Monsieur Leclerc's face brightened.

"Ah, with what grand pleasure shall I teach you the dance!"

But it fell dark again as he proceeded,—

"Though not one, nor two, nor three, nor four quarters shall be of value sufficient to achieve my payment."

"Then, if that troubles you, why, I should like to take some French lessons in the evening, when you don't have classes. I learned French when I was quite a girl, but not to speak it very easily; and if I could get some practice, and the right way to speak, I should be glad."

"And I shall give you the real *Parisien* tone, Mees Lucinda," said he proudly. "I shall be as if it were no more an exile when I repeat my tongue to you."

And so it was settled. Why Miss Lucinda should learn French any more than dancing was not a question in Monsieur Leclerc's mind. It is true that Chaldaic would, in all probability, be as useful to our friend as French; and the flying over poles, and hanging by toes and fingers, so eloquently described by apostles of the body, would have been as well adapted to her style and capacity as dancing. But his own language, and his own profession!—what man would not have regarded these as indispensable to improvement, particularly when they paid his board?

During the latter three weeks of Monsieur Leclerc's stay with Miss Lucinda, he made himself surprisingly useful. He listed the doors against approaching winter breezes; he weeded in the garden, trimmed, tied, trained, wherever either good office was needed, mended china with an infallible cement, and rickety chairs with the skill of a cabinet-maker; and, whatever hard or dirty work he did, he always presented himself at table in a state of scrupulous neatness. His long brown hands showed no trace of labor; his iron-gray hair was reduced to smoothest order; his coat speckless, if threadbare; and he ate like a gentleman,—an accomplishment not always to be found in the "best society," as the phrase goes: whether the best in fact ever lacks it is another thing. Miss Lucinda appreciated these traits; they set her at ease; and a pleasanter home-life could scarce be painted than now enlivened the little wooden house. But three weeks pass away rapidly; and when the rusty portmanteau was gone from her spare chamber, and the well-worn boots from the kitchen-corner, and the hat from its nail, Miss Lucinda began to find herself wonderfully lonely. She missed the armfuls of wood in her wood-box that she had to fill laboriously, two sticks at a time; she missed the other plate at her tiny round table, the other chair beside her fire; she missed that dark, thin, sensitive face, with its rare and sweet smile; she wanted her story-teller, her yarn-winder, her protector, back again. Good gracious! to think of an old lady of forty-seven entertaining such sentiments for a man.

Presently the dancing-lessons commenced. It was thought advisable that Miss Manners should enter a class, and in the fervency of her good intentions she did not demur. But gratitude and respect had to strangle with persistent hands the little serpents of the ridiculous in Monsieur Leclerc's soul when he beheld his pupil's first appearance. What reason was it, O rose of seventeen! adorning thyself with cloudy films of lace and sparks of jewelry before the mirror that reflects youth and beauty, that made Miss Lucinda array herself in a brand-new dress of yellow muslin-de laine strewed with round green spots, and displace her customary handkerchief for a huge tamboured collar, on this eventful occasion? Why, oh, why! did she tie up the roots of her black hair with an uncon-cealable scarlet string? And, most of all, why was her dress so short, her slipper-strings so big and broad, her thick slippers so shapeless, by reason of the corns and bunions that pertained to the feet within? The "instan-taneous rush of several guardian angels" that once stood dear old Hep-zibah Pynchon in good stead was wanting here; or perhaps they stood by all-invisible, their calm eyes softened with love deeper than tears, at this spectacle so ludicrous to man, beholding in the grotesque dress and adornments only the budding of life's divinest blossom, and in the strange skips and hops of her first attempts at dancing only the buoyancy of those inner wings that goodness and generosity and pure self-devotion were shaping for a future strong and stately flight upward. However, men, women, and children do not see with angelic eyes, and the titterings of her fellow-pupils were irrepressible. One bouncing girl nearly choked herself with her handkerchief, trying not to laugh; and two or three did not even try. Monsieur Leclerc could not blame them. At first he could scarce control his own facial muscles; but a sense of remorse smote him, as he saw how unconscious and earnest the little woman was, and remem-bered how often those knotty hands and knobbed feet had waited on his need or his comfort. Presently he tapped on his violin for a few moments' respite, and approached Miss Lucinda as respectfully as if she had been a queen.

"You are ver' tired, Mees Lucinda?" said he.

"I am a little, sir," said she, out of breath. "I am not used to dancing: it's quite an exertion."

"It is that truly. If you are too much tired, is it better to wait? I shall finish for you the lesson till I come to-night for a French conversation?"

"I guess I will go home," said the simple little lady. "I am some afraid of getting rheumatism. But use makes perfect, and I shall stay through next time, no doubt."

"So I believe," said monsieur, with his best bow, as Miss Lucinda departed and went home, pondering all the way what special delicacy she should provide for tea.

"My dear young friends," said Monsieur Leclerc, pausing with the uplifted bow in his hand, before he recommenced his lesson, "I have observe that my new pupil does make you much to laugh. I am not so surprise; for you do not know all, and the good God does not robe all angels in one manner. But she have taken me to her mansion with a leg broken, and have nursed me like a saint of the blessed, nor with any pay of silver, except that I teach her the dance and the French. These are pay for the meat and the drink; but she will have no more for her good patience and care. I like to teach you the dance; but she could teach you the saints' ways, which are better. I think you will no more to laugh."

"No, I guess we *won't!*" said the bouncing girl with great emphasis; and the color rose over more than one young face.

After that day Miss Lucinda received many a kind smile and hearty welcome, and never did anybody venture even a grimace at her expense. But it must be acknowledged that her dancing was at least peculiar. With a sanitary view of the matter, she meant to make it exercise; and fearful was the skipping that ensued. She *chasséd* on tiptoe, and *balancéd* with an indescribable hopping twirl, that made one think of a chickadee pursuing its quest of food on a new-ploughed ground; and some late-awakened feminine instinct of dress, restrained, too, by due economy, endued her with the oddest decorations that woman ever devised. The French lessons went on more smoothly. If Monsieur Leclerc's Parisian ear was tortured by the barbarous accent of Vermont, at least he bore it with heroism, since there was nobody else to hear; and very pleasant, both to our little lady and her master, were these long winter evenings, when they diligently waded through Racine, and even got as far as the golden periods of Chateaubriand. The pets fared badly for petting in these days: they were fed and waited on, but not with the old devotion. It began to dawn on Miss Lucinda's mind that something to talk to was preferable, as a companion, even to Fun, and that there might be a stranger sweetness in receiving care and protection than in giving it.

Spring came at last. Its softer skies were as blue over Dalton as in the wide fields without, and its footsteps as bloom-bringing in Miss Lucinda's garden as in mead or forest. Now Monsieur Leclerc came to her aid again at odd minutes, and set her flower-beds with mignonette-borders, and her vegetable-garden with salad-herbs of new and flourishing kinds. Yet not even the sweet season seemed to hurry the catastrophe, that we hope, dearest reader, thy tender eyes have long seen impending. No; for this quaint alliance a quainter Cupid waited: the chubby little fellow with a big head and a little arrow, who waits on youth and loveliness, was not wanted here. Lucinda's god of love wore a lank, hard-featured, grizzly shape, no less than that of Israel Slater, who marched into the garden one fine June morning, earlier than usual, to find monsieur in his blouse, hard at work weeding the cauliflower-bed.

"Good-mornin', sir, good-mornin'!" said Israel, in answer to the Frenchman's greeting. "This is a real slick little garden-spot as ever I see, and a pootty house, and a real clever woman too. I'll be skwitched ef it a'n't a fust-rate consárn, the hull on't. Be you ever a-goin' back to France, mister?"

"No, my goot friend. I have nobody there. I stay here. I have friend here; but there,—*oh, non! je ne reviendrai pas! ah, jamais, jamais!*"

"Pa's dead, eh? or shamming? Well, I don't understand your lingo;

but, ef you're a-goin' to stay here, I don't see why you don't hitch hosses
with Miss Lucindy."

Monsieur Leclerc looked up astonished.

"Horses, my friend? I have no horse."

"Thunder 'n' dry trees! I didn't say you hed, did I? But that comes o'
usin' what Parson Hyde calls figgurs, I s'pose. I wish 't he'd use one kind
o' figgurin' a leetle more: he'd pay me for that wood-sawin'. I didn't
mean nothin' about hosses. I sot out fur to say, Why don't ye marry Miss
Lucindy?"

"I?" gasped monsieur,—"I, the foreign, the poor? I could not to
presume so!"

"Well, I don't see 's it's sech dreffle presumption. Ef you're poor,
she's a woman, and real lonesome too: she ha'n't got nuther chick nor
child belongin' to her, and you're the only man she ever took any kind of
a notion to. I guess 'twould be jest as much for her good as yourn."

"Hush, good Is-ray-el! it is good to stop there. She would not to
marry after such years of goodness. She is a saint of the blessed."

"Well, I guess saints sometimes fellerships with sinners; I've heerd tell
they did: and, ef I was you, I'd make trial for't. Nothin' ventur', nothin'
have."

Whereupon Israel walked off, whistling.

Monsieur Leclerc's soul was perturbed within him by these suggestions. He pulled up two young cauliflowers, and reset their places with
pigweeds; he hoed the nicely sloped border of the bed flat to the path,
and then flung the hoe across the walk, and went off to his daily occupation with a new idea in his head. Nor was it an unpleasant one. The idea
of a transition from his squalid and pinching boarding-house to the delicate comfort of Miss Lucinda's *ménage*, the prospect of so kind and good
a wife to care for his hitherto dreaded future,—all this was pleasant. I
cannot honestly say he was in love with our friend: I must even confess
that whatever element of that nature existed between the two was now all
on Miss Lucinda's side, little as she knew it. Certain it is, that when she
appeared that day at the dancing-class in a new green calico flowered with
purple, and bows on her slippers big enough for a bonnet, it occurred to
Monsieur Leclerc, that, if they were married, she would take no more
lessons. However, let us not blame him. He was a man, and a poor one;
one must not expect too much from men or from poverty: if they are
tolerably good, let us canonize them even, it is so hard for the poor
creatures! And, to do Monsieur Leclerc justice, he had a very thorough
respect and admiration for Miss Lucinda. Years ago, in his stormy youth-
time, there had been a pair of soft-fringed eyes that looked into his as
none would ever look again. And they murdered her, those mad wild
beasts of Paris, in the chapel where she knelt at her pure prayers,—
murdered her because she knelt beside an aristocrat, her best friend, the
Duchess of Montmorenci, who had taken the pretty peasant from her

own estate to bring her up for her maid. Jean Leclerc had lifted that pale
shape from the pavement, and buried it himself: what else he buried with
it was invisible. But now he recalled the hour with a long, shuddering
sigh, and, hiding his face in his hands, said softly, "The violet is dead:
there is no spring for her. I will have now an amaranth: it is good for the
tomb."

Whether Miss Lucinda's winter dress suggested this floral metaphor,
let us not inquire. Sacred be sentiment, when there is even a shadow of
reality about it: when it becomes a profession, and confounds itself with
millinery, and shades of mourning, it is "bosh," as the Turkeys say.

So that very evening Monsieur Leclerc arrayed himself in his best to
give another lesson to Miss Lucinda. But, somehow or other, the lesson
was long in beginning. The little parlor looked so homelike and so pleasant, with its bright lamp and gay bunch of roses on the table, that it was
irresistible temptation to lounge and linger. Miss Lucinda had the volume
of Florian in her hands, and was wondering why he did not begin, when
the book was drawn away, and a hand laid on both of hers.

"Lucinda," he began, "I give you no lesson tonight. I have to ask.
Dear mees, will you to marry your poor slave?"

"Oh, dear!" said Miss Lucinda.

Don't laugh at her, Miss Tender-eyes. You will feel just so yourself
some day, when Alexander Augustus says: "Will you be mine, loveliest of
your sex?" Only you won't feel it half so strongly, for you are young, and
love is nature to youth; but it is a heavenly surprise to age.

Monsieur Leclerc said nothing. He had a heart, after all, and it was
touched now by the deep emotion that flushed Miss Lucinda's face, and
made her tremble so violently; but presently he spoke.

"Do not," said he. "I am wrong. I presume. Forgive the stranger."

"Oh, dear!" said poor Lucinda again. "Oh! you know it isn't that; but
how can you like *me?*"

There, mademoiselle, there's humility for you! *you* will never say that
to Alexander Augustus.

Monsieur Leclerc soothed this frightened, happy, incredulous little
woman into quiet before very long; and, if he really began to feel a true
affection for her from the moment he perceived her humble and entire
devotion to him, who shall blame him? Not I. If we were all heroes, who
would be *valet-de-chambre?* If we were all women, who would be men?
He was very good as far as he went; and, if you expect the chivalries of
grace out of nature, you "may expect," as old Fuller saith. So it was
peacefully settled that they should be married, with a due amount of tears
and smiles on Lucinda's part, and a great deal of tender sincerity on
monsieur's. She missed her dancing-lesson next day; and, when Monsieur
Leclerc came in the evening, he found a shade on her happy face.

"Oh, dear!" said she, as he entered.

"Oh, dear!" was Lucinda's favorite aspiration. Had she thought of it as an Anglicizing of *"O Dieu!"* perhaps she would have dropped it; but this time she went on headlong, with a valorous despair,—

"I have thought of something. I'm afraid I can't! Monsieur, aren't you a Romanist?"

"What is that?" said he, surprised.

"A Papist, a Catholic."

"Ah!" he returned, sighing, "once I was *bon Catholique,*—once in my gone youth; after then I was nothing but a poor man who bats for his life; now I am of the religion that shelters the stranger, and binds up the broken poor."

Monsieur was a diplomatist. This melted Miss Lucinda's orthodoxy right down: she only said,—

"Then you will go to church with me?"

"And to the skies above, I pray," said monsieur, kissing her knotty hand like a lover.

So in the earliest autumn they were married, monsieur having previously presented Miss Lucinda with a delicate plaided gray silk for her wedding attire, in which she looked almost young; and old Israel was present at the ceremony, which was briefly performed by Parson Hyde in Miss Manners's parlor. They did not go to Niagara, nor to Newport; but that afternoon Monsieur Leclerc brought a hired rockaway to the door, and took his bride a drive into the country. They stopped beside a pair of bars, where monsieur hitched his horse, and, taking Lucinda by the hand, led her into Farmer Steele's orchard, to the foot of his biggest apple-tree. There she beheld a little mound, at the head and foot of which stood a daily rose-bush shedding its latest wreaths of bloom, and upon the mound itself was laid a board, on which she read,—

"Here lie the bones of poor piggy."

Mrs. Lucinda burst into tears; and monsieur, picking a bud from the bush, placed it in her hand, and led her tenderly back to the rockaway.

That evening Mrs. Lucinda was telling the affair to old Israel with so much feeling, that she did not perceive at all the odd commotion in his face, till, as she repeated the epitaph to him, he burst out with, "He didn't say what become o' the flesh, did he?" and therewith fled through the kitchen-door. For years afterward Israel would entertain a few favored auditors with his opinion of the matter, screaming till the tears rolled down his cheeks,—

"That was the beateree of all the weddin'-towers I ever heerd tell on. Goodness! it's enough to make the Wanderin' Jew die o' larfin'."

HARRIET BEECHER STOWE

(1811–1896)

The Pearl of Orr's Island

(Boston: Ticknor and Fields), 1862.

Single-handedly Harriet Beecher Stowe has kept the category of mid-nineteenth-century American women prose writers from complete oblivion. She can be dismissed, she can be trivialized, but she can not be ignored. To paraphrase Sarah Orne Jewett's comment on *The Pearl of Orr's Island, there she is.* And because she is there, we know that women as well as men created nineteenth-century American literature.

Harriet Beecher Stowe was born on June 14, 1811, in Litchfield, Connecticut, the seventh child and fourth daughter of Roxana Foote and Lyman Beecher. When Harriet was five, her mother died. Throughout her life, however, Stowe retained a powerful impression of this mother. Perhaps inevitably, the maternal image was ambivalent. On the one hand, her mother presented an ideal of feminine submissiveness and placidity impossible to attain and certainly in conflict with Stowe's own various acts of self-assertion. On the other hand, as a female intellectual, she provided a potential identity denied Stowe by her father who could only wish, as he recognized her "genius," that she had been born a boy. On her deathbed, Roxana requested that her sons be trained as ministers. She felt no need to leave any instructions for her daughters. Nevertheless, for Stowe the question of vocation was both primary and vexed.

With the death of her mother, her father became the dominant influence in Stowe's life. Although Lyman praised his Roxana for her submission—"I never heard a murmur; and if there ever was a perfect mind as respects submission, it was hers"—he held himself to no such ideal (Fields, p. 6). In one of her earliest memories, Stowe recalls retreating to her father's study, "high above all the noise of the house . . . a refuge and a sanctuary," where, with "a kind of sheltered feeling," she sat and watched her father write, "careful never to disturb" his "holy and mysterious work" by "question or remark" (Fields, pp. 27–28). Although later Stowe would suggest to her husband that, "if I am to write, I must have a room to myself, which shall be *my* room" (Fields, p. 104), her descriptions of the actual conditions under which she wrote leave little doubt that Lyman's daughter did not inherit Lyman's privilege. Lyman's willingness to please himself while preaching selflessness for women appears in another memory, which perhaps provides the germ for chapter XIII of *The Pearl of Orr's Island:*

> My father was fond of excursions with his boys into the forests about for fishing and hunting. At first I remember these only as something pertaining to father and the older boys, they being the rewards given for good conduct. I remember the regretful interest with which I watched their joyful preparations for departure. They were going to the Great Pond—to Pine Island—to that wonderful blue pine forest which I could just see on the horizon, and who knew what adventures they might meet! (Fields, pp. 32–33).

For Harriet, left behind, there was "only a long seam on a sheet to be oversewed as the sole means of beguiling the hours of absence." Her father's child as much as, if not more than, her mother's—about to do a reading, she commented to Fields, "now I am exactly like my father . . . when he was going to preach"—Stowe managed, albeit belatedly, to accept her capacity for pleasure and self-indulgence, finding both in the Florida home of her later years.

At the age of five, Stowe began to attend a district school in Litchfield; by the age of eight, she was enrolled in Sarah Pierce's School for Young Ladies, famous in Litchfield and elsewhere for the quality of education it offered to women. Here that "passion for writing" Stowe claimed to have had from earliest childhood was indulged and developed. When she was twelve, one of her compositions was read at the annual exhibition of student work. When her father learned that the author was his daughter, he was pleased; for Stowe, "to have interested *him* was past all juvenile triumphs" (Fields, p. 30).

At thirteen, Stowe was sent to Hartford to attend her sister Catharine Beecher's recently opened female seminary. Soon after her arrival, Beecher enlisted her aid as a teacher and sought as well to dissuade her from her literary ambitions. Having studied Latin since her arrival in Hartford, Stowe became interested in poetry and began her own poetic drama: "I filled blank book after blank book . . . with this drama. It filled my thoughts sleeping and waking. One day sister Catharine pounced down upon me, and said that I must not waste my time writing poetry, but discipline my mind by the study of Butler's 'Analogy' " (Fields, p. 49).

In 1832, Lyman Beecher accepted the presidency of Lane Theological Seminary in Cincinnati, Ohio, and moved west, taking with him Catharine, who was to establish the Western Female Institue, and Harriet, who was to teach in Catharine's new school. Here Stowe first began to write for publication. Encouraged by the local literary club,

Stowe entered the competition sponsored by the *Western Monthly* whose editor, James Hall, was especially receptive to the work of women writers. Stowe won the fifty-dollar prize with "A New England Sketch," which was published in April of 1834. During the twenty-odd years before *Uncle Tom's Cabin*, Stowe published her work in numerous magazines and in various gift books and annuals. In 1843, she published a collection of her sketches; *The Mayflower*, however, was neither a commercial nor a critical success.

In 1836, Harriet Beecher married Calvin Stowe, professor of Biblical literature at Lane Theological Seminary and another transplanted New Englander. Within four years, Stowe had four children and was thoroughly enmeshed in the tangle of trying to raise her children, run a household on a modest income, keep up the energy and spirits of a moody and despondent husband, and pursue a career as a writer. In her edition of Stowe's letters, Annie Fields includes an account of Stowe's life at this time, written by a friend; it reads like the working notes for Elizabeth Stuart Phelps's *The Angel Over The Right Shoulder.*

In 1850, Calvin Stowe accepted a position on the faculty of Bowdoin College in Brunswick, Maine. Nearing the end of her seventh pregnancy, Harriet, with her children, preceded him east to set up house. Here in Brunswick, under extraordinarily difficult conditions—"nothing but deadly determination enables me ever to write; it is rowing against wind and tide"—Stowe conceived and wrote *Uncle Tom's Cabin* (Fields, p. 128). Inspired by her anger at the Fugitive Slave Law and originally imagined as running to only three or four installments, *Uncle Tom's Cabin* appeared serially in *The National Era* from June, 1851 until April, 1852. For it Stowe received $300 in serial rights. Nervous about money, Stowe refused an offer of a 50 percent royalty rate if she would assume a primary share of the initial financial risk of book publication. Published in 1852, with a 10 percent royalty rate, *Uncle Tom's Cabin* brought her within the first few months of its appearance $10,000 and international fame.

In 1852, Calvin Stowe made another move, this time to Andover, Massachusetts, to join the faculty of the Andover Theological Seminary. Stowe remained in Andover until 1864 when, on Calvin's retirement from teaching, she made a final move to Hartford, Connecticut. In 1853, Stowe published *A Key to Uncle Tom's Cabin*, an attempt to document the facts behind her fiction and to defend herself against attacks on her novel (over thirty anti-Uncle Tom novels had appeared within three years). In 1856 she published *Dred: A Tale of the Great Dismal Swamp*, a second antislavery novel, far gloomier and more foreboding than her first.

A group of fictions centering on New England forms the second major phase of Stowe's career. In the first of these, *The Minister's Wooing* (1859), Stowe explores her antipathy toward Calvinism and argues instead for a theology based on alternative feminine values. In 1862, she published *The Pearl of Orr's Island*, begun over a decade previously in Brunswick, Maine, and put aside during the move to Andover and the defense of *Uncle Tom's Cabin*. When Stowe finally determined to return to her "Maine story," agreeing to furnish it serially for the *Independent,* she did so while under contract with the *Atlantic* for another novel, *Agnes of Sorrento* (1862). When it became clear to Stowe that *The Pearl of Orr's Island* would be a larger work than she had originally imagined, she put it aside again while she finished *Agnes.* To these interruptions in its composition, many readers, including Annie Fields and Sarah Orne Jewett, have attributed their sense of the book's failure to realize its initial promise. In 1869, Stowe published *Oldtown Folks,* a book based on her husband's memories of his childhood in Natick, Massachusetts and expressing Stowe's own idealism for eighteenth- and early nineteenth-century New England. In contrast to her usual practice, Stowe took her time with this book, refusing to be pressured by publisher's deadlines: "Instead of rushing on, I have often turned back, and written over with care, that nothing that I wanted to say might be omitted" (Fields, p. 313). As a result, Stowe believed this to be, after *Uncle Tom's Cabin,* the best of her works. *Poganuc People* (1878), based on Stowe's own childhood in Litchfield, concluded the New England series.

A third group of novels, all written in the early 1870s and having as their subject contemporary urban American life, are decidedly her worst. As Ann Douglas points out in *The Feminization of American Culture* (1977), these works are characterized not only by their lack of analysis and intelligence, but also by Stowe's apparent delight in their mediocre mindlessness. In *My Wife and I* (1871), this mindlessness emerges most sharply in her portraits of contemporary feminists, which lack balance, perspective, and realism. In *Pink and White Tyranny* (1871), Stowe engages in a *tour de force* of blaming the victim. She charges women with responsibility for the "pink and white" cult that eroticized the frivolous, weak, and "feminine" woman and presumably gave her power over men; and thus she makes women responsible for all the ills that accrue to men from marrying such "tyrants." In 1875, Stowe published *We and Our Neighbors,* a sequel to *My Wife and I,* with the same narrator, Harry Henderson, a thinly disguised mouthpiece for Stowe herself.

In 1869, Stowe placed herself in the eye of a storm as extraordinary as that produced by *Uncle Tom's Cabin.* In the September issue of the *Atlantic Monthly,* she published "The True Story of Lady Byron's Life." In her essay, Stowe charged Byron with an incestuous relationship with his half-sister, Augusta, and defended Lady Byron from responsibility for the misery of Byron's life. This essay, one of the most overtly feminist pieces Stowe ever wrote and evidence of her considerable ambivalence on feminist issues, was viewed by many readers as undocumented, scandalous, and even obscene. As a result of its publication, Stowe's reputation plummeted and the *Atlantic* lost over one third of its subscribers in a single year.

Putatively written as a response to the publication of the memoirs of Byron's mistress, Stowe's piece was the culmination of a lifelong fascination with Byron. In Byron, Stowe found her ultimate antagonist—the embodiment of a masculinity used against women. Dangerous because attractive; attractive because rebellious; fallen because, in the final analysis, his rebellion was so conventional, Byron represented a power, particularly over women, that Stowe felt compelled to dismantle. For Stowe, Byron's life symbolized a pervasive and offensive double standard of morality. An archetypal bad boy, Byron was petted and rewarded for behavior that would outlaw any woman, the masculinity of his genius providing the alchemy by which sin was changed to glory. And in the history of Byron and Lady Byron, Stowe saw evidence of masculine literary dominance. In "The True Story of Lady Byron's Life," she declared that Lady Byron's only "crime" was that *"she has not spoken at all.* Her story has never been told."* In *Lady Byron Vindicated,* the expanded version of her defense, which she published in January of 1870, Stowe reiterates this point: "We have heard much mourning over the burned Autobiography of Lord Byron, and seen it treated . . . as 'the lost chapter in history.' The lost chapter in history is *Lady* Byron's Autobiography." Stowe provides that lost chapter, the woman's side of the story.

In her later years, Stowe discovered Florida and made her winter home there from 1868 to 1884. Stowe's passion for Florida might seem strange, given her devotion to New England virtues and her association of these virtues with the New England landscape and climate; yet covert attraction to the southern climate and landscape, and to its concomitant sensuality, is apparent in Stowe's work as early as *Uncle Tom's Cabin.* One book, *Palmetto Leaves,* grew out of her Florida experience.

Calvin Stowe's increasing illness mandated a return to Hartford in 1884. After his death in 1886, Stowe remained in Hartford at her home in Nook Farm (still standing today and open to visitors). Senility finally brought her prodigious career to an end. She died on July 1, 1896, at the age of eighty-five, and was buried beside her husband in the cemetery of the Andover Theological Seminary.

> I have been reading the beginning of "The Pearl of Orr's Island" and finding it just as clear and perfectly original and strong as it seemed to me in my thirteenth or fourteenth year, when I read it first. I never shall forget the exquisite flavor and reality of delight that it gave me. . . . It is classical—historical—anything you like to say, if you can give it high praise enough. I haven't read it for ten years at least, but *there it is!* Alas, that she couldn't finish it in the same noble key of simplicity and harmony; but a poor writer is at the mercy of much unconscious opposition. You must throw everything and everybody aside at times, but a woman made like Mrs. Stowe cannot bring herself to that cold selfishness of the moment for one's work's sake, and the recompense for her loss is a divine touch here and there in an incomplete piece of work (Sarah Orne Jewett to Annie Fields, July 5, 18—).

Although *The Pearl of Orr's Island* may be more complete than Jewett's reading implies, her praise appropriately directs our attention to this book. Flawed, "divine," above all, powerful, *The Pearl of Orr's*

Island is, next to *Uncle Tom's Cabin*, Stowe's most mythically charged and imaginatively compelling work. An early example of the ability of nineteenth-century American women writers to render successfully the physical texture of a region and the character produced by and reflected in it, this text is also Stowe's major attempt to address, in the arena afforded by the full-length fiction, the moral, social, and psychological issues connected with the uses of gender in mid-nineteenth-century America. Not a woman's fiction in the sense in which Nina Baym has defined the term in *Woman's Fiction, The Pearl of Orr's Island* is nevertheless profoundly woman-centered and derives its deepest meaning from Stowe's vision of the value of the feminine principle in a masculinist world.

In *The Pearl of Orr's Island* Stowe also engages the issues of women and fiction and explores the question of "what can a heroine do?" "Are there any lives of women," Mara asks, on first hearing of Plutarch. Indeed, Stowe may have had difficulty completing *Pearl*, and allowed and even welcomed those interruptions to writing it, because she had difficulty connecting the idea of a heroine with the idea of story and history. Stowe reintroduces her heroine and hero after a hiatus of ten years when the "great change in life had been consummated in both. They had parted boy and girl; they would meet man and woman" (chapter 22, not reprinted). Yet the story implicit in this language, a story of romantic love and eventual marriage, is not the story Stowe tells. In place of courtship, engagement, and marriage, Stowe offers in the second half of her book antagonism, disengagement, and alienation, the inevitable working out of the story already told in the first half of the book. Mara escapes marriage by dying. Her "triumphant" death displaces the romance convention and completes the story Stowe has to tell of the radical incompatibility of the feminine and masculine principle.

The conflict between masculine and feminine values forms the central subject of *The Pearl of Orr's Island*. Though not all men in the text are "masculine" nor all women "feminine," the primary embodiment of each set of values is a boy and a girl.

The opening image of *The Pearl of Orr's Island* asserts its theme. The story of the wreck of a homeward bound ship at the moment of entering the harbor, so commanding that it is "yet told in many a family on this coast," speaks of the limitations of masculine power. Men sail to and fro over the face of the earth, borne up by their sense of ownership and control, self-appointed heroes who identify their lives with history. But when they seek to return home, as inevitably they must, they discover themselves subject to forces they cannot control. Helpless, finite, contingent, they are literally brought down, and their myth of superiority is shivered as swiftly and thoroughly as the masts and riggings of their ships. On shore, the women (a category that includes the old man who has given up the sea to stay home with his wife and daughter) watch the drama of contingency, and they implicitly offer an alternative set of values symbolized by the home the men struggle to reach.

In the world of boy and girl, Mara comes first. Although her Eden, like Adam's without Eve, is incomplete and requires Moses for its completion, in Stowe's theology the primary principle is female and the original creation is woman. Moses comes to Mara as a gift from his dead mother, but Mara comes straight from God, the eternal mother, who is immanent in her. Mara, that "precious pearl cast up from the past eternity upon the wet, wave-ribbed sand of the present," has about her eyes "a strange, peculiar expression of pathos and desire, as if the spirit that looked out of them were pressed with vague remembrances of a past. . . ." Roxy, one of Mara's earthly "mothers," interprets this look: "Some say it's the mothers longin' after 'em makes 'em feel so, and some say it's them longin' after their mothers." The intensity of the mother/daughter bond, which in this text displaces the father/son paradigm of traditional Christian thought, serves to bring the worlds of heaven and earth together and provides an almost perceptible bridge between this world and the next.

Across this bridge, God speaks to Mara in a dream, giving Mara to understand that s/he has given into her keeping those other children who are "men." With the introduction of Moses into Mara's world, the struggle for salvation begins. As the patriarchal overtones of his name might suggest, Moses embodies masculine values and characteristics—willfulness, arrogance, and energy directed toward owning and controlling his world. Not surprisingly, his behavior is both antichristian and antiwoman. Since the world seems to Moses his own private oyster, he rapidly proceeds to appropriate its pearl for his use. The danger that this attitude poses to Mara, adumbrated in earlier chapters, is fully elaborated in chapter 11 (not reprinted). Imitating what he has "seen men do," Moses determines to have a romantic adventure in which he casts himself as hero/author and Mara as adulatory character. He sets out to sea in a little boat, and his conviction of glory at having at last "got Mara all to himself" is enhanced by the appearance of sharks at whom he makes "valorous plunges," which almost upset the boat. Luckily, Mara is rescued in time from the consequences of following Moses. Moses, however, feels neither guilt nor remorse. In the face of Roxy's attempted rebuke, he remains fiercely defiant: "The spirit of Sir Francis Drake and of Christopher Columbus was swelling in his little body, and was he to be brought under by a dry-visaged woman with a press-board?"

In chapter 13, Stowe explores the different worlds of boy and girl and the implications for each of their separate spheres. Moses anticipates his first voyage to the Banks, a voyage that signals his initiation into the world of men, and thus of history and heroism. His anticipation reinforces his budding self-concept: "Glorious knight he! the world all before him, and the blood of ten years racing and throbbing in his veins as he talks knowingly of hooks, and sinkers, and bait, and lines, and wears proudly the red flannel shirt which Mara had just finished for him." Compelled by this vision of possibility, Mara murmurs: " 'How I do wish I were going with you! . . . 'Pooh!' said Moses, sublimely regarding her while he settled the collar of his shirt, 'you're a girl—and what can girls do at sea? you never like to catch fish—it always makes you

cry to see 'em flop.' " Torn between her sympathy for the fish that
Moses needs to kill to prove himself a man and her desire for her hero's
glory that must be founded on their pain, Mara articulates the terms of a
larger dilemma. To worship Moses, Mara must relinquish her own morality, a morality which Stowe presents as clearly superior to his. Such
worship, then, becomes itself immoral, becomes indeed idolatry. Yet the
conventions of courtship and marriage, indeed all the conventions governing the relation of women to men, lead to this immorality. How,
then, are women to love men without sinning, and how is Stowe to
write a story that is not only outside of history but true?

A peaceful interlude, with Moses gone, allows Mara the chance to
explore her own imagination (chapter XIV, not reprinted). Her discovery of Shakespeare's *The Tempest* and her fascination with it suggests, among other things, her craving for a "sea change" capable of
magically transforming her world. Moses's homecoming, however,
brings reality back with a vengeance. Although Moses reflects merely
"animal perfection" uncomplicated by any "development of the moral,"
nevertheless it is Moses who is encouraged, supported, and attended to,
even as he wounds Mara. In the dinner that celebrates his homecoming,
"Moses bore a more prominent part in the conversation than he had
been wont to do before this voyage, and all seemed to listen to him with
a kind of indulgence elders often accord to a handsome, manly boy, in
the first flush of some successful enterprise." During all this "merry
meal," Mara sits quietly for "it was not [her] way to speak when anything thwarted or hurt her." No one encourages Mara to speak for no
one imagines that she might have a story to tell.

Perceiving Moses' deficiencies, the minister, Mr. Sewell, determines
to remedy them. Development, growth, completion govern his response
to Moses. As for Mara: "That child thinks too much, and feels too
much, and knows too much for her years! . . . If she were a boy, and
you would take her away cod-fishing, as you have Moses, the sea-winds
would blow away some of the thinking, and her little body would grow
stout, and her mind less delicate and sensitive. But she's a woman . . .
and they are all alike. We can't do much for them, but let them come up
as they will and make the best of it." The minister's program for Mara
belies his posture of non-interference, however. While Moses learns
Latin, Miss Emily instructs Mara in "female accomplishments." Deadly
to both mind and soul, these accomplishments are appropriately symbolized by Miss Emily's "triumph" in mortuary art, and by the tedium
of sewing. Luckily, the "word" intervenes to save Mara. Absorbed in
what is going on in the men's corner and inattentive to Miss Emily,
Mara follows the progress of Moses' lesson; when he gives the wrong
answer, she "involuntarily" provides the right one and the minister discovers that she knows the lesson perfectly.

Although he justifies Mara's inclusion in future lessons on the
grounds that it will be better for Moses, Sewell nevertheless feels uneasy
with his deviance from the educational norm. The reason for his un-
easiness is soon apparent. Giving Mara the chance to learn Latin forces
Moses to confront the fact that his sense of superiority has been based

not on his own abilities but on the exclusion of Mara from the race. In the final chapter of the first half of the book Stowe clarifies and extends the moral issues that concern her. What kind of relation can women form with men once they realize that men's superiority is based on the radical dishonesty of a fixed race? It is to the answer of this question that Stowe devotes the second half of her book.

Source:

The Pearl of Orr's Island (Boston: Ticknor and Fields) 1862.

Selected Primary Works:

Uncle Tom's Cabin, 1852; *Dred,* 1856; *The Minister's Wooing,* 1859; *Oldtown Folks,* 1869; *Lady Byron Vindicated,* 1870; *Pink and White Tyranny,* 1871; *Sam Lawson's Oldtown Fireside Stories,* 1872; *Poganuc People,* 1878; *Life and Letters of Harriet Beecher Stowe,* ed. Annie Fields, 1897.

Selected Secondary Works:

John Adams, *Harriet Beecher Stowe* (New York: Twayne), 1963; Elizabeth Ammons, "Heroines in *Uncle Tom's Cabin,*" *American Literature,* 49 (1977), 161–79; *Critical Essays on Harriet Beecher Stowe,* ed. Elizabeth Ammons (Boston: G. K. Hall), 1980; Jean W. Ashton, "Harriet Stowe's Filthy Story: Lord Byron Set Afloat," *Prospects,* 2 (1976), 373–84; ———, *Harriet Beecher Stowe: A Reference Guide* (Boston: G. K. Hall), 1977; Alice Crozier, *The Novels of Harriet Beecher Stowe* (New York: Oxford University Press), 1969; Charles H. Foster, *The Rungless Ladder* (Durham, N.C.: Duke University Press), 1954; Mary Kelley, "At War with Herself: Harriet Beecher Stowe as Woman in Conflict within the Home," *American Studies,* 19 (1979), 23–40; ———, *Private Woman, Public Stage* (New York: Oxford University Press), 1984; E. Bruce Kirkham, "The Source of the Shipwreck in *The Pearl of Orr's Island,*" *American Transcendental Quarterly,* 40 (1978), 365–66; ———, "The Writing of Harriet Beecher Stowe's *The Pearl of Orr's Island,*" *Colby Library Quarterly,* 16 (1980), 158–60; Ellen Moers, *Harriet Beecher Stowe and American Literature* (Hartford: Stowe-Day Foundation), 1978; Edward Wagenknecht, *Harriet Beecher Stowe: The Known and the Unknown* (New York: Oxford University Press), 1965; Forrest Wilson, *Crusader in Crinoline* (Philadelphia: J. B. Lippincott), 1941.

CHAPTER I.

ON THE ROAD to the Kennebec, below the town of Bath, in the State of Maine, might have been seen, on a certain autumnal afternoon, a one-horse wagon, in which two persons were sitting. One is an old man, with the peculiarly hard but expressive physiognomy which characterizes the seafaring population of the New England shores.

A clear blue eye, evidently practised in habits of keen observation, white hair, bronzed, weather-beaten cheeks, and a face deeply lined with the furrows of shrewd thought and anxious care, were points of the portrait that made themselves felt at a glance.

By his side sat a young woman of two-and-twenty, of a marked and peculiar personal appearance. Her hair was black, and smoothly parted on a broad forehead, to which a pair of pencilled dark eyebrows gave a striking and definite outline. Beneath, lay a pair of large black eyes, remarkable for tremulous expression of melancholy and timidity. The cheek was white and bloodless as a snowberry, though with the clear and perfect oval of good health; the mouth was delicately formed, with a certain sad quiet in its lines, which indicated a habitually repressed and sensitive nature.

The dress of this young person, as often happens in New England, was, in refinement and even elegance, a marked contrast to that of her male companion and to the humble vehicle in which she rode. There was not only the most fastidious neatness, but a delicacy in the choice of colors, an indication of elegant tastes in the whole arrangement, and the quietest suggestion in the world of an acquaintance with the usages of fashion, which struck one oddly in those wild and dreary surroundings. On the whole, she impressed one like those fragile wild-flowers which in April cast their fluttering shadows from the mossy crevices of the old New England granite,—an existence in which colorless delicacy is united to a sort of elastic hardihood of life, fit for the rocky soil and harsh winds it is born to encounter.

The scenery of the road along which the two were riding was wild and bare. Only savins and mulleins, with their dark pyramids or white spires of velvet leaves, diversified the sandy way-side; but out at sea was a wide sweep of blue, reaching far to the open ocean, which lay rolling, tossing, and breaking into white caps of foam in the bright sunshine. For two or three days a north-east storm had been raging, and the sea was in all the commotion which such a general upturning creates.

The two travellers reached a point of elevated land, where they paused a moment, and the man drew up the jogging, stiff-jointed old farm-horse, and raised himself upon his feet to look out at the prospect.

There might be seen in the distance the blue Kennebec sweeping out toward the ocean through its picturesque rocky shores, decked with cedars and other dusky evergreens, which were illuminated by the orange and flame-colored trees of Indian summer. Here and there scarlet creepers swung long trailing garlands over the faces of the dark rock, and fringes of golden rod above swayed with the brisk blowing wind that was driving the blue waters seaward, in face of the up-coming ocean tide,—a conflict which caused them to rise in great foam-crested waves. There were two channels into this river from the open sea, navigable for ships which are coming in to the city of Bath; one is broad and shallow, the other narrow and deep, and these are divided by a steep ledge of rocks.

Where the spectators of this scene were sitting, they could see in the distance a ship borne with tremendous force by the rising tide into the mouth of the river, and encountering a north-west wind which had succeeded the gale, as northwest winds often do on this coast. The ship, from what might be observed in the distance, seemed struggling to make the wider channel, but was constantly driven off by the baffling force of the wind.

"There she is, Naomi," said the old fisherman, eagerly, to his companion, "coming right in." The young woman was one of the sort that never start, and never exclaim, but with all deeper emotions grow still. The color slowly mounted into her cheek, her lips parted, and her eyes dilated with a wide, bright expression; her breathing came in thick gasps, but she said nothing.

The old fisherman stood up in the wagon, his coarse, butternut-colored coat-flaps fluttering and snapping in the breeze, while his interest seemed to be so intense in the efforts of the ship that he made involuntary and eager movements as if to direct her course. A moment passed, and his keen, practised eye discovered a change in her movements, for he cried out involuntarily,—

"*Don't* take the narrow channel to-day!" and a moment after, "O Lord! O Lord! have mercy,—there they go! Look! look! look!"

And, in fact, the ship rose on a great wave clear out of the water, and the next second seemed to leap with a desperate plunge into the narrow passage; for a moment there was a shivering of the masts and the rigging, and she went down and was gone.

"They're split to pieces!" cried the fisherman. "Oh, my poor girl—my poor girl—they're gone! O Lord, have mercy!"

The woman lifted up no voice, but, as one who has been shot through the heart falls with no cry, she fell back,—a mist rose up over her great mournful eyes,—she had fainted.

The story of this wreck of a home-bound ship just entering the harbor is yet told in many a family on this coast. A few hours after, the unfortunate crew were washed ashore in all the joyous holiday rig in which they had attired themselves that morning to go to their sisters, wives, and mothers.

This is the first scene in our story.

CHAPTER II.

DOWN near the end of Orr's Island, facing the open ocean, stands a brown house of the kind that the natives call "lean-to," or "linter,"—one of those large, comfortable structures, barren in the ideal, but rich in the practical, which the working-man of New England can always command.

The waters of the ocean came up within a rod of this house, and the sound of its moaning waves was even now filling the clear autumn star-light. Evidently something was going on within, for candles fluttered and winked from window to window, like fireflies in a dark meadow, and sounds as of quick footsteps, and the flutter of brushing garments, might be heard.

Something unusual is certainly going on within the dwelling of Zephaniah Pennel to-night.

Let us enter the dark front-door. We feel our way to the right, where a solitary ray of light comes from the chink of a half-opened door.

Here is the front room of the house, set apart as its place of especial social hilarity and sanctity,—the "best room," with its low studded walls, white dimity window-curtains, rag carpet, and polished wood chairs.

It is now lit by the dim gleam of a solitary tallow candle, which seems in the gloom to make only a feeble circle of light around itself, leaving all the rest of the apartment in shadow.

In the centre of the room, stretched upon a table, and covered partially by a sea-cloak, lies the body of a man of twenty-five,—lies, too, evidently as one of whom it is written,—"He shall return to his house no more, neither shall his place know him any more." A splendid manhood has suddenly been called to forsake that lifeless form, leaving it, like a deserted palace, beautiful in its desolation.

The hair, dripping with the salt wave, curled in glossy abundance on the finely-formed head; the flat, broad brow; the closed eye, with its long black lashes; the firm, manly mouth; the strongly-moulded chin,—all, all were sealed with that seal which is never to be broken till the great resurrection day.

He was lying in a full suit of broadcloth, with a white vest and smart blue neck-tie, fastened with a pin, in which was some braided hair under a crystal. All his clothing, as well as his hair, was saturated with sea-water, which trickled from time to time, and struck with a leaden and dropping sound into a sullen pool which lay under the table.

This was the body of James Lincoln, ship-master of the brig Flying Scud, who that morning had dressed himself gayly in his state-room to go on shore and meet his wife,—singing and jesting as he did so.

This is all that you have to learn in the room below; but as we stand there, we hear a trampling of feet in the apartment above,—the quick yet careful opening and shutting of doors,—and voices come and go about the house, and whisper consultations on the stairs. Now comes the roll of wheels, and the Doctor's gig drives up to the door; and, as he goes creaking up with his heavy boots, we will follow and gain admission to the dimly-lighted chamber.

Two gossips are sitting in earnest, whispering conversation over a small bundle done up in an old flannel petticoat. To them the doctor is about to address himslf cheerily, but is repelled by sundry signs and sounds which warn him not to speak.

Moderating his heavy boots as well as he is able to a pace of quiet, he advances for a moment, and the petticoat is unfolded for him to glance at its contents; while a low, eager, whispered conversation, attended with much head-shaking, warns him that his first duty is with somebody behind the checked curtains of a bed in the farther corner of the room. He steps on tiptoe, and draws the curtain; and there, with closed eye, and cheek as white as wintry snow, lies the same face over which passed the shadow of death when that ill-fated ship went down.

This woman was wife to him who lies below, and within the hour has been made mother to a frail little human existence, which the storm of a great anguish has driven untimely on the shores of life,—a precious pearl cast up from the past eternity upon the wet, wave-ribbed sand of the present. Now, weary with her moanings, and beaten out with the wrench of a double anguish, she lies with closed eyes in that passive apathy which precedes deeper shadows and longer rest.

Over against her, on the other side of the bed, sits an aged woman in an attitude of deep dejection, and the old man we saw with her in the morning is standing with an anxious, awe-struck face at the foot of the bed.

The doctor feels the pulse of the woman, or rather lays an inquiring finger where the slightest thread of vital current is scarcely throbbing, and shakes his head mournfully.

The touch of his hand rouses her,—her large, wild, melancholy eyes fix themselves on him with an inquiring glance, then she shivers and moans,—

"Oh, Doctor, Doctor!—Jamie, Jamie!"

"Come, come!" said the doctor, "cheer up, my girl; you've got a fine little daughter,—the Lord mingles mercies with his afflictions."

Her eyes closed, her head moved with a mournful but decided dissent.

A moment after she spoke in the sad old words of the Hebrew Scripture,—

"Call her not Naomi; call her Mara, for the Almighty hath dealt very bitterly with me."

And as she spoke, there passed over her face the sharp frost of the last winter; but even as it passed there broke out a smile, as if a flower had been thrown down from Paradise, and she said,—

"Not my will, but thy will," and so was gone.

Aunt Roxy and Aunt Ruey were soon left alone in the chamber of death.

"She'll make a beautiful corpse," said Aunt Roxy, surveying the still, white form contemplatively, with her head in an artistic attitude.

"She was a pretty girl," said Aunt Ruey; "dear me, what a Providence! I 'member the wedd'n down in that lower room, and what a handsome couple they were."

"They were lovely and pleasant in their lives, and in their deaths they were not divided," said Aunt Roxy, sententiously.

"What was it she said, did ye hear?" said Aunt Ruey.

"She called the baby 'Mary.'"

"Ah! sure enough, her mother's name afore her. What a still, softly-spoken thing she always was!"

"A pity the poor baby didn't go with her," said Aunt Roxy; "seven-months' children are so hard to raise."

"'T is a pity," said the other.

But babies will live, and all the more when everybody says that it is a pity they should. Life goes on as inexorably in this world as death.

It was ordered by THE WILL above that out of these two graves should spring one frail, trembling autumn flower,—the "Mara" whose poor little roots first struck deep in the salt, bitter waters of our mortal life.

CHAPTER V.

IT did live. The little life, so frail, so unprofitable in every mere material view, so precious in the eyes of love, expanded and flowered at last into fair childhood. Not without much watching and weariness. Many a night the old fisherman walked the floor with the little thing in his arms, talking to it that jargon of tender nonsense which fairies bring as love-gifts to all who tend a cradle. Many a day the good little old grand-mother called the aid of gossips about her, trying various experiments of catnip, and sweet fern, and bayberry, and other teas of rustic reputation for baby frailties.

At the end of three years, the two graves in the lonely graveyard were sodded and cemented down by smooth velvet turf, and playing round the door of the brown house was a slender child, with ways and manners so still and singular as often to remind the neighbors that she was not like other children,—a bud of hope and joy,—but the outcome of a great sorrow,—a pearl washed ashore by a mighty, uprooting tempest. They that looked at her remembered that her father's eye had never beheld her, and her baptismal cup had rested on her mother's coffin.

She was small of stature, beyond the wont of children of her age, and moulded with a fine waxen delicacy that won admiration from all eyes. Her hair was curly and golden, but her eyes were dark like her mother's, and the lids drooped over them in that manner which gives a peculiar expression of dreamy wistfulness.

Every one of us must remember eyes that have a strange, peculiar expression of pathos and desire, as if the spirit that looked out of them were pressed with vague remembrances of a past, or but dimly com-prehended the mystery of its present life. Even when the baby lay in its cradle, and its dark, inquiring eyes would follow now one object and now another, the gossips would say the child was longing for something, and Miss Roxy would still further venture to predict that that child always would long and never would know exactly what she was after.

That dignitary sits at this minute enthroned in the kitchen corner, looking majestically over the press-board on her knee, where she is press-ing the next year's Sunday vest of Zephaniah Pennel. As she makes her heavy tailor's goose squeak on the work, her eyes follow the little delicate fairy form which trips about the kitchen, busily and silently arranging a little grotto of gold and silver shells and sea-weed. The child sings to herself as she works in a low chant, like the prattle of a brook, but ever and anon she rests her little arms on a chair and looks through the open kitchen-door far, far off where the horizon line of the blue sea dissolves in the blue sky.

"See that child now, Roxy," said Miss Ruey, who sat stitching beside her; "do look at her eyes. She's as handsome as a pictur', but 't a'n't an ordinary look she has neither; she seems a contented little thing; but what makes her eyes always look so kind o' wishful?"

"Wa' n't her mother always a-longin' and a-lookin' to sea, and watchin' the ships, afore she was born?" said Miss Roxy; "and did n't her heart break afore she was born? Babies like that is marked always. They don't know what ails 'em, nor nobody."

"It's her mother she's after?" said Miss Ruey.

"The Lord only knows," said Miss Roxy; "but them kind o' children always seem homesick to go back where they come from. They're mostly grave and old-fashioned like this 'un. If they gets past seven years, why they live; but it's always in 'em to *long*; they don't seem to be really unhappy neither, but if anything's ever the matter with 'em, it seems a great deal easier for 'em to die than to live. Some say it's the mothers longin' after 'em makes 'em feel so, and some say it's them longin' after their mothers; but dear knows, Ruey, what anything is or what makes anything. Children's mysterious, that's my mind."

"Mara, dear," said Miss Ruey, interrupting the child's steady look-out, "what you thinking of?"

"Me want somefin'," said the little one.

"That's what she's always sayin'," said Miss Roxy.

"Me want somebody to pay wis'," continued the little one.

"Want somebody to play with," said old Dame Pennel, as she came in from the back-room with her hands yet floury with kneading bread; "sure enough, she does. Our house stands in such a lonesome place, and there a'n't any children. But I never saw such a quiet little thing—always still and always busy."

"I'll take her down with me to Cap'n Kittridge's," said Miss Roxy, "and let her play with their little girl; she'll *chirk* her up, I'll warrant. She's a regular little witch, Sally is, but she'll *chirk* her up. It a'n't good for children to be so still and old-fashioned; children ought to be children. Sally takes to Mara just 'cause she's so different."

"Well, now, you may," said Dame Pennel; "to be sure, *he* can't bear her out of his sight a minute after he comes in; but after all, old folks can't be company for children."

Accordingly, that afternoon, the little Mara was arrayed in a little blue flounced dress, which stood out like a balloon, made by Miss Roxy in first-rate style, from a French fashionplate; her golden hair was twined in manifold curls by Dame Pennel, who, restricted in her ideas of ornamentation, spared, nevertheless, neither time nor money to enhance the charms of this single ornament to her dwelling. Mara was her picture-gallery, who gave her in the twenty-four hours as many Murillos or Greuzes as a lover of art could desire; and as she tied over the child's golden curls a little flat hat, and saw her go dancing off along the sea-sands, holding to Miss Roxy's bony finger, she felt she had in her what galleries of pictures could not buy.

It was a good mile to the one story, gambrel-roofed cottage where lived Captain Kittridge,—the long, lean, brown man, with his good wife of the great Leghorn bonnet, round, black bead eyes, and psalm-book, whom we told you of at the funeral.

The Captain, too, had followed the sea in his early life, but being not, as he expressed it, "very rugged," in time changed his ship for a tight little cottage on the sea-shore, and devoted himself to boat-building, which he found sufficiently lucrative to furnish his brown cottage with all that his wife's heart desired, besides extra money for knick-knacks when she chose to go up to Brunswick or over to Portland to shop.

The Captain himself was a welcome guest at all the firesides round, being a chatty body, and disposed to make the most of his foreign experiences, in which he took the usual advantages of a traveller. In fact, it was said, whether slanderously or not, that the Captain's yarns were spun to order; and as, when pressed to relate his foreign adventures, he always responded with, "What would you like to hear?" it was thought that he fabricated his article to suit his market. In short, there was no species of experience, finny, fishy, or aquatic,—no legend of strange and unaccountable incident of fire or flood,—no romance of foreign scenery and productions, to which his tongue was not competent, when he had once seated himself in a double bow-knot at a neighbor's evening fireside.

His good wife, a sharp-eyed, literal body, and a vigorous church-member, felt some concern of conscience on the score of these narrations; for, being their constant auditor, she, better than any one else, could perceive the variations and discrepancies of text which showed their mythical character, and oftentimes her black eyes would snap and her knitting-needles rattle with an admonitory vigor as he went on, and sometimes she would unmercifully come in at the end of a narrative with,—

"Well, now, the Cap'n's told them ar stories till he begins to b'lieve 'em himself, *I think.*"

But works of fiction, as we all know, if only well gotten up, have always their advantages in the hearts of listeners over plain, homely truth; and so Captain Kittridge's yarns were marketable fireside commodities still, despite the scepticisms which attended them.

The afternoon sunbeams at this moment are painting the gambrel-roof with a golden brown. It is September again, as it was three years ago when our story commenced, and the sea and sky are purple and amethystine with its Italian haziness of atmosphere.

The brown house stands on a little knoll, about a hundred yards from the open ocean. Behind it rises a ledge of rocks, where cedars and hemlocks make deep shadows into which the sun shoots golden shafts of light, illuminating the scarlet feathers of the sumach, which threw themselves jauntily forth from the crevices; while down below, in deep, damp, mossy recesses, rose ferns which autumn had just begun to tinge with yellow and brown. The little knoll where the cottage stood, had on its right hand a tiny bay, where the ocean water made up amid picturesque rocks—shaggy and solemn. Here trees of the primeval forest, grand and lordly, looked down silently into the waters which ebbed and flowed daily into this little pool. Every variety of those beautiful evergreens which feather the coast of Maine, and dip their wings in the very spray of its ocean foam, found here a representative. There were aspiring black spruces, crowned on the very top with heavy coronets of cones; there were balsamic firs, whose young buds breathe the scent of strawberries; there were cedars, black as midnight clouds, and white pines with their swaying plumage of needle-like leaves, strewing the ground beneath with a golden, fragrant matting; and there were the gigantic, wide-winged hemlocks, hundreds of years old, and with long, swaying, gray beards of moss, looking white and ghostly under the deep shadows of their boughs. And beneath, creeping round trunk and matting over stones, were many and many of those wild, beautiful things which embellish the shadows of these northern forests. Long, feathery wreaths of what are called ground-pines, ran here and there in little ruffles of green, and the prince's pine raised its oriental feather, with a mimic cone on the top, as if it conceived itself to be a grown-up tree. Whole patches of partridge-berry wove their evergreen matting, dotted plentifully with brilliant scarlet berries. Here and there, the rocks were covered with a curiously inwoven tapestry of moss, overshot with the exquisite vine of the Linnea borealis, which in early spring rings its two fairy bells on the end of every spray; while elsewhere the wrinkled leaves of the mayflower wove themselves through and through deep beds of moss, meditating silently thoughts of the thousand little cups of pink shell which they had it in hand to make when the time of miracles should come round next spring.

Nothing, in short, could be more quaintly fresh, wild, and beautiful than the surroundings of this little cove which Captain Kittridge had thought fit to dedicate to his boat-building operations,—where he had set up his tar-kettle between two great rocks above the highest tide-mark, and where, at the present moment, he had a boat upon the stocks.

Mrs. Kittridge, at this hour, was sitting in her clean kitchen, very busily engaged in ripping up a silk dress, which Miss Roxy had engaged to come and make into a new one; and, as she ripped, she cast now and then an eye at the face of a tall, black clock, whose solemn tick-tock was the only sound that could be heard in the kitchen.

By her side, on a low stool, sat a vigorous, healthy girl of six years, whose employment evidently did not please her, for her well-marked black eyebrows were bent in a frown, and her large black eyes looked surly and wrathful, and one versed in children's grievances could easily see what the matter was,—she was turning a sheet! Perhaps, happy young female reader, you don't know what that is,—most likely not; for in these degenerate days the strait and narrow ways of self-denial, formerly thought so wholesome for little feet, are quite grass-grown with neglect. Childhood nowadays is unceasingly fêted and caressed, the principal difficulty of the grown people seeming to be to discover what the little dears want,—a thing not always clear to the little dears themselves. But in old times, turning sheets was thought a most especial and wholesome discipline for young girls; in the first place, because it took off the hands of their betters a very uninteresting and monotonous labor; and in the second place, because it was such a long, straight, unending turnpike, that the youthful travellers, once started thereupon, could go on indefinitely, without requiring guidance and direction of their elders. For these reasons, also, the task was held in special detestation by children in direct proportion to their amount of life, and their ingenuity and love of variety. A dull child took it tolerably well; but to a lively, energetic one, it was a perfect torture.

"I don't see the use of sewing up sheets one side, and ripping up the other," at last said Sally, breaking the monotonous tick-tock of the clock by an observation which has probably occurred to every child in similar circumstances.

"Sally Kittridge, if you say another word about that ar sheet, I'll whip you," was the very explicit rejoinder; and there was a snap of Mrs. Kittridge's black eyes, that seemed to make it likely that she would keep her word. It was answered by another snap from the six-year-old eyes, as Sally comforted herself with thinking that when she was a woman she'd speak her mind out in pay for all this.

At this moment a burst of silvery child-laughter rang out, and there appeared in the door-way, illuminated by the afternoon sunbeams, the vision of Miss Roxy's tall, lank figure, with the little golden-haired, blue-robed fairy, hanging like a gay butterfly upon the tip of a thorn-bush. Sally dropped the sheet and clapped her hands, unnoticed by her mother, who rose to pay her respects to the "cunning woman" of the neighbor-hood.

"Well, now, Miss Roxy, I was 'mazin' afraid you wer'n't a-comin'. I'd just been an' got my silk ripped up, and did n't know how to get a step farther without you."

"Well, I was finishin' up Cap'n Pennel's best pantaloons," said Miss Roxy; "and I've got 'em along so, Ruey can go on with 'em; and I told Mis' Pennel I must come to you, if 't was only for a day; and I fetched the little girl down, 'cause the little thing's so kind o' lonesome like. I thought Sally could play with her, and chirk her up a little."

"Well, Sally," said Mrs. Kittridge, "stick in your needle, fold up your

sheet, put your thimble in your work-pocket, and then you may take the
little Mara down to the cove to play; but be sure you don't let her go near
the tar, nor wet her shoes. D'ye hear?"

"Yes, ma'am," said Sally, who had sprung up in light and radiance,
like a translated creature, at this unexpected turn of fortune, and performed the welcome orders with a celerity which showed how agreeable
they were; and then, stooping and catching the little one in her arms,
disappeared through the door, with the golden curls fluttering over her
own crow-black hair.

The fact was, that Sally, at that moment, was as happy as human
creature could be, with a keenness of happiness that children who have
never been made to turn sheets of a bright afternoon can never realize.

The sun was yet an hour high, as she saw, by the flash of her shrewd,
time-keeping eye, and she could bear her little prize down to the cove,
and collect unknown quantities of gold and silver shells, and star-fish,
and salad-dish shells, and white pebbles for her, besides quantities of
well-turned shavings, brown and white, from the pile which constantly
was falling under her father's joiner's bench, and with which she would
make long extemporaneous tresses, so that they might play at being
mermaids, like those that she had heard her father tell about in some of
his sea-stories.

"Now, railly, Sally, what you got there?" said Captain Kittridge, as he
stood in his shirt-sleeves peering over his joiner's bench, to watch the
little one whom Sally had dumped down into a nest of clean white shavings. "Wal', wal', I should think you'd a-stolen the big doll I see in a
shop-window the last time I was to Portland. So this is Pennel's little
girl?—poor child!"

"Yes, father, and we want some nice shavings."

"Stay a bit, I'll make ye a few a-purpose," said the old man, reaching
his long, bony arm, with the greatest ease, to the farther part of his
bench, and bringing up a board, from which he proceeded to roll off
shavings in fine satin rings, which perfectly delighted the hearts of the
children, and made them dance with glee; and, truth to say, reader, there
are coarser and homelier things in the world than a well-turned shaving.

"There, go now," he said, when both of them stood with both hands
full; "go now and play; and mind you don't let the baby wet her feet,
Sally; them shoes o' hern must have cost five-and-sixpence at the very
least."

That sunny hour before sundown seemed as long to Sally as the whole
seam of the sheet; for childhood's joys are all pure gold; and as she ran up
and down the white sands, shouting at every shell she found, or darted up
into the overhanging forest for checkerberries and ground-pine, all the
sorrows of the morning came no more into her remembrance.

The little Mara had one of those sensitive, excitable natures, on which
every external influence acts with immediate power. Stimulated by the

society of her energetic, buoyant little neighbor, she no longer seemed wishful or pensive, but kindled into a perfect flame of wild delight, and gambolled about the shore like a blue and gold-winged fly; while her bursts of laughter made the squirrels and blue jays look out inquisitively from their fastnesses in the old evergreens. Gradually the sunbeams faded from the pines, and the waves of the tide in the little cove came in, solemnly tinted with purple, flaked with orange and crimson, borne in from a great rippling sea of fire, into which the sun had just sunk.

"Mercy on us—them children!" said Miss Roxy.

"*He's* bringin' 'em along," said Mrs. Kittridge, as she looked out of the window and saw the tall, lank form of the Captain, with one child seated on either shoulder, and holding on by his head.

The two children were both in the highest state of excitement, but never was there a more marked contrast of nature. The one seemed a perfect type of well-developed childish health and vigor, good solid flesh and bones, with glowing skin, brilliant eyes, shining teeth, well-knit, supple limbs,—vigorously and healthily beautiful; while the other appeared one of those aerial mixtures of cloud and fire, whose radiance seems scarcely earthly. A physiologist, looking at the child, would shake his head, seeing one of those perilous organizations, all nerve and brain, which come to life under the clear stimulating skies of America, and, burning with the intensity of lighted phosphorus, waste themselves too early.

The little Mara seemed like a fairy sprite, possessed with a wild spirit of glee. She laughed and clapped her hands incessantly, and when set down on the kitchen-floor spun round like a little elf; and that night it was late and long before her wide, wakeful eyes could be veiled in sleep.

"Company jist sets this 'ere child crazy," said Miss Roxy; "it's jist her lonely way of livin'; a pity Mis' Pennel had n't another child to keep company along with her."

"Mis' Pennel oughter be trainin' of her up to work," said Mrs. Kittridge. "Sally could oversew and hem when she wa' n't more'n three years old; nothin' straightens out children like work. Mis' Pennel she jist keeps that ar child to look at."

"All children a'n't alike, Mis' Kittridge," said Miss Roxy, sententiously. "This 'un a'n't like your Sally. 'A hen and a bumble-bee can't be fetched up alike, fix it how you will!'"

CHAPTER VII.

DURING the night and storm, the little Mara had lain sleeping as quietly as if the cruel sea, that had made her an orphan from her birth, were her kind-tempered old grandfather singing her to sleep, as he often did,—with a somewhat hoarse voice truly, but with ever an undertone of protecting love.

But toward daybreak, there came very clear and bright into her child-ish mind a dream, having that vivid distinctness which often characterizes the dreams of early childhood.

She thought she saw before her the little cove where she and Sally had been playing the day before, with its broad sparkling white beach of sand curving round its blue sea-mirror, and studded thickly with gold and silver shells. She saw the boat of Captain Kittridge upon the stocks, and his tar-kettle with the smouldering fires flickering under it; but, as often happens in dreams, a certain rainbow vividness and clearness invested everything, and she and Sally were jumping for joy at the beautiful things they found on the beach.

Suddenly, there stood before them a woman, dressed in a long white garment. She was very pale, with sweet, serious dark eyes, and she led by the hand a black-eyed boy, who seemed to be crying and looking about as for something lost. She dreamed that she stood still, and the woman came toward her, looking at her with sweet, sad eyes, till the child seemed to feel them in every fibre of her frame. The woman laid her hand on her head as if in blessing, and then put the boy's hand in hers, and said, "Take him, Mara, he is a playmate for you;" and with that the little boy's face flashed out into a merry laugh. The woman faded away, and the three children remained playing together, gathering shells and pebbles of a wonderful brightness. So vivid was this vision, that the little one awoke laughing with pleasure, and searched under her pillows for the strange and beautiful things she had been gathering in dreamland.

"What's Mara looking after?" said Sally, sitting up in her trundle-bed, and speaking in the patronizing motherly tone she commonly used to her little playmate.

"All gone, pitty boy—all gone!" said the child, looking round regret-fully, and shaking her golden head; "pitty lady all gone!"

"How queer she talks!" said Sally, who had awakened with the project of building a sheet-house with her fairy neighbor, and was beginning to loosen the upper sheet and dispose the pillows with a view to this species of architecture.

"Come, Mara, let's make a pretty house!" she said.

"Pitty boy out dere—out dere!" said the little one, pointing to the window, with a deeper expression than ever of wishfulness in her eyes.

"Come, Sally Kittridge, get up this minute!" said the voice of her mother, entering the door at this moment "and here, put these clothes onto Mara, the child must n't run round in her best; it's strange, now, Mary Pennel never thinks of such things."

Sally, who was of an efficient temperament, was preparing energeti-cally to second these commands of her mother, and endue her little neigh-bor with a coarse brown stuff dress, somewhat faded and patched, which she herself had outgrown when of Mara's age; with shoes, which had been coarsely made to begin with, and very much battered by time; but, quite to her surprise, the child, generally so passive and tractable, opposed a most unexpected and desperate resistance to this operation. She began to cry and to sob and shake her curly head, throwing her tiny hands out in a wild species of freakish opposition, which had, notwithstanding, a quaint and singular grace about it, while she stated her objections in all the little English at her command.

"Mara don't want—Mara want pitty boo des—and *pitty* shoes."

"Why, was ever anything like it?" said Mrs. Kittridge to Miss Roxy, as they both were drawn to the door by the outcry; "here's this child won't have decent every-day clothes put on her,—she must be kept dressed up like a princess. Now, that ar's French calico!" said Mrs. Kittridge, holding up the controverted blue dress, "and that ar never cost a cent under five-and-sixpence a yard; it takes a yard and a half to make it, and it must have been a good day's work to make it up; call that three-and-sixpence more, and with them pearl buttons and thread and all, that ar dress never cost less than a dollar and seventy-five, and here she's goin' to run out every day in it!"

"Well, well!" said Miss Roxy, who had taken the sobbing fair one in her lap, "you know, Mis' Kittridge, this 'ere 's a kind o' pet lamb, an old-folks' darling, and things *be* with her *as* they be, and we can't make her over, and she's such a nervous little thing we must n't cross her." Saying which, she proceeded to dress the child in her own clothes.

"If you had a good large checked apron, I wouldn't mind putting that on her!" added Miss Roxy, after she had arrayed the child.

"Here's one," said Mrs. Kittridge; "that may save her clothes some."

Miss Roxy began to put on the wholesome garment; but, rather to her mortification, the little fairy began to weep again in a most heart-broken manner.

"Don't want che't apon."

"Why don't Mara want nice checked apron?" said Miss Roxy, in that extra cheerful tone by which children are to be made to believe they have mistaken their own mind.

"Don't want it!" with a decided wave of the little hand; "I 's too pitty to wear che't apon."

"Well! well!" said Mrs. Kittridge, rolling up her eyes, "*did* I ever! no, I never did. If there a'n't depraved natur' a-comin' out early. *Well*, if she says she's pretty now, what 'll it be when she 's fifteen?"

"She'll learn to tell a lie about it by that time," said Miss Roxy, "and say she thinks she 's horrid. The child *is* pretty, and the truth comes uppermost with her now."

"Haw! haw! haw!" burst with a great crash from Captain Kittridge, who had come in behind, and stood silently listening during this conversation; "that 's musical now; come here, my little maid, you *are* too pretty for checked aprons, and no mistake;" and seizing the child in his long arms, he tossed her up like a butterfly, while her sunny curls shone in the morning light.

"There's one comfort about the child, Miss Kittridge," said Aunt Roxy; "she's one of them that dirt won't stick to. I never knew her to stain or tear her clothes,—she always come in jist so nice."

"She a'n't much like Sally, then!" said Mrs. Kittridge. "That girl 'll run through more clothes! Only last week she walked the crown out of my old black straw bonnet, and left it hanging on the top of a blackberry-bush."

"Wal', wal'," said Captain Kittridge, "as to dressin' this 'ere child,—why, ef Pennel's a mind to dress her in cloth of gold, it's none of our business! He's rich enough for all *he* wants to do, and so let's eat our breakfast and mind our own business."

After breakfast Captain Kittridge took the two children down to the cove, to investigate the state of his boat and tar-kettle, set high above the highest tide-mark.

The sun had risen gloriously, the sky was of an intense, vivid blue, and only great snowy islands of clouds, lying in silver banks on the horizon, showed vestiges of last night's storm. The whole wide sea was one glorious scene of forming and dissolving mountains of blue and purple, breaking at the crest into brilliant silver. All round the island the waves were constantly leaping and springing into jets and columns of brilliant foam, throwing themselves high up, in silvery cataracts, into the very arms of the solemn evergreen forests which overhung the shore.

The sands of the little cove seemed harder and whiter than ever, and were thickly bestrewn with the shells and sea-weed which the upturnings of the night had brought in. There lay what might have been fringes and fragments of sea-gods' vestures,—blue, crimson, purple, and orange sea weeds, wreathed in tangled ropes of kelp and sea-grass, or lying separately scattered on the sands. The children ran wildly, shouting as they began gathering sea-treasures; and Sally, with the air of an experienced hand in the business, untwisted the coils of ropy sea-weed, from which every moment she disengaged some new treasure, in some rarer shell or smoother pebble.

Suddenly, the child shook out something from a knotted mass of sea-grass, which she held up with a perfect shriek of delight.

It was a bracelet of hair, fastened by a brilliant clasp of green, sparkling stones, such as she had never seen before.

She redoubled her cries of delight, as she saw it sparkle between her and the sun, calling upon her father.

"Father! father! do come here, and see what I've found!"

He came quickly, and took the bracelet from the child's hand; but, at the same moment, looking over her head, he caught sight of an object partially concealed behind a projecting rock. He took a step forward, and uttered an exclamation,—

"Well, well! sure enough! poor things!"

There lay, bedded in sand and sea-weed, a woman with a little boy clasped in her arms! Both had been carefully lashed to a spar, but the child was held to the bosom of the woman, with a pressure closer than any knot that mortal hands could tie.

Both were deep sunk in the sand, into which had streamed the woman's long, dark hair, which sparkled with glittering morsels of sand and pebbles, and with those tiny, brilliant, yellow shells which are so numerous on that shore.

The woman was both young and beautiful. The forehead, damp with ocean-spray, was like sculptured marble,—the eyebrows dark and decided in their outline; but the long, heavy, black fringes had shut down, as a solemn curtain, over all the history of mortal joy or sorrow that those eyes had looked upon. A wedding-ring gleamed on the marble hand; but the sea had divorced all human ties, and taken her as a bride to itself. And, in truth, it seemed to have made to her a worthy bed, for she was all folded and inwreathed in sand and shells and sea-weeds, and a great weird-looking leaf of kelp, some yards in length, lay twined around her like a shroud.

The child that lay in her bosom had hair, and face, and eyelashes like her own, and his little hands were holding tightly a portion of the black dress which she wore.

"Cold,—cold,—stone dead!" was the muttered exclamation of the old seaman, as he bent over the woman.

"She must have struck her head there," he mused, as he laid his finger on a dark, bruised spot on her temple. He laid his hand on the child's heart, and put one finger under the arm to see if there was any lingering vital heat, and then hastily cut the lashings that bound the pair to the spar, and with difficulty disengaged the child from the cold clasp in which dying love had bound him to a heart which should beat no more with mortal joy or sorrow.

Sally, after the first moment, had run screaming toward the house, with all a child's forward eagerness, to be the bearer of news; but the little Mara stood, looking anxiously, with a wishful earnestness of face.

"Pitty boy,—pitty boy,—come!" she said often; but the old man was so busy, he scarcely regarded her.

"Now, Cap'n Kittridge, do tell!" said Miss Roxy, meeting him in all haste, with a cap-border stiff in air, while Dame Kittridge exclaimed,—

"Now, you don't! Well, well! did n't I say that was a ship last night? And what a solemnizing thought it was, that souls might be goin' into eternity!"

"We must have blankets and hot bottles, right away!" said Miss Roxy, who always took the earthly view of matters, and who was, in her own person, a personified humane society. "Miss Kittridge, you jist dip out your dishwater into the smallest tub, and we'll put him in. Stand away, Mara! Sally, you take her out of the way! We'll fetch this child to, perhaps. I've fetched 'em to, when they 's seemed to be dead as door-nails!"

"Cap'n Kittridge, you 're sure the woman's dead?"

"Laws, yes; she had a blow right on her temple here. There 's no bringing her to till the resurrection."

"Well, then, you jist go and get Cap'n Pennel to come down and help you, and get the body into the house, and we'll attend to layin' it out by and by. Tell Ruey to come down."

Aunt Roxy issued her orders with all the military vigor and precision of a general in case of a sudden attack. It was her habit. Sickness and death were her opportunities; where *they* were, she felt herself at home, and she addressed herself to the task before her with undoubting faith.

Before many hours a pair of large, dark eyes slowly emerged from under the black-fringed lids of the little drowned boy,—they rolled dreamily round for a moment, and dropped again in heavy languor.

The little Mara had, with the quiet persistence which formed a trait in her baby character, dragged stools and chairs to the back of the bed, which she at last succeeded in scaling, and sat opposite to where the child lay, grave and still, watching with intense earnestness the process that was going on.

At the moment when the eyes had opened, she stretched forth her little arms, and said, eagerly, "Pitty boy, come,"—and then, as they closed again, she dropped her hands with a sigh of disappointment. Yet, before night, the little stranger sat up in bed, and laughed with pleasure at the treasures of shells and pebbles which the children spread out on the bed before him.

He was a vigorous, well-made, handsome child, with brilliant eyes and teeth, but the few words that he spoke were in a language unknown to most present. Captain Kittridge declared it to be Spanish, and that a call which he most passionately and often repeated was for his mother. But he was of that happy age when sorrow can be easily effaced, and the efforts of the children called forth joyous smiles. When his playthings did not go to his liking, he showed sparkles of a fiery, irascible spirit.

The little Mara seemed to appropriate him in feminine fashion, as a chosen idol and graven image. She gave him at once all her slender stock of infantine treasures, and seemed to watch with an ecstatic devotion his every movement,—often repeating, as she looked delightedly around, "Pitty boy, *come.*"

She had no words to explain the strange dream of the morning; it lay in her, struggling for expression, and giving her an interest in the new-comer as in something belonging to herself. Whence it came,—whence come multitudes like it, which spring up as strange, enchanted flowers, every now and then in the dull, material pathway of life,—who knows?

It may be that our present faculties have among them a rudimentary one, like the germs of wings in the chrysalis, by which the spiritual world becomes sometimes an object of perception,—there may be natures in which the walls of the material are so fine and translucent that the spiritual is seen through them as through a glass darkly. It may be, too, that the love which is stronger than death has a power sometimes to make itself heard and felt through the walls of our mortality, when it would plead for the defenceless ones it has left behind. All these things *may* be,—who knows?

※　※　※　※　※　※

"There," said Miss Roxy, coming out of the keeping-room at sunset; "I would n't ask to see a better-lookin' corpse. That ar woman was a sight to behold this morning. I guess I shook a double handful of stones and them little shells out of her hair,—now she reely looks beautiful. Captain Kittridge has made a coffin out o' some cedar-boards he happened to have, and I lined it with bleached cotton, and stuffed the pillow nice and full, and when we come to get her in, she reely will look lovely."

"I s'pose, Mis' Kittridge, you'll have the funeral tomorrow,—it's Sunday."

"Why, yes, Aunt Roxy,—I think everybody must want to improve such a dispensation. Have you took little Mara in to look at the corpse?"

"Well, no," said Miss Roxy; "Mis' Pennel's gettin' ready to take her home."

"I think it's an opportunity we ought to improve," said Mrs. Kittridge, "to learn children what death is. I think we can't begin to solemnize their minds too young."

At this moment Sally and the little Mara entered the room.

"Come here, children," said Mrs. Kittridge, taking a hand of either one, and leading them to the closed door of the keeping-room; "I've got somethin' to show you."

The room looked ghostly and dim,—the rays of light fell through the closed shutter on an object mysteriously muffled in a white sheet.

Sally's bright face expressed only the vague curiosity of a child to see something new; but the little Mara resisted and hung back with all her force, so that Mrs. Kittridge was obliged to take her up and hold her.

She folded back the sheet from the chill and wintry form which lay so icily, lonely, and cold. Sally walked around it, and gratified her curiosity by seeing it from every point of view, and laying her warm, busy hand on the lifeless and cold one; but Mara clung to Mrs. Kittridge, with eyes that expressed a distressed astonishment. The good woman stooped over and placed the child's little hand for a moment on the icy forehead. The little one gave a piercing scream, and struggled to get away; and as soon as she was put down, she ran and hid her face in Aunt Roxy's dress, sobbing bitterly.

"That child'll grow up to follow vanity," said Mrs. Kittridge; "her little head is full of dress now, and she hates anything serious,—it's easy to see that."

The little Mara had no words to tell what a strange, distressful chill had passed up her arm and through her brain, as she felt that icy cold of death,—that cold so different from all others. It was an impression of fear and pain that lasted weeks and months, so that she would start out of sleep and cry with a terror which she had not yet a sufficiency of language to describe.

"You seem to forget, Mis' Kittridge, that this 'ere child a'n't rugged like our Sally," said Aunt Roxy, as she raised the little Mara in her arms. "She was a seven-months' baby, and hard to raise at all, and a shivery, scary little creature."

"Well, then, she ought to be hardened," said Dame Kittridge. "But Mary Pennel never had no sort of idea of bringin' up children,—'t was jist so with Naomi,—the girl never had no sort o' resolution, and she just died for want o' resolution,—that's what came of it. I tell ye, children's got to learn to take the world as it is; and 't a'n't no use bringin' on 'em up too tender. Teach 'em to begin as they've got to go on,—that's my maxim."

"Mis' Kittridge," said Aunt Roxy, "there's reason in all things, and there's difference in children. 'What's one's meat's another's pison.' You could n't fetch up Mis' Pennel's children, and she could n't fetch up yourn,—so let's say no more 'bout it."

"I'm always a-tellin' my wife that ar," said Captain Kittridge; "she's always wantin' to make everybody over after her pattern."

"Cap'n Kittridge, I don't think *you* need to speak," resumed his wife. "When such a loud providence is a-knockin' at *your* door, I think you'd better be a-searchin' your own heart,—here it is the eleventh hour, and you ha'n't come into the Lord's vineyard yet."

"Oh! come, come, Mis' Kittridge, don't twit a feller afore folks," said the Captain. "I'm goin' over to Harpswell Neck this blessed minute after the minister to 'tend the funeral,—so we'll let *him* preach."

CHAPTER XIII.

Zephaniah Pennel was what might be called a Hebrew of the Hebrews.

New England, in her earlier days, founding her institutions on the Hebrew Scriptures, bred better Jews than Moses could, because she read Moses with the amendments of Christ.

The state of society in some of the districts of Maine, in these days, much resembled in its spirit that which Moses labored to produce in ruder ages. It was entirely democratic, simple, grave, hearty, and sincere,—solemn and religious in its daily tone, and yet, as to all material good, full of wholesome thrift and prosperity. Perhaps, taking the average mass of the people, a more healthful and desirable state of society never existed. Its better specimens had a simple Doric grandeur unsurpassed in any age.

The bringing up a child in this state of society was a far more simple enterprise than in our modern times, when the factitious wants and aspirations are so much more developed.

Zephaniah Pennel was as high as anybody in the land. He owned not only the neat little schooner, "Brilliant," with divers small fishing-boats, but also a snug farm, adjoining the brown house, together with some fresh, juicy pasture-lots on neighboring islands, where he raised mutton, unsurpassed even by the English South-down, and wool, which furnished homespun to clothe his family on all everyday occasions.

Mrs. Pennel, to be sure, had silks and satins, and flowered India chintz, and even a Cashmere shawl, the fruits of some of her husband's earlier voyages, which were, however, carefully stowed away for occasions so high and mighty, that they seldom saw the light.

Not to wear best things every day, was a maxim of New England thrift, as little disputed as any verse of the catechism; and so Mrs. Pennel found the stuff gown of her own dyeing and spinning so respectable for most purposes, that it figured even in the meeting-house itself, except on the very finest of Sundays, when heaven and earth seemed alike propitious.

A person can well afford to wear homespun stuff to meeting, who is buoyed up by a secret consciousness of an abundance of fine things that could be worn, if one were so disposed, and everybody respected Mrs. Pennel's homespun the more, because they thought of the things she did n't wear.

As to advantages of education, the island, like all other New England districts, had its common school, where one got the key of knowledge,— for having learned to read, write, and cipher, the young fellow of those regions commonly regarded himself as in possession of all that a man needs, to help himself to any further acquisitions he might desire.

The boys then made fishing voyages to the Banks, and those who were so disposed took their books with them. If a boy did not wish to be bored with study, there was nobody to force him; but if a bright one saw visions of future success in life lying through the avenues of knowledge, he found many a leisure hour to pore over his books, and work out the problems of navigation directly over the element they were meant to control.

Four years having glided by since the commencement of our story, we find in the brown house of Zephaniah Pennel, a tall, well-knit, handsome boy of ten years, who knows no fear of wind or sea—who can set you over from Orr's Island to Harpswell, either in sail or row-boat, he thinks, as well as any man living—who knows every rope of the schooner "Brilliant," and fancies he could command it as well as "father" himself—and is supporting himself this spring, during the tamer drudgeries of driving plough, and dropping potatoes, with the glorious vision of being taken this year on the annual trip to "the Banks," which comes on after planting. He reads fluently,—witness the "Robinson Crusoe," which never departs from under his pillow, and Goldsmith's "History of Greece and Rome," which good Mr. Sewell has lent him,—and he often brings shrewd criticisms on the character and course of Romulus or Alexander into the common current of every-day life, in a way that brings a smile over the grave face of Zephaniah, and makes Mrs. Pennel think the boy certainly ought to be sent to college.

As for Mara, she is now a child of seven, still adorned with long golden curls—still looking dreamily out of soft hazel eyes into some unknown future not her own. She has no dreams for herself—they are all for Moses.

For his sake she has learned all the womanly little accomplishments which Mrs. Kittridge has dragooned into Sally. She knits his mittens and his stockings, and hems his pocket-handkerchiefs, and aspires to make his shirts all herself. Whatever book Moses reads, forthwith she aspires to read too, and though three years younger, reads with a far more precocious insight.

Her little form is slight and frail, and her cheek has a clear transparent brilliancy quite different from the rounded one of the boy; she looks not exactly in ill health, but has that sort of transparent appearance which one fancies might be an attribute of fairies and sylphs. All her outward senses are finer and more acute than his, and finer and more delicate all the attributes of her mind. Those who contend against giving woman the same education as man, do it on the ground that it would make the woman unfeminine—as if Nature had done her work so slightly that it could be so easily ravelled and knit over. In fact, there is a masculine and a feminine element in all knowledge, and a man and a woman put to the same study extract only what their nature fits them to see—so that knowledge can be fully orbed only when the two unite in the search and share the spoils.

When Moses was full of Romulus and Numa, Mara pondered the story of the nymph Egeria—sweet parable, in which lies all we have been saying.

Her trust in him was boundless. He was a constant hero in her eyes, and in her he found a steadfast believer as to all possible feats and exploits to which he felt himself competent, for the boy often had privately assured her that he could command the Brilliant as well as father himself.

Spring had already come, loosing the chains of ice in all the bays and coves round Harpswell, Orr's Island, Maquoit, and Middle Bay. The magnificent spruces stood forth in their gala-dresses, tipped on every point with vivid emerald; the silver firs exuded from their tender shoots the fragrance of ripe pine-apple; the white pines shot forth long weird fingers at the end of their fringy boughs; and even every little mimic evergreen in the shadows at their feet was made beautiful by the addition of a vivid border of green on the sombre coloring of its last year's leaves. Arbutus, fragrant with its clean, wholesome odors, gave forth its thousand dewy pink blossoms, and the trailing Linnea borealis hung its pendent twin bells round every mossy stump and old rock damp with green forest mould. The green and vermilion matting of the partridge-berry was impearled with white velvet blossoms, the checkerberry hung forth a translucent bell under its varnished green leaf, and a thousand more fairy bells, white or red, hung on blueberry and huckleberry bushes. The little Pearl of Orr's Island had wandered many an hour gathering bouquets of all these, to fill the brown house with sweetness when her grandfather and Moses should come in from work.

The love of flowers seemed to be one of her earliest characteristics, and the young spring flowers of New England, in their airy delicacy and fragility, were much like herself—and so strong seemed the affinity between them, that not only Mrs. Pennel's best India china vases on the keeping-room mantel were filled, but here stood a tumbler of scarlet rock columbine, and there a bowl of blue and white violets, and in another place a saucer of shell-tinted crow-foot, blue liverwort, and white anemone, so that Zephaniah Pennel was wont to say there was n't a drink of water to be got, for Mara's flowers; but he always said it with a smile that made his weather-beaten, hard features look like a rock lit up by a sunbeam. Little Mara was the pearl of the old seaman's life, every finer particle of his nature came out in her concentrated and polished, and he often wondered at a creature so ethereal belonging to him—as if down on some shaggy sea-green rock an old pearl oyster should muse and marvel on the strange silvery mystery of beauty that was growing in the silence of his heart.

But May has passed; the arbutus and the Linnea are gone from the woods, and the pine tips have grown into young shoots, which wilt at noon under a direct reflection from sun and sea, and the blue sky has that metallic clearness and brilliancy which distinguishes those regions, and the planting is at last over, and this very morning Moses is to set off in the Brilliant for his first voyage to the Banks.

Glorious knight he! the world all before him, and the blood of ten years racing and throbbing in his veins as he talks knowingly of hooks, and sinkers, and bait, and lines, and wears proudly the red flannel shirt which Mara had just finished for him.

"How I do wish I were going with you!" she says. "I could do something, could n't I—take care of your hooks, or something?"

"Pooh!" said Moses, sublimely regarding her while he settled the collar of his shirt, "you're a girl—and what can girls do at sea? you never like to catch fish—it always makes you cry to see 'em flop."

"Oh, yes, poor fish!" said Mara, perplexed between her sympathy for the fish and her desire for the glory of her hero, which must be founded on their pain; "I can't help feeling sorry when they gasp so."

"Well, and what do you suppose you would do when the men are pulling up twenty and forty pounder?" said Moses, striding sublimely. "Why, they flop so, they'd knock *you* over in a minute."

"Do they? Oh, Moses, *do* be careful. What if they should hurt you?"

"Hurt *me!*" said Moses, laughing; "that's a good one. I'd like to see a fish that could hurt *me.*"

"Do hear that boy talk!" said Mrs. Pennel to her husband, as they stood within their chamber-door.

"Yes, yes," said Captain Pennel, smiling; "he's full of the matter. I believe he'd take the command of the schooner this morning if I'd let him."

The Brilliant lay all this while courtesying on the waves, which kissed and whispered to the little coquettish craft. A fairer June morning had not risen on the shores that week; the blue mirror of the ocean was all dotted over with the tiny white sails of fishing-craft bound on the same errand, and the breeze that was just crisping the waters had the very spirit of energy and adventure in it.

Everything and everybody was now on board, and she began to spread her fair wings, and slowly and gracefully to retreat from the shore.

Little Moses stood on the deck, his black curls blowing in the wind, and his large eyes dancing with excitement,—his clear olive complexion and glowing cheeks well set off by his red shirt.

Mrs. Pennel stood with Mara on the shore to see them go. The fair little golden-haired Ariadne shaded her eyes with one arm, and stretched the other after her Theseus, till the vessel grew smaller, and finally seemed to melt away into the eternal blue.

Many be the wives and lovers that have watched those little fishing-craft as they went gayly out like this, but have waited long—too long— and seen them again no more. In night and fog they have gone down under the keel of some ocean packet or Indiaman, and sunk with brave hearts and hands, like a bubble in the mighty waters. Yet Mrs. Pennel did not turn back to her house in apprehension of this. Her husband had made so many voyages, and always returned safely, that she confidently expected before long to see them home again.

The next Sunday the seat of Zephaniah Pennel was vacant in church. According to custom, a note was put up asking prayers for his safe return, and then everybody knew that he was gone to the Banks; and as the roguish, handsome face of Moses was also missing, Miss Roxy whispered to Miss Ruey, "There! Captain Pennel's took Moses on his first voyage. We must contrive to call round on Mis' Pennel afore long. She'll be lonesome."

Sunday evening Mrs. Pennel was sitting pensively with little Mara by the kitchen hearth, where they had been boiling the tea-kettle for their solitary meal. They heard a brisk step without, and soon Captain and Mrs. Kittridge made their appearance.

"Good-evening, Mis' Pennel," said the Captain; "I's a-tellin' my good woman we must come down and see how you's a-getting along. It's raly a work of necessity and mercy proper for the Lord's day. Rather lonesome now the Captain's gone, a'n't ye? Took little Moses, too, I see. Was n't at meetin' to-day, so I says, Mis' Kittridge, we'll just step down and chirk 'em up a little."

"I did n't really know how to come," said Mrs. Kittridge, as she allowed Mrs. Pennel to take her bonnet; "but Aunt Roxy's to our house now, and she said she'd see to Sally. So you've let the boy go to the Banks? He's young, a'n't he, for that?"

"Not a bit of it," said Captain Kittridge. "Why, I was off to the Banks long afore I was his age; and a capital time we had of it, too. Golly! how them fish *did* bite! We stood up to our knees in fish before we'd fished half an hour."

Mara, who had always a shy affinity for the Captain, now drew towards him and climbed on his knee.

"Did the wind blow very hard?" she said.

"What, my little maid?"

"Does the wind blow at the Banks?"

"Why, yes, my little girl, that it does, sometimes; but then there a'n't the least danger. Our craft ride out storms like live creatures. I've stood it out in gales that was tight enough, I'm sure. 'Member once I turned it 'tween twelve and one, and had n't more'n got asleep, afore I came *clump* out of my berth, and found everything upside down. And 'stead of goin' up-stairs to get on deck, I had to go right down. Fact was, that 'ere vessel jist turned clean over in the water, and come right side up like a duck."

"Well, now, Cap'n, I would n't be tellin' such a story as that," said his help-meet.

"Why, Polly, what do you know about it? you never was to sea. We *did* turn clear over, for I 'member I saw a bunch of sea-weed big as a peck measure stickin' top of the mast next day. Jist shows how safe them ar little fishing craft is,—for all they look like an egg-shell on the mighty deep, as Parson Sewell calls it."

"I was very much pleased with Mr. Sewell's exercise in prayer this morning," said Mrs. Kittridge; "it must have been a comfort to you, Mis' Pennel."

"It was, to be sure," said Mrs. Pennel.

"Puts me in mind of poor Mary Jane Simpson. Her husband went out, you know, last June, and ha' n't been heard of since. Mary Jane don't really know whether to put on mourning or not."

"Law! I don't think Mary Jane need give up yet," said the Captain. "'Member one year I was out, we got blowed clear up to Baffin's Bay, and got shut up in the ice, and had to go ashore and live jist as we could among them Esquimaux. Did n't get home for a year. Old folks had clean giv' us up. Don't need never despair of folks gone to sea, for they's sure to turn up, first or last."

"But I hope," said Mara, apprehensively, "that grandpapa won't get blown up to Baffin's Bay. I've seen that on his chart,—it's a good ways."

"And then there's them 'ere icebergs," said Mrs. Kittridge; "I'm always 'fraid of running into them in the fog."

"Law!" said Captain Kittridge, "I've met 'em bigger than all the colleges up to Brunswick,—great white bears on 'em,—hungry as Time in the Primer. Once we came kersmash on to one of 'em, and if the Flying Betsy had n't been made of whalebone and injer-rubber, she'd a-been stove all to pieces. Them white bears, they was so hungry, that they stood there with the water jist runnin' out of their chops in a perfect stream."

"Oh, dear, dear," said Mara, with wide round eyes, "what will Moses do if they get on the icebergs?"

"Yes," said Mrs. Kittridge, looking solemnly at the child through the black bows of her spectacles, "we can truly say:—

'Dangers stand thick through all the ground,
To push us to the tomb;'

as the hymn-book says."

The kind-hearted Captain, feeling the fluttering heart of little Mara, and seeing the tears start in her eyes, addressed himself forthwith to consolation.

"Oh, never you mind, Mara," he said, "there won't nothing hurt 'em. Look at me. Why, I've been everywhere on the face of the earth. I've been on icebergs, and among white bears and Indians, and seen storms that would blow the very hair off your head, and here I am, dry and tight as ever. You'll see 'em back before long."

The cheerful laugh with which the Captain was wont to chorus his sentences, sounded like the crackling of dry pine wood on the social hearth. One would hardly hear it without being lightened in heart; and little Mara gazed at his long, dry, ropy figure, and wrinkled thin face, as a sort of monument of hope; and his uproarious laugh, which Mrs. Kittridge sometimes ungraciously compared to "the crackling of thorns under a pot," seemed to her the most delightful thing in the world.

"Mary Jane was a-tellin' me," resumed Mrs. Kittridge, "that when her husband had been out a month, she dreamed she see him, and three other men, a-floatin' on an iceberg."

"Laws," said Captain Kittridge, "that's jist what my old mother dreamed about me, and 't was true enough, too, till we got off the ice on to the shore up in the Esquimaux territory, as I was a-tellin'. So you tell Mary Jane she need n't look out for a second husband *yet,* for that ar dream's a sartin sign he'll be back."

"Cap'n Kittridge!" said his help-meet, drawing herself up, and giving him an austere glance over her spectacles; "how often must I tell you that there *is* subjects which should n't be treated with levity?"

"Who's been a-treatin' of 'em with levity?" said the Captain. "I'm sure I a'n't. Mary Jane's good-lookin', and there's plenty of young fellows as sees it as well as me. I declare she looked as pretty as any young gal when she ris up in the singers' seats to-day. Put me in mind of you, Polly, when I first come home from the Injies."

"Oh, come now, Cap'n Kittridge! we'r' gettin' too old for that sort o' talk."

"*We* a'n't too old, be we, Mara?" said the Captain, trotting the little girl gayly on his knee; "and we a'n't afraid of icebergs and no sich, be we? I tell you they's a fine sight of a bright day; they has millions of steeples, all white and glistering, like the New Jerusalem, and the white bears have capital times trampin' round on 'em. Would n't little Mara like a great, nice white bear to ride on, with his white fur, so soft and warm, and a saddle made of pearls, and a gold bridle?"

"You hav' n't seen any little girls ride so," said Mara, doubtfully.

"I should n't wonder if I had; but you see, Mis' Kittridge there, she won't let me tell all I know," said the Captain, sinking his voice to a confidential tone; "you jist wait till we get alone."

"But, you are *sure,*" said Mara, confidingly, in return, "that white bears will be kind to Moses?"

"Lord bless you, yes, child, the kindest critturs in the world they be, if you only get the right side of 'em," said the Captain.

"Oh, yes! because," said Mara, "I know how good a wolf was to Romulus and Remus once, and nursed them when they were cast out to die. I read that in the Roman history."

"Jist so," said the Captain, enchanted at this historic confirmation of his apocrypha.

"And so," said Mara, "if Moses *should* happen to get on an iceberg, a bear might take care of him, you know."

"Jist so, jist so," said the Captain; "so don't you worry your little curly head one bit. Some time when you come down to see Sally, we'll go down to the cove, and I'll tell you lots of stories about chil'en that have been fetched up by white bears, jist like Romulus and what's his name there?"

"Come, Mis' Kittridge," added the cheery Captain; "you and I must n't be keepin' the folk up *till* nine o'clock."

"Well now," said Mrs. Kittridge, in a doleful tone, as she began to put on her bonnet, "Mis' Pennel, you must keep up your spirits—it's one's duty to take cheerful views of things. I'm sure many's the night, when the Captain's been gone to sea, I've laid and shook in my bed, hearin' the wind blow, and thinking what if I should be left a lone widow."

"There'd a-been a dozen fellows a-wanting to get you in six months, Polly," interposed the Captain. "Well, good-night, Mis' Pennel; there'll be a splendid haul of fish at the Banks this year, or there's no truth in signs. Come, my little Mara, got a kiss for the dry old daddy? That's my good girl. Well, good-night, and the Lord bless you."

And so the cheery Captain took up his line of march homeward, leaving little Mara's head full of dazzling visions of the land of romance to which Moses had gone.

She was yet on that shadowy boundary between the dreamland of childhood and the real land of life; so all things looked to her quite possible—and gentle white bears, with warm, soft fur and pearl and gold saddles, walked through her dreams, and the victorious curls of Moses appeared, with his bright eyes and cheeks, over glittering pinnacles of frost in the ice-land.

CHAPTER XV.

MRS. PENNEL, too, had seen the white, dove-like cloud on the horizon, and had hurried to make biscuits, and conduct other culinary preparations which should welcome the wanderers home.

The sun was just dipping into the great blue sea—a round ball of fire—and sending long, slanting tracks of light across the top of each wave, when a boat was moored at the beach, and the minister sprang out,—not in his suit of ceremony, but attired in fisherman's garb.

"Good-afternoon, Mrs. Pennel," he said. "I was out fishing, and I thought I saw your husband's schooner in the distance. I thought I'd come and tell you."

"Thank you, Mr. Sewell. I thought I saw it, but I was not certain. Do come in; the Captain would be delighted to see you here."

"We miss your husband in our meetings," said Mr. Sewell; "it will be good news for us all when he comes home; he is one of those I depend on to help me preach."

"I'm sure you don't preach to anybody who enjoys it more," said Mrs. Pennel. "He often tells me that the greatest trouble about his voyages to the Banks is that he loses so many sanctuary privileges; though he always keeps Sunday on his ship, and reads and sings his psalms; but, he says, after all, there's nothing like going to Mount Zion."

"And little Moses has gone on his first voyage?" said the minister.

"Yes, indeed; the child has been teasing to go for more than a year. Finally the Cap'n told him if he'd be faithful in the ploughing and planting he should go. You see, he's rather unsteady, and apt to be off after other things,—very different from Mara. Whatever you give her to do she always keeps at it till it's done."

"And pray, where is the little lady?" said the minister; "is she gone?"

"Well, Cap'n Kittridge came in this afternoon to take her down to see Sally. The Cap'n's always so fond of Mara, and she has always taken to him ever since she was a baby."

"The Captain is a curious creature," said the minister, smiling.

Mrs. Pennel smiled also; and it is to be remarked that nobody ever mentioned the poor Captain's name without the same curious smile.

"The Cap'n is a good-hearted, obliging creature," said Mrs. Pennel, "and a master-hand for telling stories to the children."

"Yes, a perfect 'Arabian Nights' Entertainment,'" said Mr. Sewell.

"Well, I really believe the Cap'n believes his own stories," said Mrs. Pennel; "he always seems to, and certainly a more obliging man and a kinder neighbor could n't be. He has been in and out almost every day since I've been alone, to see if I wanted anything. He would insist on chopping wood and splitting kindlings for me, though I told him the Cap'n and Moses had left a plenty to last till they came home."

At this moment the subject of their conversation appeared striding along the beach, with a large, red lobster in one hand, while with the other he held little Mara upon his shoulder, she the while clapping her hands and singing merrily, as she saw the Brilliant out on the open blue sea, its white sails looking of a rosy purple in the evening light, careering gayly homeward.

"There is Captain Kittridge this very minute," said Mrs. Pennel, setting down a teacup she had been wiping, and going to the door.

"Good-evening, Mis' Pennel," said the Captain. "I s'pose you see your folks are comin'. I brought down one of these 'ere ready b'iled, 'cause I thought it might make out your supper."

"Thank you, Captain; you must stay and take some with us."

"Wal', me and the children have pooty much done our supper," said the Captain. "We made a real fust-rate chowder down there to the cove; but I'll jist stay and see what the Cap'n's luck is. Massy!" he added, as he looked in at the door, "if you ha'n't got the minister there! Wal', now, I come jist as I be," he added, with a glance down at his clothes.

"Never mind, Captain," said Mr. Sewell; "I'm in my fishing-clothes, so we're even."

As to little Mara, she had run down to the beach, and stood so near the sea, that every dash of the tide-wave forced her little feet to tread an inch backward, stretching out her hands eagerly toward the schooner, which was standing straight toward the small wharf, not far from their door. Already she could see on deck figures moving about, and her sharp little eyes made out a small personage in a red shirt that was among the most active. Soon all the figures grew distinct, and she could see her grandfather's gray head, and alert, active form, and could see, by the signs he made, that he had perceived the little blowy figure that stood, with hair streaming in the wind, like some flower bent seaward.

And now they are come nearer, and Moses shouts and dances on the deck, and the Captain and Mrs. Pennel come running from the house down to the shore, and a few minutes more, and all are landed safe and sound, and little Mara is carried up to the house in her grandfather's arms, while Captain Kittridge stops to have a few moments' gossip with Ben Halliday and Tom Scranton before they go to their own resting-places.

Meanwhile Moses loses not a moment in boasting of his heroic exploits to Mara.

"Oh, Mara! you've no idea what times we've had! I can fish equal to any of 'em, and I can take in sail and tend the helm like anything, and I know all the names of everything; and you ought to have seen us catch fish! Why, they bit just as fast as we could throw; and it was just throw and bite,—throw and bite,—throw and bite; and my hands got blistered pulling in, but I did n't mind it,—I was determined no one should beat me."

"Oh! did you blister your hands?" said Mara, pitifully.

"Oh, to be sure! Now, you girls think that's a dreadful thing, but we men don't mind it. My hands are getting so hard, you've no idea. And, Mara, we caught a great shark."

"A shark!—oh, how dreadful! Is n't he dangerous?"

"Dangerous! I guess not. We served him out, I tell you. He 'll never eat any more people, I tell you, the old wretch!"

"But, poor shark, it is n't his fault that he eats people. He was *made* so," said Mara, unconsciously touching a deep theological mystery.

"Well, I don't know but he was," said Moses; "but sharks that *we* catch never eat any more, I'll bet *you*."

"Oh, Moses, did you see any icebergs?"

"Icebergs! yes; we passed right by one,—a real grand one."

"Were there any bears on it?"

"Bears! No; we did n't see any."

"Captain Kittridge says there are white bears live on 'em."

"Oh, Captain Kittridge," said Moses, with a toss of superb contempt; "if you're going to believe all *he* says, you've got your hands full."

"Why, Moses, you don't think he tells lies?" said Mara, the tears actually starting in her eyes. "I think he is *real* good, and tells nothing but the truth."

"Well, well, you are young yet," said Moses, turning away with an air of easy grandeur, "and only a girl besides," he added.

Mara was nettled at this speech. First, it pained her to have her child's faith shaken in anything, and particularly in her good old friend, the

Captain; and next, she felt, with more force than ever she did before, the continual disparaging tone in which Moses spoke of her girlhood.

"I'm sure," she said to herself, "he ought n't to feel so about girls and women. There was Deborah was a prophetess, and judged Israel; and there was Egeria,—she taught Numa Pompilius all his wisdom."

But it was not the little maiden's way to speak when anything thwarted or hurt her, but rather to fold all her feelings and thoughts inward, as some insects, with fine gauzy wings, draw them under a coat of horny concealment.

Somehow, there was a shivering sense of disappointment in all this meeting with Moses. She had dwelt upon it, and fancied so much, and had so many things to say to him; and he had come home so self-absorbed and glorious, and seemed to have had so little need of or thought for her, that she felt a cold, sad sinking at her heart; and walking away very still and white, sat down demurely by her grandfather's knee.

"Well, so my little girl is glad grandfather's come," he said, lifting her fondly in his arms, and putting her golden head under his coat, as he had been wont to do from infancy; "grandpa thought a great deal about his little Mara."

The small heart swelled against his. Kind, faithful old grandpa! how much more he thought about her than Moses; and yet she had thought so much of Moses.

And there he sat, this same ungrateful Moses, bright-eyed and rosy-cheeked, full of talk and gayety, full of energy and vigor, as ignorant as possible of the wound he had given to the little loving heart that was silently brooding under her grandfather's butternut-colored sea-coat. Not only was he ignorant, but he had not even those conditions within himself which made knowledge possible.

All that there was developed of him, at present, was a fund of energy, self-esteem, hope, courage, and daring, the love of action, life, and adventure; his life was in the outward and present, not in the inward and reflective; he was a true ten-year old boy, in its healthiest and most animal perfection. What she was, the small pearl with the golden hair, with her frail and high-strung organization, her sensitive nerves, her half-spiritual fibres, her ponderings, and marvels, and dreams, her power of love, and yearning for self-devotion, our readers may, perhaps, have seen. But if ever two children, or two grown people, thus organized, are thrown into intimate relations, it follows, from the very laws of their being, that one must hurt the other, simply by being itself; one must always hunger for what the other has not to give.

It was a merry meal, however, when they all sat down to the tea-table once more, and Mara by her grandfather's side, who often stopped what he was saying to stroke her head fondly. Moses bore a more prominent part in the conversation than he had been wont to do before this voyage, and all seemed to listen to him with a kind of indulgence elders often accord to a handsome, manly boy, in the first flush of some successful enterprise.

That ignorant confidence in one's self and one's future, which comes in life's first dawn, has a sort of mournful charm in experienced eyes, who know how much it all amounts to.

Gradually, little Mara quieted herself with listening to and admiring him.

It is not comfortable to have any heart-quarrel with one's cherished idol, and, everything of the feminine nature, therefore, can speedily find fifty good reasons for seeing one's self in the wrong and one's graven image in the right; and little Mara soon had said to herself, without words, that, of course, Moses could n't be expected to think as much of her as she of him. He was handsomer, cleverer, and had a thousand other things to do and to think of—he was a boy, in short, and going to be a glorious man and sail all over the world, while she could only hem handkerchiefs and knit stockings, and sit at home and wait for him to come back. This was about the *resumé* of life as it appeared to the little one, who went on from the moment worshipping her image with more undivided idolatry than ever, hoping that by and by he would think more of her.

Mr. Sewell appeared to study Moses carefully and thoughtfully, and encouraged the wild, gleeful frankness which he had brought home from his first voyage, as a knowing jockey tries the paces of a high-mettled colt.

"Did you get any time to read?" he interposed once, when the boy stopped in his account of their adventures.

"No, sir," said Moses; "at least," he added, blushing very deeply, "I did n't feel like reading. I had so much to do, and there was so much to see."

"It's all new to him now," said Captain Pennel; "but when he comes to being, as I've been, day after day, with nothing but sea and sky, he'll be glad of a book, just to break the sameness."

"Laws, yes," said Captain Kittridge; "sailor's life a'n't all apple-pie, as it seems when a boy first goes on a summer trip with his daddy—not by no manner o' means."

"But," said Mara, blushing and looking very eagerly at Mr. Sewell, "Moses has read a great deal. He read the Roman and the Grecian history through before he went away, and knows all about them."

"Indeed!" said Mr. Sewell, turning with an amused look towards the tiny little champion; "do you read them, too, my little maid?"

"Yes, indeed," said Mara, her eyes kindling; "I have read them a great deal since Moses went away—them and the Bible."

Mara did not dare to name her new-found treasure—there was something so mysterious about that, that she could not venture to produce it, except on the score of extreme intimacy.

"Come, sit by me, little Mara," said the minister, putting out his hand; "you and I must be friends, I see."

Mr. Sewell had a certain something of mesmeric power in his eyes which children seldom resisted; and with a shrinking movement, as if both attracted and repelled, the little girl got upon his knee.

"So you like the Bible and Roman history?" he said to her, making a little aside for her, while a brisk conversation was going on between Captain Kittridge and Captain Pennel on the fishing bounty for the year.

"Yes, sir," said Mara, blushing in a very guilty way.

"And which do you like the best?"

"I don't know, sir; I sometimes think it is the one, and sometimes the other."

"Well, what pleases you in the Roman history?"

"Oh, I like that about Quintus Curtius."

"Quintus Curtius?" said Mr. Sewell, pretending not to remember.

"Oh, don't you remember him? why, there was a great gulf opened in the Forum, and the Augurs said that the country would not be saved unless some one would offer himself up for it, and so he jumped right in, all on horseback. I think that was grand. I should like to have done that," said little Mara, her eyes blazing out with a kind of starry light which they had when she was excited.

"And how would you have liked it, if you had been a Roman girl, and Moses were Quintus Curtius? would you like to have him give himself up for the good of the country?"

"Oh, no, no!" said Mara, instinctively shuddering.

"Don't you think it would be very grand of him?"

"Oh, yes, sir."

"And should n't we wish our friends to do what is brave and grand?"

"Yes, sir; but then," she added, "it would be so dreadful *never* to see him any more," and a large tear rolled from the great soft eyes and fell on the minister's hand.

"Come, come," thought Mr. Sewell, "this sort of experimenting is too bad—too much nerve here, too much solitude, too much pine-whispering and sea-dashing are going to the making up of this little piece of workmanship."

"Tell me," he said, motioning Moses to sit by him, "how *you* like the Roman history."

"I like it first-rate," said Moses. "The Romans were such smashers, and beat everybody—nobody could stand against them; and I like Alexander, too—I think he was splendid."

"True boy," said Mr. Sewell to himself, "unreflecting brother of the wind and the sea, and all that is vigorous and active—no precocious development of the moral here."

"Now you have come," said Mr. Sewell, "I will lend you another book."

"Thank you, sir; I love to read them when I'm at home—it's so still here. I should be dull if I did n't."

Mara's eyes looked eagerly attentive. Mr. Sewell noticed their hungry look when a book was spoken of.

"And you must read it, too, my little girl," he said.

"Thank you, sir," said Mara; "I always want to read everything Moses does."

"What book is it?" said Moses.

"It is called Plutarch's 'Lives,'" said the minister; "it has more particular accounts of the men you read about in history."

"Are there any lives of women?" said Mara.

"No, my dear," said Mr. Sewell; "in the old times, women did not get their lives written, though I don't doubt many of them were much better worth writing than the men's."

"I should like to be a great general," said Moses, with a toss of his head.

"The way to be great lies through books, now, and not through battles," said the minister; "there is more done with pens than swords; so, if you want to do anything, you must read and study."

"Do you think of giving this boy a liberal education?" said Mr. Sewell some time later in the evening, after Moses and Mara were gone to bed.

"Depends on the boy," said Zephaniah. "I've been up to Brunswick, and seen the fellows there in the college. With a good many of 'em, going to college seems to be just nothing but a sort of ceremony; they go because they're sent, and don't learn anything more 'n they can help. That's what I call waste of time and money."

"But don't you think Moses shows some taste for reading and study?"

"Pretty well, pretty well!" said Zephaniah; "jist keep him a little hungry; not let him get all he wants, you see, and he'll bite the sharper. If I want to catch cod I don't begin with flingin' over a barrel o' bait. So with the boys, jist bait 'em with a book here and a book there, and kind o' let 'em feel their own way, and then, if nothin' will do but a fellow must go to college, give in to him—that'd be *my* way."

"And a very good one, too!" said Mr. Sewell. "I'll see if I can't bait my hook, so as to make Moses take after Latin this winter. I shall have plenty of time to teach him."

"Now, there's Mara!" said the Captain, his face becoming phosphorescent with a sort of mild radiance of pleasure, as it usually was when he spoke of her; "she 's real sharp set after books; she 's ready to fly out of her little skin at the sight of one."

"That child thinks too much, and feels too much, and knows too much for her years!" said Mr. Sewell. "If she were a boy, and you would take her away cod-fishing, as you have Moses, the sea-winds would blow away some of the thinking, and her little body would grow stout, and her mind less delicate and sensitive. But she's a woman," he said, with a sigh, "and they are all alike. We can't do much for them, but let them come up as they will and make the best of it."

CHAPTER XVII.

Moses felt elevated some inches in the world by the gift of a new Latin grammar, which had been bought for him in Brunswick. It was a step upward in life; no graduate from a college ever felt more ennobled.

"Wal', now, I tell ye, Moses Pennel," said Miss Roxy, who, with her press-board and big flat-iron, was making her autumn sojourn in the brown house, "I tell ye Latin a'n't just what you think 't is, steppin' round so crank; you must remember what the king of Israel said to Benhadad, king of Syria."

"I *don't* remember; what did he say?"

"I remember," said the soft voice of Mara; "he said, 'Let not him that putteth on the harness boast as him that putteth it off.'"

"Good for you, Mara," said Miss Roxy; "if some other folks read their Bibles as much as you do, they 'd know more."

Between Moses and Miss Roxy there had always been a state of sub-acute warfare since the days of his first arrival, she regarding him as an unhopeful interloper, and he regarding her as a grim-visaged, interfering gnome, whom he disliked with all the intense, unreasoning antipathy of childhood.

"I hate that old woman," he said to Mara, as he flung out of the door.

"Why, Moses, what for?" said Mara, who never could comprehend hating anybody.

"I *do* hate her, and Aunt Ruey, too. They are two old scratching cats; they hate me, and I hate them; they're always trying to bring me down, and I won't be brought down."

Mara had sufficient instinctive insight into the feminine rôle in the domestic concert not to adventure a direct argument just now in favor of her friends, and therefore she proposed that they should sit down together under a cedar hard by, and look over the first lesson.

"Miss Emily invited me to go over with you," she said, "and I should like so much to hear you recite."

Moses thought this very proper, as would any other male person, young or old, who has been habitually admired by any other female one.

He did not doubt that, as in fishing and rowing, and all other things he had undertaken as yet, he should win himself distinguished honors.

"See here," he said; "Mr. Sewell told me I might go as far as I liked, and I mean to take all the declensions to begin with,—there's five of 'em, and I shall learn them for the first lesson, and then I shall take the adjectives next, and next the verbs, and so in a fortnight get into reading."

Mara heaved a sort of sigh. She wished she had been invited to share this glorious race; but she looked on admiring when Moses read, in a loud voice, "Penna, pennæ, pennæ, pennam," &c.

"There now, I believe I've got it," he said, handing Mara the book; and he was perfectly astonished to find that, with the book withdrawn, he boggled, and blundered, and stumbled ingloriously. In vain Mara softly prompted, and looked at him with pitiful eyes as he grew red in the face with his efforts to remember.

"Confound it all!" he said, with an angry flush, snatching back the book; "it's more trouble than it's worth."

Again he began the repetition, saying it very loud and plain; he said it over and over till his mind wandered far out to sea, and while his tongue repeated "penna, pennæ," he was counting the white sails of the fishing-smacks, and thinking of pulling up codfish at the Banks.

"There now, Mara, try me," he said, and handed her the book again; "I'm sure I *must* know it now."

But, alas! with the book the sounds glided away; and "penna" and "pennam" and "pennis" and "pennæ" were confusedly and indiscriminately mingled.

He thought it must be Mara's fault; she did n't read right, or she told him just as he was going to say it, or she did n't tell him right; or was he a fool? or had he lost his senses?

That first declension has been a valley of humiliation to many a sturdy boy—to many a bright one, too; and often it is, that the more full of thought and vigor the mind is, the more difficult is it to narrow it down to the single dry issue of learning those sounds.

Heinrich Heine said the Romans would never have found time to conquer the world, if they had had to learn their own language; but that, luckily for them, they were born into the knowledge of what nouns form their accusatives in "um."

Long before Moses had learned the first declension, Mara knew it by heart; for her intense anxiety for him, and the eagerness and zeal with which she listened for each termination, fixed them in her mind. Besides, she was naturally of a more quiet and scholar-like turn than he,—more intellectually developed.

Moses began to think, before that memorable day was through, that there was some sense in Aunt Roxy's quotation of the saying of the King of Israel, and materially to retrench his expectations as to the time it might take to master the grammar; but still, his pride and will were both committed, and he worked away in this new sort of labor with energy.

It was a fine frosty, November morning, when he rowed Mara across the bay in a little boat to recite his first lesson to Mr. Sewell.

Miss Emily had provided a plate of seed-cake, otherwise called cookies, for the children, as was a kindly custom of old times, when the little people were expected.

Miss Emily had a dim idea that she was to do something for Mara in her own department, while Moses was reciting his lesson; and therefore producing a large sampler, displaying every form and variety of marking-stitch, she began questioning the little girl, in a low tone, as to her proficiency in that useful accomplishment.

Presently, however, she discovered that the child was restless and uneasy, and that she answered without knowing what she was saying. The fact was that she was listening, with her whole soul in her eyes, and feeling through all her nerves, every word Moses was saying. She knew all the critical places, where he was likely to go wrong; and when at last, in one place, he gave the wrong termination, she involuntarily called out the right one, starting up and turning towards them. In a moment she blushed deeply, seeing Mr. Sewell and Miss Emily both looking at her with surprise.

"Come here, pussy," said Mr. Sewell, stretching out his hand to her. "Can you say this?"

"I believe I could, sir."

"Well, try it."

She went through without missing a word. Mr. Sewell then, for curiosity, heard her repeat all the other forms of the lesson. She had them perfectly.

"Very well, my little girl," he said, "have you been studying, too?"

"I heard Moses say them so often," said Mara, in an apologetic manner, "I couldn't help learning them."

"Would you like to recite with Moses every day?"

"Oh, yes, sir, so much."

"Well, you shall. It is better for him to have company."

Mara's face brightened, and Miss Emily looked with a puzzled air at her brother.

"So," she said, when the children had gone home, "I thought you wanted me to take Mara under my care. I was going to begin and teach her some marking stitches, and you put her up to studying Latin. I don't understand you."

"Well, Emily, the fact is, the child has a natural turn for study, that no child of her age ought to have; and I have done just as people always will with such children; there's no sense in it, but I wanted to do it. You can teach her marking and embroidery all the same; it would break her little heart, now, if I were to turn her back."

"I do not see of what use Latin can be to a woman."

"Of what use is embroidery?"

"Why, that is an accomplishment."

"Ah, indeed!" said Mr. Sewell, contemplating the weeping willow and tombstone trophy with a singular expression, which it was lucky for Miss Emily's peace she did not understand. The fact was, that Mr. Sewell had, at one period of his life, had an opportunity of studying and observing minutely some really fine works of art, and the remembrance of them sometimes rose up to his mind, in the presence of the *chefs-d'œuvre* on which his sister rested with so much complacency. It was a part of his quiet interior store of amusement to look at these bits of Byzantine embroidery round the room, which affected him always with a subtle sense of drollery.

"You see, brother," said Miss Emily, "it is far better for women to be accomplished than learned."

"You are quite right in the main," said Mr. Sewell, "only you must let me have my own way just for once. One can't be consistent always."

So another Latin grammar was brought, and Moses began to feel a secret respect for his little companion, that he had never done before, when he saw how easily she walked through the labyrinths which at first so confused him.

Before this, the comparison had been wholly in points where superiority arose from physical daring and vigor; now he became aware of the existence of another kind of strength with which he had not measured himself. Mara's opinion in their mutual studies began to assume a value in his eyes that her opinions on other subjects had never done, and she saw and felt, with a secret gratification, that she was becoming more to him through their mutual pursuit. To say the truth, it required this fellowship to inspire Moses with the patience and perseverence necessary for this species of acquisition. His active, daring temperament little inclined him to patient, quiet study. For anything that could be done by two hands, he was always ready; but to hold hands still and work silently in the inner forces, was to him a species of undertaking that seemed against his very nature; but then he would do it—he would not disgrace himself before Mr. Sewell, and let a girl younger than himself outdo him.

But the thing, after all, that absorbed more of Moses' thoughts than all his lessons was the building and rigging of a small schooner, at which he worked assiduously in all his leisure moments. He had dozens of blocks of wood, into which he had cut anchor moulds; and the melting of lead, the running and shaping of anchors, the whittling of masts and spars took up many an hour. Mara entered into all these things readily, and was too happy to make herself useful in hemming the sails.

When the schooner was finished, they built some ways down by the sea, and invited Sally Kittridge over to see it launched.

"There!" he said, when the little thing skimmed down prosperously into the sea and floated gayly on the waters—"when I'm a man, I'll have a big ship; I'll build her, and launch her, and command her, all myself; and I'll give you and Sally both a passage in it, and we'll go off to the East Indies—we'll sail round the world!"

None of the three doubted the feasibility of this scheme; the little vessel they had just launched seemed the visible prophecy of such a future; and how pleasant it would be to sail off, with the world all before them, and winds ready to blow them to any port they might wish!

The three children arranged some bread and cheese and doughnuts on a rock on the shore, to represent the collation that was usually spread in those parts at a ship launch, and felt quite like grown people—acting life beforehand in that sort of shadowy pantomime which so delights little people.

Happy, happy days—when ships can be made with a jack-knife and anchors run in pine blocks, and three children together can launch a schooner, and the voyage of the world can all be made in one sunny Saturday afternoon!

"Mother says you are going to college," said Sally to Moses.

"Not I, indeed," said Moses; "as soon as I get old enough, I'm going up to Umbagog among the lumberers, and I'm going to cut real, splendid timber for my ship, and I'm going to get it on the stocks, and have it built to suit myself."

"What will you call her?" said Sally.

"I have n't thought of that," said Moses.

"Call her the Ariel," said Mara.

"What! after the spirit you were telling us about?" said Sally.

"Ariel is a pretty name," said Moses. "But what is that about a spirit?"

"Why," said Sally, "Mara read us a story about a ship that was wrecked, and a spirit called Ariel, that sang a song about the drowned mariners."

Mara gave a shy, apprehensive glance at Moses, to see if this allusion called up any painful recollections.

No; instead of this, he was following the motions of his little schooner on the waters with the briskest and most unconcerned air in the world.

"Why did n't you ever show me that story, Mara?" said Moses.

Mara colored and hesitated; the real reason she dared not say.

"Why, she read it to father and me down by the cove," said Sally, "the afternoon that you came home from the Banks; I remember how we saw you coming in; don't you, Mara?"

"What have you done with it?" said Moses.

"I've got it at home," said Mara, in a faint voice; "I'll show it to you, if you want to see it; there are such beautiful things in it."

That evening, as Moses sat busy, making some alterations in his darling schooner, Mara produced her treasure, and read and explained to him the story. He listened with interest, though without any of the extreme feeling which Mara had thought possible, and even interrupted her once in the middle of the celebrated—

"Full fathom five thy father lies,"

by asking her to hold up the mast a minute, while he drove in a peg to make it rake a little more. He was, evidently, thinking of no drowned father, and dreaming of no possible sea-caves, but acutely busy in fashioning a present reality; and yet he liked to hear Mara read, and, when she had done, told her that he thought it was a pretty,—quite a pretty story, with such a total absence of recognition that the story had any affinities with his own history, that Mara was quite astonished.

She lay and thought about him hours, that night, after she had gone to bed; and he lay and thought about a new way of disposing a pulley for raising a sail, which he determined to try the effect of early in the morning.

What was the absolute truth in regard to the boy? Had he forgotten the scenes of his early life, the strange catastrophe that cast him into his present circumstances? To this we answer that all the efforts of Nature, during the early years of a healthy childhood, are bent on effacing and obliterating painful impressions, wiping out from each day the sorrows of the last, as the daily tide effaces the furrows on the sea-shore.

The child that broods, day after day, over some fixed idea, is so far forth not a healthy one. It is Nature's way to make first a healthy animal, and then develop in it gradually higher faculties. We have seen our two children unequally matched hitherto, because unequally developed.

There will come a time, by and by in the history of the boy, when the haze of dreamy curiosity will steam up likewise from his mind, and vague yearnings, and questionings, and longings possess and trouble him, but it must be some years hence.

Here for a season we leave both our child friends, and when ten years have passed over their heads,—when Moses shall be twenty, and Mara seventeen,—we will return again to tell their story, for then there will be one to tell. Let us suppose in the interval, how Moses and Mara read Virgil with the minister, and how Mara works a shepherdess with Miss Emily, which astonishes the neighborhood,—but how by herself she learns, after divers trials, to paint partridge, and checkerberry, and trailing arbutus,—how Moses makes better and better ships, and Sally grows up a handsome girl, and goes up to Brunswick to the high school,—how Captain Kittridge tells stories, and Miss Roxy and Miss Ruey nurse and cut and make and mend, for the still rising generation,—how there are quiltings and tea-drinkings and prayer-meetings and Sunday sermons,— how Zephaniah and Mary Pennel grow old gradually and graciously, as the sun rises and sets, and the eternal silver tide rises and falls around our little gem, Orr's Island.

MARY ABIGAIL DODGE
[GAIL HAMILTON]
(1833–1896)

My Garden
Atlantic Monthly, 9 (May), 1862.

Mary Abigail Dodge took the second half of her pen name, Gail Hamilton, from the place of her birth, Hamilton, Massachusetts. Born there on March 31, 1833, she was the youngest of the six living children of Hannah Stanwood and James Dodge. Dodge adored her mother who, according to Janice Pulsifer, was a "great reader" and "wrote letters as chatty and sprightly as those of her daughter" (Pulsifer, p. 166): after her mother's death in 1868, she and her sister Augusta wrote for private circulation a *Memorial to Mrs. Hannah Stanwood Dodge* (1869). Before marriage, her mother taught school and Dodge's own affection for school may have derived in part from its association with her mother: "Fifteen minutes before nine, on the 25th of May, 1835, at the patriarchal age of two years and two months, I first entered a village schoolhouse. It was the great era of my life" (*Gail Hamilton's Life in Letters*, p. 7). Augusta comments at length on her sister's academic precocity in the brief biographical sketch that prefaces her edition of the letters. She concludes with a reference to Dodge's first composition, written "when a brother, seven years her senior, was required to write a composition" and "she asked permission for the same privilege (?) and wrote, 'The Character of a Good Scholar!' " (*Life in Letters*, pp. 9–10).

At twelve, Dodge was sent for one year to a boarding school in Cambridge, Massachusetts, and the following year she entered the Ipswich Female Seminary, completing its three year course of study and graduating in 1850 at the age of seventeen. She taught at Ipswich until 1854, when she moved to Hartford, Connecticut, teaching first at the Hartford Female Seminary and later at the Hartford High School for Boys.

In January of 1856, when she was twenty-two, Dodge, at the urging of a cousin, sent a letter to Gamaliel Bailey, editor of *The National Era*, the paper that had published *Uncle Tom's Cabin* and Alice Cary's poetry and early prose, enclosing some samples of her writing. Bailey, delighted and impressed, accepted the material for immediate publication, and encouraged her to "send me whatever you please in your best style of prose sketches," for which he would pay fifty dollars (*Life in Letters*, p. 118). Two years later, in 1858, Dodge moved to Washington, D.C., to become governess to Bailey's children and to begin the transition from full-time teaching to full-time writing. By all accounts an extraordinary teacher, Dodge had nevertheless long desired to give more of her time to writing. As early as 1854, she wrote her parents, "remember that to be a good writer, one must have time to think and correct and alter, and how do you suppose I can teach all day and then have energy for mind work in the evening?" (*Life in Letters*, p. 57). In 1856, she articulated her dilemma even more clearly: "A year of leisure would be the most valuable present any one could make me just now. I never can do anything in the way of writing so long as I have to teach. That is a settled thing in my mind. No man can serve two masters" (*Life in Letters*, p. 129).

Settled in Washington, Dodge began to write for a variety of journals, including the *Independent*, the *Congregationalist*, and the *Atlantic Monthly*, in addition to the *Era*. By 1860, when she returned to Hamilton to help care for her elderly parents, she no longer had to teach for a living. By 1864, she could write:

> The money that I have received and have not spent is in government bonds, and safely deposited in Boston. This is almost entirely what I have received from my books. The magazine papers keep me in bread and butter and calicoes, and keep me "handsomely." I don't go into furs and diamonds and laces quite so much as I might like if I had the purse of Fortunatus in my pocket; but those are only luxuries, and I have everything that is necessary, and I treat myself to that best luxury of giving, upon every occasion. The sale of my books goes on (*Life in Letters*, p. 410).

The first of these books to provide money for "saving" appeared in 1862, when she was nearly thirty, *Country Living and Country Thinking*, and from then until the time of her death Dodge's output was steady. Her carefully nurtured economic independence enabled her to refuse offers of work that could be accepted only "at the expense of both my character and my reputation as a writer" (*Life in Letters*, p. 411). "Excellence," she wrote, "is far more valuable to me than money," and she once told her sister that she only wrote children's stories in a hurry; on articles "I spend a great deal of care and time, revise and correct till even you would be satisfied" (*Life in Letters*, pp. 411, 189). On occasion, she succumbed to the pressure to be an editor; from 1865 to 1867 she edited, with Lucy Larcom and John Trowbridge, the magazine *Our Young Folks*, and in 1870 she was manager of *Wood's Household Magazine*.

In 1867, Dodge discovered, "quite accidentally," that her publisher, James T. Fields, had regularly assigned her a smaller royalty than he accorded other authors. After months of futile and disheartening effort to clarify and resolve the issue, Dodge changed publishers and wrote her own account of the situation, *Battle of the Books*, published in 1870 and designed to assist other writers in their dealings with publishers. In 1868, she published *Woman's Wrongs: A Counter-Irritant*, one of a series of books that focused on the issues of nineteenth-century feminism, arguing against women's confinement to the domestic sphere and for women's economic independence through education and careers. Earlier, in "Men and Women" *(Country Living and Country Thinking)*, she had specifically urged women to consider the career of writing, despite a "certain prejudice against female writers . . . fine, subtle, impalpable, but real" that distorted the reading and criticism of women's books. Aiming to displace those male authorities annually invited to address audiences of schoolgirls on the subject of their appropriate "sphere," she exhorts, "Girls, do not be deceived. Write. . . . The more a man tells you not to write, the more do you write."

In 1871, Dodge began spending her winters in Washington, D.C., in the household of Representative James G. Blaine, whose wife was her first cousin. She may have helped to ghostwrite Blaine's congressional speeches, and she openly assisted him in writing *Twenty Years in Congress* (1884–86). After his death in 1893, she accepted the role of official biographer, spending the last years of her life gathering information for and working on the *Biography of James G. Blaine*. She undertook this task against the advice of her family, who felt she had already done enough for Blaine, and in her edition of the letters, Augusta implies that this work killed her. Dodge suffered a paralytic stroke that left her unconscious for weeks after completing all but the last chapter. Harriet Prescott Spofford, her close friend of many years, finished the biography and it was published in 1895.

Dodge eventually recovered sufficiently to write one last book, *X Rays*, privately published in 1896, which offered to interested readers an account of her experience while presumed dead. She died on August 17, 1896, at the age of sixty-three, in Hamilton, and was buried there. Augusta, with whom Dodge made her home in the years following their mother's death, living with her in Hamilton except during the winter months, paid tribute to her sister's memory by presenting a stained glass window to the First Congregational Church of Hamilton. She also gave the town $1000 "for a free reading room, and adjunct to the public library, to be called the Gail Hamilton Room" (Pulsifer, p. 168).

In addition to her collections of essays on life in the country, based on her experiences in Hamilton, and to her volumes designed to improve the condition of women, Dodge wrote several books for children; one travel book, *Wool Gathering* (1867); and one novel, *First Love is Best* (1877). Religion, a major and continuing source of interest, forms the theme of several other volumes. Most notable of these are *Stumbling Blocks* (1864), *Sermons to the Clergy* (1876), and *A Washington Bible Class* (1891). Refusing to confine herself to her "sphere" because "I like

everything that is outside of it," Gail Hamilton insisted that her mind be
free to encounter, reflect on, and jab at all topics of current interest:
"Wherever I see symptoms of a pie, thither shall my fingers travel.
Wherever a windmill flaps, it shall go hard but I will have a tilt at it"
(Skirmishes and Sketches, pp. 432–33). The result is a writer hard to
classify, except among the category of "readable" authors—the term is
Edwin Percy Whipple's writing of Gail Hamilton in "American Literature, 1776–1876" (Harper's, 1876)—or perhaps as a cultural critic-at-
large.

    Fierce in her determination to separate the public and the private
self, Dodge refused to answer any letters about her work that were addressed to Mary Abigail Dodge rather than to Gail Hamilton, and she
forbade the publication during her lifetime of any biographical details
that were not part of her public, author self. Although her commitment
to pseudonymity evidently had its origins in this desire to separate the
public and the private self rather than in any desire to circumvent conventional expectations of and responses to women's writing, Dodge
knew that her decision would produce in her readers an extraordinary
itch to identify the actual gender behind the sexually indeterminate pen
name. Unlike Sara Parton, who chose a pen name, Fanny Fern, designed
to draw attention to the fact of her femininity and then to subvert the
expectations it elicited, Dodge chose to play in a different way with her
readers' assumptions about the connection between gender and style.
Writing home in 1859, she quotes from a letter she has received: "And
the wonderful Gail Hamilton. 'Is it a man or a woman?' is a standing
topic of discussion with my brothers and sisters. For myself, I have long
since made up my mind that Gail is feminine. We like her immensely"
(Life in Letters, p. 232).

    Shortly after the Atlantic publication of "My Garden," Fields wrote
Dodge that her essay was "a hit number one. Crowds of inquiries for
the author's name beseech me, but I cry 'mum' to the myriads" (Battle
of the Books, p. 182). In the opening paragraphs of "My Garden," Gail
Hamilton toys with this itch to determine authorial identity, using it to
raise some serious questions about gender and reading and gender and
writing. Declaring that her honest admission of femaleness puts her at a
"signal disadvantage," she further asserts that her readers are dependent
on her honesty for their possession of information deemed crucial to the
reading process. Although readers might want to "know at the outset
whether the story-teller is a man or a woman" because "the two sexes
awaken two entirely distinct sets of feelings," Gail Hamilton suggests
that the basis for this distinction is questionable. Her style itself will not
provide the necessary clues, for "where an ordinary woman will leave
the beaten track, wandering in a thousand little by-ways of her own
. . . I march straight on . . ." Caroline Kirkland draws attention to her
feminine style of digression, but Gail Hamilton does not write like a
woman. Yet, as she magnanimously admits, she is one. What, then,
becomes of the assertion that gender and style are inevitably connected,
that the shape of the sentence reveals the shape of the body, and that the

writing of men and the writing of women require different readers and readings? By the time she has finished her opening digression and begun on her "true" theme, she has disarmed her readers of certain conventional assumptions and forced them into an original relationship with herself.

Her choice of theme presses the issue further. Designed as a comic exposure of illusions about the self, not the least of which is that of bounteous bestower of rural harvests on friends denied the fruits of nature, "My Garden" is equally designed to dispel cultural illusions about woman's nature. Essentially feminine—witness the "pretty conceits" she imagines writing to accompany her gifts of fruit and flowers and the equally "pretty" language that accompanies her "papers of precious seeds"—this myth of the self as Lady Bountiful derives from the illusion that neither knowledge nor labor but only nature is needed to give a woman the luxury of this role. By the end of a summer in contact with hard facts and hard work, the role of Lady Bountiful has been relinquished in favor of the "fiendish delight" of offering visitors inedible cherries and the "morbid pleasure" of watching the ensuing conflict between spirit and flesh.

This transformation has a large cultural context. Nineteenth-century works, such as Celia Thaxter's *An Island Garden* (1894), articulated the associations between women, gardens, and art that are embodied in such twentieth-century works as Alice Walker's "In Search of Our Mothers' Gardens." In this context, "My Garden" disrupts conventional assumptions about gender and style by demonstrating that women can make of a garden an awful mess as easily as they can make of it an art work. That women are not naturally fruitful, that they have no inherent ability to make things grow, that a garden can symbolize a woman's ignorance and incompetence as readily as it can her creative self denied expression elsewhere is the burden of Gail Hamilton's comic self-exposure.

But if women have no innate affinity for gardens, neither are they by nature prevented from learning what men know or doing men's work. Although men have the advantage of having been in the garden, and elsewhere, first, and although this fact presents a "circumstance" with which a woman must reckon, men's superiority is not innate. In her piece on Gail Hamilton in *Eminent Women of the Age*, Fanny Fern (Sara Parton) gleefully reveals Halicarnassus to be Dodge's brother and not the "poor devil" of a husband conjured up by male critics. Unfortunately, Halicarnassus was born before Gail Hamilton, a fact that forces her into a permanent state of "belatedness." Yet there are better and worse ways of dealing with such hard facts. Useless, unquestionably, is the strategy of pretending that it does not count. First on the spot, Halicarnassus knows his stuff, and the narrator's refusal to avail herself of his knowledge, her insistence on seeing the fact of his knowledge as her primary antagonist, betrays her into the deadend of " 'Nothing,' I answered, with that well-known accent which says, 'Everything! and I mean to keep doing it,' " and the absurdity of sneaking about the grounds with her pockets full of seeds, dropping them "surreptitiously as occasion offered." The results of this strategy of defiance are pre-

sented in "simple language . . . both for an encouragement and a warning." In truth, however, there is little encouragement except in the form
of the warning: if you want to make a garden, ask the man who knows
how and then learn to kill bugs yourself—"take 'em right between your
thumb and finger and crush 'em!"

In "Men and Women," Gail Hamilton queries, "Do you ask me,
then, why I write? Because I know I shall be read by girls." For the girl
reader, there is another dimension to the encouragement couched as
warning. The first step in learning how to crush bugs is learning to say
"crush" and "bugs." The freedom to use slang constitutes a prime advantage of being first born: "Men can talk 'slang.' 'Dry up' is nowhere
forbidden in the Decalogue. Neither the law nor the prophets frown on
'a thousand of brick.' The Sermon on the Mount does not discounte-
nance 'knuckling to'; but between women and these minor immoralities
stands at invisible barrier of propriety. . . . I should like to call my
luggage 'traps,' and my curiosities 'truck and dicker,' and my weariness
'being knocked up,' as well as Halicarnassus, but I might as well rob a
bank." Yet the weight of Gail Hamilton's own stylistic example falls
clearly on the side of robbery. Rob away, is her advice; if women can
make a mess of gardening, they can surely learn to say "dry up."

Source:

Country Living and Country Thinking (Boston: Ticknor and Fields), 1862.

Selected Primary Works:

Gala Days, 1863; A New Atmosphere, 1864; Skirmishes and Sketches, 1865;
    Woman's Wrongs: A Counter-Irritant, 1868; A Battle of the Books, 1870;
    Woman's Worth and Worthlessness, 1871; Twelve Miles from A Lemon, 1874;
    Gail Hamilton's Life in Letters, ed. H. Augusta Dodge, 1901.

Selected Secondary Works:

Fanny Fern, "Gail Hamilton—Miss Dodge," Eminent Women of the Age (Hart-
    ford: S. M. Betts), 1868; Janice Pulsifer, "Gail Hamilton," Essex Institute
    Historical Collections, 104 (1968), 165–216; Harriet Prescott Spofford, A
    Little Book of Friends (Boston: Little, Brown), 1916.

Contexts:

1862—Davis, Margret Howth; Stoddard, The Morgesons

I CAN SPEAK of it calmly now; but there have been moments when the
lightest mention of those words would sway my soul to its profoundest
depths.

I am a woman. You may have inferred this before; but I now desire to
state it distinctly, because I like to do as I would be done by, when I can
just as well as not. It rasps a person of my temperament exceedingly to be
deceived. When any one tells a story, we wish to know at the outset

whether the story-teller is a man or a woman. The two sexes awaken two entirely distinct sets of feelings, and you would no more use the one for the other than you would put on your tiny teacups at breakfast, or lay the carving-knife by the butter-plate. Consequently it is very exasperating to sit, open-eyed and expectant, watching the removal of the successive swathings which hide from you the dusky glories of an old-time princess, and, when the unrolling is over, to find it is nothing, after all, but a great lubberly boy. Equally trying is to feel your interest clustering round a narrator's manhood, all your individuality merging in his, till, of a sudden, by the merest chance, you catch the swell of crinoline, and there you are. Away with such clumsiness! Let us have everybody christened before we begin.

I do, therefore, with Spartan firmness, depose and say that I am a woman. I am aware that I place myself at signal disadvantage by the avowal. I fly in the face of hereditary prejudice. I am thrust at once beyond the pale of masculine sympathy. Men will neither credit my success nor lament my failure, because they will consider me poaching on their manor. If I chronicle a big beet, they will bring forward one twice as large. If I mourn a deceased squash, they will mutter, "Woman's farming!" Shunning Scylla, I shall perforce fall into Charybdis. (*Vide* Classical Dictionary. I have lent mine, but I know one was a rock and the other a whirlpool, though I cannot state, with any definiteness, which was which.) I may be as humble and deprecating as I choose, but it will not avail me. A very agony of self-abasement will be no armor against the poisoned shafts which assumed superiority will hurl against me. Yet I press the arrow to my bleeding heart, and calmly reiterate, I am a woman.

The full magnanimity of which reiteration can be perceived only when I inform you that I could easily deceive you, if I chose. There is about my serious style a vigor of thought, a comprehensiveness of view, a closeness of logic, and a terseness of diction, commonly supposed to pertain only to the stronger sex. Not wanting in a certain fanciful sprightliness which is the peculiar grace of woman, it possesses also, in large measure, that concentrativeness which is deemed the peculiar strength of man. Where an ordinary woman will leave the beaten track, wandering in a thousand little by-ways of her own,—flowery and beautiful, it is true, and leading her airy feet to "sunny spots of greenery" and the gleam of golden apples, but keeping her not less surely from the goal,—I march straight on, turning neither to the right hand nor to the left, beguiled into no side-issues, discussing no collateral question, but with keen eye and strong hand aiming right at the heart of my theme. Judge thus of the stern severity of my virtue. There is no heroism in denying ourselves the pleasures which we cannot compass. It is not self-sacrifice, but self-cherishing, that turns the dyspeptic alderman away from turtle-soup and the *pâté de foie gras* to mush and milk. The hungry newsboy, regaling his nostrils with the scents that come up from a subterranean kitchen, does not always know whether or not he is honest, till the cook turns away for a moment, and a steaming joint is within reach of his yearning fingers. It is no credit to a weak-minded woman not to be strong-minded and write poetry. She could not if she tried; but to feed on locusts and wild honey that the soul may be in better condition to fight the truth's battles,—to go with empty stomach for a clear conscience' sake,—to sacrifice intellectual tastes to womanly duties, when the two conflict,—

> "That 's the true pathos and sublime,
>   Of human life."

You will, therefore, no longer withhold your appreciative admiration, when, in full possession of what theologians call the power of contrary choice, I make the unmistakable assertion that I am a woman.

Hope told a flattering tale when, excited and happy, but not sated with the gayeties of a sojourn among urban and urbane friends, I set out on my triumphal march from the city of my visit to the estate of my adoption. Triumphal indeed! My pathway was strewed with roses. Feathery asparagus and the crispness of tender lettuce waved dewy greetings from every railroad-side; green peas crested the racing waves of Long Island Sound, and unnumbered carrots of gold sprang up in the wake of the ploughing steamer; till I was wellnigh drunk with the new wine of my own purple vintage. But I was not ungenerous. In the height of my innocent exultation, I remembered the dwellers in cities who do all their gardening at stalls, and in my heart I determined, when the season should be fully blown, to invite as many as my house could hold to share with me the delight of plucking strawberries from their stems and drinking in foaming health from the balmy-breathed cows. Moreover, in the exuberance of my joy, I determined to go still further, and despatch to those doomed ones who cannot purchase even a furlough from burning pavements baskets of fragrance and sweetness. I pleased myself with pretty conceits. To one who toils early and late in an official Sahara, that the home-atmosphere may always be redolent of perfume, I would send a bunch of long-stemmed white and crimson rose-buds, in the midst of which he should find a dainty note whispering, "Dear Fritz: drink this pure glass of my overflowing June to the health of weans and wife, not forgetting your unforgetful friend." To a pale-browed, sad-eyed woman, who flits from velvet carpets and broidered flounces to the bedside of an invalid mother whom her slender fingers and unslender and most godlike devotion can scarcely keep this side the pearly gates, I would heap a basket of summer-hued peaches smiling up from cool, green leaves into their straitened home, and with eyes, perchance, tear-dimmed, she should read, "My good Maria, the peaches are to go to your lips, the bloom to your cheeks, and the gardener to your heart." Ah me! How much grace and gladness may bud and blossom in one little garden! Only three acres of land, but what a crop of sunny surprises, unexpected tenderness, grateful joys, hopes, loves, and restful memories!—what wells of happiness, what sparkles of mirth, what sweeps of summer in the heart, what glimpses of the Upper Country!

Halicarnassus was there before me (in the garden, I mean, not in the spot last alluded to). It has been the one misfortune of my life that Halicarnassus got the start of me at the outset. With a fair field and no favor I should have been quite adequate to him. As it was, he was born and began, and there was no resource left to me but to be born and follow, which I did as fast as possible; but that one false move could never be redeemed. I know there are shallow thinkers who love to prate of the supremacy of mind over matter,—who assert that circumstances are plastic as clay in the hands of the man who knows how to mould them. They clench their fists, and inflate their lungs, and quote Napoleon's proud boast,—"Circumstances! I *make* circumstances!" Vain babblers! Whither did this Napoleonic idea lead? To a barren rock in a waste of waters. Do we need St. Helena and Sir Hudson Lowe to refute it? Control circumstances! I should like to know if the most important circumstance that can happen to a man is not to be born? and if that is under his control, or in any way affected by his whims and wishes? Would not Louis XVI. have been the son of a goldsmith, if he could have had his way? Would Burns have been born a slaving, starving peasant, if he had been consulted beforehand? Would not the children of vice be the children of virtue, if they could have had their choice? and would not the whole tenor of their lives have been changed thereby? Would a good many of us have been born at all, if we could have helped it? Control circumstances, forsooth! when a mother's sudden terror brings an idiot child into the world,—when the restive eye of his great-grandfather, whom he never saw, looks at you from your two-year-old, and the spirit of that roving ancestor makes the boy also a fugitive and a vagabond on the earth! No, no. We may coax circumstances a little, and shove them about, and make the best of them, but there they are. We may try to get out of their way; but they will trip us up, not once, but many times. We may affect to tread them under foot in the daylight, but in the night-time they will turn again and rend us. All we can do is first to accept them as facts, and then reason from them as premises. We cannot control them, but we can control our own use of them. We can make them a savor of life unto life, or of death unto death.

Application.—If mind could have been supreme over matter, Halicarnassus should, in the first place, have taken the world at second-hand from me, and, in the second place, he should not have stood smiling on the front-door steps when the coach set me down there. As it was, I made the best of the one case by following in his footsteps,—not meekly, not acquiescently, but protesting, yet following,—and of the other, by smiling responsive and asking pleasantly,—

"Are the things planted yet?"

"No," said Halicarnassus.

This was better than I had dared to hope. When I saw him standing there so complacent and serene, I felt certain that a storm was brewing, or rather had brewed, and burst over my garden, and blighted its fair prospects. I was confident that he had gone and planted every square inch of the soil with some hideous absurdity, which would spring up a hundred-fold in perpetual reminders of the one misfortune to which I have alluded.

So his ready answer gave me relief, and yet I could not divest myself of a vague fear, a sense of coming thunder. In spite of my endeavors, that calm, clear face would lift itself to my view as a mere "weather-breeder"; but I ate my supper, unpacked my trunks, took out my papers of precious seeds, and, sitting in the flooding sunlight under the little western porch, I poured them into my lap, and bade Halicarnassus come to me. He came, I am sorry to say, with a pipe in his mouth.

"Do you wish to see my jewels?" I asked, looking as much like Cornelia as a little woman somewhat inclined to dumpiness can.

Halicarnassus nodded assent.

"There," said I, unrolling a paper, "that is *Lychnidea acuminata.* Sometimes it flowers in white masses, pure as a baby's soul. Sometimes it glows in purple, pink, and crimson, intense, but unconsuming, like Horeb's burning bush. The old Greeks knew it well, and they baptized its prismatic loveliness with their sunny symbolism, and called it the Flame-Flower. These very seeds may have sprung centuries ago from the hearts of heroes who sleep at Marathon; and when their tender petals quiver in the sunlight of my garden, I shall see the gleam of Attic armor and the flash of royal souls. Like heroes, too, it is both beautiful and bold. It does not demand careful cultivation,—no hot-house tenderness—"

"I should rather think not," interrupted Halicarnassus. "Pat Curran has his front-yard full of it."

I collapsed at once, and asked, humbly,—

"Where did he get it?"

"Got it anywhere. It grows wild almost. It's nothing but phlox. My opinion is, that the old Greeks knew no more about it than that brindled cow."

Nothing further occurring to me to be said on the subject, I waived it, and took up another parcel, on which I spelled out, with some difficulty, "*Delphinium exaltatum.* Its name indicates its nature."

"It's an exalted dolphin, then, I suppose," said Halicarnassus.

"Yes!" I said, dexterously catching up an *argumentum ad hominem,* "it *is* an exalted dolphin,—an apotheosized dolphin,—a dolphin made glorious. For, as the dolphin catches the sunbeams and sends them back with a thousand added splendors, so this flower opens its quivering bosom and gathers from the vast laboratory of the sky the purple of a monarch's robe, and the ocean's deep, calm blue. In its gracious cup you shall see—"

"A fiddlestick!" jerked out Halicarnassus, profanely. "What are you raving about such a precious bundle of weeds for? There is n't a shoemaker's apprentice in the village that has n't his seven-by-nine garden overrun with them. You might have done better than bring cart-loads of phlox and larkspur a thousand miles. Why did n't you import a few hollyhocks, or a sunflower or two, and perhaps a dainty slip of cabbage? A pumpkin-vine, now, would climb over the front-door deliciously, and a row of burdocks would make a highly entertaining border."

The reader will bear me witness that I had met my first rebuff with humility. It was probably this very humility that emboldened him to a second attack. I determined to change my tactics, and give battle.

"Halicarnassus," said I, severely, "you are a hypocrite. You set up for a Democrat—"

"Not I," interrupted he; "I voted for Harrison in '40, and for Fremont in '56, and—"

"Nonsense!" interrupted I, in turn; "I mean a Democrat etymological, not a Democrat political. You stand by the Declaration of Independence, and believe in liberty, equality, and fraternity, and that all men are of one blood; and here you are, ridiculing these innocent flowers, because their brilliant beauty is not shut up in a conservatory, to exhale its fragrance on a fastidious few, but blooms on all alike, gladdening the home of exile and lightening the burden of labor."

Halicarnassus saw that I had made a point against him, and preserved a discreet silence.

"But you are wrong," I went on, "even if you are right. You may laugh to scorn my floral treasures, because they seem to you common and unclean, but your laughter is premature. It is no ordinary seed that you see before you. It sprang from no profane soil. It came from the—the—some kind of an office at WASHINGTON, sir! It was given me by one whose name stands high on the scroll of fame,—a statesman whose views are as broad as his judgment is sound,—an orator who holds all hearts in his hand,—a man who is always found on the side of the feeble truth against the strong falsehood,—whose sympathy for all that is good, whose hostility to all that is bad, and whose boldness in every righteous cause, make him alike the terror and abhorrence of the oppressor, and the hope and joy and staff of the oppressed."

"What is his name?" said Halicarnassus, phlegmatically.

"And for your miserable pumpkin-vine," I went on, "behold this morning-glory, that shall open its barbaric splendor to the sun and mount heavenward on the sparkling chariots of the dew. I took this from the white hand of a young girl in whose heart poetry and purity have met, grace and virtue have kissed each other,—whose feet have danced over lilies and roses, who has "known no sterner duty than to give caresses," and whose gentle, spontaneous, and ever-active loveliness continually remind me that of such is the kingdom of heaven."

"Courted yet?" asked Halicarnassus, with a show of interest.

I transfixed him with a look, and continued,—

"This *Maurandia,* a climber, it may be common or it may be a king's ransom. I only know that it is rosy-hued, and that I shall look at life through its pleasant medium. Some fantastic trellis, brown and benevolent, shall knot supporting arms around it, and day by day it shall twine daintily up toward my southern window, and whisper softly of the sweet-voiced, tender-eyed woman from whose fairy bower it came in rosy wrappings. And this *Nemophila,* 'blue as my brother's eyes,'—the brave young brother whose heroism and manhood have outstripped his years, and who looks forth from the dark leafiness of far Australia lovingly and longingly over the blue waters, as if, floating above them, he might catch the flutter of white garments and the smile on a sister's lip—"

"What are you going to do with 'em?" put in Halicarnassus again.

I hesitated a moment, undecided whether to be amiable or bellicose under the provocation, but concluded that my ends would stand a better chance of being gained by adopting the former course, and so answered seriously, as if I had not been switched off the track, but was going on with perfect continuity,—

"To-morrow I shall take observations. Then, where the situation seems most favorable, I shall lay out a garden. I shall plant these seeds in it, except the vines and such things, which I wish to put near the house to hide as much as possible its garish white. Then, with every little tender shoot that appears above the ground, there will blossom also a pleasant memory, or a sunny hope, or an admiring thrill."

"What do you expect will be the market-value of that crop?"

"Wealth which an empire could not purchase," I answered, with enthusiasm. "But I shall not confine my attention to flowers. I shall make the useful go with the beautiful. I shall plant vegetables,—lettuce, and asparagus, and—so forth. Our table shall be garnished with the products of our own soil, and our own works shall praise us."

There was a pause of several minutes, during which I fondled the seeds, and Halicarnassus enveloped himself in clouds of smoke. Presently there was a cessation of puffs, a rift in the cloud showed that the oracle was opening his mouth, and directly thereafter he delivered himself of the encouraging remark,—

"If we don't have any vegetables till we raise 'em, we shall be carnivorous for some time to come."

It was said with that provoking indifference more trying to a sensitive mind than downright insult. You know it is based on some hidden obstacle, palpable to your enemy, though hidden from you,—and that he is calm because he knows that the nature of things will work against you, so that he need not interfere. If I had been less interested, I would have revenged myself on him by remaining silent; but I was very much interested, so I strangled my pride and said,—

"Why not?"

"Land is too old for such things. Soil is n't mellow enough."

I had always supposed that the greater part of the main-land of our continent was of equal antiquity, and dated back alike to the alluvial period; but I suppose our little three acres must have been injected through the intervening strata by some physical convulsion, from the drift, or the tertiary formation, perhaps even from the primitive granite.

"What are you going to do?" I ventured to inquire. "I don't suppose the land will grow any younger by keeping."

"Plant it with corn and potatoes for at least two years before there can be anything like a garden."

And Halicarnassus put up his pipe and betook himself to the house,—and I was glad of it, the abominable bore!—to sit there and listen to my glowing schemes, knowing all the while that they were soap-bubbles. "Corn and potatoes," indeed! I did n't believe a word of it. Halicarnassus always had an insane passion for corn and potatoes. Land represented to him so many bushels of the one or the other. Now corn and potatoes are very well in their way, but, like every other innocent indulgence, carried too far, become a vice; and I more than suspected he had planned the strategy simply to gratify his own weakness. Corn and potatoes, indeed!

But when Halicarnassus entered the lists against me, he found an opponent worthy of his steel. A few more such victories would be his ruin. A grand scheme fired and filled my mind during the silent watches of the night, and sent me forth in the morning, jubilant with high resolve. Alexander might weep that he had no more worlds to conquer; but I would create new. Archimedes might desiderate a place to stand on, before he could bring his lever into play; I would move the world, self-poised. If Halicarnassus fancied that I was cut up, dispersed, and annihilated by one disaster, he should weep tears of blood to see me rise, Phœnix-like, from the ashes of my dead hopes, to a newer and more glorious life. Here, having exhausted my classics, I took a long sweep down to modern times, and vowed in my heart never to give up the ship.

Halicarnassus saw that a fell purpose was working in my mind, but a certain high tragedy in my aspect warned him to silence; so he only dogged me around the corners of the house, eyed me askance from the wood-shed, and peeped through the crevices of the demented little barn. But his vigilance bore no fruit. I but walked moodily "with folded arms and fixed eyes," or struck out new paths at random, so long as there were any vestiges of his creation extant. His time and patience being at length exhausted, he went into the field to immolate himself with ever new devotion on the shrine of corn and potatoes. Then my scheme came to a head at once. In my walking, I had observed a box about three feet long,

two broad, and one foot deep, which Halicarnassus, with his usual disregard of the proprieties of life, had used to block up a gateway that was
waiting for a gate. It was just what I wanted. I straightway knocked out
the few nails that kept it in place, and, like another Samson, bore it away
on my shoulders. It was not an easy thing to manage, as any one may find
by trying,—nor would I advise young ladies, as a general thing, to adopt
that form of exercise,—but the end, not the means, was my object, and
by skilful diplomacy I got it up the back-stairs and through my window,
out upon the roof of the porch directly below. I then took the ash-pail
and the fire-shovel, and went into the field, carefully keeping the lee-side
of Halicarnassus. "Good, rich loam" I had observed all the gardening
books to recommend; but wherein the virtue or the richness of loam
consisted I did not feel competent to decide, and I scorned to ask. There
seemed to be two kinds: one black, damp, and dismal; the other fine,
yellow, and good-natured. A little reflection decided me to take the latter.
Gold constituted riches, and this was yellow like gold. Moreover, it
seemed to have more life in it. Night and darkness belonged to the other,
while the very heart of sunshine and summer seemed to be imprisoned in
this golden dust. So I plied my shovel and filled my pail again and again,
bearing it aloft with joyful labor, eager to be through before Halicarnassus should reappear; but he got on the trail just as I was whisking up-
stairs for the last time, and shouted, astonished,—

"What are you doing?"

"Nothing," I answered, with that well-known accent which says,
"Everything! and I mean to keep doing it."

I have observed, that, in managing parents, husbands, lovers,
brothers, and indeed all classes of inferiors, nothing is so efficacious as to
let them know at the outset that you are going to have your own way.
They may fret a little at first, and interpose a few puny obstacles, but it
will be only a temporary obstruction; whereas, if you parley and hesitate
and suggest, they will but gather courage and strength for a formidable
resistance. It is the first step that costs. Halicarnassus understood at once
from my one small shot that I was in a mood to be let alone, and he let me
alone accordingly.

I remembered he had said that the soil was not mellow enough, and I
determined that my soil should be mellow, to which end I took it up by
handfuls and squeezed it through my fingers, completely pulverizing it.
It was not disagreeable work. Things in their right places are very seldom
disagreeable. A spider on your dress is a horror, but a spider out-doors is
rather interesting. Besides, the loam had a fine, soft feel that was absolutely pleasant; but a hideous black and yellow reptile with horns and
hoofs, that winked up at me from it, was decidedly unpleasant and out of
place, and I at once concluded that the soil was sufficiently mellow for
my purposes, and smoothed it off directly. Then, with delighted fingers,

in sweeping circles, and fantastic whirls, and exact triangles, I planted my seeds in generous profusion, determined, that, if my wilderness did not blossom, it should not be from niggardliness of seed. But even then my box was full before my basket was emptied, and I was very reluctantly compelled to bring down from the garret another box, which had been the property of my great-grandfather. My great-grandfather was, I regret to say, a barber. I would rather never have had any. If there is anything in the world besides worth that I reverence, it is ancestry. My whole life long have I been in search of a pedigree, and though I run well at the beginning, I invariably stop short at the third remove by running my head into a barber's shop. If he had only been a farmer, now, I should not have minded. There is something dignified and antique in land, and no one need trouble himself to ascertain whether "farmer" stood for a close-fisted, narrow-souled clodhopper, or the smiling, benevolent master of broad acres. Farmer means both these, I could have chosen the meaning I liked, and it is not probable that any troublesome facts would have floated down the years to intercept any theory I might have launched. I would rather he had been a shoemaker; it would have been so easy to transform him, after his lamented decease, into a shoe-manufacturer,— and shoe-manufacturers, we all know, are highly respectable people, often become great men, and get sent to Congress. An apothecary might have figured as an M.D. A green-grocer might have been sublimated into a merchant. A dancing-master would flourish on the family records as a professor of the Terpsichorean art. A taker of daguerro-type portraits would never be recognized in "my great-grandfather *the artist.*" But a barber is unmitigated and immitigable. It cannot be shaded off, nor toned down, nor brushed up. Besides, was greatness ever allied to barberity? Shakespeare's father was a wool-driver, Tillotson's a clothier, Barrow's a linen-draper, Defoe's a butcher, Milton's a scrivener, Richardson's a joiner, Burns's a farmer; but did any one ever hear of a barber's having remarkable children? I must say, with all deference to my great-grandfather, that I do wish he would have been considerate enough of his descendants' feelings to have been born in the old days when barbers and doctors were one, or else have chosen some other occupation than bar-bering. Barber he did, however; in this very box he kept his wigs, and, painful as it was to have continually before my eyes this perpetual re-minder of plebeian great-grand-paternity, I consented to it rather than lose my seeds. Then I folded my hands in sweet, though calm satisfaction. I had proved myself equal to the emergency, and that always diffuses a glow of genial complacency through the soul. I had outwitted Halicarnassus. Exultation number two. He had designed to cheat me out of my garden by a story about land, and here was my garden ready to burst forth into blossom under my eyes. He said little, but I knew he felt deeply. I caught him one day looking out at my window with corroding envy in every lineament. "You might have got some dust out of the road; it would have been nearer." That was all he said. Even that little I did not fully understand.

I watched, and waited, and watered, in silent expectancy, for several days, but nothing came up, and I began to be anxious. Suddenly I thought of my vegetable-seeds, and determined to try those. Of course a hanging kitchen-garden was not to be thought of, and as Halicarnassus was fortunately absent for a few days, I prospected on the farm. A sunny little corner on a southern slope smiled up at me, and seemed to offer itself as a delightful situation for the diminutive garden which mine must be. The soil, too, seemed as fine and mellow as could be desired. I at once captured an Englishman from a neighboring plantation, hurried him into my corner, and bade him dig me and hoe me and plant me a garden as soon as possible. He looked blankly at me for a moment, and I looked blankly at him, wondering what lion he saw in the way.

"Them is planted with potatoes now," he gasped, at length.

"No matter," I returned, with sudden relief to find that nothing but potatoes interfered. "I want it to be unplanted, and planted with vegetables,—lettuce and—asparagus—and such."

He stood hesitating.

"Will the master like it?"

"Yes," said Diplomacy, "he will be delighted."

"No matter whether he likes it or not," codiciled Conscience. "You do it."

"I—don't exactly like—to—take the responsibility," wavered this modern Faint-Heart.

"I don't want you to take the responsibility," I ejaculated, with volcanic vehemence. "I'll take the responsibility. You take the hoe!"

These duty-people do infuriate me. They are so afraid to do anything that is n't laid out in a right-angled triangle. Every path must be graded and turfed before they dare set their scrupulous feet in it. I like conscience, but, like corn and potatoes, carried too far, it becomes a vice. I think I could commit a murder with less hesitation than some people buy a ninepenny calico. And to see that man stand here, balancing probabilities over a piece of ground no bigger than a bed-quilt, as if a nation's fate were at stake, was enough to ruffle a calmer temper than mine. My impetuosity impressed him, however, and he began to lay about him vigorously with hoe and rake and lines, and, in an incredibly short space of time, had a bit of square flatness laid out with wonderful precision. Meanwhile I had ransacked my vegetable-bag, and, though lettuce and asparagus were not there, plenty of beets and parsnips and squashes, etc. were. I let him take his choice. He took the first two. The rest were left on my hands. But I had gone too far to recede. They burned in my pocket for a few days, and I saw that I must get them into the ground somewhere. I could not sleep with them in the room. They were wandering shades, craving at my hands a burial, and I determined to put them where Banquo's ghost would not go,—down. Down accordingly they went, but not symmetrically nor simultaneously. I faced Halicarnassus on the subject of the beet-bed, and though I cannot say that either of us gained a brilliant victory, yet I can say that I kept possession of the ground; still, I did not care to risk a second encounter. So I kept my seeds about me continually, and dropped them surreptitiously as occasion offered. Consequently, my garden, taken as a whole, was located where the Penobscot Indian was born,—"all along shore." The squashes were scattered among the corn. The beans were tucked under the brushwood, in the fond hope that they would climb up it. Two tomato-plants were lodged in the potato-field, under the protection of some broken apple-branches dragged thither for the purpose. The cucumbers went down on the sheltered side of a wood-pile. The peas took their chances of life under the sinknose. The sweet-corn was marked off from the rest by a broom-stick,—and all took root alike in my heart.

May I ask you now, O friend, who, I would fain believe, have followed me thus far with no hostile eyes, to glide in tranced forgetfulness through the white blooms of May and the roses of June, into the warm breath of July afternoons and the languid pulse of August, perhaps even into the mild haze of September and the "flying gold" of brown October? In narrating to you the fruition of my hopes, I shall endeavor to preserve that calm equanimity which is the birthright of royal minds. I shall endeavor not to be unduly elated by success nor unduly depressed by failure, but to state in simple language the result of my experiments, both for an encouragement and a warning. I shall give the history of the several ventures separately, as nearly as I can recollect in the order in which they grew, beginning with the humbler ministers to our appetites, and soaring gradually into the region of the poetical and the beautiful.

BEETS.—The beets came up, little red-veined leaves, struggling for breath among a tangle of Roman wormwood and garlic; and though they exhibited great tenacity of life, they also exhibited great irregularity of purpose. In one spot there would be nothing, in an adjacent spot a whorl of beets, big and little, crowding and jostling and elbowing each other, like school-boys round the red-hot stove on a winter's morning. I knew they had been planted in a right line, and I don't even now comprehend why they should not come up in a right line. I weeded them, and though freedom from foreign growth discovered an intention of straightness, the most casual observer could not but see that skewiness had usurped its place. I repaired to my friend the gardener. He said they must be thinned out and transplanted. It went to my heart to pull up the dear things, but I did it, and set them down again tenderly in the vacant spots. It was evening. The next morning I went to them. Flatness has a new meaning to me since that morning. You can hardly conceive that anything could look so utterly forlorn, disconsolate, disheartened, and collapsed. In fact, they exhibited a degree of depression so entirely beyond what the circumstances demanded, that I was enraged. If they had shown any symptoms of trying to live, I could have sighed and forgiven them; but, on the contrary, they had flopped and died without a struggle, and I pulled them up without a pang, comforting myself with the remaining ones, which throve on their companions' graves, and waxed fat and full and crimson-hearted, in their soft, brown beds. So delighted was I with their luxuriant rotundity, that I made an internal resolve that henceforth I would always plant beets. True, I cannot abide beets. Their fragrance and their flavor are alike nauseating; but they come up, and a beet that will come up is better than a cedar of Lebanon that won't. In all the vegetable kingdom I know of no quality better than this, growth,—nor any quality that will atone for its absence.

PARSNIPS.—They ran the race with an indescribable vehemence that fairly threw the beets into the shade. They trod so delicately at first that I was quite unprepared for such enthusiasm. Lacking the red veining, I could not distinguish them from the weeds with any certainty, and was forced to let both grow together till the harvest. So both grew together, a perfect jungle. But the parsnips got ahead, and rushed up gloriously, magnificently, bacchanalianly,—as the winds come when forests are rended,—as the waves come when navies are stranded. I am, indeed, troubled with a suspicion that their vitality has all run to leaves, and that, when I go down into the depths of the earth for the parsnips, I shall find only bread of emptiness. It is a pleasing reflection that parsnips cannot be eaten till the second year. I am told that they must lie in the ground during the winter. Consequently it cannot be decided whether there are any or not till next spring. I shall in the mean time assume and assert, without hesitation or qualification, that there are as many tubers below the surface as there are leaves above it. I shall thereby enjoy a pleasant consciousness, and the respect of all, for the winter; and if disappointment awaits me in the spring, time will have blunted its keenness for me, and other people will have forgotten the whole subject. You may be sure I shall not remind them of it.

CUCUMBERS.—The cucumbers came up so far, and stuck. It must have been innate depravity, for there was no shadow of reason why they should not keep on as they began. They did not. They stopped growing in the prime of life. Only three cucumbers developed, and they hid under the vines so that I did not see them till they were become ripe, yellow, soft, and worthless. They are an unwholesome fruit at best, and I bore their loss with great fortitude.

TOMATOES.—Both dead. I had been instructed to protect them from the frost by night and from the sun by day. I intended to do so ultimately, but I did not suppose there was any emergency. A frost came the first night and killed them, and a hot sun the next day burned up all there was left. When they were both thoroughly dead, I took great pains to cover them every night and noon. No symptoms of revival appearing to reward my efforts, I left them to shift for themselves. I did not think there was any need of their dying in the first place; and if they would be so absurd as to die without provocation, I did not see the necessity of going into a decline about it. Besides, I never did value plants or animals that have to be nursed, and petted, and coaxed to live. If things want to die, I think they 'd better die. Provoked by my indifference, one of the tomatoes flared up, and took a new start,—put forth leaves, shot out vines, and covered himself with fruit and glory. The chickens picked out the heart of all the tomatoes as soon as they ripened, which was of no consequence, however, as they had wasted so much time in the beginning that the autumn frosts came upon them unawares, and there would n't have been fruit enough ripe to be of any account, if no chicken had ever broken a shell.

SQUASHES.—They appeared above-ground, large-lobed and vigorous. Large and vigorous appeared the bugs, all gleaming in green and gold, like the wolf on the fold, and stopped up all the stomata and ate up all the parenchyma, till my squash-leaves looked as if they had grown for the sole purposing of illustrating net-veined organizations. In consternation I sought again my neighbor the Englishman. He assured me he had 'em on his, too,—lots of 'em. This reconciled me to mine. Bugs are not inherently desirable, but a universal bug does not indicate special want of skill in any one. So I was comforted. But the Englishman said they must be killed. He had killed his. Then I said I would kill mine, too. How should it be done? O, put a shingle near the vine at night, and they would crawl upon it to keep dry, and go out early in the morning and kill 'em. But how to kill them? Why, take 'em right between your thumb and finger and crush 'em!

As soon as I could recover breath, I informed him confidentially, that, if the world were one great squash, I would n't undertake to save it in that way. He smiled a little, but I think he was not overmuch pleased. I asked him why I could n't take a bucket of water and dip the shingle in it and drown them. He said, well, I could try it. I did try it,—first wrapping my hand in a cloth to prevent contact with any stray bug. To my amazement, the moment they touched the water they all spread unseen wings and flew away, safe and sound. I should not have been much more surprised to see Halicarnassus soaring over the ridge-pole. I had not the slightest idea that they could fly. Of course I gave up the design of drowning them. I called a council of war. One said I must put a newspaper over them and fasten it down at the edges; then they could n't get in. I timidly suggested that the squashes could n't get out. Yes, they could, he said,—they 'd grow right through the paper. Another said I must surround them with round boxes with the bottoms broken out; for, though they could fly, they could n't steer, and when they flew up they just dropped down anywhere, and as there was on the whole a good deal more land on the outside of the boxes than on the inside, the chances were in favor of their dropping on the outside. Another said that ashes must be sprinkled on them. A fourth said lime was an infallible remedy. I began with the paper, which I secured with no little difficulty; for the wind—the same wind, strange to say— kept blowing the dirt at me and the paper away from me; but I consoled myself by remembering the numberless rows of squash-pies that should crown my labors, and May took heart from Thanksgiving. The next day I peeped under the paper, and the bugs were a solid phalanx. I reported at head-quarters, and they asked me if I killed the bugs before I put the paper down. I said no, I supposed it would stifle them,—in fact, I did not think anything about it, but if I had thought anything, that was what I thought. I was not pleased to find I had been cultivating the bugs and furnishing them with free lodgings. I went home, and tried all the reme- dies in succession. I could hardly decide which agreed best with the structure and habits of the bugs, but they throve on all. Then I tried them all at once and all o'er with a mighty uproar. Presently the bugs went away. I am not sure that they would not have gone just as soon, if I had let them alone. After they were gone, the vines scrambled out and put forth some beautiful, deep-golden blossoms. When they fell off, that was the end of them. Not a squash,—not one,—not a single squash,—not even a pumpkin. They were all false blossoms.

APPLES.—The trees swelled into masses of pink and white fragrance. Nothing could exceed their fluttering loveliness or their luxuriant prom- ise. A few days of fairy beauty, and showers of soft petals floated noise- lessly down, covering the earth with delicate snow; but I knew, that, though the first blush of beauty was gone, a mighty work was going on in a million little laboratories, and that the real glory was yet to come. I was surprised to observe, one day, that the trees seemed to be turning red. I remarked to Halicarnassus that that was one of Nature's processes which I did not remember to have seen noticed in any botanical treatise. I thought such a change did not occur till autumn. Halicarnassus curved the thumb and forefinger of his right hand into an arch, the ends of which rested on the wrist of his left coat-sleeve. He then lifted the forefinger high and brought it forward. Then he lifted the thumb and brought it up behind the forefinger, and so made them travel up to his elbow. It seemed to require considerable exertion in the thumb and forefinger, and I watched the progress with interest. Then I asked him what he meant by it.

"That's the way they walk," he replied.

"Who walk?"

"The little fellows that have squatted on our trees."

"What little fellows do you mean?"

"The canker-worms?"

"How many are there?"

"About twenty-five decillions, I should think, as near as I can count."

"Why! what are they for? What good do they do?"

"O, no end. Keep the children from eating green apples and getting sick."

"How do they do that?"

"Eat 'em themselves."

A frightful idea dawned upon me. I believe I turned a kind of ghastly blue.

"Halicarnassus, do you mean to tell me that the canker-worms are eating up our apples, and that we shan't have any?"

"It looks like that exceedingly."

That was months ago, and it looks a great deal more like it now. I watched those trees with sadness at my heart. Millions of brown, ugly, villanous worms gnawed, gnawed, gnawed, at the poor little tender leaves and buds,—held them in foul embrace,—polluted their sweetness with hateful breath. I could almost feel the shudder of the trees in that slimy clasp,—could almost hear the shrieking and moaning of the young fruit that saw its hope of happy life thus slowly consuming; but I was powerless to save. For weeks that loathsome army preyed upon the unhappy, helpless trees, and then spun loathsomely to the ground, and buried itself in the reluctant, shuddering soil. A few dismal little apples escaped the common fate; but when they rounded into greenness and a suspicion of pulp, a boring worm came and bored them, and they too died. No apple-pies at Thanksgiving. No apple-roasting in winter evenings. No pan-pie with hot brown bread on Sunday mornings.

CHERRIES.—They rivalled the apple-blooms in snowy profusion, and the branches were covered with tiny balls. The sun mounted warm and high in the heavens, and they blushed under his ardent gaze. I felt an increasing conviction that here there would be no disappointment; but it soon became palpable that another class of depredators had marked our trees for their own. Little brown toes could occasionally be seen peeping from the foliage, and little bare feet left their print on the garden-soil. Humanity had evidently deposited its larva in the vicinity. There was a schoolhouse not very far away, and the children used to draw water from an old well in a distant part of the garden. It was surprising to see how thirsty they all became as the cherries ripened. It was as if the village had simultaneously agreed to breakfast on salt fish. Their wooden bucket might have been the urn of the Danaïdes, judging from the time it took to fill it. The boys were as fleet of foot as young zebras, and presented upon discovery no apology or justification but their heels,—which was a wise stroke in them. A troop of rosy-cheeked, bright-eyed little snips in white pantalets, caught in the act, reasoned with in a semicircle, and cajoled with candy, were as sweet as distilled honey, and promised with all their innocent hearts and hands not to do so any more.

Then the cherries were allowed to hang on the trees and ripen. It took them a great while. If they had been as big as hogsheads, I should think the sun might have got through them sooner than he did. They looked ripe long before they were so; and, as they were very plenty, the trees presented a beautiful appearance. I bought a stack of fantastic little baskets from a travelling Indian tribe, at a fabulous price, for the sake of fulfilling my long-cherished design of sending fruit to my city friends. After long waiting, Halicarnassus came in one morning with a tin pail full, and said that they were ripe at last, for they were turning purple and falling off; and he was going to have them gathered at once. He had brought in the first-fruits for breakfast. I put them in the best preserve-dish, twined it with myrtle, and set it in the centre of the table. It looked charming,—so ruddy and rural and Arcadian. I wished we could breakfast out-doors; but the summer was one of unusual severity, and it was hardly prudent thus to brave its rigor. We had cup-custards at the close of our breakfast that morning,—very vulgar, but very delicious. We reached the cherries at the same moment, and swallowed the first one simultaneously. The effect was instantaneous and electric. Halicarnassus puckered his face into a perfect wheel, with his mouth for the hub. I don't know how I looked, but I felt badly enough.

"It was unfortunate that we had custards this morning," I remarked. "They are so sweet that the cherries seem sour by contrast. We shall soon get the sweet taste out of our mouths, however."

"That's so!" said Halicarnassus, who *will* be coarse.

We tried another. He exhibited a similar pantomime, with improvements. My feelings were also the same, intensified.

"I am not in luck to-day," I said, attempting to smile. "I got hold of a sour cherry this time."

"I got hold of a bitter one," said Halicarnassus.

"Mine was a little bitter, too," I added.

"Mine was a little sour, too," said Halicarnassus.

"We shall have to try again," said I.

We did try again.

"Mine was a good deal of both this time," said Halicarnassus. "But we will give them a fair trial."

"Yes," said I, sepulchrally.

We sat there sacrificing ourselves to abstract right for five minutes. Then I leaned back in my chair, and looked at Halicarnassus. He rested his right elbow on the table, and looked at me.

"Well," said he at last, "how are cherries and things?"

"Halicarnassus," said I, solemnly, "it is my firm conviction that farming is not a lucrative occupation. You have no certain assurance of return, either for labor or capital invested. Look at it. The bugs eat up the squashes. The worms eat up the apples. The cucumbers won't grow at all. The peas have got lost. The cherries are bitter as wormwood and sour as you in your worst moods. Everything that is good for anything won't grow, and everything that grows is n't good for anything."

"My Indian corn, though," began Halicarnassus; but I snapped him up before he was fairly under way. I had no idea of travelling in that direction.

"What am I to do with all those baskets that I bought, I should like to know?" I asked, sharply.

"What did you buy them for?" he asked in return.

"To send cherries to the Hudsons and the Mavericks and Fred Ashley," I replied promptly.

"Why don't you send 'em, then? There's plenty of them,—more than we shall want."

"Because," I answered, "I have not exhausted the pleasures of friendship. Nor do I perceive the benefit that would accrue from turning life-long friends into life-long enemies."

"I 'll tell you what we can do," said Halicarnassus. "We can give a party and treat them to cherries. They 'll have to eat 'em out of politeness."

"Halicarnassus," said I, "we should be mobbed. We should fall victims to the fury of a disappointed and enraged populace."

"At any rate," said he, "we can offer them to chance visitors."

The suggestion seemed to me a good one,—at any rate, the only one that held out any prospect of relief. Thereafter, whenever friends called singly or in squads,—if the squads were not large enough to be formidable,—we invariably set cherries before them, and with generous hospitality pressed them to partake. The varying phases of emotion which they exhibited were painful to me at first, but I at length came to take a morbid pleasure in noting them. It was a study for a sculptor. By long practice I learned to detect the shadow of each coming change, where a casual observer would see only a serene expanse of placid politeness. I knew just where the radiance, awakened by the luscious, swelling, crimson globes, faded into doubt, settled into certainty, glared into perplexity, fired into rage. I saw the grimace, suppressed as soon as begun, but not less patent to my preternaturally keen eyes. No one deceived me by being suddenly seized with admiration of a view. I knew it was only to relieve his nerves by making faces behind the window-curtains.

I grew to take a fiendish delight in watching the conflict, and the fierce desperation which marked its violence. On the one side were the forces of fusion, a reluctant stomach, an unwilling æsophagus, a loathing palate; on the other, the stern, unconquerable will. A natural philosopher would have gathered new proofs of the unlimited capacity of the human race to adapt itself to circumstances, from the *débris* that strewed our premises after each fresh departure. Cherries were chucked under the sofa, into the table-drawers, behind the books, under the lamp-mats, into the vases, in any and every place where a dexterous hand could dispose of them without detection. Yet their number seemed to suffer no abatement. Like Tityus's liver, they were constantly renewed, though constantly consumed. The small boys seemed to be suffering from a fit of conscience. In vain we closed the blinds and shut ourselves up in the house to give them a fair field. Not a cherry was taken. In vain we went ostentatiously to church all day on Sunday. Not a twig was touched. Finally I dropped all the curtains on that side of the house, and avoided that part of the garden in my walks. The cherries may be hanging there to this day, for aught I know.

But why do I thus linger over the sad recital? *"Ab uno disce omnes."* (A quotation from Virgil: means, "All of a piece.") There may have been, there probably was, an abundance of sweet-corn, but the broomstick that had marked the spot was lost, and I could in no wise recall either spot or stick. Nor did I ever see or hear of the peas,—or the beans. If our chickens could be brought to the witness-box, they might throw light on the subject. As it is, I drop a natural tear, and pass on to

THE FLOWER-GARDEN.—It appeared very much behind time,— chiefly Roman wormwood. I was grateful even for that. Then two rows of four-o'-clocks became visible to the naked eye. They are cryptogamous, it seems. Botanists have hitherto classed them among the Phænogamia. A sweet-pea and a china-aster dawdled up just in time to get frost-bitten. *"Et præterea nihil."* (Virgil: means, "That's all.") I am sure it was no fault of mine. I tended my seeds with assiduous care. My devotion was unwearied. I was a very slave to their caprices. I planted them just beneath the surface in the first place, so that they might have an easy passage. In two or three days they all seemed to be lying round loose on the top, and I planted them an inch deep. Then I did n't see them at all for so long that I took them up again, and planted them half-way between. It was of no use. You cannot suit people or plants that are determined not to be suited.

Yet, sad as my story is, I cannot regret that I came into the country and attempted a garden. It has been fruitful in lessons, if in nothing else. I have seen how every evil has its compensating good. When I am tempted to repine that my squashes did not grow, I reflect, that, if they had grown, they would probably have all turned into pumpkins, or if they had stayed squashes, they would have been stolen. When it seems a mysterious Providence that kept all my young hopes underground, I reflect how fine an illustration I should otherwise have lost of what Kossuth calls the solidarity of the human race,—what Paul alludes to, when he says, if one member suffer, all the members suffer with it. I recall with grateful tears the sympathy of my neighbors on the right hand and on the left,—expressed not only by words, but by deeds. In my mind's eye, Horatio, I see again the baskets of apples, and pears, and tomatoes, and strawberries,—squashes too heavy to lift,—and corn sweet as the dews of Hymettus, that bore daily witness of human brotherhood. I remember, too, the victory which I gained over my own depraved nature. I saw my neighbor prosper in everything he undertook. *Nihil tetigit quod non crevit.* Fertility found in his soil its congenial home, and spanned it with rainbow hues. Every day I walked by his garden and saw it putting on its strength, its beautiful garments. I had not even the small satisfaction of reflecting that, amid all his splendid success, his life was cold and cheerless, while mine, amid all its failures, was full of warmth,—a reflection which, I have often observed, seems to go a great way towards making a person contented with his lot,—for he had a lovely wife, promising children, and the whole village for his friends. Yet, notwithstanding all these obstacles, I learned to look over his garden-wall with sincere joy.

There is one provocation, however, which I cannot yet bear with equanimity, and which I do not believe I shall ever meet without at least a spasm of wrath, even if my Christian character shall ever become strong enough to preclude absolute tetanus; and I do hereby beseech all persons who would not be guilty of the sin of Jeroboam who made Israel to sin, who do not wish to have on their hands the burden of my ruined temper, to let me go quietly down into the valley of humiliation and oblivion, and not pester me, as they have hitherto done from all parts of the North-American continent, with the infuriating question, "How did you get on with your garden?"

CHARLOTTE FORTEN GRIMKÉ
(1837–1914)

Life on the Sea Islands
Atlantic Monthly, 13 (June) 1864.

One of the first black American women able to be self-consciously liter-ary and to aspire to excellence in literature, Charlotte Forten Grimké is a major figure in the history of women and literature in nineteenth-cen-tury America. Grimké saw her life as symbolic and wished to dedicate it to the ending of racial prejudice in the North as much as the South; the strategy she chose to accomplish her goal was literature. If she could write something noteworthy, then she would have proved how arbitrary and insubstantial the bases of racial prejudice were.

Born in Philadelphia on August 17, 1837, into a socially, politically, and intellectually influential family, Charlotte Forten Grimké was the daughter of Mary Wood and Robert Forten, and the granddaughter of James Forten, a leader of Philadelphia's black community. James Forten was an early advocate of abolition and a fierce opponent of the alterna-tive colonization movement. He insisted that black people in the United States were as American as white people and that there were no inherent differences between blacks and whites, and thus he opposed the effort to return black Americans to Africa. Because of his influence, his opposi-tion crystallized political resistance among blacks and whites to coloni-zation and turned their attention instead to the movement for the abolition of slavery.

Charlotte Forten Grimké was educated at home because her father refused to send her to the segregated school system of Philadelphia. After her mother's death in 1840, she lived alternately at her grand-father's house—James Forten, also the most successful black busi-nessman of his generation, had amassed a fortune of over $100,000 from his sailmaking operation—and at the suburban home of her aunt Harriet who served as a surrogate mother to Charlotte and who, along with her husband Robert Purvis, was also active in the abolitionist movement. Two other aunts provided Grimké with additional role models. Margaretta Forten founded a small private school for black children in Philadelphia, served as an officer in the Philadelphia Female Anti-Slavery Society, and, like her sister Harriet, was a supporter of the women's rights movement. Sarah Forten Purvis was a founder of the Philadelphia Female Anti-Slavery Society and a member of its Board of Managers. In addition, Sarah was a writer. Between 1831 and 1837, she contributed poems and essays to the *Liberator* and the *Abolitionist.*

In 1854, Grimké's father sent her to Salem, Massachusetts, a town with an integrated school system and a substantial community of free blacks with personal ties to the community in Philadelphia. Here in May of 1854 she began the journal that she continued, intermittently, until 1864. In February of 1855, she graduated with distinction from the Higginson Grammar School. Her prize-winning poem, "A Parting Hymn," was printed and distributed to the audience gathered to witness the graduation exercises. She immediately entered the Normal School at Salem, completed the one year course, and in June of 1856, nearly nineteen, was hired to teach in the Epes Grammar School, becoming the first black teacher in Salem to instruct white children. From her journal entries of the time, it appears that Grimké may have entered the profession of teaching less from inclination than from the absence of other options. A comment made shortly after she began teaching indicates her feelings: "The weather is hot; the children restless, and I find a teacher's life not nearly as pleasant as a scholar's" (*Journal,* p. 82). Another entry records the strain of an activity so clearly against the psychic grain: "A hard day at school. This constant *warfare* is *crushing,* killing me. I am desperate to-night" (*Journal,* p. 109). Predictably, such internal warfare resulted in increasing ill health. She resigned her position in March of 1858, and returned to Philadelphia. In her journal entry for October 11, 1857, Grimké posed the question, "what shall I do to be forever known?" Teaching white children in New England did not provide an answer to this question.

During the next four years, Grimké taught briefly in her aunt's school in Philadelphia, and in the winter of 1860 and again in the summer of 1861, she returned to her position in Salem. Late in 1861, Union forces captured the sea islands off the coast of South Carolina. The white population fled; the black population stayed. In this situation, northern abolitionists saw an opportunity to create a model for the transformation of former slaves into free American citizens and to prove the validity of their belief that, given sufficient encouragement, education, and economic support, black people could accomplish this transformation with ease and rapidity. Grimké enlisted in the Philadelphia Port Royal Relief Association, and on October 28, 1862 she arrived at St. Helena to begin teaching both children and adults the rudiments of literacy. Grimké recorded her response to this experience in her journal and in two articles, "Life on the Sea Islands," published in the *Atlantic Monthly* in May and June of 1864. These articles, the second of which is reprinted here, constitute her best-known and most significant published work.

Grimké left St. Helena in May, 1864; at the same time she stopped writing in her journal. During the next several years she lived in Philadelphia, occasionally teaching and continuing to write articles for the *Christian Register,* the *Boston Commonwealth,* and the *New England Magazine.* In 1871 and 1872, she assisted Richard T. Greene, noted black educator, during his principalship of the Sumner High School in Washington, D.C. In 1873, she was appointed to a clerkship in the federal Treasury Department. Having moved to Washington, she joined a local church and in 1878, at the age of forty-one, she married its pastor, Francis James Grimké, a man thirteen years younger than herself and the son and former slave of Henry Grimké, brother of Angelina and Sarah Grimké, noted abolitionists and early women's rights activists. Grimké died in Washington, D.C., on July 23, 1914, at the age of seventy-six, and was buried there.

Charlotte Forten Grimké's journal records the experience of a woman intensely aware of what it meant to be black in mid-nineteenth-century America. Her entries reveal her elation with the growing national consciousness over slavery and her excited involvement in various aspects of the abolitionist movement—she attended anti-slavery conventions, fund-raising fairs, and lectures; she joined the Salem Female Anti-Slavery Society. The journal also records her pain at the pervasive injury of racial prejudice: "I have suffered much to-day,—my friends Mrs. P and her daughters were refused admission to the Museum, after having tickets given them, solely on account of their complexion" (*Journal,* p. 58). An entry of 1855, describing her return to school, reveals her anger at the burden of self-consciousness imposed by racism: "I wonder that every colored person is not a misanthrope. Surely we have everything to make us hate mankind. I have met girls in the schoolroom— they have been thoroughly kind and cordial to me,—perhaps the next day met them in the street—they feared to recognize me; these I can but regard now with scorn and contempt,—once I liked them, believing them incapable of such meanness" (*Journal,* p. 74).

Grimké measured every person she met, every book she read, every lecture she heard, against a high standard of consciousness on the issues of slavery and racism. Of a comparable consciousness on the issue of women's rights, there is little evidence. She can view a "Chinese hammock . . . a very elegant and pleasant conveyance for those Chinese ladies who cannot walk on account of the smallness of their feet" with no sense of outrage or injury (*Journal,* p. 51). Likewise, Antoinette Brown elicits a lukewarm response because "although she said some excellent things it was plain to be seen that she did not know as much on this subject [slavery] as on that of Woman's Rights" (*Journal,* p. 77). Nevertheless, her sex as well as her race influenced both the shape of Grimké's career and her self-concept as a writer.

Ray Allen Billington summarizes Grimké's literary career in the following manner:

Such an interest in literature in that Victorian day predestined Miss Forten to try her hand at writing. From the time her "Parting Hymn" was acclaimed at the grammar-school graduation she produced a seccession of sentimental poems and essays which ranged from a hymn sung at the semiannual normal-school examination in 1856 through such poetic effusions as "The Two Voices," "The Wind Among the Poplars," "The Angel's Visit," and "The Slave-Girl's Prayer." Perhaps her literary style was best portrayed in an essay, "Glimpses of New England," which was published in the *National Anti-Slavery Standard*. . . . Perhaps wishful thinking occasioned a contemporary to remark that her writing, "for style and true poetical diction, is not surpassed by anything in the English language" (Introduction, *Journal*, pp. 25–26).

Implicit in Billington's language, though not part of his own conceptual framework, is the fact that the literature Grimké was "predestined" to try her hand at was feminine and inevitably fell into those forms and styles considered appropriate for women in the nineteenth century. References to contemporary women writers fill her journal entries—Elizabeth Barrett Browning, Harriet Beecher Stowe, Lydia Maria Child, Phyllis Wheatley, Hattie Griffiths, Susan Warner, Louisa May Alcott—and indicate that the literature that interested Grimké and provided her with models was predominantly female.

Although Grimké wished, above all else, to do something that would reflect credit on her race, her journal entries reveal a pervasive sense of failure. She is consistently self-deprecatory and disparaging in her references to her writing; she takes little satisfaction in any evidence of success and at one point she even denies that she is a writer: "Stopped at the A S Office. Mr. McK was very gracious and pleasant. Mr. S with his most fascinating smile amazed me by asking, 'Have you written any poetry lately?' I paused a moment, at a loss what to say;—then replied, 'No, sir, I *never* wrote any,' and turned away rather abruptly, to speak to someone else" (*Journal*, p. 104). Billington ascribes this pattern of self-deprecation to the "virtue" of "modesty," but it is hard not to view it in a more sinister light. Grimké's self-concept, indeed, would seem to have been shaped by the double burden imposed on black women by a culture both racist and sexist.

"Life on the Sea Islands" grew out of Grimké's assessment of the potential significance to post–Civil War America of the experiment in which she was engaged. Indicative of her ambivalence about herself as a writer, the articles were, according to John Greenleaf Whittier's headnote, originally written for "private perusal." Yet they are so carefully crafted and so imbued with a sense of history that it is difficult not to conclude that Grimké intended them for a larger audience and even for eventual publication. In a journal entry, typically self-deprecatory, Grimké comments: "This eve. finished my Journal for Mary S. Tis so voluminous, so badly written, and so stupid that I am ashamed to send it. But I suppose almost anything from this region w'ld be interesting to people at the N so it might as well go" (*Journal*, p. 151). This view of her subject and audience certainly shaped the articles Grimké wrote and influenced both her choice of material and her attitude toward what she chose to include.

In his biographical essay in *Notable American Women*, Billington suggests that, in writing the articles, Grimké adapted her responses to meet the requirements of the white northern community that formed her primary audience. As evidence, he cites the disparity between Grimké's enthusiastic journal entries on the "shouts" that formed so large a part of the indigenous black culture and her dismissal of the "shouts" in the first of the articles as a "barbarous expression of religion, handed down to them from their African ancestors, and destined to pass away under the influence of Christian teachings." In fact, however, there is little difference in either subject matter or tone between Grimké's journal entries and her articles. The only exception to this principle is her exclusion from the articles of any references to her "blues"—her "insane" disappointment when she does not receive letters from home, her depressions around teaching, her physical discomfort. Thus, if Billington is correct in his assessment of the articles, then the journal itself is a highly-censored document, written in conformity to certain notions of the acceptable and by definition excluding from record experience that would violate those conventions or subvert the political intent of the experiment.

Two selections from other sources will suggest the nature of Grimké's exclusions. In *Rehearsal for Reconstruction: The Port Royal Experiment*, Willie Lee Rose repeatedly refers to the endemic violence of the Union army toward the local black population:

> Violent examples of race hatred could be found wherever Northern troops came into contact with numbers of freedmen. Even at Port Royal, where Saxton's benevolent protectorate should have deterred overt demonstrations, there were appalling clashes. As late as February of 1863 unruly parties from several regiments, including the 9th New Jersey, the 100th New York, known as 'Les Enfants Perdus,' and the 24th Massachusetts, went berserk and terrorized St. Helena Island. They killed and stole livestock, took money from the Negroes, and culminated their outrages in burning all the Negro cabins on the Daniel Jenkins plantations. They beat Negro men and attempted to rape the women, and when the superintendents intervened the soldiers threatened to shoot them (Rose, p. 240; for further examples, see pp. 65, 177).

To this fact of island life, Grimké's account makes only the most veiled reference. In her first article, she describes her initial encounter with the army: "Some of the officers we met did not impress us favorably. They talked flippantly, and sneeringly of the negroes, whom they found we had come down to teach, using an epithet more offensive than gentlemanly." (Her journal entry identifies the epithet as "nigger.")

Equally significant, neither journal nor articles refer to the anomaly of Grimké's position at St. Helena. A free, northern, urban, middle-class black accompanying a predominantly white group of superintendents, missionaries, and teachers, she presented considerable difficulties to the local black community, which was southern, rural, and slave:

This snobbery of the plantation people was nowhere better demonstrated than at The Oaks when Charlotte Forten arrived to teach. Even Wendell Phillips could have been no more fiercely dedicated to the equality of man than was Laura Towne, who describes her difficulty in introducing the beautiful and delicate mulatto teacher into her household. "The people on our place are inclined to question a good deal about 'dat brown gal,' as they call Miss Forten. Aunt Becky required some coaxing to wait upon her and do her room. Aunt Phyllis is especially severe in the tone of her questions. I hope they will respect her. They put on this tone as a kind of reproach to us, I think." It is gratifying to note that the people at The Oaks promptly dropped their prejudice against Miss Forten's color when they discovered her talents. "When they heard her *play on the piano*," reported Thomas Wentworth Higginson a year later, "it quite put them down, and soon all grew fond of her" (Rose, pp. 161–62).

Nevertheless, the material Grimké chose for her articles commands our interest. In particular, Grimké understood the cultural imperialism implicitly involved in this white, northern experiment: "Before teaching them the 'John Brown' song, which they learned to sing with great spirit, Miss T. told them the story of the brave old man who had died for them. I told them about Toussaint, thinking it well they should know what one of their own color had done for his race. They listened attentively, and seemed to understand" (first article, not reprinted). The second article opens with another reference to white man and white song. Of course, Grimké herself had requested Whittier to write a hymn for her to teach the children; and, in her previous article, she had referred to the black "shout" as "barbarous." In this essay, however, Grimké presents the indigenous black music as powerful and compelling, and she expresses serious reservations about the wisdom of the white ministers' insistence on white music. To make her point, she devotes more attention to the black "appendix" than to the white Praise-Meeting.

The celebration of the Emancipation Proclamation provides an obvious focus for Grimké's piece. Although the first paragraph of her article ends with the hint that northern racism may well discount the value of emancipation, the description of the celebration itself is unmarked by doubt. Grimké justifies her celebratory tone by numerous references to the experience of slavery and to the extraordinary efforts black people made to get free. In her first article, Grimké mentions the story that black people "never weary of telling you"—"how Massa run when he hear de fust gun" and how the slave refused to follow, "Jus' as if I was gwine to be sich a goat!" In the second article, Grimké carefully prefaces her account of Emancipation Day with further tales of resistance and escape. Later, she interprets these impulses through a series of "casual" references which reveal the texture of life under slavery: the blindness of Maurice, caused by a blow from a relatively "good" master;

the body of old Bess that shows whip scars three and four inches long; the terror that attends the name of Old Joe Eddings—a reference, one might note, that underscores the accuracy of Harriet Jacobs's account in *Incidents in the Life of a Slave Girl.*

Grimké chooses her conclusion with equal attention to its symbolism. Grimké shared the abolitionist conviction that black Union troops presented primary proof of the capacity and right of black persons for full American citizenship. While mobs in New York City, enraged at the recent draft policies of the Lincoln government, were murdering blacks and burning their property, the fifty-fourth Regiment of Massachusetts, led by Colonel Robert Shaw, attacked Fort Wagner. Ill-fated and fatal though that engagement was, it nevertheless conclusively proved the "manhood" of blacks and, to a nation obsessed with war, such proof meant far more than any results from the social experiments of Port Royal. While much of Grimké's attention revolves around the white man in the picture, Colonel Shaw, the black troops and their symbolic dimension are clearly present. Through them and for them, Grimké makes the war real, contrasting the fact of jackets "literally cut to pieces" with the play war alluded to earlier when, anticipating a rebel "invasion," she sat up with the officers reading poetry.

Interspersed among these focal points are, of course, the materials of the travelogue—descriptive passages, word paintings, accounts of the picturesque, and not so picturesque, features of the southern scene. Grimké seeks a tone that is neither didactic nor sentimental, but is rather reportorial and official. This choice of tone allows little room for her own personality and perspective, and, as a result, the prose is restrained and the voice impersonal. Her decision is understandable, given her desire to achieve authority on a subject she saw as crucial to the future of her race. But, given the uniqueness of her position and thus potentially of her perspective, it also seems unfortunate. Yet, though neither journal nor articles engage the issue, the question of identity may well have been a serious one for Grimké and may well have affected her ability to speak personally. In the final paragraph of her second article, she contemplates with pleasure the prospect that "I shall dwell again among 'mine own people.'" However allusive the reference may be, the use of quotes betrays an awkward self-consciousness, further revealed in phrases like "dusk faces" and "long-abused race," phrases that suggest distance and detachment while at the same time they celebrate community. There is both particular pain and particular pleasure in contemplating Grimké's attempt to participate in a "shout": "The people, after 'Praise' had one of their grandest shouts, and L and I, in a dark corner of the Praise House, amused ourselves with practicing a little. It is wonderful what perfect time the people keep with hands, feet, and indeed with every part of the body. I enjoy these 'shouts' very much" (*Journal*, p. 206).

Source:

Atlantic Monthly, 13 (June), 1864

Selected Primary Works:

"Glimpses of New England," 1860; *The Journal of Charlotte L. Forten*, ed. Ray Allen Billington, 1953.

Selected Secondary Works:

Ray Allen Billington, "Introduction," *The Journal of Charlotte L. Forten* (New York: Norton), 1981; William Wells Brown, *The Black Man, His Antecedents, His Genius, and His Achievements* (New York: Thomas Hamilton), 1863; *Black Women in Nineteenth-Century American Life*, eds. Bert James Loewenberg and Ruth Bogin (University Park: Pennsylvania State University Press), 1976; Gloria C. Oden, *"The Journal of Charlotte L. Forten:* The Salem-Philadelphia Years (1851–1862) Reexamined," *Essex Institute Historical Collections*, 119 (1983), 119–36; Willie Lee Rose, *Rehearsal for Reconstruction: The Port Royal Experiment* (New York: Vintage), 1964; Edmund Wilson, *Patriotic Gore: Studies in the Literature of the American Civil War* (New York: Oxford University Press), 1962.

Contexts:

1863—Alcott, "Pauline's Passion and Punishment," *Hospital Sketches;* Chesebrough, *Peter Carradine;* Spofford, *The Amber Gods and Other Stories;* Whitney, *Faith Gartney's Girlhood*

1864—Alcott, *Moods;* Davis "The Wife's Story"; James, "A Tragedy of Error"; Thoreau, *The Maine Woods*

1865—James, "The Story of A Year"; Stoddard, *Two Men;* Mark Twain, "The Celebrated Jumping Frog of Calaveras County"; Whitman, *Drum Taps;* the *Nation*

[To the Editor of the "Atlantic Monthly."—The following graceful and picturesque description of the new condition of things on the Sea Islands of South Carolina, originally written for private perusal, seems to me worthy of a place in the "Atlantic." Its young author—herself akin to the long-suffering race whose Exodus she so pleasantly describes—is still engaged in her labor of love on St. Helena Island.

—J. G. W.]

PART II.

A few days before Christmas, we were delighted at receiving a beautiful Christmas Hymn from Whittier, written by request, especially for our children. They learned it very easily, and enjoyed singing it. We showed them the writer's picture, and told them he was a very good friend of theirs, who felt the deepest interest in them, and had written this hymn expressly for them to sing,—which made them very proud and happy. Early Christmas morning, we were wakened by the people knocking at the doors and windows, and shouting, "Merry Christmas!" After distributing some little presents among them, we went to the church, which had been decorated with holly, pine, cassena, mistletoe, and the hanging moss, and had a very Christmas-like look. The children of our school assembled there, and we gave them the nice, comfortable clothing, and the picture-books, which had been kindly sent by some Philadelphia ladies. There were at least a hundred and fifty children present. It was very pleasant to see their happy, expectant little faces. To them, it was a wonderful Christmas-Day,—such as they had never dreamed of before. There was cheerful sunshine without, lighting up the beautiful moss-drapery of the oaks, and looking in joyously through the open windows; and there were bright faces and glad hearts within. The long, dark night of the Past, with all its sorrows and its fears, was forgotten; and for the Future,—the eyes of these freed children see no clouds in it. It is full of sunlight, they think, and they trust in it, perfectly.

After the distribution of the gifts, the children were addressed by some of the gentlemen present. They then sang Whittier's Hymn, the "John Brown" song, and several of their own hymns, among them a very singular one, commencing,—

> "I wonder where my mudder gone;
>   Sing, O graveyard!
> Graveyard ought to know me;
>   Ring, Jerusalem!
> Grass grow in de graveyard;
>   Sing, O graveyard!
> Graveyard ought to know me;
>   Ring, Jerusalem!"

They improvise many more words as they sing. It is one of the strangest, most mournful things I ever heard. It is impossible to give any idea of the deep pathos of the refrain,—

> "Sing, O graveyard!"

In this, and many other hymns, the words seem to have but little meaning; but the tones,—a whole lifetime of despairing sadness is concentrated in them. They sing, also, "Jehovyah, Hallelujah," which we like particularly:—

> "De foxes hab holes,
> An' de birdies hab nes',
> But de Son ob Man he hab not where
> To lay de weary head.
>
> CHORUS.
> "Jehovyah, Hallelujah! De Lord He will purvide!
> Jehovyah. Hallelujah! De Lord He will purvide!"

They repeat the words many times. "De foxes hab holes," and the succeeding lines, are sung in the most touching, mournful tones; and then the chorus—"Jehovyah, Hallelujah"—swells forth triumphantly, in glad contrast.

Christmas night, the children came in and had several grand shouts. They were too happy to keep still.

"Oh, Miss, all I want to do is to sing and shout!" said our little pet, Amaretta. And sing and shout she did, to her heart's content.

She read nicely, and was very fond of books. The tiniest children are delighted to get a book in their hands. Many of them already know their letters. The parents are eager to have them learn. They sometimes said to me,—

"Do, Miss, let de chil'en learn eberyting dey can. We nebber hab no chance to learn nuttin', but we wants de chil'en to learn."

They are willing to make many sacrifices that their children may attend school. One old woman, who had a large family of children and grandchildren, came regularly to school in the winter, and took her seat among the little ones. She was at least sixty years old. Another woman— who had one of the best faces I ever saw—came daily, and brought her baby in her arms. It happened to be one of the best babies in the world, a perfect little "model of deportment," and allowed its mother to pursue her studies without interruption.

While taking charge of the store, one day, one of the men who came in told me a story which interested me much. He was a carpenter, living on this island, and just before the capture of Port Royal had been taken by his master to the mainland,—"the Main," as the people call it,—to assist in building some houses which were to shelter the families of the Rebels in case the "Yankees" should come. The master afterward sent him back to the island, providing him with a pass, to bring away a boat and some of the people. On his arrival he found that the Union troops were in possession, and determined to remain here with his family instead of returning to his master. Some of his fellow-servants, who had been left on "the Main," hearing that the Federal troops had come, resolved to make their escape to the islands. They found a boat of their master's, out of which a piece six feet square had been cut. In the night they went to the boat, which had been sunk in a creek near the house, measured the hole, and, after several nights' work in the woods, made a piece large enough to fit in. They then mended and sank it again, as they had found it. The next night five of them embarked. They had a perilous journey, often passing quite near the enemy's boats. They travelled at night, and in the day ran close up to the shore out of sight. Sometimes they could hear the hounds, which had been sent in pursuit of them, baying in the woods. Their provisions gave out, and they were nearly exhausted. At last they succeeded in passing all the enemy's boats, and reached one of our gun-boats in safety. They were taken on board and kindly cared for, and then sent to this island, where their families, who had no hope of ever seeing them again, welcomed them with great rejoicing.

We were also told the story of two girls, one about ten, the other fifteen, who, having been taken by their master up into the country, on the mainland, at the time of the capture of the islands, determined to try to escape to their parents, who had been left on this island. They stole away at night, and travelled through woods and swamps for two days, without eating. Sometimes their strength gave out, and they would sink down, thinking they could go no farther; but they had brave little hearts, and got up again and struggled on, till at last they reached Port Royal Ferry, in a state of utter exhaustion. They were seen there by a boatload of people who were also making their escape. The boat was too full to take them in; but the people, on reaching this island, told the children's father of their whereabouts, and he immediately took a boat, and hastened to the ferry. The poor little creatures were almost wild with joy when they saw him. When they were brought to their mother, she fell down "jes' as if she was dead,"—so our informant expressed it,—overpowered with joy on beholding the "lost who were found."

New-Year's-Day—Emancipation-Day—was a glorious one to us. The morning was quite cold, the coldest we had experienced; but we were determined to go to the celebration at Camp Saxton,—the camp of the First Regiment South-Carolina Volunteers,—whither the General and Colonel Higginson had bidden us, on this, "the greatest day in the nation's history." We enjoyed perfectly the exciting scene on board the Flora. There was an eager, wondering crowd of the freed people in their holiday-attire, with the gayest of head-handkerchiefs, the whitest of aprons, and the happiest of faces. The band was playing, the flags streaming, everybody talking merrily and feeling strangely happy. The sun shone brightly, the very waves seemed to partake of the universal gayety, and danced and sparkled more joyously than ever before. Long before we reached Camp Saxton we could see the beautiful grove, and the ruins of the old Huguenot fort near it. Some companies of the First Regiment were drawn up in line under the trees, near the landing, to receive us. A fine, soldierly-looking set of men; their brilliant dress against the trees (they were then wearing red pantaloons) invested them with a semi-barbaric splendor. It was my good fortune to find among the officers an old friend,—and what it was to meet a friend from the North, in our isolated Southern life, no one can imagine who has not experienced the pleasure. Letters were an unspeakable luxury,—we hungered for them, we could never get enough; but to meet old friends,—that was "too much, too much," as the people here say, when they are very much in earnest. Our friend took us over the camp, and showed us all the arrangements. Everything looked clean and comfortable, much neater, we were told, than in most of the white camps. An officer told us that he had never seen a regiment in which the men were so honest. "In many other camps," said he, "the colonel and the rest of us would find it necessary to place a guard before our tents. We never do it here. They are left entirely unguarded. Yet nothing has ever been touched." We were glad to know that. It is a remarkable fact, when we consider that these men have all their lives been *slaves;* and we know what the teachings of Slavery are.

The celebration took place in the beautiful grove of live-oaks adjoining the camp. It was the largest grove we had seen. I wish it were possible to describe fitly the scene which met our eyes as we sat upon the stand, and looked down on the crowd before us. There were the black soldiers in their blue coats and scarlet pantaloons, the officers of this and other regiments in their handsome uniforms, and crowds of lookers-on,—men, women, and children, of every complexion, grouped in various attitudes under the moss-hung trees. The faces of all wore a happy, interested look. The exercises commenced with a prayer by the chaplain of the regiment. An ode, written for the occasion by Professor Zachos, was read by him, and then sung. Colonel Higginson then introduced Dr. Brisbane, who read the President's Proclamation, which was enthusiastically cheered. Rev. Mr. French presented to the Colonel two very elegant flags, a gift to the regiment from the Church of the Puritans, accompanying them by an appropriate and enthusiastic speech. At its conclusion, before Colonel Higginson could reply, and while he still stood holding the flags in his hand, some of the colored people, of their own accord, commenced singing, "My Country, 't is of thee." It was a touching and beautiful incident, and sent a thrill through all our hearts. The Colonel was deeply moved by it. He said that that reply was far more effective than any speech he could make. But he did make one of those stirring speeches which are "half battles." All hearts swelled withemotion as we listened to his glorious words,—"stirring the soul like the sound of a trumpet."

His soldiers are warmly attached to him, and he evidently feels towards them all as if they were his children. The people speak of him as "the officer who never leaves his regiment for pleasure," but devotes himself, with all his rich gifts of mind and heart, to their interests. It is not strange that his judicious kindness, ready sympathy, and rare fascination of manner should attach them to him strongly. He is one's ideal of an officer. There is in him much of the grand, knightly spirit of the olden time,—scorn of all that is mean and ignoble, pity for the weak, chivalrous devotion to the cause of the oppressed.

General Saxton spoke also, and was received with great enthusiasm. Throughout the morning, repeated cheers were given for him by the regiment, and joined in heartily by all the people. They know him to be one of the best and noblest men in the world. His Proclamation for Emancipation-Day we thought, if possible, even more beautiful than the Thanksgiving Proclamation.

At the close of Colonel Higginson's speech he presented the flags to the colorbearers, Sergeant Rivers and Sergeant Sutton, with an earnest charge, to which they made appropriate replies. We were particularly pleased with Robert Sutton, who is a man of great natural intelligence, and whose remarks were simple, eloquent, and forcible.

Mrs. Gage also uttered some earnest words; and then the regiment sang "John Brown" with much spirit. After the meeting we saw the dress-parade, a brilliant and beautiful sight. An officer told us that the men went through the drill remarkably well,—that the ease and rapidity with which they learned the movements were wonderful. To us it seemed strange as a miracle,—this black regiment, the first mustered into the service of the United States, doing itself honor in the sight of the officers of other regiments, many of whom, doubtless, "came to scoff." The men afterwards had a great feast, ten oxen having been roasted whole for their especial benefit.

We went to the landing, intending to take the next boat for Beaufort; but finding it very much crowded, waited for another. It was the softest, loveliest moonlight; we seated ourselves on the ruined wall of the old fort; and when the boat had got a short distance from the shore the band in it commenced playing "Sweet Home." The moonlight on the water, the perfect stillness around, the wildness and solitude of the ruins, all seemed to give new pathos to that ever dear and beautiful old song. It came very near to all of us,—strangers in that strange Southern land. After a while we retired to one of the tents,—for the night-air, as usual, grew danger-ously damp,—and, sitting around the bright wood-fire, enjoyed the bril-liant and entertaining conversation. Very unwilling were we to go home; for, besides the attractive society, we knew that the soldiers were to have grand shouts and a general jubilee that night. But the Flora was coming, and we were obliged to say a reluctant farewell to Camp Saxton and the hospitable dwellers therein, and hasten to the landing. We promenaded the deck of the steamer, sang patriotic songs, and agreed that moonlight and water had never looked so beautiful as on that night. At Beaufort we took the row-boat for St. Helena; and the boatmen, as they rowed, sang some of their sweetest, wildest hymns. It was a fitting close to such a day. Our hearts were filled with an exceeding great gladness; for, although the Government had left much undone, we knew that Freedom was surely born in our land that day. It seemed too glorious a good to realize,—this beginning of the great work we had so longed and prayed for.

L. and I had one day an interesting visit to a plantation about six miles from ours. The house is beautifully situated in the midst of noble pine-trees, on the banks of a large creek. The place was owned by a very wealthy Rebel family, and is one of the pleasantest and healthiest on the island. The vicinity of the pines makes it quite healthy. There were a hundred and fifty people on it,—one hundred of whom had come from Edisto Island at the time of its evacuation by our troops. There were not houses enough to accommodate them, and they had to take shelter in barns, out-houses, or any other place they could find. They afterwards built rude dwellings for themselves, which did not, however, afford them much protection in bad weather. The superintendent told us that they were well-behaved and industrious. One old woman interested us greatly. Her name was Daphne; she was probably more than a hundred years old; had had fifty grandchildren, sixty-five great-grandchildren, and three great-great-grandchildren. Entirely blind, she yet seemed very cheerful and happy. She told us that she was brought with her parents from Africa at the time of the Revolution. A bright, happy old face was hers, and she retained her faculties remarkably well. Fifteen of the people had escaped from the mainland in the previous spring. They were pursued, and one of them was overtaken by his master in the swamps. A fierce grapple ensued,—the master on horseback, the man on foot. The former drew a pistol and shot his slave through the arm, shattering it dreadfully. Still, the heroic man fought desperately, and at last succeeded in unhorsing his master, and beating him until he was senseless. He then made his escape, and joined the rest of the party.

One of the most interesting sights we saw was a baptism among the people. On one Sunday there were a hundred and fifty baptized in the creek near the church. They looked very picturesque in their white aprons and bright frocks and handerchiefs. As they marched in procession down to the river's edge, and during the ceremony, the spectators, with whom the banks were crowded, sang glad, triumphant songs. The freed people on this island are all Baptists.

We were much disappointed in the Southern climate. We found it much colder than we had expected,—quite cold enough for as thick winter clothing as one would wear at the North. The houses, heated only by open fires, were never comfortably warm. In the floor of our sitting-room there was a large crack through which we could see the ground beneath; and through this and the crevices of the numerous doors and windows the wind came chillingly. The church in which we taught school was particularly damp and cold. There was no chimney, and we could have no fire at all. Near the close of the winter a stove came for us, but it could not be made to draw; we were nearly suffocated with smoke, and gave it up in despair. We got so thoroughly chilled and benumbed within, that for several days we had school out-of-doors, where it was much warmer. Our school-room was a pleasant one,—for ceiling the blue sky above, for walls the grand old oaks with their beautiful moss-drapery,— but the dampness of the ground made it unsafe for us to continue the experiment.

At a later period, during a few days' visit to some friends living on the Milne Plantation, then the head-quarters of the First South-Carolina, which was on picket-duty at Port-Royal Ferry, we had an opportunity of seeing something of Port-Royal Island. We had pleasant rides through the pine barrens. Indeed, riding on horseback was our chief recreation at the South, and we enjoyed it thoroughly. The "Secesh" horses, though small, poor, and mean-looking, when compared with ours, are generally excellent for the saddle, well-trained and very easy. I remember particularly one ride that we had while on Port-Royal Island. We visited the Barnwell Plantation, one of the finest places on the island. It is situated on Broad River. The grounds are extensive, and are filled with magnificent live-oaks, magnolias, and other trees. We saw one noble old oak, said to be the largest on these islands. Some of the branches have been cut off, but the remaining ones cover an area of more than a hundred feet in circumference. We rode to a point whence the Rebels on the opposite side of the river are sometimes to be seen. But they were not visible that day; and we were disappointed in our long-cherished hope of seeing a "real live Rebel." On leaving the plantation, we rode through a long avenue of oaks,—the moss-hung branches forming a perfect arch over our heads,—and then for miles through the pine barrens. There was an Italian softness in the April air. Only a low, faint murmur—hardly "the slow song of the sea"—could be heard among the pines. The ground was thickly carpeted with ferns of a vivid green. We found large violets, purple and white, and azaleas of a deeper pink and heavier fragrance than ours. It was leaving Paradise, to emerge from the beautiful woods upon the public road,—the shell-road which runs from Beaufort to the Ferry. Then we entered a by-way leading to the plantation, where we found the Cherokee rose in all its glory. The hedges were white with it; it canopied the trees, and hung from their branches its long sprays of snowy blossoms and dark, shining leaves, forming perfect arches, and bowers which seemed fitting places for fairies to dwell in. How it gladdened our eyes and hearts! It was as if all the dark shadows that have so long hung over this Southern land had flitted away, and, in this garment of purest white, it shone forth transfigured, beautified, forevermore.

On returning to the house, we were met by the exciting news that the Rebels were bringing up pontoon-bridges, and were expected to attempt crossing over near the Ferry, which was only two or three miles from us. Couriers came in every few moments with various reports. A superintendent whose plantation was very near the Ferry had been watching through his glass the movements on the opposite side, and reported that the rebels were gathering in large force, and evidently preparing for some kind of demonstration. A messenger was despatched to Beaufort for reinforcements, and for some time we were in a state of expectancy, not entirely without excitement, but entirely without fear. The officers evidently enjoyed the prospect of a fight. One of them assured me that I should have the pleasure of seeing a Rebel shell during the afternoon. It was proposed that the women should be sent into Beaufort in an ambulance; against which ignoble treatment we indignantly protested, and declared our intention of remaining at our post, if the Colonel would consent; and finally, to our great joy, the best of colonels did consent that we should remain, as he considered it quite safe for us to do so. Soon a light battery arrived, and during the evening a brisk firing was kept up.

We could hear the explosion of the shells. It was quite like being in the war; and as the firing was principally on our side, and the enemy was getting the worst of it, we rather enjoyed it. For a little while the Colonel read to us, in his spirited way, some of the stirring "Lays of the Old Cavaliers." It was just the time to appreciate them thoroughly, and he was of all men the fittest person to read them. But soon came a courier, "in hot haste," to make report of the doings without, and the reading was at an end. In the midst of the firing, Mrs. D. and I went to bed, and slept soundly until morning. We learned afterward that the Rebels had not intended to cross over, but were attempting to take the guns off one of our boats, which they had sunk a few days previous. The timely arrival of the battery from Beaufort prevented them from accomplishing their purpose.

In April we left Oaklands, which had always been considered a particularly unhealthy place during the summer, and came to "Seaside," a plantation on another and healthier part of the island. The place contains nearly a hundred people. The house is large and comparatively comfortable. Notwithstanding the name, we have not even a distant glimpse of the sea, although we can sometimes hear its roar. At low tide there is not a drop of water to be seen,—only dreary stretches of marsh-land, reminding us of the sad outlook of Mariana in the Moated Grange,—

"The level waste and rounding gray."

But at night we have generally a good sea-breeze, and during the hottest weather the air is purer and more invigorating than in many parts of the island.

On this, as on several other large plantations, there is a "Praise-House," which is the special property of the people. Even in the old days of Slavery, they were allowed to hold meetings here; and they still keep up the custom. They assemble on several nights of the week, and on Sunday afternoons. First, they hold what is called the "Praise-Meeting," which consists of singing, praying, and preaching. We have heard some of the old negro preachers make prayers that were really beautiful and touching. In these meetings they sing only the church-hymns which the Northern ministers have taught them, and which are far less suited to their voices than their own. At the close of the Praise-Meeting they all shake hands with each other in the most solemn manner. Afterward, as a kind of appendix, they have a grand "shout," during which they sing their own hymns. Maurice, an old blind man, leads the singing. He has a remarkable voice, and sings with the greatest enthusiasm. The first shout that we witnessed in the Praise-House impressed us very much. The large, gloomy room, with its blackened walls,—the wild, whirling dance of the shouters,—the crowd of dark, eager faces gathered around,—the figure of the old blind man, whose excitement could hardly be controlled, and whose attitude and gestures while singing were very fine,—and over all, the red glare of the burning pine-knot, which shed a circle of light around it, but only seemed to deepen and darken the shadows in the other parts of the room,—these all formed a wild, strange, and deeply impressive picture, not soon to be forgotten.

Maurice's especial favorite is one of the grandest hymns that we have yet heard:—

> "De tallest tree in Paradise
> De Christian calls de Tree ob Life,
> An' I hope dat trumpet blow me home
> To my New Jerusalem.

> CHORUS.

> "Blow, Gabriel! trumpet, blow louder, louder!
> An' I hope dat trumpet blow me home
> To my New Jerusalem!

> "Paul and Silas jail-bound
> Sing God's praise both night and day,
> An' I hope dat trumpet blow me home
> To my New Jerusalem.

> CHORUS.

> "Blow, Gabriel! trumpet, blow louder, louder!
> An' I hope dat trumpet blow me home
> To my New Jerusalem!"

The chorus has a glad, triumphal sound, and in singing it the voice of old Maurice rings out in wonderfully clear, trumpet-like tones. His blindness was caused by a blow on the head from a loaded whip. He was struck by his master in a fit of anger. "I feel great distress when I become blind," said Maurice; "but den I went to seek de Lord; and eber since I know I see in de next world, I always hab great satisfaction." We are told that the master was not a "hard man" except when in a passion, and then he seems to have been very cruel.

One of the women on the place, Old Bess, bears on her limbs many marks of the whip. Some of the scars are three and four inches long. She was used principally as a house-servant. She says, "Ebery time I lay de table I put cowskin on one end, an' I git beatin' and thumpin' all de time. Hab all kinds o' work to do, and sich a gang [of children] to look after! One person could n't git along wid so much work, so it go wrong, and den I git beatin'."

But the cruelty of Bess's master sinks into insignificance, when compared with the far-famed wickedness of another slaveholder, known all over the island as "Old Joe Eddings." There seem to have been no bounds to his cruelty and licentiousness; and the people tell tales of him which make one shudder. We were once asking some questions about him of an old, half-witted woman, a former slave of his. The look of horror and loathing which overspread her face was perfectly indescribable, as, with upraised hands, she exclaimed, "What! Old Joe Eddings? Lord, Missus, he second to none in de world but de Debil!" She had, indeed, good cause to detest him; for, some years before, her daughter, a young black girl, maddened by his persecutions, had thrown herself into the creek and been drowned, after having been severely beaten for refusing to degrade herself. Outraged, despised, and black, she yet preferred death to dishonor. But these are things too heart-sickening to dwell upon. God alone knows how many hundreds of plantations, all over the South, might furnish a similar record.

Early in June, before the summer heat had become unendurable, we made a pleasant excursion to Edisto Island. We left St. Helena village in the morning, dined on one of the gun-boats stationed near our island, and in the afternoon proceeded to Edisto in two row-boats. There were six of us, besides an officer and the boats' crews, who were armed with guns and cutlasses. There was no actual danger; but as we were going into the enemy's country, we thought it wisest to guard against surprises. After a delightful row, we reached the island near sunset, landing at a place called Eddingsville, which was a favorite summer resort with the aristocracy of Edisto. It has a fine beach several miles in length. Along the beach there is a row of houses, which must once have been very desirable dwellings, but have now a desolate, dismantled look. The sailors explored the beach for some distance, and returned, reporting "all quiet, and nobody to be seen"; so we walked on, feeling quite safe, stopping here and there to gather the beautiful tiny shells which were buried deep in the sands.

We took supper in a room of one of the deserted houses, using for seats some old bureau-drawers turned edgewise. Afterward we sat on the piazza, watching the lightning playing from a low, black cloud over a sky flushed with sunset, and listening to the merry songs of the sailors who occupied the next house. They had built a large fire, the cheerful glow of which shone through the windows, and we could see them dancing, evidently in great glee. Later, we had another walk on the beach, in the lovely moonlight. It was very quiet then. The deep stillness was broken only by the low, musical murmur of the waves. The moon shone bright and clear over the deserted houses and gardens, and gave them a still wilder and more desolate look.

We went within-doors for the night very unwillingly. Having, of course, no beds, we made ourselves as comfortable as we could on the floor, with boat-cushions, blankets, and shawls. No fear of Rebels disturbed us. There was but one road by which they could get to us, and on that a watch was kept, and in case of their approach, we knew we should have ample time to get to the boat and make our escape. So, despite the mosquitoes, we had a sound night's sleep.

The next morning we took the boats again, and followed the course of the most winding of little creeks. In and out, in and out, the boats went. Sometimes it seemed as if we were going into the very heart of the woods; and through the deep silence we half expected to hear the sound of a Rebel rifle. The banks were overhung with a thick tangle of shrubs and bushes, which threatened to catch our boats, as we passed close beneath their branches. In some places the stream was so narrow that we ran aground, and then the men had to get out, and drag and pull with all their might before we could be got clear again. After a row full of excitement and pleasure, we reached our place of destination,—the Eddings Plantation, whither some of the freedmen had preceded us in their search for corn. It must once have been a beautiful place. The grounds were laid out with great taste, and filled with fine trees, among which we noticed particularly the oleander, laden with deep rose-hued and deliciously fragrant flowers, and the magnolia, with its wonderful, large blossoms, which shone dazzlingly white among the dark leaves. We explored the house,—after it had first been examined by our guard, to see that no foes lurked there,—but found nothing but heaps of rubbish, an old bedstead, and a bathing-tub, of which we afterward made good use. When we returned to the shore, we found that the tide had gone out, and between us and the boats lay a tract of marsh-land, which it would have been impossible to cross without a wetting. The gentlemen determined on wading. But what were we to do? In this dilemma somebody suggested the bathing-tub, a suggestion which was eagerly seized upon. We were placed in it, one at a time, borne aloft in triumph on the shoulders of four stout sailors, and safely deposited in the boat. But, through a mistake, the tub was not sent back for two of the ladies, and they were brought over on the crossed hands of two of the sailors, in the "carry-a-lady-to-London" style. Again we rowed through the windings of the creek, then out into the open sea, among the white, exhilarating breakers—reached the gun-boat, dined again with its hospitable officers, and then returned to our island, which we reached after nightfall, feeling thoroughly tired, but well pleased with our excursion.

From what we saw of Edisto, however, we did not like it better than our own island,—except, of course, the beach; but we are told that farther in the interior it is much more beautiful. The freed people, who left it at the time of its evacuation, think it the loveliest place in the world, and long to return. When we were going, Miss T.—the much-loved and untiring friend and physician of the people—asked some whom we met if we should give their love to Edisto. "Oh, yes, yes, Miss!" they said. "Ah, Edisto a beautiful city!" And when we came back, they inquired, eagerly,—"How you like Edisto? How Edisto stan'?" Only the fear of again falling into the hands of the "Secesh" prevents them from returning to their much-loved home.

As the summer advanced, the heat became intense. We found it almost overpowering, driving to school near the middle of the day, as we were obliged to do. I gave up riding, and mounted a sulky, such as a single gentleman drives in at the North. It was exceedingly high, and I found it no small task to mount up into it. Its already very comical appearance was enhanced by the addition of a cover of black India-rubber cloth, with which a friend kindly provided me. Thus adorned, it looked like the skeleton of some strange creature surmounted by a huge bonnet, and afforded endless amusement to the soldiers we chanced to meet, who hailed its appearance with shouts of laughter, and cries of "Here comes the Calithumpian!" This unique vehicle, with several others on our island, kindred, but not quite equal to it, would create a decided sensation in the streets of a Northern city.

No description of life on these islands would be complete without a word concerning the fleas. They appeared at the opening of spring, and kept constantly "risin'," as the people said, until they reached a height the possibility of which we had never conceived. We had heard and read of fleas. We had never *realized* them before. Words utterly fail to describe the tortures we endured for months from these horrible little tyrants. Remembering our sufferings "through weary day and weary *night*," we warn everybody not gifted with extraordinary powers of endurance to beware of a summer on the Sea Islands.

Notwithstanding the heat, we determined to celebrate the Fourth of July as worthily as we could. The freed people and the children of the different schools assembled in the grove near the Baptist Church. The flag was hung across the road, between two magnificent live-oaks, and the children, being grouped under it, sang "The Star-Spangled Banner" with much spirit. Our good General could not come, but addresses were made by Mr. P.,—the noble-hearted founder of the movement for the benefit of the people here, and from first to last their stanch and much-loved friend,—by Mr. L., a young colored minister, and others. Then the people sang some of their own hymns; and the woods resounded with the grand notes of "Roll, Jordan, roll." They all afterward partook of refreshments, consisting of molasses and water,—a very great luxury to them,—and hardtack.

Among the visitors present was the noble young Colonel Shaw, whose regiment was then stationed on the island. We had met him a few nights before, when he came to our house to witness one of the people's shouts. We looked upon him with the deepest interest. There was something in his face finer, more exquisite, than one often sees in a man's face, yet it was full of courage and decision. The rare and singular charm of his manner drew all hearts to him. He was deeply interested in the singing and appearance of the people. A few days afterwards we saw his regiment on dress-parade, and admired its remarkably fine and manly appearance. After taking supper with the Colonel we sat outside the tent, while some of his men entertained us with excellent singing. Every moment we became more and more charmed with him. How full of life and hope and lofty aspirations he was that night! How eagerly he expressed his wish that they might soon be ordered to Charleston! "I do hope they will give *us* a chance," he said. It was the desire of his soul that his men should do themselves honor,—that they should prove themselves to an unbelieving world as brave soldiers as though their skins were white. And for himself, he was like the Chevalier of old, "without reproach or fear." After we had mounted our horses and rode away, we seemed still to feel the kind clasp of his hand,—to hear the pleasant, genial tones of his voice, as he bade us goodbye, and hoped that we might meet again. We never saw him afterward. In two short weeks came the terrible massacre at Fort Wagner, and the beautiful head of the young hero and martyr was laid low in the dust. Never shall we forget the heart-sickness with which we heard of his death. We could not realize it at first,—we, who had seen him so lately in all the strength and glory of his young manhood. For days we clung to a vain hope; then it fell away from us, and we knew that he was gone. We knew that he died gloriously, but still it seemed very hard. Our hearts bled for the mother whom he so loved,—for the young wife, left desolate. And then we said, as we say now,—"God comfort them! He only can." During a few of the sad days which followed the attack on Fort Wagner, I was in one of the hospitals of Beaufort, occupied with the wounded soldiers of the Fifty-Fourth Massachusetts. The first morning was spent in mending the bullet-holes and rents in their clothing. What a story they told! Some of the jackets of the poor fellows were literally cut in pieces. It was pleasant to see the brave, cheerful spirit among them. Some of them were severely wounded, but they uttered no complaint; and in the letters which they dictated to their absent friends there was no word of regret, but the same cheerful tone throughout. They expressed an eager desire to get well, that they might "go at it again." Their attachment to their young colonel was beautiful to see. They felt his death deeply. One and all united in the warmest and most enthusiastic praise of him. He was, indeed, exactly the person to inspire the most loyal devotion in the hearts of his men. And with everything to live for, he had given up his life for them. Heaven's best gifts had been showered upon him, but for them he had laid them all down. I think they truly appreciated the greatness of the sacrifice. May they ever prove worthy of such a leader! Already, they, and the regiments of freedmen here, as well, have shown that true manhood has no limitations of color.

Daily the long-oppressed people of these islands are demonstrating their capacity for improvement in learning and labor. What they have accomplished in one short year exceeds our utmost expectations. Still the sky is dark; but through the darkness we can discern a brighter future. We cannot but feel that the day of final and entire deliverance, so long and often so hopelessly prayed for, has at length begun to dawn upon this much-enduring race. An old freedman said to me one day, "De Lord make me suffer long time, Miss. 'Peared like we nebber was gwine to git troo. But now we's free. He bring us all out right at las'." In their darkest hours they have clung to Him, and we know He will not forsake them.

> "The poor among men shall rejoice,
> For the terrible one is brought to nought."

While writing these pages I am once more nearing Port Royal. The Fortunate Isles of Freedom are before me. I shall again tread the flower-skirted woodpaths of St. Helena, and the sombre pines and bearded oaks shall whisper in the sea-wind their grave welcome. I shall dwell again among "mine own people." I shall gather my scholars about me, and see smiles of greeting break over their dusk faces. My heart sings a song of thanksgiving, at the thought that even I am permitted to do something for a long-abused race, and aid in promoting a higher, holier, and happier life on the Sea Islands.